PLACE-NAMES OF NORTHERN IRELAND

Volume Six

COUNTY DOWN IV

NORTH-WEST DOWN / IVEAGH

Published 1996
The Institute of Irish Studies
The Queen's University of Belfast
Belfast

Research and Publication funded by the
Central Community Relations Unit

ISBN 0 85389 570 8 (hb)

ISBN 0 85389 571 6 (pb)

British Library Cataloguing-in-Publication Data.
A catalogue record for this book is available from the British Library.

Printed by W. & G. Baird Ltd, Antrim.

Place-Names of Northern Ireland

VOLUME SIX

County Down IV
North-West Down / Iveagh

Kay Muhr

The Northern Ireland Place-Name Project
Department of Celtic
The Queen's University of Belfast

General Editor: Gerard Stockman

RESEARCH GROUP

Professor Gerard Stockman

R. J. Hannan MA (1987–95)
Dr A. J. Hughes (1987–92)
Fiachra Mac Gabhann MA
Dr Patrick McKay
Dr Kay Muhr
Seán Ó Coinn BA (1993–94)
Mícheál B. Ó Mainnín MA
Dr Gregory Toner
Eilís McDaniel BA, MSc (1987–90)

Secretary: Mrs Maeve Walker.

LIST OF ILLUSTRATIONS

The townland maps have been prepared from OSNI digitized data by Kay Muhr, with the permission of the Director, Ordnance Survey of Northern Ireland.

ACKNOWLEDGEMENTS

Among my colleagues, thanks to everyone who read drafts and made suggestions, and in particular to Art Hughes, Eilís McDaniel, and Mícheál Ó Mainnín, who collected the historical forms and wrote preliminary drafts for the parishes of Aghaderg, Drumballyroney, and Moira; to Maeve Walker who accompanied me on fieldwork, and to Leslie Lucas for meticulous transcription of the tapes.

In a multi-disciplinary field of study such as place-names, consultation with outside experts is of vital importance. The Place-Name Project cannot thank by name all those who have given us of their time and knowledge, but among them I acknowledge the help of the following:

Prof. J. H. Andrews, Dr Gillian Fellows-Jensen, Prof. Peter Foote, Dr Leslie Lucas, W. C. Kerr, Dr Cathair Ó Dochartaigh, Fr Réamonn Ó Muirí, Dr Rosemary Power, J. F. Rankin, James Savage, Dr Simon Taylor, Canon R. E. Turner, Philip Wilson.

Dr Kieran Devine, Dr M. T. Flanagan, Mary Kelly, Dr Hiram Morgan, Pamela Robinson, Dr A. Sheehan, Michael Smallman of Queen's University, Belfast.

Art Ó Maolfabhail, Dónall Mac Giolla Easpaig, Pádraig Ó Cearúil, Pádraig Ó Dalaigh of the Place-Names Branch of the Ordnance Survey of Ireland, with Dr Nollaig Ó Muraíle formerly of the Place-Names Branch of the Ordance Survey of Ireland, now of the Department of Celtic, Queen's University, Belfast.

Angélique Day and Patrick McWilliams, Ordnance Survey Memoir Project, Institute of Irish Studies QUB.

Members of the Steering Committee: Michael Brand, Professor Ronnie Buchanan, Sam Corbett, Dr Maurna Crozier, Dr Alan Gailey, Dr Ann Hamlin, Dr Maurice Hayes, Tony McCusker, Dr Brian Walker.

Claire Foley, Ann Given, Dr Chris Lynn of the Archaeological Survey of Northern Ireland, now Historic Monuments & Buildings, DoE NI.

Leonard Brown, John Buckley, Chris Davidson, Geoff Mahood, Larry Toolan of the Ordnance Survey of Northern Ireland.

Dr Bill Crawford, of the Ulster Federation for Local Studies.

Clifford Harkness, of the Ulster Folk and Transport Museum.

Dr Brian Trainor of the Ulster Historical Foundation.

Richard Warner of the Ulster Museum.

Messrs Tommy Banks, Jim Blaney, Mrs S. Brush, Sam Carlisle, Adrian Clarke, Kieran Clendinning, Ernie Copeland, Johnny Farrell, Ernie Gordon, Pat and Gerry Hanna, John Ingham, John Lennon, W. N. McFadden, John McGrehan, Séamas and Sarah McElroy, Leo and Deirdre McNeill, Mrs Muriel McVeagh, Mrs Alice O'Hare, Mary Rose Quinn, Dr Nini Rodgers, Canon Patrick Synott, the late Miss Margaret Taylor, and all others who assisted with fieldwork and in any other way in the locality.

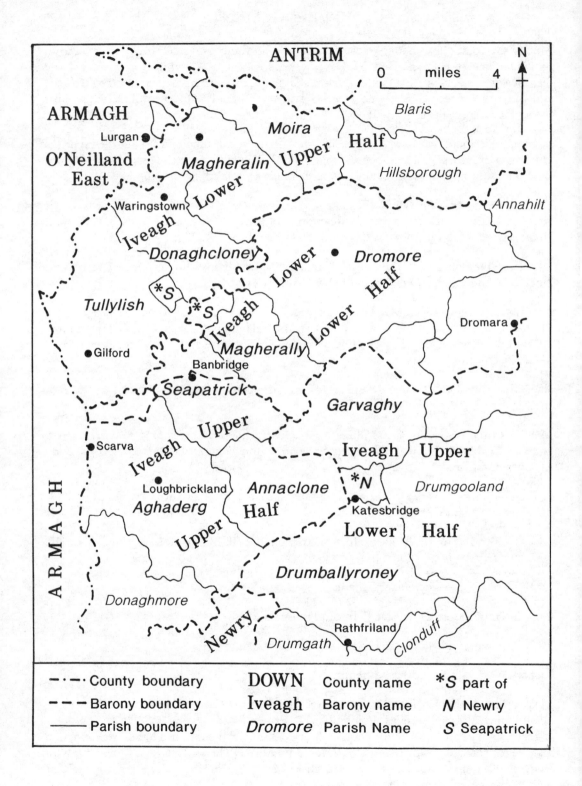

ANTRIM

0 miles 4
N

ARMAGH

Blaris

Lurgan

Moira

O'Neilland
East

Magheralin

Upper Half

Hillsborough

Waringstown

Lower

Annahilt

Iveagh

Donaghcloney

Lower

Dromore

*S

Tullylish

*S

Lower Half

Iveagh

Dromara

Magherally

Gilford

Banbridge

Seapatrick

Garvaghy

Scarva

Iveagh Upper

Iveagh Upper

Loughbrickland

Annaclone

*N

Drumgooland

ARMAGH

Aghaderg

Half

Katesbridge

Upper

Lower Half

Drumballyroney

Donaghmore

Rathfriland

Newry

Drumgath

Clonduff

- · - · County boundary   **DOWN** County name   *S part of

- - - Barony boundary   *Iveagh* Barony name   N Newry

──── Parish boundary   *Dromore* Parish Name   S Seapatrick

CONTENTS

GENERAL INTRODUCTION

BRIEF HISTORY OF PLACE-NAME STUDY IN IRELAND

Place-name lore or *dindsenchas* was a valued type of knowledge in early Ireland, to be learnt by students of secular learning in their eighth year of study. Stories about the origin of place-names appear regularly in early Irish literature. At the end of the epic "Cattle Raid of Cooley" the triumphal charge of the Brown Bull of Cooley around Ireland is said to have given rise to names such as Athlone (Irish *Áth Luain*), so called from the loin *(luan)* of the White-horned Bull slain by the Brown Bull. In the 10th, 11th and 12th centuries legends about the naming of famous places were gathered together into a number of great collections. Frequently, different explanations of the same name are offered in these legends, usually with no preference being expressed. In an entry on the naming of *Cleitech*, the palace on the Boyne of the early king *Muirchertach mac Erca*, five separate explanations of the name are offered, none of which can be correct in modern scholarly terms. Place-name study was cultivated as a branch of literature.

Knowledge of Irish place-names was of practical importance during the English conquest and exploration of Ireland in the 16th century. Recurring elements in the place-names were noted by surveyors, and a table giving a few English equivalents appears on some maps of this period. There was concern that Irish names were "uncouth and unintelligible". William Petty, the great 17th-century surveyor and map-maker, commented that "it would not be amiss if the significant part of the Irish names were interpreted, where they are not nor cannot be abolished" (Petty 1672, 72–3). However, although the English-speaking settlers created many new names, they did not usually change the names of the lands they were granted, and the names of land units remained as they were, albeit in an anglicized form.

Interest in the meaning of Irish place-names developed further towards the end of the 18th century. The contributors to William Shaw Mason's *Parochial Survey of Ireland* often included a table explaining their local townland names, and this aspect was retained in the Statistical Reports compiled by the officers of the Royal Engineers on the parishes they surveyed for the first six-inch survey of Ireland in the late 1820s and early 1830s. Information on the spelling of place-names for the maps was collected in "name-books", and the Ordnance Survey was concerned to find that a variety of anglicized spellings was in use for many Irish place-names. The assistant director, Thomas Larcom, decided that the maps should use the anglicized spellings that most accurately represented the original Irish (Andrews 1975, 122) and he employed an Irish scholar, John O'Donovan, to comment on the name-books and recommend standard forms of names. O'Donovan was sent to the areas being surveyed to talk to local inhabitants, where possible Irish speakers, to find out the Irish forms. These were entered in the name-books, but were not intended for publication.

In 1855, a reader of *Ulster Journal of Archaeology* calling himself "De Campo" asked "that a list of all the townlands should be given in their Irish and English nomenclature, with an explanation of their Irish names" (*UJA* ser. 1, vol. iii, 25 1b). Meanwhile William Reeves, the Church of Ireland Bishop of Connor, had decided to compile a "monster Index" of all Irish townlands, which would eventually include the etymology of the names, "where attainable" (Reeves 1861, 486). Reeves' project was cited favourably by William Donnelly, the Registrar General, in his introduction to the first Topographical Index to the Census of Ireland: "It would greatly increase the value of a publication of this nature if it were accompanied by a glossary or explanation of the names, and an account of their origin" *(Census 1851* 1, 11–12).

However, it was left to another scholar, P. W. Joyce, to publish the first major work dealing exclusively with the interpretation of Irish place-names, and in his first chapter he acknowledges his debt to both O'Donovan and Reeves (*Joyce* i 7–8, 10). At this period the progress made by Irish place-name scholarship was envied in England (Taylor 1896, 205). The high standard of Joyce's work has made him an authority to the present day, but it is regrettable that most popular books published since on Irish place-names have drawn almost entirely on the selection and arrangement of names discussed by Joyce, ignoring the advances in place-name scholarship over the last hundred years (Flanagan D. 1979(f); 1981–2(b)).

Seosamh Laoide's *Post-Sheanchas*, published in 1905, provided an Irish-language form for modern post towns, districts and counties, and research on place-names found in early Irish texts resulted in Edmund Hogan's *Onomasticon Goedelicum* (1910). Local studies have been published by Alfred Moore Munn (Co. Derry, 1925), and P. McAleer (*Townland Names of County Tyrone*, 1936). The idea of a comprehensive official survey was taken up again by Risteard Ó Foghludha in the introduction to his *Log-ainmneacha* (1935). A Place-Names Commission was founded in Dublin in 1946 to advise on the correct forms of Irish place-names for official use and this was followed by the Place-Names Branch of the Ordnance Survey. They have published the Irish names for postal towns (*AGBP* 1969), a gazetteer covering many of the more important names in Ireland (*GÉ* 1989), a townland survey for Co. Limerick (1990), and most recently bilingual lists of the place-names of a number of individual Irish counties.

John O'Donovan became the first professor of Celtic in Queen's University, Belfast, and in the 20th century members of the Celtic Department continued research on the place-names of the North of Ireland. The Ulster Place-Name Society was founded by the then head of department, Seán Mac Airt, in 1952 (Arthurs 1955–6, 80–82). Its primary aims were, (a) to undertake a survey of Ulster place-names; and (b) to issue periodically to members a bulletin devoted to aspects of place-name study, and ultimately to publish a series of volumes embodying the results of the survey. Several members undertook to do research on particular areas, much of which remains unpublished (Deirdre Flanagan on Lecale, and Dean Bernard Mooney on the names of the Diocese of Dromore).

The primary objective of the Ulster Place-Name Society was partly realized in 1987, when the Department of Celtic was commissioned by the Department of the Environment for Northern Ireland to do research into, "the origin of all names of settlements and physical features appearing on the 1:50,000 scale map; to indicate their meaning and to note any historical or other relevant information". In 1990, under the Central Community Relations Unit, the brief of the scheme was extended: to include work on all townlands in Northern Ireland, and to bring the work to publication. Although individual articles have already been published by various scholars, the *Place-Names of Northern Ireland* series is the first attempt in the North at a complete survey based on original research into the historical sources.

METHOD OF PLACE-NAME RESEARCH

The method employed by the Project has been to gather early spellings of each name from a variety of historical records written mainly in Irish, Latin and English, and arrange them in chronological order. These, then, with due weight being given to those which are demonstrably the oldest and most accurate, provide the evidence necessary for deducing the etymology. The same name may be applied to different places, sometimes only a few miles apart, and all forms are checked to ensure that they are entered under the correct modern name. For example, there are a number of references to a place called *Crosgare* in 17th-century sources, none of which refer to the well-known town of Crossgar in Co. Down, but to a townland also called Crossgar a few miles away near Dromara. Identification of forms is most readily facilitated by those sources which list adjoining lands together or give the name of the landholder. Indeed, one of the greatest difficulties in using Irish sources and some early Latin or English documents is the lack of context which would enable firm location of the place-names which occur in them.

Fieldwork is an essential complement of research on earlier written sources and maps. Sometimes unrecorded features in local topography or land use are well-known to local inhabitants. More frequently the pronunciation represented by the early written forms is obscure, and, especially in areas where there has been little movement of people, the traditional local pronunciation provides valuable evidence. The members of the research team visited their respective areas of study, to interview and tape-record informants recommended by local historical societies etc., but many others met in the course of fieldwork kindly offered their assistance and we record here our gratitude. The local pronunciations have been transcribed in phonetic script and these are given at the end of each list of historical forms. The tapes themselves will become archive material for the future. The transcription used is based on the principles of the International Phonetic Alphabet, modified in accordance with the general practice in descriptions of Irish and Scottish Gaelic dialects. The following diagram illustrates the relative position of each of the vowels used:

Front	Central	Back	
i		ʌu	High
ï			
e		o	High-mid
	ə	o̧	
ɛ		ɔ	Low-mid
a		ɑ	Low

Although this research was originally based on the names appearing on the 1:50,000 scale map, it soon became clear that many townland names, important in the past and still known to people today, were not given on the published version. Townlands form the smallest unit in the historical territorial administrative system of provinces, counties, baronies, parishes, and townlands. This system, which is that followed by the first Ordnance Survey of Ireland in its name-books, has been used in the organization of the books in this series. The names of all the relevant units are explained in Appendix B. Maps of the relevant barony and parish divisions within the county are supplied for the area covered in each book, to complement the published 1:50,000 series, and to make the historical context more accessible.

In the process of collecting and interpreting early forms for the *Place-Names of Northern Ireland* each researcher normally works on a group of parishes. Some books will, therefore, have joint authorship, and there may be differences of style and emphasis in the discussions within and between books. It seemed better to retain individuality rather than edit everything into committee prose. The suggested original Irish forms of the place-names were decided after group discussion with the general editor. In cases of joint authorship the members of the group responsible for the text of each book will be distinguished by name on the contents page.

All the information in this book is also preserved in a computer database in Queen's University Belfast. It is hoped that this database will eventually become a permanent resource for scholars searching for examples of a particular type of name or name element. Modern map information, lists of the townlands making up historical parishes and baronies, historical sources and modern Irish forms are all available on separate files which can be searched and interrelated. The database was designed by Eilís McDaniel, and the Project gratefully acknowledges her continuing interest.

LANGUAGE

Since Ulster was almost wholly Irish-speaking until the 17th century, most names of town-lands are of Irish-language origin. Some early names were also given Latin equivalents for use in ecclesiastical and secular documents but few probably ever gained wide currency. Norse influence on northern place-names is surprisingly slight and is largely confined to coastal features such as **Strangford Lough** and **Carlingford Lough.** The arrival of the Anglo-Normans in the 12th century brought with it a new phase of naming and its influence is particularly strong in east Ulster, most notably in the Barony of Ards. Here, the names of many of their settlements were formed from a compound of the owner's name plus the English word *tūn* "settlement" which gives us Modern English "town". Names such as **Hogstown** and **Audleystown** have retained their original form, but a considerable number, such as **Ballyphilip** and **Ballyrolly,** derive from forms that were later gaelicized.

By the time of the Plantation of Ulster in the 17th century the system of townland units and their names already existed and this was adopted more or less wholesale by the English and Scots-speaking settlers. These settlers have, nevertheless, left their mark on a sizeable body of names, particularly those of market towns, country houses, villages and farms which did not exist before the 17th century. What made the 17th-century Plantation different from the earlier ones was its extent and intensity, and it was the first time that the Irish language itself, rather than the Irish aristocracy, came under threat. The change from Irish to English speaking was a gradual one, and Irish survived into the 20th century in parts of Antrim and Tyrone. However, the language shift, assisted by an official policy that discriminated against Irish, eventually led to the anglicization of all names to the exclusion of Irish versions.

SPELLING AND PRONUNCIATION

Most of the historical sources used in this series were originally handwritten and this inevitably led to a considerable number of errors, both by contemporary copyists and by modern editors. Many of the documents, particularly grants, were copied time and again, while other sources sometimes only survive in late copies or published calendars. Mistakes could occur in any transcription but were particularly likely when the language or names being copied were unfamiliar. There is a long history of confusion in the Roman alphabet between letters of the type *i, u, n, m, w. U* and *n* are frequently confused, as are *m* and *w*. Where two or more of these letters occur together, the minims (vertical strokes) may be read in different combinations: the simple pair *ui* may be read as *iu, ni, in, m,* or *w*. Another common error is the confusion of long *s* (ſ) and *f*. The name **Ballyhaft** (par. Newtownards, Dn) is frequently spelt in 17th-century sources with *s* instead of *f* and the modern form of the name may result from confusion of the written forms. In early sources, horizontal strokes (suspension strokes) could be written over a vowel as shorthand for a following *n* or *m*, but they were easily overlooked by scribes or editors. Spellings such as *Ballemulle* for **Ballymullan** (par. Bangor, Dn) may be explained in this way.

As well as taking account of spelling mistakes, there is sometimes difficulty in interpreting just what the spellings were intended to represent. For example, *gh*, which is usually silent in modern English dialects (e.g. night, fought) often retained its original value in the 17th century and was pronounced like the *ch* in Scots *loch* and *nicht*. Thus, *gh* was the obvious way to represent the Irish sound in words like *mullach* "summit", although both the English and Irish sounds were being weakened to [h] in certain positions at the time.

In Irish the spelling *th* was originally pronounced as in modern English *thick*, but in the 13th century it came to be pronounced [h]. The original Irish sound was anglicized as *th* or as *gh* at different periods, but where the older form of the spelling has survived the sound *th* has often been restored by English speakers. In names such as **Rathmullen** and **Rathfriland,** where the initial element represents *ráth* "a ringfort", the *th* has almost invariably been re-established.

It is clear that some spellings used in place-names no longer signify what they did when first anglicized. The *-y* in the common elements "bally-" and "derry-" was selected to represent the final vowel in the corresponding Irish words *baile* and *doire* (the same sound as the *a* in "above") but this vowel is now usually pronounced as a short *ee* as in English words such as *happy, sorry.* In modern Ulster English, the vowel in words ending in *-ane,* such as *mane, crane,* is a diphthong, but in the 17th century it was pronounced as a long *a.* Thus, Irish *bán* "white" was usually represented in anglicized forms of names as *bane* as, for example, in the names **Kinbane** (Ant.) and **Carnbane** (Arm.) and this is frequently how the names are still pronounced locally.

SOURCES

The earliest representations of Irish place-names are found in a broad range of native material, written mostly in Irish although occasionally in Latin, beginning in the 7th or 8th centuries. The Irish annals, probably begun about 550 AD (Byrne 1973, 2) but preserved in manuscripts of much later date, contain a large number of place-names, particularly those of tribes, settlements, and topographical features. Tribal names and those of the areas they inhabited frequently appear among genealogical material, a substantial proportion of which is preserved in a 12th-century manuscript, Rawlinson B 502, but is probably much older. Ecclesiastical records include martyrologies or calendars giving saints' names, often with the names and locations of their churches. The Latin and Irish accounts of the life of St Patrick, which depict him travelling around Ireland founding a series of churches, contain the first lists of place-names which refer to places owned by a particular institution. Later Irish saints' lives also may list lands dedicated to the founder of a church. Medieval Irish narrative shows a great interest in places, often giving, for example, long lists of place-names passed through on journeys. Although many of these sources may date back to the 7th or 8th centuries, the copies we have often survive only in manuscripts of the 12th century and later, in which the spelling may have been modernized or later forms of names substituted.

The administrative records of the reformed Church of the 12th century are among the first to provide detailed grants of land. There are also records from the international Church, such as the papal taxation of 1302–06 (*Eccles. Tax.*). These records are more productive for place-name study, since the names are usually of the same type (either parishes or other land units owned by the church) and are usually geographically related, making them easier to identify with their modern counterparts. However, the place-names in these documents are not usually spelled as they would be in Irish.

Paradoxically, perhaps, the 17th-century Plantation provides a massive amount of evidence for the place-names of Ulster. Grants to and holdings by individuals were written down by government officials in fiants, patents and inquisitions (in the latter case, the lands held by an individual at death). A series of detailed surveys, such as the *Escheated Counties* maps of 1609, the *Civil Survey* of 1654–6, and Sir William Petty's Down Survey (*DS (Par. Maps), Hib. Del.* and *Hib. Reg.*), together with the records of the confiscation and redistribution of land found in the *Books of Survey and Distribution* (*BSD*) and the *Act of Settlement* (*ASE*), meant that, for the first time, almost all the names of smaller land units such as townlands were recorded. Unfortunately the richness of these resources has been depleted by two serious fires among the Irish public records, one in 1711 and the other in the Four Courts in Dublin in 1922. As a result, some of the original maps, and the Civil Survey covering the north-eastern counties, are lost, and the fiants, patents, inquisitions and Act of Settlement now only exist in abridged form in calendars made by the Irish Record Commission in the early 19th century. These calendars were criticized even at the time of publication for their degree of précis and for inaccurate transcription of names.

After the 17th century, little surveying of an official nature was carried out in Ireland, despite the clearance of woods and bogs and reclamation of waste land. The best sources for the 18th century, therefore, are family papers, leases, wills and sometimes estate maps, most of which remain unpublished. It became clear in the early 19th century that much of the taxation system was based on records that were out of date. The Ordnance Survey came to Ireland in 1824 and began in 1825 to do the first large-scale (six inches to the mile) survey of the country. Most of the variant spellings which they collected in their name-books were of the 18th or early 19th centuries, though in some cases local landowners or churchmen allowed access to earlier records, and these again provide a convenient and invaluable source of place-names. Minor names were also recorded in the descriptive remarks of the namebooks, in the fuller treatment of local names (water features, ancient monuments, church sites and other landmarks) in the associated Ordnance Survey Memoirs (*OSM*) and in the Ordnance Survey Revision Name-Books (OSRNB), dating from the second half of the 19th century.

Early maps are an extremely valuable source, since they show the geographical relationship between names that is often crucial for identification purposes, and in many cases they are precise enough to locate lost townlands or to identify the older name of a townland. In parts of Ulster, maps by 16th-century surveyors may antedate texts recording place-names, thus providing the earliest attestation of the names in those areas.

However, maps have their own problems. Like other written texts they often copy from each other, borrowing names or outline or both. Inaccuracies are frequent, especially in the plotting of inland water features, whether due to seasonal flooding, or the lack of a vantage point for viewing the course of a river. Frequently the surveyor of the ground was not the person who drew or published the surviving map. The great continental and English map and atlas publishers, such as Ortelius, Mercator and Speed, all drew on earlier maps, and this custom undoubtedly led to the initiation and prolongation of errors of form and orthography. Sixteenth-century maps of Lough Neagh, for example, regularly show rivers entering the lake on the south between the Blackwater and the Bann where there are known to be none (Andrews 1978, plate 22). Unsurveyed territory was not always drawn to scale. Modern Co. Donegal, for example, is usually drawn too large on 16th-century maps, while Co. Derry is frequently shown too small. The *Escheated County* maps appear to have been partly drawn from verbal information and, in the map for the barony of Armagh, the draughtsman has produced a mirror image reversing east and west (Andrews 1974, 152).

William Petty's Down Survey provided the standard map of Ireland for the 17th century. In the 18th and early 19th centuries various individuals produced local county maps: Roque (1760) Co. Armagh; Lendrick (1780) Co. Antrim; Sampson (1814) Co. Derry; Sloane, Harris, Kennedy and Williamson (1739–1810) Co. Down; Knox and McCrea (1813) Co. Tyrone. These were consulted for the place-names on their own maps by the Ordnance Survey in the 1830s. Apart from published maps, a number of manuscript maps, some anonymous, others the original work of the 16th-century surveyors Lythe and Jobson, still exist. Richard Bartlett and Thomas Raven left important manuscript maps of Ulster from the early 17th century.

HOW TO USE THIS SERIES

Throughout the series, the editors have tried to adhere to the traditional territorial and administrative divisions used in Ireland, but this has not always proved possible. The convenient unit on which to base both research and publication has been the civil parish and all townland names and minor names are discussed under the relevant parish, regardless of whether they are in the same barony or county. Each book normally deals with the parishes in one or more barony, but where the barony is too large they are split into different books, some of which may contain material from geographically adjacent baronies. Every effort has been made to accommodate the historical system in a series of volumes of regular size. Each parish, barony and county is prefaced by an introduction which sets forth its location and history, and discusses some of the sources from which the older spellings of names have been extracted.

Within each parish, townland and other names are arranged in alphabetical order in separate sections following a discussion of the parish name. The first section deals with townland names. The second section deals with names of towns, villages, hills and water features which appear on the OS 1:50,000 map, but which are not classified as townlands. This section may also include a few names of historical importance which do not appear on the map but which may be of interest to the reader. Lesser names on the 1:50,000 are only treated if relevant material has been forthcoming. An index of all the names discussed in each book is given at the back of the relevant volume.

Each name to be discussed is given in bold print on the left-hand side of the page. Bold print is also used elsewhere in the text to cross-refer the reader to another name discussed in the series. The four-figure grid-reference given under each place-name should enable it to be located on modern Ordnance Survey maps.

Beneath the map name[1] and its grid reference, all the pre-1700 spellings that have been found are listed, together with their source and date, followed by a selection of post-1700 forms. Early Irish-language forms are placed above anglicized or latinized spellings because of their importance in establishing the origin of the name. Irish forms suggested by 19th- and 20th-century scholars are listed below the historical spellings. Irish-language forms collected by O'Donovan in the last century, when Irish was still spoken in many parts of the North, require careful assessment. Some may be traditional, but there are many cases where the suggestion made by the local informant is contradicted by the earlier spellings, and it is clear that sometimes informants merely analysed the current form of the name. The current local pronunciation as collected by the editors appears below these Irish forms in phonetic script.

Spellings of names are cited exactly as they occur in the sources. Manuscript contractions have been expanded within square brackets, e.g. [ar]. Square brackets are also used to indicate other editorial readings: […] indicates three letters in the name which could not be read, while a question mark in front of one or more letters enclosed in square brackets, e.g. [?agh], denotes obscure letters. A question mark in round brackets before a spelling indicates a form which cannot be safely identified as the name under discussion.

The dates of all historical spellings collected are given in the right-hand column, followed, where necessary, by c when the date is approximate. Here, we have departed from the normal practice, employed elsewhere in the books, because the database would otherwise have been unable to sort these dates in numeric order. In Latin and English sources a *circa* date usually indicates an uncertainty of a year or two. Irish language sources, however, rarely have exact dates and *circa* here represents a much longer time-span, perhaps of one or two centuries where the dating is based purely on the language of a text. Where no date has been established for a text, forms from that text are given the date of the earliest MS in which they appear. Following normal practice, dates in the Irish annals are given as in the source, although this may give certain spellings an appearance of antiquity which they do not deserve. The Annals of the Four Masters, for example, were compiled in the early 17th century using earlier material, and many of the names in the text were modernized by the compilers. Moreover, annals were written later for dates before the mid-6th-century, and the names, let alone the spellings, may not be that old. Another difficulty with dates concerns English administrative sources. The civil year in England and Ireland began on March 25th (Lady Day) until the year 1752, when the calendar was brought into line with changes made in the rest of Europe in 1582. Thus, the date of any document written between 1st of January and 24th of March inclusive has had to be adjusted to reconcile it with the current system by adding a year.

The original or most likely original Irish form of a name, where one is known to have existed, is given in italics on the top line to the right of the current spelling, with an English translation below. This includes Norse, Anglo-Norman and English names for which a Gaelic form once existed, as well as those of purely Irish origin. *Loch Cairlinn,* for example, was used by Irish-speakers for *Carlingford Lough* and this, rather than the original Norse, is printed on the top line. Although the name may have originally been coined at an early period of the language, standard modern Irish orthography is employed throughout, except in rare cases where this may obscure the meaning or origin of the name. The rules of modern Irish grammar are usually followed when not contradicted by the historical evidence. Where some doubt concerning the origin or form of a name may exist, or where alternatives may seem equally likely, plausible suggestions made by previous authorities, particularly the *OSNB* informants, are given preference and are printed at the top of the relevant entry. Nevertheless, where there is firm evidence of an origin other than that proposed by earlier scholars, the form suggested by our own research is given prominence.

Names for which no Irish original is proposed are described according to their appearance, that is, English, Scots etc. The form and meaning is usually obvious, and there is no evidence that they replace or translate an original Irish name. Names which are composed of two elements, one originally Irish and the other English or Scots, are described as hybrid forms. An important exception to this rule is names of townlands which are compounded from a name derived from Irish and an English word such as "upper", "east" etc. In these cases, the original Irish elements are given on the right-hand side but the later English appendage is not translated.

In the discussion of each name, difficulties have not been ignored but the basic consideration has been to give a clear and readable explanation of the probable origin of the name, and its relationship to the place. Other relevant information, on the language of the name, on other similar names, on historical events, on past owners or inhabitants, on physical changes or local place-name legends, may also be included, to set the name more fully in context.

The townland maps which appear at the beginning of each parish show the layout of all the townlands in that parish. They are based on printouts from the Ordnance Survey's digitized version of the 1:50,000 map.

The rules of Irish grammar as they relate to place-names are discussed in Appendix A, and the historical system of land divisions in Ulster is described in Appendix B. The bibliography separates primary sources and secondary works (the latter being referred to by author and date of publication). This is followed by a glossary of technical terms used in this series. The place-name index, as well as providing page references, gives the 1:50,000 sheet numbers for all names on the published map, and sheet numbers for the 1:10,000 series and the earlier 6-inch county series for townland names. The index of Irish forms gives a semi-phonetic pronunciation for all names for which an Irish form has been postulated.

SUGGESTIONS FOR FURTHER INVESTIGATION

A work like this on individual names cannot give a clear picture of any area at a particular time in the past. Any source in the bibliography could be used, in conjunction with townland or other maps, to plot the references to a particular locality at that date, or to lands with a particular owner. Also the Public Record Office of Northern Ireland holds a considerable amount of unpublished material from the eighteenth century and later, which awaits investigation for information on place-names arising at that period.

Although fieldwork forms an integral part of place-name research, it is difficult for a library researcher to acquire the familiarity with an area that the local inhabitants have. Local people can walk the bounds of their townlands, or compare boundary features with those of the early 6-inch maps. Written or tape-recorded collections of local names (especially those of smaller features such as fields, rocks, streams, houses, bridges, etc.), where exactly they are to be found, how written and pronounced, and any stories about them or the people who lived there, would be a valuable resource for the future. The Place-Name Project will be happy to talk to anyone engaged on a venture of this kind.

Footnote

(1) On the OS maps apostrophes are sometimes omitted, e.g. Mahulas Well, Deers Meadow. In this series they have been inserted when there is evidence to indicate whether the possessive is singular or plural, e.g. Mahula's Well, Deers' Meadow.

Kay Muhr
Senior Research Fellow

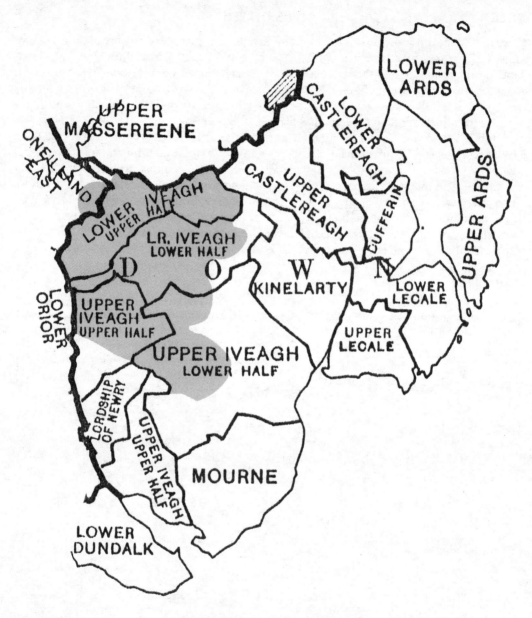

Map of Baronies in Co. Down

Ards Lower
Ards Upper
Castlereagh Lower
Castlereagh Upper
Dufferin
Iveagh Lower, Lower Half
Iveagh Lower, Upper Half
Iveagh Upper, Lower Half
Iveagh Upper, Upper Half
Kinelarty
Lecale Lower

Lecale Upper
Lordship of Newry
Mourne

Districts treated at one time as being in Co. Down are shown around the left-half margin of the map. The area described in this volume, all in the old barony of Iveagh (and comprising parts of Iveagh Lower, Lower and Upper Half, and of Iveagh Upper, Lower and Upper Half), has been shaded to highlight its position.

INTRODUCTION TO COUNTY DOWN

The division of Ireland into counties was effected under English rule and is the most recent tier in the territorial administrative system of province, county, barony, parish and townland. The counties of Ulster as they now stand were established in the early 17th century, but were built up out of pre-existing smaller districts, some of which were preserved as baronies within the county. County Down in bounded by the sea to the south, east and north-east, but, although some of its inland boundary markers are notable geographical features, the area they delimit has partly been decided by historical events.

The *Ulaid* were once the most powerful tribal group in the north of Ireland and it is from them that the province of Ulster derives its name (Flanagan D. 1978(d)). However, in the 4th and 5th centuries they were driven eastwards into the modern counties of Antrim and Down under pressure from the *Uí Néill* and the *Airgialla*. In the south the new boundary between the Ulaid and the Airgialla may have been marked by the erection of the Danes' Cast along the marshes between the northern limit of the Newry River and the ford of the Bann at Banbridge. Of the chief Ulaid tribes, *Uí Echach Coba* were located along this borderland and *Dál nAraide* east of Lough Neagh and the lower Bann. A third tribe, *Dál Fiatach*, the "true Ulaid", settled in Lecale and in the vicinity of Strangford Lough. Their capital at *Dún dá Lethglas* (modern Downpatrick) was to become an important ecclesiastical centre. Other less important kingdoms within the reduced Ulster were the *Conaille Muirthemne* in north Louth (the Cooley peninsula) and *Dál Riata* in the Glens of Antrim.

From the 6th to 10th centuries the kingship of the Ulaid was shared by Dál Fiatach, Dál nAraide and Uí Echach Coba, but in the 8th century Dál Fiatach extended their influence northward over the area east of Lough Neagh. After the Anglo-Norman invasion the whole area east of the Upper and Lower Bann became the feudal Earldom of Ulster. However, the influence of the local Dál Fiatach church was increased in 1186 when the Norman John de Courcy transferred the relics of three of the greatest Irish saints, Patrick, Brigid and Columcille, to Downpatrick cathedral. The diocese of Down, the boundaries of which were settled in the 12th century, was centred on this famous church and stretched as far north as the contemporary territorial limits of Dál Fiatach, though limited on the west by the Uí Echach diocese of Dromore. Through their ruling family of *Mac Duinnshléibhe* (MacDonlevy) Dál Fiatach retained some power as "king of the Irish of Ulidia" (*rex Hibernicorum Ulidiae*) until the late 13th century, though after their extinction the Gaelic title of *rí Ulad*, or "king of Ulster" (the province of the Ulaid), was claimed by the expanding *Cenél nEógain* to the west (Byrne 1973, 128–9).

Under the feudal Earldom of Ulster, English shire government was established in the territory of the Ulaid. It was divided into various native and other areas: the "bailiwicks of Antrim, Carrickfergus, *Art, Blathewyc, Ladcathel*" in 1226, the "counties of *Cragfergus,* Antrim, *Blathewyc, Dun* and *Coulrath*" in 1333 (*Inq. Earldom Ulster* i 31, ii 136, 141, iii 60, 63, iv 127). In 1549 the area was described as "the county of Ulster, that is to say the baronies of the *Grenecastle, Dondalk, Lacayll, Arde, Differens, Gallagh, Bentry, Kroghfergous, Maulyn, Twscard* and *Glyns*" (*Cal. Carew MSS* 1515–74, 223–4). In 1571 a commission was set up "to survey the countries of Lecale, the *Duffrens, M'Carton's country, Slaighte M'Oneiles* country, *Kilvarlyn, Evaghe, M'Ghenes'* country, *Morne,* the lands of the *Nury,* and *O'Handlone's* country, and to form them into one county, or to join them to any neighbouring counties or baronies" (*Fiants Eliz.* §1736). This led to the separation from Antrim of the modern county of Down, containing the baronies of Lecale, Dufferin, Kinelarty (McCartan's country), Castlereagh (part of the Clandeboy O'Neill's country), Iveagh (Kilwarlin and Magennis' country), Mourne and Newry. However *O'Handlone's country* became part of Co. Armagh.

The county name, appearing as *Dun* in 1333, derives like that of the diocese from the Dál Fiatach capital *Dún dá Lethglas*. In the Norman and post-Norman period, Downpatrick usually appears in Latin and English documentation as *Dunum, Dun* or *Down(e)*, and in Irish writing of the medieval period the common form is *Dún*, never *Dún Pádraig* (Flanagan D. 1971, 89). In the *Ordnance Survey Memoirs* it is noted that Downpatrick was "more commonly called by the country people Down", and "even today *Down* rather than *Downpatrick* is the local usage" (*ibid.*). Thus, when the modern county was established at the end of the 16th century, Down was still the name of the shire town. The form *Downpatrick*, which had no currency before the early 17th century, became more popular from 1617 onwards, perhaps due to the creation in that year of the Manor of Downpatrick (*ibid.*). However it never influenced the county name.

The county boundaries were not settled all at once. Jobson's set of Ulster maps (c. 1590) and Norden's map of Ireland (1610) show the names and bounds of the three counties of Antrim, Down and Armagh. Both cartographers still include in Down the Cooley peninsula (now in Co. Louth) and also Loughgilly, O'Hanlon's chief seat in the barony of Orior (Co. Armagh). According to Jobson, Armagh extended across the outflow of the Bann into Lough Neagh to include Clanbrassil (later the Barony of Oneilland East) and Down included Killultagh on the east bank of Lough Neagh (later the barony of Upper Massareene in Co. Antrim). A document in the state papers of 1603 refers to "*Downe* county alias *Leycaile*" (which includes *Cowley* and *Omethe* in modern Co. Louth), but gives *Kilulto* as a separate "country" (*Cal. Carew MSS* 1601–3, 451). In 1605 Killultagh was annexed to Co. Antrim (*CSP Ire.* 1603–6, 321). In the same year an inquisition on Clandeboy stated that the most noted boundary between the parts of it called Killultagh and Upper Clandeboy (later Castlereagh) was the river Lagan (*Inq. Ult. (Down)* §2 Jac. I), and the Lagan remains the boundary between Cos Antrim and Down to this day.

The land east of the Upper Bann on the shore of Lough Neagh, known as Clanbrassil, was traditionally Uí Echach Coba or Magennis territory. In 1605 *Clanbrassilagh* "which before lay doubtful between it and the county of Down" was formally annexed to the new county of *Ardmaghe* (*CSP Ire.* 1603–6, 318), becoming eventually the barony of Oneilland East. A dispute arose between John Brownlow and Capt. Edward Trevor in 1612 concerning the ownership of six townlands in Kilmore, a district between Clanbrassil and Killultagh. Brownlow had been granted the area as lying in Co. Armagh while Trevor had been granted exactly the same lands as lying in Co. Down (*Ulst. Plant. Paps.* 266, §60). The plantation commissioners found that the land was in Co. Armagh and awarded it to Brownlow, compensating Trevor with other lands. Sir Arthur Magennis then claimed the area from Brownlow as part of his own property in Co. Down, but the commissioners refused to recompense him unless he could prove title, and the lands remained in Brownlow's possession (*ibid.* 269, §61). Modern Co. Down has retained one townland still called Kilmore, a strip of land connecting it with Lough Neagh, although Kilmore is part of the civil parish of Shankill, all the rest of which is in Co. Armagh. The artificiality of the county boundary in this area continued to cause problems: Sir William Petty in his barony and county maps (*Hib. Reg.* c. 1657; *Hib. Del.* c. 1672) thought that the Bann formed the northern boundary between Cos Down and Armagh, and placed the Armagh parishes of Seagoe and Shankill to the west of the river instead of to the east. The diocese of Dromore, however, reflects the earlier boundary between Uí Echach Coba and Airgialla, in that it includes Seagoe and Shankill and follows the river Bann all the way to Lough Neagh (see **Iveagh**).

The date at which the southern border of Co. Down was settled is difficult to ascertain from the sources. The ancient territory of the Ulaid had stretched as far south as the river Boyne, and even after the Ulaid were driven east by the Uí Néill the Conaille tribe of north

Louth remained part of the Ulaid confederation. The feudal Earldom of Ulster covered the same area, so that in 1549 the "county of Ulster" still extended from the north Antrim coast to Dundalk (*Cal. Carew MSS* 1515–74, 223–4, quoted above). In 1552 the royal grant of Newry, Mourne, Carlingford, Omeath and Cooley to Sir Nicholas Bagenal preserves the cohesion of the older territory, but already the first two areas were said to be in the county of Down or in *Ullestere*, and the others in the county of Louth (*CPR Ed. vi*, 387–90). The latest documentary reference to Cooley being part of Co. Down is in the Carew MSS for 1603, though it is shown on Jobson's and Norden's maps (all quoted above). However, in an earlier document in the Carew collection (1596) the northern limit of Co. Louth in the English Pale is given as "the *fues* and o'hanlon's country" (i.e. Co. Armagh, as at present) (Falkiner 1904, 141). By the time of the Plantation this is also the border of the re-established province of Ulster.

The barony of Iveagh in AD 1603 from Richard Bartlett's map *A generalle description of Vlster*; another version of the cover map (*Bartlett Maps (Esch. Co. maps)* 1,2).

THE BARONY OF IVEAGH

Iveagh was the largest barony in Co. Down, stretching from Lough Neagh to Rosstrevor, and from Poyntzpass to Newcastle. It was divided in the early 17th century into Lower (northern) and Upper (southern) Iveagh by a line running east to west between Dromara and Banbridge. Since then each half-barony has also been divided into Upper and Lower halves, the northern part by another roughly east to west line, dividing Hillsborough from Dromore; the southern part by a line roughly running north to south, curving round Knock Iveagh and passing through Katesbridge and Rathfriland. Thus Iveagh became four baronies (see the barony map of Co. Down facing the county introduction, p.xviii). Most of the parishes are in one barony only, but Aghaderg, Garvaghy and Seapatrick are in both Upper and Lower Iveagh.

Iveagh has had to be also divided up in the books of the place-name series. The parishes of Clonallan, Donaghmore, Drumgath and Kilbroney are in volume i, Clonduff and Kilcoo in volume iii (*PNI*). The present book contains eleven parishes in the north and west of Co. Down. Because the initial division of Iveagh cut across some parishes, the order of parishes in this volume follows alphabetical order within Iveagh as a whole, rather than its later divisions. The eastern parishes of Hillsborough, Dromara, Drumgooland and Maghera, with Annahilt, Blaris, Magheradrool and Kilmegan partly in Iveagh, will be dealt with later in the series.

The bounds of Iveagh are largely determined by physical features. To the west lies the Newry River, extending northwards along the low-lying and boggy valley, in Irish called *Gleann Rí*, through which the Newry Canal now runs. Part of this boundary was marked in ancient times by an earthwork now known as the **Danes' Cast** (*PNI* i 40–2, 109–11). The northern limit followed the river Lagan, as far east as its tributary now called the Ravernet River, which forms the north-eastern boundary of the barony. Slieve Croob is also on the eastern boundary, and south of it the Ballybunion River. Iveagh reaches the sea at Newcastle and Rosstrevor, with the barony of Mourne in between, the dividing line marked by some of the western peaks, such as Slieve Bearnagh, Slieve Meelmore, Slieve Muck, Pigeon Rock Mountain and Shanlieve (*PNI* iii). The Lordship of Newry forms an independent barony dividing the upper part of Upper Iveagh into two distinct halves (see the barony map, xviii). The bounds of Iveagh were described in 1584 (*Fiants Eliz.* §4327), and again in the Civil Survey of 1654–6 where the division between Upper and Lower Iveagh is outlined in detail (*Civ. Surv.* x §§72,73).

Iveagh	*Uíbh Eachach*	
	"descendants of Echu"	
1. la hUibh Eachdach, Magh Roth	AFM i 38 (prehist.)	3549
2. la hUibh Eachdach	AFM i 294	689
3. (?)hin Druim moccu Echach	Muirchú (Bieler) 102 §I 23	700c
4. nepotes Ecach	AU (Mac Airt) 214	761
5. H. Echoch Cobho	AU (Mac Airt) 228	776
6. nepotes Echdach Cobho	AU (Mac Airt) 256	801
7. la Hu Echach	AU (Mac Airt) 300	842
8. dUibh Corbmaic Ua nEathach Cobha	AFM ii 628	931
9. Domhnall mac Aenghusa tighearna Ua nEathach	AFM ii 676	956
10. Aodh Ua hAitidhe rí Ua nEathach Cobha	AFM ii 688	965

11. Domhnall H. hAitidh rí H. nEchach	AU (Mac Airt) 416	981
12. Indred H. nEchach	AU (Mac Airt) 428	999
13. Gairbith rí H. nEchdach	AU (Mac Airt) 432	1004
14. Artan rioghdhamhna Ua nEathach	AFM ii 754	1004
15. Hu Echach, for Ultu 7	AU (Mac Airt) 434	1005
16. Echmilid H. Atidh rí H. nEchach	AU (Mac Airt) 436	1005
17. Muirchertach m. Artan ridomna H. nEchoch	AU (Mac Airt) 444	1013
18. (?)Ruaidhri Ua hAillelláin tigherna Ua nEathach	AFM ii 794	1019
19. Mac Concuailnge ri .h. nEachach	AU (Mac Airt) 466	1028
20. i nHuib Echach	AU (Mac Airt) 468	1031
21. in Huibh Eachach Ulad	AU (Mac Airt) 478	1041
22. Aiteidh H. hAiteidh ri H. nEchach Ulad	AU (Mac Airt) 482	1046
23. ria nUib Eachach	AU (Mac Airt) 490	1054
24. Echmhiledh H. Aiteidh rí H. nEchach	AU (Mac Airt) 502	1065
25. for Uib Echach	AU (Mac Airt) 520	1086
26. i nHu Echach Ulad	AIF 252	1096
27. hUa Echach, itir Ulto 7	TBC (Rec. I) 1.4154	1100c
28. d'Uib Echcach Ullad	AIF 256	1101
29. ridomna H. nEachach	AU (Mac Airt) 538	1102
30. hui Eachach	AU (Mac Airt) 554	1113
31. maidm Cinn Daire for Uibh Echach Uladh	AU (Mac Airt) 562	1118
32. Cluain Dallain i nDál Echach i fail Chuain Snama Ech	CSH 120,20	1125c
33. Hūi Echdach (> Conall)	CGH 137 140b23	1125c
34. de forslointib Hūa nEchach	CGH 157,15	1125c
35. Hūi Echach Ulad (Clann Conaill Cernaich)	CGH 157,46	1125c
36. Genelach hūa nEchach	CGH 161bc47	1125c
37. Eochu Coba a quo Hūi Echach Coba	CGH 162a43	1125c
38. condrecat Hūi Echach & Dál nAraide	CGH 162a56	1125c
39. Genelach hūa nEchach Coba	CGH 162b13	1125c
40. i Mag Cobha. . . . giallu H. nEchach	AU (Mac Airt) 574	1128
41. la hUíb Echach Cláir Coba	Clann Ollaman 64 §20	1160c
42. la cloinn Aedha do Uibh Eachdach Uladh	AFM iii 6	1173
43. Genélach Cloindi Echach m. Conla	Descendants Ir xiv 115	1200c
44. Tomas mac Airten ri h. nEchach Ulad	A. Conn. 300	1347
45. Ó nEachach Cobha, Uirríogha	Topog. Poems 1.383	1350c
46. Flaith ar Cloinn uasail Aedha/Mág Aonghusa	Topog. Poems 1.391	1350c

47. Mo Lipa i n-Uib Echach Ulad	Fél. Óeng. Feb 18 p76n	1400c
48. Adam mac Gilli Mure ri h. nEchach	A. Conn. 400	1407
49. Aed mac Airtt Meg Aengusa ri h. nEchach	A. Conn. 438	1418
50. Rosa Mag Aengusa adbar rig h. nEchach	A. Conn. 474	1434
51. a crich Meg Aengusa	A. Conn. 486	1444
52. i n-Uaib Echach Ulad, ó Laind Ronain Fhind	Fél. Óeng. May 22 p134n	1453
53. ar Íbh Eachach Uladh, Ceart Í Néill	LCABuidhe 42 §3 (Ceart UN)	1500c
54. ar Íbh Eachach fhéin .i. ar MhagAonghusa	LCABuidhe 42 §3 (Ceart UN)	1500c
55. Lámh dhearg Éireann Uíbh Eachach	RIA Cat. 862 (poem)	1595c
56. Teallach féile Uíb Echach	Teallach Uí Echach 92	1628
57. muinter . . . Íbh Eathach	Cín Lae Ó M. 19 lch14, 29, 43	1645c
58. tigherna Íbh Eathach	Cín Lae Ó M. 6 lch2, 10 lch6	1645c
59. E. Cobha ó ráitear Iath Eathach (Uladh)	TCD Gens 142/7 §§259,280	1666c
60. Art (d.1629) . . . tighearna Íath Eathach Cobha	TCD Gens 146a §276	1666c
61. for Uí Eachach Uladh	LCABuidhe 1	1680c
62. tiarna Uíbh Éathach	Mac Cumhaigh (b) 81 poem 1.53	1760c
63. clanna Aonghusa as tír Uíbh Éathach	Mac Cumhaigh (b) 124 poem 21.190	1769c
64. Oneac, regis	Newry Char. (Flanagan)	1157c
65. Oneach (x2)	Newry Char. (Flanagan)	1157c
66. Claneda Oneachulad, Magnus Magangasa dux	Newry Char. (Flanagan)	1157c
67. Oueach (x2)	Newry Char. (Mon. Ang.) 1133–4	1157c
68. Claneda Oveachulad	Newry Char. (Mon. Ang.) 1134	1157c
69. omnes ecclesias . . . Uuech	Pontif. Hib. i 127 §59	1204
70. Oveagh (Mackouecan)	Pipe Roll John 58	1211c
71. Oueh	Cartae Dun. 422 §10	1227c
72. Oweagh	Reg. Swayne 103	1500c
73. McGynnose his countrye . . . Iveache wherein the Myorie	Knox Hist. 298 (Ed VI ms)	1552
74. Yueage, Magynows	Mercator's Ire.	1564
75. McGenis, Magenes	Goghe's Map	1567
76. Iviegh, MacGennis	Nowel's Ire. (1)	1570c
77. Evaghe, McGhenes' country	Fiants Eliz. §1736	1571
78. Yueage	Ortelius Map	1573
79. whole country of Eveaghe	Fiants Eliz. §2565	1575
80. Mac Gynis lande called Iveache	S–E Ulster Map	1580c
81. Yuaugh	Ulster Map [1580c]	1580c
82. whole country of Iveaghe	Fiants Eliz. §4218	1583
83. entire country & territory of Iveaghe alias the country of Magnisse	Fiants Eliz. §4327	1584

84. Iveagh (x2)	Fiants Eliz. §4327	1584
85. in Eveaghe, Co. Down	Fiants Eliz. §4788	1585
86. Evagh othw Maginis countrey	Bagenal's Descr. Ulst. 151	1586
87. his country of Iveagh	Fiants Eliz. §5044	1587
88. Magenes	Dartmouth Map 6	1590
89. Magenis, Euaghe	Jobson's Ulster (TCD) 17	1590
90. in Eveagh alias McGennyes country	Fiants Eliz. §5767	1592
91. Evagh	Mercator's Ire.	1595
92. Evaugh	Mercator's Ulst.	1595
93. McGennes, Euagh	Boazio's Map (BM)	1599
94. Evaghe, McGenes	Bartlett Map (BM)	1600
95. Evaghe McGenis his Contrie	Bartlett Map (TCD)	1601
96. of Eveaghe	Fiants Eliz. §6724	1602
97. Evagh or McGenis his Contrye	Bartlett (Esch. Co. Maps) 1	1603
98. Evaghe or McGenis his contrie	Bartlett (Esch. Co. Maps) 2	1603
99. Evagh mGenis his contrye, the ancyent name Maghra yllie	Bartlett (Esch. Co. Maps) 2	1603
100. Evaugh	CPR Jas I 38b	1604
101. in Evagh al. Magenis's countrie	Inq. Ult. (Down) §2 Jac. I col.e	1605
102. Evagh	CPR Jas I 87a et pass.	1605
103. Evagh othw. Maginisse country	CPR Jas I 146b	1609
104. Iveagh, county of	CPR Jas I 394ab	1609
105. Iveagh	CPR Jas I 395a,396a et pass.	1609
106. Iveagh, territory of	CPR Jas I 195ab	1610
107. Euagh or McGennys contry	Norden's Map	1610c
108. Iveagh barony/territory	CPR Jas I 190ab,191a	1611
109. Iveagh barony	CPR Jas I 194b	1611
110. Evagh/ Magenisse's country	CPR Jas I 197a	1611
111. Iveagh territory	CPR Jas I 235ab et pass.	1612
112. Evaagh	CPR Jas I 267b	1614
113. Iveagh, country of	CPR Jas I 304b 1623	
114. in Evagh, Kilowen in	Inq. Ult. (Dn) §15 Jac. I col. c	1624c
115. de Iveagh	Inq. Ult. (Dn) §13 Car. I et pass	1629
116. de Iveagh	Inq. Ult. (Arm.) §36 Car. I et p.	1639
117. Iveagh, Clountagh in	Civ. Surv. x §73, see below	1655c
118. Iveach (Iveagh, map)	Harris Hist. 79 1744	
119. Uíbh Eadhach	OSNB Inf. E18.13	1834c
120. Uí Eathach "race of Eochy" a tribe name	J O'D (OSNB) E18.13	1834c
121. 'aï've:	Local pronunciation	1995

Lower Iveagh

1. la hUa nAidith & la hiochtar Ua nEchdach	AFM ii 796	1020
2. infra territor' de Iveaghe	Inq. Ult. (Down) §14 Car. I	1630
3. (the) Lower Iveagh	Civ. Surv. x §§72–3	1655c
4. Lower Eveagh	Civ. Surv. x §§70,72	1655c
5. barony of lower Iveagh	Inq. Ult. (Down) §1 Interregnum	1658

6. Lower Evagh Barony	Census 78	1659c
7. Lower Evagh Bar.	BSD 68ff.	1661
8. Lower Euagh Bar.	BSD 81f.	1661
9. Lower Evagh	Hib. Del. Down	1672c
10. Upper & Lower Evagh	Lamb Maps	1690c
11. Lower Iveach	Harris Hist. 84	1744
12. Lower Iveagh	Wm. Map (OSNB) E8.59	1810

Upper Iveagh

1. Upper Iveagh	Civ. Surv. x §§70,72–3	1655c
2. (the) Upper Iveagh	Civ. Surv. §73	1655c
3. Iveagh, Mountaines of	Inq. Down (Reeves1) 95	1657
4. Upper Eveagh, The Barony of	Hib. Reg. Up. Iveagh	1657c
5. upper barrony of Iveagh	Inq. Ult. (Down) §1 Interregnum	1658
6. Upper Iveagh Barony	Census 72	1659c
7. Upper Evagh Bar.	BSD 104ff.	1661
8. Upper Evagh	Hib. Del. Down	1672c
9. Upper Iveach	Harris Hist. 78	1744

The name Iveagh derives from *Uíb Echach*, later spelled *Uíbh/Íbh Eachach/ Eathach* (forms 55,62), the dative or locative form of the tribal name *Uí Echach* "grandsons/descendants of *Echu*". *Ua* or *Ó* "grandson", plural *Uí*, as used in surnames, is often prefixed by *h* in the early spellings, some of which show the Old Irish accusative plural *Uu* (forms 7,15). The use of dative *Uíbh* for all grammatical cases of this name can be traced in Irish from about AD 1600 (forms 55–8,62–3,119). In early historical times Uí Echach were one of the tribes of the confederation of the *Ulaid* "Ulstermen", after whom the province of Ulster is named (Flanagan 1978(d)). Uí Echach shared the kingship of east Ulster with *Dál Fiatach*, the historic *Ulaid*, and with *Dál nAraide* of south Antrim, who like Uí Echach belonged to the ethnic group called *Cruthin*. The large number of Irish references reflect the historical importance of Uí Echach. After 1610 only a selection is given of the many references to the anglicized name Iveagh, in order to demonstrate its use as a territorial name and its 17th–century subdivision into Lower and Upper Iveagh.

The *Uí Echach* were known more fully as *Uí Echach Coba* to distinguish them from other tribes called Uí Echach, to the east in the Ards peninsula (*Uí Echach Arda*), and to the west in Airgialla. The epithet *Coba* was taken from the area they inhabited, the plain to the east of the Danes' Cast, known in Irish literature at first as *Cuib* (*TBC Rec. I* ll.1488,1524,1534, 4153). Kings of Iveagh in the 8th and 9th centuries are usually called simply *rex Coba* "king of *Cuib*" in the annals (*AU* 735,739,776,853,882) and a king of *Cuib/Coba* appears in the Book of Rights, where the line *ríg Coba chuib*, translated "of the king of victorious Mag Coba", indicates confusion as to the correct form of the place-name (*Lebor na Cert* 86,90). Later it was called *Mag Coba, Má Cobha* "the plain of *Cuib*" or "of *Cobha*", understood as the name of the legendary slave who cleared it (*LL L.Gabála* i l.1677; *L. Gabála* v 62 §424, 84 §445; *Met. Dinds* 122–5). There is a rare word *cob* meaning "victory" in early Irish poetry, while some other Irish texts explained *cuib* as "hound" (*DIL* sv.).

Early sources indicate that *Cuib* included Sheeptown north of Newry (*TBC Rec. I* l.1524; *PNI* i 37, 43). A reference to Dromore's patron saint Colmán being in *Cuib*, (*L.Lec.* 125v b9) shows that the area stretched as far north as Dromore, and the plain called *Magh Rath* (Moira) was also located in *Cuib* (*LL (L.Gabála)* l.1916; *L. Gabála* v 430, poem xci l.3139).

In the medieval period the territorial name *Mag Coba* also continued in use. Donaghmore parish to the north of Newry was called *Domhnach Mór Maighe Cobha* (*PNI* i 85). There are references to the building and rebuilding of an Anglo-Norman castle at *Má Cobha* or *Moycove*, most likely **Ballyroney** followed by **Seafin** castles close to each other on the Bann (*ASCD* 198,219; Lawlor 1938, 88).

The tribal name *Uí Echach* or *Uí Echach Cobha* (Iveagh 5,6,8,10, 37,39,41) only came into regular use after the Dál Fiatach tribe of Uí Echach in the Ards peninsula, sometimes called Uí Echach Uladh, were eclipsed in the 9th century. Since *Druim Moccu Echach*, "*Droim*/ridge of the descendants of Echu", in *Muirchú*'s Life of Patrick (Iveagh form 3) is said to be among the Ulaid, it must refer to Dál Fiatach rather than **Dromore** in Iveagh. However, after the 9th century *Uí Echach Uladh* "Uí Echach of the Ulaid" (Iveagh forms 21,22,26,28,31,35,42,44,47,53,61) also came to mean Uí Echach in (east) Ulster, i.e. Iveagh, rather than Uí Echach in the Ards.

Who was Echu? The personal names *Echu* (gen. *Echach*) and *Echaid* (gen. Echdach) became confused very early, and it is difficult to separate the ancestor called *Echu Coba* "Echu of *Cuib*" from the 6th-century historical king *Echaid mac Condlae* of the main Dál nAraide line, who is treated as the ancestor of Uí Echach in some texts (*AU* 553 AD). This indicates the close historical relationship between Uí Echach and Dál nAraide. However the earlier *Echu Coba* has two places in the *Dál nAraide* genealogy, both associated with *Crond Ba Drui*, "Cronn who was a druid", a prehistoric king of Ulster, dated shortly before the Ulaid kings were expelled from Navan or *Eamhain Macha* (*CGH* 157.14; 162a35).

This uncertainty whether Echu Coba belongs to Ulster history or prehistory makes one suspect the influence of mythology, the story of that king Echu whose lands were drowned by **Lough Neagh** "Echu's lake", changing the topography and scattering the ancient population of Ulster (*Laud Gens* 307–9; *Aided Echach meic Maireda SG* i 233–7; *Met. Dinds* iv 62–9). *Uí Echach* or *Tuath Echach* of Airthir, south-west of Armagh city, also seem to have associated themselves with king Echu, in their territory beside the river Blackwater, "old Echu's stream", *sruth sein-Echach* (*Cath Aen. Macha* 154 §7, *Cath Leit. Ruibhe* 6 §3).

Other significant names in the legendary and early historic genealogy of Uí Echach Cobha are Conall (see **Clanconnell**), and Sárán, from whom the MacArtans of Kinelarty in Co. Down are later supposed to derive (*Céitinn* iv 25). This blood relationship is not corroborated in early sources, although the Macartans shared the lordship of the territory of Iveagh in the 14th century (44, cf 14, 17).

As with other early tribes Uí Echach subdivided into various septs. The dominant group from medieval times were the Magennises, whose surname derives from *Mac Óengusa* "son of Angus". The Uí Echach genealogies (*CGH* 161 bc 55) list an Óengus as son of *Aitíd mac Laigne*, who was king of Ulster until AD 898 (*AU (Mac Airt)* i 349), and Óengus son of Aitíd is given by Keating as the ancestor of the Magennis family (*Céitinn* iv 24,94). Both the older tribal name Iveagh and the contemporary chieftain's surname of Magennis were used to refer to the barony in 16th and early 17th-century maps and written sources (forms 51, 73–7, 80, 83, 86, 88–90, 93–5, 97–9, 101, 103, 107, 110).

The later Magennis chief seat was at **Rathfriland**, on the border of the parishes of Drumballyroney and Drumgath, while there was a tradition that the family were buried at Clonallan and Clonduff to the south (*PNI* i 55, iii 69). Three miles north of Rathfriland is the hill of **Knock Iveagh** which provides a view of the whole barony. The 16th-century cartographer, Richard Bartlett, who was interested in the inauguration sites of Irish chieftains, wrote beside Knock Iveagh on one of his maps: "*Lis-ne Ree* where the McGenis is made" (*Bartlett Maps (Esch. Co. Maps)* 2). It seems likely that *Lis-ne Ree* derives from an original Irish *Lios na Rí* "fort of the kings", but of the two modern places called **Lisnaree** in or near the barony, the closer is in the Lordship of Newry several miles further south (*PNI* i 31), while the other is in Seapatrick parish near Banbridge. Another possible inauguration site was the stone called *Cusleac Aonguis* "the footstone of Aongus" on a hill in Warrenpoint (Haughton Crowe 1969, 57). *Aongus*, or Angus, seems to refer to the founder of the Magennis surname.

However it was some time before the Magennis surname was in general use. In the 12th century the Magennis chief was described as being of *Clann Aodha*, "*Aodh*/Hugh's offspring" (*Newry Charter* 64–5, 42, cf.46) from a great-grandson of Angus, while it seems that another group (possibly the original main line) continued to refer themselves back to Aitíd (see **Muntereddy**). A third division, possibly of the 13th century, is that of the MacRory Magennises of **Kilwarlin**. An unpublished 17th-century manuscript of northern genealogies in Trinity College Dublin derives these three groups, called *Clann Aodha, Muintir Ghleann Eideadha, Muintir Coille Bairrline*, from three sons of Art an Lámhaigh Magennis, about 1400 (*TCD Gens* §261), but it is likely the divisions are older.

As well as being tribal rulers, and patrons of Gaelic poets, many Magennises also became churchmen, either in the local diocese of Dromore or further afield. The family maintained its importance in the 16th and early 17th centuries, keeping their lands together by submitting to the English policy of surrender and regrant[1], but several members, including Arthur Viscount Magennis, were implicated in the rebellion of 1641 (*Wars Co. Down* 75, 77–81) and their lands confiscated. Notable new landholders in the 17th century were John Barrett, William Hawkins, Arthur Hill, John Magill, George Rawdon, George Sexton, Edward Trevor, William Waring and Marmaduke Whitchurch, but none of them held more than parts of the original territory of Iveagh.

1. *Fiants Eliz.* §4218, §4327 (all Iveagh); §4649, §4650; *CPR Jas I* 181b, 396a (separating Kilwarlin from southern Iveagh).

NATIVE SUBDIVISIONS/SOURCES

At the time of the Plantation Iveagh was a coherent unit, and many of the Plantation documents provide information about the whole area. The lands of Iveagh were first surrendered by Sir Hugh Magennis and regranted to him by Queen Elizabeth in 1583 (*Fiants Eliz.* §4218, §4327). The surrender refers first to the "whole country of *Iveaghe*", and then lists some names of places within it:

> the lands of Raphrilan, the Narrowe water, Loughbreclyn, Corgirry, Deyne, Loghan, Clare, Ballelaghe, Myra, Dyrry, Loghaghrye, Begnive, Dycovead, Ballyrony, Clanbarde, Ryaghe, Castellwellan, Ballaghbege alias Shyleke, and Ballywolinge.

> "the lands of Rathfriland, Narrow Water, Loughbrickland, Corgary, Loughadian, Loughans, Clare, Ballylough, Moira, Islandderry, Lough-aghery, Begny, Deehommed, Ballyroney, Ballyward, Loughislandreavy, Castlewellan, Ballaghbeg, and Milltown".

This list is repeated with some differences in the regrant, where it is followed by a boundary description of the whole barony, by means of places which are at the furthest points from each other on the map. Kilwarlin (here represented by Loughaghery) was already a separate territory, surrendered and regranted in 1585 by and to Ewer McRorie (Magennis) (*Fiants Eliz.* §§4649–50).

7

In 1609 the government drew up a schedule for dividing and controlling the whole territory of Iveagh, making some of the Magennis families freeholders directly from King James I, and confirming others as tenants of the Magennis chief. This is published in the calendar of the patent rolls of James I (*CPR Jas I* 394b–396a, enrolled in 1617). The grants were made in 1611 (*CPR Jas I* 190ab, 193a). From this Schedule it becomes clear that the places in the 1583 list were the focal points of districts held by some of the Magennis septs, many of them based on castles or crannogs. These secular districts were not the same as parish divisions. The 13 freeholders represent Loughbrickland, Corgary (**Clanagan**), Clare (**Clanconnell**), Moira, Islandderry (**Lequirin**, divided in 3), Castlewellan (**Watertirry**), and Milltown (**Clanawly**, 2 divisions), from the 1583 list, with Shankill in Aghaderg, **Glasquirin**, Islandmoyle, Kilmore and **Muntereddy**, not in the Fiant (*CPR Jas I* 394b–395a). The 11 Magennis tenancies include Loughadian, Ballylough, Deehommed, Ballyward, and Ballyroney (*CPR Jas I* 395a). Most of the freeholders were Magennises (but McManuses in Kilmore, O'Lawrys in Moira), while Magennis chief tenants included McaWards in Ballyward, O'Roneys in Ballyroney, and O'Laghnans in Ballyloughlin, Maghera.

Sir Art Magennis seems generally to have kept Rathfriland, Narrow Water (the **Legan**), Loughans (in Tullylish), Begny (in Dromara, district of **Tullyomy**), Loughisland-reavy (a lake north of the village of Kilcoo), and Newcastle (*Ballaghbeg*) in his own hands (*CPR Jas I* 189a, 235a). The same details appear in the inquisitions after their deaths on the holdings of Sir Art, who died in 1617, and his son Sir Hugh (*Aodh*) (*Inq. Ult. (Down)* §13 Car. I, §85 Car. I). By 1666 most of Sir Art's lands were held by John Hawkins as "the manor of Rathfryland" (*ASE* 273b–74a).

Kilwarlin was granted direct to Brian MacRory Magennis (*CPR Jas I* 396a, 181b) but the eight towns of *Tullyomy* were transferred to Sir Art. Kilwarlin was dealt with in a series of inquisitions after Brian's death in 1631 (*Inq. Ult. (Down)* §§22–5,28,31,59–60 Car. I). It came into the possession of the Hills of Hillsborough.

The 17th-century genealogical manuscript in Trinity College Dublin follows the pedigree of the Magennis chief with those of other branches of the family. These pedigrees can be matched with the patronymics of the Magennis freeholders and chief tenants appearing in the 1609 Schedule of Iveagh and other Plantation documents. The comparison reveals that, apart from the branches in Kilwarlin and Muntereddy, the Magennis holders of the districts of Castlewellan, Clanawly, Clanconnell, Corgary, Glasquirin, Islandmoyle, Lequirin, Loughadian, Loughbrickland and Shankill were regarded with their chief as *Clann Aodha*, being great-grandsons of different sons of Aodh son of Art an Lámhaigh (*TCD Gens* 141a–146). However Aodh Magennis died in 1418, and four generations, usually reckoned as 25 years, would not span the time between 1400 and 1600.

Names of districts in Iveagh

Since some of these district names survive as townlands, and others are obsolete, historical forms are not listed here for reasons of space.

| **Ballylaghnan** | *Baile Uí Lachtnáin* |
| | "O'Laghnan's holding" |

In 1609 Shane O'Laghnan held 3 townlands, including that now called **Ballyloughlin** in Maghera parish, from Sir Art Magennis (*CPR Jas I* 395a). Woulfe says that *Ó Lachtnáin* was known in the 16th century in Co. Down, "often corrupted to Ó Lochláin, anglicized Loughlin" (Woulfe 1923, 578–9).

Ballyroney   *Baile Uí Ruanadha*
                                            "O'Roney's holding"

In 1609 Hugh McNeece McRowry *O'Ronow* held 7 townlands from Sir Art, six in Drumballyroney parish as well as Drumadonnell in Drumgooland. Another family of O'Roneys held the 7 townlands of Deehommed, in Dromara and Drumgooland, from Sir Art (*CPR Jas I* 395a,190b, listed as Sir Art's 189a).

Ballyroney refers originally to the group of townlands held by the family, and only later to the townland of **Ballyroney**, which formerly had its own name *Baile an Chaisleáin Ghlais* "townland of the grey castle".

Ballyward   *Baile Mhic an Bhaird*
                                            "McaWard's holding"

This division consisted of four townlands in Drumgooland parish, held from Sir Art Magennis in 1609 by Shane McEvard or McEward (*CPR Jas I* 395a). The family of *Mac an Bhaird* "son of the bard" were well-known as poets (*De Script. Hib.* 92). The name has often been anglicized as Ward. Although one of the townlands is now called **Ballyward**, *baile* probably referred originally to the entire holding.

Clanagan   *Clann Aogáin*
obs.   "descendants of Aogán"

Ten townlands in Donaghmore parish (*PNI* i 87, 112–3) were held in 1609 by Murtagh McEnaspicke Magennis, son of the mid-16th-century conforming bishop Gelasius Magennis of Dromore (*CPR Jas I* 394b; *TCD Gens* §271). The name *Clann Aogáin* comes from *Aodhagáin*, diminutive of *Aodh* "Hugh", but this person has not been identified.

Clanawly   *Cineál nAmhalaidh*
obs.   "Aulay's kindred"

Clanawly consisted of 16 townlands, 13 in Clonallan, two in Drumgath and one in Kilbroney parishes (*PNI* i 51–2, 116,118, 147). 1n 1609 seven were held by John and eight by Hugh McCon McGlassny Magennis (*CPR Jas I* 394b; *TCD Gens* §265). As *Ceinél . . . nAmholgaidh*, Clanawly anciently belonged to the family of McYawnie or *Méig Dhuibh Eamhna* (*Topog. Poems* 15 1.399). The genealogy of the McYawnies has not been preserved, and Amhal[gh]adh, probably their ancestor, is unknown.

Clanbrassil   *Clann Bhreasail*
obs.   "Breasal's offspring"

Clanbrassil was a district name used for the area east of the outflow of the upper Bann into Lough Neagh, now part of Co. Armagh, but originally part of Iveagh and still part of the diocese of Dromore, containing the mediaeval parishes of Seagoe and Shankill. Clanbrassil was not the same as *Uí Bhreasail (Macha)*, a tribe of the Airthir much nearer Armagh (Mooney 1952–3(b), 11; 1954(a), 6–10). The name is used for a district connected with Iveagh in *Ceart Uí Néill* and 17th century Irish texts (*LCABuidhe* 44 §9; 160 1.214).

The origin of two groups called *Clann Breasail* "offspring of Breasal" can be found in Co. Down in the mid 8th century. One possible eponymous ancestor was Breasal, son of Fergus king of Uí Echach Coba, who died in AD 685 (*AU*), and whose son fought as king in 714 (*AU, A. Tigern.*). In the Annals of the Four Masters, compiled in the 17th century, this Breasal's sons are referred to as *Clann Breasail*, "chieftains of Uí Echach of the Ulaid" (*toisecha Ua nEthach Uladh, AFM* i 310, AD 712). Another slightly later Breasal (d.750 AD) was a son of Aed Róin king of Dál Fiatach, and ancestor of "*Clann Breasail in Sliabh Garbhraighe*" (*Descendants Ir* xiv 82). The first group would be in Iveagh, the second presumably further east in Co. Down, although the mountain (*sliabh*) of Garbhraige has not been located.

The district name Clanbrassil was regularly shown on maps c. 1600 (*Jobson, Bartlett, Speed, Norden*). The name was also extended to cover the Co. Armagh stretch of the Upper Bann (*Banbrasill flu.*, 1609) and Turlough *Brassilough* O'Neill, who lived in the area. The county boundary and thus the extent of the district was long uncertain, for example a reference in 1615 to Knockmenagh, a townland now in Armagh between Portadown and Lurgan (J 0455), being in "*Clanbrassel* territory in Armagh & Down Cos" (*CPR Jas I* 299b). For the most part the name Clanbrassil was equivalent to the barony of Oneilland East, Co. Armagh.

Clanbrassil McGoolechan   *Clann Bhreasail Mhic Dhúileacháin*
obs.   "Doloughan's Clanbrassil"

In the late 16th century a district called *Clanbrassil McGoolechan* is said to have been in Co. Down. In 1586 Bagenal said that Clanbrassil in Co. Armagh bordered Lough Neagh, but he described *Clanbrasell McGoolechan* in Co. Down between Kinelarty and Lecale, as "a very fast country of wood and bogg, inhabited with a sept called the Kellies, a very savage and barborous people, geven altogether to spoile and roberies" (*Bagenal's Descr. Ulst.* 151–2). The distinction is made explicit in 1598, where Clanbrassil in Co. Down was apparently near Clandeboy:

> Clonebrassil McBoolechan, so called for difference between this and another Countrie of the same name in the Countie of Armagh, is a verie vast countrie of wood and bogg, inhabitted with a sept called the O'Rellies (recte, Kellies) (*Descr. Ire.* 9).

Clanbrassel with the epithet *McGoolechan* does not appear on maps, but the family of *Kellies* was shown on maps c. 1600 considerably east of Clanbrassil by Lough Neagh (*Jobson's Ulster* TCD 17; *Bartlett: TCD, Esch. Co. Maps* 1; *Speed: Ulster, Antrim & Down; Norden*). Knox (*History of Co. Down* 294) considered that Clanbrassil was formed of "coterminal portions of the two counties" Down and Armagh. However the map evidence indicates that at least by the late 16th century Clanbrassil and Clanbrassil McGoolechan were geographically distinct.

The epithet *Macgoolechan* seems to be the Irish surname *Mac Dúilecháin*. In the 14th century this family were called chieftains of *Clann Breasail* (*Topog. Poems* 15 1.403) and, as *Mac Suileacháin*, were one of three chief families of Iveagh mentioned in *Ceart Uí Néill* (*LCABuidhe* 42 §3; Ó Doibhlin 1970, 338–9). Their land was known by their name as *terra... Maccollocan* in 1204 (*Pontif. Hib.* i 128 §60) and there are other 13th-century references, such as the soldiers in 1211 AD who went into *Oveagh* (Iveagh) to plunder *Mackou[l]ecan* (*Pipe Roll John* 58). The family seem to have lost their importance later: they are not in the annals and there is no extant pedigree for *Mac Dúileacháin*. 17th-century sources on Co. Down give the surname with both *Mac* and *Ó*: O *Magullaghan* (*Wars Co. Down* 77b) and *O'Dollehan* (*Sub. Roll Dn* 277). It apparently survives as the surname now known in Down as Doloughan

(*Desc. Ire.* 6n), and there is a townland of **Ballydollaghan** in Drumbo. The later surname Kelly seems to be that which occurs widely in townland names in Iveagh, possibly deriving from *Clann Cheallaigh*, "Ceallach's offspring", at Drumbo, contemporary with *Clann Breasail* of Dál Fiatach (*Descendants Ir* xiv 80).

Clanconnell   *Clann Chonaill*
obs.   "offspring of Conall"

Clanconnell "offspring of Conall" was once well-known as a district name in the area of the parishes of Donaghcloney and Tullylish (*Fiants Eliz.* §4327, AD 1584), and Harris gave it as the ancient name of Waringstown (*Harris Hist. 104*). It included 15 modern townlands, eight of Donaghcloney and seven of Tullylish. **Clare** in Tullylish seems to have been the chief townland, and was referred to as "of *Clinconnel*" as late as 1821 (*Irish Wills Index* 134). The name has no evident connection with Glasney McAugholy Magennis, the holder of the land in 1609 (*CPR Jas I* 394b; *TCD Gens* 145a §266), and local tradition in 1691 explained Clanconnell as: "so called from one Conel who was the first proprietor thereof, containing between 23 and 24 townlands" (*Atkinson's Donaghcloney* 131). (In the 17th century, unusually, names are given for all the sessiagh units, which explains the different number of land units now and in 1691).

The eponymous Conall thus has to be sought in earlier sources. Although several other Conalls, down to the mid-9th-century, are mentioned in east Ulster in the Ulster genealogies (*Descendants Ir* xiv 122–3), the most obvious candidate is Conall who was father of Fothad, who died in 552 AD (*AU*) and through whom the main Uí Echach line descended. This Conall was sometimes called son of Coelbad, sometimes son of Eochu Coba son of Crund Ba Druí (*CGH* 161bc43, 162b33).

Traditionally the tribe called *Conaille Muirthemne* in Co. Louth descended from the Ulster-cycle hero Conall Cernach, who was considered as the ancestor of *Clann Conaill* which included Conaille, Dál nAraide, Uí Echach and other Cruthin tribes (*CGH* 157.47). However the genealogies sometimes say that the Conaille took their name from Conall son of Eochu Cobha above (McCann 1952–3(b), 32 n.9: ref. *CGH* 162b33, 162c20), putting Conaille in closer relationship with Uí Echach Cobha. This cannot be true in the historical sense, but may reflect political theory. Both groups boasted of their Ulster cycle ancestry, so that in the early 16th century the Magennis chief could claim to be "chief of the offspring of Conall Cernach" (*A. Conn.* 640, AD 1522).

The district name Clanconnell, on the border of the reduced Ulster, may also recall the legendary descent of the Magennises from Conall Cernach. Several local names seem to make reference to the Ulster Cycle, as may be the case with **(Lough) Brickland, Edentiroory, Rossconnor** and **Tirfergus**.

Glasquirin   *Glaschuibhreann*
obs.   "green division"

Glasquirin, based around the townland of Ballycross in Magherally parish, was a district of 8 townlands: four in Magherally, to the north Ballygunaghan in Donaghcloney with Drumnavaddy in Seapatrick, and detached to the west the Seapatrick townlands of Ballykeel and Drumnagally. It was held in 1609 by Con Boy McPhellomie McHugh Magennis (*CPR Jas I* 395a), and last referred to in 1692 (*Rent Roll Down* 11).

The name Glasquirin seems to be related in form to **Lequirin** to the north. The first element is apparently the adjective *glas* "green", as in the recurring compound place-name

11

Glassdrummon *Glasdromainn* "green ridge" (*Joyce* ii 281–2). The spelling *-quyverin* occurring for Lequirin (form 1,5) suggests the second element is *cuibhreann* "division" (*DIL*). *Cuibhreann* now means "a cultivated field" in Tyrone and Donegal (O'Kane 1970, 139,117; *Dinneen, Ó Dónaill*), but the basic meaning is probably more appropriate here.

| **Islandmoyle** | *An tOileán Maol* |
| | "the bare island" |

The "island of Islandmoyle" and five townlands adjoining in Clonduff parish, were held in 1609 by Rowrie Oge McRowrie McCollo McHugh Magennis (*PNI* iii 71,89; *CPR Jas I* 395a; *TCD Gens* §272). The word "island" in the name of the chief townland of the district suggests there may once have been a crannog, presumably in Islandmoyle Lough.

| **Killowen** | *Cill Eoghain* |
| | "Eoghan's church" |

As a district Killowen [kï'loən] referred to seven townlands along the coast in the south of Kilbroney parish, alienated by Donal and James *McYawne* to Nicholas Bagenal in 1568 (*PNI* i 131, 146–8). The lands were held from the Bishop of Dromore in the Schedule of Iveagh (*CPR Jas I* 395b). Killowen has been used in recent times as the name of a village (J 2017) and as part of the townland name Killowen Mountains.

| **Kilmore** | *Coill Mhór* |
| | "big wood" |

The large townland of **Kilmore** connects Co. Down with Lough Neagh, although it forms part of the Armagh parish of Shankill to the south and is adjacent to **Killultagh** "the Ulster wood" in Co. Antrim to the north (see the introduction to Co. Down). However in 1609 this area contained four subdivisions held by Sir Art Magennis, while six other townlands adjacent in Co. Armagh, but called "parcel of Killmore . . . in Iveagh", were assigned to Edward Trevor from Murtagh Modderagh McManus (*CPR Jas I* 395a, 396a, cf. *Inq. Ult. (Down)* §85 Car. I). There are no ecclesiastical associations.

| **Kilwarlin** | *Coill Bhairrline* |
| | "Bairrlin's wood" |

The large district of Kilwarlin ['kïl'wɑrlïn] was based on Hillsborough, extending into Annahilt, Blaris, Dromore, Dromara and Moira parishes. The name is still in use, in the name of a road, a house and several churches in the Blaris – Hillsborough – Moira area, along the M1 motorway between the Dublin turn at Sprucefield and Moira. In 1840 a new parish called Upper and Lower Kilwarlin was divided from Hillsborough by the Church of Ireland.

The lands within Kilwarlin are listed several times between 1575 and 1635, comprising about 48 units (*Fiants Eliz.* §4650; *CPR Jas I* 181b, 396a; *Inq. Ult. (Down)* §31 Car. I), and there is a map of 1640 surveyed at the take-over of the estate by Sir Arthur Hill (*Map Kilwarlin*). Not all the names in the list can be identified, while the map shows several names, some now also obsolete, which are not in the list. The old Kilwarlin included **Tullyomy**, which was a sub-district of eight townlands in Dromore and Dromara.

Kilwarlin is all in Lower Iveagh, but the later division into Upper and Lower halves runs east and west and cuts across it (Hillsborough, Blaris and Moira in the upper half, Annahilt, Dromara and Dromore in the lower). However the Kilwarlin boundaries coincide with barony bounds in two places, since it apparently included exactly the Iveagh parts of Blaris (Iveagh Lower, Upper half) and of Dromara (Lower Iveagh, Lower half).

Kilwarlin was held by the MacRory Magennises, who, according to the late genealogy, divided from the main Rathfriland line at Cathbharr son of Art an Lámhaigh at the end of the 14th century (*TCD Gens* 144a §261; another son Rory died in 1400 *AFM*; *EA* 389). However, as early as AD 1260 two Magennis chiefs, *Kaffor* and *Rochery* (Cathbharr and Rory), were fined by the Normans (*Exch. Accounts Ulster* 157). The name *Rudhraighe* (whence *Rúraí*, Rory) appears frequently in the pedigree and it is not clear which one is the founder of the line. No doubt reference was also intended to *Rudraige*, the supposed ancestor of the Ulster Cycle heroes, as well as of Uí Echach and Dál nAraide (Byrne *Clann Ollaman* 58; cf. **Loughbrickland, Clanconnell**).

The earliest reference to Kilwarlin is the anglicized form *Kilvarlyn* in 1571 (*Fiants Eliz.* §1736). Kilwarlin is the usual spelling, occasionally *Kilwarnan* etc. (e.g. in 1612 *Killwarnan, woody country of . . .*, *CSP Ire.* 1611–4 p254). Despite its being a Magennis district there are only two references to Kilwarlin in Irish-language sources, both late 17th century (*Muintir Coille Bairrline, TCD Gens* 144a §261e; *dhá chreich Choille Bairrlinne, LCABuidhe* 160 l.210). The name clearly includes the element *coill* "wood", and it adjoined the other "woods" of **Killultagh**, "wood of the Ulstermen" (south Co. Antrim), and **Kilmore** "big wood" (northwest Co. Down). *Bairrlinn* may be a personal name but there is no other instance of it.

The Legan
obs.

An Lagán
"the low-lying district"

The Legan contained 23 townlands, twelve in Clonallan, eight in Kilbroney parish, and three in Warrenpoint, based on the castle at Narrow Water (*PNI* i 49–51, 129, 161). All but two were held in 1609 by the chief, Sir Art Magennis (*TCD Gens* §259).

Lequirin
obs.

Liathchuibhreann
"grey division"

Lequirin consisted of 13 townlands in the west of Dromore and east of Magheralin, six in Dromore and seven in Magheralin parishes. However it was separated into two halves by the eastern townlands of Clanconnell, and Coolsallagh and Drumskee held by Sir Art Magennis. The northern half was larger (9 townlands) while the southern part consisted of four townlands all in Dromore. The church townland of Quilly which is next to these was also associated with Lequirin, indicating that the district may once have been larger geographically (*CPR Jas I* 193a). In 1609, as well as being in detached portions, Lequirin was divided between three Magennis holders. Art Oge McGlasney Magennis (the son of the holder of **Clanconnell**; *CPR Jas I* 394b; *TCD Gens* §266)) got the centre of Lequirin, based on Islandderry in Dromore, with four townlands in Magheralin, as a freehold held from the King, James I. Brian McDonell McBrien Magennis and Donell Oge McEdmond Boy Magennis (*CPR Jas I* 395a; *TCD Gens* §267) were tenants of Sir Art and each got a a mixture of four townlands to the north and south of Islandderry. It looks as if the original district of Lequirin had been deliberately broken up, and it is not referred to again after 1612.

From the earliest form *Leighquiverin*, which shows an internal *v* (*CPR Jas I* 395a, AD 1609), the name Lequirin seems to consist of a noun *cuibhreann* "division" and a prefixed adjective, *liath* "grey", a parallel formation to Glasquirin above. Other lost names in Iveagh appear to contain the same element *cuibhreann*: *Levallyquiverrenderne... Quiverringarrough* (*CPR Jas I* 395b).

Loughadian *Loch an Daingin*
"lake of the stronghold"

Loughadian, held in 1609 by Bryan McArte McEver Magennis (*CPR Jas I* 395a; *TCD Gens* §270), consisted of five townlands including that of **Loughadian** in the parish of Aghaderg.

Loughbrickland *Loch Bhricleann*
"Bricriu's lake"

Loughbrickland, named after an Ulster Cycle hero (*FB*), was held in 1609 by Art Oge McBryane Oge McBriane McEdmond Boy Magennis (*CPR Jas I* 394b; *TCD Gens* §269). It consisted of 10 townlands, four including **Brickland** east of the lake called **Lough Brickland** in Aghaderg parish, together with six to the north in Seapatrick parish.

Moira *Maigh Rath*
"plain of fords/wheels(?)"

The district of Moira held by the O'Laverys consisted of 14 sessiaghs in the old parish of Magheralin, now 14 modern townlands: ten in the parish of **Moira** created in 1725, four in Magheralin. The chief land unit was Risk in Moira.

Muntereddy *Muintir Aidídh*
obs. "Aidídh's people"

Muntereddy contained 7 townlands in Kilcoo (*PNI* iii 99, 101 n3), held in 1609 by Brian McHugh McAgholy Magennis (*CPR Jas I* 193a; written *Muinntir Ghleanna Eideadha*, *TCD Gens* §261). The eponymous ancestor Aidídh was king of Uí Echach and east Ulster at the end of the ninth century, and father of Angus from whom the Magennis surname derives. Before the younger branch took over, the family of *Ó hAidídh* (O'Haddy) were probably the chief family of Iveagh (**Iveagh** forms 10,11,16,22,24).

Shankill *Seancholl*
"old hazel"

Shankill, held in 1609 by Ever McArte McRowrie Magennis (*CPR Jas I* 394b; *TCD Gens* §270), consisted of 12 townlands: five, including the townland of **Shankill**, in Aghaderg parish, six in Annaclone, and one in the parish of Seapatrick.

Tullyomy *Tulaigh Ómaí*
obs. "hillock of the untilled plain"(?)

Tullyomy was a subdistrict of **Kilwarlin**, consisting of 8 townlands in Dromore and Dromara parishes, based on Begny in Dromara. It was transferred in 1609 from the Kilwarlin Magennises to Sir Art Magennis in Rathfriland (*CPR Jas I* 396a), and was last heard of in 1613 (*Ulst. Roll Gaol Deliv.* 262).

Watertirry *Uachtar Tíre*
obs. "upper part of the land"

Watertirry consisted of "the castle, island and 11 towns or townlands" around Castlewellan, nine townlands in Drumgooland and two in Kilmegan parish, held in 1609 by Ever McPhelimy Magennis (*CPR Jas I* 193a; *TCD Gens* §268). It was important enough earlier to be referred to with its kings in the Irish annals (*AU,AFM* 1046, 1054, 1061 AD), and was shown as *Water-tiry* on Mercator's map of Ulster in 1595.

The Diocese of Dromore: Parishes and Church Lands

The 1609 Schedule of Iveagh also included the lands inherited from the medieval church by the Church of Ireland bishops of Dromore (*CPR Jas I* 395a–396b). At that time tenants of church lands included many family names which appear among the medieval clergy, and in place-names in the diocese: McBredan, McBrin (Byrne), McCormick, McDonegan, McGinn, McGowan, McGivern, McKey, McAteer, O'Kerny, O'Roney, O'Sheil (*Swanzy's Dromore*). Church lands can be traced in a series of grants to and from the bishop (*CPR Jas I* 190b–191a,191b,266a,309a; *Inq. Ult. (Down)* §4 Jac. I) and in Bishop Buckworth's account in 1622 (*Buckworth*). Although many were taken over by secular landlords in the interim the remaining church lands were listed in the report of Her Majesty's Commissioners to Parliament before the dis-establishment of the Church of Ireland in 1868 (*Parl. Rept* 1868 x 574).

The diocese of Dromore seems at first to have been part of that of Down, but in the late 12th century there is the first reference to "O'Roney bishop of Iveagh", *Uroneca episcopo de Uvehe* (*EA* 192), and it seems likely that the office was created for the people of Uí Echach, distinguished from the Normanized diocese of Down. The area covered by the diocese is similar to but larger than the barony of Iveagh, and reflects the earlier extent of *Uí Echach Coba* influence to the south and north. The north-western boundary of the diocese follows the river Bann from Knock Bridge, on the modern boundary with Co. Armagh, all the way to Lough Neagh, and includes the parishes of Seagoe and Shankill (including Montiaghs) in the district of **Clanbrassil**, now the barony of Oneilland East. Clanbrassil was traditionally part of *Uí Echach* but was annexed to the new county of Armagh in 1605. It remains, however, in the diocese of Dromore. North of Moira across the Lagan is the parish of Aghalee which is also in the diocese. It was part of Iveagh in 1584 but was annexed in 1605 to Co. Antrim (barony of Upper Massereene).

In the south, Mourne was disputed between the dioceses of Down and Dromore throughout much of the medieval period, while Newry was included in Dromore until the 16th century. By the 18th century, however, the Lordship of Newry and the barony of Mourne had come to be regarded as forming an "exempt jurisdiction" as far as the established church was concerned (*PNI* iii 5–6). In 1869 both were restored to the Anglican diocese of Dromore, although in the Roman Catholic administrative system Mourne is now in the diocese of Down. In the 1950s Dean Bernard Mooney collected a large amount of information on the place-names of the diocese in a manuscript which is deposited in Ballynahinch public library (*Mooney (MS)*).

The monastery at Dromore, the later episcopal seat, is referred to in the Annals from AD 841 (*AFM*), later than the killing of an abbot at Tullylish in 809, but earlier than De Courcy's attack on the sanctuary at Magheralin in 1178 (*Misc. Ir. Annals*). Other churches are mentioned in the Irish martyrologies, where saints Beoán and Meallán were located at Loughbrickland (Aghaderg), Molioba at Annahilt, and Brónach and Conall were connected with Kilbroney and Clonallan (*PNI* i 132–4, 54–5).

The medieval parishes seem to have been based on these early churches. The earliest surviving list of the parishes of Dromore diocese is in the Papal Taxation of c. 1306, edited with commentary by William Reeves (*EA* 102–19). It does not contain all the modern names, but two lists of parishes dated to 1422 and 1546 are included in the register of Archbishop Dowdall of Armagh (*EA* 315–8; *Reg. Dowdall* ii 275ff), and there was an inquisition of parishes in 1657 (*Inq. Down*). The medieval parishes of Dromore were continued by the established Church of Ireland, and with the addition of Moira and Montiaghs in the 18th century were used as civil administrative divisions, although other boundary changes by the churches are not reflected in the civil parishes.

THE PARISH OF AGHADERG

Aghaderg is on the western boundary of Co. Down, beside the marshy valley, once called *Gleann Rí* (*PNI* i 40–2), which became the route of the canal from Newry to Lough Neagh and later of the Belfast–Dublin railway line. There are 30 townlands. Most of the parish is in the barony of Iveagh Upper, Upper Half (12,841 acres, *Knox Hist.* 321), with the two north-ernmost townlands, Drummiller and Ballyvarley west of Banbridge, in the barony of Iveagh Lower, Lower Half (1075 acres). Aghaderg parish, in the words of the Ordnance Survey Memoir (*OSM* xii 3a), "consists of a succession of hills with very little variation of height". The parish slopes east to west, and the highest part is in the north-east, where Derrydrummuck townland rises to 579 feet.

The landscape on the west must have changed considerably from past times: "Tradition says that the whole of the valley or morass through which the canal runs from Newry to Lough Neagh was so thickly wooded that a man could walk on the tops of the trees" (*OSM* xii 4a). (This traditional saying is also recorded of other places, notably along the course of the Lower Bann). The geography of Aghaderg has in large part formed its history. It is or has been on the boundary between the territories of Ulaid and Airgialla, of Magennis and O'Hanlon, the dioceses of Dromore and Armagh, the counties of Down and Armagh. The ancient route from Tara in the midlands to the north coast, *Slige Midluachra*, passed through the parish, as the A1 still does (Hamilton 1913–4; Lawlor 1938, 3–6, map), while later the canal, taking advan-tage of the valley on the west which was a barrier to land traffic, turned it into a route by water between Newry and Lough Neagh. According to tradition King William III and his army camped along the road here in 1690 on their way to the Battle of the Boyne, commemorated by King William's Oak which was in Scarva demesne, and by the mock battle which is still held on the 12th of July (*Harris' Hist.* 84; *OSM* i 5a, xii 6a; *Armagh Misc.* viii 201–3).

In 1744 Harris mentioned "three incumbred Passes through Boggs, Woods and morassy Grounds . . . affording a bad and dangerous Communication between . . . Armagh and Down", two of which, *Pointz's alias Fenwick's Pass* and *Scarvagh Pass*, are in the parish of Aghaderg (*Harris' Hist.* 85). The crossing of *Gleann Rí* from Scarva southwards was heavily defended in the past by the surviving linear earthwork now called the Danes' Cast, north and south of the water barrier formed by Lough Shark and Loughadian. The Danes Cast was possibly erected in the 5th century, and may relate to the retreat eastwards of the original Ulaid "people of Ulster" from Armagh into modern Co. Down (Mallory & McNeill 1991, 152). There are many forts in the parish, some with townlands named after them, including multivallate Lisnagade east of Scarva. Although the chief Ulaid tribe, Dál Fiatach, were active in Lecale by the 6th century they are unlikely to have consolidated their new power base in Downpatrick immediately (Co. Down introduction, xix). The strategic importance of Aghaderg, and the local names **Dromorebrague** and **Water Hill**, make this area a pos-sible site for the initial Dál Fiatach capital in Down, which was called *Óchtar i nDruimnib Breg*, in Modern Irish *Uachtar i nDromanna Breá*, i.e. a place called *Uachtar* in a district called *Dromanna Breá* (*Descendants Ir* xiii 336). The later spelling *Uachtar* is used of a place on a journey in one Ulster cycle tale (*Imm. Dá T.* §5).

Another connection with the Ulster cycle appears in the lake in the middle of the parish, **Lough Brickland**, apparently named after the trouble-making warrior Bricriu (*FB*). The lake was also the site of a Magennis castle, and *Mag Aenghusa*, probably the chief, was attacked and defeated there in 1424 (*AFM*). Lough Brickland is the place-name in this parish which appears most frequently in early sources.

Tamhlacht Menan and *Tamhlacht Umhail*, the churches of the 7th-century Beoán and Meallán named in the martyrologies, were located at Lough Brickland, and in ordinary

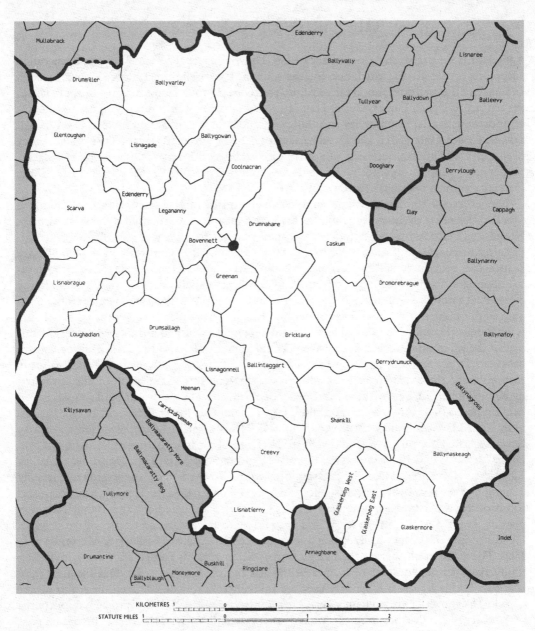

KILOMETRES

STATUTE MILES

Parish of Aghaderg
Barony of Iveagh Upper, Upper Half
Barony of Iveagh Lower, Lower Half★ (2 townlands)

Townlands	Creevy	Glaskermore	Scarva
Ballintaggart	Derrydrummuck	Glenloughan	Shankill
Ballygowan	Dromorebrague	Greenan	
Ballynaskeagh	Drummiller★	Legananny	*Town*
Ballyvarley★	(shared with Tullylish)	Lisnabrague	Loughbrickland
Bovennett	Drumnahare	Lisnagade	
Brickland	Drumsallagh	Lisnagonnell	Based upon Ordnance Survey 1:50,000
Carrickdrumman	Edenderry	Lisnatierny	mapping, with permission of the
Caskum	Glaskerbeg East	Loughadian	Director of the Ordnance Survey of
Coolnacran	Glaskerbeg West	Meenan	Northern Ireland, Crown copyright reserved.

18

speech the name Loughbrickland has often been used for the parish name. Aghaderg is the name of the medieval and civil parish, named earliest in 1413 (*Reg. Fleming*). It was one of the prebends of the diocese, along with Dromore parish, Magheralin, Donaghcloney, Dromara, and Clonallan (*EA* 316–8). The current Church of Ireland parish church, 17th-century with later additions, is in the north-east corner of Bovennett townland in the village of Loughbrickland, but 1834 local tradition said it had been moved by Sir Marmaduke Whitchurch "from Aghaderg about half a mile north-west (actually *south*-west) of the place" (*OSM* xii 4b). Old residents of Drumsallagh in 1795 described the ruins of a Franciscan friary "within about 200 yards of the old church of *Aghderg* in the said townland", stones from which had been used to build the church in Loughbrickland (Cahill 1985, 120). It looks as if the name belonged to the old church site.

A late tract on the Three Collas, the traditional 4th-century conquerors of Airgialla in mid Ulster, located their final victory over the Ulaid not at *Achadh Leithdheirg* in north Co. Monaghan, with the rout extending to *Gleann Rí*, but at "the battle of Aghaderg on this side of *Gleann Rí*" (*Cath Achaidh Dheirg don taobh abhus do Ghleann Righe, LCABuidhe* 50). O'Laverty (Bk i Introduction xiv) accepted this as meaning that *Achadh Leithdhearg* was "Aghaderg in the barony of Iveagh", but in fact the story is most likely a northern attempt to locate a famous event at a more familiar local site. For the battle traditions at Aghaderg, see the discussion of the parish name below.

Some other passes between Magennis' country and Orior were mentioned in the bounds of Iveagh as laid down in 1584: "the river or passage of *Hawallan*", "the ford *Harey*". *Ha* usually represents Irish *áth* "ford". North of these on the border, but south of the "water of *Scarvagheyedoo*" (**Scarva**), is the "moor of *Moyne Inirrye*" (*Fiants Eliz.* §4327), which is shown on some Bartlett maps: *Moenynnie* (*Esch Co. Map* 1), *Mome-yme or "the strange marish"* (*Esch Co. Map* 2: between the headwater of the Newry River, called *Owen Glin Ree fl.*, and the head of a tributary of the Cusher). In 1744 Harris referred to a rivulet from the bog near *Pointz's Pass* as:

> called in Irish *Ellin-money*, or "the wonderful bog", from the nature of its current, that immediately upon its rising separates into two branches [one going to Lough Neagh, the other to Newry] (*Harris' Hist* 115).

Although *Ellin-money* looks more like *Oileán Mónadh* "island of the bog", it seems that the original name must have been *Móin na nIonadh* "bog of wonders", as in **Moneyneany** in the parish of Ballynascreen, Co. Derry (*PNI* v 29–30). Local information in 1834 said that oak trees had been found buried in Scarva bog "with their tops all one way in one part of the bog and in another part with their tops in an opposite direction, following the course of the stream which here runs different ways north and south" (*OSM* xii 3b–4a). The difficulty of making out the watershed in this low-lying area caused confusion in early maps, some of which show one river from Newry to Lough Neagh. A map of about 1690, a preliminary survey for the Newry canal, shows a string of loughs and bogs linked by streams, and the 1:10,000 map shows bogs in most of the townlands to this day. **Loughadian** townland was named from a lake now drained.

Before the Plantation most of the area was divided into three main native (Magennis) holdings (*CPR Jas I* 394b–395a). *Loughbrickland* (10 townlands, partly in Seapatrick parish) and *Shanchall* (12 townlands, partly in Annaclone parish) were held from the King. *Loughdegan* (5 western townlands around Loughadian) was held from Sir Art Magennis. The two *lough*-names seem to be centred on crannog sites. Most of the land units in these holdings can be identified with modern townlands.

Loughbrickland, held in 1609 by Art Oge McBryane Oge McBriane McEdmond Boy Magennis, consisted of 10 towns: Brickland, Caskum, Coolnacran, Drumnahare, together with, in Seapatrick, Ballydown, Balleevy, Ballyvally, Lisnaree, Tullyear and *Dromynleckawly*, probably the older name of Dooghary. As well as Loughbrickland Castle, this holding also controlled the fords over the Bann at and near Banbridge. By 1633 eight of the 10 townlands, including all in Aghaderg, had been transferred by Art MacBrian Magennis to Marmaduke Whitchurch or Whitechurch (*Inq. Ult. (Down)* §§39 Car.I, 62 Car. I; *CPR Jas I* 409b).

Loughadian, *Loughdegan,* held in 1609 by Bryan McArte McEver Magennis, consisted of 5 towns: Loughadian, Lisnagade, Lisnabrague, and *Clandeknaverly* and *Nemeagh*, apparently older names for Scarva and Edenderry townlands. In 1618 (*Inq. Ult.* xliii, *CPR Jas I* 305a) Lisnagade and *Clonknaverly* had been acquired by Sir Edward Trevor, along with Drumsallagh, while George Sexton held *Ballymeagh*. In 1629 these were listed as having been Sir Art Magennis' lands (*Inq. Ult. (Down)* §13 Car.I, listed as his son's 1639) but by 1632 some of them had been passed to George Sexton (*Inq. Ult. (Down)* §30 Car. I). By 1641 the resident landlord was Capt. Henry Smith (*Wars Co. Down* xi 59).

Shankill, held in 1609 by Ever McArte McRowrie Magennis, consisted of 12 towns. Five were in Aghaderg: Shankill, Ballynaskeagh, Creevy, Derrydrummuck, *Dromore* which is Dromorebrague, and six in Annaclone: Ballynafern, Ballynafoy, Ballynagross, Ballynanny, Cappagh and Clay. The last townland was Tullyconnaught in the parish of Seapatrick.

Glassney Roe Magennis held Ballymacinratty in Donaghmore and two other denominations, one of which is Meenan and the other probably an earlier name for Lisnagonnell in this parish. The southernmost townland of Aghaderg is Lisnatierny, originally one of the ten townlands of **Clanagan**, parish of Donaghmore (*PNI* i 87, 112–3), held in 1611 by Murtagh McEnaspicke Magennis.

A number of scattered townlands, namely Ballyvarley and Drummiller in the north of the parish and in Lower Iveagh, with Glenloughan, Ballygowan, and Glaskerbeg and Glaskermore, belonged to Sir Art Magennis of Rathfriland. For lands of his called *Creevy* and *Aghnekenny* see **Drummiller** in the parish of Tullylish.

Aghaderg parish also contained land belonging to the see of Dromore. In the earliest list (*CPR Jas I* 395b, 1609 AD) these lands were allocated by the bishop to Capt. Edward Trevor. The grant in 1611, after Carnew in Garvaghy parish, continues:

> Levally-Idongill otherwise Igonvile, Levallyquiverinderry, Knockegan otherwise Quivernigarrough, Levallyshanmullagh, Levallyenlearge, Dromese, Ballyvickey-Leggannanagh, Bovened, Clowennycarrowen, Downaghillie otherwise Carroragh, Dromshallagh (*CPR Jas I* 191a).

The list then returns to Kilkinamurry in Garvaghy, the next townland to Carnew. The modern townlands of Legananny, Bovenett and Drumsallagh are recognizable towards the end of the quotation above, but the other names are unknown, although names containing the elements *levally* and *carrow*, referring to divisions of townlands (*leathbhaile, ceathrú*), might be more likely to be lost. The part of Garvaghy following was also granted to Sir Edward Trevor, rents payable to the bishop. The bishop also held Greenan and Ballintaggart.

None of the landlords remained the same. Although Bovennett, Greenan, Drumsallagh and Legananny were in Bishop Percy's Manor of Dromore in 1795 (Cahill 1985, 121), there were no Church of Ireland lands in Aghaderg in 1868 (*Parl. Report* 574). Resident gentlemen in 1777 were Fivey of *Loughdyon*, Dawson of Union Lodge, Reilly of Scarva; and Gordon of Ballintaggart (*Taylor and Skinner* maps 22,4). In the early 19th century the main proprietors were Reilly of Scarva (House), Fivey in Lisnabrague (Union Lodge), Trevor in Lisnagade (House), Whyte in Coolnacran (Loughbrickland House). Tenants mostly held direct from them (*OSM* xii 6a, 10a).

PARISH NAME

Aghaderg *Achadh Dearg*
J 0941 "red field"

1. (?)ar bhrú Uchdearc	AFM ii 1082 see n.p	1147
2. Cath Achaidh Dheirg . . . taobh abhus do Ghleann Righe	LCABuidhe 50	1680c
3. (?)Hacyglid, ecclesia de	Eccles. Tax. 112–3	1306c
4. Achdyryg, vicar.	Reg. Fleming 152 §210	1413
5. preb. of Achadeyrg	Cal. Papal Letters vii 122	1419
6. Achadirg, prebenda de	Annates Ulst. 289	1420
7. Aghadeyrge, ecclesia de	Reg. Dowdall 275 §129	1422
8. Aghudyrke, perp. vicar.	Reg. Swayne 61	1427
9. Achedyrke, vicar.	Reg. Swayne 183	1440
10. preb. of St Congal Achadradeug	Cal. Papal Letters xvi §336	1495
11. Aechderdoch, perp. vicar.	Annates Ulst. 292	1505
12. Aechdirdoch, annates of	Annates Ulst. 293	1505
13. Achadeyrg, prebendary of	Annates Ulst. 119n	1530c
14. Achaderyge, prebend, vicar of	Reg. Dowdall 80 §113	1546
15. Acaderige	CPR (Tresham) 286 §34	1547c
16. T. Aghaderick	Bartlett Map (BM)	1600
17. Temple Aghadericke	Bartlett Map (Greenwich)	1602
18. Achedericke	CPR Jas I 85a	1605
19. Aguaderrey	Speed's Ulster	1610
20. Aghaderick	CPR Jas I 190a	1611
21. Aghadricke	CPR Jas I 190b	1611
22. Achaderricke	OSM xii 1a	1634
23. p'ish of Aghederick	Wars Co. Down xi 60	1641
24. Aghaderick	Inq. Down (Reeves1) 77	1657
25. Aghaderrig	Hib. Reg. Upr Eveagh	1657c
26. Aghaderig	Hib. Reg. Lr Evagh	1657c
27. Aghedericke	Census 73	1659c
28. Aghaderigg parish	BSD 105,106	1661
29. Aghaderrick als Loughbrickland	Trien. Visit. (Bramhall) 14	1661
30. Rector de Aghederrick als Loughbrickland	Trien. Visit. (Bramhall) 14	1661
31. Aghederrick	Trien. Visit. (Margetson) 24	1664
32. Aghadarrige parish	BSD 119	1666
33. Aghaderge	ASE 61b §39	1667
34. Aghaderrig	Hib. Del. Down	1672
35. Aghadericke Rectoria	Trien. Visit. (Boyle) 46	1679
36. Aghadericke vicaria	Trien. Visit. (Boyle) 47	1679
37. Aghaderrig	Lamb Maps Co. Downe	1690c

38. I was made for Aghoderick church [bell]	OSM xii 4b	1698
39. Audory	Deeds & Wills (Mooney) 1	1729
40. Aghaderig	Harris Hist. 83	1744
41. Aghaderrig or Loughbricklan	OSM xii 1a	1744?
42. Aghederrig	OSM xii 1a	1755
43. parish of, old church of, Ahaderig	Statist. Sur. Dn 302,303	1802
44. Aghaderrick	Civ. & Ecc. Top. (OSNB) NB62	1806
45. Aughaderg	Wm. Map (OSNB) NB62	1810
46. [Agh-a-der-'rig]	OSNB Pron. NB62	1834c
47. aith "ford" + dearg "red"	OSM xii 1a	1834
48. Áth Dearg "red ford"	J O'D (OSNB) NB62	1834c
49. Aghaderg "The Red Ford" Athderg	Knox Hist. 355	1875
50. Ath-derg "red ford"	Joyce iii 27	1913
51. ˌɑhəˈdɛrg	Local pronunciation	1991

The two earliest possible forms of the name are both open to doubt. Reeves (*EA* 204), O'Donovan (*AFM* ii 1082 n.p) and Hogan (*Onom. Goed.* 660b) identified *Uchderc*, the site of a battle in AD 1147, between the Ulaid and Cenél nEogain allied with Airgialla, as Aghaderg. Battles often took place in boundary areas between the factions involved (Ó Riain 1974(a), 67–80). However Dean Mooney has pointed out that the subsequent rout of the Ulaid to Dundrum makes more sense if *Uchderc* were on the southern approach to Down in the area of the Crown Mound north-east of Newry, more accessible to a large army but still fairly close to the boundary (Mooney 1955(a), 1). *Áth Duma* "the ford of the mound" is an 8th-century battle-site probably in the same area (*AU* 761 *Uí Echach* against *Ulaid*, 776 §9 *Uí Echach Cobha* against *Airthir*). Nevertheless the prehistoric battle in which the Ulaid were defeated by the Three Collas was relocated at Aghaderg (form 2), and there were local traditions of battles (see below and **Drummiller**).

If the location of *Uchderc* is accepted the form is still problematic. If the name, which is uninflected in the source, is taken as copied from an earlier text, and could be modernized as *Ucht Dearg* "red hill-breast" or the like, it could be linked to the next oldest form *Aghdyryg*. In 1795 the local explanation of the parish name involved the old church in **Drumsallagh**. "Tradition received in this country" was that several holy men had been killed by the Danes, who destroyed both church and monastery, and that the place was afterwards called *Aghdurg*, "the red or bloody ford" on the boundary stream running close by the site. This name eventually became the name of the parish. This account implies the holy men were equated with the saints Beoán and Mellán at Lough Brickland named in the martyrologies, and that their festival was still kept annually (Cahill 1985, 21).

The replacement church in Loughbrickland village was also dedicated to St Mellán, and in 1834 the local explanation of the parish name was either "red ford" or "red hill" (*OSM* xii 1a). However all the other spellings have a vowel after *Agh-*, suggesting *achadh* "field" rather than *ucht* "hill-breast" or *áth* "ford".

The second element is probably *dearg* "red", and the final syllable appearing as *-rig* in some forms up to 1834 could be explained as the epenthetic vowel pronounced in Irish between the *r* and *g* of *dearg* ['d'ɛrəg]. Thus the name would be *Achadh Dearg* "red field", the Irish form given in the 17th century (*LCAB*). However Dean Mooney (*op. cit.*) preferred to explain the second element as *dairthech* "oak-house", an early word for a church. He adduced the forms with final *-gh*, *-y* as evidence for an original form *Achadh Dairthighe*, "field of the church", since these forms would not be a natural development of *dearg* with a hard *g*. The spellings with *-k,-g* however are generally older, *y* could be a misreading of *g*, and the unusual forms are mostly from one record from the Vatican or maps deriving from Speed. *Dearg* is well supported, a sound change from [ɣ'] to [g] is less likely, and it frequently happens, despite Dean Mooney's misgivings, that there is no ecclesiastical reference in a parish name.

The second form, *Hacyglid*, appears in the papal taxation of Irish parishes c. 1306 AD (*Eccles. Tax.*). Reeves gives no reason for equating *Hacyglid* with Aghaderg, and it seems his identification is based on its place in the list of names rather than on the form itself (*EA* 112n). I suspect interference from *Tamhlacht Gliadh*, the old name of Ballymore parish, which appears in the Armagh part of the taxation as *Thamelache Dalig'*, or from the parish of Aghalee, in the Down part of the taxation as *Achelo* (*CDI* 1302–7 203, 207). Reeves also interpreted the church lands of *Laireacht Dyke* (1427 AD) as Aghaderg, but the forms show that this was **Lenaderg** in Tullylish (*EA* 112, 114, 309; Mooney 1955, 2). It is clear from later references that Aghaderg was an important parish, held by a prebend of Dromore cathedral (forms 5,6,13,14), and associated with Tullylish which was a luminary, i.e. its revenues provided the cathedral with altar candles. Neither Aghaderg nor Tullylish was named as such in the Papal taxation.

TOWNLAND NAMES

Ballintaggart   *Baile an tSagairt*
J 1139   "townland of the priest"

1.	Shane Mc Brynn of Balletullenegrott	CPR Jas I 195b	1610
2.	Ballentollenegrott otherwise Ballentegart (Bp)	CPR Jas I 191a	1611
3.	Ballentollenegrott othw Ballentegart, to Shane McBrin	CPR Jas I 191a	1611
4.	Ballentollenegrott, Shane McBrin of	CPR Jas I 191a	1611
5.	Shane M'Bryan of Ballintegart, gent	Ham. Copy Inq. [1623] xxix	1623
6.	Ballintegett (gleabe)	Hib. Reg. Upr Eveagh	1657c
7.	Ballytagart	Census 73	1659c
8.	Ballintegert	BSD 105	1661
9.	Ballentegart (par. Donnoghclony)	ASE 61b §35	1666
10.	Ballintagart	ASE 112a §34	1667
11.	Ballintegart	Rent Roll Down 12	1692
12.	B. Tagirt	Harris Hist. map	1743
13.	Ballintagart	Vestry Reg. (OSNB) NB62	1747
14.	Ballintegart	Vestry Reg. (OSNB) NB62	1754
15.	Ballintagairt	Map of Down (OSNB) NB62	1755
16.	Ballintaggart	Vestry Reg. (OSNB) NB62	1768
17.	Ballintaggart	Wm. Map (OSNB) 62	1810
18.	Ballenteggart	County Warrant (OSNB) 62	1827
19.	Ballintegart	Reg. Free. (OSNB) NB62	1830
20.	Ballentaggart	Bnd. Sur. (OSNB) NB62	1830c
21.	Ballintaggart	Wm. Little (OSNB) NB62	1834c
22.	[Bal-lin-'teg-gart]	OSNB Pron. 62	1834c
23.	Baile-an-tsagart "The priest's townland"	OSM xii 1b	1834

24. Baile an tSagairt "Priest's Town"	J O'D (OSNB) NB62	1834c
25. Baile an tSagairt	Mooney 1	1950c
26. 'balïn'tagərt	Local pronunciation	1991

This townland belonged to the Bishop of Dromore, so that the obvious interpretation as *Baile an tSagairt*, "the priest's townland", is probably correct. Between 1611 and 1623 (at least) it was held by Shane McBrin, gent., a member of the family of *Mac* or *Ó Broin*, many of whom were churchmen in the 15th and 16th centuries, and after whom the church townland of **Ardbrin** in Annaclone may have been named. They were abbots of Newry in the 15th century (Mac Niocaill 1959, 175) and in 1427 Maurice *Mac[B]ryn* was the erenagh of church lands in *Laireachtdyke* (**Lenaderg** in Tullylish parish (*Reg. Swayne* 73)). In 1609 Gilleduffe *McBrien* held the church townland of Tullyorior in Garvaghy parish. *Mac Broin* was anglicized in Co. Down as Burns or Byrne (Bell 1988, 26).

Ballintaggart became secular land in the later 17th century and was held by Capt. John Magill of **Gilford**, parish of Tullylish (form 10). It is difficult to know what weight to put on the early 17th-century alias form (1–4): if not simply a miss-spelling, *tulach* "knoll" may have been an alternative element.

Ballygowan
J 1044

Baile na nGabhann
"townland of the smiths"

1. Ballynegowen	CPR Jas I 396a	1609
2. Ballynegowne	CPR Jas I 235a	1612
3. Ballenegoan	CPR Jas I 305a	1623
4. Ballygoan Hill	CPR Jas I 305a	1623
5. Ballinegowne	Inq. Ult. (Down) §13 Car.I	1629
6. Ballygowen	Civ. Surv. x §72	1655c
7. Ballingowin	Hib. Reg. Upr Eveagh	1657c
8. Ballygone	Census 73	1659c
9. Ballingowne (x2)	BSD 106	1661
10. Ballyngowen	BSD 106	1661
11. Ballingowne	Mooney MS 2	1668
12. Ballingoneen	Hib. Del. Co. Downe	1672c
13. Ballygowne	ASE 274a 29	1681
14. Ballygowan	Vestry Reg. (OSNB) NB62	1747
15. Ballygowne	Map of Down (OSNB) NB62	1755
16. Ballygowan	Wm. Map (OSNB) NB62	1810
17. Ballygowan	Reg. Free. (OSNB) NB62	1829c
18. Ballygowən	Bnd. Sur. (OSNB) NB62	1830c
19. Ballygowan	Wm. Little (OSNB) NB62	1834c
20. Baile-Uí-Ghobhann "O'Gowan's Town"	J O'D (OSNB) NB62	1834c
21. Baile Mhic Gabhann	Mooney 2	1950c
22. Baile an Ghabhann "Townland of the smith"	Mooney 2	1950c
23. Baile Mhic Gabhann	GÉ 21	1989
24. ˌbalə'gauən ˌbalï'gauən	Local pronunciation	1991

24

From the early forms with *na* the second element appears to have been derived from a plural noun: *Baile na nGabhann* "townland of the smiths". However, since these forms are all from related documents (*CPR Jas I, Inq. Ult.*) and the article eventually disappears entirely, the name may have been *Baile an Ghabhann* "townland of the smith". The smith was an important member of society and is frequently referred to in place-names, for example **Ednego**, probably "the hill-face of the smith", in the parish of Dromore. There was also a well-known surname *Ó Gabhann* "grandson of a smith", anglicized O'Gowan. The townland of **Ballygowan** in Kilkeel parish seems to include the surname, recorded locally in 1552 (*PNI* iii 23). A family of *O Gowan* had held lands in Newry before they reverted to the Crown (*CPR Jas I* 495a). There is no early reference to anyone of the surname in the parish of Aghaderg. If this place-name had ever included the surname, as suggested by O'Donovan, it would seem that the syllable *Ó* had been re-interpreted as the article *na*.

Ballygowan is a fairly common townland name, also found in Drumbeg, Comber/ Killinchy, and Moira parishes in Co. Down, and generally explained by O'Donovan as "O'Gowan's town". The history of **Ballygowan** in Moira, given an alias *Smithestowne* in 1631, seems similar to this, although it was close to church land in Dromore parish with an obsolete name for which the spellings suggest the surname *Mac an Ghabhann* "son of the smith", anglicized Magowan (see **Magherabeg**). Rather than being craftsmen by profession this family were "professors of history" (*De Script. Hib.* 91). There were clergy of the name in the diocese, for example, a vicar of Donaghcloney in 1427 (*Swanzy's Dromore* 113). There are no spellings with *mac* in the townland name in Aghaderg.

Ballynaskeagh	*Baile na Sceach*	
J 1338	"townland of the thornbushes"	

1. Ballyneskeagh (Shanchall)	CPR Jas I 394b	1609
2. Ballyneskeagh (Shanchall)	CPR Jas I 190a	1611
3. Ballineskeaghe	Inq. Ult. (Down) §7 Jac. I	1618
4. Ballinaskeagh al. Ballincrou	Hib. Reg. Upr Eveagh	1657c
5. Ballisciagh	Census 73	1659c
6. Ballinecrough	BSD 105	1661
7. Ballincrea	Hib. Del. Co. Downe	1672c
8. Ballyneskeagh al. Ballynecrough	ASE 274a 29	1681
9. Ballinasceagh	Vestry Reg. (OSNB) NB62	1747
10. B.neskeagh	Map of Down (OSNB) NB62	1755
11. Ballyneskeagh	Wm. Map (OSNB) NB62	1810
12. Ballynaskeagh	Reg. Free. (OSNB) NB62	1829
13. Ballinaskeagh	Bnd. Sur. (OSNB) NB62	1830
14. Ballinaskeagh	Wm. Little (OSNB) NB62	1834c
15. [Bal-lin-as-'key/kay]	OSNB Pron. NB62	1834c
16. Baile na Sceach "town of briars or thorns"	J O'D (OSNB) NB62	1834c
17. Baile-na-sceach "townland of the whitethorn bushes"	Joyce iii 114	1913
18. Baile na Sceiche/Sceach "place of the thorn bush"	Mooney 1	1950c
19. Baile na Sceach	AGBP 112	1969
20. Baile na Sceach	GÉ 24	1989

21. ˌbalənəˈskɛi	Local pronunciation	1991
22. ˌbalnəˈske:	Local pronunciation	1991
23. ˌbɛlənəˈske	Local pronunciation	1991

This townland was part of Shankill district. From the evidence of the early spellings the name was most likely derived from *Baile na Sceach* "townland of the thornbushes". The modern Irish form has been established as *Baile na Sceach* (*AGBP* 112), but the *OSNB* pronunciation ['kay] or ['key] and the modern pronunciation [e:] might indicate the genitive singular *sceiche*. An isolated hawthorn was often left alone because of fairy associations, and might grow into a considerable tree. The alternative form given in a few cases following Petty (forms 4, 6–8) might be *Baile na Croiche* "townland of the cross/gallows", but the evidence is scant.

Ballyvarley
J 0945

Baile Uí Mhearlaigh
"O'Marley's townland"

1. Ballivarly	CPR Jas I 396a	1609
2. Ballyvarlye	CPR Jas I 235a	1612
3. Ballivarley	Inq. Ult. (Down) §13 Car. I	1629
4. Balleevarly	Inq. Ult. (Down) §85 Car. I	1639
5. Ballyvarly	Civ. Surv. x §72	1655c
6. Aguekem, Ballimearly	Hib. Reg. Lr Evagh	1657c
7. Ballimearly	BSD 78	1661
8. Ballybarliecreen	Sub. Roll Down 273	1663
9. Ballyvarley	ASE 46b 26	1666
10. Ballimeary	Mooney MS 3	1666
11. Ballymearly	Mooney MS 3	1666
12. Ballyvarly, Crever, Aghenkenny	Rent Roll Down 7	1692
13. Ballyvarley	Vestry Reg. (OSNB) NB62	1754
14. B'varly	Map of Down (OSNB) NB62	1755
15. Ballyvarley	Wm. Map (OSNB) NB62	1810
16. Ballyvarley	Reg. Free. (OSNB) NB62	1829
17. Ballyvarley	Bnd. Sur. (OSNB) NB62	1830c
18. Ballyvarley	Wm. Little (OSNB) NB62	1834c
19. Baile Mharla "town of the marl or Marley's town"	J O'D (OSNB) NB62	1834c
20. Baile Uí Mhearlaigh	Mooney 3	1950c
21. ˌbaləˈva:rlï	Local pronunciation	1991
22. ˌbɛləˈvarlï	Local pronunciation	1991

Ballyvarley was held by Sir Art Magennis and passed to Patrick Deery, along with other townlands in the area, in 1639 (4). The place-name seems to contain the surname now known as Marley, *Baile Uí Mhearlaigh*. The name has been discussed most fully by MacLysaght (1964, 109) who says he has no doubt there was a distinct Oriel sept, from 17th-century references in the hearth-money rolls of Cos Armagh and Monaghan, and in Louth in the Dowdall deeds. In the 1659 "census" *O Marly* is listed as a principal Irish name in north Co. Armagh (*Census* 40, barony of *Oneyland*). Mooney claimed that the "name appears among pre-reformation clergy in Dromore", but I have not seen it (*Mooney MS* 3). It is not mentioned in Ulster in the *Calendar of Patent Rolls of James I*. The 18th-century road-maps of *Taylor and Skinner* (map 22, 1777) show the Revd Dean Marlay at Loughgilly. Our colleague Pat McKay says there are Marleys in Portadown, and this is borne out by the 1994 Northern Ireland telephone directory. For the additional names in forms (6,8,12) see **Drummiller** in Tullylish.

	Bovennett	Both Bheinéid	
	J 0942	"Bennett's hut"	
1.	Bovenned (Edw. Trevor)	CPR Jas I 395b	1609
2.	Bovened (Bp Dromore)	CPR Jas I 191a	1611
3.	Bovennet	Vestry Reg. (OSNB) NB62	1747
4.	Bovenet	Vestry Reg. (OSNB) NB62	1754
5.	Bovenit	Map of Down (OSNB) NB62	1755
6.	Bovenit	Wm. Map (OSNB) NB62	1810
7.	Bovennett	Newry Tel. (OSNB) NB62	1830
8.	Bovinett	Vestry Reg. (OSNB) NB62	1834c
9.	Bovenett, pronounced Bovenit	OSM xii 2	1834
10.	[Bo-'ven-net]	OSNB Pron. NB62	1834c
11.	Both Bheinit "Bennett's booth or hut"	J O'D (OSNB) NB62	1834c
12.	Both-Bheneit "Bennet's booth"	Joyce iii 147	1913
13.	'bɔvənət 'həus	Local pronunciation	1991
14.	ˌbə'vɛnət	Local pronunciation	1995

Bo- as an initial syllable in Irish place-names frequently represents *both* "hut" plus a personal name: **Bovevagh** Co. Derry, *Boith Mhéabha* "Méabh's hut" (*GÉ* 192); **Bohoona** Co. Galway, *Both Chuana* "Cuana's booth" (*Joyce* iii 143). Bovennett is a small townland, of 128 acres. It was church land but there are only two 17th-century forms (1,2), so that it may well have begun as a subdivision of a larger unit. Alternatively there may be other references to it under a different name not yet recognized. See **Drumsallagh** below. Woulfe gives *Beinéid*, *Bionáid* as a personal name, and mentions Bennett as a surname brought into Ireland and "now common in many parts of the country" (Woulfe 1923, 229). MacLysaght gives Bennett as "a prominent Anglo-Irish family in Kilkenny . . . The name appears as MacBennett in Oriel". "Later in the 17th century we find the name, as MacBennett as well as Bennett, occurring frequently in Co. Armagh. Art Bennett (fl. 1825) the poet-satirist was an Armagh man" (MacLysaght 1985, 16; 1982, 33; Ó Buachalla 1979). As with **Ballyvarley**, there is no record of a person of the name living in the townland.

	Brickland	Baile Bhricleann	
	J 1140	"*Bricriu's* townland"	
1.	Bryklyn	Mercator's Ire.	1595
2.	Brickland, the castle and town of	CPR Jas I 394b	1609
3.	Ballybrickland	CPR Jas I 394b	1609
4.	Ballybrickland, Arte Oge McBrien Magenis of	CPR Jas I 195b	1610

5. Ballibrickland (Loughbrickland)	CPR Jas I 190a	1611
6. the castle of Brickland	CPR Jas I 190a	1611
7. Brickland otherwise Loughbrickland, the castle of	CPR Jas I 409b	1618
8. Ballibrickland	CPR Jas I 409b	1618
9. Brickland al Loughbrickland al Ballybrickland	Inq. Ult. (Down) §39 Car. I	1633
10. Brickland al. Loughbrickland al. Ballebrickland	Inq. Ult. (Down) §62 Car. I	1635
11. Loghbrickland	Census 73	1659c
12. Brecklin	Lamb Maps Co. Downe	1690c
13. Tent of the Castle, town and lands of Brickland, and the Tythes of Toone in the Princt of Ballybrickland in the Territory of Eveagh	Rent Roll Down 11	1692
14. Bricklan	Harris Hist. 116	1744
15. Brickland	Vestry Reg. (OSNB) NB62	1747
16. Brickland	Map of Down (OSNB) NB62	1755
17. Brickland	Reg. Free. (OSNB) NB62	1830
18. Brickland	Bnd. Sur. (OSNB) NB62	1830c
19. Brickland	Wm. Little (OSNB) NB62	1834c
20. Breac-chluain "spotted meadow or bog-land"	J O'D (OSNB) NB62	1834c
22. 'brïklǝn	Local pronunciation	1991

The 17th-century forms are predominantly *Ballybrickland*, but there is a tendency to drop the prefix *Baile* when the Magennis castle is being referred to (2,6,7,13). Presumably in Irish this could be *Caisleán Bhricleann* "Bricriu's castle" but, when this name was anglicized, "Brickland" was understood as being a place-name itself. Brickland is not an English place-name, as it might appear, but represents the genitive case of a rare Old Irish personal name *Bricriu* (a nasal stem), with later change of the second *r* to *l* (*Joyce* i 48).

Since the name is so uncommon it is likely that its occurrence here, and in **Lough Brickland** lake to the north-west of the townland, is intended to indicate the site of a tale in the Ulster Cycle, *Fled Bricrenn* "Bricriu's Feast", where Conchobar king of Ulster and his warriors were invited to feast in Bricriu the trouble-maker's hall at *Dún Rudraige* "Rudraige's hill-fort" (*FB* §1). This place-name has been connected with the site of the castle at Dundrum, where the inner bay and shore were *Loch* and *Trácht Rudraige* "Rudraige's lough, strand" (*O'Laverty* i 69). However, although names involving their legendary ancestor *Rudraige* (later *Rúraí*, "Rory") are connected with the tradition that Uí Echach and the related Dál nAraide were the true *Ulaid* (**Kilwarlin, Edentiroory**), there is no need for the place-names to be close together.

The site of the castle here has been lost, but the townland of Brickland contains **Water Hill Fort**, a rath with internal ditch on top of a steep ridge 470 feet high, overlooking **Loughbrickland** lake and its crannog, and with a good view in all directions, particularly to the west into Co. Armagh (*ASCD* 154).

Carrickdrumman

J 0838

Carraig Dhromainne
"rock of the ridge"

1. Carrick Drummond	Vestry Reg. (OSNB) NB62	1747
2. Corackdruman	Vestry Reg. (OSNB) NB62	1754
3. Carrickdrummon	Map of Down (OSNB) NB62	1755
4. Carrickdrummond	Wm. Map (OSNB) NB62	1810
5. Carrickdrummon	Bnd. Sur. (OSNB) NB62	1830c
6. Carrickadrummon	Wm. Little (OSNB) NB62	1834c
7. Carrick	Bassett's Down 257	1886
8. Carraig Dromainn "rock of the ridge or long hill"	J O'D (OSNB) NB62	1834c
9. ˌkɑrək'dromən	Local pronunciation	1991
10. 'kjɑrk'dromən	Local pronunciation	1991

There are no early forms for this name, since Carrickdrummond was originally a subdivision of Ballymacaratty More in the parish of Donaghmore to the south (*Cowan's Donaghmore* 42n; *PNI* i 94). It is not clear what rock gave it its name but there is a farm called "The Rocks" on the eastern boundary with Ballymacaratty More (OS 1:10,000 sheet 237). The second element is clearly *dromainn* "ridge". The usual genitive of *dromainn* is *dromainne*, but no final vowel appears in the 17th-century forms of Aughnadrumman in Moira, and a nasal genitive *dromann* may also be possible here.

Caskum

J 1242

An Choiscéim
"the footstep/path"

1. Keskein (Loughbrickland)	CPR Jas I 394b	1609
2. Seskum	Ancient Patent (OSNB)	1610
3. Leskem (Loughbrickland)	CPR Jas I 190a	1611
4. Dromynacarcaskem [recte Caskem?]	CPR Jas I 409b	1618
5. Caskeame	Inq. Ult. (Down) §39 Car. I	1633
6. (?)Seskin	Inq. Ult. (Down) §62 Car. I	1635
7. Cassgem	Census 73	1659c
8. Ballynkeskeane, a sessiagh of	BSD 106	1661
9. Keskane	Sub. Roll Down 276	1663
10. (?)Ballyncasslane (Aghadarrige)	BSD 119	1666
11. Keskem or Keskein	Deeds & Wills (Mooney) 5	1719
12. Keskin al Keskem	Deeds & Wills (Mooney) 5	1719
13. Caskum	Vestry Reg. (OSNB) NB62	1754
14. Caskum	Map of Down (OSNB) NB62	1755
15. Caskum	Wm. Map (OSNB) NB62	1810
16. Kescum	County Warrant (OSNB) NB62	1827
17. Caskum	Reg. Free. (OSNB) NB62	1829
18. Kescum	Reg. Free. (OSNB) NB62	1829
19. Kescum	Bnd. Sur. (OSNB) NB62	1830c
20. Caskum	Wm. Little (OSNB) NB62	1833c

21.	Cos cham "crooked leg"	J O'D (OSNB) NB62	1834c
22.	An Coiscéim "a path, a pad"	Joyce iii 420	1913
23.	'kaskəm	Local pronunciation	1994

An Choiscéim, literally "foot-step", seems the most likely interpretation of the spellings. There is a townland of Coskeam in Co. Clare which appears to be the same word. Hogan has two examples from medieval literature: *Coiscéim Easa Ruaid, Coiscéim na Féindi* "foot-step of Assaroe, foot-step of the warrior-band" (*Acallam (Stokes)* l.6898, p.331). Joyce says that *céim* is "often applied topographically to a narrow pass or roadway between rocks or hills", and that the compound with *cos* "foot" is also applied to "a narrow road or pass", giving as examples Kishkeam and Cushcam in Cork and Waterford (*Joyce* ii 386). However Cushcam has subsequently been analysed as *Cois Chaim*, the form suggested by O'Donovan here (*L. Log. P. Láirge* 27). Caskum lies in hilly ground a mile east of the main road north to Banbridge. There are two minor roads which cross the townland from west to east. The more northerly rejoins the main road to Dromore, the southern one goes to Annaclone, passing between a rath, shown on the 1:50,000 map just north of Clover Hill, and the hill-fort in Dromorebrague.

Coolnacran   *Cluain Chrannacháin*
J 1043   "meadow of the wooded place"

1.	Cloncharcharm	CPR Jas I 394b	1609
2.	Cloncranchann (Loughbrickland)	CPR Jas I 190a	1611
3.	Cloncranchan	CPR Jas I 409b	1618
4.	Cloncranaghan	Inq. Ult. (Down) §39 Car.I	1633
5.	Cloncronaghan	Inq. Ult. (Down) §62 Car.I	1635
6.	(?)Derrychoole	BSD 106	1661
7.	Cloncranchy	Sub. Roll Down 11	1663
8.	Clonecrannagh, Ballyncaslane and	BSD 119	1666
9.	Cloncranchan al. Clonronlagan		
	al. Colenecran al. Colenecrawen	Deeds & Wills (Mooney) 5	1719
10.	Clonranachan, Clonronahan	Deeds & Wills (Mooney) 6	1720
11.	Clonronahan	Deeds & Wills (Mooney) 5	1722
12.	Collenecrannon als Cloneranehan		
	als Colencrawn	Deeds & Wills (Mooney) 5	1722
13.	Colenacran	Vestry Reg. (OSNB) NB62	1754
14.	Colnacran	Map of Down (OSNB) NB62	1755
15.	Colnacrane	Ir. Wills Index 67	1765
16.	Coolnacran	Vestry Reg. (OSNB) NB62	1768
17.	Colnacran	Wm. Map (OSNB) NB62	1810
18.	Colenacran	County Warrant (OSNB) NB62	1827
19.	Colenacran	Reg. Free. (OSNB) NB62	1829
20.	Coolnacran	Bnd. Sur. (OSNB) NB62	1830c
21.	Colenacran	OSM xii 2	1834
22.	Colnacran	Vestry Reg. (OSNB) NB62	1834c
23.	Coolnecrann	OSNB 13	1834c
24.	['Cool-na-cran]	OSNB Pron. NB62	1834c
25.	Cúl-na-crann "behind the trees"	OSNB Inf. NB62	1834c

26. Cúil na gCrann		
"corner/angle/balk of the trees"	J O'D (OSNB) NB62	1834c
27. Cúl-na-gcrann "corner of the trees"	Joyce iii 247	1913
28. Cúil na gCrann "corner of the trees"	Mooney 5	1950c
29. Cluain Chrannachain	Mooney 5	1950c
30. ˌkulnəˈkrɑn	Local pronunciation	1991

This name has a very diverse collection of early spellings, from which it appears that the elements *cluain* "meadow", *cúil* "recess", *crann* "tree" (*crannachán* "(little?) wooded place") and *doire* "oakwood" have all been involved. The early forms (1–8) seem to represent *Cluain Chrannacháin* "the meadow of the wooded place", the 18th-century forms (9, 12 on), perhaps influenced by the possible alias *Derrychoole*, may stand for *Cúil na gCrann* "corner of the trees" as suggested by Mooney. Alternatively the earlier form *Cluain Chrannacháin* could have developed into the later Coolnecran if *Cloncrannaghan* metathesized into *Colnacrannaghan*, *-crannaghan* became shortened to *-crannan* with the weakening of [x], and lost its final *-an* by haplology, ending up as *Colnacran*.

Creevy
J 1137

An Chraobhaigh
"the bushy place"

1. Ballycrevie (Shanchall)	CPR Jas I 394b	1609
2. (?)Ballynecrivie (Sir A. Magenis)	CPR Jas I 396a	1609
3. Ballycrevie (Shanchall)	CPR Jas I 190a	1611
4. (?)Ballynecrivie (Sir A. Magenis)	CPR Jas I 235a	1612
5. Ballycreevie (Shanechall)	Inq. Ult. (Down) §7 Jac. I	1618
6. (?)le sessiagh . . . de Creevy 40a	Inq. Ult. (Down) §85 Car.I	1639
7. Creeny	Hib. Reg. Upr Eveagh	1657c
8. Creevy	Census 73	1659c
9. Crevey (Up. Evagh)	BSD 106	1661
10. (?)Creeue (Lr. Evagh)	BSD 78	1661
11. (?)Creny	Hib. Del. Co. Downe	1672c
12. Crevy	ASE 274a 29	1681
13. Cervery	Rent Roll Down 11	1692
14. Creevey	Vestry Reg. (OSNB) NB62	1747
15. Crevey	Vestry Reg. (OSNB) NB62	1754
16. Creevy	Wm. Map (OSNB) NB62	1810
17. Creevy	Reg. Free. (OSNB) NB62	1829
18. Creevy	Bnd. Sur. (OSNB) NB62	1830c
19. Crewy	OSM xii 1b	1834
20. Creevey	Wm. Little (OSNB) NB62	1834c
21. Craobhach "bushy land"	J O'D (OSNB) NB62	1834c
22. Craobhach	Mooney 5	1950c
23. ˈkriːvï	Local pronunciation	1991

The early 17th-century forms for Creevy prefix the name with *Ballyne-*, showing that the name was then used with the article. Only those forms which are associated with the district of Shankill definitely refer to this townland, but they are enough to establish the Irish form.

The early 17th-century spellings marked with a query (2,4,6;10,11) are from the list of lands owned by Sir Art Magennis, where they follow the name of Ballyvarley in the north of Aghaderg. Sir Art's townland of **Lisnacreevy** in Drumballyroney was also listed as *Ballynecreevie* etc., but next to Tirfergus in that parish. Since the queried forms could also be mistaken for Lisnacreevy they are also given there. However documents later in the 17th century resolve the confusion. The inquisition on Sir Hugh Magennis' lands in 1639 refers to *le sessiagh, vil' et ter' de Creevy 40 acres* next to Drummiller in this parish, and *Ballelesnecreevy* next to Imdel in Drumballyroney (*Inq. Ult. (Down) §85 Car. I*). A land unit called *Creeve* was shown on Petty's map of Co. Down (form 11) in the southern part of Lower Iveagh near Banbridge, and was listed as *Creeue* in *Aghaderigg* parish in Lower Iveagh (form 10). Most of Aghaderg, including the current townland of Creevy, is in Upper Iveagh. The Creevy which belonged to Sir Art Magennis was not modern Creevy in Aghaderg, but a lost name in the north of the parish, bordering Tullylish.

| **Derrydrummuck** | *Doire Droma Muc* |
| J 1340 | "oakwood of the ridge of (the) pigs" |

1.	Derudmuke al. Derrivermucke (Shanchall)	CPR Jas I 394b	1609
2.	Derrydrommuck othw Derryvormuck (Shanchall)	CPR Jas I 190a	1611
3.	Derrydromuck al. Derryvermack	Inq. Ult. (Down) §7 Jac. I	1618
4.	Derridromocke	Hib. Reg. Upr Eveagh	1657c
5.	Derry Drummucke	Census 73	1659c
6.	Derryromacke	BSD 105	1661
7.	Doredromock	Hib. Del. Co. Downe	1672c
8.	Derridrumucke pt	ASE 274a 29	1681
9.	Derredromack	ASE 255a	1681
10.	Derrydrumnemuck	Rent Roll Down 11	1692
11.	Derrydromack	Rent Roll Down 12	1692
12.	Derrydrummock	Vestry Reg. (OSNB) NB62	1747
13.	Derrydrumuck	Vestry Reg. (OSNB) NB62	1754
14.	Derrydrummuck	Map of Down (OSNB) NB62	1755
15.	Derrydrummuck	Wm. Map (OSNB) NB62	1810
16.	Derrydrumuck	County Warrant (OSNB) NB62	1827
17.	Derrydrumock/Derrydrumuck	Reg. Free. (OSNB) NB62	1829
18.	Derrydrummuck	Bnd. Sur. (OSNB) NB62	1830c
19.	Derrydrummuck	Wm. Little (OSNB) NB62	1833c
20.	Doire Druma Muc "Derry or oak-wood of the pigs"	J O'D (OSNB) NB62	1834c
21.	Doire-droma-muice "of the pig's hill-ridge/pig's back"	Joyce iii 295	1913
22.	Doire Droma Muc	Mooney 7	1950c
23.	ˌdɛrïdrọˈmǫk	Local pronunciation	1991
24.	ˌdərïˈdrọmǫk	Local pronunciation	1991

Derrydrummuck was in the Magennis district of Shankill and is the highest part of the parish, rising to 579 feet (*OSM* xii 8a). One of the spellings, in 1692 (form 10), adds the article *ne* between *drum* and *muck*, so that it appears that at least at that date the name was understood in Irish as "the oakwood of the ridge of the pigs". It is more difficult to understand the early 17th-century alternative forms *Derryvormuck* etc., where the syllable following *Derry* has been lenited: *Doire Bhuair Muc* "oakwood of pigs' dung", or *Doire Mhór Muc* "large oakwood of pigs" would need *doire* to be dative, or possibly feminine. Swine were taken to the woods in autumn to feed on acorns, which formed an important resource for early animal husbandry.

Wallace's Hill Head is in the south-west (OS 1:10,000 sheet 237), near where there was a standing stone called "Conn's Stone" on the border with the north-east corner of Shankill (*PSAMNI* 112). The stone is not in the *Archaeological Survey of Co. Down*, nor on recent maps, and there is no evidence as to who Conn might have been.

Dromorebrague
J 1341

Droim Mór Breá
"big ridge of the high ground"

1. (?)Cairell a Raith Droma Breg	Descendants Ir xiii 322 (verse)	1200c
2. (?)a nDruimnib Breag	Descendants Ir xiii 336,338	1200c
3. Ballydromore (Shanehall)	CPR Jas I 394b	1609
4. Ballydromore (Shanchall)	CPR Jas I 190a	1611
5. Ballydromore	Inq. Ult. (Down) §7 Jac.I	1618
6. Dromorebreagh	Inq. Ult. (Down) §88 Car. I	1640
7. Drumore Breege	Census 73	1659c
8. Dromoreabreage	Vestry Reg. (OSNB) NB62	1747
9. Dromoreabreag	Vestry Reg. (OSNB) NB62	1754
10. Dromore-breaga	Map of Down (OSNB) NB62	1755
11. Dromorebreague	Vestry Reg. (OSNB) NB62	1768
12. Dromoreabreage	Wm. Map (OSNB) NB62	1810
13. Breagh Ir.	Wills Index 64	1817
14. Dromorebreda	Bnd. Sur. (OSNB) NB62	1830c
15. Dromorebreda	Wm. Little (OSNB) NB62	1833c
16. Dromorebreda, generally called Brague	OSM xii 2a	1834
17. the townland of Brague	OSM xii 4b	1834
18. sometimes written Dromorebrega	OSM xii 2a	1834
19. Brague school in Dromore Brague townland	OSM xii 11b	1837
20. Dromorebrague Fort	OSM xii 8a	1837
21. Druim Mór Bréige "false or pseudo Dromore"	J O'D (OSNB) NB62	1834c
22. Druim Mór Bréagtha "great hill of playing games"	Mooney 7	1950c
23. 'bre:g	Local pronunciation	1991
24. drọ,mo:r'brɛ:g	Local pronunciation	1991

Dromorebrague must be the townland of Shankill district called in the early 17th century *Ballydromore*, although it is now known locally just as Brague. There is a hill-fort at 489 feet near the north-east boundary of the parish (*ASCD* 148). The townland is high ground and *Droim Mór* "big ridge" would need no explanation as the basic name of the place. The two place-names in this parish including the element *brague* have been understood as containing *bréige*, the genitive of *bréag* "a lie", and thus having the sense of an adjective "false" (Glancy 1956, 78). The term *buachaill bréige* "false lad" was often used for a standing stone which might look like a person when seen from far off (*Joyce* ii 435; Ó Ceallaigh 1952–3(b) 36–7). If Dromorebrague were *Droim Mór Bréige* "false Dromore" it would be a parallel to the popular interpretation of **Armaghbrague** in Co. Armagh.

In the case of Armaghbrague there was a story in local tradition explaining that it was called "false Armagh" because St Patrick had intended to build his first church on top of the hill there, but a bull knocked what was built down each night and forced him to move to Armagh city (MacNeill 1962, i 59; *Joyce* ii 436). "False Armagh" makes no topographical sense, since no one approaching on the main road from the south could mistake the height of Carrickatuke (1304 feet) for the cathedral hill in Armagh, 9 miles on. "False Dromore", if used also to refer to a diocesan capital, is slightly more plausible, since the rising ground at Dromorebrague was visible from the main road 12 miles south of Dromore and had a fort on top, like Maypole Hill north of the cathedral in the town.

The *-brague* element has also been studied by Dean Mooney. He thought that this name was rather *Droim Mór Bréagtha* "big ridge for playing games", where *-brague* represented the genitive of *bréagadh*, "deceiving" and thence "beguiling", used in this case of a hill where people once assembled to play games (Mooney 1956(a), 26–7). In **Lisnabrague** the element might refer to the tricks played by the fairy people (*Mooney MS* 11). However, this would strain the meaning of *bréagadh*, and *bréagtha*, pronounced [bˈrˈɛːkə], would be unlikely to be anglicized *brague*.

The townland is known as Brague locally, and this is as old as the early 19th century (forms 13,16,23: *OSM* xii 2,11). The area of Armaghbrague was likewise known as The Brague (Arthurs 1952–3(c), 29; MacNeill 1962, ii 475,476,477). It is possible that *-brague* could represent the genitive singular or plural *breagh* (standard *breá*) of *brí* "height, plateau", with final [ɣ] delenited to [g] in the modern form. This occurs sometimes in the Irish of Donegal, especially when [ɣ] is at the end of monosyllables (Quiggin 1906, 139 §429).

Dromorebrague (less likely Lisnabrague, which is on low ground) might then be part of the district *Droim Breá* or *Dromanna Breá* "ridge (or ridges) of the height (or heights)", which was the earliest settlement of Dál Fiatach in east Ulster (forms 1,2). The element *brí* makes the name very similar to that of the early Meath kingdom of *Brega* "heights" which, since it lay partly north of the Boyne, was partly in the ancient province of Ulster (Byrne 1973, 46,83). *Ad Dorsos Breg* "to the ridges of Brega" was used in the 8th-century *Liber Angeli* (Bieler, 184 §7) as the south bound of St Patrick's see, with *Brí Erigi*, possibly Slieve Croob, as the east bound, repeated in Irish as *co Dromma Breg* in the 9th-century Life (*Trip. Life (Stokes)* 352, 234). Byrne regards the mention of "*Druimne Breg*" in these bounds as chosen to include the territory still inhabited by the Ulaid (1973, 83).

Dobbs considered that Dál Fiatach moved east from Co. Armagh to settle, not in Louth and Meath, but in Co. Down, and that the place (2) where the sons of their ancestor Muiredach Muinderg divided their inheritance *a nDruimnib Breag* "on the ridges of *Breagh*" was in east Co. Down, their later power-base (*Descendants Ir* xiii 337n). However it is more likely that they first established themselves in the area of Aghaderg, immediately behind the Danes' Cast (O'Rahilly 1946, 498–9). After *Ráith Dromma Breg* "the rath of *Droim Breá*", the next-named tribal capital, *Lethead*, could have been at the townland of **Leode** on a hill in the parish of Clonduff, between Mayobridge and Hilltown (*Descendants Ir* xiii 322–4 n.3, *PNI* iii 91–2). On the other hand the epithet *na lear* "of the seas" in the verse account in the same document has meant that *Lethead* has been taken by Byrne as Knocklayd hill in north Co. Antrim, at the opposite end of Ulaid territory from *Brega* (Byrne 1973, 109; *Clann Ollaman* 83 nn.16,18).

Drummiller   *Droim Iolair*
J 0745   "eagle's ridge "

1. Ballylisdromiller	CPR Jas I 396a	1609
2. Ballylisdromiller	CPR Jas I 235a	1612
3. Ballylissdromiller	Inq. Ult. (Down) §13 Car.I	1629
4. Drommiller	Inq. Ult. (Down) §85 Car. I	1639
5. Dromiller	Civ. Surv. x §72	1655c
6. Dromiller	Civ. Surv. x §73	1655c
7. 1 sessiagh of Drumiller	Hib. Reg. Lr Evagh	1657c
8. 2 sessiaghs of Drummiller	Hib. Reg. Lr Evagh	1657c
9. Drumiller 2 sessiagh	BSD 78	1661
10. Drummiller (manor of Gilford)	ASE 112a 34	1667
11. Drumiller	Hib. Del. Co. Down	1672c
12. D.miller	Lamb Maps Co. Down	1690c
13. Drummiller	Vestry Reg. (OSNB) NB62	1747
14. Drumiller	Vestry Reg. (OSNB) NB62	1754
15. D-miller	Map of Down (OSNB) NB62	1755
16. Tullyhoe	Rocque's Map (Coote)	1760
17. Drummiller	Wm. Map (OSNB) NB62	1810
18. Drumillar	Reg. Free. (OSNB) NB62	1830
19. Drummiller	Bnd. Sur. (OSNB) NB62	1830c
20. Drummillar	Wm. Little (OSNB) NB62	1834c
21. Druim Iolair "ridge or long hill of the eagle"	J O'D (OSNB) NB62	1834c
22. Druim Iolair "ridge of the eagle"	J O'D (OSNB) E61 (Tullylish)	1834c
23. Iolar "the eagle's ridge"	Knox Hist. 353	1875
24. ˌdrə'mələr	Local pronunciation	1991

Within Iveagh there are townlands of Drummiller in the parishes of Donaghmore (*PNI* i 100–1), Dromore and Aghaderg. This one is divided between Aghaderg and Tullylish parishes, although the whole townland was reckoned to be in the barony of Iveagh Lower, Lower half. It belonged at the beginning of the 17th century to Sir Arthur Magennis, but came into the hands of John Magill and was made part of his manor of Gilford in 1680 (*ASE* 112a). There may have been names for the subdivisions, discussed under Tullylish.

The first element is clearly *droim* "ridge", but since this word ends in *m* it is difficult to distinguish whether the second element might be the genitive of *muilleoir* "miller" or *iolar* "eagle". There is a stream running west from Drummiller Lough in the townland, but no record of any water-mill. Likewise there is no evidence for the original [u] vowel of the first syllable which any name containing *muilleoir* might be expected to retain in early anglicized forms (Toner 1991–3, 55).

Since the townland is higher ground in what was once a desolate and boggy area (the townland of **Loughans** to the north was impassable even in the 18th century) *Droim Iolair*

35

"eagle's ridge" seems more likely. The first three references to Drummiller call it *Ballylisdromiller*, but the *lios* cannot now be identified, although in 1834 there was an old fort with a ditch "on top of the highest hill" in the townland, and a "very remarkable cairn" (*OSM* xii 7; *OSNB*), both now destroyed. John O'Donovan was taken to see the cairn, "a large mount of loose stones in a very barren valley . . . much decreased by carrying stones from it to build houses in the neighbourhood". He recorded the local tradition that "a battle was fought in the valley, and that this *kern* of stones was piled over the slain as a monument" (*OSL Dn* 29). However O'Laverty's *Carn Eochy* identified with Drummiller seems to be a mistake for *Carn Achaidh Leithdheirg* (*O'Laverty* i intro. xiv, see **Aghaderg**). Close by the cairn were some "wretched cabins", and the haunted ruins of a house called Tally-ho, possibly the same as "*Tullyhoa* near Gilford" which according to Knox had been an abbey (*Knox Hist.* 353,403).

Drumnahare	*Dromainn an Choirthe*	
J 1142	"ridge of the standing-stone"	

1. Drominaeer	CPR Jas I 394b	1609
2. Drominakar (Loughbrickland)	CPR Jas I 190a	1611
3. Dromynacarcaskem	CPR Jas I 409b	1618
4. Domencarr 60a	Inq. Ult. (Down) §39 Car.I	1633
5. Dromenecarr	Inq. Ult. (Down) §62 Car.I	1635
6. Druma Chara	Census 73	1659c
7. Drumnehare	Deeds & Wills (Mooney) 9	1714
8. Drumynaear or Dromynacar	Deeds & Wills (Mooney) 9	1719
9. Drumnekarr or Drimnekarr al. Drummaharr or Drumnehar	Deeds & Wills (Mooney) 9	1719
10. Druimnahare	Vestry Reg. (OSNB) NB62	1747
11. Drumnahar	Map of Down (OSNB) NB62	1755
12. Drumnahare	Wm. Map (OSNB) NB62	1810
13. Drumnahare	County Warrant (OSNB) NB62	1827
14. Drumnahare	Reg. Free. (OSNB) NB62	1829
15. Drumnahare	Bnd. Sur. (OSNB) NB62	1830c
16. Drumnahare	Wm. Little (OSNB) NB62	1834c
17. Druim na h-Aér "ridge of the air"	J O'D (OSNB) NB62	1834c
18. Druimeann Uí Charra/Chairre "Carr's Hill"	Mooney 9	1950c
19. Druimne Earracha	Mooney 9	1950c
20. ˌdrọmnəˈhɛːr	Local pronunciation	1991

The earlier spellings of Drumnahare (1–9) seem to indicate the alternation of hard *c* with its lenited form [x] or [h]. Mooney suggested that the name was based on a surname, *Ó Cairre* or *Ó Carra* (18). In the 13th century the family of *Ó Cairre* shared the rulership of southern Tyrone (*Cineál nAonghusa*) with the McCanns (Simms 1978, 72). There was an *O'Corra* family of Lissan parish Co. Tyrone (*Joyce* iii 483), anglicized as O'Corr in the 17th-century sources (*CPR Jas I*). Woulfe (1923, 452,481) says all of these are variants (e.g. *Ó Cairre* in *AFM* for *Ó Carra*) of "a common Ulster surname", but it is not specifically recorded in this area.

In the local area in 1618 a man called Neale *O'Hyer* demonstrated the bounds of the church townland of Drumsallagh for Sir Edward Trevor and Sir George Sexton and Sir Art Magenis (*Inq. Ult.* xliii), and Teige *O'Hoyre* of *Balleenlogh*, probably Ballylough in Donaghmore, was acquitted in 1613 (*Ulst. Roll Gaol Deliv.* 263). By the mid-19th century the English form O'Hare was the most common surname in Upper Iveagh and especially in Donaghmore (Bell 1988, 209). It is usually thought to be an anglicization of the Orior surname *Ó hÉir / Ó hÍr* (Woulfe 1923, 571), which would not explain the early forms with [k] here.

A more likely explanation is that Drumnahare is *Dromainn an Choirthe* "ridge of the standing stone", referring to the standing stone at 300 feet above Loughbrickland lake, apparently marking a single burial (*ASCD* 95–6, grid-reference 111415, 5'x3', illustrated plate 11 no.271). This element seems also to appear in **Tamnaharry** in Clonallan, where there is also a standing stone (*PNI* i 80–1).

Drumnahare was part of the Magennis district of Loughbrickland. When he was made a freeholder in 1609, Art Oge Magenis of Loughbrickland agreed to "give to the rector of *Aghaderick* and his successors for ever the moiety of one of the said townlands next to the said church (Aghaderg parish), which should be assigned to it by the bishop of Dromore" (*CPR Jas I* 190a). It is not clear what happened, since "noe gleab" was known in 1657 (*Atkinson's Dromore* 134). At the same date land called *The Gleab* was noted on Petty's map of Upper Iveagh which appears to be located in the south of Brickland townland (between Derrydrummuck and Shankill). This could have been Art Oge's gift, but is nowhere near the old church. By 1837 there was a Glebe school and house, inhabited by the Rev. Lefroy (*OSM* xii 10a,11). The place now called Aghaderg Glebe is in Drumnahare townland south-east of Loughbrickland village.

Drumsallagh
J 0940

Droim Saileach
"willow ridge"

1.	Dromohallagh	CPR Jas I 395b	1609
2.	Dromshallagh	CPR Jas I 191a	1611
3.	Dromsallagh	Inq. Ult. (Down) xlii	1618
4.	Dromsallagh	CPR Jas I 305a	1623
5.	little brook of Dromsallagh	CPR Jas I 305a	1623
6.	Dromsallagh, fort in Lislonan wood in	CPR Jas I 305a	1623
7.	Dromsallagh (Sir Edw. Trevor)	CPR Jas I 305a	1623
8.	Dromsalagh	Census 73	1659c
9.	Drumsallagh	BSD 106	1661
10.	Dromsallagh	Sub. Roll Down 276	1663
11.	Drumsallagh	Vestry Reg. (OSNB) NB62	1754c
12.	Drumsallagh	Map of Down (OSNB) NB62	1755
13.	Drumsallagh	Wm. Map (OSNB) NB62	1810
14.	Drumsallagh	Reg. Free. (OSNB) NB62	1829
15.	Drumsallagh	Bnd. Sur. (OSNB) NB62	1830c
16.	Drumsallagh	Wm. Little (OSNB) NB62	1833c
17.	[Drum-'sal-lagh/ -salla]	OSNB Pron. NB62	1834c
18.	Druim Salach "miry or dirty ridge"	J O'D (OSNB) NB62	1834c
19.	ˌdrọm'sɑləx	Local pronunciation	1991
20.	ˌdrọm'salə	Local pronunciation	1991

Drumsallagh belonged to the bishop of Dromore, sublet to Sir Edward Trevor. From the bounds between the lands held by Sir Edward Trevor and Sir George Sexton, detailed in 1618 (forms 3–7), it seems that Drumsallagh must have been much larger than its current area, since it adjoined both Lisnagade and Ballygowan to the north, and Meenan (*Mynnye*) and Ballymacaratty to the south. Of the intervening townlands, Legananny is not mentioned in the bounds, although it is mentioned with Bovenett, and Drumsallagh, in the list of church lands (*CPR Jas I* 191a). Neither Legananny nor Bovennett is mentioned regularly in the 17th-century sources, and the simplest explanation would be that both were often included in Drumsallagh. Edenderry may appear in the bounds of Drumsallagh as "the hill of *Edendaran* in the *Meagh*", mearing with Lisnagade.

Drumsallagh contained the site of the early parish church (*EA* 112–3n). Atkinson was misled by his etymology of **Shankill** as "old church" into locating the church south of the lake (*Atkinson's Dromore* 224). However in 1834 the standing stones called the Three Sisters, in Greenan townland near the eastern border of Drumsallagh, were "by some supposed to have been the site of the ancient glebe and near the old church" (*OSM* xii 7b). Correspondence in 1795 between Bishop Percy and Dr Shiel, the Vicar-General, about ecclesiastical remains in Drumsallagh, has now been printed, and reveals the details (Cahill 1985). Shiel was told that the site of a Franciscan monastery, not abandoned till 1641, was "within about 200 yards of the old church", which was then in ruins. Stones from the Friary had been used to build the 17th-century church in Loughbrickland village, and subsequently, about 1755, the rest of the stone had been used for a bleach green beside a "large rivulet" running near the monastery (in fact the western boundary of the townland). An old man "above ninety" called Patrick Fegan, whose ancestors for many generations had lived in Drumsallagh, remembered the walls standing, a spring in the courtyard called the Fryars' Well, and avenues between the monastery and old church to the daughter church in Loughbrickland. The church site beside the stream, the original **Aghaderg**, has been forgotten, but the remains of the monastery are marked on the OS 1:10,000 map in the north of the townland (sheet 237, J 0941; *ASCD* 302).

The first element must be *droim* "ridge" as in various townland names in the parish. There are three possibilities for the second element: *salach* "dirty", *sealbhach* "rich in cows" (as in **Ballysallagh** in Dromore), or *saileach, salach*, genitives of *sail* "willow". There is no evidence of a lost *-bh-*, and the historical forms consistently spell the second element as *-sallagh*, which might indicate *salach* "dirty" rather than *saileach* "of willow". *Saileach* can be anglicized *-sillagh* and *-sallagh*, but there are no place-names spelt *-sillagh* in Cos Antrim or Down. Since willow was mentioned in 1834 ("oak and fir and sometimes sally") among the species of trees found in the bogs (*OSM* xii 3b), *Droim Saileach* "ridge of willow" may be most likely here, like **Coolsallagh** in Dromore.

Edenderry	*Éadan Darach*	
J 0843	"hill-face of (the) oak-tree"	
1. Nemeagh (Loughdegan)	CPR Jas I 395a	1609
2. Nemeagh (Loughdegan)	CPR Jas I 190b	1611
3. ditch Lemneneigh, in English		
the Horse-leap	Inq. Ult. (Down) xliii	1618
4. hill called Lenneneigh	Inq. Ult. (Down) xliii	1618
5. Ballymeagh	Inq. Ult. (Down) xliii	1618
6. Lisnecnow in the Meagh	Inq. Ult. (Down) xliii	1618
7. hill Edendaron in the Meagh	Inq. Ult. (Down) xliii	1618
8. the lands of the Meagh	Inq. Ult. (Down) xliii	1618

9. ditch Lemnemeigh, in English the Horse-Leap	CPR Jas I 305a	1623
10. Lymnemeagh hill	CPR Jas I 305a	1623
11. Ballymeagh (Sir Geo. Sexton)	CPR Jas I 305a	1623
12. Lisnecnow in the Meagh	CPR Jas I 305a	1623
13. Edendaran Hill in the Meagh	CPR Jas I 305a	1623
14. the townland of the Meagh	CPR Jas I 305a	1623
15. Nemyagh	Inq. Ult. (Down) §13 Car.I	1629
16. Ballynemeighe x 2	Inq. Ult. (Down) §30 Car.I	1632
17. The Meagh town	Magennis Paps (O'Sullivan) 68	1632
18. Nemeagh	Inq. Ult. (Down) §85 Car. I	1639
19. Edendarrowe, Ballyneneh	Mooney MS 9	1666
20. Edendarrowe and Ballyneineh	BSD 119	1666
21. Edendery	Vestry Reg. (OSNB) NB62	1754
22. Edenderry	Wm. Map (OSNB) NB62	1810
23. Edenderry	Reg. Free. (OSNB) NB62	1829
24. Edenderry	Bnd. Sur. (OSNB) NB62	1830c
25. Edenderry	Wm. Little (OSNB) NB62	1834c
26. Eadan Doire "brae or hill-brow of the oakwood"	J O'D (OSNB) NB62	1834c
27. Eadan Dair-mhaighe	Mooney 9	1950c
28. ˌidən'dɛrï	Local pronunciation	1991

The name Edenderry generally follows the Aghaderg townlands of Ballyvarley and Ballygowan in the lists of Sir Art Magennis' lands, but this refers to the contiguous townland of Edenderry in Seapatrick parish just west of Banbridge. The townlands grouped in the early 17th century under Loughadian, further south in Aghaderg, include *Nemeagh* between forms for Lisnabrague and Lisnagade townlands, the position of this Edenderry. The text on the bounds of Drumsallagh which refers to *Edendaran Hill in the Meagh* proves this identification, and along with forms like *Ballymeagh* shows that the basic name was originally *An Mhaigh* "the plain", with *na maí*, earlier *na maighe*, "of the plain" following *baile* "townland" and possibly *léim* "leap". The form *Nemeagh* seems to have had initial *Bally* removed. However the form *Lemnemeigh* has more likely arisen from confusion with *Léim an Eich* "leap of the steed", as confirmed by the English translation "the Horse-leap". This name is no longer known, but places called "leap" usually have a story attached of how a hero cleared a near-impossible gap (*Joyce* i 170–1).

In the absence of historical forms Edenderry might be assumed to be *Éadan Doire* "hill-face of (the) oakwood", although on the evidence of two forms (7,13, reading -*ou* for -*on*) Mooney suggested *Éadan Dair-mhaighe* "hill-face of the oak-plain". It is more likely, reading -*oh*,-*ah* for -*on*,-*an*, that these spellings represent *Éadan Darach* "hill-face of the oak-tree" (as with Sligo from *Sligeach*), later replaced by the more familiar Edenderry.

Glaskerbeg East and West	*Glascar Beag*	
J 1237, 1337	"little green meadow/rock-shelf"	
1. Glaskar (Sir A. Magenis)	CPR Jas I 395b	1609
2. Ballyglaskar two townlands (Sir A. Magenis)	CPR Jas I 189a	1611

3. Glaskar 2 townlands	CPR Jas I 235a	1612
4. Glaskerbeg	Inq. Ult. (Down) §13 Car.I	1629
5. Glascorr, Donald Magennis of	Wars Co. Down x 77a,77b	1641
6. Gascar, Donald oge Magennis of	Wars Co. Down x 78a	1641
7. Glascor, Donald oge Magennis of	Wars Co. Down x 79a	1641
8. Glascorry, Donald oge Magennis of	Wars Co. Down x 80a	1641
9. Glaskerbeg als. Glotguruater	Hib. Reg. Upr Eveagh	1657c
10. Glaskerbegg	Census 73	1659c
11. Glaskerbegg	BSD 105	1661
12. Glaskerbeg	Hib. Del. Co. Down	1672c
13. Glaskerbegg	ASE 274a 29	1681
14. Glaskerbegg	Rent Roll Down 11	1692
15. Glassgariter als Glascarbeg	Rent Roll Down 9	1692
16. Glaskerbeg	Vestry Reg. (OSNB) NB62	1747
17. Glaskerbeg	Wm. Map (OSNB) NB62	1810
18. Glaskerbeg	County Warrant (OSNB) NB62	1827
19. Gaskerbeg	Reg. Free. (OSNB) NB62	1829
20. Toddstown (Glaskerbeg)	OSNB NB62	1834c
21. 'gla:skər'bɛ:g	Local pronunciation	1991

The two townlands called Glasker were owned by Sir Art Magennis, but the position of the name in the list of his holdings gives no indication of their location. However, there are no other Glasker townlands in Co. Down or in the rest of Ireland. Joyce gave the etymology as *glas-sceir* "green rock" (*Joyce* iii 364), referring to his treatment of the word *sceir, sceire* "sharp sea rock, reef". "There are several places far removed from the coast whose names contain the word" (*Joyce* i 420).

However *sceir*, a Scandinavian loan, borrowed into Scots from Norse as "skerry", is not to be found in the dictionary of early Irish (*DIL*). It does include, however, various extended meanings of the word *scor* "unyoking", for example *scor .i. cluain* "i.e. a meadow", or "encampment". The meaning "meadow" for *scor* would fit well with *glas* "green", although it does not appear in later dictionaries. Glasscloon, from *Glaschluain* "green meadow", is a common townland name. Later dictionaries give the sense "shelf of rock" for *scor*, although its exact derivation is unclear (*O'Reilly, Dinneen, Ó Dónaill*). The suggested compound *glas-scor* may mean "green meadow" or "green rock-shelf".

The Glaskers are on two low hills and the whole is bordered on the north, east and south by streams. Locally Glaskermore and Glaskerbeg are called Back Glasker and Front Glasker. One small rock outcrop is marked in Glaskermore (OS 1:10,000 sheet 238). Glaskerbeg was said to be 105 acres in 1681. The division into Glaskerbeg East (281 acres) and West (250 acres) first appeared in the 1851 census, although they were referred to as Glaskerbeg Large (282 acres) and Little (249 acres) in 1834 (*OSM* xii 2b). Glaskermore was said to be 244 acres in 1681, and 578 acres in the 1971 townland index.

Glaskermore *Glascar Mór*
J 1336 "big green meadow/rock-shelf"

1. Ballyglaskar two townlands	CPR Jas I 189a	1611
2. Glaskar 2 townlands	CPR Jas I 235a	1612
3. Glasscarrs, lez 2	Inq. Ult. (Down) §13 Car.I	1629

4. Glaskarmore	Hib. Reg. Upr Eveagh	1657c
5. Glasskemore	Census 73	1659c
6. Glaskermore	BSD 105	1661
7. Glassgarrieighter	BSD 119	1666
8. Glaskermore	Hib. Del. Co. Down	1672c
9. Glaskermore	ASE 274 a 29	1681
10. Glasskermore	Rent Roll Down 11	1692
11. Glaskerymore	Vestry Reg. (OSNB) NB62	1747
12. Glasker-beg & more	Map of Down (OSNB) NB62	1755
13. Glaskermore	Wm. Map (OSNB) NB62	1810
14. Glaskermore	Reg. Free. (OSNB) NB62	1829c
15. Glaskermore (big)	Bnd. Sur. (OSNB) NB62	1830c
16. Glaskermore	Wm. Little (OSNB) NB62	1834c
17. Glas Sceir "green rock"	J O'D (OSNB) NB62	1834c
18. Glas Sceir "green rock"	Joyce iii 364	1913
19. ˈglaːskərˈmoːr	Local pronunciation	1991

For discussion see **Glaskerbeg** above.

Glenloughan
J 0744

Cluain Locháin
"meadow of the small lake"

1. Clonloghan, the sessiagh of	CPR Jas I 396a	1609
2. Clonleghan sessiagh	CPR Jas I 235a	1612
3. Clon-lowghan	Inq. Ult. (Down) xliii	1618
4. Clonlawghan	CPR Jas I 305a	1623
5. Clonloghan, le sessiagh de	Inq. Ult. (Down) §13 Car.I	1629
6. le sessiagh sive 1/3 de Clonloghan, 40a	Inq. Ult. (Down) §85 Car.I	1639
7. Clonloghan	Civ. Surv. 72	1655c
8. Clanloghane, the sheesheagh of	Hib. Reg. Upr Eveagh	1657c
9. Clonloghan	Hib. Del. Co. Down	1672c
10. Sessiagh-Clonloghan	ASE 274a §29	1681
11. Clonloghagh	Rent Roll Down 9	1692
12. Seisiogh Clonoghan	Rent Roll Down 9	1692
13. Glenloughan	Map of Down (OSNB) NB62	1755
14. Glenloughan	Vestry Reg. (OSNB) NB62	1768
15. Glenloughan	Wm. Map (OSNB) NB62	1810
16. Glenloghan	Bnd. Sur. (OSNB) NB62	1830c
17. Clanloughin al. Glenloughan	Mooney MS 12	1834
18. Glenlougher	Mooney MS 12	1834
19. large pillar Cloughmore "the big stone"	OSM xii 7a	1834
20. Gleann Lochain "valley of the small lough"	J O'D (OSNB) NB62	1834c
21. ˌglɛnˈlɔxən	Local pronunciation	1991

It seems that Glenloughan was originally the name of a sessiagh of 40 acres (1,2,5,6,8,10,12), not a full townland. It belonged to Sir Art Magennis, and was listed next to *Ballylisdromiller*, Drummiller, in a group of townlands belonging to him in the north of the parish. The spellings make it clear that the voicing of initial *c-* to *g-* in this name is very recent, so that the first element was *cluain* "meadow" rather than *gleann* "valley". The second element seems to be *lochán* "lakelet", although the forms with *aw,ow* (3,4) might indicate *lóchán* "chaff", which would give the townland a similar meaning to *Cluain Chnámharlaigh* "meadow of the stalk" beside it (see **Scarva**). There is no lake at present, although there is some marsh in the north-west. The townland contains a standing stone Cloughmore, in Irish *Cloch Mhór* "big stone", near the northern border (marked on OS 1:50,000 sheet 20; *OSM* xii 7a, 3a).

Greenan　　　　　　　　　　　　*Grianán*
J 1041　　　　　　　　　　　　　　"eminent place"

1. Levallygrenan, Patrick O'Massey of　CPR Jas I 395b　　　1609
2. Grenan, Patrick O'Muskey of　　CPR Jas I 195b　　　1610
3. Grenan, To Pat O'Mulsley/Mulstey
　of, the half town . . . Levallygrenan
　(Bp)　　　　　　　　　　　　CPR Jas I 191a　　　1611
4. Grynan　　　　　　　　　　Census 73　　　　　1659c
5. Grenan　　　　　　　　　　Vestry Reg. (OSNB) NB62　1747
6. Greenen　　　　　　　　　Vestry Reg. (OSNB) NB62　1754
7. Greenon　　　　　　　　　Map of Down (OSNB) NB62　1755
8. Greenan　　　　　　　　　Wm. Map (OSNB) NB62　1810
9. Greenan　　　　　　　　　Reg. Free. (OSNB) NB62　1829
10. Greenan　　　　　　　　Bnd. Sur. (OSNB) NB62　1830c
11. Greenan　　　　　　　　Wm. Little (OSNB) NB62　1834c
12. The Three Sisters, Greenan　OSM xii 7b　　　1834

13. Grianán "sunny land, solarium,
　fort on a hill"　　　　　　J O'D (OSNB) NB62　1834c
14. Grianán "sandy place"　　Mooney 11　　　　1950c

15. 'gri:nən　　　　　　　　Local pronunciation　1991

Greenan townland lies to the west of the northern end of Lough Brickland. The common place-name *Grianán* (**Greenan** *PNI* i 28) seems to indicate a place or hill that faces the sun (*grian*) or has a good view or was used for public assembly (Ó Maolfabhail 1974). There is a hill in the south of the townland, on which are the standing stones called the Three Sisters, beside a minor road. The old church site was nearby in Drumsallagh, which borders Greenan.

In the 1611 list of church lands *Levallygrenan*, apparently meaning "the half-townland of" Greenan, is said to belong to the bishop, and further down the page "the half-town called *Levallygrenan*" is let to Patrick O'Mulstey of *Grenan* (form 3). Since the modern extent is only 196 acres it seems likely that Greenan was originally a half-townland. As with Shane McBrin, who held the church townland of Ballintagart, the tenant came from the family of *Ó Maoilsté*, now McStay, which had produced many churchmen, including parish clergy in Aghaderg in 1415 and 1505 (*Atkinson's Dromore* 226). **Carrickmacstay** in the parish of Clonallan (*PNI* i 69) was also named after them.

42

A townland called *Ballygrenan* belonging to Sir Art Magennis, listed in the documents next to Seafin in Drumballyroney, can be safely equated with **Grallaghgreenan** in that parish.

Legan(anny	*Lag an Eanaigh*	
J 0942	"hollow of the marsh"	

1. Legganannagh	CPR Jas I 395b	1609
2. Ballyvickey-Leggannanagh	CPR Jas I 191a	1611
3. Legganamig	Census 73	1659c
4. Laganawagh	Sub. Roll Down 276	1663
5. Legananey	Vestry Reg. (OSNB) NB62	1747
6. Legganany	Map of Down (OSNB) NB62	1755
7. Leganany	Vestry Reg. (OSNB) NB62	1768
8. Legganany	Wm. Map (OSNB) NB62	1810
9. Leganany	Reg. Free. (OSNB) NB62	1829
10. Legananny	Reg. Free. (OSNB) NB62	1830
11. Legananny	Bnd. Sur. (OSNB) NB62	1830c
12. Legananny	Wm. Little (OSNB) NB62	1834c

13. Lag an Eanaigh "hollow of the marsh/cut-out bog"	J O'D (OSNB) NB62	1834c
14. Lag an Eanaigh	Mooney 11	1950c

15. ˌlɛgəˈnanï	Local pronunciation	1991
16. ˌlïgəˈnɑnï	Local pronunciation	1991

Legananny was originally another church townland (forms 1,2) and lies north of the main church townland of **Drumsallagh**. The name seems to be *Lag an Eanaigh* "hollow of the marsh", referring to Legananny Moss in the west of the townland. It is thus different from **Legananny** in Drumgooland, which seems to be named from a local megalith *Liag an Eanaigh*, "stone of the marsh", although the Irish goddess Áine has also been suggested (O'Rahilly 1946, 518). Dunboy House in the townland seems to have a Gaelic name *Dún Buí*, "yellow hillfort". Its origin is unknown but it is possibly a name imported from elsewhere.

Lisnabrague	*Lios Rátha Bréige*	
J 0741	"fort/enclosure of deceit"	

1. Lissrabregie (Loughdegan)	CPR Jas I 395a	1609
2. Lisrabregie (Loughdegan)	CPR Jas I 190b	1611
3. Liserabregh	Inq. Ult. (Down) §13 Car. I	1629
4. Lissrabregie	Inq. Ult. (Down) §30 Car. I	1632
5. Lisrabregie town	Magennis Paps (O'Sullivan) 68	1632
6. Lisravesse	Inq. Ult. (Down) §85 Car. I	1639
7. Lisnabreage	Vestry Reg. (OSNB) NB62	1754
8. Lisnabreague	Wm. Map (OSNB) NB62	1810
9. Lissanebreage	OSL Dn 32 (Bell's map)	1815c
10. Lissabrague	County Warrant (OSNB) NB62	1827

11. Lisnabrague	Bnd. Sur. (OSNB) NB62	1830c
12. Lisnabrague	Wm. Little (OSNB) NB62	1834c
13. Lios na Bréige "fort of the falsehood"	J O'D (OSNB) NB62	1834c
14. Lios-na-bréige "fort of the falsehood"	Joyce iii 477	1913
15. Lios Rátha an Bhréagtha "fort of deceit"	Mooney 11	1950c
16. Lios na mBreac	Mooney 11	1950c
17. Lios na mBréag	Mooney 11	1950c
18. ˌlïsnə'bre:g	Local pronunciation	1991

Dean Mooney in his article on the element *brague* commented that the forms for Lisnabrague, **Lisnatierney** also in the parish and **Lisnaward** in the parish of Dromore, all originally began *lios rátha* "enclosure of the rath", as can be seen from the forms (Mooney 1956(a), 25). Another example is *Lisremoylan* in **Annaghanoon**. Joyce mentioned combinations of *lios, dún* and *ráth*:

> either the first is used adjectivally, . . . or it is a mere explanatory term used synonymously with the second . . . or such a name might originate in successive structures (*Joyce* i 282).

There is no surviving fort in the townland to illustrate the meaning here.

The final element Mooney took as *bréagtha*, the genitive of *bréagadh* "deceiving, beguiling" and thence "playing": "probably refers to tricks played by fairies" (*Mooney MS* 11). Alternatively, there is a standing stone in the townland south-east of Lough Shark (*ASCD* 96, grid-reference 076413, 5'6" x 3') which might have been referred to as a "false man" *fear* or *buachaill bréige* (*Joyce* ii 435). Although this townland is less on the "upland" the second element could also be a form of *brí* "height", which may have been a district name in the past, as suggested above for **Dromorebrague**, locally Brague. However the 17th-century forms for Dromorebrague do not show a final vowel, unlike -*bregie* in the three earliest forms here. The most likely Irish form seems to be *Lios Rátha Bréige*, though it is unclear what "enclosure of the fort of the deceit" might mean.

Lisnabrague House, an 18th-century building, was formerly Union Lodge, the residence of the Fivey family (*ASCD* 369; *OSM* xii 6a,10a; *Taylor and Skinner* map 22).

Lisnagade	*Lios na gCéad*	
J 0844	"fort of the hundreds"	
1. Ballylissnegead (Loughdegan)	CPR Jas I 395a	1609
2. Ballylisnegeade (Loughdegan)	CPR Jas I 190b	1611
3. Lysnegeado	Inq. Ult. (Down) xliii	1618
4. Lisnegeade	Inq. Ult. (Down) xliii	1618
5. Lysnegeade	Inq. Ult. (Down) xliii	1618
6. Lisnegeade x3	CPR Jas I 305a	1623
7. Dromenyskie hill in Lisnegad	CPR Jas I 305a	1623
8. Lisnegead, the Dingle under the fort of	CPR Jas I 305a	1623
9. Lisnegeade (Sir Edw. Trevor)	CPR Jas I 305a	1623

10. Ballylissnegade	Inq. Ult. (Down) §13 Car.I	1629
11. Ballelesnegede	Inq. Ult. (Down) §84 Car.I	1639
12. Lissegead	Civ. Surv. x §72	1655c
13. Lishnegade	Census 73	1659c
14. Lissnegead	BSD 106	1661
15. Lisnegead	Vestry Reg. (OSNB) NB62	1747
16. Lisnagade	Vestry Reg. (OSNB) NB62	1754
17. Lisnegead	Map of Down (OSNB) NB62	1755
18. Lisnagead fort . . . probably of the Danes	Statist. Sur. Dn 276	1802
19. Lisnagade	Wm. Map (OSNB) NB62	1810
20. Lisnagade	Bnd. Sur. (OSNB) NB62	1830c
21. townland of Lisnagad	OSM xii 4b	1834
22. Lisnagade	Wm. Little (OSNB) NB62	1834c
23. Lios na gCéad "fort of the hundreds"	J O'D (OSNB) NB62	1834c
25. Lios na gcéad "fort of the hundreds: a place of meeting"	Joyce iii 477	1913
26. ˌləsnəˈgjeːd	Local pronunciation	1991

This townland takes its name from the magnificent triple-ringed fort within it, the "largest and most strongly entrenched rath in Ulster, if not in Ireland" (*PSAMNI* 111), which was excavated in 1953. It was part of the district of Loughadian. Both from the 17th-century historical spellings and apparently 18th-century local tradition the name seems to be *Lios na gCéad* "fort of the hundreds". One explanation was that over a hundred other earthworks could be seen from its top (*Mooney MS* 14). The hundreds could refer to numbers of troops, or even to the land measure *céad*, "one eighth of an Irish acre" (*Ó Dónaill*). The only parallel form in Hogan's *Onomasticon* is *Lecc na Cét* "flagstone of the hundreds" (*Onom. Goed.*, *Book of Lismore*). However translated, Lisnagade sounds like a late popular name and the original name may have been lost. There are two other named forts to the north-west, Lisnaweelan (OS 1:10,000 sheet 220, called -*welan*, *ASCD*) and Lisnavaragh, and three other earthworks in the townland (*ASCD* 149–50 Lisnagade and Lisnavaragh, 166, plate 28). Dean Mooney suggested *Lios an bhéartha* (r.*bhearrtha*) "fort of (sheep) clipping" for Lisnavaragh (*Mooney MS* 14).

Lisnagonnell
J 1039

Lios na gCoinneal
"fort of the candles"

1. Ballynlishdowneverr	CPR Jas I 395a	1609
2. (?)Ballylisidimehevaghe	CPR Jas I 395b	1609
3. Ballinlishdownever	CPR Jas I 190b	1611
4. (?)Ballylisidunehevagh	CPR Jas I 191a	1611
5. (?)Ballylisdunehevaghie	CPR Jas I 309a	1616
6. Ballinlishedownevery	Inq. Ult. (Down) §13 Car. I	1629
7. Ballelesdumvarry	Inq. Ult. (Down) §85 Car. I	1639
8. Lisseginnell	Inq. Ult. (Down) §89 Car. I	1640
9. Ballindenver	Inq. Ult. (Down) §89 Car. I	1640
10. Lissenginne	Hib. Reg. Upr Eveagh	1657c

11. Lisnagonnell	Mooney MS 13	1659
12. Lishnegunnall	Census 73	1659c
13. Lisnagill	BSD 105	1661
14. Lissnekinnell (par. Aghaderge)	ASE 61b §35	1666
15. Lissanagill al. Lislacnell	ASE 112a §34	1667
16. Lisnegill	Hib. Del. Co. Down	1672c
17. Lisnagill als Lissnamell	Rent Roll Down 12	1692
18. Lisnagunnen	OSM xii 2b	1727
19. Lisnagunnell (will)	OSNB NB62	1727
20. Lisnagannon	Vestry Reg. (OSNB) NB62	1747
21. Lisnagenell	Vestry Reg. (OSNB) NB62	1754
22. Lisnaginel	Map of Down (OSNB) NB62	1755
23. Lisnagonnell	Wm. Map (OSNB) NB62	1810
24. Lisnagannon/Lisnagunnell	Reg. Free. (OSNB) NB62	1830
25. Lisnegannell	Bnd. Sur. (OSNB) NB62	1830c
26. Lisnagannel so pronounced	OSM xii 2b	1834
27. Lisnagannell	Wm. Little (OSNB) NB62	1834c
28. [Lis-na-'gan-nell]	OSNB Pron. NB62	1834c
29. Brown Bog (Lisnagonnell)	OSNB NB62	1834c
30. Lisnagonnell	J O'D (OSNB) NB62	1834c
31. Lisnagannel	Ir. Wills Index 87	1841
32. Lisnagannon	Bassett's Down 257	1886
33. Lisgannon and Lisnagonnell	UJA ser.2 i 153–4	1895
34. Lios na g-Coinneall "fort of the candles"	J O'D (OSNB) NB62	1834c
35. Lios na gCoinneal "fort of the lights"	Mooney 13	1950c
36. ˌlïsnə'gɔnəl	Local pronunciation	1996

The earlier forms given above relate to a land unit in this area, associated with Meenan, the neighbouring townland on the west, and Ballymacinratty beyond it. The 1640 inquisition on the lands of Glasney Roe Magennis of Meenan describes him conceding *Ballindenver*, Meenan and Ballymacinratty to his eldest son Donald in 1610, but in 1630 conceding Ballymacinratty and Lisnagonnell to his second and third sons Hugh and Arthur. The text does not explain further, but it is most likely that the inquisition refers to the same three lands each time, and that *Ballindenver* and Lisnagonnell are equivalent. The earlier forms may be derived from *Baile Lis Dúin Eimhire* "townland of the enclosure of Eimhear's fort", possibly another reference to the Ulster cycle, since Eimhear the wife of Cú Chulainn appears with Bricriu in the story of Bricriu's Feast (*FB*). Joyce's comment on combinations of *lios* and *ráth* (*Joyce* i 282, see **Lisnabrague** above) also covers the use of *lios* before *dún*, as for example in Lisdoonvarna Co. Clare. The doubtful forms (2,4–5), which seem also to begin *lios dúin*, are more likely, from their context, to relate to **Knockgorm** in Garvaghy parish.

Lisnagonnell is a folkloric name given after the place became uninhabited: *Lios na gCoinneal* "fort of the candles". According to Mooney they were "no doubt mysterious fairy lights" (*Mooney MS* 13), from lights seen in a fort at night when the fairies are at work there, as with Lisgonnell in Tyrone (*Joyce* i 192, iii 478).

There were "two small earthen forts" in the townland, which in 1894 was called both *Lisgannon* and Lisnagonnell. During the 19th century one James McKeag and his grandson

James Buchanan or M'Whanan uncovered four dug-out canoes in a bog, which must once have been a lough covering 40 acres. The largest was 25 feet long, made of an oak probably four feet in diameter. The inhabitants also pointed out a spot in the centre of the bog called "the island", which had been surrounded by stakes, and where crocks, brass pins and animal bones had been found. However they were not convinced that this had been a crannog residence in a lake, believing rather that the boats had been there from the time of Noah's Flood! (Lett, H.W. 1895, 153–4; *ASCD* 184a no.735).

References to the name as *Lis(na)gannon* appear first in the 18th century (18, 20, 24, 32, 33). This form could result from interchange of final *-l* and *-n*, as for example *Kilsaran* in the parish of Dromore, becoming modern **Killysorrell**. The syllable *-na-* must be the Irish article in both versions of the name. Both *Lisgannon* and Lisnagonnell may refer to either fort or to the crannog.

Lisnatierny
J 1037

Lios Rátha an Tiarna
"fort/enclosure of the lord"

1. Ballylissraniteirne	CPR Jas I 395a	1609
2. Ballisrahirny	CPR Jas I 396a	1609
3. Ballylisrahintierne (Clanagan)	CPR Jas I 190a	1611
4. Ballelisrantearne	Mooney MS 14	1630
5. Lisraterny, Irrial & Connell Magennis of	Wars Co. Down x 80	1641
6. Lisratierny	Inq. Ult. (Down) §106 Car. I	1650c
7. Lisraturny	Inq. Ult. (Down) §106 Car. I	1650c
8. Lesinterny	Hib. Reg. Upr Eveagh	1657c
9. Lishratyerny	Census 73	1659c
10. Listratierna	BSD 105	1661
11. Listratierna	Mooney MS 13	1666
12. Lissenterine	ASE 112a §34	1667
13. Lisnenterine	Rent Roll Down 12	1692
14. Lisnaterney	Vestry Reg. (OSNB) NB62	1747
15. Lisneterney	Vestry Reg. (OSNB) NB62	1754
16. Lisnatirny	Map of Down (OSNB) NB62	1755
17. Lisnaturney	Wm. Map (OSNB) NB62	1810
18. Lisnatierny	Bnd. Sur. (OSNB) NB62	1830c
19. Lisnatierney	Wm. Little (OSNB) NB62	1834c
20. Lios na dTighearna "fort of the Lords"	J O'D (OSNB) NB62	1834c
21. Lios-na-dtighearnaigh "fort of the lords"	Joyce iii 482	1913
22. ˌlïsnə'te:rnï	Local pronunciation	1991
23. ˌlïsnə'ti:rnï	Local pronunciation	1991

Lisnatierny in the south of the parish was part of the district of Clanagan, most of which was in the parish of Donaghmore (*PNI* i 87). Forms from the 18th century onwards give the impression that the original Irish was *Lios na dTiarna*, "fort of the lords". However the form

Lisraturny (1–7) indicates *lios* prefixed to *ráth* again, as in **Lisnabrague** (*Joyce* i 282), and the final element looks more like a genitive singular form: "enclosure of the fort of the lord". Once, perhaps, the original significance had been forgotten, *lios rátha* pronounced [ˌlïsrə] could become *lios na* [ˌlïsnə] by interchange of *n* and *r*. There is no further information on the original "lord", and the later meaning "fort of the lords" can be compared with the townlands called **Lisnaree** "fort of the kings", which are possibly late romantic names rather than old tradition. However, in this case, the terms *lios* and *ráth* seem to refer to **Tierny Fort**, a part translation of the name which is "a large planted fort . . . on the summit of a large hill" (350 feet, *Mooney MS* 14), shown on the 1:50,000 map (*ASCD* 160). The Fort House is beside it.

Loughadian	*Loch an Daingin*	
J 0740	"lake of the stronghold"	

1. Deyne (+Loghan)	Fiants Eliz. §4218	1583
2. (?)Deyrloghan	Fiants Eliz. §4327	1584
3. Loghdegan	CPR Jas I 395a	1609
4. Loughedegan, Brian McArt Magenis of	CPR Jas I 195b	1610
5. Loughdegan	CPR Jas I 190b	1611
6. Loghdingyn	Inq. Ult. (Down) §13 Car. I	1629
7. Loghadeggen/ Loghadeggan	Inq. Ult. (Down) §30 Car. I	1632
8. Loghadeggan	Inq. Ult. (Down) §30 Car. I	1632
9. Loughadegin, house and town	Magennis Paps (O'Sullivan) 68	1632
10. Loghedrane	Inq. Ult. (Down) §85 Car. I	1639
11. Loughedeyne	Wars Co. Down xi 59	1641
12. Loghdein	Census 73	1659c
13. Loghdyan	Sub. Roll Down 276–7	1663
14. Loghedine	BSD 119	1666
15. Lough Adiaen (lake)	Map Newry Canal	1690c
16. Loghadaine	Ir. Wills Index 95	1735
17. L.Dian	Harris Hist. map	1743
18. Lough-Dian	Harris Hist. 85,151	1744
19. Loughadine	Vestry Reg. (OSNB) NB62	1747
20. Loughadian	Vestry Reg. (OSNB) NB62	1754
21. Loughadyan	Kennedy Map (OSNB) NB62	1755
22. Loughadyan	Vestry Reg. (OSNB) NB62	1768
23. Loughdyon	Taylor and Skinner map 22	1777
24. Loughadian	Wm. Map (OSNB) NB62	1810
25. Loughadian	Bnd. Sur. (OSNB) NB62	1830c
26. Loughadian	Wm. Little (OSNB) NB62	1834c
27. Loch Doimhin "deep lough"	J O'D (OSNB) NB62	1834c
28. Lough a' daingin "lake of the fortress"	Mooney 13	1950c
29. ˌlɔxəˈdaiən	Local pronunciation	1991

Loughadian was the chief townland of a district called by the same name. A lake called *Lough Adiaen* is shown on the late 17th-century map (15), and Harris (18) mentions *Lough-*

Dian as a lake. Stuart's *History of Armagh* says the lake had been drained about 70 years previously (i.e. about 1750; *OSM* xii 3b), and no lake is shown at *Loughdyon* by Taylor and Skinner (23, 1777 AD).

However, when described in 1834, it had been "a lake long since that period, though now dry and used for pasture" (*OSM* xii 3b). Joyce stated, "The lake is now meadowland" (*Joyce* iii 488), while Knox listed it among lakes which had become morasses in Co. Down (*Knox Hist.* 311). This fact, along with the evidence of spelling and pronunciation, makes unlikely O'Donovan's suggestion that it could be *Loch Doimhin* (or *Domhain*) "deep lough".

Mooney's interpretation (28) is no doubt correct, following the comment of Joyce: "*Daingean* [is] often softened to *dian*" (*Joyce* iii 488). It can refer to "an ancient circular fort or a more modern fortress or castle", and is pronounced and written *dian* in the north (*Joyce* i 306–8). According to the *Ordnance Survey Memoir*, there was a crannog on the lake, which had been the find spot of a dugout boat (*ASCD* 144b, 184).

This fortification must have been important enough to be referred to as a *daingean* "stronghold", used as the name of the district in the *Fiants* where *Deyne* is followed by the name of Loughans in Tullylish (1,2). Subsequently the name given to the lake, "lough of the stronghold", was used for both townland and native district. Other examples of *daingean* in Ulster townland names are **Lisadian** "fort of the stronghold", in the parish of Hillsborough, Co. Down, and in Eglish and Loughgilly parishes, Co. Armagh.

Meenan	*Minín*	
J 0939	"grassy patch"	
1. (?)i Tamlachta Mennann		
ic Loch Bricrend	Fél. Óeng. Oct 26 p228n	1400c
2. (?)hi Tamlachta Menna		
in Huibh Echach Ulad	Fél. Óeng. Oct 26 p228n	1400c
3. (?)ó Thamhlacta Menainn		
in Úibh Eacdach Uladh	Mart. Gorm. Oct 26 p204n	1630c
4. (?)Tamhlachta Menainn	Mart. Don. 285	1630c
5. Ballyneenmine		
(Glassney Roe Magenise)	CPR Jas I 395a	1609
6. Ballymeminny,		
Glasny Roe Magenis of	CPR Jas I 195b	1610
7. Ballenemunie,		
Glassney Roe Magenis of	CPR Jas I 190b	1611
8. the landes of the Mynnye		
(Glasney Roe Magneis)	Inq. Ult. (Down) xliii	1618
9. the lands of the Mynnye		
(Glasney Roe Magenis)	CPR Jas I 305a	1623
10. Ballynemyne	Inq. Ult. (Down) §13 Car.I	1629
11. Ballenemynnyn	Inq. Ult. (Down) §85 Car.I	1639
12. Beemne,Glasney Roe Magneisse of	Inq. Ult. (Down) §89 Car. I	1640
13. Ballebemne	Inq. Ult. (Down) §89 Car. I	1640
14. Loghmonen	Hib. Reg. Upr Eveagh	1657c
15. Loghmoneen	Hib. Del. Co. Down	1672c
16. Ballyloghmynyn	ASE 274a §29	1681
17. Minion	Vestry Reg. (OSNB) NB62	1747

18. Menon	Vestry Reg. (OSNB) NB62	1754
19. Minian	Vestry Reg. (OSNB) NB62	1768
20. Meenan	Wm. Map (OSNB) NB62	1810
21. Minnin	Ir. Wills Index 92	1819
22. Meenan	Bnd. Sur. (OSNB) NB62	1830
23. Meenan, so pronounced	OSM xii 3	1834
24. Minine or Minen or Minian or		
Meenan or Meenin	OSM xii 3	1834
25. ['Meenan] last syll. v. indistinct	OSNB Pron. NB62	1834c
26. Mionán "a kid"	J O'D (OSNB) NB62	1834c
27. An Mínín/Maoinín		
"the grassy patch"	Mooney 15	1950c
28. 'mi:nən	Local pronunciation	1991

According to the Irish martyrologies, two saints Beoán and Meallán, associated with the seventh-century St Fursa, were buried at *Tamlachtae Mennann*, a church at Lough Brickland (forms 1,2,3,4). The identification with modern Meenan was put forward by Reeves (*EA* 113n) and taken up by Hogan (*Onom. Goed.* 620b). Pádraig Ó Riain, in his discussion of the Life of St Fursa (Ó Riain 1989, 2 n.10), also accepted this identification. However, Meenan is out of sight of Lough Brickland, unless *Loch Bricrenn* was already used as a district name, and furthermore *Mennann* would be pronounced ['mɛnən] or ['manən]. Despite the superficial resemblance of *Tamhlachtae Mennann* or *Menna* to Meenan, the early church or churches at or near **Lough Brickland** are probably better sought in Greenan or Drumsallagh townlands, which are both attested as belonging to the church. Greenan overlooks the lake and had a tradition of an ancient glebe, while the old parish church was in Drumsallagh.

Some of the 17th-century spellings of Meenan seem to be connected with the word for bog, *móin*, possibly *móinín* "little bog". Petty's maps show a lake *Loghmonen*, described in 1894 as a "bog, which every winter resumes the character it . . . formerly had of a lake", in which a dugout canoe of oak had been found (Lett 1895, 154). However most of the spellings indicate *mínín, maoinín* "grassy patch or stretch" (*Dinneen*).

Scarva   *Scarbhach*
J 0643   "shallow place, rough ford".

1. Na Sgarbhátha (gen. case?)	Omeath Infs (GJ) 157	1901
2. the water of Scarvagheyedoo	Fiants Eliz. §4327	1584
3. the Skarvagh	Inq. Ult. (Down) xliv	1618
4. the Skarvagh	CPR Jas I 305a	1623
5. the bridge of the Skarrow	Wars Co. Down xi 64	1641
6. Skarowagh, a foord called	Civ. Surv. x §72	1655c
7. foord Skarowagh, glin flush	Civ. Surv. x §72	1655c
8. Scarvagh al Glanflush	Civ. Surv. x §73	1655c
9. Scarvagh Passe	Map Newry Canal	1690c
10. Scarvagh Pass	Harris Hist. map	1743
11. Scarvagh Pass (antiently called		
Bealach-Ultagh)	Harris Hist. 84,85	1744

12. great bog about Scarvagh antiently called Glan-flush	Harris Hist. 270	1744
13. Scarvagh	Vestry Reg. (OSNB) NB62	1747
14. Scarva	Vestry Reg. (OSNB) NB62	1754
15. Scarva	Statist. Sur. Dn 196,206,276	1802
16. Scarva	Wm. Map (OSNB) NB62	1810
17. Scarva Pass	Wm. Map (OSNB) NB62	1810
18. Scarvagh Pass	Atkinson's Tour (OSNB) NB62	1823
19. Scarva	Reg. Free. (OSNB) NB62	1829
20. Scarvagh	Bnd. Sur. (OSNB) NB62	1830c
21. Scarvagh Village	Bnd. Sur. (OSNB) NB62	1830c
22. Scarva alias Clonknaverly	OSNB NB62	1834c
23. Scarva	Wm. Little (OSNB) NB62	1834c
24. Village of Scarva	J O'D (OSNB) NB62	1834c
25. Scarbha "the point of partition of waters"	OSM xii 3a	1834
26. part of the bog called Glen Flusk	OSM xii 4b	1834
27. Scarva alias Clonknaverly	OSM xii 7a	1834
28. Scarva bog . . . part called Glen Flusk	OSM xii 4a	1834
29. Scairbheach "a shallow ford"	J O'D (OSNB) NB62	1834c
30. An Scarbhach "place of shallows /rough shallow ford"	J O'D (OSNB) NB62	1834c
31. An Scrabh-achadh Dubh	Post-Sheanchas 112	1905
32. Scarbh "shallow place, ford"	Onom. Goed. 592	1911
33. Scarbhach (gen. scarbhaigh)	AGBP 119	1969
34. Scarbhach/Scarva	Éire Thuaidh	1988
35. Scarbhach	GÉ 154	1989
36. 'skarvə	Local pronunciation	1991

Scarva was originally the name of a ford not a townland, now used as equivalent to the older townland name of *Clondeknaverly*, part of the district of Loughadian: "In the old deeds it is called Scarvagh alias Clonknaverly" (*OSM* xii 3a; forms 22,27). For *Clonknaverly* see below. The early forms above (2–11) all refer to the crossing place, over an interlinked chain of bogs, lakes and streams shown on the 1690 map (9). The 1641 account of the drowning of 120 settlers at the "bridge of the *Skarrow*" (5) may well be a transfer of the better-attested massacre at the bridge in Portadown, but the name itself indicates that there was some water to cross at Scarva before the canal was built (*Wars Co. Down* xi 64,59). The *Ordnance Survey Memoir* quoted an "autograph manuscript of General Vallency" in which he stated: "by *Scarbha* I understand 'the point of partition in water' from *scaroim* 'to separate' and *agh* 'a ford'". "This derivation agrees with the peculiar situation of the place, as the water flows from hence northward to Lough Neagh and southward to Newry" (*OSM* xii 3a). The letter was shown by Mr Reilly of Scarva to John O'Donovan, who commented, "This, like all Vallancey's derivations, is forced to agree with the locality" (*OSL Dn* 31). Vallancey's etymology combines tradition about the place (see **Moyne Inirrye**, parish introduction) with the basic meaning of the name: *sca(i)rbh* fem., derivative *sca(i)rbhach* masc. "shallow shingly ford". The form of the name used by two Omeath Irish speakers about 1900 is similar to the 1584 form (1,2), but for the final element *dubh*, "black". As suggested by the collector/editor it may be genitive (1), but it could also be plural *Na Scairbheacha* "the rough fords" (*Dinneen*).

1. Clandeknaverlie (Loughdegan)	CPR Jas I 395a	1609
2. Clandeknaverly (Loughdegan)	CPR Jas I 190b	1611
3. Clonknaverly	Inq. Ult. (Down) xliii	1618
4. Clonknaverly	CPR Jas I 305a	1623
5. Clonknaverly (Sir Edw. Trevor)	CPR Jas I 305a	1623
6. Clandeknaverly, Ballylissnegeade &	Inq. Ult. (Down) §13 Car. I	1629
7. Clandeknaverly	Inq. Ult. (Down) §85 Car. I	1639
8. Cloanknaverley	BSD 106	1661
9. Clonknaverly "a pagan oracle or speaking pillar of stone"	OSM xii 3a	1834
11. Clann-mhaicne-Mhearlaigh	Mooney 15,16	1950c

The 17th-century name of the townland, *Clonknaverly*, was possibly *Cluain Chnámharlaigh* "meadow of the stalk", from *cnámharlach* "skeleton, stalk". Mooney also suggested *Cluain Mhaicne Mhearlaigh*, "meadow of the offspring of Mearlach", related to the family name in **Ballyvarley** above.

Shankill   *Seancholl*
J 1238   "old hazel"

1. Shanchall	CPR Jas I 394b	1609
2. Ballyshanshall	CPR Jas I 394b	1609
3. Shanhole and Ballyshanhole	Ancient Patent (OSNB) NB62	1610
4. Ballyshancole and Shancole	Ancient Patent (OSNB) NB62	1610
5. Ballyshanchell, Ever McArte Magenis of	CPR Jas I 195b	1610
6. Shanchall (precinct of)	CPR Jas I 190a	1611
7. Ballyshamchall	CPR Jas I 190a	1611
8. Ballyshanchall	CPR Jas I 190a	1611
9. Shanehall	Inq. Ult. (Down) §7 Jac. I	1618
10. Balleshanechall	Inq. Ult. (Down) §7 Jac. I	1618
11. Shanckall, lands in	CPR Jas I 373b	1618
12. precinct of Shanechall	Inq. Ult. (Down) §7 Jac. I	1618
13. Shannahall, Ever . . . Magenis late of	CPR Jas I 423b	1619
14. Shanchill	Inq. Ult. (Down) §88 Car. I	1640
15. Shankall, Brian McEver Magennis of	Wars Co. Down x 80a	1641
16. Shannahall	Hib. Reg. Upr Eveagh	1657c
17. Seuchall	Census 73	1659c
18. Shanhall	BSD 106	1661
19. Shanahall	Hib. Del. Co. Down	1672c
20. Shankall	ASE 274a 29	1681
21. Shankall	Rent Roll Down 11	1692
22. Shankhill	Map of Down (OSNB) NB62	1755
23. Shankil	OSNB NB62	1784
24. Shankhill	Statist. Sur. Dn	1802

25. Shankill	Wm. Map (OSNB) NB62	1810
26. Shankill	Reg. Free. (OSNB) NB62	1829
27. Shankhill	Bnd. Sur. (OSNB) NB62	1830c
28. Shankhill	Wm. Little (OSNB) NB62	1834c
29. Shankhill (x 7)	Bassett's Down 257	1886
30. Seinchill "old church"	J O'D (OSNB) NB62	1834c
31. Sean-chill "old church"	Mooney 15,16	1950c
32. 'ʃaŋkəl	Local pronunciation	1991

This townland was the chief unit in the district of *Shanchall*, consisting of 12 townlands. The terrain provided a natural place of dominance, since the townland "rises towards the centre, forming a large and high hill which commands an extensive prospect of the surrounding country" (*OSNB* 62). However the hill is not mentioned in the townland name. O'Donovan (30), followed by Atkinson (*Atkinson's Dromore* 224) and Mooney (31), assumed the name meant "old church", *seanchill*, but there is no old church site in the townland, nor was it church land. However all but one of the pre-1750 spellings have an -*a*- in the second syllable (compare the parish name **Shankill** in Co. Armagh, which is regularly spelled -*kill*). This makes both *cill* "church" and *coill* "wood" unlikely as the second element, but it could be *coll* or its variant *call* "hazel" and thus *Seanchall, Seancholl* "old hazel". The tree may have been a local emblem, like the trees that grew at the inauguration sites of **Crew Hill** Co. Antrim and **Tullaghoge** Co. Tyrone. Those trees were cut down by enemies as an insult to the tribe they belonged to (*AU*, 1099 and 1111 AD).

The additional syllable in some of the forms (*Shannahall*) is the epenthetic vowel which normally develops in Irish between *l,n,r* and a following consonant. The later spellings (22–29) and the current pronunciation show assimilation to the more common place-name *Seanchill* (30,31).

OTHER NAMES

Dane's Cast   *Gleann na Muice Duibhe*
J 0634, 0640, 0743   "glen of the black pig"

1. (?)Gort mBúraig	TBC Rec. I 1.4154	1100c
2. (?)co Fergna mac Findchona co Búrach	TBC (LL) 1.4093	1160c
3. (?)Fergna mac F rí Búraig Ulad	TBC (LL) 1.4525	1160c
4. (?)rí Búraig Ulad	Mesca Ulad 1.325	1160c
5. Gleann na Muice Duibhe "the glen of the black pig"	Stuart's Armagh 583	1819
6. The Dowagh	OSL Dn 34 (notes)	1810c
7. the Dowagh or Danes Cast	OSM xii 6	1815
8. the Danes Cast / the Race of the Black Pig	OSM Dn Misc. 6	1834
9. Danes Cast (Lisnabrague, Scarva)	OSNB NB62	1834c
10. 'diənz 'kjɑst	Local pronunciation	1990

The form and extent of the defensive linear earthwork now known as the Danes Cast, which once extended between Lisnagade in this parish and Aghyalloge in Co. Armagh three miles south-west of Newry, has been described earliest by Dubourdieu (*Statist. Surv. Dn* 1802) and Bell (*Newry Magazine* 1815, reprinted by *Stuart's Armagh* 1819 App. iii 583ff; *OSL Dn* 32–4; *Emania* vi 17).

Surviving sections of the Danes Cast are shown on the 1:50,000 map in the townlands of Scarva and Lisnabrague, and the name has already been discussed in Book 1 with reference to the section of earthwork in the parish of Donaghmore. It was known as the Black Pig's Glen in Drummiller townland, a name connected with the legend that other earthworks in south Ulster were dug by supernatural pigs (*PNI* i 109–11; Lett 1897, 68). The name "Black Pig's Dyke" was also known in Annaclone parish.

The Danes Cast is much earlier than the Danes with whom it has been associated in English, and has been tentatively dated to the 5th century A.D. (Mallory and McNeill 1991, 150–1). It has been asserted that it is not mentioned in early Irish literature, though implicitly avoided in the campaign of *Táin Bó Cuailnge* (Dobbs 1912, 340).

However, it is possible that a feature called *Gort mBúraig*, named at the end of version I of *Táin Bó Cuailnge* (form 1), made by the Brown Bull before its death at *Druim (> Droim) Tairbh* "the Bull's Ridge", "between Ulaid and Uí Echach", could refer to part of the earthwork. Thus the early story might have explained it as the work of a supernatural bull, later altered in folk tradition to a supernatural pig, a creature which also appears in the early literature (*SMMD I* §5). The word *búrach* meant both "attack" and "trench" (*DIL*), the bull *concechlaid búrach* "dug a búrach" in Cooley (*TBC Rec. I* 1.966, translated there "pawed the earth"), and the Ulster Cycle hero Fergna is twice called *rí Búraig Ulad* "king of *Búrach Ulad*" (forms 3,4). The kingdom is probably that of *Mag Coba*, later *Uí Echach*, **Iveagh**. "The Ulstermen's trench" would seem a good name for the earthwork along the border established between the Ulaid confederation and Airgialla, and *Gort mBúraig* would be "the enclosure of the trench". *Gort* "field" probably refers to an earthwork in the name *Gort na Morrígna* "field of the Morrígan (war-goddess)". *Druim Tairbh* has not been located, but Uí Echach must have meant *Uí Echach Coba*, Iveagh, west of Dál Fiatach or Ulaid (O'Rahilly 1946, 347). The Ulster Cycle was remembered in the area, as seen in Stuart's discussion of the earthwork (quoted *OSL Dn* 32–4) "which some deem the work of a demon, others of the O'Hanlons, and others again of Mabhe Cruachan, an enchantress".

Lough Brickland lake   *Loch Bricleann*
J 1141   "Bricriu's lake"

1.	ic Loch B[r]icrenn, i Tamlachtain Umail	Mart. Tal. Oct 26 p84	830c
2.	Orgain Locha Bricrenn	AFM i 446	832
3.	Orggain Locha Bricerna	AU (Mac Airt) 290	833
4.	Raoineadh oc Loch Bricrend	AFM ii 754	1004
5.	Roiniudh ic Loch Bricrenn	AU (Mac Airt) 434	1005
6.	ic Loch Bricrend, i Tamlachta Mennann	Fél. Óeng. Oct 26 p228n	1400c
7.	Caislén Locha Bricrenn, caislén Mhég Aengusa	AFM iv 862	1424
8.	Locha Bricrenn, a Tamlachtu a farrud	Fél. Óeng. Oct 26 p226n	1453c
9.	i lLoch Bricrenn, iuxta Tamlachtain mic ua Caill	Fél. Óeng. Oct 26 p226n	1453c

10. ag Loch Bricrend i nUibh Eachach Uladh	Mart. Don. Oct 26 p284	1630c
11. Loch Bricirnne (ref. 832 AD)	Céitinn iii 164–5	1633c
12. go Loch Briclinn	Meath (McDonnell) 38	1854c
13. L. Bryklyn (lake and island)	Mercator's Ulst.	1595
14. Ca. & Lo. Brecklin (+island)	Bartlett Map (BM)	1600
15. Ca. & Lough Brecklin (+island)	Bartlett Map (TCD)	1601
16. Ca. & Lo. Breckline (+island)	Bartlett Map (Greenwich)	1602
17. Castle & Lo. Brecklme (+island)	Bartlett Maps (Esch. Co. Maps) 2	1603
18. Ca. & Lo. Brecklim (+island)	Bartlett Maps (Esch. Co. Maps) 1	1603
19. Co. & Lo. Bricklin	Norden's Map	1610
20. L.(+island); L. Bricklan (town)	Harris Hist. map	1743
21. Lough-Bricklan	Harris Hist. 151	1744
22. Loughbricklan "the lake of speckled trouts"	Harris Hist. 83,84	1744
23. Lough-breac-lan "lake of speckled trouts"	Statist. Sur. Dn 304	1802
24. Loch Bricreann	J O'D (OSNB) NB62	1834c
25. Loch Bricleann	GÉ 127	1989

Loughbrickland town	*Loch Bricleann*	
J 1042	"Bricriu's lake"	
1. Loch Briclionn	Omeath Infs (GJ) 157	1901
2. Loughbricklin, Arthur oge (Magenis) of	Fiants Eliz. §1583	1570
3. Loughbreclyn	Fiants Eliz. §4218	1583
4. town of . . . Lugbreghen	Fiants Eliz. §4327	1584
5. Loughbrickland	CPR Jas I 394b	1609
6. Ca. Lough Brecklin	Speed's Ulster	1610
7. C. Logh Brecklin	Speed's Ireland	1610
8. Loughbrickland	CPR Jas I 190a	1611
9. Loughbricklane	CPR Jas I 194b	1611
10. Loughbrickland	CPR Jas I 373b	1618
11. Brickland oth. Loughbrickland, the castle of	CPR Jas I 409b	1618
12. Brickland al. Loughbrickland al. Ballybrickland	Inq. Ult. (Down) §39 Car. I	1633
13. Loughbrickland	Inq. Ult. (Down) §62 Car. I	1635
14. Brickland al. Loughbrickland al. Ballebrickland	Inq. Ult. (Down) §62 Car. I	1635
15. Loghbrickland	Inq. Ult. (Down) §91 Car. I	1640
16. Loughbrickland, Aghederrick als	Trien. Visit. (Bramhall) 14	1661
17. L. Bricklan; L.(+island)	Harris Hist. map	1743
18. Loughbricken, a small town	UJA ser.3 48 (1985) 114	1760
19. Loughbrickland	Taylor & Skinner 15	1777

20.	Loughbrickland <Lough breaclan	Statist. Sur. Dn 304	1802
21.	Loughbrickland	Wm. Map (OSNB) NB62	1829
22.	Loughbrickland	Reg. Free. (OSNB) NB62	1830c
23.	Loughbrickland	Bnd. Sur. (OSNB) NB62	1834c
24.	Lougbrickland	Wm. Little (OSNB) NB62	1834c
25.	Loch Bricleann	AGBP 117	1969
26.	Loch Bricleann/Loughbrickland	Éire Thuaidh	1988
26.	ˌlɔx'brïklən	Local pronunciation	1991
27.	ˌlɔx'brəklənd	Local pronunciation	1991

Lake

Although forms 3,11 (lake) might suggest a tribal name, *Bricirne*, formed like *Lathairne* **Larne**, Lough Brickland probably consists of *Loch* plus a personal name. Despite Harris' imaginative suggestion (lake 22) "from *breac* 'speckled or parti-coloured' and *lan* bearing the sense of 'full'", the lake seems to take its name from *Bricriu*, one of the characters in the Ulster Cycle, who appears in *Táin Bó Cuailnge* and in the story of the feast in his own hall (*FB*). The change from *-cr-* to *-cl-* is later than 1633, the date of the latest written Irish-language form (lake 11), but *Loch Briclionn* was the form used orally about 1900 by Irish speakers in Omeath (lake 12, town 1). It is an example of the fairly frequent interchange of *l,n,r* in Irish, and here *-l-* is dissimilated from the *r-* in the first syllable of the name. The lake is clearly the primary feature, but its name has been used less specifically to locate: (i) early churches in the area around it (the later church lands were all west of the lake), (ii) the parish of Aghaderg, (iii) the Magennis district north and east of the lake based on the crannog in the lake and a castle somewhere on the bank, (iv) the townland of **Brickland** to the south and (v) the village of Loughbrickland to the north. The final *-d* in these names is a common addition in anglicized spellings (*OSM* xii 1b), as in **Rathfriland**, although not used by Harris (lake 20-22).

The island in the lake is visible from the main Belfast-Newry road. The *Ordnance Survey Memoir* recorded, "There is a small green island in the centre of the lake which tradition says was formed on a frame of wood and formerly floated up and down the lake" (*OSM* xii 3a). The Archaeological Survey (*ASCD* 184b no.738) confirms that the island was a crannog, and says that "A house in the lake at Loughbrickland was occupied by rebels in 1642". However the site on the north shore given for the Magennis castle on the OS 6-inch map has not been confirmed, although the castle is regularly mentioned in the sources. Lough, island and castle were important enough to be shown on early maps, while Harris was the first to show the lake separately from the town of Loughbrickland (lake 20, town 17). Speed's maps show the castle at the north end of a lough on which is marked an island (town 6-7). This is the site of the modern town (6,7), although Speed may not have intended an exact position. Bartlett's maps generally show the castle to the west of the lough and island (lake 14,18), north-west in 1601 (lake 15), south-west in 1603 (lake 17). From forms (town 11,12,14), or **Brickland** forms (2,6,7,13), given the alias Loughbrickland, it looks as if the castle may have been in the townland of Brickland on the south shore of the lake.

Town

Nevertheless the Magennis castle, wherever situated, was probably the antecedent of the modern village called Loughbrickland, half a mile north of the lake, at the junction of the townlands of Coolnacran, Bovenett, Greenan and Drumnahare. The parish church is said to have been moved into the village in the 17th century, when the area had been taken over by Sir Marmaduke Whitchurch (*Atkinson's Dromore* 224, though Whitchurch's connection began as a commissioner on the 1609 schedule). Although it was on the main road between Newry and Belfast, the settlement of Loughbrickland remained small. In 1834 it was "not a market town" but had monthly fairs (*OSM* xii 9a, 4a).

| **Lough Shark** | *Loch Seirce* | |
| J 0641 | "lake of the love-story" | |

1. Loughseirke	Inq. Ult. (Armagh) §20 Car. I	1633
2. Lough Shirke	Map Newry Canal	1690c
3. L.Shark	Harris Hist. map	1743
4. Lough-Shark	Harris Hist. 85,151	1744
5. Lough Shirk	Rocque's Map (Coote)	1760
6. "lake of the affections"	J O'D (OSNB) NB62	1834c
7. "lake of love/ of the pair of lovers"	Mooney 14	1950c
8. 'lɔx 'ʃark	Local pronunciation	1996
9. 'aktən 'lɔx	Local pronunciation	1996

Despite its size, 79 acres, and its position on the county boundary between Down and Armagh, there are few references to Lough Shark, which became the principal reservoir for the summit level of the Newry Canal (*OSM* xii 3). In recent times it has more often been referred to as Acton Lough, from the village nearest to it in Co. Armagh (9). Harris derived the name Lough Shark "from an abundance of pike, often known by the name of Shark, found in it" (*Harris' Hist.* 85). The Gaelic word order makes an English etymology unlikely, but there are problems with providing an Irish one.

O'Donovan suggested *Loch Searc* "lake of the affections", without further comment (6). Mooney suggested the same word, translating "lake of the (pair of) lovers" (7) and wondering if there could have been a local story, based on an elopement or a drowning tragedy. *Searc* is the common title of a class of love stories in early Irish (*LL* iv 837). The earlier spellings seem to indicate *Loch Seirce*, "lake of the love-story", like Sherky Island off Kerry for which Joyce gave the Irish form *Oileán na Seirce* "island of love": "I have not heard the legend, but there was one" (*Joyce* iii 554). *Searc* also occasionally appears in early Irish as a personal name, but is not attested in this area. The Irish form of Shercock in Co. Cavan has been established as *Searcóg* (*GÉ* 271).

| **Poyntz Pass** | An English form | |
| J 0539 | gaelicized *Pas an Phointe* | |

1. Pas a'Phuinte	Omeath Infs (GJ) 157	1901
2. Poyns pass over a great bog	Civ. Surv. 69 x §77	1655c
3. Poynes Pass	Map Newry Canal	1690c
4. Poins	Lamb Maps Co. Down	1690c
5. Pointz's Pass	Harris Hist. map	1743
6. Pointz's alias Fenwick's Pass	Harris Hist. 85	1744
7. Poyntz Pass	Rocque's Map (Coote)	1760
8. Points Pass	Taylor & Skinner 22	1777
9. Pointz/Fenwick Pass	Civ. & Ecc. Top. (OSNB) NB62	1806

10. Poyntz Pass	Wm. Map (OSNB) NB62	1810
11. Pointz Pass	Atkinson's Tour (OSNB) NB62	1823
12. Pointz Pass	Bnd. Sur. (OSNB) NB62	1830
13. Village of Pointz Pass, Pointz is a family name	J O'D (OSNB) NB62	1834c
14. Pas an Phointe	GÉ 145	1989
15. 'pɔïnts 'pɑs	Local pronunciation	1991

In 1837 20 houses of Poyntzpass were situated in the south-west of this parish (*OSM* xii 9a), the rest of the town being in the Armagh parish of Ballymore. The town takes its name from Charles Pointz (*Pointes* or *Poyntes*) who was granted land in the early 17th century across the county boundary in Orior, Co. Armagh, which was created the manor of Acton in 1618 (*CPR Jas I* 184b, 299b, 412a). The earliest reference to this place-name is in the *Civil Survey* barony bounds of 1654-6 (2), and *Poynes Passe* is shown on the late 17th-century map of the route for the Newry Canal (3). It was also sometimes called Fenwick's Pass (6,9).

The name is entirely of English origin, but the Irish form given is a part-translation used by Irish speakers in Omeath about 1900, "well tested", "a genuine name, but arises from folk's etymology, as if the English were Point's Pass, whereas it was so named from Lieut Poyntz, an Elizabethan soldier" (*Omeath Infs (GJ)* 157n).

Tierny Fort
J 1037

A hybrid form
see **Lisnatierny** townland

1. Tierny Fort (Lisnatierny)	OSNB NB62	1834c
2. Lisnatirney Fort, a Danish earthwork	Bassett's Down 256	1886
3. 'ternï 'forθ	Local pronunciation	1991

Water Hill Fort
J 1140

Uachtar
"upland"

1. (?)iar nUachtur	Imm. Dá T. §5 (LL l.24225)	1160c
2. (?)ba si a raith, Ochtar a nDruimnib Breag	Descendants Ir xiii 336	1200c
3. (?)Ba ssí a raind, Óchtar Cuillche no Cholland i ndrumnib Breg	CGH LL 330c16	1200c
4. (?)Ba ssí a raith, Ochtar Cuillche no Calland i nDrumnib Breg	CGH 330c16 Lec,BB	1200c
5. Watery Fort	OSNB NB62	1834c
6. earthwork called "the watery fort"	Bassett's Down 256	1886
7. 'wɔːtərï 'fɔrt	Local pronunciation	1996

Water Hill Fort (misprinted as Water Hill *Foot* on 1:50,000 sheet 20) is a hill-top rath 70 feet across on a hill 470 feet high in Brickland townland south-east of Lough Brickland. It has its bank outside the ditch like a henge monument, making it comparable on a smaller scale to **Navan** fort near Armagh (*ASCD* 154 §460, fig.94). The deep ditch is water-logged round a central mound. The place has been called *Watery Fort* locally since the 19th century (5-7), when it provided "an extensive prospect of the area", and was used for Roman Catholic worship (*OSNB* 44). The view includes the crannog on Lough Brickland, the summit of Knock Iveagh, and a wide sweep of Co. Armagh.

There are no earlier forms, but if "Watery" is a reinterpretation from an earlier Water Hill or Water Fort, this place could be the site of *Uachtar* "upland", the chief fort of the ruling Ulaid dynasty of Dál Fiatach after their resettlement in east Ulster (2): "That was their fort, *Uachtar* on the ridges of *Brí/Breá*" (*Descendants Ir* 336 l.15; cf. **Dromorebrague**). Other copies of the Ulster genealogies give *Uachtar* epithets which do not appear elsewhere in the literature (forms 3,4). However on its own *Uachtar* appears in one Ulster cycle tale in a list of places passed through on a journey from Scotland via mid Co. Antrim to Navan, between the Bann and *Uí Bhreasail Macha* near Armagh (1). The element *uachtar* has been anglicized "water" in the obsolete district of **Watertirry** in south Co. Down (*EA* 351), and in the Co. Antrim townland **Ballywatermoy** (*PNI* iv 196), but there, as in the parish name **Kilwaughter**, the *-ch-* may still be [x] in local pronunciation. The parish of **Witter** in the Upper Ards is also from *uachtar* (*PNI* ii 121–2).

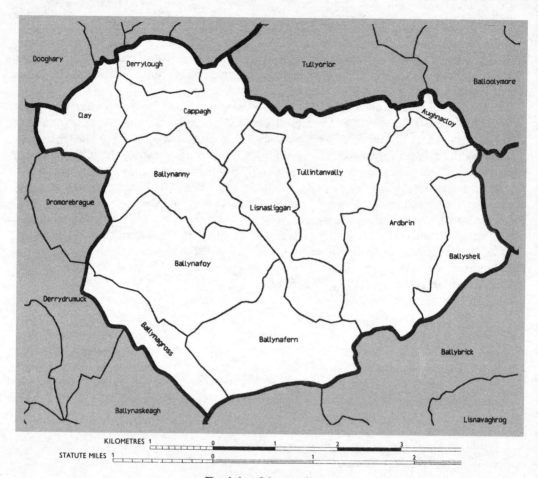

KILOMETRES 1 0 1 2 3

STATUTE MILES 1 0 1 2

Parish of Annaclone
Barony of Iveagh Upper, Lower Half

Townlands
Ardbrin
Aughnacloy
Ballynafern
Ballynafoy
Ballynagross
Ballynanny
Ballysheil

Cappagh
Clay
Derrylough
Lisnasliggan
Tullintanvally

60

THE PARISH OF ANNACLONE

The parish was first referred to in AD 1422, as *Enaghluan* (*Reg. Dowdall*). There is no town-land bearing the parish name, but Annaclone is the name of the village, partly in the town-land of Ardbrin, which contains the First *Anaghlone* Presbyterian church (OS 1:10,000 sh. 238). In 1834 the parish church "rebuilt in 1806" was in Ardbrin "rather at the eastern end and at the foot of a low hill" (*OSM* xii 17a,14b), presumably in the graveyard close to the present Church Bog, although the present Church of Ireland church is in the townland of Lisnasliggan. In 1657 there were "ten townes and one third part of a towne, the church ruinated" (*Inq. Down* 1657, *Atkinson's Dromore* 140). There are 12 townlands, no smaller divisions being known in the parish (*OSM* xii 16a). Earlier six western townlands, Ballynafern, Ballynafoy, Ballynagross, Ballynanny, Cappagh and Clay, possibly also Derrylough, were part of the district of **Shankill** in **Aghaderg** parish held by one group of the Magennises, while the east was owned by the Bishop of Dromore (*CPR Jas I* 394b, 395a).

There were apparently six church lands in 1609. Ardbrin, Lisnasliggan and Tullintanvally were held by McGiverns, and three denominations, *Scatarick*, *Ardaragh alias Dromecrosspatrick*, and *Tollegillgawneth alias Averleigh*, were held by O'Sheils. Both of these families had earlier connections with the parish. In 1427 the church lands were held by Canon Peter *Mcgyryn* (McGivern, form 2), and Odo *O'Syagill* (O'Sheil) was rector in 1527 (form 3). The land unit *Tollegillgawneth* is explained as being "Annaclone" (*CPR Jas I* 191a); it may have been the north end of Ardbrin in which the church was, since modern Ardbrin is an unusually large townland of 1008 acres (*OSM* xii 16a). Likewise Ardbrin now contains, at the eastern end of the Blue Hill, the hill of **Skateridge**. In the 17th century Skateridge was used as the name of a land unit, and explained by the alias Ballysheil, now the townland immediately east of Ardbrin (*BSD* 117). The borders of these lands have clearly been changed. The whole parish was mapped by Petty, which enables one to see the layout of the townlands c. 1657. At that date Ardbrin is shown very large, next to a long thin Tullintanvally, while Ballysheil and Ballybrick, to the south in Drumballyroney, are both omitted and seem to be included in Ardbrin.

By 1658 the O'Sheils had to forfeit Aughnacloy (the later name of *Ardaragh*, *EA* 311) and Skateridge, meaning the hill in Ardbrin and the townland of Ballysheil (*Inq. Ult. (Down) Interregnum*). Aughnacloy and Ballysheil were still church lands in the early 19th century (*OSM* xii 16a), although not in Bishop Buckworth's 1622 list, and were listed as belonging to the Church of Ireland in 1868 (*Parl. Rept*). In 1611 Patrick McGivern was only granted half the townland of Lisnasliggan by the bishop, and in 1657 "one halfe towne of land" called Lisnasliggan was the glebe of the parish (**Lisnasliggan** forms 3,4). In 1834 the Marquis of Downshire owned the three townlands once held from the bishop by the McGiverns, although 124 acres of Lisnasliggan had been given by his grandfather to be the Church of Ireland glebe (*OSM* xii 16a, 15b). The present church was built on this land in 1860 (*Atkinson's Dromore* 237).

O'Donovan received much local information from Mrs Con Magennis of Ardbrin, 70-year-old sister of Dean McArdle, parish priest of Loughbrickland: "although she is not the lady of Iveagh, I am fully persuaded that no Con Magennis ever had for wife a more civilized or more elegant woman . . . She understands Irish very well, and is now the only repertory of the traditions and legends of Iveagh" (*OSL Dn* xiv, xxi 63). Mrs Magennis also gave him information on the names of Drumballyroney parish, but unfortunately not much of her wider repertoire seems to have been written down. Constantine (Connie) Magennis of Skateridge, who died in 1978 aged 83, was probably the last representative of this family, and he and his sisters kept up some of the old traditions, including a "Black Pig's Dyke" located in Ballysheil, east of their house in Ardbrin (cf. **Dane's Cast**).

The present chief local informants have been Leo and Deirdre McNeill, who knew Connie Magennis well, and Mr Adrian Clarke, who are working together on a history of the parish.

PARISH NAME

Annaclone *Eanach Luain*
J 1841 "marsh of the haunch-like hill"

1. Enaghluan	Reg. Dowdall §129 275	1422
2. Enaghluan	Reg. Swayne 76	1427
3. Anaghluan	Reg. Cromer ii §57	1527
4. Anagh or Anaghlowan	Reg. Cromer ii §91	1528
5. Enaghluayn	EA 258n	1542
6. Enaghlayne	CPR (Tresham) ii 28	1542c
7. Enaghlayne [Fiants Hen. VIII]	Mooney MS 17	1543
8. Enaghluan	Reg. Dowdall §113 80	1546
9. T Anaghclone	Bartlett Maps (Esch. Co. Maps) 2	1603
10. Anechloin	Jas I to Dromore Cath. 314	1609
11. Anaghcloine	Speed's Ulster	1610
12. Tollegillenegawnathe al. Annathloan	CPR Jas I 191a	1611
13. Tollygillenegawneth al. Anaghclowane	CPR Jas I 191a	1611
14. Anacloan parish	Inq. Down (Reeves1) 91	1657
15. Anaghcloane	Hib. Reg. Up. Iveagh	1657c
16. Anaghclon	Census 75	1659c
17. Annaghclon Parish	BSD 117	1661
18. Rector de Annaghcloane	Trien. Visit. (Bramhall) 15	1661
19. Vicaria de Annaghclone	Trien. Visit. (Bramhall) 16	1661
20. Anacloane	Trien. Visit. (Margetson) 25	1664
21. Anaclone Rectoria	Trien. Visit. (Boyle) 47	1679
22. (?)Annagh	Lamb Maps Co. Downe	1690c
23. Anaghclone (+ church)	Harris Hist. map	1743
24. Anacloan	Dubourdieu's Map (OSNB) E18	1802
25. Anaghclone	Civ. & Ecc. Top. (OSNB) E18.172	1806
26. Anaghlone	Newry Tel. (OSNB) E18.172	1830
27. Anacloan	Bnd. Sur. (OSNB) E18.172	1830c
28. Anaclone	Wm. Little (OSNB) E18.172	1834c
29. Annaclone	J O'D (OSNB) E18.172	1834c
30. Anacloan or Annaghlone	Lewis' Top. Dict. i 25b	1837
31. Anaghlone, parish of	Wars Co. Down xii 5n	1906
32. 1st/2nd Anaghlone Presbyterian Church	OS 1:10,000 sh.238	1984

32. Eanach Cluaine "Marsh of the Lawn or insulated meadow"	J O'D (OSNB) E18.172	1834c
33. Anacloan, Eanach Cluana "marsh of the meadow"	Joyce iii 37	1913

34. Eanach Cluana/Annaclone	Éire Thuaidh	1988
35. Eanach Cluana	GÉ 102	1989
36. ˌanəˈkloːn	Local pronunciation	1995

The parish name is attested from 1422, but there is no evidence before 1603 for the *c* in the modern name. The first element *Enagh* later *Anagh* is clearly derived from *eanach* "marsh". The second element has been generally taken as a form of *cluain* "meadow", following O'Donovan (form 32), but the medieval spelling has also survived to the present in the name of the First and Second *Anaghlone* Presbyterian churches (form 31). Although it may have been re-interpreted later, the second element seems to have begun as the word *lón/luan* "haunch" (*DIL* 2 *lón*). The spellings of the final element with *i,y* here (5,6,7,10,11) would indicate a singular form *Eanach Luain* "marsh of the haunch". Athlone has long been understood as *Áth Luain*, interpreted as the "ford of the haunch" which fell from the corpse of the Whitehorned bull of *Táin Bó Cuailnge* (*TBC Rec. I* 1.4147), or occasionally as a personal name (*Onom. Goed.* 65a). However, more recent discussion of the names **Malone**, Belfast, and **Loan** townland, parish of Craigs Co. Antrim, has suggested that *lón* in place-names is usually a metaphor for a feature of the landscape, a "haunch-shaped hill" (Uí Fhlannagáin 1970(k), 22; *PNI* iv 206–7).

Since Annaclone is not a townland name it is hard to be sure which area "the marsh of the haunch" describes, although Church Bog beside the former church site in Ardbrin is the most likely. The parish is a mixture of hills, bogs, and pasture-land. In 1834 the name Annaclone was used for the parish church then in Ardbrin and the Presbyterian meeting houses in Tullintanvally and Ballynanny (*OSM* xii 17a). The name Annaclone is now used for the small village on the road between Loughbrickland and Katesbridge, in the townlands of Ardbrin and Tullintanvally, which seems to have grown up later near the meeting house in Tullintanvally. If the marsh is Church Bog the haunch-like hill is probably the ridge now known as the Blue Hill which stretches across Ardbrin and **Tullintanvally**.

Forms 37–40 below are an alternative name (cf. 12,13), probably representing *Tulaigh Ghiolla na nGamhnach*, "hillock of the cowherd" (*Mooney MS* 17). It appeared in the 17th-century patents for a local land unit, held from the bishop by the O'Sheils, probably the northern part of Ardbrin which contained the old parish church.

37. Tollegillegawneth al. Averleigh	CPR Jas I 395a	1609
38. Tollegillenegawnathe al. Annathloan	CPR Jas I 191a	1611
39. Tollygillygawnagh	CPR Jas I 191a	1611
40. Tollygillenegawneth al. Anaghclowane	CPR Jas I 191a	1611

TOWNLAND NAMES

Ardbrin
J 1941

Ard Brain
"Bran's height"

1. Ardbrin	CPR Jas I 395a	1609
2. Ardbrin	CPR Jas I 191a	1611
3. Arbrin Ardbrin	CPR Jas I 191a	1611
4. Ballylissardbryn	Inq. Ult. (Down) §39 Car. I	1633
5. (?)Ballyilanbegg, Balleaghan	Inq. Ult. (Down) §62 Car. I	1635
6. Lipardbrenn	Hib. Reg. Up. Iveagh	1657c

7. Lisard brin	Census 75	1659c
8. Lissardbrin	BSD 117	1661
9. Lippardbren	Hib. Del. Down	1672c
10. Ardburin	Tombstone (OSNB) E18.172	1806
11. Ballyardbrin	Wm. Map (OSNB) E18.172	1810
12. Ardbrin	Tombstone (OSNB) E18.172	1811
13. Church Bog in Ardbrin	OSM xii 14a,16b	1834
14. Ardbrin sometimes Ballyardbrin	OSM xii 16a	1834
15. Ard Broinn "Altitudo Branni"	OSL Dn xxi 63	1834
16. Ard Broin "Bran's hill or height"	J O'D (OSNB) E18.172	1834c
17. Ard Brain "the heights of Byrne"	J O'D (OSNB) E18.172	1834c
18. Ardbrin "Bran's height or Byrne's height"	Joyce iii 41	1913
19. ard'brïn	Local pronunciation	1995
20. ar'brən	Local pronunciation	1995

Ardbrin is the largest townland in the parish, measuring 1008 acres. It was a church townland, held by McGiverns in the early 17th century. However the O'Sheil holding of *Tulligilligawneth* may well have occupied the northern end where the parish church was, and the hill of Skateridge in the east was once part of **Ballysheil**. Between 1633 and 1672 *Lissardbrin* and similar forms appear (4,6–9: *p* is a misreading of *ʃ*), and the *lios* was probably the still-conspicuous Logan's Forth on a southern spur of the Blue Hill. There is no evidence for a syllable between *Ard-* and *-brin*, and O'Donovan translated the name simply as "Bran's hill or height" (16). *Bran*, an old word meaning "raven", was more commonly used in Irish as a personal name. In 1834 Ardbrin contained the residence of O'Donovan's Irish-speaking informant Mrs Con Magennis (*OSL Dn* 63), probably the large farmhouse of Connie Magennis and siblings now derelict at Skateridge in the townland.

However local people in the 1830s understood Ardbrin as "called from a family of name Byrne long resident in it" (17). Byrne is an anglicization of the surname *Ó Broin*, of Leinster origin but subsequently widespread (MacLysaght 1957, 68–9), which was well-known in the area. In 1444 John *O'Brynd* was rector of Magheradrool (*Swanzy's Dromore*), in 1619 there was Edmond *O'Brine* in Co Down (*CPR Jas I* 413b). A name spelt MacBrin or MacBrien was also known in Co. Down and was also further anglicized as Burns or Byrne (Bell 1988, 26). The surname with either *mac* or *ó* seems to have been used by the same family, who had a long connection with the church in Co. Down. In 1427 they provided the erenagh of church lands in **Lenaderg** in Tullylish parish (*Reg. Swayne* 73), and many had become churchmen in the 15th and 16th centuries. In 1609 members of the family held the church townlands of **Ballintaggart** in Aghaderg, and **Tulliorior** in Garvaghy adjoining this parish. The name could have begun as *Ard Uí Bhroin* "Ó Broin's" or "Byrne's height", with loss of the middle syllable, but more likely local people understood it as this because of their familiarity with the surname.

Aughnacloy
J 1942

Áth na Cloiche
"ford of the stone"

1. Ardar[r]agh al. Dromecrospatrick	CPR Jas I 394b	1609
2. Ardarragh al. Downecrospatricke	CPR Jas I 191a	1611

3. Anacly (hill)	Hib. Reg. Up. Iveagh	1657c
4. Aghnecloy	Inq. Ult. (Down) §1 Interreg.	1658
5. Aghvacloye	BSD 117	1661
6. Aghvacloy	DS (Mooney) 17	1661
7. Aghnacloy	Wm. Map (OSNB) E18.172	1810
8. Aghnacloy	Bnd. Sur. (OSNB) E18.172	1830
9. Aughnacloy	Wm. Little (OSNB) E18.172	1834c
10. Ath na Cloiche "Ford of the stone"	J O'D (OSNB) E18.172	1834c
11. Achadh na Cloiche	Mooney 93	1950c
12. ˌaxnəˈklɔï	Local pronunciation	1995

Aughnacloy is a small townland (114 acres) on the east bank of the Bann, which divides it from the rest of the parish, although the boundary follows an oxbow loop to the west now detached from the river. It was described as 40 acres in 1658 (4). There are few early forms of this name, but *Anacly* on Petty's barony map (3) would seem to indicate *áth* "ford" as the first element (10). The ford (on the Bann) may have been either that at **Poland's Bridge**, which is now slightly north of the townland boundary, or at Radcliff's steps, now removed, on the southern boundary. However the later spellings with *Agh-* and the current pronunciation [ax] make *achadh* "field" equally likely (11). There is no remarkable stone at present. Dean Mooney followed Reeves (*EA* 311) in linking Aughnacloy with earlier *Ardarragh al. Dromecrospatrick* (forms 1,2). These names probably represent *Ard an Rátha* "height of the rath" or *Ard Darach* "height of the oak", depending on how the name was stressed, and *Dún* or *Droim Croise Phádraig* "hillfort/ridge of Patrick's cross". There is no surviving cross, although the townland was church land.

Ballynafern
J 1739

Baile na Fearna
"townland of the alder"

1. Ballynefarin (in Shanchall)	CPR Jas I 394b	1609
2. Ballinefarin (12 towns, precinct of Shanchall)	CPR Jas I 190a	1611
3. Ballynafarrin (in Shanechall)	Inq. Ult. (Down) §7 Jac. I	1618
4. Ballynafarney, Arthur Magneisse of	Wars Co. Down xii 5(n)	1642
5. Ballinofarny	Hib. Reg. Up. Iveagh	1657c
6. the halfe towne of Ballyfearn	Census 75	1659c
7. Ballynefarny	BSD 117	1661
8. Ballinafarny	Hib. Del. Down	1672c
9. Ballyfarme	Rent Roll Down 12	1692
10. Ballynaferne	Wm. Map (OSNB) E18.13	1810
11. Ballynafern	Tombstone (OSNB) E18.172	1819
12. Ballynaferin	Newry Tel. (OSNB) E18.172	1830
13. Ballynafern	Bnd. Sur. (OSNB) E18.13	1830c
14. [Bal-ly-na-ferin]	OSNB Pron. E18.172	1834c
15. Smith Point & The Ethere (boggy places)	Mooney 22	1950c
16. Baile na Fe(a)rna "Town of the Alder"	J O'D (OSNB) E18.172	1834c

17. Baile-na-bhfearn "the town of the fearns/alder trees"	Joyce iii 110	1913
18. Baile na fearthaine "Town of the rain"?	Mooney 21	1950c
19. ˌbɑlnəˈfɛːrn	Local pronunciation	1995
20. ˌbɛlïnəˈfɛrn	Local pronunciation	1995

The name Ballynafern seems to be derived from *baile* followed by the article followed by a final element, which has two syllables in the earliest forms (1–3). The Ordnance Survey Name-book records five syllables in the early 19th-century pronunciation *Bal-ly-na-ferin* (14), sometimes reflected in the spelling (12), which made Dean Mooney suggest *Baile na Fearthainne* "townland of the rain". However -*fern* is now pronounced as one syllable and O'Donovan's suggestion of the original meaning is here followed. *Fearn* "alder", now masculine in gender, was originally feminine and remains feminine in Scottish Gaelic. Fernhill House in the townland seems to have been named from an English folk-etymology of Ballynafern.

Ballynafoy · *Baile na Faiche*
J 1540 · "townland of the green"

1. Ballinefoy (in Shanchall)	CPR Jas I 394b	1609
2. Ballynefey (in Shanchall)	CPR Jas I 190a	1611
3. Belenefoy	Hib. Reg. Up. Iveagh	1657c
4. Ballynefoy and qr of Ballynegross	Census 75	1659c
5. Ballynafoy	BSD 117	1661
6. Ballinafoy	Hib. Del. Down	1672c
7. Ballynefoy	ASE 274a 29	1681
8. B.Nafoy	Lamb Maps Co. Downe	1690c
9. Ballynefeigh	Rent Roll Down 11	1692
10. Bellanafau	Ir. Wills Index 100	1720
11. Ballynafoy	Tombstone (OSNB) E18.172	1818
12. Ballynafoy	Bnd. Sur. (OSNB) E18.172	1830c
13. Ballynafoy Hill 612 feet	OSM xii 13b	1834
14. Baile na faithche "town of the green"	J O'D (OSNB) E18.172	1834c
15. ˌbalnəˈfɔːi	Local pronunciation	1991
16. ˌbɑlnəˈfɑi	Local pronunciation	1994
17. ˌbɛlnəˈfɔï	Local pronunciation	1995

Ballynafoy Hill at 612 feet is the highest point in the parish "from which on a clear day the mountains of Tyrone, Derry and Antrim may be seen" (*OSM* xii 13a). There is a standing stone now lying near the summit and a rath close by on the south-eastern slope, as well as another lower down. "Town of the green (fair-green)" was the interpretation suggested by John O'Donovan (14), and the green might be the space in front of a rath, or a playing-field or assembly site, which was quite often a prominent hill. This hill-top could have been a meeting-point for the Magennis district of Shankill (forms 1,2). Cave Hill in the south of the townland is doubtless the site of a cave which was "about 30 yards in length . . . a fine spring well in the interior" (*OSM* xii 15a).

Ballynagross
J 1439

Baile na gCros
"townland of the crosses"

1.	Ballynecrosse (in Shanchall)	CPR Jas I 394b	1609
2.	Ballynecrosse (in Shanchall)	CPR Jas I 190a	1611
3.	3 qrs Ballynecrosse (in Shanechall)	Inq. Ult. (Down) §7 Jac. I	1618
4.	(?)Ballinegrosse, O Magullaghan of	Wars Co. Down x 77	1641
5.	(?)Ballynegross	Wars Co. Down x 78	1641
6.	Ballinogrosse	Hib. Reg. Up. Iveagh	1657c
7.	a qr of Ballynegross	Census 75	1659c
8.	one qr of Ballynegross	Census 75	1659c
9.	Ballynagrosse	BSD 117	1661
10.	Ballilogrosse/Ballilagrosse [Petty]	Mooney MS 19	1661?
11.	Ballinagrosse	Hib. Del. Down	1672c
12.	3 qrs Ballynecrosse	ASE 274a 29	1681
13.	3 qrs Ballynecross	Rent Roll Down 11	1692
14.	Ballynagross	Wm. Map (OSNB) E18.13	1810
15.	Baile na gcros "Town of the crosses"	J O'D (OSNB) E18.172	1834c
16.	ˌbalïnəˈgrɔs	Local pronunciation	1995

In the early 17th century Ballynagross, then spelt *Ballynecrosse*, was one of the 12 town-lands of Shankill (forms 1,2,3). This enables the forms to be distinguished from those of the townland of Ballycross in Glasquirin in Magherally. Another differentiating feature is the mapping of the Shankill townlands by Petty, which links them rather than Glasquirin with people accused of rebellion in 1641. Because of this, forms 4,5 probably belong here. The spellings in *-gross*, occurring from 1641 on, indicate more than one cross in Ballynagross, since in Irish nasalization occurred after the article in the genitive plural. However it is not clear what the "crosses" were: no suitable ancient monuments or crossroads appear on the modern map.

Ballynanny
J 1441

Bealach an Eanaigh
"routeway of the marsh"

1.	Ballaghanaghtymacart	CPR Jas I 394b	1609
2.	Ballaghannaghmiacart	CPR Jas I 190a	1611
3.	Ballaghamaccarte	Inq. Ult. (Down) §7 Jac. I	1618
4.	Ballinary	Hib. Reg. Up. Iveagh	1657c
5.	Ballynany	Census 75	1659c
6.	Ballynary	BSD 117	1661
7.	B'nary	Hib. Del. Down	1672c
8.	Ballynany	Rent Roll Down 12	1692
9.	Ballynanny	Tombstone (OSNB) E18.13	1809
10.	Ballynaney	Wm. Map (OSNB) E18.172	1810
11.	Ballinany	Tombstone (OSNB) E18.13	1824
12.	Baile an Eanaigh "Town of the marsh"	J O'D (OSNB) E18.172	1834c
13.	Bealach Aonaigh Mc Airt	Mooney 24	1950c
14.	Eanach Mac Airt	Mooney 24	1950c

15. ˌbɛləˈnanï	Local pronunciation	1991
16. ˌbaləˈnanï	Local pronunciation	1991

Ballynanny is to be identified with the early 17th-century name (forms 1–3) *Ballaghanaghtymacart, Ballyhannaghmiacarte, Ballaghmaccarte*, which was part of Shankill and held by Ever McArte McRowrie Magennis. The final element of these forms seems to be *Mac Airt* "of the sons of Art", possibly a surname, "of the MacArts". Ever (*Eimhear*) Magennis was himself called *Mac Airt* "son of Art", but Art was the name of his father as given in the Magennis genealogy (*TCD Gens* §270). This Art seems too recent to appear in the place-name, but most of the Magennis pedigrees go back to an ancestor called *Art an Lámhaigh*, and the name Art was in frequent use among the various branches. Thus *Mac Airt* probably refers to a group of the Magennises. The surname MacArt is often ephemeral (MacLysaght 1985, 39; Woulfe 1923, 306), but there is a reference to a 17th-century *McArte* in Co. Down (*CPR Jas I* 28a), and others in Antrim and Tyrone.

For the first element, the early forms seem to indicate either *Baile* "townland" or *Bealach* "routeway" (anglicized *Ballagh-*), with the more common element *baile* predominant later. The townland contains, on the old road from Tullintanvally, the Sentry-box crossroads at which the B-road from Banbridge to Rathfriland crosses the minor road to Loughbrickland, and the ancient *bealach* is likely to have been the Loughbrickland road. The spelling *a* in the third syllable, confirmed by the modern pronunciation, suggests *eanach* "marsh" for the second element. There is some marsh by the stream which forms the northern boundary. It looks as if the name *Eanach Mhic Airt* "MacArt's marsh" already existed when *Bealach* was prefixed to it, as *eanach* (spelt *-an(n)agh-*) is apparently not inflected. The full 17th-century name may even have been *Bealach Eanach Ti Mhic Airt* "routeway through the marsh of MacArt's house" (form 1). When the name was shortened to *Baile an Eanaigh*, "townland of the marsh" *eanach* (*-any*) appears in its correct genitive form.

Ballysheil
J 2040

Baile Uí Shiail
"O'Sheil's townland"

1. Ballyoheele al. Siatrick	BSD 117	1661
2. Syapatrick al. Ballyoheele	S & D Ann. (Mooney) 23 (f. 83)	1661?
3. Ballysheal	Wm. Map (OSNB) E18.13, 172	1810
4. Ballysheal	Bnd. Sur. (OSNB) E18.13, 172	1830c
5. Ballysheil	J O'D (OSNB) E18.172	1834c
6. Baile (Ui) S(h)iadhail "O'Sheil his town"	J O'D (OSNB) E18.172	1834c
7. ˈbɑliˈʃil	Local pronunciation	1991

Ballysheil has been misprinted on the OS 1:50,000 map as *Ballyshell*. The name **Skateridge**, now a hill in the adjacent townland of Ardbrin, was used as a land unit including current Ballysheil until the late 17th century, as revealed by an alias form in 1661 (form 1). This unit was church land in the 17th century, held with Aughnacloy by the O'Sheil family. Although the O'Sheils had to forfeit Aughnacloy and *Skeatricke* in 1658, from then on the townland name included their surname. It is not clear when the hill called Skateridge became part of Ardbrin townland, and there was still a Cormicke *O'Sheill* of *Scatricke* in 1663 (*Sub. Roll Dn* 277). *Ballysheal* had become the recognized spelling of the townland when O'Donovan altered it to Ballysheil to indicate the connection with the family, by that time generally spelt as Sheil with "but one *l*" (*OSNB*).

The family of O'Sheil, earlier *Ó Siadhail*, were famous in Ireland as doctors (*De Script. Hib.* 92; Brady 1947, 50–1). There was another Ballysheil in Co. Offaly where the O'Sheils of that district were hereditary physicians to the MacCoghlans (AD 1548, *AFM* v 1508 n.b). In Dromore diocese they were prominent as clergy during the late 15th and 16th centuries, different members of the family being connected in AD 1526–7 with the churches of Donaghcloney, Tullylish and Annaclone (*Swanzy's Dromore; Reg. Cromer* 208,213,223). Members of the family were pardoned as followers of the Magennises in 1602 and 1610 (*Fiants Eliz.* §6616; *CPR Jas I* 175a, 195b) and of *Slught O'Neales*, the O'Neills in Castlereagh (*CPR Jas I* 86b–87a). By 1659 the surname was most common in Orior Co. Armagh, eastern Fermanagh and in Co. Donegal (*Census* 32,120,59,64).

Cappagh   *An Cheapaigh*
J 1542   "the tilled plot"

1. Killkappie (in Shanchall)	CPR Jas I 394b	1609
2. Killkappie (in Shanchall)	CPR Jas I 190a	1611
3. Killcappie (in Shanechall)	Inq. Ult. (Down) §7 Jac. I	1618
4. The Rapagh	Hib. Reg. Up. Iveagh	1657c
5. Cappy	Census 75	1659c
6. Rapagh	BSD 117	1661
7. Cappagh	ASE 274a 29	1681
8. Cappagh	Rent Roll Down 11	1692
9. Cappagh	Wm. Map (OSNB) E18.172	1810
10. Cappy	Reg. Free. (OSNB) E18.172	1829
11. Cappa	Wm. Little (OSNB) E18.172	1834c
12. [Kap-pa]	OSNB Pron. E18.13	1834c
13. Cappy (rec. form Cappagh)	J O'D (OSNB) E18.172	1834c
14. Cappy, Corbet (x 3)	Bassett's Down 252	1886
15. Cappagh, Corbet	Bassett's Down 253	1886
16. Ceapaidh "a plot of land laid out for tillage"	Mrs Con Magennis (OSNB) E18.172	1834c
17. Ceapach "a Plot"	J O'D (OSNB) E18.172	1834c
18. Coill Ceapaigh "wood of [illeg.]"	Mooney 24	1950c
19. 'kjapï	Local pronunciation	1995
20. 'kɛpï	Local pronunciation	1995

Some of the 17th-century forms for Cappagh show copyists' corruptions of *c/r* or *K/R*, but the basic form is clearly an anglicized form of *Ceapach*, explained by Mrs Con Magennis as "a plot of land laid out for tillage" (16). The term meant originally "piece of ground where trees have been felled" from *cepp* "stump" (*DIL*, which quotes O'Donovan's supplement to *O'Reilly's* dictionary, where O'Donovan seems to have used this information from Mrs Magennis). The early forms like *Kilkappie* (1–3) will therefore represent *Coill Cheapaí* "wood of the cleared plot". The element *coill* was probably abandoned as the rest of the wood was cut down. The current pronunciation seems to reflect the dative *Ceapaigh*, but although O'Donovan recommended that *Cappy* be accepted as the official form (13) the spelling

Cappagh was retained by the Ordnance Survey. As a single element the word *ceapach* would have been used with the article, and the English article appears in the form *The Rapagh* from Petty's barony map, although it is not used with the name today. The *R* in this spelling must have been misread from capital *K*. Cappagh was also in the Magennis district of Shankill (forms 1–3). A lost monument called Cappagh Fort, at 412 feet on the hill in the north-east, was once a "commanding feature" (*OSNB; OSM* xii 13a).

Clay   *An Chléith*
J 1342   "the hurdle"

1.	Ballyclerhie (in Shanchall)	CPR Jas I 394b	1609
2.	Ballicleihie (12 towns, precinct of Shanchall)	CPR Jas I 190a	1611
3.	Cleyhey (in Shanechall)	Inq. Ult. (Down) §7 Jac. I	1618
4.	Clay	Hib. Reg. Up. Iveagh	1657c
5.	Cleay	Census 75	1659c
6.	Cley	BSD 117	1661
7.	Clay	Hib. Del. Down	1672c
8.	Cley	ASE 274a 29	1681
9.	Sley	Rent Roll Down 11	1692
10.	Clea	Wm. Map (OSNB) E18.172	1810
11.	Cloy	Reg. Free. (OSNB) E18.172	1829
12.	Clay	Bnd. Sur. (OSNB) E18.13	1830c
13.	Clay generally . . . the Clay	OSM xii 16a	1834
14.	An Cliath	Mrs Con Magennis (OSNB) E18	1834c
15.	Cliath "a hurdle"	J O'D (OSNB) E18.172	1834c
16.	Cliathach "Place of hurdles'	Mooney 299	1950c
17.	ðə ˈkle:	Local pronunciation	1995

The interpretation of the name Clay is clear enough, the earliest form *Ballicleihie* (1609) showing the genitive case of *cliath* "a frame or hurdle". The basic meaning of *cliath* is "frame-work", from which it has been used to mean wattled fencing, hurdles, ribcage, a harrow and so on. In the Irish name for the city of Dublin, *Baile Átha Cliath* "town of the wattled ford", the reference seems to have been to a structure consolidating the roadway through the ford, as suggested for **Thornyford** in Magheralin. The exact meaning in this name is unclear, although a stream forms the north-west boundary of the townland. The suggested form is dative/locative, though Mrs Con Magennis suggested *An C(h)liath* (nominative). Local usage in 1834, as today, includes the article in English as in Irish: The Clay (forms 13,14,17).

Derrylough   *Doire Locha*
J 1543   "oakwood of the lake"

1.	(?)Deyrloghan	Fiants Eliz. §4327	1583c
2.	(?)Dromneleckawly	Inq. Ult. & CPR Jas I Mooney 299	1950c
3.	Derrilagh	Hib. Reg. Up. Iveagh	1657c
4.	Dereylogh a qr	Census 75	1659c
5.	Derrylogh	BSD 117	1661

6. Derrylogh	Sub. Roll Down 276	1663
7. Derelagh	Hib. Del. Down	1672c
8. Derrylough	Wm. Map (OSNB) E18.13, 172	1810
9. Derrylough	Bnd. Sur. (OSNB) E18.13, 172	1830c
10. [Der-ry-'lough]	OSNB Pron. E18.172	1834c
11. Doire loch	Mrs Con Magennis (OSNB) E18.172	1834c
12. Doire-locha	J O'D (OSNB) E18.172	1834c
13. Doire Locha "Oakwood of the lake"	Mooney 299	1950c
14. Doire Loch "Black oakwood'	Mooney 300	1950c
15. ˌdɛrï'lɔx	Local pronunciation	1995

Derrylough is a small townland of 222 acres and the most northerly townland of the parish. The interpretation of the name seems clear enough, although there is now no lake visible on the maps. The queried 16th-century form (1) is more likely to have arisen from the names of two Magennis districts, *Deyr* (read *Deyn*) for **Loughadian**, *Loghan* for **Loughans**, on the boundary between Cos Down and Armagh. The name Derrylough therefore does not appear before 1657 (form 3). Dean Mooney pointed out that *Dromnelekawly* in Loughbrickland district in the Inquisitions and Patents seems to substitute for both this name and that of **Dooghary** in the parish of Seapatrick (2). He also thought that if Dooghary were *Dubhdhoire* "black oakwood" and Derrylough contained the old word *loch* "black" their current names might have the same meaning (2,14; *Mooney MS* 299). The townland of Dooghary is slightly further west and, although not now contiguous to Derrylough, could have been in the past.

Lisnasliggan   *Lios na Sliogán*
J 1741   "fort of the shells"

1. Lisnesleggan	CPR Jas I 395a	1609
2. Lisnesleggan (to manor of Dromore)	CPR Jas I 191a	1611
3. half td Lisnesleggan	CPR Jas I 191a	1611
4. Lisneslligan, one half towne of land (glebe)	Inq. Down (Reeves1) 91	1657
5. Lissonsligan	Hib. Reg. Up. Iveagh	1657c
6. Lisconsligan with Glebe	Hib. Reg. Up. Iveagh	1657c
7. The Glabe	Census 75	1659c
8. a qr of Lisneslickan	Census 75	1659c
9. a qr of Lisneslickan and a qr of Ballynefearn (2nd ref.)	Census 75	1659c
10. Lissnesliggan	BSD 117	1661
11. Lisnesligan	Sub. Roll Down 277	1663
12. Lissonsligan	Hib. Del. Down	1672c
13. Lisnasligan	Tombstone (OSNB) E18.13	1806
14. Lisnasligan	Wm. Map (OSNB) E18.13	1810
15. Lisnasligan	Tombstone (OSNB) E18.13	1812
16. Lios na Sligean "fort of the shells"	Mrs Con Magennis (OSNB) E18.172	1834c

17. Lios-na-sliogán "of the shells /thin slaty stones"	Joyce iii 482	1913
18. sliogán "shell, husk, hull" – slatey stones?	Mooney 29	1950c
19. ˌlïsnəˈslïgən	Local pronunciation	1991

Lisnasliggan was part of the church lands in the east of the parish. No *lios* survives within the present boundary; or within the 17th-century boundary as reconstructed below. The Irish form suggested was the interpretation of Mrs Con Magennis, with the final element explained by Dean Mooney as possibly meaning "of the slatey stones". This is quite likely, as in 1834 Ballynagross was described as containing "slaty rock . . . of a brittle or rotten description" (*OSNB*). However, shells were used in early Ireland as manure (*DIL* sv *slice*). In the 18th century the fresh-water mussels of the Bann were well-known and were fished for pearls around Banbridge, although "As an article of food it gained popularity only among the peasantry, for the reason that it required very high flavouring to make it palatable" (*Bassett's Down* 231–3). Deposits of shells might have been found within the lost monument. In 1834 there were still "seven ancient forts" in Lisnasliggan (*OSNB*). Of the "5 and 20 of the old forts" recorded in the parish (*OSM* xii 15a) hardly any remain.

From forms (1–4) it seems that in 1609 the townland had been divided by the bishop, half let to Patrick McGivern, half allocated as the parish glebe. Petty showed the main area of Lisnasliggan as it exists today west of an area called Glebe, which was listed as such in 1659 (forms 5–6,7). In 1834 the glebe was 124 acres (*OSNB*), and was regarded as a part of Lisnasliggan which had been given to the Established Church by the grandfather of the then owner, the Marquis of Downshire (*OSM* xii 16a, 15b). Since Lisnasliggan had earlier been church land, the granting of the glebe may have been a condition of the change of ownership. The current Church of Ireland church seems to have been built on the post-plantation glebe, abandoning the old church site in the townland of Ardbrin.

On Petty's barony map the river Bann was shown as dividing the parish of Annaclone from the townland of **Tullyorior** in Garvaghy, whereas it now runs through Tullyorior. Petty thought the Bann was a boundary in several places where it was not, most notably the county boundary between Down and Armagh. However the map of Upper Iveagh showed part of Lisnasliggan on the east bordering the Bann and Tullyorior, where Tullyorior is now bordered by Tullintanvally. It appears from the sources that the original boundaries of Lisnasliggan must have been redrawn. Petty showed the Church of Ireland Glebe in the middle of Lisnasliggan, dividing it into two parts. Lisnasliggan now adjoins Ballynafern in the south, but Petty showed this area, which, although unnamed by Petty, is probably modern Annaghanarva, as the south end of Tullintanvally.

Tullintanvally
J 1741

Tulaigh an tSeanbhealaigh
"hillock of the old road"

1. Ballytollyntanvallagh	CPR Jas I 395a	1609
2. Balletollenleanvallegh, Shane Oge Maguirin of	CPR Jas I 195b	1610
3. Ballytollintanvallagh (to manor of Dromore)	CPR Jas I 191a	1611
4. Tullytanvally	Hib. Reg. Up. Iveagh	1657c
5. Tollymtenvolly	Census 75	1659c

6. Tollentanvally	BSD 117	1661
7. Tullyvally	Sub. Roll Down 276	1663
8. Tullantavelly	Sub. Roll Down 277	1663
9. Tullitunvally	Hib. Del. Down	1672c
10. Terrantenvalley	Mooney MS 38	1810
11. Tanvelly, Tanvelley	Newry Tel. (OSNB) E18.172	1829
12. Tullintanvally generally . . . Tanvally	OSM xii 14b,16a	1834
13. McClory's Bog in Tullintanvally	OSM xii 14a,17a	1834
14. Hillis' Fort in Tullintanvally	OSM xii 15a	1834
15. McClory's Bog, Brown Bog	OSNB E18.172	1834c
16. Tanvally	Wm. Little (OSNB) E18.172	1834c
17. [Tull-in-'tan-valley]	OSNB Pron. E18.172	1834c
18. Tanvally Fort near the church	Lewis' Top. Dict. i 25b	1837
19. Tanvally	Ir. Wills Index 98	1856
20. Tulaigh an tSeanbhaile	Mrs Con Magennis (OSNB) E18.172	1834c
21. Tul an t-seanbhaile "hill of the old town"	Joyce iii 588	1913
22. Tulach an tSeanbhealaigh "the hill of the old road"	Mooney 37	1950c
23. ˌtan'valï	Local pronunciation	1991
24. ˌtolǝntan'valï	Local pronunciation	1994

Since 1834 Tullintanvally has been "used indiscriminately with Tanvally" (*OSNB*), and the short form is used most often by current informants. Mrs Con Magennis understood the name as ending with *baile* "town(land)", while "hillock of the old road" was the interpretation of Dean Mooney, who pointed out that "traces of the old road from Downpatrick to Armagh remain" (*Mooney MS* 37). Mooney left no fuller notes or sketches in his manuscript. Tullintanvally is now crossed by three roads from east to west, and has Poland's Bridge across the Bann in its north-east corner. However the old road as remembered locally, and as walked by Leo McNeill, went along the ridge of the Blue Hill, from Skateridge in the east to Monteith chapel in the west, and then linked the Guard House with the Sentry-box on the road to Lough Brickland. *Baile* "town, townland" is always spelt *bally* or *Balli-*. Early 17th-century forms such as *Ballitollintanvallagh* indicate *bealach* "road" as the likely final element, although the final *-gh* is ungrammatical if intended to indicate [x] as in *bealach*, instead of genitive *bealaigh*. The hill or *tulach* was no doubt that now called the Blue Hill.

Tullintanvally was originally a church townland, held in the early 17th century by the McGiverns (2). In 1837 "Tanvally fort near the church", probably on the border with Ardbrin, was "one of the largest and most perfect in this part of the country" (18). The Ordnance Survey Memoir mentions Hillis' Fort, presumably named from the family of William Hillis who had a "most comfortable farmhouse" in the townland (*OSM* xii 14b,15a). This contained a cave or souterrain, and a story was told how people trying to dig open the fort at night were frightened off by the sound of horses rushing at them from every side. These forts are not marked on modern maps, although there are still Hillises in the parish.

The townland still contains McClory's Bog near the village of Annaclone (forms 13,15), although it was already dug out in 1834 (*OSM* xii 14a,17a). McClory is derived from *Mac*

Labhradha, "a rare Ulster surname" (Woulfe 1923, 385). It is still prevalent locally, but the 51 examples in the 1993 Northern Ireland telephone directory are all in the area of Iveagh. It was borne by Alice, grandmother of the Brontë sisters (Haughton Crowe 1969, 32–3).

OTHER NAMES

Annaghanarva	*Eanach an Arbha*	
J 1739	"marsh of the corn"	
1. ˌanəxənˈɑrvə	Local pronunciation	1995
2. ˌanəkinˈɑrvə	Local pronunciation	1995

An Irish name but not a townland name, Annaghanarva is in the south of Lisnasliggan townland, possibly the area which is shown as the south end of Tullintanvally on Petty's map. Although now understood as the name of a hill, overlooking Monteith, it may have been the name of a sessiagh. There are no earlier spellings, but Annaghanarva apparently derives from *Eanach an Arbha* "marsh of the corn". *Arbha* is an old genitive of *arbhar* "corn", and is as common in place-names as its other genitive *arbhair*. Joyce gave the example Meenanarwa near Fintown in Co. Donegal (*Joyce* ii 318–9) where, however, the final -*r* still exists in the local pronunciation in Irish (O'Kane, J. 1970, 99).

Glebe Bog	An English form	
J 1642		
1. Glebe Bog	OSM xii 14a	1834
2. Glebe Bog	OSNB E18.172	1834
3. the Glebe and Glebe house		
(Lisnasliggan)	OSNB E18.172	1834c
4. a glebe of 124 Irish acres		
(Lisnasliggan)	OSNB E18.172	1834c
5. ðə ˈglaïb	Local pronunciation	1995
6. ˈglib ˈbɔg	Local pronunciation	1995

Glebe Bog is situated at the junction of the townlands of Ballynanny, Cappagh and the north end of **Lisnasliggan**, half of which townland was the parish glebe in 1657. Much of Glebe Bog was already pasture in 1834 (*OSM* xii 14a). The Glebe itself was shown with bog to the south on Petty's barony map of Upper Iveagh, and was listed as a land unit c. 1659 (Lisnasliggan forms 6,7). The bog shown by Petty is unlikely to be the current Glebe Bog, and is probably McClory's Bog in the middle of Tullintanvally. In 1834 the Glebe was 124 Irish acres of Lisnasliggan, as given by Lord Downshire to the rectory of Annaclone. It also contained the Rector's house and a school (*OSM* xii 15b,17b). The Glebe is still pronounced the old way (5), unlike **Glebe Bog**.

Guard House	An English form	
J 1641		
1. ðə ˈgjɑːrd həus	Local pronunciation	1994

The building known as the Guard House is across the "old road" through Tullintanvally from Downpatrick to Armagh from the Drilling Field, now the site of Ballynanny Presbyterian church, where the Protestant settlers of the area used to exercize in the 17th century as the Annaghlone Volunteers. Aubrey Jelly, 93, who gave this information to Adrian Clarke, now lies buried in this churchyard. A little further along the road is the Sentry Box. From this hillside there is a good view of the valley, covering northern and eastern approaches.

McClory's Bog   An English form

1. ˌmək'lɔrïz 'bɔg   Local pronunciation   1991

See **Tullintanvally** townland.

Monteith   Of uncertain origin
J 1740

1. Monteith's Lough	Wm. Map (OSNB) E18.172	1810
2. Monteith Lough / Lake	OSM xii 13b,14b	1834
3. Monteith Bog	OSM xii 14a	1834
4. John Montouth who erected the mill	OSNB E18.13	1834c
5. Monteith's Lough (mill-dam)	J O'D (OSNB) E18.172	1834c
6. Monteith's Lough	OSM xii 16b	1837
7. ˌmɔn'tiθ	Local pronunciation	1991

The name Monteith now belongs to a village in the south of Tullintanvally, consisting of an old mill and school called Monteith, new housing called Frazer Park, and St Colman's Roman Catholic church. The *Ordnance Survey Memoir* refers to a lough "the only one in the parish" and an extensive bog of the name. The lake had originally covered most of the bog, in all 60 acres, but in 1834 there was apparently a crannog, "a high bank called the Island, built on piles as most of these islands are" which appeared at the north end when the lough was drained for turf-cutting in summer. This custom is still remembered.

Local tradition in 1834 was undecided if the name was a surname (still known further north in Co. Down) or the Irish word *móinteach* "bog" as in the **Montiaghs** parish near Lough Neagh (*OSM* xii 13b). As it stands the name looks closer to the Scottish surname Monteith, which derives from a place called Monteith in south-west Perthshire (Black 1946, 608a). Willie Sawey who died about 30 years ago used to point out a derelict house on the right of Monteith Road going south as the dwelling of a water-bailiff of the name. Monteith Road used to be called Lough Road, but all that remains of the lough is a bog and some marshy ground on each side of the stream which forms the townland boundary around St Colman's church.

Mount Hill   An English form
J 1742

1. 'məunt 'hïl   Local pronunciation   1991

Mount Hill on the boundary between the townlands of Tullintanvally and Tulliorior may possibly have been the *tulach* "hillock" which forms the first element in Tullyorior. The *tulach* of Tullintanvally and the *Ard*, "height", of Ardbrin seem to have been the hill known locally as the Blue Hill.

Poland's Bridge   An English form
J 1942

1. Poland's Steps & Radcliff's Steps	OSM xii 13b	1834
2. 'po:lənd 'brədʒ	Local pronunciation	1991
3. 'po:lṇz 'brïdʒ	Local pronunciation	1994
4. ˌðə 'polənz 'brïdʒ	Local pronunciation	1994

In 1834 there were two fords across the Bann in the parish, Poland's and Radcliff's Steps, both with stepping stones for pedestrians, and the first also with planks laid across piers so that people could cross even after heavy rain (*OSM* xii 13–14). Thus the name Poland antedates the building of the bridge, which now crosses from Tullintanvally in Annaclone to the east part of Tullyorior in Garvaghy. The ford at Poland's Bridge may have originally been in **Aughnacloy** above. Radcliff's Steps are not named on maps, but a generation ago a shoemaker called Ratcliffe lived across the river from a footbridge shown in the south of Aughnacloy (OS 1:10,000 sheet 221). The family of McPoland are known in the area, although the bridge which is now called The Polands Bridge is not specifically connected with them.

Skateridge   *Scátraic* (?)
J 1940   "conspicuous place"

1. Scattrick (to manor of Dromore)	CPR Jas I 191a	1611
2. Scattricke	CPR Jas I 191a	1611
3. Skeatricke	Inq. Ult. (Down) §1 Interreg.	1658
4. Siatrick al. Ballyoheele	BSD 117	1661
5. Scatricke	Sub. Roll Down 277	1663
6. Sciathrach "Shields" (play on family name)	Mooney 24	1950c
7. 'sketrïtʃ	Local pronunciation	1995

Skateridge is the name of a hill in Ardbrin townland, the eastern extremity of the Blue Hill. Although it is shown on the modern 1:50,000 map, the name was maintained locally by one family only, that of Mr Connie Magennis who died in old age in 1978. The hill rises to 301 feet, not high enough to be noted under the hills of the parish in the Ordnance Survey Memoir, although the ridge forms the course of the old road. In the early 17th century Skateridge was used as a townland name, apparently including Ballysheil, now the next townland to the east. The family of O'Sheil held the land for most of the 17th century (see **Ballysheil**), and Connie Magennis and his brothers and sisters used the name for their farm by the old road. Despite the 17th-century forms of this place-name it is difficult to suggest an etymology.

Hogan gives various examples of place-names containing the element *sciath* "shield"; such as **Lisnaskea** in Fermanagh, *Sciathbaile Mic Murchadha* and *Sciath Gabra* which is Skea Castle, the Maguires' inauguration place (*Onom. Goed.* 592b). Dean Mooney's suggestion was *Sciathrach* "place of shields", as a play on the anglicized form of the family name, which was sometimes spelt as Shields. However it is unlikely that a townland name in Irish would have originated so late as to be based on a pun from English.

There are two other similar names in Co. Down. In the townland of Kilfeaghan, parish of Kilbroney, there is a minor name spelled Seatritch Hollow on the map (1:10,000 sheet 284), but pronounced [skatritʃ], so that *e* is apparently a spelling mistake for *c*, i.e. *Scatritch*. There are no early forms for this name. **Sketrick** Island in Strangford Lough, on which was a medieval castle (parish of Ardquin, *PNI* ii 25–6), was called *Skaterick* in the 17th century. The earliest form was *Scatra* in 1178 AD. O'Donovan related the name to a place in the locality called in Irish in 1470 *Caislén Sgath Deircce* (*AFM* iv 1066), which he translates as "castle of the red shelter". The author in this series suggested the Irish form *Oileán Scathdeirge*, and translated it tentatively as "red-pointed island".

Another possible Irish origin is *scadharc* "mirror, looking-glass" (*Dinneen*), masculine, but earlier variable, a compound of *scáth* "shelter, shade" and *derc* "socket, eye", which was originally neuter and later feminine. The dictionary of early Irish (*DIL*) gives one example of the earlier spelling *Scadarc* standing alone as a place-name in a poem from the Early Irish tale *Bórama Laigen*: *dar Scadarc . . . do-ria mac meic Muiredaig* "over *Scadarc* will go Murrough's grandson" (*SG* 373.9, *LLec*). Hogan has a reference to *Scadarc* in the prose of the same text (*ac Scadairc i ndesciurt Hua Cendselaig*, *LL* 301b, v 1.38462), which may be Skeirke in Co. Laois where "the height at the church commands an extensive view" (*Onom. Goed.* 591b). The word appears in a later literary place-name *Tipra na Scath-deirce* "well of the looking-glass" (*DIL* from *Acallam (Stokes)* 1.4527). As well as being a metaphor for still water, the use of *scadharc* in place-names may sometimes reflect the alternative meaning of "spectacle, sight" (*DIL*); i.e. a "conspicuous place".

Scadharc in some of these examples is feminine, with dative *scadhairc*. As David Greene pointed out, the expected early Irish form would actually be *scáterc*, reflected in one early source (*Ériu* 35 (1985) 195; *Thes. Pal.* ii 227.26), where the internal consonant cluster *thd[h]* has given unlenited *t* rather than *dh*, as in the recurring place-name **Leitrim** from *Liath-dhroim*. If it is the word in Sketrick, Skateridge, the second syllable of dative *Scátairc* has been metathesized to give *Scátraic*. Sketrick castle would be a prominent object seen across Strangford Lough, and the hill at Skateridge has a good view to the north. A further possibility, returning to the original compound *scáth-derc*, is that the place-name could mean "sheltering hollow" or "cave", the later meaning of *dearc* (see **Lenaderg** in Tullylish).

It is possible that the place-name was not originally Irish, especially in Strangford Lough which itself bears a Viking name, although much more unlikely inland. The final syllable could be Norse *hryggr* "ridge", often anglicized in English place-names as *-rick*, the same word as English ridge. *Skata*, the fish called "skate", is used, "probably because it is very flat", as an element in place-names in Shetland, but Skateridge and Sketrick are not notably flat (G. Fellows-Jensen, pers. comm.). *Skothryggr* "humpback ridge" is a possible compound in Norse, but it does not explain the 3-syllable form *Skaterick* or why the vowel in the first element of the Irish place-names is always *-a-* not *-o-* (P. Foote, pers. comm.). Nevertheless interchange of stressed *a* and *o* is a long-established feature in Irish (O'Rahilly 1932, 192–3).

The Sentry Box
J 1541

An English form

1. a house called Sentrybox	OSM xii 15a		1834
2. ðə'sɛntrï ˌbɑks	Local pronunciation		1994

In 1834 Sentrybox was the name of a house situated in the townland of Ballynanny, at the crossroads of the "main road from Banbridge to Rathfriland" with the "main road from Loughbrickland to Castlewellan" (form 1, *OSM* xii 15a). The house is still there and the name as The Sentrybox is also used for the crossroads, although the road to Loughbrickland is now classified as a minor road. The name refers to the local 17th-century Protestant militia called the Annaghlone Volunteers, who used to exercise up along the old road from the Sentrybox in a field called the Drilling Field, opposite the **Guard House**. Behind the Sentrybox there is a field called the Sentry Field, which contains a souterrain. Local lore has it that some sheep disappeared down the cave and were later found grazing on the Knock Hill (**Knock Iveagh**).

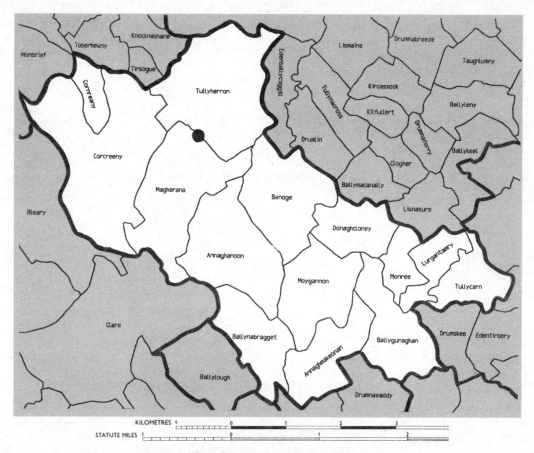

KILOMETRES 1   0   1   2   3

STATUTE MILES 1   0   1   2

Parish of Donaghcloney

Barony of Iveagh Lower, Upper Half

Townlands
Annaghanoon
Annaghmakeonan
Ballygunaghan
Ballynabragget
Banoge
Corcreeny
Cornreany
Donaghcloney

Lurgantamry
Magherana
Monree
Moygannon
Tullycarn
Tullyherron

Town
Waringstown

THE PARISH OF DONAGHCLONEY

Donaghcloney lies along the Lagan in the barony of Iveagh Lower, Upper Half. The parish is generally flat, Tullycarn 296 feet in the south-east and Cornreany 268 feet in the west being the most conspicuous hills (*OSM* xii 56a). The present local informant was Mr E.F. Copeland of Blackskull, local historian, artist and poet.

The parish name is attested from 1422 in the registers of the Archbishops of Armagh, and in 1526 the prebend of *Domnachclone* was Cormac *O'Shiegell*, presumably one of the local family of O'Sheils whose name is preserved in **Ballysheil** townland, parish of Annaclone (*Reg. Cromer* 208). In 1657 the parish was reckoned as nine towns and one sessiagh (*Inq. Down* 137), while the current number of townlands is 14. The townland bearing the parish name was originally church land, held by the McBredan family of Magheralin (*CPR Jas I* 191a). There is an excellent local history of the parish by E.D. Atkinson, whose appendix of sources includes the Donaghcloney Vestry Book, and the Clanconnell and Waring papers (*Atkinson's Donaghcloney*, 1898, 114–9,131–5).

With part of the neighbouring parish of Tullylish it formed the territory of **Clanconnell**, held in 1609 by Glasney McAugholy Magennis (*CPR Jas I* 394b, 193a; *Inq. Ult. (Down)* §9 Car. I). Eight modern townlands were included in Clanconnell: Annaghanoon, Banoge, Corcreeny, Magherana, Tullyherron, and, detached in the east, Lurgantamry, Monree, and Tullycarn. Landholding in Clanconnell in the early 17th century was distinguished by land units grouped in threes, probably sessiaghs, although described in the patents etc. in the formula "the town of *X* with the hamlets of *Y* and *Z*". Lurgantamry and its two divisions all became modern townlands but the subdivisions of the others have disappeared. Petty's barony map of Lower Iveagh shows clearly that in the 17th century bog and wood must have provided physical boundaries between the different divisions.

Three contiguous townlands in the south, Annaghmakeonan, Ballynabragget and Moygannon, belonged to Sir Art Magennis, and one, Ballygunaghan, was part of another Magennis district called **Glasquirin** (Magherally and Seapatrick parishes).

After 1641 the Magennis proprietors who had been implicated in the rebellion had to forfeit their lands, including locally Donald Shane Magennis and Fferdoragh McManus, Hugh and Donald Conor Magennis of *Linan* (Annaghanoon); Murtagh McGlasny, Phelim McGlasny and Glasny Oge Magennis of Clanconnell; and Brian mac Edmund Boy Magennis of Clare, the old centre of Clanconnell in Tullylish (*Wars Co. Down* x 79–81). Much of the land in the east of the parish was acquired by William Waring of Waringstown: the two subdivisions of Anaghanoon, part of Magherana, Corcreeny and two subdivisions, Tullyherron and one subdivision, and one subdivision of Banoge (*ASE* 49b 19). The Warings continued to be influential in the parish, and the Rev. Holt Waring supplied comments on the correct spelling of the place-names in the Donaghcloney name book (*OSNB* E2).

Other settlers who gained lands in Clanconnell were John Magill, who acquired Cornreany and Tullycarn, Bannog sessiagh and mills, two subdivisions of Banoge, a quarter of Moygannon, subdivisions of Tullyherron etc., and half of Ballynagarrick in Tullylish, mostly previously mortgaged to him by the Clanconnell Magennises; and George Rawdon, who acquired part of Magherana, and several townlands in Tullylish (*ASE* 61b, 1666 AD). Magill also got *Donoghclony* and *Moorelt* (Monree), and several townlands, mostly from Sir Art Magennis, in the south of Tullylish (*ASE* 112a, 1667 AD). In 1777 Magill Esq. had a house at Tullycarn, close to the main Magill seat of Gillhall (*Taylor & Skinner* map 18).

In the Book of Survey and Distribution *Lurgantawry*, *Bannoge* and *Morree* (or half-sessiaghs of the last two) were listed in Magheralin as well as under Donaghcloney (*BSD* 74-6). In the 1715 parish register of Magheralin four townlands, Banoge, Lurgantamry, Monree and Tullycarn, were still included in that parish. The Donaghcloney Vestry Book shows that several of the 17th-century subdivisions continued in use until the 19th century.

PARISH NAME

Donaghcloney   *Domhnach Cluana*
J 1353   "the church of the meadow"

1. Domhnach Cluana	Cín Lae Ó M. 22	1645c
2. Donnaghclona cum capellis	Reg. Dowdall §129 275	1422
3. preb. of par. church of St Mowus de Dompnachcluana	Cal. Papal Letters vii 264	1422
4. Dompnachcluana	Reg. Swayne (EA) 107n	1427
5. Dompnaghcluana	Reg. Swayne 82	1427
6. prebend of Domnuchdoluana[?]	Cal. Papal Letters xvi 330	1495
7. Domnachclone	Reg. Cromer ii §47	1526
8. prebenda de Downachclone	EA 313	1526
9. Donachilone	Reg. Cromer ii §84	1528
10. Downagh Clona	Reg. Dowdall §113 80	1546
11. Donaclona	EA 107n King's Bks	1601c
12. Templ: Donoghclone	Bartlett Maps (Esch. Co. Maps) 2	1603
13. Donoghoclooney	Atkinson's Donaghcloney 75	1608
14. Donachglonie	Jas I to Dromore Cath. 314	1609
15. Donnoghclownagh, Shane & Jenkin McBriden of	CPR Jas I 195b	1610
16. Donochelon	Speed's Ulster	1610
17. Downaghclonagh	Inq. Ult. (Down) §30 Car. I	1632
18. Dawnaghclonagh	Inq. Ult. (Down) §30 Car. I	1632
19. Donaghclony two towns	Magennis Paps (O'Sullivan) 68	1632
20. Donoghclony (parish)	Inq. Down (Reeves1) 85	1657
21. 2 tns of Donaghclony	Hib. Reg. Lr. Iveagh	1657c
22. Donaghclony	Par. Map (Mooney) 335	17thc
23. Donnaclony	Census 79	1659c
24. Donaghglony Parish	BSD 77	1661
25. Donaghglony	S & D Ann. (Mooney) 335 (28)	17thc
26. Donaghclony	BSD 77	1661
27. Donaghclony	Trien. Visit. (Margetson) 24	1664
28. Donaghclony	Trien. Visit. (Margetson) 26	1664
29. Donoghclony 178a	ASE 112a 34	1667
30. Donaghclony	Hib. Del. Down	1672c
31. Donoghcloney	Trien. Visit. (Boyle) 46	1679
32. Donoghcloney vicaria	Trien. Visit. (Boyle) 48	1679
33. Donaghcloney	Trien. Visit. (Boyle) 48	1679
34. Donacloney	Atkinson's Donaghcloney 31	1682
35. Donagholeny	Rent Roll Down 7	1692
36. Donogh Clony	Harris Hist. map	1743
37. Donochlony (on bell)	OSM xii 60a	1750c
38. Donaghclony	Wm. Map (OSNB) E2	1810

39. Donacloney	Custom of County (OSNB) E2	1834c
40. [Don-a-'clo-ny]	OSM xii 57a	1834
41. Domhnach Cluaine, Dominica campi		
"church of the lawn or meadow"	J O'D (OSNB) E2	1834c
42. Domhnach Cluanach		
"church of the meadow"	Mooney 335	1950c
43. Domhnach Cluana/Donaghcloney	Éire Thuaidh	1988
44. Domhnach Cluana	GÉ 89	1989
45. ˌdɔnəˈklonï	Local pronunciation	1992
46. ˌðə ˈklonï	Local pronunciation	1992

The name Donaghcloney belongs to the parish, the townland which contained the parish church, and a village in the townland. The parish church was moved in the 17th century to Waringstown, but "was formerly situated in the graveyard near Donaghcloney bridge" (*OSM* xii 60a), beside which another church was built in 1894. Atkinson explained the parish name from the site of the ancient church "on a slight eminence rising out of a water meadow on the right bank of the river Lagan" (*Atkinson's Dromore*, 194). He then continued with an apparent citation of local tradition: "Here it is said that St Patrick himself, one Lord's Day, traced out with his pastoral staff, the Bachall Jesu, the foundations". Certainly the term *domhnach* indicates an early church, as well as meaning the "Lord's Day", but the ruined foundations Atkinson described are not dated or mentioned in the archaeological survey (*ASCD*). The second element, from *cluain* "meadow", has been thought to be the same as that in the preceding parish of **Annaclone**. However the final vowel of genitive *cluana* only appears in the forms for Donaghcloney, and Annaclone seems originally to have ended with *luan* "haunch". If *Eanach Cluana* were still to be suggested for Annaclone, Donaghcloney would have to be *Domhnach Cluanaí*, a genitive based on the later dative *cluanaidh*.

The townland bearing the parish name was church land, held in the early 17th century by the family of McBredan, with three other denominations probably including **Ballymacbredan** in Magheralin parish (15). However these church lands were granted by the bishop to George Sexton, and were no longer listed as church lands in 1622 (17–19). By 1667 *Donoghclony* belonged with other lands in the area to Sir John Magill (*ASE*, form 29), and the parish contained no lands belonging to the Church of Ireland in the Parliamentary Reports of 1833 and 1868.

The village of Donaghcloney is beside the Lagan in the centre of the townland. It is known as *The Cloney* locally, and has been "many's a year". Although the *gh* was no longer pronounced in Donaghcloney in 1834 (40), Mr Copeland says Donagh Cottage in the townland is still called ['dɔnəx].

TOWNLANDS

Annaghanoon	*Eanach an Uain*	
J 1153	"marsh of the lamb"	
1. Balliannaghonowen in Clanconnell		
+ 2 hamlets Loynnan Kinnoge	CPR Jas I 193a	1611
2. Ballyannaghan Leynan Kynoge	Inq. Ult. (Down) §9 Car. I	1627
3. MacGlasny Magenis of Linen	Wars Co. Down xi 61	1641

4. Leenan Aghnehan Kenoge	Atkinson's Donaghcloney 22	1650c
5. Leenan Aghnehan Kenoge	Hib. Reg. Lr. Iveagh	1657c
6. Anaghnoan	Census 79	1659c
7. Leenan Aghnehan	BSD 77	1661
8. Aghananeone al. Aghnehan	ASE 123a 37	1667
9. Lenan Ardnehan Kenoge	Hib. Del. Down	1672c
10. 2 sess. of td Anaghanowan = Leenan, Kinoge	Atkinson's Donaghcloney 133	1691
11. Anaghanoon (?sess.)	Atkinson's Donaghcloney 133	1691
12. (?)Aghananeronane	Rent Roll Down 8	1692
13. Aghnanoone als Aghnehur, ½ sessgh	Rent Roll Down 8	1692
14. (?)Aghnenan	Rent Roll Down 9	1692
15. Anaghanown	Ir. Wills Index 78	1700
16. Anaghnowan al. Lisremoylan and Leenan	Atkinson's Donaghcloney 46	1703
17. Annaghanoon, Annaghanowen	Deeds & Wills (Mooney) 335	1720c
18. Anaghanoon	Map of Down (OSNB) E2	1755
19. Anaghanoon	Vestry Bk D'cloney 114	1772
20. Anagahanoon	Vestry Bk D'cloney 114	1785
21. Anahanoon	Vestry Bk D'cloney 115	1805
22. Anaghanoon	Wm. Map (OSNB) E2	1810
23. [Annagha'noon]	OSM xii 58b	1834
24. Eanachán Úna "Winifred's little marsh"	J O'D (OSNB) E2	1834c
25. Eanach an Uain "marsh of the lamb"	Mooney 335	1950c
26. Eanachán Uain "lamb's bog"	Mooney 335	1950c
27. ˌɑnəxəˈnun	Local pronunciation	1992

Since there appears to be a close connection between the name Annaghanoon and the minor name Lambs Island in the townland they will be dealt with together here. Although the townland name was sometimes shortened to *Aghnehan* in the mid-17th century, there are sufficient long forms to suggest that *Annaghanowen* was in Irish *Eanach an Uain* "marsh of the lamb". The biggest marsh lies between low hills in the centre of the townland. The shorter historical forms which begin with *Agh-* all come from Petty and related sources, and may simply have been copied from each other. Alternatively, they may have had *achadh* "field" as the first element, rather than "marsh", and may have referred to part of the same place. Whichever was the case it is the long form Annaghanoon which has survived to the present.

The place-name **Lambs Island** refers to a farm by a fort on a high knoll in the south of the townland, which is mainly marshy and low-lying (*ASCD* 161a, 369a). Lambs Island is probably a translation of the townland name, and an example of *eanach* "marsh" being translated as "island", as with *Anaghbawn* now **Islandbawn** Co. Down. Further examples include *Annaghbeg*, anglicized as The Island, and **Annasamry** townland which contains Summer Island, in Newry and Loughgall parishes, Oneilland West, Co. Armagh (Ó Mainnín 1989–90, 204–5). The semantic shift seems to be from the meaning "marsh" to "land surrounded by marsh". The surname Lamb has not been found locally in the 17th century. The earliest example of the place-name found so far is Lambs-Island in 1777 (*Taylor & Skinner* map 45), and it was used as an address distinct from Annaghanoon in 1890.

In 1609 the townland name was associated with two "hamlets", *Loynnan* and *Kinnoge*, which were also shown on Petty's barony map c. 1657. *Linan* appeared as the address of three Magennis rebels in 1641, and both units were named as sessiaghs in the 1691 confirmation of Clanconnell lands to William Waring. In 1703 *Anaghnowan alias Lisremoylan* and *Leenan alias Lynan* were mentioned in a land agreement between Magennis and Waring, but neither Linan nor Kenoge appears subsequently. Linan may have been *Líonán* "a ravine", and seems to have been in the north-west of the townland, although I cannot identify the feature. Kenoge appears to have a diminutive ending, and may be from *cionóg* "a speck" (*Dinneen*). Joyce says that *Keenoge*, a diminutive of *caonach* "moss", is "met with pretty often in some of the Ulster and Leinster counties" (*Joyce* ii 337).

Atkinson suggested that *Lisremoylan* could be the old name for the fort on present-day Lambs Island (*Atkinson's Donaghcloney* 78). The name *Lisremoylan* appears to begin with *lios rátha* "fort-enclosure of the fort", as do the townland names **Lisnabrague, Lisnatierny** in Aghaderg, **Lisnaward** in Dromore. Joyce considered that when synonyms for "fort" were combined, "either the first is used adjectivally,... or it is a mere explanatory term used synonymously with the second... or such a name might originate in successive structures" (*Joyce* i 282). The latter part of *Lisremoylan* may represent *Ráth Maoláin* "fort of the low rounded hill", like the town of Rathmullan in Donegal (*GÉ* 265). There is no early record of the surname *Ó Maoláin*/Mullan in the area, apart from Mullan's Corner, the local name of the stepped crossroads with the dual carriageway south of Dromore between Blackscull and Katesbridge.

Annaghmakeonan
J 1251

Eanach Mhic Eoghanáin
"McKeonan's marsh"

1. Ballyannaghanckeonan half td	CPR Jas I 396a	1609
2. Ballyanaghmickeonan (half td)	CPR Jas I 235a	1612
3. Ballynaghwickeonan	Inq. Ult. (Down) §13 Car. I	1629
4. Anaghmackeonan	Inq. Ult. (Down) §85 Car. I	1639
5. Aghnaghmakeena	Atkinson's Donaghcloney 22	1650c
6. AnamcKeona	Hib. Reg. Lr. Iveagh	1657c
7. Anaghmakeona	OSNB E2	17thc
8. Anaghmakona	BSD 76	1661
9. Ahanankonan al. Aghanankehane	ASE 123a 37	1667
10. Anaghinkeon	Hib. Del. Down	1672c
11. Annochmecownan	Ir. Wills Index 72	1719
12. Anough mcCounan	Ir. Wills Index 69	1746
13. Anamakeonan	Map of Down (OSNB) E2	1755
14. Annamakeownan	Vestry Bk D'cloney 114	1786
15. Anaghmacownan	Vestry Bk D'cloney 114	1789
16. Annamacownan	Vestry Bk D'cloney 114	1790
17. Anamakeonan	Wm. Map (OSNB) E2	1810
18. Makeonan Bog	OSM xii 57b	1834
19. [Annaghma'keonan]	OSM xii 59a	1834
20. Eanach Mic Eoghanáin "MacKeonan's marsh"	J O'D (OSNB) E2	1834c

21. Eanach Mac Eoghanáin "Paludaus		
campestris filiorum Eogan"	J O'D (OSNB) E2	1834c
22. Eanach Mhic Comhghan-ain	Mooney 329	1950c
23. ˌɑnəxməˈkjonən	Local pronunciation	1992
24. ˈkjonən	Local pronunciation	1996

Annaghmakeonan was held by Sir Art Magennis (1–4), but had passed by 1667 to Benjamin Newton (form 9). The earliest instances of the name, in 1609 and 1612, call it a half-townland. The forms obviously include the surname McKeonan, a name which is not attested in Woulfe (1923). The family also gave their name to the townland of **Ballymakeonan** in Magheralin, the parish which adjoins Donaghcloney to the north. Nicholas *McOwenan* had surrendered his townland of *Ballyvickonenan* in 1609. A Nicolas Oge *Maconan* lived near Lurgan in 1641 (*Atkinson's Donaghcloney* 21), and Mooney had seen the name spelt *Mac Cohenan* in a 17th-century document (*Mooney MS* 329). However there is no surviving evidence for the family in this place. John O'Donovan listed them among the "old families of Ulster": "*Mac Eoghanáin*, now McConan and McKeonan. This family is almost extinct" (*OSL Dn* 44).

On the 1:50,000 map and in local usage (24) the name is reduced to Keonan, following a trend seen in the place-name *Makeonan Bog* referred to in 1834 (form 18).

Ballygunaghan *Baile Uí Dhuinneagáin*
J 1451 "O'Donegan's townland"

1. Ballyagonygan (in Ballynecrosse)	CPR Jas I 395a	1609
2. Balliagonigan	CPR Jas I 190a	1611
3. Ballygomgan	Inq. Ult. (Down) §34 Car. I	1632
4. Ballygonygan	Atkinson's Donaghcloney 22	1650c
5. Balligonioan	Hib. Reg. Lr. Iveagh	1657c
6. Balligonygan unforfeited	Par. Map (Mooney) 337	17thc
7. Ballygonigon	Census 79	1659c
8. Ballygonniga	BSD 77	1661
9. Ballygonniga	S & D Ann. (Mooney) 338 (29)	17thc
10. Ballygonigan	OSNB E2	17thc
11. Balligonioan	Hib. Del. Down	1672c
12. (?)Ballynagany	Rent Roll Down 7	1692
13. Ballygonaghan	Map of Down (OSNB) E2	1755
14. Ballyguniaghan	Vestry Bk D'cloney 114	1771
15. Ballygonahan (?-akan)	Wm. Map (OSNB) E2	1810
16. Ballygunaghan	Vestry Bk D'cloney 116	1821
17. Ballynagunikan	Bnd. Sur. (OSNB) E2	1830c
18. Ballynagunikan	OSM xii 58b	1834
19. Ballynagunaghan [Ballynaguni'kan]	OSM xii 59a	1834

20. Baile Guineachain "Gonaghan's town"		
	J O'D (OSNB) E2	1834c
21. Baile Ó gConachain "O'Conaghan's town"	Joyce iii 91	1913

86

22.	Baile Mhic Dhonnagáin	GÉ 21	1989

| 23. | ˌbaliˈgɔnəhən | Local pronunciation | 1992 |
| 24. | ˌbaliˈɣɔnəxən | Local pronunciation | 1992 |

Ballygunaghan is the most easterly townland of Donaghcloney. It has the river Lagan as its northern border, and is the only townland in the parish to form part of the Magennis district of **Glasquirin**, which extended south into **Magherally** and Seapatrick parishes. The townland name is attested from 1609, when it was one of eight towns held by Con Boy McPhelim McHugh Magennis from the King. By 1632 (form 3) he had transferred five of these, including Ballygunaghan, to Sir Faithful Fortescue, whose name is still used for part of the townland (see **Fortescue** under Other Names). The area is now most frequently known as **Blackskull**. The forms for Ballygunaghan indicate a possible surname, and Joyce suggested *Baile Ó gConachain* "O'Conaghan's town" (*Joyce* iii 91). Woulfe gives this surname as *Ó Connacháin* (Woulfe 1923, 478). The surname *Ó Donnagáin* or *Ó Duinneagáin*, which also forms part of the Moira townland of **Balloonigan**, seems more probable. In **Balloonigan** the lenited *Dh* of *Uí Dhuinneagáin* disappeared and two syllables were elided to give the present form of the name. However, in the name Ballygunaghan the *D* of *Duinneagán* may retain its lenited form [ɣ] in modern pronunciation (24), or be delenited [g] in spelling and pronunciation (23), since [ɣ] represents the lenition of both *d* and *g* in Irish. In contrast to **Balloonigan**, the internal -*g*- became [x], spelt *gh*, although recorded as pronounced as [k] in 1834 (*OSM* xii 59a).

These two townlands named after the family were both secular lands. There is an early 15th-century ecclesiastical reference to "the (Archbishop's) lands of *O'Donnacon*", which connects the family with the Church (*Reg. Swayne* 45,97, 1426-8). The surname *Mac Donnagáin* occurs regularly connected with the diocese and is probably a variant of the same name. Florence *MacDonegan* was bishop of Dromore in 1309, and there were numbers of McDonegan clergy in the diocese in the 14th and 15th centuries (*Swanzy's Dromore*). Patrick McDonegan held the church lands of **Tullylish** in the early 17th century, and McDonegans also held some other unlocated church lands which passed to Edward Trevor (*CPR Jas I* 195a,395b,191a).

Ballynabragget
J 1151

Baile na Brád
"townland of the gorge"

1.	Ballynebrade	CPR Jas I 235b	1612
2.	Ballynebraide	Inq. Ult. (Down) §13 Car. I	1629
3.	Ballinbrahada x5	Maġennis Paps (O'Sullivan) 63n193	1632
4.	Ballenibrade	Inq. Ult. (Down) §85 Car. I	1639
5.	Ballibraggett	Atkinson's Donaghcloney 22	1650c
6.	Ballibraggett	Hib. Reg. Lr. Iveagh	1657c
7.	Ballybragget	OSNB E2	17thc
8.	Ballibraggett	Par. Map (Mooney) 332	17thc
9.	Ballybrogatt	Census 79	1659c
10.	Ballibraggett	BSD 76	1661
11.	B'bragett	Hib. Del. Down	1672c
12.	Tullylough al. Ballybraggett	Deeds & Wills (Mooney) 331	1714
13.	Ballinlogh al. Ballybrogitt al. Ballybragett al. Ballynebragett	Deeds & Wills (Mooney) 331	1719

14. Ballynabraggit	Map of Down (OSNB) E2	1755
15. Ballynebraget	Ir. Wills Index 52	1791
16. Ballynabragett	Wm. Map (OSNB) E2	1810
17. Ballynabragget so pronounced	OSM xii 59a	1834
18. Baile na Bragoide "town of the ale or beer"	J O'D (OSNB) E2	1834c
19. Baile-na-bragoide "the town of the bragget, ale/beer"	Joyce iii 109	1913
20. Baile na Brághad "townland of the gorge/sheltered land facing cliff"	Mooney 331	1950c
21. Baile na Brogóide	GÉ 22	1989
22. 'balnə'bragət	Local pronunciation	1991
23. ˌbɑlņə'brakət	Local pronunciation	1991
24. ðə 'bragət	Local pronunciation	1992

The initial *baile* of Ballynabragget is clear, but there is debate about the second element. The earliest instance of the place-name is in AD 1612 (1), where the three contiguous townlands *Ballinlagh* (**Ballylough** in Seapatrick), *Ballymoygannane* (Moygannon) and *Ballynebrade* were granted by Sir Arthur Magennis to Brian Carragh Magennis. A different name *Ballykedromade* appears with the other two in the calendared version of the Schedule of Iveagh early in 1609 (*CPR Jas I* 394-5), but the report of a court case between Brian Magennis and Whitchurch in 1632 gives eight names of lands, called four townlands, allotted to Brian Magennis, beginning *Ballinlogh, Ballinbrahada, Ballenmoy* (form 3, Thrift MSS T.356). *Ballenibrade* (form 4), given in the same group among Sir Art's townlands, makes four forms with final *-bra(i)de* before 1639.

However, later forms, from c. 1650 on, spell the second element *-bragget*, which is now pronounced with [g] or even [k], while the name is sometimes abbreviated to The Bragget only in current local usage (24). *Bragóid*, the name for a type of beer, was borrowed into early Irish and appears in Cormac's Glossary: *brocoit .i. sainlind* "bragget, that is, a special ale" (*DIL* s.v. *brocóit*). This word was enthusiastically accepted by Joyce (*Baile na Bragóide*, 18) and *AGBP* and *GÉ* (*Baile na Brogóide*, 19).

On the evidence of the earlier spellings without internal *-g- bragóid* cannot be correct. The form chosen above is genitive of *bráid* fem. "neck", earlier *brágha*, gen. *bràghad*. Dean Mooney suggested *Baile na Brághad* "townland of the neck or gorge" (20), and *brágha* can also mean "sheltered land breasting a cliff or rock" (*Dinneen*). When the name was written down in the 17th century it seems the lenited *g* [ɣ] was only faintly articulated, and so could be written as *h* (form 3) or omitted (1,2,4) as in modern Irish. On the other hand [ɣ] might be heard as a sound related to [g] and written down accordingly. The modern form and pronunciation(s) reflect this written tradition. The original name must refer to a topographical feature, which is now difficult to identify.

Banoge
J 1254

An Bhánóg
"the green patch (of ground)"

1. Ballinebanogie in Clanconnell, 2 hamlets Derryhurke Lurgeneniagh	CPR Jas I 193a	1611

2. Ballinebonogie Derrehursk Lurgenagh	Inq. Ult. (Down) §9 Car. I	1627
3. Banoge Derriherisk Edengreogan	Atkinson's Donaghcloney 22	1650c
4. Banoge Derryherisk Edengreogan	Hib. Reg. Lr. Iveagh	1657c
5. Banoge	Par. Map (Mooney) 331	17thc
6. Bannoge ½ Sessiogh	BSD 73	1661
7. Bannoge Derryherish Edengreogan	BSD 76-77	1661
8. Bannog Derryhirke Edentegreene	ASE 61b 35	1666
9. Banoge Dereherick	Hib. Del. Down	1672c
10. Banog sessiah (Magill)	Atkinson's Donaghcloney 132	1691
11. Banog = 3 sessiaghs:		
Edengren Deri-herk Banog	Atkinson's Donaghcloney 133	1691
12. Banmogs, sessiagh of;		
Edengreeny Derrykirke	Rent Roll Down 8	1692
13. Banoge al. Edendegreene	Lodge (Mooney) 331 (III 68)	1701
14. Banoge now Banagh	Reg. Magheralin (OSNB) E8.59	1715
15. Banagh	Vestry Bk D'cloney 114	1778
16. Banogh	Vestry Bk D'cloney 114	1782
17. Banog	Vestry Bk D'cloney 114	1791
18. [Ban'oag]	OSM xii 59a	1834
19. "little lea field"		
(uncroppped grassland)	Atkinson's Donaghcloney 79	1898
20. Bánóg "small enclosed space,		
courtyard"	Mooney 331	1950c
21. Beannóg "small ben or peak"	Mooney 332	1950c
22. bɑ'nog	Local pronunciation	1991
23. 'banok	Local pronunciation	1992

After forming most of the southern boundary of Donaghcloney townland, the Lagan runs through Banoge, and then forms the eastern boundary of Edenballycoggill to the north. Two mills had been erected in Banoge sessiagh by 1666 (*ASE* 61b). The basic element is the Irish adjective *bán* "white" with a diminutive suffix (20), originally stressed on the first syllable, as preserved by some local informants (23). The word can mean "a small enclosed space", but the sense "green patch" is also supported by Atkinson, "a little lea field, i.e. uncropped grassland" (form 19). The townland is low-lying by the river, and there is no feature likely to be called a "little peak" (21). *Bánóg* is used with the article in forms 1,2: *Baile na Bánóige* "townland of the green patch".

In 1609 the townland name was associated with two "hamlets", *Derryhirke* and *Lurgeneniagh*. The first could be *Doire Thoirc* "oakwood of the boar", the second *Lorgain an Eich* "ridge of the steed". *Derryhirke* appears throughout the 17th century and on Petty's maps. The name *Lurgeneniagh* became obsolete, but in 1691 Mr Waring was confirmed in *Banog*, consisting of the three sessiaghs of *Banog*, *Deriherk* and *Edengren*. This last denomination was in Magennis hands in 1641 (*Wars Co. Down* x 81), and appears as *Edengreogan* next to *Derryherisk* on Petty's barony map, and as *Banoge alias Edendegreene* in a deed of 1701 (forms 4,13). However only the name Banoge survived to the present.

Corcreeny
J 0855

Corr Chríonaigh
"hill of the dry branches"

1. Ballychorchryny in Clanconnell, 2 hamlets Aghevackan Killileyny	CPR Jas I 193a	1611
2. Ballecharchuy Aghavackane Killeberry	Inq. Ult. (Down) §9 Car. I	1627
3. Corcreeny Killeloan	Atkinson's Donaghcloney 22	1650c
4. td of Corcreeny and BallymcIteere (M'lin)	Civ. Surv. x §73	1655c
5. Creeve Corcrevy	Hib. Reg. Lr. Iveagh	1657c
6. Corkrery	Census 79	1659c
7. Corcreevy Killeloan	BSD 76-77	1661
8. Corcreeny al Corcrney 231 acres, agkimacon[?] Killeloan	Atkinson's Donaghcloney 144	1662
9. Corcreny	ASE 49b 19	1666
10. Corcreeny	ASE 49b 19	1666
11. Corcreny Aghimecam pts of Killeon al. Killeen	Lodge (Mooney) 336	1666
12. Corcrevy	Hib. Del. Down	1672c
13. Corcreeny town (Waring)	Atkinson's Donaghcloney 132	1691
14. td Corcreeney (Waring) 3 sess: Corcreeney Killilean Aghimacan	Atkinson's Donaghcloney 133	1691
15. Currereeny Aghameacam Killdon, pt of same als pt of Corcreeny	Rent Roll Down 6	1692
16. Corcreeny	Map of Down (OSNB) E2	1755
17. Corrcreany	Vestry Bk D'cloney 114	1771
18. Corncreeny	Vestry Bk D'cloney 114	1778
19. Corncraneny	Vestry Bk D'cloney 114	1780
20. Cornacreevy	Deeds & Wills (Mooney) 336	1796c
21. Corcreeny	Wm. Map (OSNB) E2	1810
22. Corkreany	Clergyman (OSNB) E2	1834c
23. Cor crianaighe "round hill of the withered trees or grass"	J O'D (OSNB) E2	1834c
25. Cor-crionaigh "round hill of the withered trees/grass/brambles"	Joyce iii 254	1913
26. ˌkɔrˈkrenï	Local pronunciation	1992

The first part of the name Corcreeny is probably *corr* "a round hill", possibly followed by *críonach* "faggots", which can be either masculine or feminine, derived from the adjective *críon* "withered, decayed". Spellings of the name vary little, with an *e* or *ee* in the second syllable in all except the earliest, although the current local pronunciation is [e] rather than [i]. The vowel makes it unlikely that the second element is the tribal name *Cruthin* or *Cruithne*, as one would expect early spellings to give *u*. Place-names like **Duncroon**, Co. Derry, (*Dún Cruithne*) and **Crown Mound**, Newry, (*Áth Cruithne*, *PNI* i 43) commemorate the border between this people, who are not to be confused with the Scottish Picts, and other tribes. Uí Echach were Cruthin in origin, and the river **Bann** had been the boundary between them and Airgialla in this area (*Geneal. Tracts* 72 §112). However the word *críonach* is the most likely possibility. *Críonach* appears by itself as a place-name as the site of a battle in 1086, apparently in Meath (*AU*).

In 1609 Corcreeny was associated with two "hamlets", *Aghevackan*, from *Achadh an Mheacain* "field of the parsnip", and *Killileyney*. These appear to be unknown after the 17th century. The name *Killeloman* is shown south of Corcreeny and north of Bleary on Petty's barony map, between a bog, probably Clare Bog, on the east and a wooded area to the west beside the Bann. It seems unlikely that the element *Kill-* referred to a church site as this was not church land; and it is more likely that it represented *coillidh*, originally dative of *coill* "wood", as in **Quilly** and **Skillyscolban** in Dromore. *Killileyney* possibly represents *Coillidh Léana* "wood of the water-meadow", while *Killeloman* may be *Coillidh Lomáin* "wood of the stripped tree-trunk, or outcrop of rock". In the mid-17th century Petty gave a description of the parish: "The quallity of the soyle is arable meadow and pasture, with much mossy and boggie ground on which grow many large timber trees, but great parte of them are ould and rotten" (*Atkinson's Donaghcloney* 22).

Cornreany
J 0855

Corrán Raithní
"crescent/hill of bracken"

1. Cornreaney	Atkinson's Donaghcloney 55	1657
2. Corranraine	ASE 61b 35	1666
3. Corenrane	Lodge (Mooney) 345	1701
4. Cornreany	Map of Down (OSNB) E2	1755
5. Cornreany	Atkinson's Donaghcloney 92	1772
6. Cornreany	Wm. Map (OSNB) E2	1810
7. Carn Raithnigh "ferny carn"	J O'D (OSNB) E2	1834c
8. kɔːˈrini	Local pronunciation	1996

Cornreany is on a noticeable hill, 268 feet, in the west of the parish. The townland has no forms before 1657 and is not mentioned as a part of Clanconnell, although by 1628 it had been rented with *Tollycarny* (Tullycarn) in the east of the parish, where the Magills had Tullycairn House in 1777, by Captain John Magill from Art Oge son of Glassney Magennis (form 2, 1666). From its position on the north bound of Corcreeny townland, which surrounds it on three sides, it looks as if it may have once been a subdivision of **Corcreeny**, though hardly an alternative to one of the two lost names there, which were held in 1666 by William Waring (*ASE* 49b). The "bracken" element is from modern *raithneach* rather than the older form *raithean* suggested for **Taughrane, Tullyrain**.

Donaghcloney
J 1353

Domhnach Cluana
See the parish name

Lurgantamry
J 1453

Lorgain an tSamhraidh
"summer ridge"

1. Ballylurganetawrie in Clanconnell 2 hamlets Tullycarny Morigh	CPR Jas I 193a	1611
2. Ballelargantaury Tullecarny Moryagh	Inq. Ult. (Down) §9 Car. I	1627
3. Lurgentory Mooree	Atkinson's Donaghcloney 22	1650c
4. Lurgan teaury	Census 79	1659c
5. Lurgantawry	BSD 73	1661

6. Lurgentory	BSD 76	1661
7. Largintory	ASE 123a 37	1667
8. Lurgan Taurey (Waring) 3 sess:		
Lurgan Taurey, Moree, Tulicarn	Atkinson's Donaghcloney 133	1691
9. Lurgintory	Rent Roll Down 8	1692
10. Lurgantamry	Reg. Magheralin (OSNB) E8.59	1715
11. Lurgantamry	Map of Down (OSNB) E2	1755
12. Lurgantamey	Vestry Bk D'cloney 114	1774
13. Lurgantamery	Ir. Wills Index 74	1805
14. Lurgantamry	Wm. Map (OSNB) E2	1810
15. Lurgán t-Samhraidh "Summer hill"	J O'D (OSNB) E2	1834c
16. Lurgan Teamhrach	Mooney 342	1950c
17. ˌlọrgən'tɑmrï	Local pronunciation	1991
18. ˌlọrgən'taمərï	Local pronunciation	1991

The first element of Lurgantamry is clearly *lorga* fem., dative *lorgain*, a "shin-shaped ridge". The most obvious etymology is *Lorgain an tSamhraidh* "ridge of the summer", referring to upland seasonal pasture. Other place-names with the element "summer" seem to refer to summer pasture (*Joyce* iii 468–9). Form (1) suggests the presence of the article, but the name may have been *Lorgain tSamhraidh* (15), with *t* prefixed to *s* in imitation of the treatment of *s* after the singular article *an*. The map shows, bordered east and south by the Lagan, a ridge with a rath on it, probably a good viewing-point. The early Irish place-name element *Temair*, *Tara*, as in the Ards peninsula (*PNI* ii 131), seems to mean "hill with a view", and *Lorgain Teamhrai* "Tara ridge" could also be suggested. *Temair* was originally a feminine *i*-stem, becoming a consonant-stem with dative singular *Temraig* (*DIL* sv.). For it to appear in this place-name one has to postulate that this could develop into a new *a*-stem, *Temrach*, dat. *Temraig*, gen. *Temraige*, which last would be *Teamhrai* in modern spelling. However the early forms for Tara in the Ards provide no evidence for such a change.

The two early hamlets both became townlands in their own right, **Monree** west of Lurgantamry, and **Tullycarn** to the east of the Lagan. According to local information, since the naming of Monree Road the name Monree is used more often than Lurgantamry.

Magherana
J 1054

Machaire an Átha
"plain of the ford"

1. Ballymagherynagh in Clanconnell:		
2 hamlets Corriroge Donugalman	CPR Jas I 193a	1611
2. Ballinghernynagh Correogh		
Dougallman	Inq. Ult. (Down) §9 Car. I	1627
3. Magherenagh	Atkinson's Donaghcloney 22	1650c
4. Magherenagh	Hib. Reg. Lr. Iveagh	1657c
5. Mahernac	Census 79	1659c
6. Maghernagh	BSD 76	1661
7. pt td Mageranagh	Atkinson's Donaghcloney 144	1662
8. Magherana	ASE 49b 19	1666
9. Magherenaw	ASE 61b 39	1666
10. Magherenagh	Hib. Del. Down	1672c

11. Magherana town (Waring)	Atkinson's Donaghcloney 132	1691
12. pt tn Magherna = qr Dongalman (Rawden)	Atkinson's Donaghcloney 132	1691
13. pt tn Magherna = 3 sess (Waring): 3 qrs Dongalman, Magherna, Cororog	Atkinson's Donaghcloney 132	1691
14. Maghereneman	Rent Roll Down 6	1692
15. Maghorana, part of	Rent Roll Down 6	1692
16. Maghernaw al. Mayernane	Mooney MS 343	no d.
17. Magherynana	Map of Down (OSNB) E2	1755
18. Magherhana	Wm. Map (OSNB) E2	1810
19. [Magheran'a]	OSNB Pron. E2	1834c
20. [Magheran'a]	OSM xii 59a	1834
21. Machaire an átha "plain of the ford"	J O'D (OSNB) E2	1834c
22. Machaire an eanaigh	J O'D (OSNB) E2	1834c
23. Machaire-n'-atha "of the ford"	Joyce iii 496	1913
24. ˌmɑxərəˈnɑː	Local pronunciation	1991

In both the name-book and the *Ordnance Survey Memoir* (forms 19,20) the stress in pronunciation was said to be on the last syllable of Magherana. This pronunciation is so far resisting changes introduced by incomers to the area, and indicates the etymology "plain of the ford". A small stream runs through this townland and the town of Waringstown, and was large enough to support a mill in 1834 (*OSM* xii 58a). I do not know where the ford was. Petty's map of the area shows large areas of bog, and it is possible that the "ford" was the route for crossing this marshy area, as well as the stream itself.

Magherana was originally in Clanconnell, but by 1666 part of the townland had been acquired by George Rawdon (form 9). In 1609 the townland name was associated with two "hamlets", *Corriroge* and *Donugalman*. There is not sufficient evidence to establish the original forms of these names, but a case could be made for *Corr Riabhóg* "round hill of the drills" or "pipits", and *Dún na gColmán* "fort of the pigeons". *Corriroge* does not appear after the 17th century, but the name *Dongalman* or *Dongalvan* was heard by Atkinson in late 19th-century oral tradition as the name of an ancient lost grave-yard in a field in the townland (*Atkinson's Donaghcloney* 14,76) although it is not church land. This site is not on current maps, nor is it mentioned by the Archaeological Survey (*ASCD*).

Monree
J 1453

Móin Fhraoigh
"heather moor"

1. Morigh (hamlet)	CPR Jas I 193a	1611
2. Moryagh	Inq. Ult. (Down) §9 Car. I	1627
3. Mooree	Atkinson's Donaghcloney 22	1650c
4. Moore (Donaghglony)	BSD 76	1661
5. Morree half sessiagh (M'lin)	BSD 74	1661
6. Moree (sess. of Lurgan Taurey)	Atkinson's Donaghcloney 133	1691
7. (?)Moorall [Mocrall?]	Rent Roll Down 7	1692
8. Munree	Reg. Magheralin (OSNB) E8.59	1715
9. Monree	Map of Down (OSNB) E2	1755
10. Munree	Atkinson's Donaghcloney 93	1773

11. Monree	Vestry Bk D'cloney 115	1788
12. Monree	Wm. Map (OSNB) E2	1810
13. Móin righ "the King's bog"	J O'D (OSNB) E2	1834c
14. 'mǫnri:	Local pronunciation	1991
15. mɔn'ri:	Local pronunciation	1992

The river Lagan divides Monree, originally a hamlet of **Lurgantamry** (1), from Ballygunaghan on the south-east. Monree was formerly a sessiagh, in 1661 (forms 4,5) half in each of the two parishes of Donaghcloney and Magheralin, which explains its appearance in the Magheralin parish register (8). It is not until the 18th century that *n* appears in the historical forms (8), although *móin* seems a likely part of the etymology. Possibly an abbreviation for *n* was omitted, or the name was earlier *Maigh Fhraoigh* "heather plain". The more local pronunciation (15) keeps the original stress in the two-word Irish form. A rath was described in 1834 as on the boundary of Donaghcloney with Monree: "a large Danish fort... site of the old church" (*OSM* xii 59a). The fort is still there, but is included in Monree, near Monree House, and is separate from the site of the church.

Moygannon
J 1252

Magh gCeannann
"plain of the white-faced cows"
or "white-speckled plain"

1. Baeenmoygarran	CPR Jas I 395a	1609
2. Ballymoygannane	CPR Jas I 235b	1612
3. Ballymoyganan	Inq. Ult. (Down) §13 Car. I	1629
4. Ballymaganan	Inq. Ult. (Down) §30 Car. I	1632
5. Ballenmoy	Magennis Paps (O'Sullivan) 63n193	1632
6. Maganan	Magennis Paps (O'Sullivan) 68	1632
7. Ballimoyganna	Atkinson's Donaghcloney 22	1650c
8. Ballimoygunna	Hib. Reg. Lr. Iveagh	1657c
9. Megonan	Census 79	1659c
10. Ballimoyganna	BSD 76	1661
11. Ballymoyganna	S & D Ann. (Mooney) 345 (27)	17thc
12. Moygan	Sub. Roll Down 273	1663
13. qr of Maganan called Anagare	ASE 61b 35	1666
14. Ballymoyganna or gunna	ASE 112a 34	1667
15. Ballimoyguna	Hib. Del. Down	1672c
16. Mogenan	Ir. Wills Index 16	1727
17. Moygannon	Map of Down (OSNB) E2	1755
18. Megannon	Vestry Bk D'cloney 114	1776
19. Moygannon	Wm. Map (OSNB) E2	1810
20. Magh Geannainn "Gannon's plain" Campus Geanainn	J O'D (OSNB) E2	1834c
21. ˌmɔi'gjanən	Local pronunciation	1992

The earliest clear instance of Moygannan is in 1612 (form 2), where *Ballinlagh* (Ballylough townland in Seapatrick parish), *Ballymoygannane* and *Ballynebrade* were granted to Bryan Carragh by Sir Arthur (Art) Magennis. The same three townlands are grouped together in other sources, thus proving the identity of *Baeenmoygarran* and *Ballenmoy* (forms 1,5). *Ballenmoy* "townland of the plain" shows that the townland could be known by its first modern element only.

Sir Art Magennis also held another townland called **Moygannon** in south Down, in the parish of Kilbroney (*PNI* i 150), where the forms from 1570 to 1629 AD have a vowel after *Moy-*, indicating that the name contains the surname *Ó Canann*. The Donaghcloney forms provide no evidence for *Ó*, although *Ó Canann* may have been part of this name too. Hogan gives various place-names containing the personal name *Geanann*, including *Magh Geanainn*, a legendary plain now covered by Loch Erne (*Céitinn* ii 126), and *Dún Geanainn*, Dungannon, Co. Tyrone (*GÉ* 218). Dungannon is explained as "the fort of Geanann"; he appears as a character in late Ulster cycle tales, a son of Cathbhadh the druid (*Battle of Airtech* §18n; *Cath Aen. Macha* §3; *Cóir Anmann* §245).

The forms spelt *Megonan, Maganan, Mogenan, Megannon* (4, 6, 9, 13, 16, 18), possibly pronunciation spellings, indicate that the first element might represent *magh* (later *má*), the early Irish nominative of *maigh* "plain". The initial *g* of *-gannon* might also arise from nasalization of *c* after *magh*, an old neuter (cf. **Moyallen** in Tullylish), and the adjective *ceannann* "marked with white" (from *cenn* "head", *finn* "white") would also fit the forms. As a noun it means an animal with a white face, or "blaze". There is also a reference to a battle in 786 AD "at *Cenu*", *bellum Cenond*, between Uí Echach and Conaille (*AU*), which could be part of the name *Magh gCeanann*, although Hogan identified *Cenu* with Canonstown in Co. Louth (*Onom. Goed.* 228).

Tullycarn	*Tulaigh Chairn*	
J 1553	"hillock of (the) cairn"	

1. (?)ac tulaig chais chernaig	Lebor na Cert 8–9 1.108		1050c
2. Tullycarny, hamlet of			
Ballylurganetawrie, Clanconnell	CPR Jas I 193a		1611
3. Tullecarny	Inq. Ult. (Down) §9 Car. I		1627
4. Tullicarr, McConwell & Magennis of	Wars Co. Down x 81		1641
5. Tullecarne	Atkinson's Donaghcloney 22		1650c
6. Tullaghkearne	Atkinson's Donaghcloney 22		1650c
7. Tullicarne	Hib. Reg. Lr. Iveagh		1657c
8. Tullecarne	Hib. Del. Down		1672c
9. Tullicarne	S & D Ann. (Mooney) 347 (28)		17thc
10. Tulicarn sess of Lurgan Taurey	Atkinson's Donaghcloney 133		1691
11. Tullycarne, sessiagh of	Rent Roll Down 8		1692
12. Tullycarne	Reg. Magheralin (OSNB) E8.59		1715
13. Tullycarn	Map of Down (OSNB) E2		1755
14. Tullycarn	Vestry Bk D'cloney 115		1795
15. Tullycarn	Wm. Map (OSNB) E2		1810
16. Tullycairn(e)	Vestry Bk D'cloney 116		1829
17. Tullycarn [Tully'cairn]	OSM xii 59a		1834
18. Tulach an Chairn "hill of the			
carn or sepulchral heap"	J O'D (OSNB) E2		1834c

20. Tulach Mhic Chearnaigh		
"Kearney's Hill"	Mooney 347	1950c
21. ˌt̪ɔliˈkjɛːrn	Local pronunciation	1992
22. ˌt̪ɔliˈkjɑːrn	Local pronunciation	1992

In 1609 the townland name *Ballylurganatawrie* (Lurgantamry) in Clanconnell was associated with two "hamlets", *Tullycarny* and *Morigh*, which are also shown on Petty's barony map, and in 1691 *Lurgan Taurey*, containing the sessiaghs of *Lurgan Taurey, Moree* and *Tulicarn*, was confirmed in the possession of Mr Waring. In this case all three sessiaghs have become modern townlands, **Lurgantamry, Monree** and Tullycarn, all fairly small, of 267 acres and under.

Tullycarn is the most easterly townland of the parish, with its western boundary formed by the river Lagan. The older local pronunciation is represented by form (21) but is giving ground to (22). Tullycarn House, still inhabited by a Magill in 1834, is on a low hill of 296 feet (*OSM* xii 57a). There is no evidence of a cairn on it now, but there could have been before the house was built, to give the name *Tulaigh Chairn* "hillock of the cairn". Another possibility is *Tulaigh Uí Chearnaigh* "O'Kearney's hillock". The surname O'Kearney or McKearney is attested in Co. Down in the early 17th century (*CPR Jas I* 195a,395b) as the holder of three townlands in the parish of Donaghmore to the south. James *O'Kerny* was bishop of Connor 1324-51 AD (*EA* 257), while much earlier *Mattach Dungan Omungan OKerny* appeared with a MacArtan and Magennises in a list of local chieftains fined in 1260–1 (*Exch. Accounts Ulst.* 157b). A final -*y* appears in the two earliest forms (2,3): 1611,1627), and the mid-17th century forms have a final -*e*, suggesting, but insufficient proof of, the second syllable of *Chearnaigh*.

The doubtful form (1) is mentioned as the place where the Ulaid entertained the king of Cashel in a poem in the 11th-century "Book of Rights" (*Lebor na Cert*), first edited by O'Donovan. It was translated by O'Donovan as "at Cearnach's hill, Tullycarney in the Co. of Down" (p.39), but by the later editor, Dillon, as "at the pleasant triumphant hill". From the rest of the poem it seems more likely to be a place-name, not necessarily this townland, though Tullycarn is the nearest match to "*Tullycarney* in Co. Down". There are two townlands called **Tullycarnan**, a **Kearney** and a **Carneyhill** in Lecale and the Ards (*PNI* ii 134,61-2,188-9), and Tullycarnet in Knockbreda, while as minor names there are **Kearney's Hill** in Bangor (*PNI* ii 174) and **Carney Hill** in Moira and Drumgooland. If an eponymous chieftain called *Cearnach* had a hill-fort in Ulaid territory we do not know where it was.

Tullyherron   *Tulaigh Chaorthainn*
J 1056   "hillock of rowan"

1. Ballyhollyhirrine in Clanconnell:		
2 hamlets Tullyrappane Gortmeyrie		
	CPR Jas I 193a	1611
2. Balleholli-Jarry Tullerappan Gurtmeny	Inq. Ult. (Down) §9 Car. I	1627
3. Tulleherin Gortmoyry Taunaghrappan	Atkinson's Donaghcloney 22	1650c
4. sess Gortmoira in td Tullyherron	Atkinson's Donaghcloney 55	1657
5. Tulleherin Gortmoyry		
Tannough-vappan	Hib. Reg. Lr. Iveagh	1657c

96

6.	Tolleherim	Census 79	1659c
7.	Tulleherin Tannarippan Gortmoyrey	BSD 76	1661
8.	Tulleherin	S & D Ann. (Mooney) 349 (27)	17thc
9.	Tulleherrin 74a, half Taniarappan (Waring)	Atkinson's Donaghcloney 145	1662
10.	Tulleherem (+ Townerappan half)	ASE 49b 19	1666
11.	half-tn Tulliherrin = sess Tulliherrin, half Tannerappan	Atkinson's Donaghcloney 132	1691
12.	Tulleherum, half Rappan	Rent Roll Down 6	1692
13.	Tullykern Tullykerrin Tullyherin	Deeds & Wills (Mooney) 349	18thc
14.	Tullyheron	Vestry Bk D'cloney 114	1790
15.	Tullyherim	Clergyman (OSNB) E2	1834c
16.	Tulaig Chaorthainn "hill of the rowan tree"	J O'D (OSNB) E2	1834c
17.	Tulach Uí hEaradháin "O'Heron's hill"	Mooney 349	1950c
18.	ˌt̯o̯liˈhɛrən	Local pronunciation	1992

The first element in Tullyherron is clearly *tulach* fem. "a hillock/small hill". O'Donovan suggested for the second element the word *caorthann* "rowan tree", a derivative of which appears in the name of the townland of **Kernan** in Tullylish. The earliest spellings of both names have the stressed vowel of this element as *i* (*-hirrine*, *-kirinan*). Neither name shows any evidence of the Irish *th* in the historical forms, but this is to be expected in East Ulster Irish. The *h* in Tullyherron would represent the *ch* of *Chaorthainn*, lenited after *Tulaigh*. The name was sometimes even spelled with *k* in 18th century deeds collected by Dean Mooney, though *k* could be a misreading of *h* (form 13).

This explanation is more likely than Mooney's (form 17), involving the family of *Ua hEaradháin*, later *Ó hEaráin*, anglicized O'Heron or Haran, who were chieftains of *Uí Bhreasail Macha* in Co. Armagh (Woulfe 1923, 562; *AFM* ii 792–3, 1017 AD). There is another townland of Tullyherron in Loughgilly parish co. Armagh, with forms very similar to here. The O'Heron family were closely related to *Ó Gairbhíth* (Arthurs 1954(c), 48–9; cf. **Ballymoney**, Magherally). Hugh *O'Hawran* appears associated with Sir Art Magennis in the 17th century (*CPR Jas I* 299a, 1616), although Woulfe gives *Ó hAmhráin*, usually anglicized with a *-v-* e.g. Havern, as a family "anciently chiefs of Dál Fiatach; still extant in East Ulster" (Woulfe 1923, 553). The man surnamed Heron or Herne c. 1610 in Aghivillan Co. Armagh, which is also called Richmount in the parish of Drumcree, just west of Portadown, seems to be a settler, newly granted the land (*CPR Jas I* 165a, 299b). The *h* of the surname would not appear in the genitive, so the *h* in the place-name would have to be explained as a reflex of the *ch* of *tulach*, which usually appears in place-names in its dative form *tulaigh*. Neither of these explanations would account for the form *Balliholli-jarry* (form 2) which must be a mistranscription.

In 1609 the townland name was associated with two "hamlets", *Tullyrappane* and *Gortmeyrie*. These names appear on Petty's maps, and were used as addresses in the *Vestry Book of Donaghcloney* in the early 19th century, but they are not on modern maps. They may represent *Tulaigh Chnapán* "lumpy hillock" and *Gort Meidhre* "field of merriment".

OTHER NAMES

Blackskull   An English form
J 1451

1. Blackskull	Atkinson's Donaghcloney 84	1898
2. Baile Mhic Dhonnagáin	GÉ 21	1989
3. ˌblakˈskọl	Local pronunciation	1992
4. ˌðə ˈskọl	Local pronunciation	1992

The village of Blackskull is in, and has locally replaced the name of, the townland of **Ballygunaghan,** and thus in 1969 the Irish-language form for the village post office was given as *Baile Mhic Dhonnagáin* (*AGBP*). Atkinson explained the use of the name Blackskull for the southern part of Ballygunaghan from an inn with a negro-head sign, which by his day had become the post office (*Atkinson's Donaghcloney* 84). Mr Copeland of Blackskull explains the sign from the murder of a black man:

> The officer arrived with his batman and he told him to go and stay with the horses while he went in to order a meal. And the man didn't return so he went out to look for him only to discover that the poor fellow had got his head beheaded and stuck up above the door... people outside were chanting, "the Black Skull Inn", "the Black Skull Inn".

The post office has now been closed, and Mr Copeland regretted he had not been able to keep the date stamp, which "adhered to the original spelling, *skull*", rather than Blackscull, which appears on local road-signs. The village is now known locally as "The Skull" (3). According to Atkinson an earlier name for the area had been The **Fortescue** (see below).

Cambray House   An English form
J 1055

1. ˌkjemˈbraiə ˈhəus	Local pronunciation	1992

Cambray House is on the northern outskirts of Waringstown, and several streets around it now also bear the name, spelt Cambrai. The local pronunciation is like that of Cambrai St on the Crumlin Road. *Cambrai* is a town in northern France, the Flemish name of which, *Kameryk*, gave the English word *cambric* "a fine white linen or cotton fabric" (*Longman Dict.* 230b). The name Cambray House probably refers to the linen trade, set up in Waringstown by Samuel son of William Waring in the early 18th century after travelling in Holland and Belgium. "The first piece of Irish diaper was made here" (*Bassett's Down* 277). The diaper made in Waringstown is probably also the origin of the name Diaper Hill south of the town. In 1834 most houses in the parish had a third downstairs room, the "shop", to contain the loom, for "damask, cambric, duck and linen" (*OSM* xii 58b).

Donaghcloney Village   *Domhnach Cluana*
J 1353   See the parish name

Fortescue   An English form
J 1451

98

1. Fortesque	OSM xii 61b	1834
2. the Fortescue	Atkinson's Donaghcloney 84	1898
3. 'fɔrtïskju:	Local pronunciation	1992

According to Atkinson (2), Fortescue was an alternative name for the south part of Ballygunaghan, which had been owned in the early 17th century by Sir Faithful Fortescue. He was constable of Carrickfergus, and appears regularly in the patent rolls of James I (*CPR Jas I* 95a, 363b,366a,367b, 487a,577b). By 1632 Sir *Fidelis* (the Latin translation of his name) Fortescue had obtained Ballygunaghan, and Ballycross, Drumnavaddy, Tonaghmore and Mullaghfernaghan in Magherally, from Con Boy Magennis of Glasquirin, and in 1621 Ballykelly in Seapatrick from Edmund Boy Magennis (*Inq. Ult. (Down)* §§34-5 Car. I).

In 1834 there was a school called *Fortesque* (*OSM* xii 61b), remembered by Mr Copeland: "Fortescue school is still there, now a church hall, but the little triangle of ground, roughly two acres, is called Fortescue".

Harrymount
J 1056

An English form

1. Harrymount	Atkinson's Donaghcloney 56	1709
2. Harrymount, Perrymount	Sloane map	1739
3. Harry Mt, Perry Mt	Harris Hist. map	1743
4. Harry Mt, Jennings Esq.	Taylor & Skinner 18	1777
5. Harrymount	OSNB E8.59	1834c
6. 'harï,məunt	Local pronunciation	1992
7. 'pɛrï,məunt 'dʒənï,məunt	Local pronunciation	1992

Harrymount and Jennymount in the townland of Tullyherron are English names from the recurring Christian name Henry (pet-name Harry) and the surname of the Jenny family. The Jennys were 17th-century settlers, but the earliest reference to the house name Harrymount is to a burglary of the Rev. Henry Jenny's house in 1709 (1). In 1750 a Henry Jenny gave a bell inscribed with his name to the parish church (*OSM* xii 60a; *Atkinson's Dromore* 197). In 1777 *Harry Mt* was occupied by *Jennings* Esq. (form 4, *sic*). I have no early reference to Jennymount, but in 1739 another house nearby had the analogous name *Perrymount*, but was occupied in 1777 by Arnold Esq. (*Taylor & Skinner* map 18). The surname Perry appears in the Donaghcloney Vestry Book in 1788 (Monree) and 1798 (Ballygunaghan) (*Vestry Bk D'cloney* 114,115).

Holdens Valley

An English form

1. Brown of Holdings Valley	Ir. Wills Index 17	1788
2. Brown of Holding's Valley	Vestry Bk D'cloney 114	1794
3. Holdens Valley	Atkinson's Donaghcloney 72	17??
4. 'holdənz 'vali	Local pronunciation	1996

I can find no reference to explain the 18th-century name *Holding's Valley* in the townland of Magherana, which may have been connected with the linen trade. It appears to contain a surname, now spelt Holden in Ulster: there may be a connection with the Norman-Welsh family of Howlin in Co. Kilkenny but it is more likely to have arrived in the Plantation (MacLysaght 1982, 132). However the late 18th-century occupant was John Brown (1, 2). In 1801 the *Vestry Book of Donaghcloney* gave John Brown's address just as Magherana (114–5). In 1834 a John Brown had a bleach green in the townland of Donaghcloney (*OSM* xii 58a).

Keonan	See **Annaghmakeonan** (townland)	
J 1251		

Lambs Island	An English form	
J 1152	See **Annaghanoon** (townland)	
1. (?)Anaghnowan al. Lisremoylan	Atkinson's Donaghcloney 46,[78]	1703
2. Lambs-Island	Taylor & Skinner 45	1777
3. Lamb's Island	Vestry Bk D'cloney 118	1890
4. 'lɑːmz 'əilənd	Local pronunciation	1992

Maggie's Steps	An English form	
J 1452		
1. Maggie's Steps	Atkinson's Dromore 197	1925
2. 'magïs 'staps	Local pronunciation	1992

This place in Ballygunaghan was described in 1925: "there is also a holy well close to a ford over the Lagan called Maggie's Steps" (form 1). The ford is marked on OS 1:10,000 sh. 202. Mr Copeland explained further:

> I wrote a poem once on Maggie, Maggie's Steps. Maggie must have been a brawny lass, for in the old story told by my grandparents, she was running across the stones one day and she tripped, her foot slipped on one stone and the mark of her foot is on one stone, her elbow took another stone, and the pitcher she was carrying hit the third stone, and there's the round circle of the base of the pitcher where it hit the stone.

Waringstown	An English form	
J 1055		
1. Warings-towne	Brownlow LB 20	1667
2. Waringstown	Brownlow LB 131	1687
3. Warrenstowne	Atkinson's Donaghcloney 42	1690
4. Waringstowne in Clinconnell	Atkinson's Donaghcloney 43	1691
5. Waringstown	Atkinson's Donaghcloney 57	1742
6. Waring's Town	Harris Hist. map	1743
7. Waringstown antiently called Clan-Connell	Harris Hist. 104	1744
8. Waringstown	Map of Down (OSNB) E2	1755
9. Revd Holt Warring of Warringstown	Vestry Bk D'cloney 115	1795
10. Waringstown x9	Vestry Bk D'cloney 115	1800+
11. Waring'stown	Statist. Sur. Dn 195,316,317	1802
12. Waringstown	Wm. Map (OSNB) E2	1810

13. Waringstown	Ir. Wills Index 95	1829
14. ['Ware-ing] always long	OSNB Pron. E2	1834c
15. named from Waring family, formerly		
Clan Connel	OSM xii 59b	1837c
16. Baile Varing	J O'D (OSNB) E2	1834c
17. Baile an Bhairínigh/Waringstown	Éire Thuaidh	1988
18. Baile an Bhairínigh	GÉ 11	1989
19. 'wɛrïŋz,təun	Local pronunciation	1994

Waringstown is in the north of Magherana, on the border with Tullyherron, and was apparently known at first by the district name of **Clanconnell** (4, 7), as commemorated in a local housing development. It got its English name from the 17th-century settler, William Warren or Waring (or from his son, *Bassett's Down* 277). After the rebellion of 1641, in which the sons of Glasney McAgholy Magennis of Clanconnell took part, their lands were confiscated and shared among the Cromwellian soldiers in lieu of pay. The soldiers' lands were bought up by their captains, and the eastern part of Donaghcloney had been sold to Waring by 1659 (*Census* 79; *ASE* 49b 19). His fortified house (erected in 1666) in Magherana remained in the family, and became the centre of the weaving village of Waringstown, which in 1777 still also contained the residence of a Magennis Esq. (*Taylor and Skinner* map 18). The parish church was moved to Waringstown from the old site in Donaghcloney. Waring's house was built on the site of an old fort, where in 1834 it was still the custom of the local young men to gather on Easter Monday to "play common" (hurley) (*OSM* xii 58a). The Warings continued in occupation and several became prominent figures: members of parliament (17th and late 19th century) and Anglican clergymen (Archdeacon of Dromore 1683 AD, Dean of Dromore 1842 AD; *Atkinson's Dromore* 194-5, 125, 115).

In March 1834 John O'Donovan visited the Rev. Holt Waring, rector of Shankill, and local "lord of the soil", who was extremely proud of his family and its traditions (*OSL Dn* x 25, xi 26). Waring's comment "Correct, I believe, H. W." appears several times in the name book, and Tullyherron was dismissed as "the present vulgar name" because *Tullyherim* appeared in old deeds (*OSNB* E2). When O'Donovan told the Rev. Archbold, "rector of Rathmullen and one of the magistrates of the Co. Down", that Waring wanted the town mapped as "Waringstown... pronounced *Ware-ing's town*", Archbold told O'Donovan that *Warring* was the spelling used "in all the records and grants" (cf. *ASE* 49b), "Mr Warring has no right to alter his name", and "if I humour the whims of any old pedant [i.e. by altering place-name spellings on the map] I shall hear from himself". O'Donovan's own comment at the time was:

> No person in the County of Down heard the little town ever called any name but Warringtown (*a* short), nor would you be understood if you called it *Ware-ing'stown* (*OSL Dn* xxviii 82, xxx 84–5).

Nevertheless Rev. Waring seems to have had his way in the modern spelling. He also insisted his family had no connection with the family of Warren, although William *Warren* (of Leenan, *Atkinson's Donaghcloney* 144) and *Warrenstowne* (form 3) were used as alternative spellings in the late 17th century.

Waring seems to have had no connection with Warrenpoint in Co. Down (*PNI* i 161–2) but both Waringfield in Moira (*Bassett's Down* 277) and **Waringsford** in Garvaghy contain the same surname.

Parish of Dromore

Townlands
Backnamullagh
Balleny
Ballykeel
Ballymacormick
Ballymaganlis
Ballynaris
Ballysallagh
Ballyvicknacally
Bishopscourt
Coolsallagh
Drumaghadone
Drumaknockan
Drumbroneth
Drumlough
Drummiller
Drumskee
Edenordinary
Edentiroory
Edentrillick
Ednego
Greenan
Greenoge
Growell
Islandderry
Killysorrell
Kinallen
Lappoges
Lisnaward
Listullycurran
Lurganbane
Magherabeg
Quilly
Skeagh
Skillyscolban
Tullindoney
Tullyglush
Tullymacarath

Town
Dromore

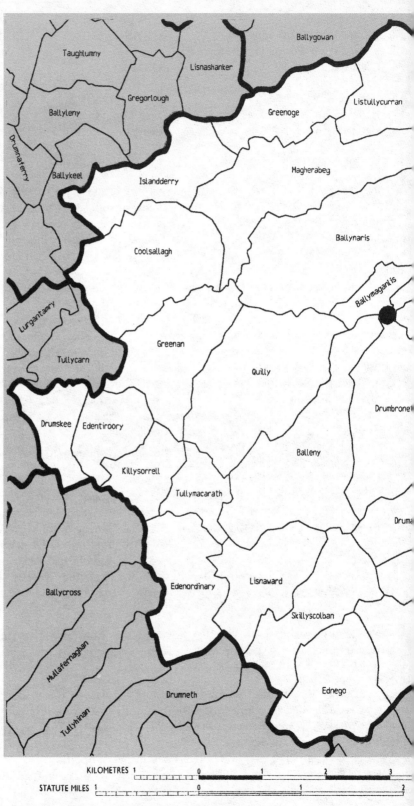

KILOMETRES

STATUTE MILES

103

THE PARISH OF DROMORE

Dromore is the name of an early monastery, a parish, a diocese corresponding to the baronies of Iveagh, and the town around the cathedral church. The patron saint of Dromore, *Colmán mac Conrathain*, is dateable only to "some time in the Heroic Age of the Old Irish Christianity" (Kenney 1929, 465), possibly the 6th century, and his pedigree connects him directly with Fiachu Araide of Dál nAraide, rather than through the related local tribe of *Uí Echach Cobha* or **Iveagh** (*CSH* 99). The Latin life of Colmán is "short and fabulous" and does not give any specific information about the place or the saint. The Book of Lecan refers to him as *Colmán... i Cuib* "Colmán in **Iveagh**" (*L. Lec.* 125v b9). The martyrologies commemorate him on June 7th under a pet-form of his name, *Mocholmóg Droma Móir* "My little Colmán of Dromore", and give his tribal background as *Moccu Arti* (forms 3,21: *Fél. Óeng., Mart. Gorm.*). Another church in the area was called *Lann Mocholmóg*, but the saint there was associated with Camas in Dál nAraide and called Colmán of the Gáilinne (O'Rahilly T.F. 1946, 460-1). Another Colmán was associated with the church of Kilkeel (*PNI* iii 5). At Dromore there is a 10th- or 11th-century cross (*ASCD* 129), which formerly stood in the town marketplace, and an earlier cross-inscribed stone "pillow" associated with St Colmán. There was also a well dedicated to St Colmán in the grounds of the bishop's palace, although in 1609 the dedication of the cathedral was changed from St Colmán to Christ the Redeemer (*Atkinson's Dromore* 88–9,161,35).

The succession of abbots to Colmán's monastery at Dromore appears in the annals from the 9th century (AD 841/2, 903 *AU* only, 909, 972), and later an *airchinneach*, erenagh or "steward" of Dromore is mentioned (AD 1006, 1143, 1159; *EA* 305–6; *Atkinson's Dromore* 109). Some monasteries were as often referred to by the founder's name as by the place where they were situated. The "coarbs of Finnian and Mocholmóg" mentioned in AD 992, 1018/9, and 1043 (*AFM*), or "of Mocholmóg and Comhgall" in AD 953 (*AU*) and 1068 (*AFM*) (forms 3,12-13 below), suggest that Dromore had links in east Down, with the monasteries founded by St Finnian at Movilla or by St Comhgall in Bangor (*PNI* ii 233-5, 141). The recurrence of the family name *Mac An Bheccánaigh* as coarb of Mocholmóg and Comhgall in 1068 and erenagh of Dromore in 1143 confirms the connection (forms 13–17). After this period there are no further references to the monastery of Dromore.

The abbot who died in AD 972, Mael-Brighde, is also called a bishop (10). He may have functioned only within the monastery, but Riagán who died in 1101 as "bishop of Dromore and the province of Ulaid" (*espoc Droma Moir 7 coicidh Uladh*, form 14 *AU*) appears to have had wider responsibilities. The diocese of Dromore is coterminous with the territory of Iveagh, and was probably set up on the basis of the monastery to serve the Gaelic lordship as distinct from the Norman rulers of east Down. A late-12th-century charter of the monastery of Nendrum in Strangford Lough was witnessed by "O'Roney bishop of Iveagh", the first evidence for the modern diocese (*coram Uroneca episcopo de Uvehe*, *EA* 192 v; dated 1178-84 but possibly a decade later). Gerard from Mellifont became bishop in 1227, Florence MacDonegan canon of Dromore became bishop in 1369, but most of the following bishops were Franciscan or Carmelite friars from outside Iveagh until Arthur Magennis in the mid-16th century (*EA* 307-8). The parish of Dromore was first mentioned as such in 1306 and 1309 (forms 32,33).

The Norman motte and castle, repairs, soldiers and supplies, were referred to in 1212 AD, along with *Rath* (**Dundrum**) and *Maincove* (probably **Seafin** motte in Drumballyroney) (forms 27-30). Dromore is on one of the main routes north from the Bann crossing at Banbridge, from which one went either along the east of Lough Neagh (*Slige Midluachra*), or via Dromore, then Hillsborough and Blaris to the coast, crossing the mouth of the Lagan at Belfast (*Cal. Carew MSS* i (1556) 262; *SMMD II* 48-9; *S.E. Ulster Map 1580c*). There is a short study of the town by T.D. Vaughan (1960).

Its early strategic importance was based on the fordability here of the river Lagan, which flows over solid rock from opposite the Motte to the road-bridge at the far end of the town. The first bridge was built in 1611 (Vaughan 1960, 131,134). The town grew up along the fordable part of the Lagan, in the area where the current extremities of the townlands of Ballymaganlis, Ballymacormick, Balleny and Drumbroneth meet. The town was described by Petty in 1657: "There is no building in the parish, only Dromore it being a market town hath some old thatched houses and a ruined church standing in it" (*Atkinson's Dromore* 162). The current church seems to have been rebuilt on the early site. The Lagan flows through the parish from east to west and forms the boundary of many of its townlands.

Dromore is a large parish of 38 townlands (called 31 and a half in 1657), including parts of other pre-plantation divisions. As might befit the spiritual centre of Iveagh, the largest proportion belonged to the church (forms 43,50). Adding two townlands once included in Magherally (*Buckworth (Atkinson)* 127), the bishop held 16 modern townlands: Balleny, Ballymacormick, Ballymaganlis, Ballynaris, Ballysallagh, Ballyvicknacally, Drumbroneth, Drumaghadone, Drumiller, Ednego, Lisnaward, Lurganbane, Magherabeg, Quilly, Skillyscolban, and Tullyglush. All but Ballymaganlis and Ballynaris were unwisely let by the bishop to William Worseley at the beginning of the 17th century, but were forfeit to the King and regranted to the bishop in 1616. By 1868, when the Church of Ireland was disestablished, there were only 13 church townlands, so that in the intervening period the church seems to have lost hold of Lisnaward, Magherabeg and Tullyglush (*Parl. Rep. 1868* 574–7, see Garvaghy parish).

Twelve townlands in the east of the parish were part of the MacRory Magennis holding of **Kilwarlin**: Backnamullagh, Ballykeel (Loughaghery), Drumaknockan, Drumlough, Edentrillick, Growell, Kinallen, Lappoges, Listullycurran, Skeagh and Tullindony, along with the lost townland of *Leclerin* between Backnamullagh and Drumaknockan (*Fiants Eliz.* §4650; *CPR Jas I* 181b, 396a; *Map Kilwarlin*). Kinallen, Skeagh and Tullindoney in the southeast were in the subdivision of *Tullyomy*, which was separated from Kilwarlin in the early 17th century, and granted instead to Sir Art Magennis (*CPR Jas I* 396a, 181b, 235a). They do not appear on the 1640 *Map of Kilwarlin* showing the lands of Kilwarlin held by Arthur Hill, consolidated after the rebellion into the manor of Hillsborough.

Sir Art held three scattered townlands in the west of the parish, Coolsallagh, Drumskee and Lisnaward, this last apparently divided between him and the bishop. Bishop Buckworth was to complain in 1622 that Sir Art had been granted various lands "of right anciently belonging to the Church" (*Atkinson's Dromore* 132).

In the west of the parish also were parts of the Magennis district of **Lequirin**; Islandderry the chief townland and Greenoge to the north of Coolsallagh; Greenan, Edentiroory, Tullymacarath and Edenordinary to the south of it. Between Edentiroory and Tullymacarath is the modern townland of Killysorrell, which is not mentioned till 1659. It may have had an earlier name. In 1609 Lequirin was divided between three Magennis holders. Art Oge McGlasney Magennis (the son of the holder of **Clanconnell**) got Islandderry and four townlands to the west in Magheralin, held from the King. From Sir Art Magennis, Brian McDonell McBrien Magennis got Edentiroory, Greenan and Tullymacarath further south in Dromore, and Donell Oge McEdmond Boy Magennis held Greenoge next to Islandderry and Edenordinary further south. Islandderry was owned by Alexander Waddell in 1659, and by 1668 he also had Ballykeel.

In 1837 the parish was described as "a well-cultivated and fertile country. In many parts, particularly on the west side of the parish, the scenery is picturesque, this part being well-wooded" (*OSM* xii 76b). It is hilly in the east but the ground is lower along the Lagan and towards the west. There are still many patches of bog. There were no Irish-speakers in 1834: "The old native who could speak Irish in this parish was an old woman who is just dead" (*OSNB* E125). The current informants were Mrs Muriel McVeigh of Garvaghy who lived in Kinallen and now lives in Drumbroneth, and Mr John McGrehan of the Cock Crow Knowe.

PARISH NAME

Dromore　　　　　　　　　　　　　*Droim Mór*
J 2053　　　　　　　　　　　　　　　"big ridge"

1. (?)hin Druim moccu Echach	Muirchú (Bieler) 102 §I 23	700c
2. Moc[h]olmóc Dromma móir	Mart. Tal. 48, June 7	830c
3. (feil Choluimb... maccu Artai	Fél. Óeng. 139, June 7	830c
4. abb Droma móir lá hUibh Eachdach	AFM i 462	841
5. abbas Droma Moer la hU Echach	AU (Mac Airt) 300	842
6. Corbmac, abb Droma móire	AFM ii 564	903
7. Cormac ancorita, princeps Droma Moir	AU (Mac Airt) 356	908
8. Mae!maedhocc, abb Droma móir, dég	AFM ii 580	909
9. Maolmoedhoc princeps (ab) Drommór	Fragment. Ann. 178 §450	909c
10. espoc 7 abb Droma móir Mocholmócc	AFM ii 696	972
11. airchinneach Droma Moir Mocholmócc	AFM ii 756	1006
12. (comharba Findéin 7 Mocolmócc	AFM ii 842	1043
13. (Mac an Bheccánaigh comharba Mocholmócc 7 Comhghaill	AFM ii 894-5	1068
14. espoc Droma Moir & coicidh Ulad	AU (Mac Airt) 536	1101
15. Mocholmoc Dromma Moir (Dál nAraide)	CSH 17 §99	1125c
16. Colman Dromma Moir	CSH 141 §707.132	1125c
17. Mac an Bheacanaigh airchindech Dromamoir	AFM ii 1070	1143
18. Dromamoyr, Angen herennanus	Newry Char. (Flanagan) 3	1157c
19. Dromamoir	Newry Char. (Mon. Ang.) 1134	1157c
20. Colman Droma moir i Cuib	L.Lec. 125v b9	1397c
21. Mo Cholmóc Droma Moir ind hUaib Echach Ulad	Fél. Óeng. 144n (June 7)	1453
22. (?)a nDruim-mor [2 O'Neills hanged]	AU iii 570-572n	1528
23. mo Cholmoc Dhromma Móir, Columbanus espoc mac ú Arti ó Dhruim mór mo-Colmóc i n-Uibh Eachach Uladh	Mart. Gorm. 112 June 7 n.	1630c
24. Mocholmog of Druim Mocholmog/ Druim Mor in Uí Echach	Mart. Don. 149	1630c
25. Droim Mór Íbh Eathach	Cín Lae Ó M. lch 24	1645c
26. Mocholmog Droma Móir	TCD Gens 147a §280	1666c
27. Drunmor (castle repairs)	Pipe Roll John 56	1211c
28. Drummor et Maincoue (castles)	Pipe Roll John 60	1211c

29. Drummor, patriam de Drummor	Pipe Roll John 60	1211c
30. Drummor (castle larder)	Pipe Roll John 60	1211c
31. decano et capitulo Drumerensibus	Pontif. Hib. ii 101 §259	1245
32. Drummore, ecc'ia de	Eccles. Tax. 102-3	1306c
33. eccles. S Colmani de Drumore	EA 311 (Edw. II)	1309
34. Dromore	Reg. Sweteman 50 §221	1368
35. bishopric, diocese of Dromore	Reg. Fleming §34	1407
36. procurationes Dromorensis; eccl. Dromor.	Reg. Dowdall §129 275	1422
37. Dromore (clerics of)	Reg. Swayne 45	1426
38. Dromorensis	Annates Ulst. 290	1480
39. primate custos of diocese of Dromore	Reg. Cromer ii 342 §46	1526
40. diocese/ cathedral cleric of Dromore	Reg. Cromer ii 342 §47	1526
41. Dromemoer	SMMD II 48-9	1565
42. Drommore	Ulster Map [1580c]	1580c
43. Drommore	S-E Ulster Map	1580c
44. Dromore (on river to L. Coyn)	Mercator's Ulst.	1595
45. Drommor sedes Episc./ fort Drommor	Bartlett BM	1600c
46. Dromoore sedes Episc.	Bartlett TCD	1601
47. maneria de Dromore	EA 309 King's Bks	1601c
48. terr. de Dromore xiv vill. terr.	EA 309 King's Bks	1601c
49. Droomore sedes Episc.	Bartlett Maps (Esch. Co. Maps) 1	1603
50. Dromoore sedes Episc.	Bartlett Maps (Esch. Co. Maps) 2	1603
51. ecclesia... de Drumore	Jas I to Dromore Cath. 104n,314	1609
52. chief parcels of Dromore al. Ballymagalge	CPR Jas I 395b	1609
53. Dromore (+church)	Speed's Ulster	1610
54. lands of Dromore al. Ballengalgae	CPR Jas I 190b	1611
55. the aforesaid lands of Dromore al. Ballenegalga	CPR Jas I 190b	1611
56. Dromore (+ 13 tds)	Buckworth (EA) 310	1622
57. tenement(s) in Dromore x8	Buckworth (Atkinson) 128-9	1622
58. Colmanus Drumorensis Episcopus	Acta SS Bolland. (EA) 304 Jun.7	1643+
59. Dromore	Inq. Down (Reeves1) 89	1657
60. Drummore	Hib. Reg. Lr. Iveagh	1657c
61. Drummore towne (pop. 178)	Census 79	1659c
62. Drummore (parish)	Census 78	1659c
63. Dromoore parish (5 times)	BSD 67-71	1661
64. Rector de Dromore	Trien. Visit. (Bramhall) 15	1661
65. Drumore	Sub. Roll Down 274	1663
66. Dromore	Trien. Visit. (Margetson) 26	1664
67. Dromore rectoria	Trien. Visit. (Boyle) 46	1679
68. Dromore	Rent Roll Down 5	1692
69. Dromore	Harris Hist. (map)	1743
70. Drommore, a poor market-town	UJA ser.3 48 (1985) 114	1760
71. Druim Mór "a high narrow ridge of hills"	J O'D (OSNB) E125	1834c
72. Droim Mór/Dromore	Éire Thuaidh	1988

73. Droim Mór	GÉ 94	1989
74. drə'moːr	Local pronunciation	1991

Although the name *Droim Mór* "big ridge" is used earliest to refer to St Colman's monastery, the church site and the town which has grown up around it are in a hollow between the hills. However, Harris in 1744 was happy to explain the name of the town as "'the great back of a hill', being a cluster of houses spread on the side of a hill" (*Harris' Hist.* 98). There is a ridge to the north of the town and another, Barban Hill, to the south (1:10,000 sheet 202). There is a rath in the north-west of the town on Maypole Hill, just above the cathedral, and between it and the main Belfast-Dublin road. The next earliest site, the Anglo-Norman motte, is on a spur close to the north bank of the river Lagan (*ASCD* 203). Only the top has been excavated, but if the motte has been built on a native foundation this could also be the *droim* of the name.

Despite Bieler's suggestion, it is unlikely that form 1 above, from Muirchú's Life of St Patrick, could refer to Dromore in **Iveagh** (*Muirchú (Bieler)*, index 257). *Druim Moccu Echach* "ridge of the descendants of Echu" is described as "a wild place high up in the hills" where St Patrick found Mac Cuill of the Grecraige who became Bishop Maughold of the Isle of Man. However, since it is located among the Ulaid, which at this date would mean Dál Fiatach, the name probably refers to Uí Echach of the Ards, although an identification with Nendrum is also unlikely (*ASCD* 292b). The abbot of Colmán's monastery of Dromore is sometimes referred to by the name of the founding saint rather than the place (12,13). I have included the reference from the Newry charter (18,19) with the Irish forms as it clearly shows the Irish genitive inflection; however, in the late *Fragmentary Annals, Drummor* is uninflected even in an Irish text (9).

As a land unit the name Dromore is linked with *Ballenegalga*, now the townland of **Ballymaganlis**. There is no townland bearing the parish name.

TOWNLAND NAMES

Backnamullagh
J 2255

Originally two names:
Bac "balk" and
Mullach "summit, hill"

1. Ballichorenvally Ballienvacky (in Kilwarlin)	Fiants Eliz. §4650	1585
2. Ballychorenvally Ballyenvickie in Kilwarlin	CPR Jas I 396a	1609
3. (?)Lecleryn, Moylagh, Killynlettin (Sir Art Magenis)	CPR Jas I 395b	1609
4. (?)Levallyshanmullagh... Balleyvickey (Bishop)	CPR Jas I 395b	1609
5. Ballichorenvalie Ballienvackie (in Kilwarlin)	CPR Jas I 181b	1610
6. (?)Levallyshanmullagh... Balleyvickey (Bishop)	CPR Jas I 191a	1611
7. (?)Lecklerim, Moylagh, Killymattin, half tds (Sir Art Magenis)	CPR Jas I 235a	1612

8. Ballivack or Leighballivack and Ballimoiluge al Leighvallymolagh or Leighvallymoilugh (in Kilwarling) (from Bp)	CPR Jas I 266a	1614
9. Lecklern, Moylagh (sessiaghs de)	Inq. Ult. (Down) §13 Car. I	1629
10. Levallyvacke & Levallymoylagh, 60a in vil. de (Kilwarlin)	Inq. Ult. (Down) §46 Car. I	1633
11. Ballichorawallie Ballyenvacky (Kilwarlin)	Inq. Ult. (Down) §60 Car. I	1635
12. Lecklearan, Backan Mullagh	Map Kilwarlin	1640
13. Vickonmollagh	Census 78	1659c
14. Vack & Mullagh	BSD 71	1661
15. Back & Moyla; Back & Mulla	Deeds & Wills (Mooney) 93	18thc
16. Backnamullogh	Wm. Map (OSNB) E125	1810
17. Backnamulloch	Ir. Wills Index 5	1830
18. Baic na Mullach "bend of the summits"	J O'D (OSNB) E125	1834c
19. Bac na Mullach "the angular hollow of the hilltops"	Mooney 93	1950c
20. ˌbaknəˈmoləx	Local pronunciation	1991

This modern townland is in the north of Dromore parish, and lay between the church lands of Dromore and the McRory Magennis holding of Kilwarlin based on Hillsborough. From the early 17th-century forms it is clear that there were originally at least two names in the area, belonging to or divided among the Church and two different Magennis proprietors. **Grallaghgreenan** in Drumballyroney, and **Drumo & Drumcrow** and **Edenballycoggill** in Magheralin are other townlands which have combined the names of more than one unit.

In the Schedule of Iveagh Sir Art Magennis held a sessiagh or half-townland called *Moylagh* (3, 7, 9), regularly listed next to the lost name *Leclerin*, which seems to have been used for part of **Edentrillick**, the townland next to Backnamullagh on the east (cf. 12). In the lists of the lands originally held by the McRory Magennises of Kilwarlin the names *Ballychorenvally, Ballienvacky* regularly follow each other (1, 2, 5, 11). The Bishop of Dromore also had two land-units called *Levallyshanmullagh* and *Ballyvickey* (4,6: granted to Edward Trevor). The prefixes Bally (*baile*) and Levally (*leathbhaile*) indicate "townland" and "half-townland", but in another grant in 1614 the bishop's lands were called both (8). The 1633 inquisition informs us that by 1618 Edward Trevor had obtained 60 acres in the "townland of *Levallyvacke & Levallymoylagh*" from Brian McRory Magennis of Kilwarlin (form 10). This is the first instance in which the two halves clearly form a unit name, and without the *Levally* prefix would be very close to forms (14, 15) and the modern version. The English ampersand & seems to have been written out as *an[d]* in forms (12, 13), reinterpreted as the Irish article and metathesized to give Back*na*mullagh as the current form.

The earlier history could be as follows. *Seanmhullach* "old hill" and *Bac* "balk" could be townlands disputed or divided between the McRory Magennises and the bishop. With *baile* "townland" prefixed the names appeared in the genitive. *Bac* is confused between masc. *an bhaic* and fem. *na baice*, while *-chorenvally* could possibly be a corruption of *-seanmhullaigh* i.e. *-shanmully*, reading *c* for short *s*, and repeated in later copies of the same document. When *levally* "half-townland" was prefixed to the name in the recurring list of bishop's lands the rest of the name was not inflected. However, when granting this piece of land more modern forms of the name were used, dropping the element *sean* "old" and any inflections, to make clear that the bishop's lands were half-townlands "in Kilwarlin" (8) and that the McRory Magennis unit was one townland made up of two halves (10).

There is a strong impression that two (half-)townlands have been combined, but which halves? For instance, were the land units obtained by Trevor in 1611–18 (forms 6, 10) four pieces held by two different proprietors, or was he being careful to confirm his acquisition of two pieces by agreement with both the bishop and McRory Magennis in a case of disputed ownership? *Back* seems to have been both Kilwarlin and bishop land, but since *Ballychorawallie* in Kilwarlin last appeared in 1635 *Mullagh* was possibly shared between the bishop and Sir Art Magennis.

The townland of Backnamullagh is now a normal-sized 450 acres. Treating the two parts of the name separately, *bac* is "a balk, bend, step", usually in place-names a field-bank, angular enclosure, or bend in a river. There is no stream in this area. *Bacc* "angle, bend, corner" was neuter or masculine in Old Irish (*DIL*), and is now normally masculine (*Ó Dónaill*), although *Dinneen* gives feminine as an alternative, and this is apparently found in the name **Cullybackey** *Cúil na Baice* (*PNI* iv 199). The masculine genitive is *baic*, so that the forms apparently with the masculine article *Ballienvackie, Ballyenvickie* have to be explained with the longer form *bacadh: Baile an Bhactha* "townland of the balk" or even as originally *Baile an Bhacaigh* "townland of the lame man, or beggar".

The current form of the second part of the name looks like *mullach* "summit", as in the church unit *Levallyshanmullagh*, which apparently ends *Seanmhullach* "old summit", less likely "of the old summits". The apparent diphthong in the spellings *moylagh, moiluge* could represent plural *maoileacha*, or *maolach* a derivative, of *maoil* "bald, a bare-topped round hill". However, since **Mullaghdrin** in Dromara is spelled *-mollagh-* in the early lists of Kilwarlin townlands, *moilagh* more likely arose from a misreading of *ll*.

Balleny	*Baile Uí Éinigh*	
J 1851	"Heaney's townland"	

1. Ballyanyne	CPR Jas I 395b	1609
2. Ballyanyne	CPR Jas I 190b	1611
3. Ballyannie al. Ballyanine	CPR Jas I 266a	1614
4. Ballyanine	CPR Jas I 309a	1616
5. Ballyannum	Buckworth (EA) 310	1622
6. Ballehenny	Magennis Paps (O'Sullivan) 63 §93	1632
7. Balliany	Hib. Reg. Lr. Iveagh	1657c
8. Ballyanny	Census 78	1659c
9. Ballyany	BSD 68	1661
10. Ballyany	Sub. Roll Down 274	1663
11. Balliany	Hib. Del. Down	1672c
12. Ballyeany, the Deary lands	Reg. Deeds abstracts i §387	1727
13. Ballany	Ir. Wills Index 4	1742
14. Belleny	Ir. Wills Index 100	1765
15. Balleny	Wm. Map (OSNB) E125	1810
16. [ball-'ea-ny]	OSNB Pron. E125	1834c
17. Bellany	Ir. Wills Index 4	1842
18. Tagne's fort	Mooney 96	1950c

19. Baile Ennaidh/Eghnigh "Enna's town"	J O'D (OSNB) E125	1834c
20. Baile (Uí) Theangana "Tagney's/ Tangney's town"	Mooney 95	1950c
21. ˌbəˈlenï	Local pronunciation	1991

Balleny townland belonged to the church until 1868, and its northern end borders the Lagan in the town of Dromore. The first element seems to be *baile*, but the final syllable [ə] of that word may have been elided before an initial vowel in the second element. Possibilities might be *baile* plus genitive *eanaigh* "townland of the marsh" (like **Ballinanny** in Annaclone) or *baile* plus genitive *aonaigh* "townland of the fair" (like **Enagh** in Garvaghy). It could be a contracted form of *Baile Léana* "townland of the wet meadow", but there is also a townland of **Ballyleny** which seems to have this origin nearby in Magheralin. Although the modern forms are different, the names are sometimes confused by people in the area, and Balleny may be referred to as the West End (of Dromore).

O'Donovan suggested that the second element was the genitive of a personal name (form 19). It could also be the genitive of a surname formed with *Ó* and a forename beginning in a vowel. Woulfe gives a surname *Ó hEighnigh* from 12th-century Fermanagh and East Armagh, later *Ó hÉinigh*, anglicized as Heaney etc. (Woulfe 1923, 565–7). In fact *Munterheny*, the "family of *Ó hÉinigh*", had held the church lands of Ballymore parish Co. Armagh (Tanderagee) on the border with Down, and an *O'Heany* is mentioned in Co. Down in 1609 and 1612 (*CPR Jas I* 375a, 228a). The place-name Balleny would have preserved the older pronunciation [ɔ'he:nï] of this surname, which may also form part of the name **Killaney** in Garvaghy.

There is a final *-n* in some of the early forms, which has led Dean Mooney to postulate a different surname *Baile Uí Theangana* (20), based on the minor name Tagne's Fort which he recorded in the townland. Three raths are marked in the south of the townland on the OS 1:10,000 map, but none of them is named. This surname is peculiar to Co. Kerry (Woulfe 1923, 651) and thus seems unlikely, while there is no evidence of internal [h] from Irish *th*. A possible explanation of the *-n* is that the surname *Ó hAonáin* or *Ó hÉanáin* (also known in Down, apparently part of the townland name **Tullyhinan** in Magherally) was assimilated to (O') Heaney.

Ballykeel
J 2752

Baile Caol
"narrow townland"

1. Ballykyle in Kilwarlin	CPR Jas I 194b	1611
2. Ballikeeleloghaghery al. Ballikeele of the mill	Inq. Ult. (Down) §31 Car. I	1632
3. Keele	Census 78	1659c
4. Ballykeele, Loghaghry (manor of Hillsborough)	CSP Ire. 1660-2 p459	1661
5. Ballykeeleloghalery	BSD 70	1661
6. Ballykeel	Sub. Roll Down 275	1663
7. Ballykeele	ASE 174a 38	1668
8. B:keele	Hib. Del. Ulster	1672c
9. Ballikeele	Hib. Del. Down	1672c
10. Ballykeel, Loghahery [Comm. Grace]	Mooney MS 95	1684

11. B.keele	Lamb Maps Co. Downe	1690c
12. Ballykeele	Rent Roll Down 5	1692
13. Ballykeeloghagherry	Rent Roll Down 9	1692
14. McKearly of Bellyceell	Ir. Wills Index 94	1731
15. Ballykeale al Longaghry	Reg. Deeds abstracts iii §96	1787
16. Ballykeel	Wm. Map (OSNB) E125	1810
17. Baile Caol "narrow town"	J O'D (OSNB) E125	1834c
18. Baile caol-loch eachraidhe	Mooney 95	1950c
19. An Baile Caol/Ballykeel	Éire Thuaidh	1988
20. ˌbaliˈkil	Local pronunciation	1991

Ballykeel is the easternmost townland of Dromore and was part of Kilwarlin. It seems to have been known by the name of the lough it borders, **Lough Aghery**, up to 1632. Subsequently the name of Lough Aghery was used as an epithet (2, 4, 5, 10, 13, 15), as was Kilwarlin (1), to distinguish this "narrow townland" from other townlands of the same name: **Ballykeel** just west of Banbridge in the parish of Seapatrick; **Ballykeel** of *Clanawly* in the parish of Donaghmore; **Ballykeel Edenagonnell** and **Ballykeel Artifinny** in the neighbouring parish of Hillsborough. Ballykeel Lough has now become an alternative name for Lough Aghery.

Ballymacormick
J 2254

Baile Mhic Cormaic
"townland of McCormick"

1. Ballymackormocke	CPR Jas I 395b	1609
2. BallemcCormock, Cahell McDermot McCormock of	CPR Jas I 195b	1610
3. Ballymccarmick	CPR Jas I 190b	1611
4. Ballymccarmick	CPR Jas I 191a	1611
5. half of BallymcCarmick farthest from Dromore	CPR Jas I 266a	1614
6. Ballymccormucke	CPR Jas I 309a	1616
7. Ballymccarmick	Buckworth (EA) 310	1622
8. Ballimiconnisky	Hib. Reg. Lr. Iveagh	1657c
9. Bally McCormack	Census 78	1659c
10. Ballymcomisty	Par. Map (Mooney) 96	1660c
11. Ballimacomisky	BSD 68	1661
12. Ballimicomisky	Hib. Del. Down	1672c
13. Ballymaccormick	Wm. Map (OSNB) E125	1810
14. Baile mhic Chormaic "McCormack's Town"	J O'D (OSNB) E125	1834c
15. ˌbaləməˈkɔrmək	Local pronunciation	1991

This townland name obviously contains a surname. Despite the misreading (8,10–12) in Petty and related documents of an anglicized form of *Mac Con Uisce* "son of water dog", later anglicized as Waters, (as in the alias of **Edenordinary**), Ballymacormick clearly indicates the surname *Mac Cormaic* "son of Cormac". According to Woulfe this family name was "a common surname in all parts of Ireland" (Woulfe 1923, 344). There was an early family called *Ó Cormaic* "grandson of Cormac" in Iveagh. In 931 AD the poet Bard Bóinne was killed by the *Uí Corbmaic* of Iveagh (*AFM* ii 628). O'Donovan placed the O'Cormicks around Newry, since the charter of Newry abbey in 1156–7 located the foundation in their land, in Latin *terra(m) O Cormaic*. The annals mention the family in the early 12th century: in 1104 *Cormac Ó Cormaic*, chief of the *Monaig*, died, and the year before *In Gilla Guit Ó Cormaic* was killed in a raid on *Mag Coba*, Iveagh (*AU*). Woulfe noted that *Ó Cormacáin* was the name of "an ecclesiastical family who were erenaghs of Iniscourcey" (Inch, Co. Down). "The name... was often shortened to Ó Cormaic, and is now in many places disguised under the anglicized form of MacCormack" (Woulfe 1923, 480–1).

Ballymacormick was church land, belonging to the Bishop of Dromore, so that it is likely that a family called *Mac Cormaic* held it in return for service to the church. There were *Mac Cormaic* abbots of Bangor in 1170 and 1212 (*AU*), and *Giolla Domhnaill Mac Carmuic* who was "bishop of the Ulaid" died in 1175 (*AFM* iii 18). The bishop of Raphoe who died in 1515 was a *Mac Cormaic* (*AU*). Thomas *MacCarmuyc* was Dean of Dromore in 1539, which made him rector and prebend of Dromara (*Anal. Hib.* i 297-8). There were McCormicks in this townland in 1610 when Cahell McDermot *McCormock* had to surrender his lands to Timothy Castletowne, sheriff of Down (*CPR Jas I* 195b). In the schedule and grant Ballymacormick was handed over to William Worseley (returned to the bishop in 1616, *CPR Jas I* 309a), while Cahell *McCormocke* was allocated *Ballkylelekerin* and was granted *Ballyleatrome*, apparently Leitrim in Drumgooland (*CPR Jas I* 395a, 191a). In 1623 Patrick McCormick held the church townland of Skillyscolban in Dromore (*Montgomery MSS* xxix).

By 1659 McCormick or McCormack was a "principall Irish name" in Co. Antrim, Castlereagh, the Ards, and Lower Iveagh (*Census* 3, 7, 19, 90, 95, 81). In 1837 McCormick was one of the Roman Catholic surnames to be found in the vicinity of Slieve Croob (*OSM* xii 67b). The surname McCormick also appears in the lists of Protestant clergy of the diocese of Dromore in the 18th and 19th centuries (*Swanzy's Dromore, Atkinson's Dromore*). There is another townland called **Ballymacormick** in the parish of Bangor in Co. Down (*PNI* ii 156–7).

Ballymaganlis	*Baile Mhig Amhalaidh*	
J 2053	"McGawley's townland"	

1. chief parcels or portions of Dromore al. Ballymagalge and Ballyenaries	CPR Jas I 395b	1609
2. Ballengalgae, Dromore othw.	CPR Jas I 190b	1611
3. lands of Dromore al. Ballenegalga	CPR Jas I 190b	1611
4. small town of Balleinagauley	Inq. Down (Atkinson) 139	1657
5. Ballimaganley	BSD 68	1661
6. Ballymaganly	DS (Mooney) 95	1661?
7. Ballymagarly	Sub. Roll Down 274	1663
8. (?)"the Deary lands"	Reg. Deeds abstracts i §387	1727
9. Ballymagennis [old plan of Bp]	OSNB E125	n.d.
10. Ballymeganlis	Bnd. Sur. (OSNB) E125	1830c
11. Ballymaganlis	OSM xii 72b, 73a	1834
12. Baile meig Ainleis "Meganlis'town"	J O'D (OSNB) E125	1834c

13. Baile Mic Ainleis "Maganless' town"	Joyce iii 104	1913
14. Baile Mhig Chuindlis "MacCandless' town"	Mooney 95	1950c
15. Baile Mhac Sheanlaoich > MacCanly & Cantly	Mooney 95	1950c
16. ˌbaləmə'ganləs	Local pronunciation	1991

Ballymaganlis is not on the 1:50,000 map, and no longer exists separately as a townland. It is given no acreage in the 1961 *Topographical Index*, but was 115 acres in 1851. It is now part of the urban district of Dromore, and contains a large part of the town, including the old cathedral, from the river Lagan north to the bypass of the main Belfast-Dublin road. Although used in the *Ordnance Survey Memoir*, the name is now generally forgotten locally, and remembered only by Ballymaganlis House and Park.

It was church land, described in 1657 as "the small town of *Balleinagauley* through the middle whereof the river runneth, in the year 1640 possessed by the Bishopp, but of late years farmed out with the tythes and the Gleabe" (*Inq. Down (Atkinson)* 139). Ballymaganlis is now all to the north of the Lagan. The form *Balleinagauley* (4) appears to be connected with *Ballynagalge*, the earlier alias name for the bishop's land within (the town of) Dromore (1–3). At this stage the second element did not look like a surname, nor did it have a final -s.

In forms such as *Ballymaganley* (5,6) the second element looks like a surname, and Mooney suggested *Mac S(h)eanlaoich*, attested as McGanly in Roscommon c. 1594 and which was a "principal Irish name" around Mullingar c. 1659 (*Census* 5260). However the forms in -*anly* (5-7) and -*alga* (1-3) might be reconciled by considering the Irish surname *Mac/Mag Amhalghaidh* (now *Amhalaidh*), anglicized as MacAuley, McGawley or Gawley (Woulfe 1923, 307,414). The *n* of forms 5–7 could be an attempt to spell the strong nasal quality of *mh*. McCawleys are widespread, and there are now Gawleys in Cos Down and Fermanagh (NI telephone directory 1994). The name is possibly related to the obsolete district of **Clanawly** *Cineál nAmhalaidh* "kindred of Amhalghadh" in Co. Down (*PNI* i 51–2), and the Fermanagh barony of **Clanawley**, where there was a surname *Mac Amhlaoibh*, equivalent to the Scottish MacAulay (Woulfe 1923, 307–8). People called *McCawlie* were pardoned as associates of the Magennises in 1602 (*Fiants Eliz.* §6616). By the 19th century the place-name had acquired a final -*s* (like **Ballynaris**), which could be an English plural from the "chief parcels or portions of Dromore" (forms 9–11).

By this date the name was understood as containing the surname McCandless, *Mac Cuindlis*, which Woulfe refers to Ó *Cuindlis*, "the name of a literary family in Connacht, who had a share in compiling the Book of Lecan" (Woulfe 1923, 112, 347, 489). The name was fairly numerous in Ulster (MacLysaght 1985, 36). According to J.R. Ward's Fair Sheets, a Presbyterian called Samuel McCandles was schoolmaster in 1837 in the neighbouring townland of Ballyvicknacally (*OSM* xii 78a), and McCandless is still a common surname around Dromore (NI telephone directory, 1994). It appears on the map again in McCandless Terrace just south of the Diamond in Skeagh townland (OS 1:10,000 sheet 202). However no early local reference to the McCandless family has been found, which suggests that the current form is a late re-interpretation of the original name.

Ballynaris *Baile an Árais*
J 1954 "townland of the building"

1. Ballyenaries	CPR Jas I 395b	1609

2. Ballynaries (twice)	CPR Jas I 190b	1611
3. Ballynories	Inq. Ult. (Down) §4 Jac. I	1616
4. Ballinaries	CPR Jas I 309a	1616
5. Ballynoris	Buckworth (EA) 310	1622
6. Balleneris	Magennis Paps (O'Sullivan) 63 §93	1632
7. Ballimery	Hib. Reg. Lr. Iveagh	1657c
8. Ballynoris	Census 78	1659c
9. Ballymery al. Ballymory	Par. Map (Mooney) 97	1660c
10. Ballymery	BSD 68	1661
11. Balynaries	Sub. Roll Down 274	1663
12. Ballimery	Hib. Del. Down	1672c
13. Ballyneross	Ir. Wills Index 97	1763
14. Ballynares	Deeds & Wills (Mooney) 97 [Will]	1772
15. Ballynaries	Civ. & Ecc. Top. (OSNB) 98	1795
16. Ballynarist	Deeds & Wills (Mooney) 97 [Will]	1801
17. Ballynaris	Wm. Map (OSNB) E125	1810
18. [Bally-'nay-ris]	OSNB Pron. E125	1834c
19. Baile Néiris "Nare's Town"	J O'D (OSNB) E125	1834c
20. Baile Uí Naradhaigh > Nary/Neary	Mooney 97	1950c
21. ˌbalïˈnarəs	Local pronunciation	1991

Ballynaris was a church townland until 1868. In 1837 it contained the bishop's palace: "a plain building, very well situated, as it commands a view of the country round for many miles" (*OSM* xii 76). Ballynaris including Bishopscourt is a big townland of 988 acres, north of the Belfast-Dublin road which bypasses Dromore, with the Lagan as its southern bound. It could be *Baile an Árais* "townland of the building", with the Irish palatal *s* [ʃ] spelled as English *s* not *sh*, as in Divis from *Dubhais*, Stranmillis from *Sruthán Milis*. The townland of **Bishopscourt** in Dunsfort parish in Lecale got its name from the residence of the bishop of Down, replacing the older name of *Lismullan* (*EA* 37n, 171, 174, 175). However the residence of the bishops of Dromore seems to have been in the town. Bishop Buckworth's new house was destroyed in 1641, and after 1695 the bishop lived for some time in Magheralin before the new residence was built in the late 18th century, too late to be the origin of the townland name (*Atkinson's Dromore* 37, 53, 63, 68).

The final *-s* does not appear on the Petty maps or in the related 1661 *BSD* form (10) although Petty gives the name *Ballimery* twice, north-east and west of Dromore (*Hib. Del. Down*). Possibly the modern anglicized form is plural, meaning two parts of *Baile an Aoire* "townland of the herdsman", where Petty's spelling *-e-* represents Irish *ao* as in **Enagh** in Garvaghy from *aonach*. There are other examples (eg. **Lappoges**) where an English plural *-s* has been added to the Irish form of the place-name. Both O'Donovan and Mooney suggested that Ballynaris includes a surname (19, 20) and Mooney also mentioned anglicized surnames with a final *-s*, such as Burns for *Ó Broin* (*Mooney MS* 97). There is no evidence for this happening with *Nary*. Woulfe lists the Connaught and Leinster surname *Ó Naradhaigh* which would give O'Nary (Woulfe 1923, 624), but I have found no evidence for it in Co Down. MacLysaght has (O) Neary "a north Connacht name" (MacLysaght 1985, 233; 1982, 166).

Ballysallagh   *Baile Sealbhach*
J 2151   "townland of herds"

1. Ballinaboshalagh	CPR Jas I 395b	1609
2. Ballynaboshallagh	CPR Jas I 190b	1611
3. Ballyshallagh al.		
Ballenaboshallagh	CPR Jas I 266a	1614
4. Ballynaboshulaghy	Inq. Ult. (Down) §4 Jac. I	1616
5. Ballinaboshalagh	CPR Jas I 309a	1616
6. Ballysallagh	Buckworth (EA) 310	1622
7. Ballishallagh	Hib. Reg. Lr. Iveagh	1657c
8. Ballysallogh	Census 78	1659c
9. Ballyhallagh	BSD 68	1661
10. Ballishallagh	Hib. Del. Down	1672c
11. Ballysallogh	Wm. Map (OSNB) E125	1810
12. Baile salach "dirty town"	J O'D (OSNB) E125	1834c
13. B. saileach "sallows"	J O'D (OSNB) E125	1834c
14. Baile na bó-sheala		
"of the herd of cows"	Mooney 97	1950c
15. Baile S(h)eallach		
"td of cattle-herds"	Mooney 97	1950c
16. Baile Salach	GÉ 26	1989
17. ˌbalïˈsaləx	Local pronunciation	1996

Ballysallagh was a church townland until 1868, held in 1609 by William Worseley (1). O'Donovan suggested the etymology *Baile Salach* "dirty town" from the later spellings (12). Up to 1616 (1-5) there was a further internal element in the forms, *nabo*, apparently *na mbó* "of the cows". This cannot be the land-unit term *ballybo*, which was not used in the Schedule of Iveagh (compare *CPR Jas I* 394-6 with 165, Co. Armagh), and does not appear as *nabo* with the article. The meaning of the element *bó* here and the spelling *sh* in the earlier forms suggests that the final element might be *sealbhach* "a flock", which can also mean as an adjective "wealthy", "possessing herds". A compound *bó-shealbhach* "(possessing) herds of cows" is unlikely as it would be stressed on the element *bó*, which is the very one that disappears, and the *s* of *sealbhach* would be lenited and pronounced as [h]. Could it be that two alternative names, *Baile na mBó* "townland of the cows" and *Baile Sealbhach* "townland of herds", have been combined in the early forms here, with the name *Baile Sealbhach* becoming the dominant one later? It is clear from the difference in spelling of the second element of **Coolsallagh** below that this was not *Baile Saileach* "townland of willow", since for Ballysallagh the early spellings have *sh*, most likely representing Gaelic [ʃ], and no raising of the first vowel to *i*.

Ballyvicknacally   *Baile Mhic na Caillí*
J 2153   "townland of the son of the hag"

1. Ballyvickencally al. Ballynakally	CPR Jas I 395b	1609
2. Ballivickenkally al. Ballinakally	CPR Jas I 190b	1611

3. half of Ballyvicknecally al. Ballinacally lying farthest from Dromore	CPR Jas I 266a	1614
4. Ballyvickencallye al. Ballynekalye	Inq. Ult. (Down) §4 Jac. I	1614
5. Ballyvickencally al. Ballynakally	CPR Jas I 309a	1616
6. (?)Aucknakelly	Buckworth (EA) 310	1622
7. (?)Vickmekeay	Buckworth (Atkinson) 129	1622
8. (?)Ballymacnegolly, O'Kellie of	Wars Co. Down x 77	1641
9. (?)Ballymacnegally, Walsh of	Wars Co. Down x 78	1641
10. Balliuskinekelly	Hib. Reg. Lr. Iveagh	1657c
11. Ballivismekelly	BSD 67	1661
12. Vicknekelly	Sub. Roll Down 274	1663
13. Balliviskmkelly	Hib. Del. Down	1672c
14. McCollogh of Beliveeknekely	Ir. Wills Index 85	1720
15. Ballyvicnakelly	Wm. Map (OSNB) E125	1810
16. Ballyvicknakelly	Ir. Wills Index 54	1813
17. Ballyvicknakelly (> Rec. form)	Bnd. Sur. (OSNB) E125	1830
18. a hill called The Cailleach's Hill or The Hag's Hill in the townland.	OSNB E125	1834c
20. Ballyvicknakelly	Ir. Wills Index 58	1856
21. Baile mhic na caillighe "town of the son of the hag"	J O'D (OSNB) E125	1834c
22. ˌbalï,vəknəˈkalï	Local pronunciation	1991
23. ˌbalï,vəknəˈkɛlï	Local pronunciation	1991

Ballyvicknacally, church land till 1868, stretches east from the town of Dromore along the north bank of the Lagan, including the Norman motte and a rath on Cannon Hill. The explanation c. 1834 was, "There is a hill in the townland called "The Cailleach Hill" or "Hag's Hill"", and the suggested Irish form was *Baile Mhic na Caillighe* (>*Cailli*) "town of the son of the hag" (form 21). The five earliest forms have an alias which could be interpreted as *Baile na Cailli* "townland of the hag", and it looks as if the name was already understood as referring to a *cailleach*, usually a supernatural figure. Most of the historical forms begin with *baile*, with only three (6, 7, 12) to suggest that *vick* may not represent "son" but some topographical element such as *bíog* "leap". The lenition of this element, seen in the majority of the historical forms, might result from following the dative of *baile*, but the lenition of *mic* to *mhic* is also the treatment one would expect in recent Irish of a fixed surname in the genitive.

Despite a vague local tradition of an old woman and her son who lived on this hill, the name is more likely to include a family name. Based on the shorter early 17th-century alias forms (*Ballynakally*, 1–5) one could suggest *Mac Ceallaigh*, taking *na* as a corruption of *mc*. *Mac Ceallaigh* is attested also in **Carnacally** in Newry (*PNI* i 11), **Ballykelly** and **Drumnagally** townlands in Seapatrick, and *Ó Ceallaigh* possibly in **Tirkelly** in Drumballyroney, and **Clontonakelly**, divided between the parishes of Hillsborough and Drumbo. Woulfe gives *Mac Ceallaigh* in Cos Galway and Leitrim, and also in the Isle of Man (Woulfe 1923, 330), sometimes confused with *Ó Ceallaigh* (Roscommon, Meath, Loughinsholin barony in Co. Derry etc., Woulfe 1923, 330, 457–8). *Clann Ceallaigh* at Drumbo are mentioned in the Ulster genealogies as descended from Bécc king of Dál

Fiatach who died in 718 AD (*Descendants Ir* xiv 80). The district inhabited by *Slut Kellies* (*Sliocht Ceallaigh*, "progeny of Ceallach") was shown nearby to the north on 16th-century maps (see **Clanbrassil McGoolechan**, Iveagh). A yeoman called Tirlogh, with William, Rory mac Cullo, Cullo, Patrick, Richard, Neill Duff, Edmond and Donald *O'Kellie* of this townland were all named as rebels in 1641 (forms 8,9); and there is some evidence that *Ó* and *Mac* could interchange in surnames in Co Down (Ó Casaide 1929, 5n; cf. form 14).

If the surname *Ó* or *Mac Ceallaigh* is correct, the surviving forms could represent a local reinterpretation of the name, or even a nickname, which meant "son of the hag/nun". A possible alternative surname which contains the extra syllable would be McEnkelly, which is close to the early 17th-century spellings like *Ballyvickencally* (1, 2, 4, 5). McEnkelly derives from *Mac Con Choille(adh)* "son of *Cú Choille(adh)*" or "hound of the woods", and was often anglicized as Woods. It was known in Derry and Tyrone (Woulfe 1923, 338). According to probably 12th-century tradition, *Cú Choilleadh*, ancestor of the family, cleared the plains of Larne and Moylinny in Co. Antrim in the late 7th century (Arthurs 1956(a), 24). *Baile Mhic Con Choille* could be metathesized to give Ballyvicknacally. However the vowel in *coill-* is unlikely to have given *a*, and this family had no particular connection with Dromore or Co. Down.

Coolsallagh   *Cúil Saileach*
J 1754   "recess of willow"

1.	Ballykowsillagh, Ballygarrimarckes	CPR Jas I 395b	1609
2.	Ballycowlsillagh	Inq. Ult. (Down) 22	1612
3.	Ballycowlsillagh, Ballygarrymarkes	CPR Jas I 235a	1612
4.	Ballycowlesillagh, Ballygarrymerkes	Inq. Ult. (Down) §13 Car. I	1629
5.	Cowlesillagh & Garremarkes	Inq. Ult. (Down) §85 Car. I	1639
6.	Culsillagh, Ptk Moder McConwall of		
		Wars Co. Down x 81	1641
7.	Coolesillagh & Garrimarky	Hib. Reg. Lr. Iveagh	1657c
8.	Cowgillaghe	Census 78	1659c
9.	Coolesillagh & Garmarky	BSD 69	1661
10.	Coolisilagh	Sub. Roll Down 273	1663
11.	Coolesillagh & Garmarky	ASE 112a 34	1667
12.	Coolesillagh & Garimarkie	Hib. Del. Down	1672c
13.	Coolesellogh, Garramarky	Rent Roll Down 7	1692
14.	Culsallagh	Wm. Map (OSNB) E125	1810
15.	Cúl Salach "dirty corner or angle"	J O'D (OSNB) E125	1834c
16.	Cul Selleach (?saileach) "corner willows"	J O'D (OSNB) E125	1834c
17.	Cúil Saileach "corner of willow trees"		
		Mooney 99	1950c
18.	ˌkul'sɔləx	Local pronunciation	1991
19.	ˌku'sala	Local pronunciation	1991

Coolsallagh, in the west of the parish and divided by the Lagan, belonged originally to Sir Art Magennis. For most of the 17th century (forms 1,3–5, 9, 11, 13) it was listed next to

Garrymarkes, now lost, which is shown beside it on Petty's maps (7, 12). The early forms all prefix *Bally*, as often happens in documents. The final *-l* of *cúil* "a corner" is not always pronounced, presumably as *l* may be lost before another consonant in English, such as northern English *fause* for *false*, but is attested in most of the forms. Mooney has examples of lost *l* in place-names such as **Aughnamoira** from *Achadh na Maolrátha* (*PNI* i 57), or the family name McStay from *Ó Maoilsté(ighe)* (Mooney 1952-3(d), 57), as in Carrickmacstay (*PNI* i 69).

The second element now looks like that of **Ballysallagh** above, but the early forms spell the first syllable with an *i* not an *a*. The spelling *-sillagh* probably represents the raising/fronting of the vowel before Gaelic palatal [l'] as in *saileach* "of willow", which makes the broad *l* of *salach* unlikely, and there are no *sh* spellings to suggest a slender *s* as in *sealbhach*. Presumably the willows grew beside the Lagan which flows through the townland. *Garrimarkes*, possibly *Garraí Marcais* "Marcus' enclosure", may have been the part of Coolsallagh south of the Lagan. In later times the townland contained the Earl of Clanwilliam's residence of **Gill Hall**.

Drumaghadone	*Dromnach an Damháin* (?)	
J 2050	"ridge of the young stag/ox; kidney-shaped ridge "	

1. Ballydromaughadowan	CPR Jas I 395b	1609
2. Ballydromnaghadowan	CPR Jas I 190b	1611
3. Ballidromnaghadowan	CPR Jas I 266a	1614
4. Ballydromnaghadowan	Inq. Ult. (Down) §4 Jac. I	1614
5. Ballydromnahadowan	CPR Jas I 309a	1616
6. Drumnaghadowan	Buckworth (EA) 310	1622
7. Dromaghodowam	Hib. Reg. Lr. Iveagh	1657c
8. Drumna Iadowan	Census 78	1659c
9. Dromaghodowan	BSD 68	1661
10. Drumaghdowen	Sub. Roll Down 274	1663
11. Drumaghoclowan	Hib. Del. Down	1672c
12. Drumaghadine	Wm. Map (OSNB) E125	1810
13. Dromaghadone	Bnd. Sur. (OSNB) E125	1830c
14. Dromach a'dúna "back or rising ridge of the fort"	J O'D (OSNB) E125	1834c
15. Drom(n)ach a'dóin "ridge of the fort"	Mooney 101	1950c
16. ˌdrǫmaxǝ'doːn	Local pronunciation	1991
17. ˌdrǫmǝ'doːn	Local pronunciation	1991

Drumaghadone was bishop land until 1868, and according to Dean Mooney contained the remains of a castle, a tower anciently resided in by the bishops, and two forts (15). Three forts are shown on 1:10,000 sheet 202, but only "enclosures" are mentioned by the Archaeological Survey (*NISMR* sh.28 sites 3,7,8).

The townland is all on a ridge south of the Big Bog. Ignoring the early 17th-century addition of *baile*, the first element is probably a derivative of *droim* "a ridge" such as *drom(n)ach* (forms 2-5). The early 17th-century spellings have *dromnagh*, those later *dromagh* or *drumagh*. There are ancient fortifications in the townland, and *dún* "a (hill)-fort" has been suggested for the second element, but it seems unlikely that this should be spelt in English as *dowan*. Williamson's form ending in *-dine* (12) might suggest *daingean*, but it is an isolated instance, and late. It is possible that the final syllable, which now bears the stress, could be the adjective *domhain* "deep" qualifying a noun represented by the syllable spelt *agh*. The name could have been *Droim (an) Átha Domhain* "ridge of (the) deep ford", but the ford would have to be through the Big Bog since there are no streams in the townland. No modern road crosses the bog, but a lane heads into it at the west end of Drumaghadone, possibly to meet another on the north side of the bog south-east of Barronstown Hall (1:10,000 sheet 202, J 198504). However such a minor feature is unlikely to have been the origin of the townland name.

The diminutive *damhán* can mean "little ox" or "little stag", but also "spider", which has an alternative spelling *dubhán* (*Dinneen*). There was confusion in sound between the two words which could have resulted in the spelling *-dowan* here. *Dubhán* now spelled *duán* can also mean "hook" or "kidney" (*Ó Dónaill*). There was an early church called *Droim Dubháin* (*Fél. Óeng* 110). The noun is based on the adjective *dubh* "black" and could refer to other black things such as soil. The Irish form could have several different translations.

Drumaknockan
J 2553

Dromainn an Chnocáin
"ridge of the little hill"

1. Ballydromeneknockan (in Kilwarlin)	Fiants Eliz. §4650	1585
2. Ballydromenknockan in Kilwarlin	CPR Jas I 396a	1609
3. Ballydromeneknockan (in Kilwarlin)	CPR Jas I 181b	1610
4. Drumenknockan al. Ballydrumeneknockan	Inq. Ult. (Down) §31 Car. I	1632
5. Ballydromenecnakan	Inq. Ult. (Down) §60 Car. I	1635
6. Drumnaknockan	Census 78	1659c
7. Dromneknockan (manor of Hillsborough)	CSP Ire. 1660-2 p459	1661
8. Droneknockan	BSD 70	1661
9. Drumineknockan	Hib. Del. Down	1672c
10. Dronekouckan	S & D Ann. (Mooney) 101 (70)	1690c
11. Drumnenocken	Wm. Map (OSNB) E125	1810
12. Drumnaknockan	J O'D (OSNB) E125	1834c
13. Druim na gcnocán "ridge of the hillocks"	J O'D (OSNB) E125	1834c
14. Druimeann a'Chnocáin	Mooney 101	1950c
15. ˌdrọməˈnɔkən	Local pronunciation	1991
16. ˌdrəməˈnakən	Local pronunciation	1991

Drumaknockan is a hilly townland in Kilwarlin in the north-east of the parish. Spellings before 1630 indicate that the first element is the derivative *dromainn* "ridge, mound", from *droim* "ridge". The second element is the genitive of *cnocán* i.e. *cnoc* "hill" with the diminutive -*án* ending. The early anglicized form (1, 3, 4 alias, 5) would have been pronounced [ˌdrɔmənəˈnɔkən], and the first [ən] syllable, i.e. the -*ainn* ending of *Dromainn*, has been later dropped by haplology.

| **Drumbroneth** | | *Droim Bróncha* | |
| J 2051 | | "(St) Brónach's ridge" | |

1.	Balydrombroneth	CPR Jas I 395b	1609
2.	Ballydrombroneth	CPR Jas I 190b	1611
3.	Ballidrombroneth	CPR Jas I 266a	1614
4.	Ballydrombroneth	Inq. Ult. (Down) §4 Jac. I	1614
5.	Ballydrombroneth	CPR Jas I 309a	1616
6.	Drumbroneth	Buckworth (EA) 310	1622
7.	Drumfony	Hib. Reg. Lr. Iveagh	1657c
8.	Drumfrony	BSD 68	1661
9.	Drumfrony	DS (Mooney) 101	1661?
10.	Drumbrony	Sub. Roll Down 274	1663
11.	Drumforny	Hib. Del. Down	1672c
12.	Drumbrony	Harris Hist. map	1743
13.	Drumbrony	Wm. Map (OSNB) E125	1810
14.	Drumbrony	Bnd. Sur. (OSNB) E125	1830c
15.	Drumbroneth is the usual	OSNB Pron. E125	1834c
16.	Drumbroneth	J O'D (OSNB) E125	1834c
17.	Druim Bronaighe "Bronach's ridge"		
		J O'D (OSNB) E125	1834c
18.	Druim Bronthacht "exposed bare ridge" (<fornocht)		
		Mooney 101	1950c
19.	ˌdrəmˈbroːnəθ	Local pronunciation	1991

Drumbroneth was church land until 1868. *Droim* "a ridge" seems to be the first element. All the spellings from the early 17th century end in -*th*, but the two English sounds spelt *th* ([θ] or [ð]) did not exist in the Irish of the period. Particularly in lists of church lands, *th* may be used in alternation with *gh* to spell [x], as with the lost name *Tollegillegawneth* in **Annaclone**, representing *Tulaigh Ghiolla na nGamhnach* "hillock of the cowherd", and **Fedany** and **Killaney** in Garvaghy, **Drumneth** in Magherally.

Dean Mooney suggested that the second element might represent *fornocht* "very bare", with the [f] nasalized to [v] by *droim*, an old neuter, and *Droim bhFornocht* metathesized to *Droim bhFronocht* in pronunciation (form 18). An identically-formed place-name *Druimfornact* does appear in the *Newry Charter* of 1157, later spelled *Drumfronett*, but now called **Croreagh** (*PNI* i 18, which quotes a third similarly-formed name, *AFM* i 320). The spellings of the Newry name illustrate the change *for* to *fro*, though not *f->v->b*.

Another possibility might be *Droim Brónach* "sorrowful ridge", but even more likely is *Droim Bróncha* "St Brónach's ridge", referring to the patron saint of **Kilbroney** (*PNI* i 132–5). *Bróncha* pronounced ['broːnəxə] is the earliest genitive of *Brónach*, attested in *Kylbronca* in the 15th century (*PNI* i 133, form 13) and the form *Cill Broncha* given by the

OSNB informant ((*PNI* i 134, form 52). Possibly there was a chapel dedicated to the saint on the road into Dromore. The later spellings *Drumfrony, Drumbrony* would represent *Droim B(h)rónaí*, formed with the other genitive of Brónach (earlier *Brónaighe*) like modern Kilbroney, *Cill Bhrónaí*.

Drumbroneth stretches south from the river Lagan within the town of Dromore, opposite Dromore motte, as far as the Big Bog. The road runs south up a hill and forks just below the summit, with more rising ground beyond. The left-hand fork goes to the **Diamond**, while on the right is the terrace of houses called the **Cockcrow Knowe**, often used locally instead of the townland name.

Drumlough	*Dromlach*	
J 2655	"ridgy place, ridge"	
1. Ballidromelaghe (in Kilwarlin)	Fiants Eliz. §4650	1585
2. Ballydromelagh in Kilwarlin	CPR Jas I 396a	1609
3. Drumlagh al. Ballydrumlagh	Inq. Ult. (Down) §31 Car. I	1632
4. Ballydrommellagh	Inq. Ult. (Down) §60 Car. I	1635
5. Drumlogh	Inq. Ult. (Down) §95 Car. I	1640
6. Drumlagh	Census 78	1659c
7. Drumlagh & Edentrillick	BSD 71	1661
8. Drumlough	Reg. Deeds abstracts iii §63	1781
9. Drumlogh	Reg. Deeds abstracts iii §63	1781
10. Drumloch	Civ. & Ecc. Top. (OSNB) E125	1806
11. Drumlough	Wm. Map (OSNB) E125	1810
12. ['Drumlogh / Drum-'lough]	OSNB Pron. E125	1834c
13. Druim a'locha "ridge/hill of the lough"	J O'D (OSNB) E125	1834c
14. 'drɔmlɔx	Local pronunciation	1991

Drumlough in the far north-east of the parish was part of Kilwarlin. From the written forms it could be *Droim an Locha* "ridge of the lake", as suggested by John O'Donovan, and a Drumlough Moss is shown in the townland on the 1:10,000 map. Drumlough Bog was the largest in the parish in 1834–7 (*OSM* xii 70b, 73b). However Mrs McVeigh distinguished the pronunciation of this townland ['drɔmlɔx] from **Drumlough** [drɔm'lɔx] in Drumgath, near Rathfriland (*PNI* i 122). Since the modern pronunciation always has the stress on the first syllable, and there is no record of an actual lake in the townland, it is more likely that this is one word, a collective noun *dromlach* meaning "ridgy place, ridge" (*Ó Dónaill*).

Drummiller	*Droim Iolair*	
J 2352	"eagle's ridge"	
1. Ballydromiller	CPR Jas I 395b	1609
2. Ballydromiller	CPR Jas I 190b	1611
3. Ballidromiller	CPR Jas I 266a	1614
4. Ballydromiller	Inq. Ult. (Down) §4 Jac. I	1614
5. Ballydromiller	CPR Jas I 309a	1616

6. Dromiller	Buckworth (EA) 310	1622
7. Drumiller	Hib. Reg. Lr. Iveagh	1657c
8. Dromiller	Census 78	1659c
9. Drumiller	BSD 67	1661
10. Drummeller	Rent Roll Down 8	1692
11. Drummiller	Wm. Map (OSNB) E125	1810
12. "miller's ridge"	J O'D (OSNB) E125	1834c
13. Druim Muilleóir/-ora "miller's ridge"	Mooney 103	1950c
14. drə'mīlər	Local pronunciation	1991

Drummiller was church land, situated south-east of Dromore town beside the river Lagan. The river runs through the middle of the townland, but there is a ford of stepping-stones just south of Drummiller House. The three townlands called **Drummiller** in Iveagh (Donaghmore, Aghaderg/Tullylish, and the present one) are the only examples in Ireland. If there was a water-mill on the river, *Droim Muilleora* "miller's ridge" seems as likely a meaning as the alternative *Droim Iolair* "eagle's ridge". However, one might expect the original *u* vowel of *muilleoir* to appear in the earlier anglicized spellings, as happens with names containing *muileann* "mill", and there is no evidence for a final vowel (*PNI* i 100–101). Local information and the OS 1:10,000 map sheet show that part of this townland is still "wild and rocky" in the west near Lagan Green, and there is an isolated ridge in the south between Lough Moss and the Black Bog.

Drumskee *Droim Sceiche*
J 1552 "ridge of the thornbush"

1. Ballydruminskie	CPR Jas I 395b	1609
2. Ballydrominiskie	CPR Jas I 235a	1612
3. Balledromeniske	Inq. Ult. (Down) §13 Car. I	1629
4. Dromsky 60a	Inq. Ult. (Down) §85 Car. I	1639
5. Dronskyagh	Inq. Ult. (Down) §85 Car. I	1639
6. Drumskea	Hib. Reg. Lr. Iveagh	1657c
7. Drumskea (Drummore parish, Verner)	Census 78	1659c
8. Drumskee (Dromoore parish)	BSD 70	1661
9. Drumskey half-td 128a (Verner)	ASE 123 a 37	1667
10. (?)Drumniskeagh, halfe Town	Land Rent Roll Down 4	1692
11. Drumsky 1/2 town	Rent Roll Down 8	1692
12. Dromskee	Reg. Deeds abstracts i §466	1732
13. Drumskee	Wm. Map (OSNB) E125	1810
14. Druim Sceiche "hill of the thorn"	J O'D (OSNB) E125	1834c
15. Druim-sceithe "of the whitethorn bush"	Joyce iii 337	1913
16. ˌdrọm'ski:	Local pronunciation	1992

Drumskee is the most westerly townland in Dromore parish, bounded on the north-west by the Lagan. It was held in 1609 by Sir Art Magennis. Drumskee House is on a ridge with bog to the east. A stream which once supported a mill flows from the Big Bog, through the townland and into the Lagan, forming the townland boundary for short parts of its course. The early forms (1–3) suggest that the name could once have been *Droim an Uisce* "ridge of the water", but by 1639 the shorter spellings *Dromsky* and *Dronskyagh* (4, 5, both listed with Lisnaward, Sir Art's next townland to the south) indicate the modern stress on the final syllable. This makes it likely that the final element was then the genitive of *sceach* "thornbush". If this was the case in the early 17th century the first element seems to have been *dromainn* "ridge" (forms 1–3) as with **Drumaknockan** above, and later simply *droim*.

After 1659 *Drumskea* was owned by John Verner, but the forms could be easily confused with an alias name and division, called *Ballydromneskie* in 1611, of **Ballydugan** townland in Tullylish, which passed via George Rawden to Daniel Monroe (*ASE* 61b, 92a). (Although the parishes of Tullylish and Dromore are in different halves of Lower Iveagh, this distinction is not mentioned in the 17th-century sources). Like the Dromore townland, this seems to have been *Droim na Sceiche* "ridge of the thorn-bush".

Edenordinary   *Éadan Ordoire*
J 1750   "hill-face of the great oakwood"

1. Balliderryvickaniskie al. Edenorderie	CPR Jas I 395a	1609
2. Ballidirrinvickinuskie al. Edenorderrie	CPR Jas I 235b	1612
3. Ballyderryvicknuskie al. Roddenerdery	Inq. Ult. (Down) §13 Car. I	1629
4. Ballyderrevick Commusky al. Edenorderry	Inq. Ult. (Down) §85 Car. I	1639
5. Edenordry, Phelim Magennis of	Wars Co. Down x 81	1641
6. DerimcCumisky	Hib. Reg. Lr. Iveagh	1657c
7. Edenardry	Census 78	1659c
8. Edenordery al. Derimc vinsky	BSD 70	1661
9. Edenoedeinn	Sub. Roll Down 273	1663
10. Derrymackinnisky al. Edenordery	ASE 82b §40	1666
11. Edenordinary 77a, Derrincumskey 96a	ASE 112a 34	1667
12. DeremcCumisky	Hib. Del. Down	1672c
13. Derrynmackminisky als Edenderry	Rent Roll Down 4	1692
14. Edenordmurry, Derrynemeasky	Rent Roll Down 8	1692
15. Edennorderry als Derrynomisky	Rent Roll Down 10	1692
16. Ednarory	Ir. Wills Index 68	1739
17. Ednaordenery	Ir. Wills Index 97	1742
18. Ednorney	Ir. Wills Index 62	1748
19. Edenorny	Ir. Wills Index 97	1755
20. Edenornary	Map of Down (OSNB) E125	1755
21. Edenornery	Ir. Wills Index 70	1773
22. Edenarrary	Ir. Wills Index 96	1795
23. Edenordinary	Ir. Wills Index 96	1802
24. Edenirrary	Ir. Wills Index 71	1806

25. Edenordinary[?]	Wm. Map (OSNB) E125	1810
26. Edenornary	Ir. Wills Index 67	1818
27. Edonorury, Rury commonly	Custom of County (OSNB) E125	1834c
28. Edenorny	Ir. Wills Index 51	1846
29. Éadan Rudhraighe "Rury's brae or brow/front of a hill"	J O'D (OSNB) E125	1834c
30. Eadan Rudraighe "Collis Rudricii"	J O'D (OSNB) E125	1834c
31. Eadan Odhar (n)Doire "(pale) grey hill-brow of the oakwood"	Mooney 103	1950c
32. ˈidənˈɔrdnərï	Local pronunciation	1991

Edenordinary was part of the old Magennis district of Lequirin, held from Sir Art Magennis in 1609. *Derrymackinnisky*, the alias or contiguous name in early sources, is clearly *Doire Mhic Con Uisce* "the oakwood of Mac Con Uisce", literally "the son of the water-hound". This is a Monaghan surname frequently understood as *Mac an Uisce* "son of the water", and anglicized as Waters (Woulfe 1923, 343). Thomas *McAnuskye* was pardoned in Co. Down in 1620 (*CPR Jas I* 474b).

The current name is not so simple. The *n* in *ordinary* does not appear before 1667 (form 11), was often omitted in local spellings, and may be discounted as an attempt to make the form closer to an English word. "Eden" in place-names is usually *éadan* "(hill-)face", and the final element *dary* is probably *doire* "oakwood". It is most likely that the middle element formed a compound with *doire*, and therefore bore the stress, otherwise one would expect the usual anglicization *derry* to be more clearly preserved. The most plausible form, *ard-doire* "high wood" is not supported by the spellings, which all have *o* in this syllable. Confusion of the prefixes *or* "front" (leniting) with *for* originally "on", now "over-, super-, great" might give a form *(f)ordoire* (cf. *fordoras* "lintel") or *(f)ordhoire* "great oak-wood". A form without *f-* and with unlenited *d* would be very close to *-orderrie* in the early anglicized spellings. Mooney's suggestion *Éadan Odhardhoire* (31), "hill-brow of the dun oak-wood", might have been anglicized *Edenorgarry*. A place in Tyrone called *Doire Odhar* was mentioned by Joyce (ii 285), but not the compound form suggested here. The short form *Rury* c. 1834 (27) may refer to **Edentiroory**, one townland away to the south.

Edentiroory
J 1551

Éadan Tí Rúraí
"hill-face of Rory's house"

1. Ballyedentirorie al. Ballydullaghan in Leighquirin	CPR Jas I 395a	1609
2. Ballyedentyrory al. Ballydullaghan	CPR Jas I 190b	1611
3. Ballyedenterory al. Ballydallaghan	Inq. Ult. (Down) §13 Car. I	1629
4. Edentorory	Hib. Reg. Lr. Iveagh	1657c
5. Edentorory	BSD 69	1666
6. Edentorory	ASE 123a 37	1667
7. Edentorory	Hib. Del. Down	1672c
8. Edentory	Hib. Del. Ulster	1672c
9. Edentory	Lamb Maps Co. Downe	1690c
10. Edentowny	Rent Roll Down 8	1692

11. Edenterory	Reg. Deeds abstracts i §446	1732
12. Edinorory[?]	Wm. Map (OSNB) E125	1810
13. Edentarury	Bnd. Sur. (OSNB) E125	1830c
14. Edenterury	OSNB E125	1834c
15. Éadan Tighe Rudraige "Brae of the house of Rury"	J O'D (OSNB) E125	1834c
16. Collis domus Rudricii "Rury"	J O'D (OSNB) E125	1834c
17. Éadan Tigh Ruaidhri "Hill brow of Rory's house"	Mooney 105	1950c
18. ˌidəntəˈruːrï	Local pronunciation	1992
19. ˈruːrï ˈhəl	Local pronunciation	1992

Edentiroory is in the western part of Dromore and part of Lequirin, so there is no territorial connection with the MacRory Magennises of Kilwarlin. However the personal name Rury or Rory seems definitely part of the name and, despite the Oroory Hill and Road so-named on road signs and shown on the OS 1:10,000 map, "Roory Hill" is the local abbreviation (19). The usual Gaelic origin of Rory is *Ruairí*, earlier *Ruaidhrí* "great king" (17), but the Magennis genealogies use *Rughraidhe*, which can be modernized as *Rúraí* (*TCD Gens* §262). *Rud(h)raig(h)e* (15), which may have been originally a tribal name, appears in the Ulster genealogies (*CGH* 156a 55n; *Descendants Ir* xiii 320, xiv 50,52,60) as the name of the grandfather of King Conchobhar mac Neasa of the Ulster Cycle, considered as the common ancestor of the tribes of Dál nAraide, Uí Echach and Conaille, which were later known as *Clanna Rudhraighe*, "Rúraí's offspring" (*Top. Poems* 1.666; *Céitinn* ii 98, 258; *TCD Gens* §§277, 280). In Iveagh *Rúraí* appears to have been deliberately preferred to *Ruairí* (cf. Ó Corráin and Maguire 1981, 158). The name Edentiroory can be included with other place-names in Iveagh which seem intended to bring to mind the heroes of the Ulster Cycle in early Irish literature (see **Brickland**, Aghaderg).

The alias name *Ballydullaghan* used in the early 17th century probably incorporates the family name Ó Dúlacháin, earlier Ó Dubhlacháin, which according to MacLysaght (1985, 92) was "An Oriel name mainly found in Co. Louth". *Méig Dhúileacháin* were attested in north Co. Down in the district called **Clanbrassil MacGoolechan** (*Top. Poems* 1.403; *Desc. Ire. 1598* 6n). The surname *Magullaghan*, probably from *Mac Dhúlacháin*, was listed in Ballynagross, Annaclone parish, in 1641 (*Wars Co. Down* 77), and an Owen *O'Dollehan* lived in˙Grallaghgreenan, Drumballyroney in 1663 (*Sub. Roll Down* 277). The surname is now Doloughan locally.

Edentrillick
J 2455

Éadan Trilic
"hill-face of the dolmen"

1. Balliedentrillicke Ballylickreyleyn (in Kilwarlin)	Fiants Eliz. §4650	1585
2. Ballyedentrillicke Ballylikreylen in Kilwarlin	CPR Jas I 396a	1609
3. Ballyedentrillicke Ballilikreilen (in Kilwarlin)	CPR Jas I 181b	1610
4. Edentrillick al. Ballyedenericke 80a	Inq. Ult. (Down) §31 Car. I	1632
5. Leclerim (Ptk Oge McEnereny)	Inq. Ult. (Down) §67 Car. I	1634c

6. Ballydentrillick, Ballylybrenan	Inq. Ult. (Down) §60 Car. I	1635
7. one fifth... Edentrillick	Inq. Ult. (Down) §95 Car. I	1640
8. Edentrillick	Census 78	1659c
9. Edentrilicke al. Letlerim al. Copponagh (manor of Hillsborough)	CSP Ire. 1660-2 p459	1661
10. Edentrillick	BSD 70	1661
11. Edentrillick (Drumlagh &)	BSD 71	1661
12. Lecleran Collenmaxhill	Hib. Del. Down	1672c
13. Leclearyn Edentrillick	S & D Ann. (Mooney) 105 (f.19)	1690c
14. Edentrillick al. Lisclerin	Deeds & Wills (Mooney) 106	1711
15. Edintrillick	Reg. Deeds abstracts i §373	1726
16. Edentrillic	Wm. Map (OSNB) E125	1810
17. Edentrillick al. Leclern	Mooney MS 106	1811
18. Eadan trí liag "brae of the three stones" collis trium lapidum	J O'D (OSNB) E125	1834c
19. Éadan Trilic	GÉ 101	1989
20. ˌidən'trələk	Local pronunciation	1991

Edentrillick between Drumaknockan and Backnamullagh was part of Kilwarlin, as was the lost unit called *Ballylickreyleyn* listed next to it from 1585-1610 AD (1–3). Edentrillick's present figure-of-eight shape seems likely to include another lost unit called *Leclerin*, which was shown in this position on the 1640 *Map of Kilwarlin*. However earlier forms of this name indicate that a half-townland or sessiagh so-called was held by Sir Art Magennis alongside his *Moylagh* from 1609 to 1629 (**Backnamullagh** forms 3, 7, 9, 12). If, by metathesis of *r* and *l*, *(Bally)lickreyleyn* is the the same name as *Lecleryn* etc., we may have another example of boundary lands being disputed between Sir Art and the Kilwarlin Magennises (see **Backnamullagh**).

The first element of Edentrillick, which contains a hill of 570 feet, is the common *éadan* "face/brow (of a hill)". The second element is an archaeological term, an early compound of the numeral *tri* "three" and *lia(c)* "a standing stone", with the stress on the first syllable. *Trilic* occurs in other place-names such as **Trillick** in Co. Tyrone, referred to in the Annals of Ulster in AD 814 and in the martyrologies of Gorman and Donegal (*AU; Mart. Gorm; Mart. Don.*). The word seems to mean "portal tomb" or "dolmen", a megalithic burial chamber formed of large upright stones supporting a capstone (Mallory and McNeill 1991, 63). Unfortunately the Archaeological Survey of Co. Down has no record of a megalith in this townland. The name on Petty's map of Co. Down, *Collenmaxhill* (12), seems to be a corruption of an owner's name, since "Col. Maxwell" appears on the 1640 *Map of Kilwarlin*.

Ednego	*Éadan an Ghabhann*
J 1948	"hill-face of the smith"

1. Ballyedenegan	CPR Jas I 395b	1609
2. Ballyedenegan	CPR Jas I 190b	1611
3. Ballyedenagone	CPR Jas I 266a	1614
4. Ballyednegon	CPR Jas I 309a	1616
5. Ballyednegon	Buckworth (EA) 310	1622
6. Edendegon	Hib. Reg. Lr. Iveagh	1657c

7. E Anigon	Census 78	1659c
8. Edendegan	BSD 69	1661
9. Edenclegon	Hib. Del. Down	1672c
10. Ednegone	Reg. Deeds abstracts i §387	1727
11. Ednegone	Wm. Map (OSNB) E125	1810
12. Ednego	Bnd. Sur. (OSNB) E125	1830c
13. Eadan a'ghabhann "the smith's brae or brow of a hill"	J O'D (OSNB) E125	1834c
14. Eadan Uí Ghobhann "O'Gowan's hill-face"	Mooney 103	1950c
15. 'ɛdnïgo	Local pronunciation	1991

Ednego was a church townland until 1868. In 1609 and 1611 it was listed next to *Ballyvickegowan,* now **Magherabeg,** which clearly contained the surname *Mac an Ghabhann* "son of the smith". The surname *Ó Gabhann* also existed in Co. Down, and either it or the noun "smith" appears in **Ballygowan** townlands in Aghaderg, Moira, and Saintfield parishes. The final element in this name is not so clear, but there is a final *-n* in the forms until the 19th century, which could represent the n-stem ending of *gabha* "a smith" in the genitive case, while the modern final *-o* could reflect a later stage when *gabha* had become indeclinable. The townland name is now stressed on the first syllable in local pronunciation, although the original stress would have been on the last syllable, representing the element *Gabhann.* The final *-n* could have been lost after the stress shifted to the first syllable of Ednego. The shift of stress may have been caused by hybrid names like Ednego Close in the townland, where the stress in English falls on the second word. Ednego Close was explained to me as an old cluster village inhabited by Scottish settlers, now almost gone.

Greenan
J 1652

Grianán
"eminent place"

1. Ballyegrenan in Leighquirin	CPR Jas I 395a	1609
2. Ballygrenan, Brian McD McBrian Magenis of	CPR Jas I 195b	1610
3. Ballegrenan (in Leighquirrin)	CPR Jas I 190b	1611
4. Ballygrenan	Inq. Ult. (Down) §13 Car. I	1629
5. Grenan, Fergus Magennis of	Wars Co. Down x 80	1641
6. Greenan, Fergus Magennis of	Wars Co. Down x 81	1641
7. Greenan	Hib. Reg. Lr. Iveagh	1657c
8. Grenan	Census 78	1659c
9. Grenan	BSD 69	1661
10. half Greenan	BSD 71	1661
11. Greenans	Sub. Roll Down 273	1663
12. Greenan	ASE 112a 34	1667
13. Upper Greenan (part)	ASE 123a 37	1667
14. Grenan	Hib. Del. Down	1672c
15. Greenan	Rent Roll Down 7	1692
16. Uppergrenan, part of ½ town	Rent Roll Down 8	1692
17. Greenan	Wm. Map (OSNB) E125	1810

18. Grianán "a solarium/palace on a hill; splendid place"	J O'D (OSNB) E125	1834c
19. 'grinən	Local pronunciation	1991

Grianán is a well known place-name term for a sunny hill-face or top, possibly with a good view: an "eminent place" (Ó Maolfabhail, 1974). Greenan Hill in the north overlooking the river Lagan is probably the origin of the name, though the hill in the south, west of Greenan House, is higher (110 metres to 90 metres) and has a rath near the summit. In the north-east of the townland by a ford in the Lagan is a cairn and Dumb Fort, opposite Phil's Fort in Ballynaris. Goose Island in the Lagan does not seem to contain any antiquity.

This was the first unit in the part of Lequirin held by Brian McDonell McBrien Magennis from Sir Art Magennis, and Fergus Magennis of Greenan was cited as a rebel in 1641 (forms 5,6). There is some evidence for a subdivision of Upper Greenan in the late 17th century (forms 10,13,16).

Greenoge　　　　　　　　*Grianóg*
J 1856　　　　　　　　　　"eminent place"

1. Ballygrinnocke in Leighquirrin	CPR Jas I 395a	1609
2. Balligrinnock, Donell Oge Magenis of	CPR Jas I 195b	1610
3. Ballecrinock in Leighguyrrin	CPR Jas I 235b	1612
4. Ballyrinnock, D. Magenis of	CPR Jas I 235b	1612
5. Greneoge	CPR Jas I 373b	1618
6. Ballycrunocke	Inq. Ult. (Down) §13 Car. I	1629
7. Ballycreenoge	Inq. Ult. (Down) §85 Car. I	1639
8. Greeneoge	Hib. Reg. lr. Iveagh	1657c
9. Greenog	Census 78	1659c
10. Greeneoge	BSD 69	1661
11. Greneoge	ASE 112a 34	1667
12. Greneoge	Hib. Del. Down	1672c
13. Greneoge	Rent Roll Down 7	1692
14. Greenoge	Wm. Map (OSNB) E125	1810
15. Grianóg "a little sunny hill"	J O'D (OSNB) E125	1834c
16. gri'no:g	Local pronunciation	1991

Greenan and Greenoge townlands are only two and a half miles apart, and are both in the Magennis territory of Lequirin, so it is understandable that the names might be treated as a pair. Greenoge townland is hilly, with the summits surmounted by farms: Rosemount, Purdys Close and Sylvan Hill. The similar name Greenock on the Clyde in Scotland is in Scottish Gaelic *Grianaig*. Greenock and two other Scottish examples are described as "dative of *grianàg*, a sunny knoll, parallel to the masculine *grianàn* of the same meaning" (Watson 1926, 201). *Grianàn* "eminent place" seems to be based on the word for "sun" *grian*, but there is another word *grian* meaning "gravel" from which place-names could be derived. Additionally, although the spellings with initial *C-* (after *baile*) in three early 17th-century forms (3, 6, 7) suggest that the original forms of Greenan and Greenoge might not be so close, Hogan has no record of *cruinneog* "a round bundle" in place-names (*Onom. Goed.*). On balance it appears that the two related terms *Grianán* and *Grianóg* were used here simply to differentiate the townlands, and the desire to avoid confusion seems also the most likely reason why Greenoge is now stressed on the second syllable (16).

Growell　　　　　　　　　　　　　*Grothal*
J 2753　　　　　　　　　　　　　　　　"gravel"

1. Balligrombolke (in Kilwarlin)	Fiants Eliz. §4650	1585
2. Ballygrombou in Kilwarlin	CPR Jas I 396a	1609
3. Balligromvowe (in Kilwarlin)	CPR Jas I 181b	1611
4. Growlle al. Ballygranbowe al. Ballygrowlle	Inq. Ult. (Down) §31 Car. I	1632
5. Growle	Inq. Ult. (Down) §31 Car. I	1632
6. Balligrombowe	Inq. Ult. (Down) §60 Car. I	1635
7. Growle	Census 78	1659c
8. Growle (manor of Hillsborough)	CSP Ire. 1660–2 p459	1661
9. Growle	BSD 70	1661
10. Growell	Wm. Map (OSNB) E125	1810
11. Growle al. Growell	Mooney MS 108	1811
12. Grawl pronounced Grole	OSNB Pron. E125	1834c
13. pronounced today Grow-ell	Mooney 107	1950c
14. Grothal "gravel"	J O'D (OSNB) E125	1834c
15. Griothal, greitheal "coarse sand or gravel"	Mooney 107	1950c
16. Baile griain buidhe	Mooney 107	1950c
17. 'groəl	Local pronunciation	1991

Growell townland in the east of the parish was part of Kilwarlin. The present name only came into use after 1632, but it seems to be a version of a word meaning "gravel". There is a late borrowing from English, *graibél* (*DIL*), *graibhéal, gairbhéal* (*Ó Donaill*), and Joyce gave the form *gairbhéal* "pronounced *gravale*" as the name of a mountain in Wicklow (Joyce ii 375). There is also a native word beginning with palatalized *gr*: *griothal, greitheal, greifeal* (*Dinneen, Ó Donaill*). There is no evidence of palatalization in this townland name and any internal consonant in Irish has been lost. However, there is a Scottish Gaelic form *grothal* meaning "gravel" (*Dwelly*), so that the initial palatalized consonants of *griothal* may have changed to give *grothal* in east Ulster too, as suggested by John O'Donovan (form 14). Alternative possibilities are *grothal* or *glothar* "death-rattle" (*Dinneen, Ó Donaill*), although one would expect these to follow an element such as *baile* "town(land)".

Dean Mooney attempted to explain the forms pre-1632, when *Growlle* first appears, as based on *grian* also meaning "gravel" with a qualifying adjective "yellow" (16), but four of the five forms have *grom*, possibly a spelling for *droim* "ridge" (*droim bó* "ridge of (the) cow"). **Drumadoney** in Dromara has an alias *Ballegranendonny* in one Kilwarlin inquisition, where *gran* seems also to represent *droim* (*Inq. Ult. (Down)* §30 Car. I). Growel rises to 500 feet and slopes steeply into Lough Aghery to the south (*OSM* xii 70a).

Islandderry　　　　　　　　　　*Oileán an Doire*
J 1554　　　　　　　　　　　　　　"island of the oakwood"

1. Ballinderry (Lequirin)	CPR Jas I 394b	1609
2. Ballinderrie, Arte... Magenis of	CPR Jas I 193a	1611
3. Ballyenderry (5 towns, island, lough)		
	CPR Jas I 193a	1611
4. Iland-Derry	CPR Jas I 373b	1618
5. Ilanddery	Inq. Ult. (Down) §106 Car. I	1650c
6. Ilandery	Hib. Reg. Lr. Iveagh	1657c
7. Ilanderry	Census 78	1659c
8. Ilandery	BSD 69	1661
9. Islandeery	Sub. Roll Down 272	1663
10. Islandeine	Sub. Roll Down 273	1663
11. Island-Derry	ASE 174a 38	1668
12. Ilandery	Hib. Del. Down	1672c
13. Islanderry	Rent Roll Down 5	1692
14. Isle Derry	Harris Hist. map	1743
15. Island Derry, Waddel Esq.	Taylor & Skinner 285b	1777
16. Ilinderry	Ir. Wills Index 90	1789
17. Islandderry	Wm. Map (OSNB) E125	1810
18. Oileán a'Doire "Island of the oakwood" Insula roboreta	J O'D (OSNB) E125	1834c
20. "a clear dry spot in the midst of a woody swamp"	J O'D (OSNB) E125	1834c
21. ˌəilən'dɛrï	Local pronunciation	1992

Following the 1609 Schedule of Iveagh, King James granted in 1611: "to Arte Oge McGlasney Magenis, of *Ballinderrie*, gent., in Iveagh territory: The five towns of *Ballyenderry*, with the island and lough thereof" (2,3). This must be Islandderry, where Islandderry Lough still exists but has been reduced by drainage. The other names seem to be Lisnasure, Ballymacanally, Drumnaferry and Ballykeel townlands, all in the parish of Magheralin to the west. It appears that Islandderry was the chief portion of **Lequirin** (1), although by 1609 the district was divided between three Magennis holders.

Art Oge's father was Glasney (*Glaisne*) Magennis, who in 1608 was considered a potential rival to the chief (*BM Cat.* i 395n), and the 1611 grant confirmed Glasney as Lord of **Clanconnell**. However, in 1641 Arthur Oge McGlasney Magennis and two brothers from Clanconnell were named as rebels (*Wars Co. Down* 81a). By 1659 *Ilanderry* was held by "Alexr. Waddell, gent", and a Major Waddell held it at the time of the first Ordnance Survey.

A crannog is marked on Islandderry Lough on the 1:50,000 map, from a report that worked timbers were found on the site (*ASCD* 184), and the reference above suggests the island was a valued possession. John O'Donovan was apparently not thinking of the lough with its island or crannog in his additional note (form 20) on the Irish word *oileán* as "a clear dry spot in the midst of a woody swamp". In the early 19th century, however, both "island" and "derry" were used of patches of good land in boggy areas (Ó Mainnín 1989–90; *OSM* vi 4b Artrea). Nevertheless the original meaning of the Irish words suits best here. Islandderry House, "one of the great houses of this particular area", has now become a dairy labelled "Island Dairy", to the irritation of some local residents.

Killysorrell
J 1651

Coill Során
"wood of wire-worms"

1. Kilsaran	Hib. Reg. Lr. Iveagh	1657c
2. Kilfarran	Census 78	1659c
3. Killsaran	BSD 69	1661
4. Killsaran	ASE 82b 40	1666
5. Killsaran (part)	ASE 123a 37	1667
6. Kilsaran	Hib. Del. Down	1672c
7. Kilsarran (part)	ASE 112a 34	1679
8. (?)Killsoakan	Rent Roll Down 4	1692
9. Killsarran	Rent Roll Down 8	1692
10. Killsarum, part of 1/2 town	Rent Roll Down 8	1692
11. Kilsarran al. Kilsarrell	Deeds & Wills (Mooney) 112	1720
12. Killsarran al. Killsarell	Reg. Deeds abstracts i §466	1732
13. Killysorall	Wm. Map (OSNB) E125	1810
14. Kilsorrell	Bnd. Sur. (OSNB) E125	1830c
15. ['sarrell]	OSNB Pron. E125	1834c
16. Killysorrell	J O'D (OSNB) E125	1834c
17. Coill Uí Suarghaill "O'Sorrell's wood"	J O'D (OSNB) E125	1834c
18. Coill Suirn/Sairn "Wood of the kiln"	Mooney 112	1950c
19. Cill Saráin "Sarán, a man's name"	Mooney 111	1950c
20. ˌkəlïˈsɔrəl	Local pronunciation	1991
21. ˌkəlˈsɔrəl	Local pronunciation	1991

Killysorrell is on the western border of Dromore. All the forms are dated 1657 and later, and it is not known where this land unit fitted in the pre-plantation system, although the townlands round about were in Lequirin. There is no evidence before 1810 (13) for the second syllable of *killy*, although the current pronunciation sometimes contains it (20). The first element is no doubt *coill* or possibly *coillidh* "wood", as in the townland of **Quilly** which it borders. The form of the second element with final *-ll* seems to be 18th-century, all earlier spellings ending in varieties of *-saran*. Dean Mooney suggested *Coill Suirn* "wood of the kiln", which he thought would have an epenthetic vowel pronounced [ə] between the final *r* and *n* (form 18). This is unlikely. A kiln could refer to charcoal-burning when the area was still under wood, but would probably be anglicized *-surn*. Another possible second element is *során* "wire-worm", referring to pests in the soil.

A surname *Ó Sáráin* occurs in **Tullysaran** in Eglish near Armagh, and there is also a parish Kilsaran *Cill Sáráin* "Sárán's church" in Co Louth (*Liosta Log. Lú* 36). A man with the personal name Sárán and his son Mongán appear in the Uí Echach genealogy in the 6th century AD, but Byrne considers these two names or generations "superfluous" (*CGH* 161bd40; *Clann. Ollaman* genealogy facing p.56). Sárán mac Coilboth appears as an early king of east Ulster in the Dál nAraide genealogy (*CGH* 157.15) and in the Life of St Patrick (*Trip. Life (Stokes)* ii 349 (*Notulae*), i 164). Keating gave this Sárán as a brother of the Uí Echach ancestor Conall, and as the ancestor of the MacArtans (*Céitinn* iv 25,95). Several names in Sir Art Magennis' property seem to recall figures of historical legend (**Tirfergus, Rossconor**) and Killysorrell could also be *Coill Sáráin* "Sárán's wood".

| **Kinallen** | *An Cionn Álainn* | |
| J2549 | "the beautiful headland" | |

1. Ballinekenalen (in Kilwarlin)	Fiants Eliz. §4650	1585
2. Ballynellellenellen in Kilwarlin	CPR Jas I 396a	1609
3. Ballynekenalin in Tullyomy	CPR Jas I 396a	1609
4. Ballynekenalin in Tullyomie	CPR Jas I 235a	1612
5. Ballinkinnallen	Inq. Ult. (Down) §13 Car. I	1629
6. Kinallin	Hib. Reg. Lr. Iveagh	657c
7. Kinmmallin	Census 78	1659c
8. Kynallin	BSD 70	1661
9. Kinnalen	Sub. Roll Down 273	1663
10. Kinallin	ASE 112a 34	1667
11. Kinallin	Hib. Del. Down	1672c
12. Kinallin	Rent Roll Down 7	1692
13. Kinallin	Wm. Map (OSNB) E125	1810
14. Ceann Álainn "a beautiful head or hill"	J O'D (OSNB) E125	1834c
15. Cionn Álainn, An	GÉ 62	1989
16. kə'naln̦	Local pronunciation	1991

Kinallen was part of Kilwarlin, in the district of *Tullyomy*, and is also now the name of a village at a cross-roads within the townland. It is surrounded on three sides by the Lagan, described in 1834 as "Kinallen Hill in the south-east... about 628 feet above the sea, falling in the distance of a mile 316 feet into the river Lagan, by which its base is bounded" (*OSM* xii 70a). Ardtanagh Hill to the south (in Dromara) is higher, but there is little in the forms to suggest any other interpretation than the description of the hill suggested above. The steep slope is to the north, below Kinallen Hill Head.

The complimentary adjective *álainn* "beautiful" also occurs in Tullyallen parish in Louth where *Tulaigh Álainn* "beautiful hillock" was used by Omeath Irish speakers (*Liosta Log. Lú* 20,43). There are also townlands of Tullyallen in Cos Armagh, Monaghan and Tyrone. However **Moyallan** *Maigh Alúine* in Tullylish contains a different word, and neither is the same as the Hill of Allen in Kildare (*Almhu* gen. *Almhaine, Onom. Goed.* 29b).

| **Lappoges** | *Leapacha na bhFiann* | |
| J 2551 | "beds of the warrior bands" | |

1. (?)cath Lapaist in Carn Cantain	LL 41c/ i l.5813	1160c
2. Ballilappaghnevien (in Kilwarlin)	Fiants Eliz. §4650	1585
3. Ballylappaghnevien in Kilwarlin	CPR Jas I 396a	1609
4. Ballylappaghnyvien (in Kilwarlin)	CPR Jas I 181b	1610
5. Ballilappaghnevrien	Inq. Ult. (Down) §60 Car. I	1635
6. Loppairvian, Tullindeny al.	CSP Ire. 459	1661
7. Lappenevine	BSD 70	1661
8. Lappags	Deeds & Wills (Mooney) 113	1737

9. Lappags	Wm. Map (OSNB) E125	1810
10. Leapokes	Bnd. Sur. (OSNB) E125	1830c
11. Leapokes	OSM xii 72a	1834
12. Leapockes, proper name Drumadoney	OSNB E125	1834c
13. Lopanavian (ancient doc)	Clergyman (OSNB) E125	n.d.
14. Lepanavian "the beds of the Fians/ Fingalians" cromlechs so-called by the peasantry	J O'D (OSNB) E125	1834c
15. Lappoughs al. Lappoghs al. Lepanevian	Deeds & Wills (Mooney) 113	1836
16. Leappocks	Ir. Wills Index 17	1851
17. Leppocks	Ir. Wills Index 17	1851
18. Leapoga "little beds or ridges"	J O'D (OSNB) E125	1834c
19. Leapthacha + Eng. pl. s: popular name for dolmens	Mooney 113	1950c
20. 'li:poks	Local pronunciation	1991
21. 'li:pọgz	Local pronunciation	1991

Lappoges is in the east of the parish in Kilwarlin. The name was prefixed by *Baile-* in the early 17th century, and the modern name consists of what was then only the second element. Although the later spellings are very variable, the early forms such as *Ballylappaghnevien* (2) make the etymology *Leapacha na bhFiann* clear. The "beds of (Finn mac Cumhail's) warrior bands" are still there, in the form of a chambered long cairn which only partly survives to the present day (*ASCD* 75). This term, linking megalith and legend, is already referred to as a common popular name for monuments by Keating in the 17th century, similar to the tradition that Finn's betrothed bride Gráinne slept in chambered tombs with her lover Diarmaid as they fled from Finn around Ireland (*Céitinn* ii 348, 324). Despite the later abbreviation Mooney found the full form of the name still remembered in a deed in 1836 (form 15).

The English plural *-s* was added to the first element *Leapacha* apparently in the 18th century, giving the form we have today. The early spellings give the first vowel as *a* and indicate the fricative [x] at the end of the word with *gh*. A fricative is still suggested by the spelling *Leapoughs* insisted upon by my older informants, although they now pronounce it as a [k]. The first vowel seems to have been raised to [i] in the 19th century, giving the pronunciation [li:poks]. The spelling *Lepokes* was suggested by the boundary surveyor, and the received form was given as *Leapokes* (*OSNB* 1834c), eventually standardized to the older form Lappoges.

Hogan (*Onom. Goed.* 476a) suggested that a place called *Lapast* (form 1), site of a 9th-century battle between Ulaid and Uí Echach Cobha, might have been Lappoges, but, although the general area is plausible, the earlier forms of the name provide no support for his guess.

Lisnaward   *Lios Rátha an Bhaird*
J 1850   "enclosure of the poet's fort"

1. BallymcOwen (Bishop)	CPR Jas I 395b	1609
2. Lisnereward (Sir Art)	CPR Jas I 395b	1609

3. Levallylisnareward al. Ballyfeaghan, BallymcOwen (Bp)	CPR Jas I 190b	1611
4. Lisroreward (Sir Art)	CPR Jas I 235a	1612
5. BallymcOwen al. Leighvallyseaghan al. Leighvallytheaghan al. Lisrareward (Bp)	CPR Jas I 266a	1614
6. Ballymcowen al. Leighvallyseaghan (Bp)	CPR Jas I 309a	1616
7. Ballymac[ ] (Bp)	Inq. Ult. (Down) §4 Jac I	1616
8. Lissrareward, sess de (Sir Art)	Inq. Ult. (Down) §13 Car. I	1629
9. Lissrarevard, half vil' de, 60a	Inq. Ult. (Down) §85 Car. I	1639
10. Lissrareward	Inq. Ult. (Down) §85 Car. I	1639
11. Lissureward	Hib. Reg. Lr. Iveagh	1657c
12. Lisnereward	Census 78	1659c
13. Lyssureward	BSD 70	1661
14. Lisnarnard	ASE 82b 40	1666
15. Lisureward al. Lisnereward	ASE 213a 5	1669
16. Lisureward	Hib. Del. Down	1672c
17. Lissureward	ASE 112a 34	1679
18. Lissurewaird als Lissneereward	Rent Roll Down 4	1692
19. Lissnaroard	Rent Roll Down 4	1692
20. Lissureward	Rent Roll Down 8	1692
21. Lissareward al. Lissnereward	Deeds & Wills (Mooney) 114	1711
22. Lisnereward	Ir. Wills Index 7	1739
23. Lisnaward	Wm. Map (OSNB) E125	1810
24. Lisnaward	Bnd. Sur. (OSNB) E125	1830c
25. Lios na mbard "fort of the bards"	J O'D (OSNB) E125	1834c
26. Lios-na-mbard "fort of the bards"	Joyce iii 482	1913
27. Liosán a'Bhaird	Mooney 113-4	1950c
28. Lios Rátha a' Bhaird	Mooney 13	1950c
29. ˌlïsnə'wɔːrd	Local pronunciation	1991

The modern name Lisnaward seems to have been contracted in the late 18th century from *Lisnereward*, which belonged to Sir Arthur Magennis in 1609 (form 2), and was described as a half-townland in 1639 (form 9). The first element is clearly *lios* "fort/enclosure" and the last *bard* "poet", but there is doubt whether the poet element is genitive singular, *an Bhaird*, or plural, *na mBard*. Dean Mooney's suggestion in his manuscript (form 27) represents *Liosán an Bhaird* "the little enclosure of the bard", implying that *r* had replaced one of the *n*s in the early anglicized spellings (forms 2, 3). In a different part of the manuscript and in print he interpreted the name as *Lios Rátha an Bhaird* "enclosure of the poet's fort", comparing it with other examples of *lios rátha*: **Lisnabrague, Lisnatierny** in Aghaderg (form 28; Mooney 1956(a), 25). Joyce mentioned combinations of *lios, dún* and *ráth*: "either the first is used adjectivally... or it is a mere explanatory term used synonymously with the second... or such a name might originate in successive structures" (*Joyce* i 282). The development in the anglicized spelling therefore seems to have been from a hypothetical *Lisrahenward* to *Lisraneward* to *Lisnereward* (forms 2, 3) by metathesis of *r* and *n*, or to

Lisrareward (forms 4, 5) by assimilation of *n* to *r*. Neither form dominates, and *r* and *n* could also have been confused in writing. Eventually the name lost an internal syllable by haplology, to give Lisnaward.

One might suspect a connection with the poet family of *Mac an Bhaird* "son of the bard" who were settled on Magennis lands in Drumgooland (**Ballyward**), but there is no evidence for the surname here. Another place, the notable fort of **Listullyard** in Seapatrick parish, is now also sometimes called Lisnaward (Crowe 1969, 26; fieldwork).

Lisnaward, or part of it, is also mentioned among the church lands in the early 17th century, with an alias or division *Bally McOwen* (forms 3, 5, 6) "McKeown's townland". The two names occur separately in the 1609 schedule when William Worseley got *Ballymcowen* from the Bishop (1). The surname McOwen was mainly found in Munster, but there were McOwens among the *Slught Neills* in north Co. Down in 1605 (*CPR Jas I* 86b–87a). In 1428 a clergyman called Philip *McKewyn* was in charge of the tithes and rents of church lands in Garvaghy and Seapatrick parishes, and was called "learned in law" at a collation to Dromore in 1438 (*Reg. Swayne* 101, 177).

Another alias for the "half town of *Lisnareward*" is *Ballyfeaghan* (form 3), which recurs beginning not with *baile* "townland" but with *leathbhaile* "half townland" (forms 5, 6). The second element in these instances begins with *s* and *th* but may well represent *Féichín*, a personal name well known as a saint's name: "Féichín's townland". The church townland of **Killfeaghan** in Kilbroney was understood by a local Irish speaker in 1834 as *Cill Fiacháin* "Fiachán's church", and Fiachán could be an Ulster variant of Féichín (*PNI* i 144–6). There may once have been a church site here.

The latest reference to these alternative names is in 1616. Thus the townland may have originally been divided into two or three parts. It is now 416 acres and contains three raths, including an elevated one at Mitchell's Hill Head which overlooks a crannog on Toad Island, mentioned in 1834: "Lisnaward, partly a mill-dam and partly a swamp, should perhaps be considered as a lake... and has a large island near its southern extremity" (*OSM* xii 70b; *ASCD* 185). The mill-dam supplies Millfield and the swamp is now called the Big Bog (see **Drumaghadone**). The present *lios* name was presumably based on one of the surviving raths, but the boundaries of the other divisions are unknown.

Listullycurran
J 2055

Lios Tulaigh Uí Chorráin
"fort/enclosure of Ó Corráin's knoll"

1.	Ballitollochorran (in Kilwarlin)	Fiants Eliz. §4650	1585
2.	Ballychollochoran in Kilwarlin	CPR Jas I 396a	1609
3.	Ballichollacharan (in Kilwarlin)	CPR Jas I 181b	1610
4.	Ballytullowrorane	Inq. Ult. (Down) §22 Car. I	1631
5.	Ballytullocorreran	Inq. Ult. (Down) §31 Car. I	1632
6.	Ballichollothorane	Inq. Ult. (Down) §60 Car. I	1635
7.	Listollicarreran	Hib. Reg. Lr. Iveagh	1657c
8.	Listillicarran	Census 78	1659c
9.	Lissullicorrean	Par. Map (Mooney) 114	1660c
10.	Listully Corrane al. Listulley Correran (manor of Hillsborough)	CSP Ire. 1660-2 p459	1661
11.	Lussellicorrean	BSD 69	1661
12.	Listollicoriran	Hib. Del. Down	1672c
13.	Tully-corecan	Hib. Del. Down	1672c

14. Lissarrevareram als Listullycurrenan

	Rent Roll Down 4	1692
15. Listullycorran	Wm. Map (OSNB) E125	1810
16. Listullycorrane al. Correran al.		
Corran	Mooney MS 114	1811
17. Listullycurran	Bnd. Sur. (OSNB) E125	1830c
18. genl name Lisnacurran	Custom of County (OSNB) E125	1834c
19. Lios Tulaigh Corráin "Fort of		
Curran's hill"	J O'D (OSNB) E125	1834c
20. Lios Tulaighe Uí Chorraidhín	Mooney 113	1950c
21. ˌləstọli'kọrn̩	Local pronunciation	1991
22. ˌləsˌtọli'kɔrən	Local pronunciation	1991

Listullycurran on the northern border of the parish was part of Kilwarlin. The early 17th-century forms all have *baile* "settlement, townland" instead of *lios* "enclosure, fort". *Lios* is frequently used in the north for the circular enclosures called *ráth* elsewhere, but in some names it appears likely to have the general meaning "settlement" (cf **Tullymacarath**). There is no rath marked on the OS 1:10,000 map (sheet 183), but there is a farm called Fort Hill, after which a road has been named, which may preserve the memory of one.

The element *tully* (*tulach* "hillock") is in the modern form, so that the *c* of some earlier spellings can be explained simply as a misreading of handwritten *t*. The reverse has happened in form (6), and *r* has been misread as *c* in the final element in form (13). Most of the forms suit a derivation from the widespread Irish surname *Ó Corráin*, often anglicized Curran (19). Some forms show an extra syllable, as in 1632 -*correran* (5, 7, 12, 16). This may have developed from doubling of the *co-* syllable, which was misread as *ro-* in 1631 (form 4). However *Ó Corráin* is itself a variant of *Ó Corraidhín*, a form still used in the south of Ireland (Woulfe 1923, 481–2), and the palatal *dh* may be represented by the extra *r* here, since the sounds are very close in some Gaelic dialects (Donegal, Wester Ross: Quiggin 1906, 99). The same form of the surname seems to be preserved in the townland of **Ballygorian** in Clonduff (*PNI* iii 78), and there was a 17th-century *McCurrerane* in Co. Fermanagh (*CPR Jas I* 144a).

Lurganbane	*An Lorgain Bhán*
J 2252	"the white ridge"

1. Ballynalurgenbane	CPR Jas I 395b	1609
2. Ballynalurgenbane	CPR Jas I 190b	1611
3. Ballinelurganebane	CPR Jas I 266a	1614
4. Ballynalurgenbane	Inq. Ult. (Down) §4 Jac. I	1616
5. Ballynalurgenbane	CPR Jas I 309a	1616
6. Lurgenbane	Buckworth (EA) 310	1622
7. Lurgan-bane	Hib. Reg. Lr. Iveagh	1657c
8. Larganbane	Census 78	1659c
9. Lurganbane	BSD 67	1661
10. Lurganbane	BSD 68	1661
11. Lurgenbane	Sub. Roll Down 274	1663
12. Lurgenbane	Hib. Del. Down	1672c
13. Lurganban	Wm. Map (OSNB) E125	1810

14. Lurganban	Bnd. Sur. (OSNB) E125	1830c
15. -bawn	Custom of County (OSNB) E125	1834c
16. Lurganbane	J O'D (OSNB) E125	1834c
17. Leargan Bán "white hill side"	J O'D (OSNB) E125	1834c
18. Leargán bán "white hill"	Mooney 114	1950c
19. ˌlərgən'baːn	Local pronunciation	1991

Lurganbane lies east of Dromore town on a low ridge along the south bank of the Lagan. *Baile* is prefixed to the earlier forms, which in Irish would give *Baile na Lorgan Báine*, pronounced with a final vowel. This does not occur, but the long vowel of Irish *bán* "white" is preserved, as often happens, in the local pronunciation (19). From the Irish *Lorgain Bhán* one might expect the spelling to be *Lurganvane*, as *lorgain* is a feminine noun, but in some Irish place-names the lenition from [b] to [v] is not shown in the anglicized spelling (see **Corbally** in Garvaghy). Lurganbane was church land belonging to the Bishop of Dromore.

Magherabeg	*Machaire Beag*
J 1955	"small plain"

1. Ballyvickegowan cont. 2 towns viz. Ballyreogh al. Ballimagerybegg	CPR Jas I 395b	1609
2. Ballyvickegowan, Ballyreogh al. Ballymagheriebegg	CPR Jas I 190b	1611
3. Ballyvickegowne al. Ballyreagh or Ballinemagheriebegg	CPR Jas I 266a	1614
4. Ballyveagh al. Ballymeagherybeg	Inq. Ult. (Down) §4 Jac. I	1616
5. Ballyvickgowan cont. the 2 towns of Ballireagh al. Ballymagheribeg & Ballinaries	CPR Jas I 309a	1616
7. Maheribeg	Buckworth (EA) 310	1622
8. Magherybeg	Hib. Reg. Lr. Iveagh	1657c
9. Magherabegg	Census 78	1659c
10. Mgherobegg	BSD 69	1661
11. Magherabeg	Sub. Roll Down 274	1663
12. Magherybeg	Hib. Del. Down	1672c
13. Magherabeg	Wm. Map (OSNB) E125	1810
14. Machaire Beag "small plain" parva planities	J O'D (OSNB) E125	1834c
16. Machaire Beag/ Béitheach	Mooney 115	1950c
17. ˌmɑxərə'bɛːg	Local pronunciation	1991

Although Magherabeg is now a large townland of 864 acres, the etymology is clearly *Machaire Beag* "small plain". *Machaire* is usually masculine and there is no evidence in the forms that it might be feminine in this name, *Machaire Bheag*. It was church land belonging to the Bishop of Dromore.

From the evidence of forms 1–5 (AD 1609–1616) Magherabeg was only one of the names for this townland, which was also called *Ballyreagh, Baile Riabhach* "brindled townland" and *Ballyvickegowan, Baile Mhic an Ghabhann* "McGowan's townland", a surname meaning "son of the smith". The family were known as professional historians, *ollamhain seanchais* (*De Script. Hib.* 91; *AFM* iii 626, 1364 AD, iv 868, 1426 AD). A man surnamed *McaGowan* was in 1427 vicar of the parish of Donaghcloney (*Swanzy's Dromore* 113), so that McGowans are attested locally as an ecclesiastical family. The McGowans of the Ards were associated in 1744 with the Clandeboy O'Neills (*Cloinn Mhic Í Ghabhanna, O'Neill Fun. Oration* 266), and John O'Donovan found the surname McGowan "in Newry and other towns in the Co. Down... There were McGowans and O'Gowans". There is also evidence that the family of O'Gowan (*Ó Gabhann* "grandson of a smith") had a long history in Co. Down (see **Ballygowan**).

Magherabeg is near the northern boundary of Dromore parish, and only Greenoge, once part of the Magennis territory of Lequirin, divides it from the Moira townland of **Ballygowan**, which was part of Kilwarlin. It is unlikely that Ballygowan had any connection with *Ballyvickegowan*, since Kilwarlin and Lequirin are treated in the grants as entirely secular territories, and *Ballyvickegowan* was church land, containing "the two towns" of Magherabeg and *Ballyreagh* (forms 1, 2). Subsequently Magherabeg "small plain" has become the name for this larger unit. **Ballynaris** to the south is another large church townland, now 988 acres, which may also have been two originally. The apparent connection between Magherabeg and Ballynaris in 1616 (form 5) may be caused by a wrongly-inserted ampersand.

| **Quilly** | *An Choillidh* | |
| J 1852 | "the wood" | |

1. Ballinequilly al. Cully (Bp)	CPR Jas I 395b	1609
2. Ballynequillie al. Cullie (Bp)	CPR Jas I 190b	1611
3. Leighquirrine al. Cuillie, parcel/circuit of land	CPR Jas I 193a	1611
4. Ballynequilly al. Cully (Bp)	CPR Jas I 191a	1611
5. Ballinequilly al. Cullin al. Cully	CPR Jas I 266a	1614
6. Ballinequilly al. Cully (Bp)	CPR Jas I 309a	1616
7. Quilly	Buckworth (EA) 310	1622
8. Quilly	Hib. Reg. Lr. Iveagh	1657c
9. Quilly	Census 78	1659c
10. Quilley	BSD 68	1661
11. Quilie	Sub. Roll Down 274	1663
12. Quillie	Hib. Del. Down	1672c
13. pt of Quilly	Reg. Deeds abstracts i §387	1728
14. Queely	Ir. Wills Index 81	1795
15. Quilly	Wm. Map (OSNB) E125	1810
16. Coillidh "woods"	J O'D (OSNB) E125	1834c
17. Coilleach/Cuailleach < cuaille fem. "tall branchless tree"	Mooney 115	1950c
18. 'kwəlï	Local pronunciation	1991
19. 'kọlï 'bọrn	Local pronunciation	1992

Quilly is now a large townland of 814 acres. The name is once used as an alias for the district named Lequirin (2), a Magennis holding of townlands apparently based on the crannog at **Islandderry**. The townland of Quilly, however, belonged to the Bishop of Dromore (1, 2, 4–7). In 1728 part of it was held from the Bishop by Thomas Knox along with the church lands of Magherally (form 13). Quilly and "Quilly Holme" were recorded as church land in 1868.

Baile appears as a prefix with some early 17th-century forms (1, 2, 4–6), followed by what looks like the genitive singular feminine of the article. The spelling of the following element begins with *qui*, but *cu* in the alias forms without *baile*, indicating a broad consonant, *cu* or *co*, at the beginning of the Irish word. The local pronunciation with [kw] is probably reinforced by the modern spelling, but did not appear in the pronunciation of Quilly Burn (form 19), which is more like *cully*. *Coill* "wood" with its two-syllable genitive *na coille(adh)* would suit the spellings if the *quilly* element were always genitive (from *Baile na Coille, Baile na Coilleadh*), but since *baile* may not be original it seems better to suggest the longer form *coillidh* (an old dative) which provides two syllables in the nominative.

The Quilly Burn referred to by Mr Copeland (19, see Donaghcloney parish) is not named on the maps but is presumably the stream which forms the northern boundary between Quilly and Greenan, entering the Lagan in Greenan.

| **Skeagh** | *An Sceach* | |
| J 2150 | "the hawthorn bush" | |

1. Skiaghlatdana (in Kilwarlin)	Fiants Eliz. §4650	1585
2. Skeagh Latdana in Kilwarlin	CPR Jas I 396a	1609
3. Ballyskeaghletanan in Tullyomy	CPR Jas I 396a	1609
4. Ballyskeoglatanan in Tullyomie	CPR Jas I 235a	1612
5. Balleskeogeletannan	Inq. Ult. (Down) §13 Car. I	1629
6. Skiaghlatdana	Inq. Ult. (Down) §60 Car. I	1635
7. Skeoge	Hib. Reg. Lr. Iveagh	1657c
8. Skoage	Census 78	1659c
9. Skeoge	BSD 70	1661
10. Skeoge	Hib. Del. Down	1672c
11. Sheoge 422a	ASE 112a 34	1679
12. Skeoge	Lamb Maps Co. Downe	1690c
13. Skeog	Ir. Wills Index 83	1748
14. Skeagh	Wm. Map (OSNB) E125	1810
15. Skeagh	Bnd. Sur. (OSNB) E125	1830c
16. ch... guttural	OSNB Pron. E125	1834c
17. Sceach "a thorn, whitethorn"	J O'D (OSNB) E125	1834c
18. Scéichach "place of whitethorns"	Mooney 117	1950c
19. Sceach a'teannáil "thorn bush of the ceremonial fire"	Mooney 117	1950c
20. ske:x	Local pronunciation	1991
21. ski:	Local pronunciation	1991

Skeagh is on a ridge running from east to west. It formed part of the old division of Kilwarlin called *Tullyomy*, granted in 1609 to Sir Art Magennis. In the early 17th century the name had been longer, with *-latdana* or *-letanan* qualifying Skeagh (forms 1-6). *Baile* was prefixed in the lists of Sir Art Magennis' lands (3–5), but since 1657 (form 7) only the *skeagh* element appears in the name.

Despite the frequent late 17th-century spellings with [g] the modern pronunciation (16,20) provides ample evidence for a final fricative [x]. The pronunciation of this name was one of the indications by which incomers to the area could be distinguished by the locals, but now younger local people may also say "skee" (form 21). The suggested Irish form is *An Sceach* "the thorn bush". Perhaps because *sceach* had originally been qualified by a further element the name is not used with the article in English, unlike the minor name **The Skeagh** in Drumballyroney. Skagh townland in Co. Limerick has also been reduced from a longer name (Ó Maolfabhail 1990, 244b). The spellings like *Skeoge* (7–13) may show that the diminutive form *sceitheog* was also in use for a time.

The first part of *-latdana* or *-letanan* qualifying *Sceach* (forms 1–6) might be *leacht* "a grave", possibly referring to an ancient monument, beside which a "fairy" thorn might have grown. The final element might be a personal name, possibly even that of the goddess *Anu, Danu*, gen. *Anann, Danann*, who appears in other place-names (*Onom. Goed.* 324b). There is a rath at 400 feet in the east called Cromie's Fort (*ASCD* 167; 1:10,000 sheet 203), and two other raths due west of the farm called Altafort. In the west of the townland there are two raths on Skeagh Hill (*ASCD* 182), and one beside Diamond View Road. Dean Mooney's suggestion (form 19), a metathesized form of *Sceach an Teannáil* "thorn of the ceremonial fire" (*Dinneen*), seems unlikely linguistically, though Joyce gives various names including *teine-aoil* "limekiln" or *teannál* "bonfire", this last probably referring to the lighting of St Johns's Eve fires on hills at midsummer (ii 229). Skeagh also contains a stepped cross-roads called **The Diamond**, an English name unlikely to be connected with *-letanan*.

Skillyscolban
J 1949

Coillidh Scolbán
"wood for thatching pegs"

1.	Ballykilloohalbane	CPR Jas I 395b	1609
2.	Ballykilleskolbane	CPR Jas I 190b	1611
3.	Ballikilloskolbane	CPR Jas I 266a	1614
4.	Ballikilleskolbane	CPR Jas I 309a	1616
5.	Killescolvane	Buckworth (EA) 310	1622
6.	Killestolbane	Buckworth (Atkinson) 128	1622
7.	Killescolban	Ham. Copy Inq. [1623] xxix	1623
8.	Killescolbane	Hib. Reg. Lr. Iveagh	1657c
9.	Kiliscolban	Census 78	1659c
10.	Killesolbane	BSD 68	1661
11.	Killescolban	Sub. Roll Down 274	1663
12.	Kilsolban	Hib. Del. Down	1672c
13.	Kiliscolbin	Ir. Wills Index 21	1783
14.	Killscolven	Ir. Wills Index 33	1800
15.	Killyscolbans	Wm. Map (OSNB) E125	1810
16.	Skillyscolban	Bnd. Sur. (OSNB) E125	1830c
17.	skill is always pronounced	OSNB Pron. E125	1834c
18.	Coill Uí Scolbáin "O'Scolban's wood"	J O'D (OSNB) E125	1834c
19.	Coill scolbán "wood of the scollops"	Mooney 117	1950c

20. ˌskəliˈskɔːlvən   Local pronunciation   1991
21. ˈskɔːlvən   Local pronunciation   1991

Skillyscolban was a church townland, held by Patrick McCormick (see **Ballymacormick**) in 1623, but no longer listed as such by 1868. The forms show that the initial *s* is not original: it first appears, by way of alliteration with the second element, in the boundary survey of 1830 (form 16). There is no reference to a church site, and *Killy* is probably *coillidh* "wood" as in **Killysorrell, Quilly**. *Scolb*, here with a diminutive *-án* ending, is a piece of wood used to peg down thatch, and the word has been borrowed into English as *scollop* (19; *OSM* xxvii 1b). The first element of the place-name is often not used locally, and the place is called Scolvan (21). The current pronunciation with [v] not [b] is reflected in the spelling in 1622 and 1800 (forms 5, 14; 20); it could have developed from a mis-reading of *b* as *v*, but *b* is preserved in most of the written forms.

Tullindoney	*Tulaigh an Domhnaigh*	
J 2351	"church/Sunday hillock"	

1. Ballitollydony (in Kilwarlin)	Fiants Eliz. §4650	1585
2. Ballytobbdony in Kilwarlin	CPR Jas I 396a	1609
3. Ballytullydowny in Tullyomy	CPR Jas I 396a	1609
4. Ballytullydowny in Tullyomie	CPR Jas I 235a	1612
5. Tulledonney al. Ballytulledonney	Inq. Ult. (Down) §31 Car. I	1632
6. Tollindony	Hib. Reg. Lr. Iveagh	1657c
7. Tollandony	Census 78	1659c
8. Tullindeny al. Loppairvian (manor of Hillsborough)	CSP Ire. 1660–2 p459	1661
9. Tollindony	BSD 70	1661
10. Tullidonny	Hib. Del. Down	1672c
11. Tullandony	Wm. Map (OSNB) E125	1810
12. Tullydowney Tullindony Tullandony		
	Mooney MS 120	1811
13. Tulaigh an Domhnaigh "Sunday hill"		
	J O'D (OSNB) E125	1834c
14. (?)Tulach an dúna	Mooney 119	1950c
15. ˌt̪ɔlənˈdoːnï	Local pronunciation	1991

Tullindoney is on a long narrow ridge above the river Lagan, with no ancient monuments marked on the 1:10,000 map (sheet 203). The first part of the name is clearly the dative/locative of *tulach* "hillock, knoll". The spelling of the second is the usual anglicization of the word *domhnach*, which is an Irish borrowing of Latin *dominica*, "belonging to the Lord", used both of early church sites and of Sunday, the "Lord's Day". The "Book of the Angel" claimed all places called *domhnach* as having a special connection with St Patrick (*Liber Angeli (Bieler)* 188–9). Tullindoney townland was part of Kilwarlin, in the district of **Tullyomy**, with no ecclesiastical associations, and it is disappointing that no traditions remain of an old church, or of a site such as a well or a mass rock more recently visited on Sunday, to identify the meaning of *domhnach* here. Mooney's suggestion *Tulaigh an Dúna* "hillock of the (hill-)fort" seems unlikely because of the final syllable of *-dony*. Although *dún* had two genitives, *dúin* and *dúna*, only *-down(e)* appears in the forms for **Ballydown**, *Baile an Dúin*, in Seapatrick. The related word *dúnadh* "encampment" would give a final syllable, but Irish *Tulaigh an Dúnaidh* would be more likely to be anglicized Tullindooney. For the alias *Loppairvian* (8) see **Lappogues** townland.

Tullyglush J 2049	*Tulaigh Ghlais* "green hillock"		
1. Ballytullyglasse	CPR Jas I 395a	1609
2. Ballytullyglasse	CPR Jas I 190b	1611
3. Ballytollyglas	CPR Jas I 191a	1611
4. Ballytullyglasse	CPR Jas I 191b	1611
5. Ballitulliglasse or Ballitalliglasse	CPR Jas I 266a	1614
6. Balletulleglas	Inq. Ult. (Down) §85 Car. I	1639
7. Tolliglisse	Hib. Reg. Lr. Iveagh	1657c
8. Tuliglish	Census 78	1659c
9. Tullyglish	Wm. Map (OSNB) E125	1810
10. Tullyglush hill... 567 feet	OSM xii 70b	1834
11. -glush is the usual pronunciation	OSNB Pron. E125	1834c
12. Tullyglush Glushgrove	Ir. Wills Index 66	1853
13. Tulaigh glaise "hill of the brook"	J O'D (OSNB) E125	1834c
14. Tulaig Glas "green hill"	J O'D (OSNB) E125	1834c
15. Tulach na gclais	J O'D (OSNB) E125	1834c
16. Tulaigh-glaise "of the streamlet"	Joyce iii 590	1913
17. ˌtoli'gloʃ	Local pronunciation	1991

Tullyglush is adjacent to Garvaghy parish, the boundary being the Gall Bog. It seems that Tullyglush was originally a church townland, associated with others to the south and east in **Garvaghy**. This group was disputed between the bishop (forms 3, 5) and Sir Art Magennis (1, 2, 4, 6).

The first indication that the final consonant is [ʃ], English *sh*, occurs in the 1659 spelling (form 8); before this spellings in *-sse* do not indicate the quality of the *s* and may indicate an additional final vowel [ə]. *Tully* is from *tulach* "a hillock", presumably from its dative form *tulaigh*, so that the dative singular of the adjective *glas* "green" agreeing with it would give *Tulaigh Ghlais*. Another possibility, as suggested by O'Donovan and Joyce (13, 16), is *Tulaigh* with the genitive of the noun *glas* "a stream", *Tulaigh Ghlaise*. There is no evidence for the article between the elements of the name. There is a hill in Tullyglush, but no streams big enough to be shown on the 1:50,000 map. The house name Glushgrove (12) seems to have fallen out of use.

Tullymacarath J 1751	*Tulaigh Mhic an Reachtaí* "McEnratty's hillock"		
1. Ballylirstrillyvickenratty al. Hullymackenrattie in Leighquirin	CPR Jas I 395a	1609
2. Ballilistullyvickenratty al. Ballyhullymackenrattie	CPR Jas I 190b	1611

3. Ballilistolly, Holiemichen-Ratty al. Ballimuckenrattie or Ballitollyholymickenratty	CPR Jas I 266a	1614
4. Ballyvickenratty	Inq. Ult. (Down) §13 Car. I	1629
5. Ballylissetullyvicenraty al. Ballyhullymacenratty	Inq. Ult. (Down) §13 Car. I	1629
6. Ballymacinratty	Inq. Ult. (Down) §85 Car. I	1639
7. Balleleskullyvickenratty al. Balhullvickenratty	Inq. Ult. (Down) §85 Car. I	1639
8. Tullimuke and Raty	Hib. Reg. Lr. Iveagh	1657c
9. Tolle McAnratty	Census 78	1659c
10. Tullimisk & Ratty	BSD 71	1661
11. Tullimick Ratty	Hib. Del. Down	1672c
12. Tullymacrat	Wm. Map (OSNB) E125	1810
13. Tullymackeratt	Ir. Wills Index 50	1813
14. Tullymackeratt	Ir. Wills Index 50	1821
15. Tullymacarat	Bnd. Sur. (OSNB) E125	1830c
16. Tullymacaret	OSM xii 73a	1834
17. [Tully-mac-a-'rath]	OSNB Pron. E125	1834c
18. Tullymacarath	OSM xii 77b	1837
19. [Tullymaca-rat] stress on the last	Mooney 117-8	1950c
20. Tulaigh Mic Rait "MacRat" ref. McIlratty	J O'D (OSNB) E125	1834c
21. Tulach Mhic Ratha/Mhic an Reachtaigh	Mooney 117	1950c
22. ˌto̞lïmakəˈrat	Local pronunciation	1991
23. ˌto̞lïməˈkarət	Local pronunciation	1992

Tullymacarath was part of the Magennis district of **Lequirin** and contains the village of Gowdystown on its eastern border. The name is apparently from *tulach* "hillock" plus a surname formed with *mac*. The final *th* of the modern spelling is attested neither in the historical spellings nor in modern speech, which all have [t], followed in the 17th-century forms by a vowel. In the 1950s, according to Mooney, it was "pronounced and spelled locally Tullymacarette, with the stress on the first syllable, but older people call it Tullymaca-rat, with the stress on the last" (*Mooney MS* 117–8). Both pronunciations ([məˈkarət] and [makəˈrat]) are still known locally (22, 23).

The first might suggest the surname was *Mac Anrachtaigh*, possibly related to Ó hAnrachtaigh anglicized Hanratty, the surname of chiefs of *Uí Meith Macha* in Monaghan and common in Co. Armagh (Woulfe 1923, 555). The pronunciation with final stress, still thought to be older locally, and spellings such as *-vickenratty* or *and Raty* (forms 1–11) suggest the surname *Mac an Reachtaí* "son of the law-giver", attested in Co. Down in a 1617 pardon as *McEnrattie* (*CPR Jas I* 320b). The 17th-century forms were very difficult to separate from those for **Ballymacinratty More** and **Beg** in Donaghmore parish, which clearly contain the same surname (*PNI* i 93-5).

The forms for Tullymacarath also show confusion in the first element. *Baile* has been added to *tulach*, and *lios* "fort/enclosure", but possibly also "settlement", appears between them in some forms pre-1639. There is a rath shown on the 1:10,000 map to the east of Tullymacarette Primary School.

OTHER NAMES

Altafort   An English form (?)
J 2350

  1. ˈaltəˌfort   Local pronunciation   1991

Altafort is the name of a house belonging to the Heron family, beside two raths in Skeagh townland. In 1886 the magistrate William Heron lived at Mount Alta, Dromore (*Bassett's Down* 59b). Although these may not be the same house, the names are clearly related. Mount Alta is probably based on Latin *Mons Alta* (correctly *altus*) "high mountain", so that Altafort suggests "the high place by the fort". It is unlikely to be Irish *Allt an Phoirt* "glen of the harbour/camp".

Barronstown   An English form
J 1951

  1. ˈbarənsˌtəun   Local pronunciation   1991

The name Barronstown is applied to Barronstown House and Barronstown Hall and the road passing them in Balleny townland. The surname Barron (rarely Baron) is now uncommon and scattered, the nearest modern bearer being in Hillsborough.

Beattiestown   An English form
J 1452

  1   ˈbitïzˌtəun   Local pronunciation   1992

Although not marked on maps, the name of this settlement near him in Drumskee was known to Mr Copeland of Blackscull in Donaghcloney:

> In Drumskee there used to be a row of houses on the side of the road and it was called Beattie's Town because Beatties had lived there for almost 500 years. And they were of Scottish descent and my grandfather was called Beattie; he was one of that line and he said that they were all workers in leather, leather beaters, only that the Scottish people referred to them as leather beatties. And that Beattie stuck till the day, there's still some about the day. I have an uncle up the road there at 96.

There were Beatties in the *Vestry book of Donaghcloney* from 1811 (115–6), and a Mr Beatty of Donaghcloney townland helped the Ordnance Survey with their enquiries (*OSNB* E2). "The term *town* is affixed on very slight grounds. Two families of the same name residing near each other, on a public road, might give such names... and three would certainly do so" (*Surnames Down*, 83).

Bulls Brook   An English form

  1. Bulls Brook (Lappoges)   OSNB E125   1834c
  2. the river called Bulls Brook
     (Lurganbane)   OSNB E125   1834c

145

3. 'bulz'bruk	Local pronunciation	1996

Bullsbrook is given on the map as the name of a house/farm in Tullindoney, but form (2) makes it clear the name belonged first to the boundary stream between Tullindoney and Drummiller, which flows into the Lagan a little to the north of the house.

The Cockcrow Knowe   An English form
J 2052

1. ðə 'kɔkro 'nəu	Local pronunciation	1991

The Cockcrow Knowe, where Mr McGrehan was born, was a settlement of labourers' cottages in the townland of Drumbroneth, on the hill above Dromore where two roads meet. He explained the name as "something to do with King William" who was there when the cock crew and was supposed to have said "The cock crows now, we had better go on", and because of this it was called "the Cock Crow Knowe". It was called "a townland within a townland" in the account by Roy Gamble who grew up there (Gamble 1991, 35–7). The name is well-known, and is used locally rather than the townland name Drumbroneth, although the distinctive whitewashed houses were gradually left empty and have now been demolished.

The Diamond   An English form
J 2250

1. ðə 'daimənd	Local pronunciation	1991
2. ðə 'dəïmən 'həl	Local pronunciation	1991

The Diamond is a stepped crossroads on elevated ground (the Diamond Hill) in the middle of **Skeagh** townland, where roads to Kinallen and Tullyglush branch off from the road into Dromore. It is also used as a district name, the part running south down to Garvaghy being called the Near Diamond, and the part on the north side of the Diamond Hill the Far Diamond. There are seven places called The Diamond on the OSNI 1:50,000 map, in Cos Antrim, Armagh and Tyrone, mostly at cross-roads, including another in Co. Down in Magheralin, townland of Tullynacross, where a road and a lane intersect. There is also a 5-pointed crossroads in Drumballyroney called Diamond on the map, but known locally as The Diamond.

Gill Hall   An English form
J 1653

1. Gill Hall	Harris Hist. map	1743
2. Gill-hall	Harris Hist. 101	1744
3. Gillhall; El Clanwilliam	Taylor & Skinner 5a	1777
4. Gillhall	Statist. Sur. Dn 24	1802
5. Gillhall House and demesne	OSM xii 71a,72a	1834
6. Gill Hall (Greenan,Coolsallagh)	OSNB E125	1834c
7. Gillhall House and demesne	OSM xii 73b,76b	1837
8. ˌgəl'hɔːl	Local pronunciation	1992

146

The site of Gill Hall, in Coolsallagh townland beside the Lagan, is still well known, although the house itself is gone and is no longer named where its parkland is shown on the map. The woods surrounding it were described in the 1830s, when the house itself was "an old house of no architectural beauty" and "an extensive and manorial-like building" (*OSM* xii 71a, 72a, 76b). According to Mr Copeland of Donaghcloney it was locally called Gill Hall Castle, and Moles Wood, White Hill and Bell's Hill Planting (this last in Greenan) were all part of the demesne.

In the Cromwellian settlement Captain John Magill acquired an estate which he made into the manor of **Gilford**, based on the market town beside the Bann in Tullylish parish to which he gave his name (*ASE* 112a). His own dwelling in Dromore parish he named Gill Hall. This passed through the female line to John Meade, who became Baron Gilford and in 1776 first Earl of Clanwilliam. It was mentioned by Harris (*Hist.* 101). Later the house was inhabited by the agent to the estate. It retained its early 18th-century fittings, but was "empty and dilapidated" when described c. 1966 (*ASCD* 364–6). It was subsequently burned down. Another place-name connected with the Magill surname was McGill's Dam, a pool in Lisnaward townland, at the south end of the Big Bog, which supplied the water to Millfield.

The story of the Beresford ghost, which appeared to a visitor in the house, was recounted by Atkinson (*Dromore* 163–4) and the room in which this was supposed to have happened was known locally. Mr Copeland also saw the ghosts of the Big House, at the place where the servants entered, Agnew's Corner:

> Well, I was walking down the road one Sunday morning at five o'clock and I came round the corner and there at that gate in Gilhall wall, six old ladies standing dressed in black, black bonnets and each with a prayer book in her hand. I was going to walk straight into them. So I got off the footpath and kept looking at them, and looking and looking. And a fellow said to me, "Do you see something?" And I says, "Do you not see them?" They just disappeared.

Glenlagan	*Gleann an Lagáin*	
J 2450	"valley of the Lagan (river)"	
1. ˌglɛnˈlɛːgən	Local pronunciation	1991

The river **Lagan** flows through the parish of Dromore and has given rise to various names for houses on its banks: Glenlagan and Lagandale in Kinallen, Lagan Green ['lɛgən 'grin] in Drummiller. The name Glenlagan uses Irish word order and may have been based on an original Irish form as given above. If so the name Lagandale, belonging to another house further downstream, is more or less a translation into English. However the name Glenlagan may have been coined to give a more Irish flavour, like the name Glenbanna which was a house in Lawrencetown near the Bann (*Bassett's Down* 267). The river name **Lagan** is discussed in the section dealing with Moira parish.

Gowdystown	An English form	
J 1751		
1. ˈgəudïzˌtəun	Local pronunciation	1991

Like Connollystown in Ballynaris and **Beattiestown** in Drumskee, the original cluster of houses at Gowdystown in Tullymacarath was presumably occupied by an extended family of the same surname. New houses have been recently built in Gowdystown, but there is no-one left of the name. The surname Gowdy, a variant of Scottish Goldie (Black 1946, 321a), is now mostly found in the greater Belfast area, including Dromore and Magheralin (NI Telephone Directory, 1994). Watsonsgrove in the east of Ballyvicknakelly seems to be another of these settlements.

Lough Aghery	*Loch Eachrai*	
J 2853	"lough of the herd of horses"	

1. Loghaghrye	Fiants Eliz. §4218	1583
2. Dirrylowghaghry	Fiants Eliz. §4327	1583c
3. Loughaghry in Kilwarlin	Fiants Eliz. §4650	1585
4. Loghaghtery in Kilwarlin	CPR Jas I 396a	1609
5. Loghagherie in Kilwarlin	CPR Jas I 181b	1610
6. Ballikeeleloghaghery al Ballikeele	Inq. Ult. (Down) §31 Car. I	1632
7. Ballikeeleloghaghery	Inq. Ult. (Down) §31 Car. I	1632
8. Loghaghry	Inq. Ult. (Down) §60 Car. I	1635
9. Loghaghry	CSP Ire. 459	1661
10. Loghalery	Hib. Del. Down	1672c
11. Lough-Aghree	Harris Hist. 149	1744
12. Killeloghaghlery	DS (Mooney) 113	17thc
13. Lough Aghree	Civ. & Ecc. Top. (OSNB) E125	1806
14. Lough Aghery	Wm. Map (OSNB) E125	1810
15. Lough Aghry	OSM xii 70b	1834
16. Lough Aghery, Upper and Lower Isles	OSM xii 73b	1837
17. Loch Eachraidhe "Lake of the horses"	J O'D (OSNB) E125	1834c
18. ˌlɔx ˈaxrï	Local pronunciation	1991

Lough Aghery is now a lake containing two crannogs on the north-west side of the townland of Ballykeel (*ASCD* 184), but the name was also used as a townland name in 17th-century land grants, equivalent to **Ballykeel** (1–8). As with **Loughadian, Loughbrickland** in Aghaderg, **Loughorne** in Newry (*PNI* i 32), the crannog in the lake seems to have been the notable settlement of the townland. Presumably the epithet *Eachrai* indicates that horses were once pastured beside the lough. A less colourful possibility would be *eachréidh*, which means simply "plain" (*Ó Dónaill*).

Sometimes *Loughaghery* was combined with the current townland name Ballykeel (6, 7). Since this was a common townland name, different epithets were used to distinguish the various ones: Ballykeel Loughaghery, **Ballykeel** in **Clanawly** (*PNI* i 118–9), in **Glasquirin** (Seapatrick), in **Lequirin** (Magheralin). The queried form *Derryloughaghry* comes from a list of these districts within Iveagh held by the Magennises. *Derry* in this list refers to the district of Lequirin, centred on **Islandderry** in the west of the parish of Dromore. It is nothing to do with the townland of Derry in Dromara, near Lough Aghery, even though next on the list is *Begnive*, Begny in Dromara, which borders Derry on the south.

The lake is now sometimes named from the townland "Ballykeel Lough", and the relationship of this name to Lough Aghery has become confused in local usage, with Lough Aghery thought to be a different lake or further away.

McAdams Cross Roads   An English form
J 2435

  1. Crois Mhic Ádhaimh   GÉ 80   1989

  2. mə'kadəmz 'krɔs 'rodz   Local pronunciation   1996

McAdams Cross Roads near Watsonsgrove is not named on the 1:50,000 map but was translated into Irish because it had a post office (*AGBP, GÉ*). The surname McAdam can be of either Irish or Scottish origin (MacLysaght 1985, 1).

River Lagan   *Abhainn an Lagáin*
see Moira parish   "river of the hollow/lowlying area"

Thornyford Bridge   An English form
J 1654

  1. (?)Áth an Ornaimh   CMR II 226 (verse)   1721c
  2. Thornyford (Coolsallagh)   OSNB E125   1834c

  3. 'θɔrnï 'ford   Local pronunciation   1992
  4. 'θɔrnïford 'brïdʒ   Local pronunciation   1992

This is a bridge over the Lagan in the townland of Coolsallagh. Although the name Thornyford is written on maps as one word Mr Copeland spoke it as two (3), and explained it as given below:

> Possibly before the bridge was built [there could] have been a ford, a dry ford type of thing across the river, and they may have used hawthorn there as a bedding for stones, they did that sort of thing.

An attempt has been made to connect Thorny Ford with *Áth an Ornaimh*, a ford named in a poem in the story of the Battle of *Magh Rath*, **Moira** (form 1, only found in a paper MS: 23 K 44, dated 1721–2). However in the article, an anonymous review of Reeves' *Ecclesiastical Antiquities* (*EA*), the Irish name is given as *Áth Ornaidh* (*UJA* 1855, 294n). Although *Ornaidh* might be anglicized *Orny*, there is no manuscript authority for this spelling, and it is unlikely that the sound *th* [θ] in *Áth* would have been preserved in the name from early Irish, even though the road to Moira passes Thornyford Bridge.

Hanna disagreed with the identification (1856, 58, 61) and, in arguing that *Magh Rath* was near Newry, equated *Áth an Ornaimh* with the historical name *Ath Ername* near **Sheeptown** (*PNI* i 37–8). This was in turn rebutted by Mooney (1952–3(b), 13).

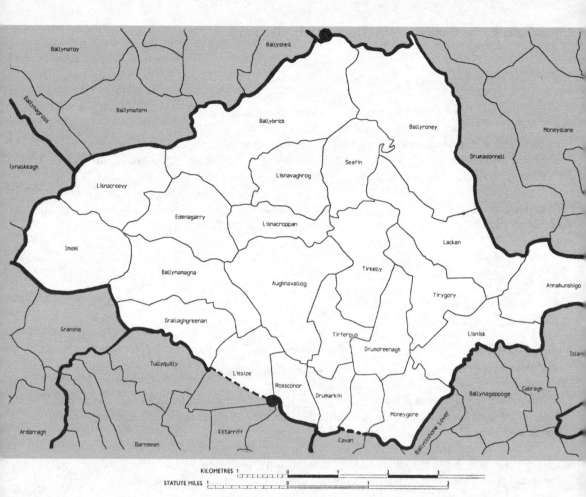

Parish of Drumballyroney
Barony of Iveagh Upper, Lower Half

Townlands
Annahunshigo
Aughnavallog
Ballybrick
Ballynamagna
Ballyroney
Cavan (shared with Clonduff)
Drumarkin
Drumdreenagh
Edenagarry
Grallaghgreenan
Imdel
Lackan
Lisnacreevy

Lisnacroppan
Lisnavaghrog
Lisnisk
Lissize (shared with Drumgath)
Moneygore
Rossconor
Seafin
Tirfergus
Tirkelly
Tirygory

Towns
Katesbridge (part)
Rathfriland (part)

Based upon Ordnance Survey 1:50,000 mapping, with permission of the Director of the Ordnance Survey of Northern Ireland, Crown copyright reserved.

150

THE PARISH OF DRUMBALLYRONEY

There are 23 townlands in the parish, no other divisions being known (*OSM* iii 17b). The 1657 inquisition says there were then 21 *townes*, although the names are not given there (*Atkinson's Dromore* 135). In 1659 Drumarkin, Grallagh(greenan), and Tirfergus were reckoned as half-towns (*Census* 76). Earlier **Imdel** was counted as two townlands (*CPR Jas I* 189a, 1611). Alternatively, the townlands of Cavan and Lissize, shared with Clonduff and Drumgath parishes, may not have been included in the reckoning (*PNI* i 123, iii 83–4, where the cross-reference to Cavan in Drumballyroney should be omitted). The river **Bann** (*PNI* iii 175–7) flows through the parish from south to north, forming the boundary between the townlands that lie along its course. It was shallow in this parish but "subject to sudden and heavy floods" (*OSM* iii 11). The river **Muddock** (*PNI* iii 182) forms part of the south-east boundary of the parish, between this and Clonduff (*OSM* iii 14b; *Inq. Ult.* xlii; *CPR Jas I* 304b).

When John O'Donovan came to the parish in 1834, in association with the Ordnance Survey, he had unsatisfactory interviews with Dubourdieu the rector, and with Mackay the parish priest "altho' a native and an Irish scholar". Eventually the place-names were pronounced for O'Donovan by "Old Hennan of Lisnacroppan and two other old natives" (*OSNB* E63). "Old Hennan" (Heenan) was a well-off farmer, nearly 90 years of age, with "much animal spirits and surprizing energy, but very hard of hearing", who told O'Donovan that "Irish was the first language that I ever spoke" (*OSL Dn* 61). He gave local Irish forms for many of the names, which O'Donovan generally accepted. Mrs Con Magennis of Annaclone, another Irish-speaker, also assisted.

The earliest place-name recorded in the parish is that of the Anglo-Norman castle of *Moycove*, 1188–1261 AD (the plain of *Magh Cobha*, see **Iveagh**). This was identified by Lawlor with two sites, the stone castle at **Seafin** beside the Bann, but probably at first the motte and bailey on the other side of the river in **Ballyroney** townland half a mile downstream (Lawlor H. 1938(b), 88).

At its southern end Drumballyroney includes part of the Magennis chief seat of Rathfriland. In the early 17th century Sir Art Magennis held the *four towns of Rathfriland* (probably **Cross, Kiltarriff** and **Lissize** (*PNI* i 115; discussed 121–3) with Rossconor in this parish), while the names of other townlands in this parish were scattered through the list of his possessions: Ballybrick, Ballynamagna, and Edenagarry; Annahunshigo, Grallaghgreenan, Imdel, Lisnacreevy, Lisnisk, Monygare, Seafin, and Tirfergus. Tirkelly is first mentioned, among the Magennis possessions, in 1639 (*Inq. Ult. (Down)* §85 Car. I). In effect Sir Art Magennis kept a block in the west, around Knock Iveagh, and another in the south-east of the parish, in his own hands. Sir Art Magennis and his son Sir Hugh also held the advowson of the parish (*Inq. Ult. (Down)* §§13, 85 Car. I).

Another important family in the history of Drumballyroney is that which provides part of the parish name. The family of *Ó Ruanadha* (O'Roney) were famous as poets, like the family of *Mac an Bhaird* (Macaward) in neighbouring Drumgooland (*De Script. Hib.* 92: *Aos Dána Éreann* inc. *Clann an Bhaird, Uí Ruanadha*). *Cellach Ua Ruanadha* was chief poet of Ireland at his death in 1079 (*AU*). In Iveagh the O'Roneys also distinguished themselves as churchmen, providing the first-known bishop of Iveagh in the late 12th century (*EA* 192 v). However *Eoin Ua Ruanadha* who died in 1376 was chief poet to Magennis (*AFM* iv 666–7), and it is not clear if the family came first as poets or as ecclesiastics. It has been suggested that two of the name pardoned in 1602 in Iveagh may have been poets (*Fiants Eliz.* §6616; O'Rahilly T.F. 1922, 109 §42).

In 1609 Hugh McNeece McRowry *O'Ronow* held seven townlands from Sir Art, regularly listed together: *Ballenecastleglasse, Ballneedronmey, Ballyracowlan,* Drumdreenagh, Lackan, Lisnavaghrog, Tirygory, as well as Drumadonnell in Drumgooland. Another family of O'Roneys held the seven townlands of Deehommed, in Dromara and Drumgooland, from Sir Art (*CPR Jas I* 395a,190b, as Sir Art's 189a, *Inq. Ult. (Down)* §§13,85 Car. I). In Drumballyroney the first-named land-unit seems to have been the townland now called **Ballyroney**, the site of the first castle of *Magh Cobha*, the other two **Drumarkin**, and **Lisnacroppan** (*Inq. Ult.* xlii).

The townland of Aughnavallog, which contained the parish church, was the only piece of church land, and was held in 1609 by the McKey family, who remained influential in the parish (see **Katesbridge**). The family of O'Doran, a "principall Irish name" in the Lordship of Newry in 1659 (*Census* 83; *PNI* i 137), also held land in the south-east of the parish (*Inq. Ult.* xlii, (*Down*) §85 Car. I). *Ui Dheoráin* were famous as jurists in the native legal system (*De Script. Hib.* 91: *Breitheamhuin Éreann*). Members of both families were pardoned as associates of the Magennises in 1602 (*Fiants Eliz.* §6616).

In 1681 John Hawkins held 13 townlands from the Magennis and O'Roney holdings, which became part of his "manor of Rathfryland": Ballybrick, Ballynamagna, Ballyroney (*Ballycaslane*), Drumarkin, Edenagarry, Grallaghgreenan, Imdel, Lackan, Lisnacreevy, Lissize, Tirfergus, Tirkelly, and Rathfryland (*ASE* 273b–274a). In 1834 General Meade held ten of these (excluding Ballyroney and Lackan, but including the church townland of Aughnavallog): Aughnavallog, Ballynamagna, Drumarkin, Edenagarry, Grallaghgreenan, Imdel, Lissize, Rosconnor, Tirfergus, and Tirkelly (*OSM* iii 18) along with others in the parish of Drumgath to the south, so that this part of the Magennis holding remained together. The Meade family were descendants of Hawkins (*Knox Hist.* xxi 358).

PARISH NAME

Drumballyroney *Droim Baile Uí Ruanadha*
"ridge of O'Roney's holding"

1.	(?)Dru[m]lyn, Ecclesia de	Eccles. Tax. 104	1306c
2.	Druim	Annates Ulst. 294	1422
3.	Vicarius de Drom.	Reg. Dowdall §129 275	1422
4.	perp. vic. St Patrick's Druim	Cal. Papal Letters vii 241	1422
5.	Vicarius de Droym	Reg. Dowdall (EA) 317	1546
6.	Droyn, Vicar of	Reg. Dowdall §113 80	1546
7.	Ba Rone	Bartlett Maps (Esch. Co. Maps) 2	1603
8.	Dromballyroy, vicar' de	Inq. Ult. (Down) §13 Car.I	1629
9.	Dromballyrony, vicar' sive capell' de	Inq. Ult. (Down) §85 Car.I	1639
10.	Dromballyroney	Inq. Down (Reeves1) 81	1657
11.	Dromballironow parish	Hib. Reg. Up. Iveagh	1657c
12.	Vicaria de Dromballarony	Trien. Visit. (Bramhall) 16	1661
13.	Drumballirony	Trien. Visit. (Margetson) 24	1664
14.	Drumballyrony	Trien. Visit. (Margetson) 25	1664
15.	Dromballironew	Hib. Del. Down	1672c
16.	Drumballirony Rectoria	Trien. Visit. (Boyle) 46	1679
17.	Drumballironey vicaria	Trien. Visit. (Boyle) 48	1679
18.	D.Ballirowne	Lamb Maps Co. Downe	1690c
19.	Drumballyroney	Wm. Map (OSNB) E63	1810

20. Drumballyroney	Bnd. Sur. (OSNB) E63	1830c
21. pronounced Drumballyrooney	OSL Dn 61	1834
22. Druim Bhaile Uí Ruanadha		
"ridge of O'Rooney's town"	Old Hennan and others (OSNB) E63	1834c
24. ˌdrọmˌbɑlliˈronï	Local pronunciation	1991

The parish is called *Drum* in the ecclesiastical records in 1422 and 1546 (forms 2–6), while Reeves suggested it may also have been the parish of *Drumlyn* referred to in 1306 (form 1, *EA* 105, 316, 317). The original *droim* or "ridge" may have been the hills around Knock Iveagh, the highest point in the parish, although two townlands also begin with the element *Droim-*, and the town of Rathfriland and the parish church in Aughnavallog were on hills.

The rest of the parish name, *Baile Uí Ruanadha* "settlement of O'Roney" comes from the land granted to the O'Roneys, later one of the Magennis chief tenants, though whether originally as erenaghs or poets it is difficult to say. The position of the lands of the learned family near the Magennis chief seat, and Knock Iveagh, their possible inauguration site, could indicate that the O'Roneys performed some role in the ceremony. The modern village of Ballyroney is actually in the townland of Lackan, not in the townland of Ballyroney, and it seems that Ballyroney could also be used as a district or as the parish name (*OSM* iii 10a,13a). *Baile* here could then indicate the large unit called *ballybetagh* rather than the townland unit or *ballybo*.

The etymology of Drumballyroney was known to Old Hennan in 1834 (form 22), and, less confidently, to English-speakers in the parish: "By some it is said to have taken its name from a family of the Rowans or Roney who are said to have resided here, but we have been unable to trace the derivation with certainty" (*OSM* iii 13b). However this does establish the relationship locally of the surnames (O')Roney and Rowan (not mentioned by Bell, Woulfe, or MacLysaght). There is a Rowan's Hill in the neighbouring parish of Drumgooland.

TOWNLAND NAMES

Annahunshigo
J 2536

Eanach Uinseogach
"ash-tree marsh"

1. Ballyamaghvushogagh	CPR Jas I 396a	1609
2. Ballyannaughousheyagh	CPR Jas I 235a	1612
3. Ballyunshonagh	Inq. Ult. (Down) xlii	1618
4. Ballyonshenagh	CPR Jas I 304b	1623
5. Cloghoge Hill	CPR Jas I 304b	1623
6. Ballyrunanonshogagh	Inq. Ult. (Down) §13 Car.I	1629
7. Ballyanaghunshogaghe	Inq. Ult. (Down) §85 Car.I	1639
8. Annaghunsogeaghree	Hib. Reg. Up. Iveagh	1657c
9. Adnughanshegagh	Census 76	1659c
10. Annoghunsogagh	BSD 113	1661
11. Aghnahinsegagh	ASE 91a 4	1667
12. Ana Unsoga	Hib. Del. Down	1672c
13. Aghnalinsegagh	Rent Roll Down 8	1692
14. Anahinshigo	Ir. Wills Index 3	1729

153

15. Annahunchigo	Wm. Map (OSNB) E63	1810
16. Annahinchego	County Warrant (OSNB) E63	1827
17. Annahinshigo	Ir. Wills Index 4	1828
18. Annahinchigo	Bnd. Sur. (OSNB) E63	1830c
19. [An-na-'hinch-i-go]	OSNB Pron. E63	1834c
20. Aughnahinchigo	OSL Dn 56–7	1834
21. Aughnahinchigo "field of the ash"	OSL Dn 56–8	1834
22. Áth na hUinseóige "Ford of the Ash"	Old Hennan and others (OSNB) E63	1834c
23. ˌanə'hənʃəgoː	Local pronunciation	1991
24. ˌanə'hïntʃïgo	Local pronunciation	1995

When John O'Donovan called on the rector of the parish, John Dubourdieu, in 1834 to discuss place-names they had a disagreement about the meaning of "Aughnahinchego", Dubourdieu holding that the ash was a foreign plant that could not be referred to in an Irish place-name. As O'Donovan indignantly pointed out, the evidence goes the other way and the name of the ash is fairly common in place-names (*OSL Dn* 56–7; *Joyce* i 506).

The townland is bounded on the south by the river Muddock, but, although Old Hennan suggested a form meaning "ford of the ash-tree", the historical spellings show that the first element was *eanach* "bog". On Petty's barony map bog is shown all around the townland, which was "interspersed with large portions of turf bog" (*OSNB*). The adjective *uinseogach* "of ash trees" is paralled in *fearnogach* "of alder trees" in some of the forms for **Mullaghfernaghan**, parish of Magherally, which also has varying forms of the tree-adjective. In 1618 the boundary between Sir Art Magennis' lands of Annahunshigo (form 3, representing *Baile Uinseanach* "ash-tree townland") and Lisnisk with Islandmoyle and Cabra belonging to Sir Edward Trevor was trodden by Donogh O'Doran, "beginning at the bog to the bottom of a hill called *Cloghoge* to a stone leading to the river Moddock" (*Inq. Ult.* xlii). There is a farm called Cloghead near the Muddock at the south east corner of the townland (1:10,000 sheet 239).

By the early 19th century the name had been shortened in the forms **Hunshigo** Lake, Hunshigo Bog (*OSM* iii 10b, 11a). Trees are shown growing in Hunshigo Bog on the 1:10,000 map (sheet 239).

Aughnavallog *Achadh na bhFáinleog*
J 2136 "field of the swallows"

1. D McJas McKey to have Aghevelough	CPR Jas I 395a	1609
2. James McKey of Aghevelogh	CPR Jas I 195b	1610
3. Agheveloighe	CPR Jas I 191a	1611
4. Donell McJas mKey of Agheveloigh	CPR Jas I 191a	1611
5. Aghevelogh	CPR Jas I 191a	1611
6. Daniel McKey de Aghnavallogge	Inq. Ult. (Down) §97 Car.I	1640
7. Aghyvolloy	Hib. Reg. Up. Iveagh	1657c
8. Aghinalloge	BSD 113	1661
9. Aghyvolloy	Hib. Del. Down	1672c
10. Aughnavalloge	Ir. Wills Index iv 133	1756
11. Aghnavallog	Wm. Map (OSNB) E63	1810
12. Aughnavalloge	Reg. Free. (OSNB) E63	1829

13. Aughnavollog	Bnd. Sur. (OSNB) E63	1830c
14. [Agh-na-'vol-log]	OSNB Pron. E63	1834c
15. Island Bog	OSNB E63	1834c
16. Warren Bog	OSNB E63	1834c
17. Aughnavollog	OSM iii 14a,15b,17a,18a	1834
18. Ath na Mallóg	Clergyman (OSNB) E63	1834c
19. Áth na Mallog "Ford of the bags/sacks"	J O'D (OSNB) E63	1834c
20. Áth n-Uí / Athan Uí Mhaolaodha "Malley/Molloy's ford"	Mooney 19	1950c
21. Áth n-Uí Mhaolaodhog	Mooney 19	1950c
22. ˌaxnəˈvalɔg	Local pronunciation	1995

The name Aughnavallog appears to consist of two noun elements with the article between them, although the first clear evidence of the article is form (6) in 1640. Despite the suggestion of the Irish-speaking parish priest, Fr McKey (form 18), there is no stream to suggest *Áth* "ford", and no notable routeway across the bog in the south of the townland. The first element is therefore probably *Achadh* "field". Dean Mooney suggested the rest of the name could be the genitive singular of *Ó Maol[mh]aodhóg*, a Donegal surname, first anglicized *O Mologe, O Mulm/voge* and becoming later Logue or Mulloy (*Woulfe* 1923, 604,610). The surname Loy, which could be another short form, is still found in this area.

If the final element is a noun plus article, it appears to be the genitive plural of a word beginning *f-*, possibly a feminine noun with the diminutive ending *-óg*, although the five early 17th-century anglicized spellings have final *gh*. Father McKey's suggestion *mallóg*, understood by O'Donovan as a diminutive of *mála* "a bag" (18,19), is not listed in the dictionaries. He may have meant *Áth na mBallóg* "ford of the ruins", but neither would fit the *v* of the early forms.

The vowel of the first syllable of the element is spelled *e* from 1609–11, with *o* and *a* alternating in later forms. (The 1834 *OSM* has *o*, supported by the *OSNB* pronunciation, but the 1836 account has *a*). *Ao* is anglicized *e(e)* in **Ballykeel** (<*caol*), **Enagh** (<*aonach*). However in the Irish of Tyrone vowels were "frequently shortened in stressed syllables, particularly before *l, n* and *r*" (Stockman and Wagner 1965, 185), and one example of this occurring in west Ulster dialects was the word *faoileog* "seagull" (Stockman 1986, 11). However Aughnavallog is rather far from the sea. An alternative interpretation of the vowel is to regard *o* as an English spelling of Irish *á* before *l*, misread in the earlier forms here as *e*, in which case the name could be *Achadh na bhFáinleog* "field of the swallows".

If the local Irish dialect had retained the original consonant sound [γ] of *adh*, as in the spelling *Garwaghadh* for **Garvaghy** *garbh-achadh* in 1428 (*Reg. Swayne* 101), and in stressed syllables in Tyrone Irish in the early 20th century (*Sgéalta Mh. L.* xvii §11), the name could be *Achadh na bhFáladh* "field of the fenced-in areas", with final *-dh* anglicized as *g*. However *fáladh* "fencing" is rare in a concrete sense, although it seems to occur in **Fallagloon** *Fáladh Luán* "enclosure of lambs" in the parish of Maghera, Co. Derry (*PNI* v 186–8).

Aughnavallog was the church land of the parish in the 17th century, but by 1834 had been secularized and belonged to General Meade (*OSM* iii 18b). It contained the old parish church, shown on the early *Townland Index Map* sheet 1 (1949), but on OS 1:10,000 sheet 238 only the road bears the name Church Hill Road. The old parish church of Drumgath was abandoned for a new Church of Ireland church in Rathfriland, and became the parish church for Drumballyroney also when the two parishes were united (*Atkinson's Dromore* 266–7). No glebe was known in 1657, but glebe in Aughnavallog was later granted by the lord of the soil (*OSM* iii 13), and the Glebe House near Rathfriland remains (*OSM* iii 15b).

The townland contains Island Bog on the east, "so named from a portion being cultivated near the centre" (*OSM* iii 14b), and Warren Bog on the south (*OSNB*; 1:10,000 sh. 238). In 1834 there was "A large stone (as usual called Cloughmore) standing in a field at the west end of Aughnavallog townland. It is 8 feet high... tapering to a point at the top. Tradition says it was put there by Fin McCool" (*OSM* iii 16b). This stone (*ASCD* 96), evidently *Cloch Mhór* "big stone", is marked on the 1-inch *Townland Index Map* of Down (1970, sheet 2), but not on the 1:50,000. There was also a rectilinear earthwork called Liscrum, probably *Lios Crom* "crooked fort" (*ASCD* 169).

Ballybrick
J 2140, J1938

Baile Mhic Giolla Bhric
"McGilbrick's townland"

1.	BallyMc gillevricke	CPR Jas I 395b	1609
2.	Ballyvickgillvrick	CPR Jas I 189a	1611
3.	Ballemcgillevrick	CPR Jas I 235a	1612
4.	Bally McGilbrick x2	Inq. Ult. (Down) xlii	1618
5.	Ballymcgilbricke	CPR Jas I 304b	1623
6.	Ballygilbrick	CPR Jas I 304b	1623
7.	Ballymackilbricke	Inq. Ult. (Down) §85 Car. I	1639
8.	Mc Kilbricke	Inq. Ult. (Down) §85 Car. I	1639
9.	Ballymacgillroick, Upper	Inq. Ult. (Down) §85 Car. I	1639
10.	Ballyngillurke	Inq. Ult. (Down) §13 Car.I	1639
11.	Ballimackellbrick	Hib. Reg. Up. Iveagh	1657c
12.	Bolly Mc Gillbrick, lower halfe of ye said towne	Census 75	1659c
13.	Bolly Mc Gillbrick, Upper halfe towne	Census 75	1659c
14.	Ballymack Ilbirk	BSD 113	1661
15.	Ballymack Ilbrick	BSD 114	1661
16.	Ballym' Ilebrige	Sub. Roll Down 277	1663
17.	Ballimc:keelbrick	Hib. Del. Down	1672c
18.	Ballimacilurick	ASE 274a 29	1681
19.	BallymcIllerick	Rent Roll Down 10	1692
20.	Ballymuclbrick	Ir. Wills Index 89	1730
21.	Ballybrick	Wm. Map (OSNB) E63	1810
22.	Ballybrick	Reg. Free. (OSNB) E63	1830
23.	Ballymelbrick	Reg. Free. (OSNB) E63	1830
24.	Ballymielbrick	Bnd. Sur. (OSNB) E63	1830c
25.	Ballymulbrick	OSM iii 14a,16a,17a	1834
26.	Ballymeilbrick	OSM iii 16b,18ab	1834
27.	Ballymeilbrick pronounced Ballybrick	OSM iii 18b	1834
28.	[Bal-ly-'brick] meel is never used	OSNB Pron. E63	1834c
29.	Baile Breac "town of trouts"	OSNB Inf. E63	1834c
30.	Baile Gile Bric	OSNB Inf. E63	1834c

31. Baile mic Giolla Bhric "Mac Gilbrick's town"	J O'D (OSNB) E63	1834c
32. Baile Mhic Giolla Bhric "BallyMcIlbrick"	OSL Dn 62	1834
33. Baile-Mhic-Giolla-Bhric "MacGilbrick's/MacGillavrick's town"	Joyce iii 73	1913
34. ˌbaliˈbrĭk	Local pronunciation	1995

Ballybrick is a large townland of 1,397 acres in the north of the parish. There is some evidence (forms 9,12,13) that the townland was subdivided in the past, and the name is shown twice on the 1:50,000 map, giving two grid-references: at the eastern end beside a cluster of houses on sheet 20, at the western end on sheet 29. The Bann forms the eastern boundary. Ballybrick includes Katesbridge and the site of the Shannaghan Lough named on Speed's maps (*PNI* i 35–6), marked "bog and logh" on Petty's "Upper Iveagh" (*Hib. Reg.*). In 1834 it was "said to have received its name from the fishers of the Bann who lived thereon: *Baile breac* 'town of trouts'. This is not however true as the old natives called it *Baile Gile Bric*" (*OSNB*). *Ballymielbrick* was was the first spelling suggested at this time by the Ordnance Survey (*OSNB*).

Earlier historical spellings as well as the syllable *mul, meil* persisting till the 19th century show that this name contained a surname formed with *mac* "son", as suggested by O'Donovan's informant Old Hennan (form 32). The surname McGilbrick, derived from Scottish Gaelic *Mac Gille Riabhaich* "son of the brindled lad", existed in Scotland (Black 1946, 514). However this name never seems to have become established in Ireland, and would be unlikely to give rise to the forms here.

Although place-names sometimes appear to contain surnames not otherwise recorded in the area, historical spellings can become corrupted and historical context may also provide guidance. The 1663 *Subsidy Roll*, on the same page as *Ballym'Ilebrige* (form 16), lists a man called *Art M'Ilebrige* of Barnmeen nearby in Drumgath (*PNI* i 119). The final syllable suggests the surname *Mac Giolla Bhrighde* "son of the servant of Brigid", which belonged to a family of churchmen in Donegal and Derry, a branch of which settled in Down (MacLysaght 1957, 61). A pardon of Magennis followers in 1602 included Owen and Patrick *McGilbridie* (*Fiants Eliz.* §6616) and in 1616 Rory *McGilbridey* (*CPR Jas I* 299a). There is evidence for the anglicization of the surname without *giolla* as McBride from the mid-17th century (*Census* 72; 7), although the apparent diminutive McBredan is found much earlier (see **Ballymacbredan**, Magheralin). However Bally(meil)brick is an unlikely corruption of *Baile Mhic Giolla Bhríde* "McBride's townland", especially as the surname was well-known. There is a McBrides Crossroads nearby in the townland of Moneyslane (1:10,000 sheet 239), and in 1837 McBride was a prevailing Protestant surname in the parish of Dromara (*OSM* xii 67b). The same surname under its various forms also existed in Scotland (Black 1946, 460b,515b). In providing an original Irish form for Ballybrick one is faced with the choice between an unknown surname and an unlikely corruption of one that would have been well-known.

Ballybrick was a secular townland belonging to Sir Art Magennis. "Fower acres of arable and meaddowe, whereupon standeth a great Irish howse", lying between "the lands of *Raconyglan* on one side, *Lysmaghtknock* on an other side, and *Bally McGilbrick* belonging to Sir Arthur Magneis" was adjudged part of Ballybrick in 1618 (*Inq. Ult.* xlii). When this investigation of bounds in Iveagh was entered in the patent rolls, the item was written "whereon *stood* a great Irish house" (*CPR Jas I* 304b, 1623). On the 1:10,000 map (sheet 238, *ASCD* 94 grid 192372) there is a "mound and enclosure" in the west part of Lisnacroppan near the junction of the modern boundary with Ballybrick and Lisnavaghrog, "on the highest hill in the townland" (*OSNB*). The mound 10 feet high, within an oval enclosure 180 feet long, is likely to be a barrow (*ASCD* 94, with plan). As such it could have been the inauguration site of the Magennises named by *Bartlett* on one of his maps (*Esch. Co.* 2) **Lisnaree**, with the house of a learned retainer beside it. The name *Lyssarthei* appears beside a hill with a tower on *Mercator's Ulster* map (1595). However the house site has not been located or investigated further.

Ballynamagna		*Baile na mBeagánach*	
J 1735		"townland of the O'Beggans"	
1. Ballynemeganagh		CPR Jas I 395b	1609
2. Ballynemeganagh		CPR Jas I 189a	1611
3. Ballynemeganagh		CPR Jas I 235a	1612
4. Ballinemegranagh		Inq. Ult. (Down) §13 Car.I	1629
5. Ballynemogenagh		Inq. Ult. (Down) §85 Car. I	1639
6. Ballynemagenagh		Hib. Reg. Up. Iveagh	1657c
7. Ballynemognagh		Census 75	1659c
8. Ballinnemeganah		BSD 114	1661
9. Ballinemaginagh		Hib. Del. Down	1672c
10. Ballynemeganagh		ASE 274a 29	1681
11. Ballynemegannagh		Rent Roll Down 11	1692
12. Ballynemageneth		Ir. Wills Index 80	1711
13. Ballynamagna		Wm. Map (OSNB) E63	1810
14. Ballynamagenah		Bnd. Sur. (OSNB) E63	1830c
15. Ballnamagnoh		Ir. Wills Index 81	1832
16. Ballynemagenagh		OSM iii 16a	1834
17. Ballynemagenagh, so pronounced		OSM iii 18b	1834
18. Baile na Meagana "Town of the parsnips"		J O'D (OSNB) E63	1834c
19. Baile na macánartha "townland of the young heroes"		Mooney 21	1950c
20. ˌbalənəˈmagnə		Local pronunciation	1995

This townland was held by Sir Art Magennis. Until the 19th century many forms had an extra syllable *-meganagh*. Likewise the final *-gh* appears in all the spellings until the 19th century, when it may have been still pronounced (*OSNB*), but it is not heard in the current local pronunciation.

O'Donovan thought the second element might be based on the word *meacan*, meaning various tap-rooted plants (*Dinneen*), most often "wild parsnip" (*meacan, Joyce* ii 349–50; *Joyce* iii 37 *Alt na meacan*, Altnamackan S. Armagh). There was a subdivision of Corcreeny in Donaghcloney called *Aghevackan*, probably *Achadh an Mheacain* "parsnip field". Joyce gives an example Gortnamackanee, probably *Gort na Meacanaí* "field of the parsnip place" from the derivative *meacanach*. If this element occurs in Ballynamagna, *Baile na Meacanach* (gen. plural) would have to mean the same thing as the basic word *meacan* "tap-rooted plant", although Tim Robinson translates *meacan* as "lump" in minor names in Connemara (Robinson T. 1990, 77, 120, 128).

However, other examples of anglicized names including the element *meacan* all preserve voiceless *k* or *ck* for Irish *c*, and it is difficult to explain the *g* here. A compound *beag-eanach* "little marsh" would be possible, but this name would require a plural form "townland of the little marshes" which seems odd. Another possibility, also suggested for the Dromara townland of **Begny**, otherwise explained as *Beignidh* "little thing" (*OSNB*), is that both names refer to the surname then spelt *Mac an Beccánaigh* attested among the 11th- and 12th-century clergy of the diocese (see Dromore introduction). Ballynamagna might be *Baile na mBeagánach*, "townland of the O'Beggans". Woulfe calls *Ó Beagáin* a "rare and scattered" surname (1923, 434), and as Beggan it is now found in the north mainly around Rosslea, Co. Fermanagh (N.I. telephone directory, 1995). However what seems to be the same name occurs, spelled *O'Becan*, among the lists of Magennises and associates pardoned in 1602 (*Fiants Eliz.* §6616).

Ballyroney

Ballyroney   *Baile Uí Ruanadha*
J 2237   "O'Roney's townland"

1.	Goill chaisteoil Mhaighe Cobha	AFM iii 80	1188
2.	Gaill chaislén Muighe Caba	ALC 178	1188
3.	Gaill Caisteoil Maighi-Coba	AU ii 212-3	1188
4.	castle of Oniaht	Mon. Ang. ii 1019	1200c
5.	excepto castello de Maincove	Pontif. Hib. i 128 §60	1204
6.	excepta ecclesia castelli de Maincove	Pontif. Hib. i 127 §59	1204
7.	Maincoue, Drummor et (castles)	Pipe Roll John 60	1211c
8.	Maincoue (castle larder)	Pipe Roll John 60	1211c
9.	Maincoue (castle repairs)	Pipe Roll John 56	1211c
10.	Ballenecastleglasse	CPR Jas I 395a	1609
11.	Balleencastleglasse, Hugh O'Ronowe of	CPR Jas I 195b	1610
12.	Ballycastleglasse	CPR Jas I 189a	1611
13.	Ballyronowe, Hugh McNeece McRowrie O'Ronowe of	CPR Jas I 190b	1611
14.	Ballycastleglass	Inq. Ult. (Down) §13 Car. I	1629
15.	Ballycassane, Hug' O' Rony de	Inq. Ult. (Down) §85 Car. I	1639
16.	Ballycaslan, Hugh O'Rony of	Wars Co. Down x 79a	1641
17.	Ballicaslane	Hib. Reg. Up. Iveagh	1657c
18.	Castletowne	Census 76	1659c
19.	Ballycaslane	BSD 114	1661
20.	Castletown	Sub. Roll Down 277	1663
21.	Ballicaslan	Hib. Del. Down	1672c
22.	Ballycaslane 661a	ASE 274a 29	1681
23.	Ballycaslane	Rent Roll Down 10	1692
24.	B.Roney	Harris Hist. map	1743
25.	Ballyroney	Harris Hist. 151	1744
26.	Ballyroney	Bnd. Sur. (OSNB) E63	1830c
27.	Baile Uí Ruanaidh	Old Hennan and others (OSNB) E63	1834c
28.	Baile Uí Ruanadha "O'Rooney's town"	J O'D (OSNB) E63	1834c

29. Baile-Ui-Ruanaidhe "O'Rooney's town"	Joyce iii 117	1913
30. Baile Uí Ruanaí/Ballyroney	Éire Thuaidh	1988
31. Baile Uí Ruanaí	GÉ 29	1989
32. ˌbaləˈronï	Local pronunciation	1991

The townland of Ballyroney lies on the north-east bank of the Bann a little to the north of the village of the same name. *Ba: Rone*, naming a small castle on a hill by the Bann, appeared on a Bartlett map of c. 1600 (*Bartlett Esch. Co.* map 2). In the early 17th century the name Ballyroney (form 13) seems to have been used for the district of eight townlands held by the *Ó Ruanadha* or O'Roney family, as described under the parish name. At that period the townland of Ballyroney was called *Ballenecastleglasse*, in Irish *Baile an Chaisleáin Ghlais* "townland of the grey/green castle". Later it became *Ballycaslane* and *Castletown*. The village which bears the name Ballyroney is in Lackan townland, and Harris' map in 1743 (form 24) seems to be referring to either the village or the parish. By 1834 Ballyroney had replaced Castletown as the townland name (*OSNB*).

"Castle" refers to the structure which once existed on the "remarkable rath or mound", alias motte and bailey, which survives on the north-east bank of the Bann, in the north of the townland (*OSM* iii 16b; *ASCD* 198). This earthwork, excavated in 1953, was identified by H.C. Lawlor (1938(b), 88) as the site of the first Norman castle of *Magh Cobha* (**Iveagh**). A raid by the English of *Caistéal Maighe Cobha* with Uí Echach on Tyrone was referred to in the annals for 1188 AD (forms 1, 2, 3). In Latin sources the castle of *Maincove* and its church were mentioned in 1204 (forms 5, 6), and repairs and palisading for the castle in the *Pipe Roll of King John* for 1211 (forms 7, 8, 9). A coin of King John was found on an old ground level, covered by material which indicated occupation by a local rather than an English garrison. This usage fits with the building of a new Anglo-Norman stone castle of the same name in 1252 in **Seafin** townland.

The townland of Ballyroney is divided by the Drumadonnell river flowing into the Bann, south of which (nearer Ballyroney village) are **Ballyroney Lake** and **Duggan's Hill**.

Cavan
J 2133

An Cabhán
"a round dry hill"

1. Cavan	BSD 114	1661
2. Caven	Hib. Del. Down	1672c
3. Cavan	ASE 274a 29	1681
4. Caven	Rent Roll Down 11	1692
5. Cavan	Wm. Map (OSNB) E63	1810
6. Cavan	Bnd. Sur. (OSNB) E63	1830c
7. Cnoc a'Chabháin	Old Hennan and others (OSNB) E63	1834c
8. Cabhan "a dry hill"	J O'D (OSNB) E63	1834c
9. ˈkavən	Local pronunciation	1991

Cavan in the south of the parish is shared between Clonduff (**Cavan** *PNI* iii 84–5) and Drumballyroney as given above. There are no forms for either part before 1657 and the original holder is unclear. The 1659 reference under Clonduff parish calls that part *Cauan halfe* *towne* (*Census* 76). The 1:10,000 map sheet 253 shows, near Rathfriland, Cavan Hill 110 metres high, from which Old Hennan seems to have thought this townland took its name. In 1743 Harris' map showed an oval marked *Course* north of the road, between Rathfriland and the bridge over the Bann (now McCombs Bridge) on the road to Castlewellan, which could be in the Drumballyroney part of Cavan (*Harris' Hist.*). This seems to be the place referred to c. 1834, "The Course Bog in this townland... receives its name from a race course on the south side, which has been some years broken up and under tillage" (*OSNB*). The oval is also shown, on both sides of the road, on *Taylor and Skinner*'s map 7, between a stream and the Bann, but I have not identified the site on the ground.

Drumarkin　　　　　　　　　　　*Droim Earcáin*
J 2133　　　　　　　　　　　　　　　"ridge of the piglet"

1. Ballneedronmey (O'Rony)	CPR Jas I 395a	1609
2. Ballynedromey	CPR Jas I 189a	1611
3. Ballenedrommey (Ballyronowe)	CPR Jas I 190b	1611
4. Ballinedromin	Inq. Ult. (Down) §13 Car.I	1629
5. Balledrom[ ]	Inq. Ult. (Down) §85 Car.I	1639
6. Dromorkane	Hib. Reg. Up. Iveagh	1657c
7. Dromak ½ towne	Census 76	1659c
8. Dromarkane	BSD 113	1661
9. Dromorkan	Hib. Del. Down	1672c
10. Dromarkans	ASE 273a 29	1681
11. Dromarkeens	Rent Roll Down 10	1692
12. Drumarkin part	Rent Roll Down 13	1692
13. Drinarkin	Wm. Map (OSNB) E63	1810
14. Drumarkin	Bnd. Sur. (OSNB) E63	1830c
15. Drumarkin	Tombstone (OSNB) E63	1834c
16. [Dru-'mar-kin]	OSNB Pron. E63	1834c
17. Drum Marcain "Marcán's ridge"	Old Hennan and others (OSNB) E63	1834c
18. Droim Orcan "ridge of the little pigs"	Mooney 25	1950c
19. ˌdrə'markən	Local pronunciation	1991

By a process of elimination Drumarkin seems to be the O'Roney townland called *Ballneedronmey* etc., a name not to be confused with Sir Art Magennis' own townland of **Drumena** in Kilcoo. If the identification is correct it was the O'Roneys' most southern townland. It seems likely that it was called *Baile na Droimní* or, possibly, *Baile an Droimne* "townland of the ridge". There is a small hill in the east, which is probably the ridge of the name.

The modern name first appears on Petty's barony map, but from references to a half-townland and the occasional addition of plural *-s* it seems the townland may have been in two parts. *Dromarkans* in 1681 (form 10) was 103 acres, and Drumarkin is now a small townland of 201 acres. Drumarkin seems to contain the basic element *droim*: *Droim Earcáin*. If it means "Earcán's ridge", Drumarkin may show the same personal name as in Rasharkin *Ros Earcáin* "Earcán's wood" (*Buile Suibhne* §§30, 50, n.p. 162). However it is more likely that *earcán* is a variant of the word *arcán/orcán* meaning "piglet", as suggested by Mooney (form 18), and supported by Petty's forms (6, 9).

Old Hennan suggested the second element was *Marcán*. Marcán was the name of a king of Uí Mhaine who died in 654 AD, and who was a character in early Irish literature (*Scéla Cano* ll.173,195,201,300 etc.). Marcán is a diminutive of Marc, and the earlier version of *Táin Bó Cuailnge* refers to "Marc at his knoll", *Telach Mairc*, where Cú Chulainn killed Marc in *Cuib*, now **Iveagh** (*TBC Rec. I* l.1525).

Drumdreenagh   *Droim Draighneach*
J 2235   "blackthorn ridge"

1. Ballydromgrinagh	CPR Jas I 395a	1609
2. Ballydromdrynagh	CPR Jas I 189a	1611
3. Ballydromgrinagh	CPR Jas I 190b	1611
4. Balledronenegh	Inq. Ult. (Down) §13 Car. I	1629
5. Ballydromdrinagh juxta le Bawne	Inq. Ult. (Down) §13 Car.I	1629
6. Ballydromdrinagh	Inq. Ult. (Down) §85 Car. I	1639
7. Balledromgreanagh	Inq. Ult. (Down) §85 Car. I	1639
8. Dromdrynagh	Inq. Ult. (Down) §85 Car. I	1639
9. Ballydromdrinagh	Inq. Ult. (Down) §85 Car. I	1639
10. (?)Drumgrinagh	Hib. Reg. Up. Iveagh	1657c
11. (?)Drumgrernagh	Census 76	1659c
12. (?)Drumrenagh	Census 76	1659c
13. Dromgrinagh	BSD 115	1661
14. Dromdrinagh	Sub. Roll Down 277	1663
15. D:grinagh	Hib. Del. Down	1672c
16. (?)Druingrinagh, ½	Rent Roll Down 9	1692
17. Drumdrinagh	Wm. Map (OSNB) E63	1810
18. Drumdrina	Tombstone (OSNB) E63	1819
19. Drumdrinagh	Bnd. Sur. (OSNB) E63	1830c
20. Drumgreenagh	OSNB E63	1834c
21. [Drum-'dree-nagh]	OSNB Pron. E63	1834c
22. Drum Draoigheanach "Ridge of the Blackthorns"	J O'D (OSNB) E63	1834c
23. Druim Dhraoighneach "ridge of sloe bushes"	OSL Dn 62	1834
24. Druim-draoighneach "blackthorn ridge"	Joyce iii 321	1913
25. Druim draighneach	Mooney 25	1950c
26. ˌdrọm'grəina	Local pronunciation	1991
27. ˌdrọm'grinəx	Local pronunciation	1995

Drumdreenagh, usually listed with Tirygory, was part of the O'Roney holding, which eliminates confusion with the similarly-named **Drumgreenagh** in Drumgath, which originally had the same Irish name (*PNI* i 121–2). The two forms given for 1659 are both listed as being in this parish. In the 17th century the Drumballyroney one was apparently called Drumdreenagh "next to the *bawn*" (form 5) as distinct from that "next to Barnmeen" (in Drumgath). There is no trace of a bawn, although on a 350 foot hill there is the ploughed-out site of a rath and a rectangular enclosure (*ASCD* 156 §469 pl. 30). The reference is therefore probably to the river Bann, which forms the eastern boundary of the townland.

The forms provide further evidence for the change of initial *d* > *g* in the second element, discussed under **Drumgreenagh**. The change could be the result of dissimilation of *d-d-* to *d-g-*, or of delenition of *dh* [ɣ] in the dative form to [g]. John O'Donovan said that Drumdreenagh was "always pronounced by the natives *Drumgreenagh*, but this is an attempt at anglicizing *Druim Dhraoigheanach* 'ridge of sloes'" (*OSNB; OSL Dn* 62). Charles O'Hare of *Drumgreena* was cited as a local authority for the spelling of Lissize (*OSNB*), but it is not clear whether he was from this parish or from Drumgreenagh in Drumgath. In the case of Drumdreenagh the second *d-* has remained in the accepted spelling although not in pronunciation.

OS 1:10,000 sheet 253 shows Goak Hill, apparently "cuckoo hill" from Scots *gowk*, beside a farm in the south-west of Drumdreenagh, and Hanna's Hill a little further north.

Edenagarry	*Éadan Garraí*		
J 1717	"hillface of (the) garden"		

1. Ballyeddengary	CPR Jas I 395b	1609
2. Ballyedengarry	CPR Jas I 189a	1611
3. Ballyedengarrie	CPR Jas I 235a	1612
4. Edengarry	Ulst. Roll Gaol Deliv. 264	1613
5. Ballyedingary	Inq. Ult. (Down) §13 Car.I	1629
6. Edengery	Hib. Reg. Lr. Iveagh	1657c
7. Edingarye	Census 75	1659c
8. Edengary	BSD 114	1661
9. Edengery	Hib. Del. Down	1672c
10. Edengarvy al' Edengarry	ASE 274a 29	1681
11. Edengarny als Edengarry	Rent Roll Down 11	1692
12. Eddegarry als Eddengarry, more of	Rent Roll Down 11	1692
13. Edengarey	Ir. Wills Index 92	1724
14. Ednagarey	Ir. Wills Index 92	1731
15. Edengarry	Wm. Map (OSNB) E63	1810
16. Edenagary	Tombstone (OSNB) E63	1824
17. Ednegarry	Reg. Free. (OSNB) E63	1829
18. Ednagarry	Bnd. Sur. (OSNB) E63	1830c
19. [Ed-na-'gar-ry]	OSNB Pron. E63	1834c
20. Ednagarry	OSM iii 16a	1834
21. Ednagarry so pronounced	OSM iii 18b	1834
22. Eadan a' Gharraidh	Old Hennan and others (OSNB) E63	1834c
23. ˌidnəˈgarï	Local pronunciation	1991

Edenagarry, held in 1609 by Sir Art Magennis, extends over the south slope of Knock Iveagh, and includes Knock Terrace and the summit cairn. *Éadan* "hill-face" is a common element in Ulster place-names. The exact significance of *garraí* "enclosure, garden" is unclear. The summit of Knock Iveagh is rough and unenclosed, although I am reminded of the English name "The Steeple Garden" given to the field enclosing the summit cairn on the hill of Fairymount north of Lough Ree. The present form looks as if it contains the article, but if so the received form *Ednagarry* in 1834 shows that there were then only four syllables in pronunciation (forms 19,21). From the evidence of the earlier forms it seems that the name did not contain the article, and *Éadan Garraí* pronounced as [ˌeːdanˈgari] has been metathesized as *Edna-* [ˌidnəˈgari].

Grallaghgreenan   Originally two names:
J 1835   *Greallach* "miry land" and
                                              Grianán "eminent/gravelly place"

1. (?)hic Greallaigh Dollaith	AFM i 296–7 nn.o.& q.	693
2. (?)a nGreallaig Dhollaigh	AU (Mac Airt) 154–5	695
3. (?)Bogaine ina grellaig (hi Cuib)	TBC (Rec. I) l.1526	1100c
4. (?)Grellach Dolluid	TBC (Rec. I) l.2514–5	1100c
5. (?)Amrún Fer nDea... Grellach Dolluid indiu	Comp. CC 36 §35	1100c
6. (?)dolluid forsin ngrellaig... .i. Grellach Dolluid iarum.	IT II 2, 245 §5	1392c
7. (?)Greallagh Tollye	AFM i 297 n.o. (A.Clon.)	690
8. Ballygrenan (Sir A. Magenis)	CPR Jas I 395b	1609
9. Ballygrenane (Sir A Magenis)	CPR Jas I 189a	1611
10. Ballygrenan (Sir A Magenis)	CPR Jas I 235a	1612
11. Ballygrenan (Sir A Magenis)	Inq. Ult. (Down) §13 Car.I	1629
12. Gorynan 120a (Sir A Magenis)	Inq. Ult. (Down) §85 Car. I	1639
13. Greenan alias Grallagh	Civ. Surv. x §72	1655c
14. Grellagh al. Grinen	Hib. Reg. Up. Iveagh	1657c
15. Grullagh half towne	Census 75	1659c
16. Grallagh al Greenan	BSD 113	1661
17. Grelagh	Sub. Roll Down 277	1663
18. Grenin	Hib. Del. Down	1672c
19. Gralagh alias Grenane (manor of Rathfryland)	ASE 274a 29	1681
20. Gralagh als Grenan	Rent Roll Down 11	1692
21. Grallaghgreenan	Tombstone (OSNB) E63	1800
22. Gralaghgreenan	Wm. Map (OSNB) E63	1810
23. Gralaghgreenen	Ir. Wills Index iv 9	1829
24. Grallaghgreenan	Bnd. Sur. (OSNB) E63	1830c
25. Grallough	Clergyman (OSNB) E63	1834c
26. Greallach Grianáin "miry land of the fort or palace"	Old Hennan and others (OSNB) E63	1834c
27. "miry place of the sunny house"	Joyce iii 389	
28. Greithealach + Greanán, both "gravelly place"	Mooney 27	1950c
29. ˈgraləx	Local pronunciation	1996

Ballygrenan listed next to Seafin was held by Sir Art Magennis (8–11), and the current first element *Grallagh* does not appear until c. 1655, as an alias form (13). Judging by the alias forms, Grallaghgreenan must have been two places originally: possibly *Greallach* "miry place" plus *Grianán* "eminent place", not exactly Joyce's romantic translation "sunny house" (form 27). If there is a connection between the two words, in this case *grianán* might be "gravelly place" from *grean* "gravel" (*Joyce* ii 374), rather than *grian* "sun". There is no high ground in the townland, and there are marsh and ponds at the southern point, just south-east of McGinn's Cross. A map of 1743 still shows a lake between Lissize and Grallaghgreenan (*Harris Hist.*), and Hugh McGaffin in his pamphlet on *Southern County Down* (pp.26, 31) says that this area in the townland of *Grallagh*, where there is always water beneath the vegetation, is the source of the Clanrye River. The name is now generally Grallagh in local usage.

The element *greallach* is not particularly common: 20 townlands begin *Grallagh*, and there are references to about 25 different places in texts in Irish. It has been suggested by Hogan (*Onom. Goed.* 450b) that this place was *Grellach Dolluid* "marsh of loss(?)", the scene of a battle in c. 695 AD (forms 1, 2, and most of the Irish annals) and mentioned in three Ulster Cycle tales (*Táin Bó Cuailnge* (4), *Tochmarc Emire* (5), and *Táin Bó Regamna* (6)). A more likely identification from the *Táin* is *Grellach Boguine* in *Cuib* (**Iveagh**) or on *Slige Midluachra*, the main road north past Newry (*TBC Rec. I*1.1526; Haley 1970, 102). *Grellach Boguine* has elsewhere been associated with *Bend Boguine* on the north coast (*Met. Dinds.* iv 391), but could also be "the water or passage called the *Gralaghepatrick*" between Iveagh and Bagenal's country, i.e. Newry (*Fiants Eliz.* §4327) of which Grallaghgreenan could represent the eastern end, while Ballynamagna adjoining it might then preserve the element *Boguine*. There is a townland of Drumlisnagrilly (from *greallach*) in Co. Armagh beside the Bann where the river enters from Co. Down, but that seems too far north for Bagenal.

Imdel
Of uncertain origin

J 1536

1. (?)Cassán Imduail	Mart. Tal. 26–7 Mar.28	830c
2. (?)oc Imduail	Trip. Life (Stokes) 234	900c
3. (?)Cassán ó Imduail	Mart. Gorm. 64 Mar.28n	1630c
4. (?)Iomdual, Cassán of	Mart. Don. 89 Mar.28	1630c
5. (?)co Láegairi mBuagach co hImpail	TBC (Rec. I) l.3486	1100c
6. (?)Loegaire Buadach... ó Impuil	TBC (Rec. I) l.3654	1100c
7. (?)bú Imbial (rosc)	TBC (Rec. I) l.3932	1100c
8. (?)hi Ráith Impail	TBC (Rec. I) l.3369	1100c
9. (?)co Laegaire co hImmail		
(ms Immiaille)	TBC (LL) l.4083	1160c
10. (?)ó Immail	TBC (LL) l.4387	1160c
11. (?)Loegaire ó Ráith Immil	Mesca Ulad l.601	1160c
12. Emdell	CPR Jas I 395b	1609
13. Ballyedell, 2 tds	CPR Jas I 189a	1611
14. Emdell, 2 towns	CPR Jas I 235a	1612
15. Quibdell, Brian Offegan of	Ulst. Roll Gaol Deliv. 264	1613
16. Tindell	Inq. Ult. (Down) §13 Car. I	1629
17. 2 vil. de Emdell	Inq. Ult. (Down) §85 Car. I	1639
18. Emdell	Civ. Surv. x §72	1655c
19. Imdill	Hib. Reg. Up. Iveagh	1657c

20. Imdelld	Census 75	1659c
21. Imdill	Hib. Del. Down	1672c
22. Tindell or Imdell als Emdell	ASE 274a 29	1681
23. Imdell als Emdell	Rent Roll Down 11	1692
24. Imdall	Ir. Wills Index iv 38	1757
25. Imbdell	Ir. Wills Index 4	1770
26. Imdale	Tombstone (OSNB) E63	1785
27. Imdale	Ir. Wills Index iv 38	1799
28. Emdale	Wm. Map (OSNB) E63	1810
29. Imdeal	Bnd. Sur. (OSNB) E63	1830c
30. Embdale	Clergyman (OSNB) E63	1834c
31. Emdeal pronounced Em-del	OSNB Pron. E63	1834c
32. Emdeal	OSM iii 14a,16a	1834
33. Emdeal so pronounced	OSM iii 18a	1834
34. Eemdell	Ir. Wills Index 89	1842
35. In-deal "a border/limit"	Old Hennan and others (OSNB) E63	1834c
36. Indheall "border" ?	Mooney 27	1950c
37. 'əmdəl	Local pronunciation	1950c
38. 'ɛm'de:l	Local pronunciation	1995

Imdel is an almost circular townland, consisting of a foothill of Knock Iveagh (540 feet, *OSM* iii 14a), which was held in the early 17th century by Sir Art Magennis. Imdel is the western limit of the parish, and is bordered by seven other townlands. There is no obvious Irish equivalent. The current pronunciation, possibly represented or encouraged by the early 19th-century spellings (28, 30–4), seems to have been influenced by the English word *dale*, but an older pronunciation ['əmdəl] was remembered by some people until a generation ago.

Possibly this unusual name was the original name of Knock Iveagh, a notable landmark. Hogan (*Onom. Goed.* 456a, 572b) gives Imdel townland as the equivalent of both Laegaire Buadach's dwelling of *Impail* or *(Ráith) Immail* in the Ulster cycle (forms 5–11), and of *Imdual*, home of a holy man Cassán mentioned in three Irish martyrologies (forms 1, 3–4), and the place where St Patrick rode his chariot over his sister Lupait after her love affair with Colmán son of Ailill of *Uí Bresail* (form 2). Both these places could be in the right area, although neither can be definitely connected with Imdel.

There is little information about St Cassán, although the Cassán who was son of Moenach did have a brother Lochán in Iveagh (*i nUíb Echach, CSH* 298.2, 662.238, 730; *PNI* i 147). The tribe of *Uí Bresail* were located east of the city of Armagh. In the later Ulster cycle tales, which often promote the claims of the Uí Néill rather than the Ulaid, Laegaire Buadach is located at *Loch Laeghaire*, now **Lough Mary** beside Bessie Bell mountain in Tyrone (*Onom. Goed.* 500b). Significantly, this was also the chief residence of the descendants of Laeghaire son of Niall of the Uí Néill (*Aeidhe ma chroidhe* 162–3n). However, in the earlier tales which have *Immail* an Ulaid or east Ulster location is more plausible, particularly in *Mesca Ulad* where all the participating Ulster warriors are located in the east of the province (Muhr, *Emania* 1996 forthcoming).

The initial *Im-* in all these forms could be the prefix *imb-, imm-*, leniting, which can mean "very" or simply an intensive, used in the older language and "very common in Early Modern Irish" (*DIL*, for example: *imáille* "great beauty"; *imdol/imdul* "going"; *imb-ro-ól* > *imról* which from meaning "a great draught" came to mean "abundance"; *imbuile* from *imm-*

maíle "great baldness"). As place-name examples there are *Imchiúin* "very quiet", the name of a mythical Otherworld plain, and *Imchláir*, the oldest name of the area around Donaghmore parish in Tyrone (*Onom. Goed.*), which seems to be an intensive of *clár*, "a plain".

From the spellings with either *p* or *d*, *ai* or *ua*, forms (1–4) and (5–11) could well be two different places. The first early Irish name might be from *imm-* with *dual*, meaning "hereditary possession". The later spelling would be *Iomdhual*, which by reduction of the unstressed second element might have been anglicized as Imdel, spelling *d* for *dh*, [ɣ]. In the *Ecclesiastical Taxation* of 1306 the parish of Umgall in Co. Antrim is spelled *Indel* (*EA* 4).

The forms of the second Early Irish name do not fit well together, *Impail* in the early version of the *Táin* (5, 6, 8) becoming *Immail* later (9–11). *Impail* could be the product of *imb-* followed by a word beginning *s*, possibly *sail* "prop" (*DIL; Ó Dónaill*), as in *iompodh* the verbal noun of *imm-soí* "turns", where *s* unvoices *b* to *p* (*GOI* §841). If *-p-* were a spelling of *b*, in the early language *imb-* is written before a vowel or *f*, as in *imbe* "fencing", the verbal noun of *imm-fen*. "*Imbail*" might be *imb-* with *fail* fem. "ring, enclosure", possibly confused with *fál* masc. "hedge, enclosure" (cf. *iomfhál, Dinneen*) which might account for the variant endings. Later *mb* would be spelled *mm* as in *Immail*. In either case the spelling Imdel would have to go back to a mistake in the anglicized form. The word apparently at the back of Old Hennan's mind, in Old Irish *imbel* later *imeall* (neut. > masc.) "border", would likewise not explain the *-d-* in the 17th-century forms. Carney refers Old Irish *imbel* "border" to *bel*, the root form of *bealach* "road, pass" (*DIL sv. bel*). If *imeall* were the word in the place-name, Imdel would have to be an early written form reading *d* for *b*.

The etymology has to be based on the 17th-century forms. The *t*-prefix in the form *Tindell* (16,22) suggests the name might be a masculine noun (Appendix A §2). *Tin* could also simply be a misreading of *Im*. There are two early words *imdeall*, both originally neuter: 1. the "mashing" process in brewing, occasionally by transference "a feast" (*FB* §32); and the surviving word 2. "deceit, treachery" (*DIL, Ó Dónaill*). One could postulate compounds of *imm* with *dá(i)l* fem. "meeting" or *deil* fem. "prop" (*DIL*), in both of which Irish *dh* [ɣ] would have to be anglicized as *d*. *Imdheaghail* "defence" is unlikely to have been heard as two syllables in 1600. Dean Mooney was convinced (36) that *indeall* later *inneall* fem. "arrangement", sometimes *tinneall*, but meaning "border" (usually *imeall*) as given by Old Hennan to O'Donovan (35), was the original word.

Lackan
J 2336

Leacán
"(small) flagstone"

1. (?)L. Lakon	Hondius Map	1591
2. (?)Lo. Lackan	Mercator's Ulst.	1595
3. (?)Lo. Lackan	Boazio's Map (BM)	1599
4. Ballyleakin	CPR Jas I 395a	1609
5. (?)Lo. Lackan	Norden's Map	1610c
6. Ballyleakine	CPR Jas I 189a	1611
7. Ballyleakin	CPR Jas I 190b	1611
8. Balleleakine	Inq. Ult. (Down) §13 Car.I	1629
9. Ballelarkie	Inq. Ult. (Down) §85 Car.I	1639
10. (?)Loghan	Wars Co. Down x 77	1641
11. Lacken	Hib. Reg. Up. Iveagh	1657c
12. Lackin	Census 76	1659c
13. Lakane	BSD 114	1661

14. Lakney	Hib. Del. Down	1672c
15. Lackane	ASE 274a 29	1681
16. Leckane	Rent Roll Down 10	1692
17. Leken	Ir. Wills Index 101	1736
18. Leckan	Tombstone (OSNB) E63	1777
19. Laikan	Tombstone (OSNB) E63	1799
20. Lackan	Wm. Map (OSNB) E63	1810
21. Lacken	Tombstone (OSNB) E63	1812
22. Lackin	Newry Tel. (OSNB) E63	1828
23. Leacain "a hill-side"	J O'D (OSNB) E63	1834c
24. 'lɛkən	Local pronunciation	1991
25. 'lakən	Local pronunciation	1995

Lackan was part of the O'Roney holding, and contains the modern village of Ballyroney. "A long, irregular and hilly townland. The river Bann winding through a wide and deep valley partly skirts it on the west side. Kennedy's Hill towards the centre is the highest part of the townland. There are two lakes on its SE boundary" (*OSNB*). The OS 1:10,000 sheet 239 also shows Hamilton Hill and Crabtree Hill in the townland, with some rock outcropping in the south to the west of Crabtree Hill. This may have given the townland its name. The historical forms indicate two possibilities: *Leacán* "flagstone" and *Leacain* "hillside", originally "cheek". When the genitive of the word follows *baile* it is difficult to distinguish them, but the spellings in *-an(e)* (13,14,16) point to *leacán* rather than *leacain* as suggested by O'Donovan (form 23).

Several maps c. 1600 mark a lake called *Lo. Lackan* (forms 1–4, 6). The Ordnance Survey Memoir described "the Lacken or the Flow bog" in the townlands of Lackan and Ballyroney (*OSM* iii 14b), and in 1834 Lackan Lake, clearly the **Hunshigo Lake** of 1836 and modern usage: "In it the townlands of Lackan, Annahinchigo, Lisnisk and Teerygory meet" (*OSM* iii 14a).

Lisnacreevy
J 1637

Lios na Craobhaí
"fort/enclosure of the branchy place"

1. (?)Ballynecrivie (Sir A Magenis)	CPR Jas I 396a	1609
2. Ballynecreevie (Sir A. Magenis)	CPR Jas I 396a	1609
3. Ballynecrevie	CPR Jas I 189a	1611
4. (?)Ballynecrivie (Sir A. Magenis)		
	CPR Jas I 235a	1612
5. Ballynecreevie (Sir A. Magenis)	CPR Jas I 235a	1612
6. the fields of Lisnacrewe	Ulst. Roll Gaol Deliv. 262	1613
7. Ballelissnecryvie	Inq. Ult. (Down) §13 Car. I	1629
8. Ballelesnecreevy	Inq. Ult. (Down) §85 Car. I	1639
9. Lisnecreetty	Hib. Reg. Up. Iveagh	1657c
10. Lisnecreety	BSD 114	1661
11. Lisnecretty	Hib. Del. Down	1672c
12. Lisnacreevy	ASE 274a 29	1681
13. Lissnacrevy	Rent Roll Down 10	1692
14. Lisnacreevy	Wm. Map (OSNB) E63	1810

15. Lisnacreevy	Atkinson's Tour (OSNB) E63	1823
16. Lisnacreevy	Bnd. Sur. (OSNB) E63	1830c
17. Lios a'chraobhaidhe "Fort of the bush"	Old Hennan and others (OSNB) E63	1834c
18. Lios a'chraobhaidhe "Fort of the wide branching tree"	J O'D (OSNB) E63	1834c
19. Lios na craobhaighe "Fort of the spreading tree"	Mooney 29	1950c
20. ˌlïsnəˈkrivi	Local pronunciation	1991

Lisnacreevy was held by Sir Art Magennis, but there is a complication in the earlier sources, where his possessions included two units called *Ballinecrevie* or the like. There is also a townland in Aghaderg parish now called Creevy, and Lisnashanker in Magheralin was originally *Lios na Seanchraobh* "fort of the old trees". Although the forms for these were confusingly similar, they can be distinguished by being located in the Magennis districts of Shankill and Lequirin. The problem of Sir Art's second *Ballinecrevie*, listed next to townlands in Aghaderg, is solved by Petty's map of Co. Down which shows a land unit called Creevy, now lost, near Banbridge.

As regards Lisnacreevy, the first element, *lios* "fort, enclosure", was not part of the name before 1629. The 1:50,000 map shows a rath beside a farm north of Lisnacreevy House, and on 1:10,000 sheet 238 there is another on the southern boundary with Edenagarry, though neither is described in *ASCD*. It is hard to be sure whether the second element is the word *craobh* "branch, bushy tree", or the derivative *craobhach* "place of branches" (19). The genitive of the first would have a final [ə] vowel, which might be anglicized *y*, the second would have a clearer [i] sound, which is probably what is represented here by the spelling *-ie* (forms 2, 3, 5, 7). *Lios na Craobhaí* also seems to be what is intended by form (17) suggested by Old Hennan to O'Donovan. Lisnacreevy House, on the 1:50,000 map, was inhabited by a magistrate called Corbett in 1886 (*Bassett's Down* 57).

Lisnacroppan
J 1937

Lios na gCnapán
"fort/enclosure of the lumps"

1. Ballyracowlan	CPR Jas I 395a	1609
2. Ballyracoughlane	CPR Jas I 189a	1611
3. Ballyraconlan	CPR Jas I 190b	1611
4. lands of Raconyglan	Inq. Ult. (Down) xlii	1618
5. lands of Raconyglan	CPR Jas I 304b	1623
6. Balleraconoghkan	Inq. Ult. (Down) §13 Car.I	1629
7. Balleraconnaghlan	Inq. Ult. (Down) §85 Car.I	1639
8. Kneknapan	Census 75	1659c
9. Lisnappan	BSD 113	1661
10. Lisenappan	Sub. Roll Down 276	1663
11. Lisnacrappan	Wm. Map (OSNB) E63	1810
12. Lisnacruppen	County Warrant (OSNB) E63	1827
13. Lisnacrappan	Bnd. Sur. (OSNB) E63	1830c
14. [Lis-na-'crap-pan]	OSNB Pron. E63	1834c
15. Lisnacrappan, Old Hennan of	J O'D (OSNB) E63	1834c

16. Lisnacroppan	J O'D (OSNB) E63	1834c
17. Lisnacrappen so pronounced	OSM iii 18a	1834
18. Lisnacrappin	Ir. Wills Index 96	1846
19. Lisnacrappin	Ir. Wills Index 96	1848
20. Lios a chrappáin "Lumpy fort"	OSNB Inf. E63	1834c
21. Lios a' chrappáin "Fort of the knoll or hillock"	Old Hennan and others (OSNB) E63	1834c
22. Lios na cnapóg/cnapán	Mooney 29	1950c
23. Rath Chonghaláin	Mooney 29	1950c
24. ˌləsnəˈkrɔpən	Local pronunciation	1991
25. ˌlïsnəˈkrapən	Local pronunciation	1995

Lisnacroppan can be identified as part of the holding of the family of O'Roney, since from the names mentioned in the investigation of bounds in 1618 (*Inq. Ult.* xlii) the O'Roney unit called *Raconlan*, possibly "Conlan's rath", was in the position of this townland. The current name with *lios* sounds more recent, and in the *Ordnance Survey Namebook* Lumpy Fort has been entered in the received name column, possibly as the local translation into English. There were "four ancient forts, the most westerly of which is on the highest hill in the townland" (*OSNB*). The mound and enclosing bank in the west, discussed under **Ballybrick**, is on a hill 140 metres high (*ASCD* 94), and there are two other raths in the middle of the townland (1:10,000 sheet 238). It is unclear why, given his etymology and the spellings available to him, almost all ending -*crappan*, O'Donovan changed the spelling to Lisnacroppan. In the immediate area the name is still pronounced with *a* (form 25).

Lisnavaghrog　　　　　　　　　*Lios na bhFeathróg*
J 2038　　　　　　　　　　　　　"fort/enclosure of the woodbines"

1. Ballylisnevaghorke	CPR Jas I 395a	1609
2. Ballilisnevaghorke	CPR Jas I 189a	1611
3. Ballylisnevaghorke	CPR Jas I 190b	1611
4. Lysmaghtknock	Inq. Ult. (Down) xlii	1618
5. Kisnevachorkie, Donnell Banne McBrady of	CPR Jas I 373b	1618
6. Lissmagherknocke	CPR Jas I 304b	1623
7. Ballelissnevahorke	Inq. Ult. (Down) §13 Car. I	1629
8. Ballelisnevaghirke	Inq. Ult. (Down) §85 Car. I	1639
9. Lisnevoghoge	Hib. Reg. Up. Iveagh	1657c
10. Lisnenaghough	Census 75	1659c
11. Lisnaraghoge	BSD 113	1661
12. Lisnevoghoge	Hib. Del. Down	1672c
13. Lisnavaghrog	Wm. Map (OSNB) E63	1810
14. Lisnavaghrel	County Warrant (OSNB) E63	1827
15. Lisnavaghroug	Tombstone (OSNB) E63	1829
16. Lisnamaugheral	Bnd. Sur. (OSNB) E63	1830c
17. [Lis-na-'magh-e-ral]	OSNB Pron. E63	1834c
18. Lisnavaghrog	J O'D (OSNB) E63	1834c
19. Lisnamaugheral so pronounced	OSM iii 18ab	1834

20. Lisnamaugheral	OSM iii 15b	1836
21. Lisnavaghrol	Ir. Wills Index iv 9	1846
22. Lios na bhfeathrog		
"Fort of the woodbine"	Old Hennan and others (OSNB) E63	1834c
23. Liosán a' mhaghchnuic "Fort of the		
great/prominent hill"	Mooney 31	1950c
24. ˌlisnəˈvahrɔg	Local pronunciation	1995
25. ˈmaxərəl	Local pronunciation	1995

Lisnavaghrog was part of the O'Roney holding. There is little doubt about the first element, where *lios* refers to a monument which is still well-preserved (*ASCD* 181). As described in the 1830s, "There is a very fine fort here near the road surrounded by two wide deep ditches" (*OSNB*). The site was also described by O'Donovan, who commented on the fine view from many old forts:

> My eye was caught by a beautiful fort to the east of the road. It is called in Irish *Lios na bhFeathróg* and the townland derives its name from it. It consists of two circular mounds or ramparts, and two wide and deep ditches which I found it very difficult to cross... From *Lios na bhFeathróg* you can see a great extent of country in every direction (*OSL Dn* 59).

Although I have accepted the local Irish version (22), the final element is difficult to reconcile with the historical sources. From other local information in 1834–6 the name was "*Lisnamaugheral*, so pronounced" and spelled the same (19, 20), and this was used by the Boundary Surveyor (16), and accepted as the received name in the first Name-book, until altered by John O'Donovan (form 18). A variant ending *-vaghrel* appears in forms 14, 21. Without *lios*, Magheral is the name now given to the Roman Catholic chapel in the townland, erected in the early 19th century by the Rev. James McKey. In the 1960s the primary school was referred to as Magheral, although the name Lisnavaghrog was on the official register. At that time, but no longer, the names Lisnavaghrog and (Lisna-)Magheral were regarded as alternative versions of the townland name.

In 1834 the Irish form *Lios na bhFeathróg* "fort of the woodbine" (more correctly, "woodbines") was agreed by "Mrs Con Magennis, Old Hennan, and all others who speak Irish" (22). However the term the dictionary gives for woodbine is *feithleog* or *feathlóg*, not *feathróg* (*Ó Dónaill*). After the initial *Lios* there is no *l* in the early 17th-century forms (1, 2, 3, 6, 7), which seem to show *feathróg* metathesized to *feathorg*, although the spelling *gh* might indicate *feachróg*, a variant of *feachrán* "barb". If the name began as *Lios na bhFeathlóg* it might have developed into the two variant local pronunciations by metathesis of *l,r,g* and delenition of *v* to *m*. However it seems much more likely that *Lios na bhFeathróg* developed from *Lios na bhFeathlóg* "fort of the woodbines", and that the form Lisnamagheral is from a different plant: *Lios na mBachrán* "fort of the bog-beans", with interchange of the final *-n* with *-l*. It could refer to a different fort, since there is another behind the Groves' farm on the other side of the road.

Like many *lios*-names in Co. Down, *Lios na bhFeathróg* seems to be a late descriptive name. It may be a reinterpretation of the original name of the site. Dean Mooney based his suggestion *maghchnoc* on the spelling of the final element in the 1618 investigation of bounds (forms 4, 6), where it begins with *magh* and ends in *knock(e)*. Texts on boundaries sometimes seem to preserve an independent record of the name, but "the great hill" (*DIL*) makes little sense for a foothill of Knock Iveagh, and -*nock* could have been a misreading of -*hork*.

Lisnisk   *Lios an Uisce*
J 2355   "fort/enclosure of the water"

1. Ballylisenoskie	CPR Jas I 396a	1609
2. Ballilissenuskie	CPR Jas I 189a	1611
3. Ballylissenusky	CPR Jas I 235a	1612
4. Lysneusque	Inq. Ult. (Down) xlii	1618
5. Lisneusque	CPR Jas I 304b	1623
6. Ballylissenuskie	Inq. Ult. (Down) §13 Car.I	1629
7. Lissenusky	Inq. Ult. (Down) §85 Car.I	1639
8. Liskenmusky	Inq. Ult. (Down) §85 Car.I	1639
9. Lisumsky	Hib. Reg. Up. Iveagh	1657c
10. Lisenusky	Census 76	1659c
11. Lismuisky	BSD 113	1661
12. Lissinisky	ASE 91a 4	1678
13. Limisky	Rent Roll Down 8	1692
14. Lisnisky	Harris Hist. map	1743
15. Lisnisk	Wm. Map (OSNB) E63	1810
16. [Lis-'nisk]	OSNB Pron. E63	1834c
17. Lios an Uisge "Fort of the water"	Old Hennan and others (OSNB) E63	1834c
18. Lios [na] naosg "Fort of the snipes"	Clergyman (OSNB) E63	1834c
19. ˌləsˈnəsk	Local pronunciation	1991

The townland of Lisnisk was held in 1609 by Sir Art Magennis. Old Hennan's etymology (17) corresponds to the early forms, where the four syllables of *Lios an Uisce* are evident throughout the 17th century. The townland is bounded on the south-east by the river Muddock, and on the south and west by the river Bann. "It is a very flat townland" (*OSNB*). It contains Bannfield Bog, the largest bog in the parish, very deep and wet. "In the middle there are some spots dangerous to cross and said to be more than 20 feet deep, which the inhabitants term *quaws*" (*OSM* iii 10b, 14b; cf. Irish *caoth* "boghole").

Lissize   *Lios Seaghsa*
J 1833   "enclosure of the wood/wooded height"

1. Lissyse	Hib. Reg. Up. Iveagh	1657c
2. Lyseyse	Hib. Reg. Up. Iveagh	1657c
3. Lisseis (Drumballironow)	BSD 113 (cf 110 Drumgath)	1661
4. Lysise 153a, more of the same 174a	Rent Roll Dn 10	1692
5. Lisize	Harris Hist. map	1743
6. Lissize	Wm. Map (OSNB) E63	1810
7. Lessize	Tombstone (OSNB) E63	1821
8. [Lis-'size]	OSNB Pron. E63	1834c
9. Lios Adas(?)	OSNB Inf. E63	1834c

10. Lios Size "Size's fort"	J O'D (OSNB) E63	1834c
11. Lios Shaghas "Size's fort" (Size a rare surname)	Mooney 31	1950c
12. ˌləˈsaiz	Local pronunciation	1991

Lissize was one of the "four towns of Rathfriland" held by Sir Art Magennis, and was shared between the parishes of Drumgath (*PNI* i 123) and Drumballyroney. The name does not appear before 1657, but the division is already evident in the sources, where the name is listed separately for each parish (forms 1–4). There is no longer any fort to be seen. O'Donovan and Mooney recorded the local interpretation that the place-name contains a surname, but it seems this tradition relates to the name *Sawey*, which still exists locally and is pronounced ['sai]. However it is unlikely that the possessive of a surname apparently of English origin would be included in a townland name where the word order is Irish.

Moneygore   *Mónaidh Ghabhar*
J 2233   "goats' bog"

1. Ballymondgare	CPR Jas I 395b	1609
2. Monygare	CPR Jas I 189a	1611
3. Ballyemonygare	CPR Jas I 235a	1612
4. Ballymonygard	Inq. Ult. (Down) §13 Car.I	1629
5. Monegare	Inq. Ult. (Down) §85 Car. I	1639
6. Monygar 120a	Inq. Ult. (Down) §85 Car.I	1639
7. Monygar, Ptk O'Doran de	Inq. Ult. (Down) §85 Car.I	1639
8. Monigar	Hib. Reg. Up. Iveagh	1657c
9. Mourgarr	Census 76	1659c
10. Momgarr	BSD 113	1661
11. Monygarr	Sub. Roll Down 276	1663
12. Nominegare alias Monygarre	ASE 91a 4	1667
13. Moniger	Hib. Del. Down	1672c
14. Moynegare als Monygare	Rent Roll Down 8	1692
15. Moneygor	Wm. Map (OSNB) E63	1810
16. Moneygore	Bnd. Sur. (OSNB) E63	1830c
17. Monigore	Tombstone (OSNB) E63	1834c
18. Muine Ghaur "Goat's bog" [sic]	OSNB Inf. E63	1834c
19. Muine Gabhar "brake or shrubbery of the goats"	J O'D (OSNB) E63	1834c
20. Móin na nGabhar "Goats' bog"	Mooney 33	1950c
21. ˌmɒnïˈgɔːr	Local pronunciation	1991
22. ˈmɒnïˌgɔr	Local pronunciation	1995

Moneygore belonged to Sir Art Magennis, and was held in 1630 by Patrick O'Doran. Although the Irish form of the first element is given as *muine* "brake or shrubbery" in the name-book (forms 18,19) it appears that Goats' Bog was the local understanding of the name. There is no evidence for the article between the two elements, unless the Irish form was *Móin na nGabhar* "bog of the goats", as suggested by Mooney (form 20). The 17th-century forms of **Knocknagore** in Tullylish also spell the final element *gabhar* as *-gare*. The townland is well-watered, although no bog is shown at present. "A stream running north-east through the centre divides it into two long hills. This stream enters the Bann river, which skirts the townland on the north-east side" (*OSNB*). Bannfield Bridge, in 1834 a ford called Bannfield Steps (*OSM* iii 16a), gives access to Bannfield, a farm across the Bann in Lisnisk.

Rossconor	*Ros Conchúir*	
J 2034	"Conor's wood"	
1. Rosconor	Rent Roll Down 13	1692
2. (?)Rosslenan	Rent Roll Down 10	1692
3. Rossconnor	Wm. Map (OSNB) E63	1830
4. Rosconnor	Bnd. Sur. (OSNB) E63	1830c
5. ['Ross-con-nor]	OSNB Pron. E63	1834c
6. Ros Conchobhair "Conor's point or wood"	Old Hennan and others (OSNB) E63	1834c
7. ˌrɔs'kɔnər	Local pronunciation	1995

This townland on the east side of Rathfriland, first mentioned by name in 1692, is presumably the last of the four towns of Rathfriland held by Sir Art Magennis. "The town of Rathfriland on the south-west boundary is the highest part of this townland... The greater part is divided into small square fields called Town-parks" (*OSNB*).

The name Rossconor could be *Ros Conaire* "wood of the path". However, as explained by Old Hennan, it could also contain a reference to the Ulster Cycle of early Irish literature in the name of *Conchobhar*, later *Conchúr*, the legendary king of *Emain Macha* (*TBC* passim). Many of the stories were about cattle-raiding, and another of the four towns is **Kiltarriff** "wood of bulls", also first mentioned in 1692 (*PNI* i 122-3). Poetry composed for the Magennises associated them with the ancient heroes (*Teall. Uí Echach* 92–3; *BM Cat.* i 396–7).

Although *Conchobhar/Conchúr* remained in use it was not a common name among the Magennises. In parts of Ireland *Conchobhar* developed into *Cnochúr* in Irish (cf. *Knoghor* McCarey in Co. Antrim, *CPR Jas I* 92b), but the name was generally anglicized as *Connogher* or *Connor* in 17th-century Ulster (*CPR Jas I* 32–34, 144a, 227b, 474b), and a *Concher* Boy McConwah was mentioned in Co. Down in 1618 (*Inq. Ult.* xliv).

Seafin	*Suí Finn*	
J 2138	"Finn's seat"	
1. Caislén Mhuighe Cobha	AFM iii 344	1252
2. Caislen Mhuige Cobha	ALC i 398	1252
3. Caslén Moigi Caba	A. Conn. 106	1252
4. Caislen Muighe-Cobha do dhenamh	AU ii 314-5	1252
5. Caislen Muighe-cabha do sgris	AU ii 316-7	1253
6. go Moigh Cobha gur trascradh a chaislén	AFM iii 348	1253
7. castle of Maicove	CDI ii §32,124	1252

8. de auxilio castri de Mayncove	ASCD 209	1255c
9. ad castrum de Maincoue	Anal. Hib. ii 262, 264	1255c
10. de exercitu... de Maincoue	Anal. Hib. ii 263, 264	1255c
11. de servitio de Maincoue	Anal. Hib. ii 263	1255c
12. Ballyliphyn	CPR Jas I 395b	1609
13. Ballysiffyn	CPR Jas I 189a	1611
14. Ballyseiphin [?sciphin]	CPR Jas I 235a	1612
15. Ballysiffer	Inq. Ult. (Down) §13 Car. I	1629
16. Syfin	Inq. Ult. (Down) §85 Car. I	1639
17. See Fyn	Census 75	1659c
18. Syfinn	BSD 113	1661
19. Seafine	Rent Roll Down 9	1692
20. Seafin, ruins at...	Statist. Sur. Dn 306	1802
21. Seafin	Wm. Map (OSNB) E63	1810
22. Seafin	Tombstone (OSNB) E63	1818
23. Seafin	Bnd. Sur. (OSNB) E63	1834c
24. ['Sea-fin]	OSNB Pron. E63	1834c
25. Seaphin	Ir. Wills Index iv 9	1845
26. Suidhe Finn "Finn's seat / sitting place"	Mrs Con Magennis (OSNB) E63	1834c
27. Seafin "seat of Finn"	Joyce iii 550	1913
28. si:'fən	Local pronunciation	1991
29. 'si'fin	Local pronunciation	1995

   Seafin townland in the middle of the parish contained the ruins of a castle and belonged to Sir Art Magennis. "On the top of a small hill over the river Bann on the east end of the townland of Seafin are the ancient foundations of a large castle which tradition states to have been built by Fin McCoole" (*OSM* iii 16b). Mrs Con Magennis explained her Irish form *Suidhe Finn* "Finn's seat" (26), as "i.e. Finn MacCumhail, the ruins of the castle at Seafin having been one of his military stations", and told O'Donovan a number of legends connected with the place. "These legends she does not believe, but she told them faithfully as she had heard them" (*OSL Dn* 63). It is remarkable that a 13th-century castle (see below) has been associated with one of the chief heroes of Irish legend. O'Donovan, convinced the castle was "of modern erection", preferred to think that "an old fort near the castle, now just levelled" was "the real Seafin or station of Finn" (*OSL Dn* 63).

   Since O'Donovan's time Seafin castle has been identified with the rebuilding of the Anglo-Norman castle of *Magh Cobha* (1–11; Lawlor, H. 1938 (b), 88), although it was O'Donovan who first located the plain of *Magh Cobha* in **Iveagh**, not in Tyrone (Coagh) as had been previously thought (*AFM* iii 81 n.q, 344 n.u). The Irish annals (forms 1–4) tell how the castle was built in the same year, AD 1252, as a castle at *Caeluisce* ("Narrowwater"), though it is unlikely this could be Narrow Water in south Down (*PNI* i 163–4). The castle of *Magh Cobha* was attacked and "destroyed" in 1253 by Brian O'Neill king of Cenél nEogain (forms 5, 6; Waterman 1955, 95). Latin documents refer to the repairing of the castle and the supplying of its garrison after the attack, but after 1305 there is little information. It may be significant that the Magennis chief retained Seafin with its stone castle, while granting the earlier fortification, on the opposite bank in **Ballyroney**, to the O'Roney family.

Seafin Castle (J 2138) lies on "a narrow curving promontory formed by a double bend of the river Bann, close to its junction with the Drumadonnell River" (*ASCD* 219). An interesting feature of the townland boundary east of the castle is that it follows a former course of the river Bann, an oxbow lake now lying south-east of the river among trees (OS 1:10,000 sheet 238). The name Seafin, rather than *Magh Cobha*, was established by the 17th century. The received form in the first name-books was *See-Finn*, altered to one word by O'Donovan, although the stress now is either equal or on the second syllable. There is no evidence for the comment "Now Castletown" (*OSNB*), since Castletown and *See Fyn* were both listed in c. 1659 (form 17), and *Castletown* clearly referred to **Ballyroney**.

Tirfergus	*Tír Fearghais*	
J 2134	"Fergus' land"	
1. Tyrfarish	CPR Jas I 395b–396a	1609
2. Terfurishe	CPR Jas I 235a	1612
3. 1/4 de Tarfarish	Inq. Ult. (Down) §13 Car.I	1629
4. Tyrfargus	Inq. Ult. (Down) §85 Car. I	1639
5. Tonfergus	Hib. Reg. Up. Iveagh	1657c
6. Tyrfergus 1/2 towne	Census 76	1659c
7. Tirefurgus	BSD 113	1661
8. Torfergus	Hib. Del. Down	1672c
9. Terfirgus	ASE 274a 29	1681
10. Tyrefurgus	Rent Roll Down 10	1692
11. Teerfergus	Wm. Map (OSNB) E63	1810
12. Terferguis	Tombstone (OSNB) E63	1821
13. Tierfergus	Ir. Wills Index iv 133	1833
14. Tierfergus	Tombstone (OSNB) E63	1834c
15. ['Teer-fer-gus]	OSNB Pron. E63	1834c
16. Teerfergus so pronounced	OSM iii 18a	1834
17. Tír feargaidh "Fergy's land"	Old Hennan etc. (OSNB) E63	1834c
18. Tír fearghuis (-ghusa)	Mooney 35	1950c
19. ˌtʃirˈfəːrgəs	Local pronunciation	1995

Tirfergus townland, not far north of Rathfriland, belonged to Sir Art Magennis. On the north it is bounded by Tirkelly, which is separated by the Bann from Tirygory further east. All three have the first element *tír* "land", which only appears in the names of these three townlands in Co. Down, although it is used for the names of the counties of Donegal (*Tír Chonaill*) and Tyrone (*Tír Eoghain*) and is found widely elsewhere. Dean Mooney's opinion here was that "All lands in *tír* are reclaimed bog" (*Mooney MS* 35). The second element is usually either a personal or a family name. In Tirfergus it is clearly the personal name Fergus "chosen man" (Lewis and Pedersen 1937, 21), in later Irish *Fearghas*. The subsequent loss of lenited g [ɣ] in pronunciation is clearly shown in the earliest forms here (1, 2, 3). These forms also have the final -*sh* that indicates that the genitive form used was *Fearghais* rather than the older genitive *Fearghasa*. From the mid-17th-century the accepted anglicization of the name, Fergus, reappears, although Old Hennan gave the name as a pet form, Feargaidh. *Joyce* also (ii 381) referred to "the local pronunciation of some old people as *Tirfergagh*" but the earlier spellings make it clear Fergus was the original name.

176

Fergus was "an extremely common name in the early period" (Ó Corráin and Maguire 1981, 97). However, apart from *Fergus mac Aedáin*, king of Uí Echach and of Ulster who died in 692 AD, it was not a common name for historical characters in Iveagh, although a Fergus Magennis of Greenan, Dromore, was cited in 1641 (*Wars Co. Dn* x 80a). One could suspect again the influence of the Ulster cycle, as in **Rossconor** above. Carrickfergus in Antrim, as well as having a legendary connection with king Fergus of Dál Riata who led his people over to Scotland (Boece and 17th-century local tradition, *MacDonnells Antrim* 6, 386), is also associated with the Ulster hero Fergus mac Róich in Irish literature from the 13th century on (*Cath Aen. Macha* §5; *Duan. Finn* ii 282-3). Initial *F* is often not lenited (*PNI* i 144).

There is a rath beside a farm called Heron's Hill on a hilltop in the townland (1:10,000 Sheet 253).

Tirkelly　　　　　　　　　　　*Tir Cheallaigh*
J 2136　　　　　　　　　　　　　"Ceallach's land"

1. Ballykiltykelly	Inq. Ult. (Down) §85 Car. I	1639
2. Kiltokelly	Inq. Ult. (Down) §85 Car. I	1639
3. Killkilly	Hib. Reg. Up. Iveagh	1657c
4. Terekelly	Census 75	1659c
5. Killkilly	BSD 114, 115	1661
6. Killkilly	Hib. Del. Down	1672c
7. Kilkelly	ASE 274a 29	1681
8. Killkelly	Rent Roll Down 10	1692
9. Tierkelly	Harris Hist. map	1743
10. Tierkelly, chalybeate spring at	Harris Hist. 166,170	1744
11. Teerkelly	Wm. Map (OSNB) E63	1810
12. ['Teer-kel-ly]	OSNB Pron. E63	1834c
13. Teerkelly so pronounced	OSM iii 18a	1834
14. Tír Cheallaigh "Kellagh's District"	Mrs Con Magennis (OSNB) E63	1834c
15. Coill > Tír Uí Cheallaigh "Kellagh's land"	Mooney 35	1950c
16. ˌtiːrˈkɛlï	Local pronunciation	1991

Tirkelly is bordered by the Bann on the north-east, and by a stream running into it on the south-east. It belonged to the Magennis chief, but is not in the list of Magennis lands in 1609, not being mentioned till 1639. The interpretation *Tir Cheallaigh* "Kellagh's district" was given by Mrs Con Magennis (14), anglicizing the Irish personal name *Ceallach* which was most common from the 7th to the 11th century (*AU;AFM*). In this place-name the element *tír* does not appear before 1659, and was possibly applied by analogy with Tirfergus and Tirygory to the west and east. The earliest forms suggest *Coillte Ceallaigh* "Ceallach's woods". As Mooney says, maybe "the name was changed when the woods were cut down", as in the townland of **Cappagh**, Annaclone. Some trees just east of Whitegates crossroads are the only remnant of former woods, and there is a fort called Hart's Fort (OS 1:10,000 sheet 238).

Although it is not as visible in the spellings as with Tirygory above, the second element could also be the surname Kelly, *Tír* or *Coillte Uí Cheallaigh*. The family of *Ó* or *Mac Ceallaigh* seem to appear in the district name *Slught Kellies (Sliocht Ceallaigh)* c. 1600 in north Co. Down (see **Clanbrassil McGoolechan**), and in the townlands of **Carnacally** in Newry (*PNI* i 11), and **Ballykelly** in Seapatrick.

Tirygory	*Tír Uí Ghothraidh*	
J 2335	"O'Gorry's land"	

1.	Ballyhurrygory	CPR Jas I 395a	1609
2.	Ballyhirrigorie	CPR Jas I 189a	1611
3.	Ballyhyrrygorry	CPR Jas I 190b	1611
4.	Ballyterrigory	Inq. Ult. (Down) §13 Car.I	1629
5.	Balleherregory	Inq. Ult. (Down) §13 Car.I	1629
6.	Ballytiregory	Inq. Ult. (Down) §85 Car.I	1639
7.	Ballehiregory	Inq. Ult. (Down) §85 Car.I	1639
8.	Tirgory	Inq. Ult. (Down) §85 Car.I	1639
9.	Ballytirgory	Inq. Ult. (Down) §85 Car.I	1639
10.	Terregory	Hib. Reg. Up. Iveagh	1657c
11.	Tirgory bog	Hib. Reg. Up. Iveagh	1657c
12.	Tyrgerye	Census 76	1659c
13.	Tyrygory	BSD 114	1661
14.	Teergorrie	Sub. Roll Down 276	1663
15.	Toregory	ASE 91a 4	1678
16.	Toregory	Rent Roll Down 8	1692
17.	Teerygoary/gory	Ir. Wills Index 1	1799
18.	Teeragorry	Tombstone (OSNB) E63	1800
19.	Terrygory	Wm. Map (OSNB) E63	1810
20.	Teeragory	Tombstone (OSNB) E63	1824
21.	Tiergory	Reg. Free. (OSNB) E63	1829
22.	Teeregory	Bnd. Sur. (OSNB) E63	1830c
23.	['Teer-a-'go-ry]	OSNB Pron. E63	1834c
24.	Teeregory	OSM iii 14ab,16a	1834
25.	Tirygory	OSM iii 10b,12ab	1836
26.	Tír Uí Ghoraidh "O'Gorey's land/district"	Old Hennan etc. (OSNB) E63	1834c
27.	ˌtʃərˈgɔri	Local pronunciation	1995

Tirygory was part of the O'Roney holding. Evidence of its earlier state is provided by the small canoe "found at the edge of a bog in Teeregory townland about 5 ft under the surface... on a bank of sand" (*OSM* iii 16b). Most of the spellings, and the local pronunciation in 1834 (form 23), have a vowel after the element *Tír*, and the second part of the name was interpreted by Old Hennan as a surname *Ó Goraidh,* which O'Donovan derived "from Anglo-Norman Godfrey". A surname formed with *Ó* "grandson (of)" is the most likely explanation of the second syllable. The early native name Guaire was also suggested for the final element (*OSNB*). Fiachnae mac Baedán, the king of Dál nAraide and Ulster who died in 626 AD, had a brother Guaire from whom a line descended (*Descendants Ir* xiv 115), but the name seems to have been obsolete when surnames were being formed. According to Woulfe (1923, 544) *Ó Gothraidh* was a "not uncommon surname in east Limerick and Tipperary", derived from the name Godfrey "God-peace" which was "introduced by the Danes and early adopted by the Irish". Gorrey O'Gorrey was pardoned in Fermanagh in 1606 (*CPR Jas I* 91a), but there is no early record of the surname in Co. Down. O'Donovan changed the received spelling from *Teeregory* to give his standard anglicization of Irish *tír* "land", now reduced to [tʃər] in the pronunciation of this name (27).

OTHER NAMES

Ballyroney Lake	A hybrid form
J 2237	

The townland of Ballyroney "settlement of O'Roney" is divided by the Drumadonnell river flowing into the Bann, south of which are Ballyroney Lake and Duggan's Hill. Ballyroney lake contains two islands, both tree-covered in 1834 (*OSM* iii 10b). "The island in the centre appears as a possible crannog, but there is no evidence of early occupation here" (*ASCD* 183).

Bannfield	An English form	
1. Bannfield Bog	OSNB E63	1834c
2. 'ban,fild	Local pronunciation	1995

The name of the river **Bann** has already been discussed at its source in Clonduff parish (*PNI* iii 175–7). The English derivative Bannfield began as the name of a house, situated above the flat land near the eastern bank of the river in Lisnisk townland (1:10,000 sh. 254), which has then given its name to a bog in **Lisnisk** and Tirygory (J 2335), and a bridge (J 2234) over the Bann on a minor road almost due east of Rathfriland. The bridge had not been built in 1834: "There is a ford over the same river (Bann) in Moneygore townland generally known as the Bannfield steps" (*OSM* iii 16a).

Brontë Memorial	An English form
J 1537	

The Brontë Memorial began as a ruined cottage on the slope of the hill in the north-west of Imdel townland, close to the road and stream that forms the boundary with Lisnacreevy. In the late 18th century it was occupied by Hugh Prunty, and was the birthplace in 1777 of his son Patrick. The ten children were reared in Ballynaskeagh in Aghaderg, attending the parish church, and Patrick at 16 opened a school in the parish of Drumgooland. His ability was recognized by the vicar, the Rev. Thomas Tighe, who assisted him to study at the University of Cambridge, where he graduated in 1806. As intended Patrick Brontë was ordained as an Anglican clergyman, and from 1811 spent the rest of his long life in Yorkshire where his own family grew up (*Atkinson's Dromore* 178, 225).

Thanks to enthusiasts for the writings of the Brontë sisters, the Creem family who owned the site, and the interest of the people of the neighbourhood, the tumbled walls of the cottage were partly reconstructed, and on Saturday, July 21, 1956 several hundred people assembled for the unveiling of a plaque on the site. It reads: "Patrick Brontë, father of Charlotte, Branwell, Emily and Anne, was born here on March 17, 1777."

The Gaelic surname *Ó Proinntí* was known in the 17th century in Co. Armagh, "later O Pruntys, O Prontys, Pruntys, Prentys, Prenties and Bruntys.... Just when the change took

179

place to the present conformation has not been definitely ascertained. It is interesting, however, to note that in County Armagh the O Pruntys of 1625 had become O Prentys by 1664, and Brontys by 1714... in 1714 we find a Torlagh Bronty of Armaghbrague who, indeed, may have been the elusive ancestor of the Brontes of County Down" (T.G.F. Paterson 1976, 168–174). The spelling *Bronte* was used in Co. Down, though the diaresis may have been adopted by the Rev. Patrick after his move to England (Crowe, H. 1969, 35-6). There are still Brontes in the area.

| **Crabtree Hill** | An English form | |
| J 2336 | | |

| 1. 'krabtri 'hïl | Local pronunciation | 1996 |

This is one of a group of hills round the bog between Ballyroney and Ballyward. It is 100 metres high, and is in the townland of Lackan. It appears to be named from crabapple trees, sometimes called crabtree (*Shorter OED*). A surname is also possible, although the name is not discussed in the standard works on Irish or Scottish surnames (Bell, Black, MacLysaght, Woulfe). Crabtree is a fairly rare English topographical surname, which has arisen in various places but particularly in west Yorkshire (McKinley, R. 1990, 184,63). There are two people surnamed Crabtree in the 1994 Northern Ireland telephone directory.

| **Diamond** | An English form | |
| J 1937 | | |

| 1. ðə 'daimənd | Local pronunciation | 1995 |

This Diamond is a crossroads at the forking of the B-road between Rathfriland and Banbridge at the northern end of Lisnacroppan. For discussion of the name see **The Diamond** in Dromore.

| **Duggan's Hill** | An English form | |
| J 2337 | | |

| 1. 'dugənz 'hïl | Local pronunciation | 1995 |

Duggan's Hill is one of a group of hills round the bog between Ballyroney and Ballyward, including Crabtree Hill, most of which seem to be named after owners or previous owners. Duggan's Hill is in Ballyroney townland, and the bog next to it is called Haddock's Bog. In 1834 J. Haddock Esq. of Dublin was a non-resident proprietor of the townland (*OSM* iii 18a). The surname Duggan (Dugan or Doogan) comes from Gaelic *Ó Dúgáin* from the personal name *Dúgán (Dubhagán)* "little black-haired one", and may be either Scottish or Irish (Woulfe 1923, 508–9; MacLysaght 1957, 132–3). In Ireland the family of *Ó Dubhagáin/ Ó Dúgáin* were well-known as professional historians. There is early evidence for the family in Co. Down, where two townlands seem to have been named after them: **Ballydugan** in the parishes of Tullylish and Downpatrick. In this parish there were Dugans in Imdel from the mid 18th century (*Ir. Wills Index* iv 38).

| **Glebe House** | An English form | |
| J 2034 | | |

In 1657 the church of Drumballyroney had been "situate in the middle [of the parish], only old walls" (*Inq. Down (Atkinson)* 135) and a church in Aughnavallog was shown on Petty's barony map of Upper Iveagh (*Hib. Reg.*). In 1834 the parish church was "on a small elevation in the north-east" of the townland, "on the old line between Newry and Dromara" (not the road via Rathfriland), built in 1780 or 1788 (*OSM* iii 15b, 10a). Atkinson dated the church to 1800 and said "from its position on a considerable hill... its white colour forms a conspicuous object in the landscape" (*Atkinson's Dromore* 269). Church Hill road preserves the memory of this church. No parish glebe was known in 1657 but, as happened in Annaclone, the family who became proprietors of what had originally been church land allocated some of it as glebe (*OSM* iii 15b). Although the date is not recorded in either case, this may have been a condition of the change of ownership. The Glebe House in the south of Aughnavallog was described in 1836, "built in the year 1822 by the present vicar, the Reverend John Dubourdieu, at an expense of 700 pounds" (*OSM* iii 10a).

Hunshigo Lake	A hybrid form	
J 2536	see **Annahunshigo** townland	

1. (?)L. Lakon	Hondius Map	1591
2. (?)Lo. Lackan	Mercator's Ulst.	1595
3. (?)Lo. Lackan	Boazio's Map (BM)	1599
4. (?)Lo. Lackan	Norden's Map	1610c
5. Lackan Lake	OSM iii 14a	1834
6. Hinchigo Bog	OSM iii 14b	1834
7. Hinchigo Bog 106a	OSNB E63	1834c
8. Hunshigo Lake	OSM iii 10b	1836
9. Hunshigo Bog	OSM iii 11a	1836
10. 'hïntʃïgo 'lek	Local pronunciation	1995

The first part of the name Hunshigo Lake is a shortened form of the townland name **Annahunshigo**, as attested from the early 19th century in the forms Hunshigo Lake, Hunshigo Bog (8, 9). In 1834 a man called McComb found a wooden vessel of bog butter in *Hinchigo* Bog (form 6), and this spelling is closest to the modern pronunciation (6, 7, 10). From its situation Hunshigo Lake is the same as **Lackan** Lake (5). According to the 1836 account, "It communicates with a smaller lake situated to the north-east and it has an outlet on the northern shore which falls into the Bann to the north of Roughan Steps" (*OSM* iii 10b, see **Roughan**).

Maps c. 1600 AD show part of the Bann or Newry river rising in a lake called *Lough Lackan*. Hondy's map (1) has *Coche* (*PNI* i 42–3) river along the low ground from Newry to Lough Neagh, with the lake unconnected just north of a tributary joining it from the east. Boazio's map (3) shows it in the same position, while from its course the tributary is more clearly the main Newry river. Norden's map (4) has two rivers called Bann, the western running into the Newry river. It shows Lough Brickland unconnected near the eastern, Lough Lackan unconnected near the western "Bann", just north of the east-west stretch of the Newry river. The most detailed map to show Lough Lackan is Mercator's Ulster (2), which separates the Bann and its tributary the Cusher (*Little Bann*) from the rivers flowing south to Newry. *L. Hyll* (Loughgilly?) to the west and *L.Lackan* to the east are both shown as sources of streams running into the northern bend of the Newry river, well west of the Upper Bann.

The modern Lough Lackan or Hunshigo Lake lies east of the Bann, although the drainage seems to have been altered since 1834, and the connection between lake and river is difficult to make out. Unlike Ballyroney Lough to the north, there is no tradition recorded of a crannog in the lough, which might have made it notable in the 16th century. There was a lake and crannog at Loughorne in the north of Newry parish (*PNI* i 32) next to a lost land-unit called *Lackan* quoted in conjunction with the townland of Shinn (*PNI* i 38; 1549–1638: *Mon. Hib.* 287; *CPR* Ed. VI 388; *CPR Jas I* 86a, 102b, 495a; *Inq. Ult. (Down)* §84 Car. I). A tributary of the Newry river does seem to rise in the bog that is all that is left of the lough. The identification of Lough Lackan in forms (1) to (4) remains unproven.

Katesbridge
An English form
J 2040

1.	Makey's Bridge	Harris Hist. map	1743
2.	McCay's-Bridge	Harris Hist. 145	1744
3.	McCay's-bridge	Statist. Sur. Dn 24	1802
4.	McKeys Bridge	Wm. Map (OSNB) E63	1810
5.	Kate McKey's Bridge	Atkinson's Tour (OSNB) Vol.1; 324	1823
6.	Kate's Bridge	Bnd. Sur. (OSNB) E63	1834c
7.	Kate McKey's Bridge	J O'D (OSNB) E63	1834c
8.	Kate McKay's Bridge, commonly called Kate's Bridge	OSM iii 12a (16a)	1836
9.	ˌkjets'brədʒ	Local pronunciation	1991
10.	ˌket mə'kaiz 'brədʒ	Local pronunciation	1991
11.	ˌkjets'brïdʒ	Local pronunciation	1994

The village of Katesbridge is on both sides of the Bann, joined by the bridge from which it takes its name. The bridge was described in 1836 as "a plain structure of unhewn stone", but no date of construction was mentioned (*OSM* iii 12a). The bridge was located at the: "north end of Ballymielbrick and on the Bann river between the parish of Drumballyroney and the townland of Shannaghan, a detached part of Newry lordship. The family of McKay is of old standing in this parish. They have a tradition that the family came from Scotland, to which country they had more anciently emigrated from Portugal" (*OSNB* E63). The name-book continues with further unlikely information, that the families of McGee, McKee and McKay, all connected with the Magennises, were in Irish *Clann ic Aodha, Clann ic Oi, Clann ic Céidh* (*OSNB* E63).

The earlier forms of the place-name seem to use the surname while the modern place-name uses the lady's Christian name, a transition noted in form 8, although the longer form is still known. Despite the Boundary Surveyor's form c. 1830 as *Kate's Bridge*, O'Donovan gave the received form as *Kate McKey's Bridge* (6,7). The 1:10,000 sheet 238 still calls the actual bridge Kate McKay's Bridge (*OSM* iii 16a). A story explaining the name was recorded in 1886:

> While the bridge was in progress of erection, the workmen boarded at the house of Mrs Kate McKay, in view of it, and as a reward for the trouble she had taken to ensure their comfort, it was made to serve the purpose of a memorial (*Bassett's Down* 152).

The surname McKay, MacKey or Magee is in Irish *Mac Aodha* (variant *Aoidh*) "son of Hugh". The surname is also known in Scotland, but this family seem more likely to be Irish in origin, although there are no local references before the 17th century. Members of the McKey family held the church townland of Aughnavallog from the bishop in 1609 and were there in 1640 (**Aughnavallog** forms 1, 2, 4, 6). In 1663 Patrick Duffe *Mackey* lived in *Castletown* (Ballyroney), Owen *Magee* in *Monygarr* and Daniel Magee in *Dromdrinagh* in the parish (*Sub. Roll Dn* 11–12). In 1834 the parish priest was the Rev. James McKey, who seems to have been a local man "a native and an Irish scholar". He was too feeble to talk to John O'Donovan when he visited the parish, although he suggested an Irish form for Aughnavallog (*OSNB* E63; Rev. J. McKay *OSM* iii 15b; *OSL Dn* 55,59). In 1837 *McKay* was a common Roman Catholic surname around Slieve Croob (*OSM* xii 67b).

Kennedy's Hill
J 2336

An English form

1. Kennedy's Hill	OSNB E63	1834c
2. 'kɛnədïs ˌhïl	Local pronunciation	1996

Kennedy's Hill is one of a group of hills round the bog between Ballyroney and Ballyward. It is in the townland of Lackan, as is Hamilton's Hill further south (1:10,000 sheet 239). There were Kennedys in the parish in the 18th century (*Ir. Wills Index* iv 71), still remembered now.

Knockiveagh
J 1838

Cnoc Uíbh Eachach
"hill of Iveagh"

1. K:evaghe [?]	Jobson's Ulster (BM)	1590
2. K: evaghe	Jobson's Ulster (TCD) 17	1590c
3. (?)Lyssarthei	Mercator's Ulst.	1595
4. Knock Evagh	Bartlett Map (TCD)	1601
5. Kno: Evagh, Lise-ne Ree	Bartlett Maps (Esch. Co. Maps) 2	1603
6. Knock Evah	Speed's Ulster	1610
7. Knock Evah	Speed's Antrim & Down	1610
8. KnockIveagh	CPR Jas I 189a	1611
9. Knockevagh Mountaine	Hib. Reg. Up. Iveagh	1657c
10. Knockevagh qr	BSD 115	1666
11. Knockevagh	Hib. Del. Down	1672c
12. Knockeragh al. Knockberagh	ASE 274a	1682
13. Knockeragh als. Knockberagh	Rent Roll Down 12	1692
14. Knock Iveagh	Harris Hist. map	1743
15. Knock Iveagh	Wm. Map (OSNB) E63	1810
16. Knock Iveagh	Bnd. Sur. (OSNB) E63	1830c
17. the Knock Hill (Edenagarry)	OSNB E63	1834c
18. the Knock Hill	Wars Co. Down xii 5n	1906
19. Croc Uibh Éadhach	Old Hennan and others (OSNB) E63	1834c
20. Cnoc Ua n-Eathach "Hill of the Iveaghs" Collis Iveachorum	J O'D (OSNB) E63	1834c
21. ðə 'nɔk	Local pronunciation	1995
22. ðə 'nɔk 'hïl	Local pronunciation	1995
23. ˌnɔk 'aï've:	Local pronunciation	1995

Knock Iveagh is the full name of what is known locally as the Knock Hill, with a row of houses called Knock Terrace up its southern side. The name Knock Iveagh was given beside a hill symbol on some maps c. 1600 (*Jobson, Bartlett, Speed*; forms 1, 2, 4–7). It was described in 1834: "Knock Iveagh or the Iveagh Hill in the townland of Ednagarry and Ballymulbrick near the north west end of the parish is the highest [hill], being 785 feet above the level of the sea. This hill is oval-shaped stretching east and west, rocks of granite and schist are found on this hill and near the summit project above the surface. The top is therefore uncultivated and has a barren appearance but yields some pasture" (*OSM* iii 14a). Form (17) shows the name was already abbreviated in general use, as it is at present.

Knock Iveagh is isolated, with a view that includes Slieve Gallion in Tyrone and Slemish in Co. Antrim, as well as the Belfast mountains, Slieve Croob, the Mournes and Carrickatuke. The heather-covered top is also visible from Water Hill Fort above Lough Brickland. Although not noted by the Memoir, there is a large cairn on top of the hill (Lett 1898, 67). The cairn, excavated in 1954, is 100 feet across. There had been a central burial cist, broken up by treasure-seekers at some time during the 19th century (*ASCD* 84 §164).

The summit of the hill is now in the north of Edenagarry townland, and its flanks are included in Ballybrick and Lisnacreevy. All of these townlands were held by the Magennis chief. The apparent inclusion of the name *Knock Iveagh* among Sir Art's lands in 1611 (*CPR Jas I* 189a) may be a mis-spelling of the Kilbroney townland of **Knockbarragh**, also held by Sir Art (*PNI* i 148–9). However Knock Iveagh appears separately on Petty's barony map of Upper Iveagh, shown as a stretch of land labelled *mountaine* (misread as *Wonfin* in his atlas, *Hib. Del.*), and both it and Knockbarragh must be mentioned in the two forms *Knockberagh* and *Knockeragh alias Knockberagh* given in two late 17th-century sources (forms 12, 13: *ASE* 273,274; *Rent Roll Dn* 10, 12). At any rate it is clear that Sir Art kept Knock Iveagh in his own hands.

On Bartlett's map of South Ulster, in 1603, the hill is shown as *Kno: Evagh* with the legend "*Lise ne Ree* where the McGenis is made" on its eastern side (form 5, see cover). This name may be connected with *Lyssarthei* on Mercator's map (3). There is no historical account of the Magennis inauguration, but Irish kings or chieftains were traditionally inaugurated by their hereditary poets in the presence of other retainers at a particular site in their territory (*Céitinn* iii 8–14; Hore 1857, 216–35). The site was usually an elevated place and often at an ancient monument, as at Tullaghoge in Tyrone where O'Neill's inauguration was depicted on another map of the period (Hayes McCoy 1970, plate viii c. 1602). There are two townlands called **Lisnaree** "fort of the kings" a few miles away in the parishes of Newry (*PNI* i 31) and Seapatrick (this vol.), but the most likely monument for the Magennis inauguration site, apart from the hill-top cairn, is a mound now in the townland of Lisnacroppan, but possibly once part of **Ballybrick**. Oral tradition concerning the Magennis "Coronation Stone" or *Cusleac Aonguis* "footstone of Aongus" at Clonduff was recorded by Crowe (1969, 56–7).

In 1834 O'Donovan recorded *Croc Uibh Eadhach* as the "pronunciation of the old Irish natives", including Old Hennan (19). The Irish word *cnoc* "hill" was pronounced *croc* in the north, and O'Donovan continued, "Knock in Irish signifies a low hill standing single without any continued range of hills" (*OSNB*). Despite the word order, with the epithet following the noun as in Irish, the current name of the hill does not represent a grammatically correct Irish form. "Hill of the Uí Eachach" would be *Cnoc Ó nEachach* in Irish (form 19), which would have been anglicized as "Knockoneagh". However references such as *Droim Mór Íbh Eathach* "Dromore of Iveagh" in 1645 (*Cín Lae Ó Mealláin* lch 24) show that in the 17th century the tribal name was already becoming fixed in the plural locative form which gave **Iveagh** in English.

May's Corner   An English form
J 1939

1. Mayscorner (sub po)	Bassett's Down 169	1886
2. Coirnéal Mhé	GÉ 74	1989
3. ˌmez ˈkɔrnər	Local pronunciation	1995

May's Corner is a crossroads at the north end of Knockiveagh, in Ballybrick. Because it had a post office it has been translated into Irish as *Coirneal Mhé* (*AGBP, GÉ*). No more seems to be known of the identity of May.

Millvale   An English form
J 1736

1. ˈmïlvel	Local pronunciation	1996

The name Millvale belongs to some buildings at a crossroads in Ballynamagna south of Knockiveagh, beside a small stream going south into a tributary of the Clanrye river from Rathfriland. There were a corn and two flax mills in Ballynamagna in 1834, not noted in 1836 (*OSM* iii 16a).

Muddock River   *An Mhodóg*
J 2635   "the (little) murky one"

"There is a small river called the Muddock river which enters out of Clonduff and forms the south-east boundary of the parish for about 3 miles" (*OSM* iii 14b). The Muddock rises in Clonduff and the earlier references all show it used as a boundary. The name has been discussed in the volume on The Mournes (*PNI* iii 182). The Muddock Bridge is over the Muddock in the south-east of the parish just before the river enters the Bann.

Rathfriland   *Ráth Fraoileann*
J 2133   "fort of Fraoile"

1. Rafier Iland	Dartmouth Map 5	1590c
2. Insula Magnesii	Bodley's Lecale 76	1603
3. Rathfryland	Tombstone (OSNB) E63	1717
4. Rathfryland	Harris Hist. 144,170,255	1744
5. Rathfriland	Tombstone (OSNB) E63	1784
6. Ráth Fraoileann/Rathfriland	Éire Thuaidh	1988
7. ˌraˈfrəilən	Local pronunciation	1995

The name Rathfriland, now a town, has been discussed with a fuller list of spellings in volume i of this series (*PNI* i 126–8). It was the Magennis chief seat, although neither a fort nor the identity of *Fraoile* earlier *Fraoiliu* can be discovered today. The 16th- or early 17th-century Magennis castle which would have superseded the rath was largely pulled down after the 1641 rebellion (*ASCD* 248). Forms from 1570 to 1603, to which form (1) above is an addition, imply that in the late 16th century the *th* of *ráth* was not pronounced, as might be expected in Irish. This fact enabled an almost-independent map tradition where the second part of the name seems to have been understood as equivalent to English *island* (1). The situation on a hill in the midst of bog would have encouraged this, and there is one 1603 reference to the place as *Insula Magnesii* "Magennis' Island" (*Bodley's Lecale* 76). *Th* returned to documentary tradition in 1609, as seen in the 18th-century forms above (3–5), although the form *Rafrylan* in the Civil Survey barony bounds (x §72) may have been closer to the local pronunciation. Many people still omit *th*, and the final -*d*, except when thinking about the spelling. It would only be in Anglo-Norman areas that medieval Irish *th* might be heard and preserved as [θ] by English speakers (O'Rahilly 1930, 182–4).

Roughan	*Ruachán*	
J 2237	"red bog"	
1. Roughan Steps	OSM iii 10b,16a	1836
2. Roughan mills	OSM iii 12ab,16a	1836
3. 'ruxən	Local pronunciation	1995

The place-name Roughan covers a large part of the townland of Tirygory, with Roughan Hill in the east and Roughan Bog in the south between the Bann and Hunshigo alias Lackan Lake (OS 1:10,000 sheet 239). Roughan is a recurring place-name, applied also to townlands in Cos Armagh and Tyrone, and is from *Ruachán* "reddish area", much like "Red Bog" in English. In fact the bog in Tirygory is labelled "Red Bog" on Petty's barony map of Upper Iveagh.

Roughan Bridge crosses from Drumdreenagh on the west bank of the Bann to Tirygory on the east, on the minor road towards Ballyward (grid-ref. J 2236). There was no bridge in the early 19th century and the fording place was called the *Roughan Steps* (1). "At the Roughan mills in the townland of Tirygory there are stepping stones over the river Bann, which however are so soon covered after rain that it was found necessary to establish the ferry. This was done by Mr Clarke in 1833" (*OSM* iii 12a (2)). Mills and ferry are now gone, although the Clarke family are still in the area.

The name Roughan Bridge is wrongly shown on 1:50,000 sheet 29 (J 2237) for the bridge across the Bann just south of Ballyroney village. In 1836 that bridge was called Ballyroney Bridge: "It is supposed to be several hundred years old. It is very strong in its architecture, never having given way and scarcely ever having been repaired" (*OSM* iii 11a).

Skeagh, The	*An Sceach*	
J 2239	"the hawthorn"	
1. ðə 'skɛg	Local pronunciation	1995

The area named The Skeagh is in the north of the parish, near the north-east bound of the townland of Ballyroney, beside the main A50 road between Castlewellan and Banbridge. On the 1:10,000 map there is both The Skeagh and Skeagh House (sheet 239). The name appears to be *An Sceach* "the (fairy) thorn", possibly in the diminutive form *An Sceitheog*. Local tradition does not remember an isolated thorn tree in this area, but such a tree may have been held in awe as belonging to the fairies.

KILOMETRES 1 ... 0 ... 1 ... 2 ... 3

STATUTE MILES 1 ... 0 ... 1 ... 2

Parish of Garvaghy
Barony of Iveagh Upper, Lower Half (9 townlands)
Barony of Iveagh Lower, Lower Half★ (5 townlands)

Townlands

Ballooly
Balloolymore
Carnew★
Castlevennon
Corbally
Enagh★
Fedany★

Garvaghy★
Kilkinamurry
Killaney
Knockgorm
Shanrod
Tullinisky★
Tullyorior

THE PARISH OF GARVAGHY

The parish of Garvaghy is first mentioned, as a vicarage (*vicarius*), in the Archbishop's list of Iveagh parishes in 1422. The name follows that of Dromara in the 1546 list of parish revenues in the same document, and the parish was sometimes part of the prebend of Dromara (*Reg. Dowdall* 275, 80). The "lands of *Garwaghadh* annexed to the Bishop of Dromore's table" were mentioned in 1427-8 and 1431 as let to the family of McKewyn (*Reg. Swayne* 101). Some church lands in the parish were held by the O'Sheils as "erenagh of *Cnocgwrnis*" in 1526 (*Reg. Cromer*), called the "four and a half townlands of the territory of *Knockaguerrin*" in the King's Books (*EA* 310). In 1657 "four townes of *Knockagurrin*, part of the parish, was a mensall to the Bishop". Mensal land was intended to provide food for the table, so that this district was totally devoted to the bishop's use. The four townlands, in 1622 called *Ballylysdunevaghy* (probably the townland of Knockgorm), *Ballincastlevaunan*, *Ballyyinkillichehuch*, *Ballihilli* (Castlevennon, Killaney, Balloolymore), were allocated to Bishop Todd's brother-in-law William Worseley in 1609, leased for 60 years to Edward Trevor by Bishop Buckworth in 1622, and held by a Mrs Buckworth, widow, probably a relation of the bishop, in 1657. Five other townlands were church land. In 1609 Owen O'Rony held Corbally and *Castlemyrathie* (Ballooly, since it borders Garvaghy and Fedany), Gilleduffe McBrien had Tullyorior, and Edward Trevor also had Kilkinamurry and Shanrod, as tenants of the bishop.

Five townlands in the east: Garvaghy (called *Fergone*), Carnew, Fedany, Enagh (earlier *Dromaneigh*), and Tullinisky, apparently belonged to Sir Art Magennis in 1609. In the schedule of Iveagh they were allocated with Tullyglush in Dromore to William Worseley, brother-in-law to Bishop Todd, rent payable to Sir Art (*CPR Jas I* 395a, 191b). However in two instances, one being the same grant (*CPR Jas I* 191a, 266a), this group of townlands is listed as if they also were held from the bishop, which would mean the entire parish was once church land. Nevertheless this seems to have been the case, as Bishop Buckworth complained in 1622 that "Six towne lands of Garvaghy anciently belonging to the bishopric of Dromore... are paying a chiefe rent to Sir Arthur Magennis and so are wholly aliened from the church", even though the patents included them as part of the Bishop's manor of Dromore (*Buckworth (Atkinson)* 130). He blamed John Todd's mismanagement for this instance but, since he also mentioned that the "Settlement of *Evagh*" had allowed Magennis to take over other church lands, it is likely that the lands had been appropriated when the bishop was a Magennis in the mid-16th century. Sir Arthur Magennis of Rathfriland seems to have been granted some church lands by King James (*CPR Jas I* 195b, 1611 AD).

The townland bearing the parish name or containing the parish church was usually church land, and the current parish church is in the townland of Fedany, near the border with Garvaghy townland. In 1836 the church appeared "Very ancient, at least 200 [years old], thick walls prove its antiquity" (*OSM* xii 83b). Lewis says it was originally built in 1699 (*Lewis Top. Dict.* i 651b). It may be on the earlier site, as described in 1657: "the Church half a mile from the middle of the parish towards the north-east... 60 acres of Gleabe and course lands lying upon the south west of the Church" (*Inq. Down (Atkinson)* 142). It seems that Fedany was originally church land, but the glebe must be the 60 acres which Worseley was to provide as a condition of his grant (*CPR Jas I* 191a).

Apparently Garvaghy was not a townland name originally and modern Garvaghy townland is the unit called *Ballyfergowan* in the grants. The barony bound between Upper and Lower Iveagh cuts through Garvaghy parish. Both *Fergon*, in the bounds of Lower Iveagh (*Civ. Surv.* x §73), and *Garvagh*, in the bounds of Upper Iveagh (§72), or the *hill of Garvaghy* (*Inq. Ult.* xliii), are given as bounding Ballooly, so that *Fergon* must be equivalent to the term

189

Gorvacky towne (*Census* 79). The five supposed Magennis townlands are thus in Lower Iveagh and the rest of the parish in Upper Iveagh (*Census* 79,75). The Magennis family, according to Knox the lineal representatives of the Magennises of Iveagh, held the townland of Ballooly in 1836 and provided the schoolhouse there (*OSM* xii 81b, 82a).

The parish consists of 14 townlands, the same number as in 1657 (*Inq. Down (Atkinson)* 141-2). Since all the revenue of Knockgorm district went to the bishop, the rector was supported by the tithe money from the other ten townlands. In 1834 only Knockgorm and Tullyorior were mentioned as church lands, both lost to the church by 1868. However the parish was mainly Presbyterian and Roman Catholic, as seems to be the case today (*OSM* xii 81). The main local informants were Mrs McVeigh now of Dromore, and Miss Margaret Taylor, who lived all her long life in Rookvale in the townland of Shanrod in the parish, built and named by her family. She told me about Chips Corner in Ballooly (*Ballela*) where a family called Fitzpatrick lived. "There were so many Fitzpatricks in the country they got nicknames, and the father had been a carpenter, and it was known as Chips Corner and still is".

PARISH NAME

Garvaghy	*Garbhachadh*	
J 2148	"rough field"	
1. Garwagh	Reg. Dowdall §129 275	1422
2. Garwaghadh	Reg. Swayne 101	1428
3. Garvagh	Reg. Dowdall §113 80	1546
4. rectory/vicarage of Garvaghy	CPR Jas I 190b	1611
5. Garvaghie	CPR Jas I 191a	1611
6. Garvaghy	Inq. Down (Reeves1) 95	1657
7. Garvaghy	Hib. Reg. Up. Iveagh	1657c
8. Rector de Garvaghy	Trien. Visit. (Bramhall) 17	1661
9. Garvagh	Hib. Del. Down	1672c
10. Garvaghy Rectoria	Trien. Visit. (Boyle) 47	1679
11. Garvaghy vicaria	Trien. Visit. (Boyle) 47	1679
12. Garvaghy	Lamb Maps Co. Downe	1690c
13. Garvaghy +church	Harris Hist. map	1743
14. Garvaghy	Dubourdieu's Map (OSNB) NB12	1802
15. Garvaghy	Wm. Map (OSNB) NB12	1810
16. Garvaughy	Cess Book (OSNB) NB12	1834c
17. [gar-'va-hy]	OSNB Pron. NB12	1834c
18. pronounced Garvaghy and Garvacky	OSM xii 81b	1834
19. Garbh-achadh "rough field"	J O'D (OSNB) NB12	1834c
20. Garbhachadh	GÉ 108	1989
21. ˌɡərˈvaxi	Local pronunciation	1991

The name Garvaghy appeared in 1428 in the form *Garwaghadh* (2), and this and the other forms have been generally interpreted as *Garbhachadh* "rough field", the same etymology as the town of **Garvagh** in Co. Derry, and townland of **Garvaghy** in Co. Tyrone (forms 19, 20; *GÉ* 108). The stress, which would have been on the first element, ie the adjective, has shifted to the second element, possibly influenced by the pronunciation of the phrase Garvaghy Hill

190

in English (Stockman 1991, 19b). The parish is low ground beside the Bann on the west, but the ground rises steadily to the east, where many of the townlands contain hills from 500 to 750 feet high, with boggy ground between them. The north of the parish, including the townland of Garvaghy, is bounded by the Gall Bog. Garvaghy Hill, 671 feet in the townland of the name, has an extensive view. In 1834 the parish contained "numerous small bogs and lakes" (*OSNB* 12). Three former lakes, Knockgorm, Lough Kock and Loughdoo, have now been drained, leaving only one in Shanrod townland.

TOWNLAND NAMES

Ballooly   *Baile Ailigh*
J 1947   "townland of (the) stony place"

1. Mirahe	Fiants Eliz. §1583	1570
2. Castlemyrathie	CPR Jas I 395b	1609
3. Castlemirathir or Castlenirathir	CPR Jas I 191a	1611
4. Castle Elly al Moyrather	Inq. Ult. (Down) xliii	1618
5. stone Slackneskestie	Inq. Ult. (Down) xliii	1618
6. hill Slatgillecolme	Inq. Ult. (Down) xliii	1618
7. forde Bealle-da-van	Inq. Ult. (Down) xliii	1618
8. hill called Knockenemersin in Castle Ely	Inq. Ult. (Down) xliii	1618
9. playne Tavenagh Tober	Inq. Ult. (Down) xliii	1618
10. hill Legikistie (next hill of Garvaghy)	Inq. Ult. (Down) xliii	1618
11. Loughnotowe	Inq. Ult. (Down) xliii	1618
12. to Lisneskistye first mentioned	Inq. Ult. (Down) xliii	1618
13. Castle-Ellyn al. Moyrather	CPR Jas I 305a	1623
14. Castle-Elyn	CPR Jas I 305a	1623
15. Castle-Ely	CPR Jas I 305a	1623
16. Castle-Elly	CPR Jas I 305a	1623
17. Ballyely	Civ. Surv. x §72	1655c
18. Ballyely	Civ. Surv. x §73	1655c
19. Balilye	Census 75	1659c
20. Bally Illy	BSD 116	1661
21. Castle-Elly al. Bally-Elly al. Castlemoyrather	Mooney MS 93	1722
22. Bellully	Ir. Wills Index 98	1774
23. Balloolly House, Magennis Esq.	Taylor & Skinner 285b	1777
24. Ballully	Ir. Wills Index 54	1791
25. Balliely	Statist. Sur. Dn 305	1802
26. Ballyilli-beg	Wm. Map (OSNB) NB12	1810
27. Balooly	Tombstone (OSNB) NB12	1821
28. Balleely	County Warrant (OSNB) NB12	1827
29. Balluley	Tombstone (OSNB) NB12	1827
30. Ballyilly	Bnd. Sur. (OSNB) NB12	1830c
31. Ballyelly	Custom of County (OSNB) NB12	1834c
32. Balluleybeg	Cess Book (OSNB) NB12	1834c
33. Balloolley	Post Chaise Comp. (OSNB) NB12	1834c
34. [Bal-'lel-ley]	OSNB Pron. NB12	1834c

35. Ballyilly pronounced Ball'illy	OSM xii 81b	1834
36. Ballooly or Ballyilly in Garvaghy par.	OSM xii 113b	1834
37. Mr Maginnis's of Ballyilly	OSM xii 80b	1834
38. Ballooly	OSM xii 82	1837
39. Ballyely, R. Maginnis of	Lewis' Top. Dict. i 651	1837
40. McCardle of Balleley	Ir. Wills Index 82	1853
41. Bellela, Gar[vaghy]	Bassett's Down 251	1886
42. ˌbəˈlelə	Local pronunciation	1991

Ballooly was an individual church townland, not grouped with any other in the sources. Although earlier owned by the Church of Ireland, by 1834 the landlord was a Magennis and his residence and a Roman Catholic church were situated in the townland. The name, then given as Ballooly-beg, was associated in the 19th century with that of the townland of Ballooly-more further south, in the Knockgorm group, even though the local pronunciation was different. The earlier sources give different names to the two townlands.

Ballooly was anciently *Castle-Elly(n) al. Moyrather*, as is made explicit in 1722 (form 21). A pardon was granted in 1570 to "Donald M'Brien of *Mirahe*, gent" (form 1). The McBrins frequently appear as tenants of church land, which this was, and some of the family held the townland of Tullyorior in this parish in the early 17th century. However, *Castlemyrathie* was held in 1609 by Owen *O'Rony*, and the bounds of the townland were trodden for the new tenant Edward Trevor in 1618 by Art *O'Ronow*. These two were members of the same church and literary family from whom the parish of **Drumballyroney** is named. The north side of Ballooly is the boundary between Upper and Lower Iveagh, while the townland itself lay between the four church lands of Knockgorm and the Garvaghy group (parish introduction §2).

The bounds of Ballooly were given in 1618 (forms 4–12) and enrolled in 1623, after the land had been let to Sir Edward Trevor (*CPR Jas I* 305a). A "foord called *Belandavan*" (cf. 7) was also mentioned c. 1655 in the barony bounds of Lower Iveagh (*Civ. Surv.* x §73), where it was between Ballooly and *Fergone* (**Garvaghy** townland). The north-west bound of Ballooly is now formed by a brook running from the Gall Bog, and the ford must be somewhere here. The name was possibly *Béal an Dá Bheann* "the approach to the two peaks". Garvaghy Hill (10) has two summits, but it is hard to locate the hills of *Knocknemersin* and *Legakistie* on each side of *Tamhnach Tobair* "field of the well". After Garvaghy on the northeast of Ballooly, the townlands of Fedany on the east and Shanrod on the south-east are mentioned in the bounds, and *Loughnotowe* (11) following must be **Lough Doo**, then described as "bounded with the *O'Sheales* lands" (*Inq. Ult. (Down)* xliii). Since the erenagh lands of Knockgorm were held by the O'Sheils in 1526 it is probably Knockgorm and Killaney west of Ballooly that are intended here.

The "castle" of the name *Castlemyrathie* was not used as a marker point and may have been a cashel which no longer existed as more than a heap of stones. Joyce has a note on the Irish term *caisleán*, almost always anglicized "castle", which referred to structures later than "dun, caher etc". However in Castlebar in Mayo, as here, there is no sign on the ground of the Barry castle from which the place took its name (*Joyce* i 306). One rath is shown in the middle of Ballooly on the modern maps (OS sheets 20, 221).

Presumably the second element of *Castle-elly* was continued in the later form *Ballyely*, which first appeared in the Civil Survey barony bounds c. 1655 (17, 18). *Baile Ailigh* "townland of the stony place" could refer to the remains of the castle. Similar anglicized spellings continued in use into the 19th century, as can be seen in forms 28, 30, 31 (John O'Donovan's local informants J. and D. Martin). The current local pronunciation as recorded then was *Bal-'lel-ley* or *Ball'illy* (forms 34, 35). *Ballela* is the spelling used on the modern road sign, and [ˌbaˈlelə] is the modern name of the small village, unnamed on the maps (1:50,000, 1:10,000), which contains the Roman Catholic chapel of Ballela parish. Ballooly House in the townland was also pronounced [ˌbaˈlelə] locally, but has been called Ballooly [ˌbəˈluliˈ] House by recent owners. The confusion is also apparent in the Ordnance Survey Memoir (forms 36–8), which mentioned Mr Magennis of *Ballyilly* House, proprietor of the townland and provider of the schoolhouse (*OSM* xii 80–82). Nevertheless O'Donovan accepted the form Ballooly, as found in Garvaghy graveyard and the Cess Book (forms 27, 32, 33). The spelling *oo* or *u* first appeared in the late 18th century (forms 22–24), including the earliest reference to Mr Magennis' house. See **Balloolymore**.

Balloolymore	*Baile Ailigh Mór*	
J 2043	"large townland of (the) stony place"	

1. Bally-Illy	CPR Jas I 395b	1609
2. Bally-Illie	CPR Jas I 191a	1611
3. Bally-Illy	CPR Jas I 266a	1614
4. Bally-illye	Inq. Ult. (Down) §4 Jac. I	1616
5. Bally-Illie	CPR Jas I 309a	1616
6. Ballihilli (Knockaguerin 4tds)	Buckworth (EA) 310	1622
7. (?) Ballyyinkillichehuch	Buckworth (Atkinson) 127	1622
8. Bally Illy al. Ballimy	Hib. Reg. Up. Iveagh	1657c
9. Ballilie	Census 75	1659c
10. Bally Elly & Shanread	BSD 116	1661
11. Ballimy	Hib. Del. Down	1672c
12. Ballyilly-more	Wm. Map (OSNB) NB12	1810
13. Balluley	Tombstone (OSNB) NB12	1823
14. Balloolymore	Reg. Free. (OSNB) NB12	1830
15. Ballyillymore	Bnd. Sur. (OSNB) NB12	1830c
16. Ballylymore	Reg. Free. (OSNB) NB12	1830c
17. Balleely	Clergyman (OSNB) NB12	1834c
18. Balluleymore	Cess Book (OSNB) NB12	1834c
19. Balloolley	Post Chaise Comp. (OSNB) NB12	1834c
20. [Bal-lu-ley-'more]	OSNB Pron. NB12	1834c
21. Ballyillymore pronounced Ball'illymore and Balloolymore	OSM xii 81b	1834
22. Balloolymore	J O'D (OSNB) NB12	1834c
23. Baile Ghil Shuiligh "Gilhooly's town"	J O'D (OSNB) NB12	1834c
24. Baile Ubhlaighe "the town of the apples/ Gilhooly"	Joyce iii 67	1913
25. baile aileach	Mooney 93	1950c
26. ail-mhaigh "stony place"	Mooney 93	1950c
27. bəˌluliˈmoːr	Local pronunciation	1991

Balloolymore was church land, one of the townlands of Knockgorm, the mensal lands of the bishop of Dromore. From the earliest reference in 1609 into the 19th century the second element was regularly spelt -*illie* etc. A form in -*uley* appears first in Garvaghy graveyard and in the Cess Book, while the 1830 Freehold Registry has both Balloolymore and Ballylymore (*OSNB* 12). The inhabitants by this stage generally pronounced the name as [-lu-ley] and O'Donovan adopted the spelling Balloolymore. He reported that, "The rector says that Balleely is the correct name but the rector knows nothing about it" (*OSNB* 12, 42). Dean Mooney commented on the pronunciation of Balloolymore and Ballooly townlands:

> The rector was right - naturally enough. The form in -*ooly* is a (late) 18th-century development from misreading of manuscript *ee* in 17th-century documents where *ee* looks like *oo*. The -*oo*- form began in Balloolymore, a protestant and planted townland, i.e. among people ignorant of current and traditional pronunciation. The traditional pronunciation still survives in (so-called) Ballooly (it remained in Irish hands - Magennis): it is Ballela... Ballooly has no standing in history (*Mooney MS* 93).

Despite Mooney's defence of tradition, the historical forms collected so far indicate that Mr Magennis and the McMain family of **Ballooly** were the first to use the later spelling (see above, forms 22,23). However it is only in Balloolymore that the name is generally pronounced Ballooly.

From O'Donovan on, the two names Ballooly and Balloolymore have regularly been discussed together. The surname (Mac)Gilhooly put forward by O'Donovan (23) is common in Co. Leitrim (Woulfe 1923, 375, 380). However this suggestion, like Joyce's *Baile Ubhlaighe* "town of the apples" (24), can be discounted, since the *oo* is not original, and the element following *Baile* was earlier spelled with either *e* or *i*. To explain the variant vowels, Mooney suggested the word *ulaidh* fem., meaning "monument, tomb" (variants *ailad, aulad, ilad, elad, ulad* masc. and fem., *DIL*). Joyce gives examples of the history of the word, which more recently has signified "a penitential station, a stone altar erected as a place of devotion" (*Joyce* i 338–9). According to Dubourdieu the stones of a cairn were removed in Ballooly in about 1800 (*Statist. Sur. Dn* 305). However the second element of Balloolymore is most likely *aileach* "stony, stony place" (25), as in Ballooly. Since the earlier spellings of this element are not the same for the two names, with Balloolymore being consistently spelt -*illy* rather than -*ely*, it is possible that Balloolymore contains a different word and was originally *Baile Aoiligh* "townland of manure", although this would be most likely anglicized *Balleely*. If this were so the name has either fallen together with the later spellings of Ballooly, or the pronunciation with [u] may also reflect the earlier Irish pronunciation of *ao* as [λ:].

Carnew
J 2245

Carn Aodha
"Aodh's cairn"

1. Ballycarnea	CPR Jas I 395a	1609
2. Ballycarnewe	CPR Jas I 191a	1611
3. Ballicharnewe	CPR Jas I 190b	1611
4. Ballycharnewe	CPR Jas I 191b	1611
5. Ballycarnewe	CPR Jas I 266a	1614
6. the Carnew	Inq. Ult. (Down) xlii	1618
7. the Carnew	CPR Jas I 304b	1623
8. Ballecarnane	Inq. Ult. (Down) §13 Car. I	1629
9. Ballykarnewe	Inq. Ult. (Down) §13 Car. I	1629

10. Ballecarnewe	Inq. Ult. (Down) §85 Car. I	1639
11. Carnew	Civ. Surv. x §72	1655c
12. Carnen	Civ. Surv. x §72	1655c
13. Carnitt	Census 79	1659c
14. Ennacarnew	Mooney MS 100	1717
15. Carnew	Wm. Map (OSNB) NB12	1810
16. Carnew	OSNB NB12	1834c
17. Carn Aodha "Hugh's cairn or sepulchral heap"	J O'D (OSNB) NB12	1834c
18. Carn Niadh/ Naoi	Mooney 99	1950c
19. kər'nju:	Local pronunciation	1991
20. kɑr'nju:	Local pronunciation	1994

This townland on the eastern boundary of the parish belonged to Sir Art Magennis, and contains Carnew Hill, at 753 feet the highest point in the parish. Harris' map in 1743 shows *Carny L.[ake]* in this area, but there is no lake now. The first element seems to be *carn* "cairn". The 1:50,000 map (sh. 20) shows a Carnew Fort at the foot of Carnew Hill in the north, but Dean Mooney suggested that the cairn might have been located in a field called The Cairn Park with the possible remains of a cairn in the corner (*Mooney MS* 100), not shown on this or the 1:10,000 map. The Ordnance Survey Memoir described the top of Carnew Hill as naturally rocky, while Gransha Fort on high ground at the extreme east is the meeting point of Carnew with the Dromara townlands of Aughnaskeagh and Gransha (*OSM* xii 79a). O'Donovan's suggestion (17) seems the most likely. *Aodh* (gen. *Aodha* or *Aoidh*) is often anglicized as Hugh. It was a common name in the main Magennis pedigree, but there is no indication of when or from whom the townland was named. **Balloo** in Bangor (*PNI* ii 150) is from *Baile Aodha* "Hugh's townland".

Castlevennan	*Caiseal Uí Bheannacháin* (?)	
J 1944	"O'Banahan's cashel"	
1. Ballycastlevanane	CPR Jas I 395b	1609
2. Ballycastlevanan	CPR Jas I 191a	1611
3. Ballycastlevanahan	CPR Jas I 266a	1614
4. Ballycastlevanan	CPR Jas I 309a	1616
5. Ballicastlevannan (Knockaguerin 4tds)		
	Buckworth (EA) 310	1622
6. Castlevannan	Civ. Surv. x §72	1655c
7. Castlevanan	Hib. Reg. Up. Iveagh	1657c
8. Castlevenan	Census 75	1659c
9. Castlevannan	BSD 116	1661
10. Castlevana	Hib. Del. Down	1672c
11. Castlevenan	Ir. Wills Index 90	1750
12. Castlevenin	Wm. Map (OSNB) NB12	1810
13. Castleavennon	Bnd. Sur. (OSNB) NB12	1830c
14. Castlevenan	Cess Book (OSNB) NB12	1834c
15. [Kas-tle-'ven-an]	OSNB Pron. NB12	1834c

16. Caiseal Bheannain "Benan's stone fort"	J O'D (OSNB) NB12	1834c
17. -Beanóin/ Beineáin "Benén's"	Mooney 99	1950c
18. ˌkɑsəl'vanən	Local pronunciation	1994
19. ˌkasəl'vɛnən	Local pronunciation	1995

Castlevennan was a church townland. As with *Castle-elly* (**Ballooly** above) no castle or cashel survives, although there are two surviving cashels to the south-east in the parish of Drumgooland. The interpretation of the first element seems clear enough and the stones of the cashel have probably been re-used. The second element is problematic. Earlier 17th-century forms have the form *-vanan* etc. (once *-vanahan*, in 1614 (3)), later becoming *-vennan*. A noun, personal or sept name beginning with *B-* or *M-* seems most likely. Both *b* and *m* would be lenited, if a noun or personal name, after the dative or genitive of *caiseal*, and if a surname after genitive *Uí*. In order to account for [v], the basic word would need to begin with palatalized *b* or *m*, and the vowel would have to account for the variation between *-van* and *-ven*, probably Irish *ea* which might have been pronounced [ɛa] in the 17th century, as in 20th century North Uist in Scotland.

Both O'Donovan and Mooney suggested personal names. Mooney's *Benén*, the name of a bishop-companion of St Patrick, would not account for *-vanan*. O'Donovan's *Beannán* means "little horned one" and might refer to an animal: another animal term, *meannán* "little kid", would also be possible, perhaps referring to a ruin frequented by wild goats, *Caiseal Mh/Bheannán*. However, there is an extra syllable *-vanahan* preserved only in the 1614 form (3). The surname *Ó Beannacháin*, which would fit all the forms, belonged to an old Sligo family (Woulfe 1923, 435, *Fiants Eliz.* §5815, *Census* 607), although it is unusual for [x] between vowels to be dropped to such an extent.

Corbally	*Corrbhaile*	
J 2244	"odd/noticeable townland"	

1. Corbally	CPR Jas I 395b	1609
2. Corbally, Owen O'Rowny of	CPR Jas I 195b	1610
3. Corbally	CPR Jas I 191a	1611
4. Corbally	Civ. Surv. x §73	1655c
5. Carbally	Civ. Surv. x §72	1655c
6. Corbalye	Census 75	1659c
7. Corbally	Sub. Roll Down 276	1663
8. Corbally al. Corwally	Mooney MS 99	1722
9. Carbolley	Tombstone (OSNB) NB12	1802
10. Corbally	Wm. Map (OSNB) NB12	1810
11. Carbolly	Cess Book (OSNB) NB12	1834c
12. [kor-bol-ly]	OSNB Pron. NB12	1834c
13. corrbhaile "odd town"	J O'D (OSNB) NB12	1834c
14. Cor-bhaile "odd town"	Joyce iii 253	1913
15. Cuar bhaile or corr-bhaile	Mooney 99	1950c
16. 'kọrblï	Local pronunciation	1991
17. 'kɔrbəlï	Local pronunciation	1994

Corbally was a church townland in the early 17th century. Only one reference to this place-name, a 1722 deed quoted by Mooney (form 8), shows the grammatically correct lenition of the second element: *Corbally alias Corwally*. However Corbally is a fairly common townland name; there are nine occurrences in Northern Ireland (see **Curley**, *PNI* i 18, **Corbally** *PNI* iv 176), and unlenited *b* regularly appears in anglicized forms. The word is a compound of the adjective *corr* "odd, pointed, projecting" and *baile*, and the precise meaning is unclear. O'Donovan and Joyce translated it "odd town" (forms 13, 14), while the Place-Names Office of the Ordnance Survey in Dublin have more recently translated it "noticeable town" (Ó Maolfabhail 1990, 141).

| **Enagh** | *Aonach* | |
| J 2347 | "fairground" | |

1. Balledromneigh	CPR Jas I 395a	1609
2. Ballenedromneigh	CPR Jas I 190b	1611
3. Ballenedromneigh	CPR Jas I 191b	1611
4. Ballindromneh	CPR Jas I 191a	1611
5. Ballydromneigh	CPR Jas I 266a	1614
6. Balledromnaght	Inq. Ult. (Down) §13 Car. I	1629
7. Balledromnagh	Inq. Ult. (Down) §85 Car. I	1639
8. Enoch	Census 79	1659c
9. Enagh	Sub. Roll Down 273	1663
10. Ennacarnew	Mooney MS 100	1717
11. Enagh	Wm. Map (OSNB) NB12	1810
12. Enagh	County Warrant (OSNB) NB12	1827
13. Enoch	Reg. Free. (OSNB) NB12	1829
14. Enoch	Bnd. Sur. (OSNB) NB12	1830c
15. Enoch (bounds of Fedany)	OSNB NB12	1834c
16. [E-'noch]	OSNB Pron. NB12	1834c
17. eanach "a marsh or cut out bog"	J O'D (OSNB) NB12	1834c
18. 'inəx	Local pronunciation	1991
19. 'i:nɑx	Local pronunciation	1994

The origin of the townland name Enagh is obvious from its modern pronunciation, and I suspect that the stress on the second syllable reported c. 1834 (form 16) describes the strength of the final [x]. Although O'Donovan suggested *eanach* "marsh", this is usually anglicized *annagh*, and the name here must be *aonach* "fairground" from a fair-ground site or "fair hill", not identified. However there are no sources for the name Enagh before 1659, so that it must also have had an older name. Since Enagh lies between Sir Art Magennis' townlands of Tullinisky, Fedany and Carnew it is likely to have been *Ballenedromneigh*, regularly referred to along with those townlands. This was apparently *Baile na Droimni* "townland of the ridgy place".

| **Fedany** | *Feochadánaigh* (?) | |
| J 2246 | "place of thistles" | |

1. Ballyfeideney	CPR Jas I 395a	1609

2. Ballyfoydeny	CPR Jas I 190b	1611
3. Ballyfoydeneth	CPR Jas I 191a	1611
4. Ballyfoyneth	CPR Jas I 191b	1611
5. Ballifoideneth	CPR Jas I 266a	1614
6. Ballyfoydoney	Inq. Ult. (Down) xliii	1618
7. Ballyfoydey	CPR Jas I 305a	1623
8. Ballyfodowny	Inq. Ult. (Down) §13 Car. I	1629
9. Ballyfideny	Inq. Ult. (Down) §13 Car. I	1629
10. Balleffedeyny	Inq. Ult. (Down) §85 Car. I	1639
11. Foyden	Civ. Surv. x §73	1655c
12. Foydynye	Civ. Surv. x §72	1655c
13. Phenanny	Census 79	1659c
14. Foifeine	Sub. Roll Down 273	1663
15. Fedany	Tombstone (OSNB) NB12	1767
16. Fedeny	Wm. Map (OSNB) NB12	1810
17. Fedney	Tombstone (OSNB) NB12	1814
18. Fedney	Tombstone (OSNB) NB12	1817
19. Fedney	Clergyman (OSNB) NB12	1834c
20. [Fed-ney]	OSNB Pron. NB12	1834c
21. Fedney	Ir. Wills Index 95	1849
22. feadánach "abounding in brooks or runnels"	J O'D (OSNB) NB12	1834c
23. 'fe:dnï	Local pronunciation	1991
24. 'fɛdnï	Local pronunciation	1991

Fedany was held by Sir Art Magennis in the early 17th century, but since it contains the parish church and graveyard it most likely began as a church townland. The spellings suggest a descriptive term used in nominative or dative, with *baile* prefixed ungrammatically, as often, in early 17th-century forms. John O'Donovan and Mooney suggested *feadánach* from *feadán* "a small stream" (22). It is likely that the name contained the suffix *-ach*, often meaning "place of", here spelled *-eth*. However, the vowel of the first syllable is regularly *o* in the 17th century, followed by *y* which may suggest a diphthong [ɔï]. *Fódánach*, or *Fóidíneach*, derived from *fód* "sod", would be unlikely to have given the modern local pronunciation [e:] or [ɛ]. *Feochadánach* "place of thistles" might account for the *-oy/-oi* spellings and the following development from dative *Feochadánaigh* is possible, though not totally convincing: ['f'ɔxədɑnï] > ['f'ɔ:dɑnï] (loss of [x]) > ['fɛɔdənï] > ['fɛ:dənï].

The name of the townlands of **Fofanny** in Kilcoo is based on a form of the word without the *-d-*, but also has spellings with *e* as well as *o* (*PNI* iii 110; *Joyce* ii 332, iii 353). The Subsidy Roll form (14) for this townland, listed next to Enagh, is similar to Fofanny. If *e* developed from a misreading of *o* one could suggest *Fóidíní* "small farms/parcels of land", but this does not explain final *-th*, which was often used in 17th-century names of church lands to indicate [x] (cf. **Drumbroneth**).

In the local pronunciation the vowel of the second syllable is elided, as reflected in the spelling of Fedney Hill Road in the townland. The road goes over the summit, where Miss Taylor said, "There's a most beautiful view from Fedany: you can see the Tyrone hills. It was called Lookabooty, [meaning] "look about you" ['lukə'butï], and you could see for miles".

Garvaghy   *Garbhachadh*
J 2148   See the parish name

1. Ballyfergowan	CPR Jas I 395a	1609
2. Garvagh, Owen O'Rony of	CPR Jas I 195b	1610
3. Ballyfergone	CPR Jas I 190b	1611
4. Ballyfergowan	CPR Jas I 191a	1611
5. Ballifergowen	CPR Jas I 191b	1611
6. Ballifergowan	CPR Jas I 266a	1614
7. hill of Garvaghy	Inq. Ult. (Down) xliii	1618
8. hill of Garvaghy	CPR Jas I 305a	1623
9. Ballyfergonnan	Inq. Ult. (Down) §13 Car. I	1629
10. Garvagh	Civ. Surv. x §72	1655c
11. Fergon in the Lower (Iveagh)	Civ. Surv. x §73	1655c
12. Gorvacky towne	Census 79	1659c
13. ˌgərˈvɑxï	Local pronunciation	1991
14. ˌgjərˈvɑxï	Local pronunciation	1994

As explained in the parish introduction, an examination of the various groups of town-lands in the parish leads one to believe that up to 1659 the townland of Garvaghy was the unit often referred to in the sources as *Ballyfergowan*, and *Fergone* c. 1655. This name possibly derives from *Féar Gabhann* "smith's grassland". The noun *féar* "grass, grass-land" is used with colour adjectives in the townlands of Ferbane, Fearboy and Fearglas, meaning "white, yellow and green grasslands" (*Joyce* ii 337).

The notable hill in the townland has been known since 1618 as Garvaghy Hill, and the townland now bears the same name as the parish, although the parish church is near the boundary in the adjacent townland of Fedany. Another neighbouring townland, Tullynisky, was the butt of a rhyme told by Mrs McVeigh:

Up the lane for buttermilk, down the lane for brandy,
Tul'nisky is the turdy hole, Garvaghy is the dandy.

The northern bound of the townland of Garvaghy is the road through the **Gall Bog**.

Kilkinamurray   *Coill Chon Murchaidh*
J 2343   "wood of Murchadh's hound"

1. Killcoumurragh	CPR Jas I 395b	1609
2. Kilconmurragh	CPR Jas I 191a	1611
3. Killconmeerwee	Civ. Surv. x §72	1655c
4. Collocanmurph	Civ. Surv. x §73	1655c
5. Kilconemie	Census 75	1659c
6. Kilkinamurray	Wm. Map (OSNB) NB12	1810
7. Kilknamurry	Ir. Wills Index 66	1829
8. Kilkinamurry	Bnd. Sur. (OSNB) NB12	1834c
9. the Glen meeting house	OSNB NB12	1834c
10. Bigharristown (house cluster)	OSNB NB12	1834c
11. [Kil-kin-a-'mur-ry]	OSNB Pron. NB12	1834c

12. pronounced Kilkna'murry	OSM xii 81b	1834
13. Cill cine Muireadhaigh "Church of the sept of Muireadhach"	J O'D (OSNB) NB12	1834c
14. Cill-cine-Muireadhaigh "church of the sept of Murray"	Joyce iii 405	1913
15. Coill Cinnidh Muireadhaigh	Mooney 108	1950c
16. ˌkəlknə'mọrï	Local pronunciation	1991
17. ˌkəlkənə'mərï	Local pronunciation	1991

Both in 1834 (*OSM*) and the present the second syllable of the 5-syllable modern spelling is usually omitted in pronunciation (forms 12, 16). The suggested interpretation is possible from the four syllables of the earliest attestation, *Kilconmurragh* (1, 2; reading *n* for *u*). Although it was church land the unusual barony bound spelling *Collocanmurph* (form 4) indicates *coill* "wood" rather than *cill* "church". The final element seems to have contained [x], alternating in form (4) with [f], like the anglicization of Gaelic *Murchadh* as Murphy.

A surname based on the personal name *Murchadh* is also possible. McMurphy was a principal Irish name in upper Iveagh, as was O'Murphy in Lecale, in 1659 (*Census* 77). Woulfe located the origin of both names in Tyrone (Woulfe 1923, *Ó Murchadha* of *Síol Aodha* 622, *Mac Murchadh*a of *Muinntear Birn* 394; Ó Doibhlín, É. 1971(a), 20). MacMurphy variously spelt was frequent in Armagh in the early 17th century (*CPR Jas I* 148b), having moved in to *Uí Echach* from Tyrone as early as 1152 (Simms 1978, 72). The territory of Uí Eachach of Armagh was situated along the Blackwater to the south-west of Armagh city.

Both O'Donovan and Mooney suggested that the latter part of the name was *Cine Muireadhaigh* "the sept of *Muireadhach*", from the "9th-century kings of Dál nAraidhe" (*Mooney MS* 108). However, the element *cine* would fit the spellings after 1800 better than the 17th-century forms, and the name *Muireadhach*, revived in the 9th century, was popular in the Dál Fiatach royal line, rather than in Dál nAraide and Iveagh (Byrne 1973, 285). *O'Laverty* (i lxi) thought O'Murry was often a local substitute for *Mac Giolla Muire*, more frequently anglicized as Gilmore (see **Clankilvoragh**). According to Woulfe, families with the original surname *Ó Muireadhaigh* were once rulers in Westmeath and Roscommon and there were many ecclesiastics of the name (1923, 621). In 1659 *O Murry* was a "principall Irish name" in west Co. Armagh and Castlereagh barony Co. Down (*Census* 27, 29, 90).

Neither MacMurphy nor O'Murry can be proved to have existed in this parish, although there are Murrays now in Drumballyroney, near where there is a minor name Murray's Hollows. By 1617 Kilkinamurray belonged to Edward Trevor and its earlier history is lost. There is now a church, which is the "meeting house for Covenanters" built in 1821 (*OSM* xii 80b, 84), and some houses at a crossroads between two hills (622 and 721 feet) in the townland. According to local information the area is more often known as The Glen [ðə'glɛːn]. There is a reference to Glen Meeting House in 1834 (*OSNB* 12).

Killaney	*Cill Eidhnigh* (?)	
J 1946	"ivy-covered church"	
1. Bally-Ienkillehehueh	CPR Jas I 395b	1609
2. Bally-Jenkinkilliehehneh	CPR Jas I 191a	1611
3. Bally-Jenkinkillyhehneth	CPR Jas I 266a	1614
4. Ballyibreckyllyehueh(?)	Inq. Ult. (Down) §4 Jac. I	1616

5. Bally-Jenkillehehuegh	CPR Jas I 309a	1616
6. Ballijenkillies (Knockaguerin 4tds)	Buckworth (EA) 310	1622
7. Ballyyinkillichehuch	Buckworth (Atkinson) 127	1622
8. Ballisenkilliehuch [Reg. Visit.]	Mooney MS 110	1622
9. Bally-Jenkilliehehnogh [Reg. Visit.]	Mooney MS 110	1634
10. Killiloan	Civ. Surv. x §72	1655c
11. Killilane	Civ. Surv. x §73	1655c
12. Killane	Hib. Reg. Up. Iveagh	1657c
13. Rilleni	Census 75	1659c
14. Killeane	BSD 116	1661
15. Killeny	Sub. Roll Down 277	1663
16. Killan	Hib. Del. Down	1672c
17. Killiany	Deeds & Wills (Mooney) 109	1720
18. Killeany	Wm. Map (OSNB) NB12	1810
19. Killiney	Ir. Wills Index 67	1829
20. Killeny	Bnd. Sur. (OSNB) NB12	1830c
21. Killany	Cess Book (OSNB) NB12	1834c
22. [kil-'le-ny]	OSNB Pron. NB12	1834c
23. pronounced Kill'eeny	OSM xii 81b	1834
24. Killinney	Ir. Wills Index 67	1841
25. [Kil-'lay-ny]	Mooney 110	1950c
26. Cill Éinne "Church of St. Eany or Endeus"	J O'D (OSNB) NB12	1834c
27. Cill Eithne "Church of St Ethna"	Mooney 109	1950c
28. Cill Uí hEidhnigh or hAdhnaidh	Mooney 109	1950c
29. ˌkjəl'lenï	Local pronunciation	1991
30. ˌkil'eni	Local pronunciation	1991

Killaney was church land, belonging to Knockgorm, the mensal of the bishop of Dromore. It contained a religious site which was probably once quite important. Dean Mooney observed, "There was a holed stone associated with Killaney (a cupped stone) and one called St Patrick's Chair. There was a graveyard on this hillside and a well near it on the roadside below the farmyard of the man that owns the land of St Patrick's Stone" (*Mooney MS* 110). St Patrick's Stone only is shown on the 1:10,000 sheet 221 (as on the 1-inch) to the east of Killaney House near the border with Knockgorm townland (J 190460). It is probably the stone mentioned in 1834: "a standing stone in Killeny near the Flow Bog" (*OSM* xii 81a), although St Patrick's stone is near the townland boundary on the opposite side (south-east) from the Flow Bog.

The original form of the townland name is difficult to make sense of from the long early 17th-century spellings (1–9), all of which may be related and refer to Killaney as church land. Dean Mooney suggested (*Mooney MS* 109) that these forms show confusion between *sean-chill* "old church" and the personal name *Seanicin* or Jenkin, which was used locally by the McBredan erenagh family (*CPR Jas I* 395b, 191a), resulting in an extra syllable in the first element. This seems plausible, but it is also possible that *Ballyjenkin* was an alternative name for Killaney, which appears in its present shorter form from c. 1655. However Reeves' transcription of his copy of Buckworth's list (form 6) indicates an earlier attempt to shorten the name. As for the rest of the modern name, the parish of Killaney in north Co. Down seems to go back to *Cill Eanaigh* "church of the marsh", and this townland is beside marshy ground. However, *eanach* is usually anglicized *annagh* and the local pronunciation here has [e], suggesting a different vowel in the second element.

The second element in a *cill-* name is quite likely to give the name of the original saint associated with the site. O'Donovan, working from the later forms, suggested *Cill Éinne*, a dedication to "St Eany or Endeus", but although Énda of Aran is linked by his pedigree with Airgialla (Kenney 1929, 374 §164) he had no connection with Co. Down. Mooney suggested one of the female saints called Eithne, *Cill Eithne*, which might explain the *-h-* in the penultimate syllable in the early 17th-century forms but not the clearly attested final fricative, variously spelt *h, gh, th*. Fainche, the name of a northern woman saint, would give *Cill Fhainche*, with a fricative in the final syllable but not in the first. However, the adjective *eidhneach* "ivy-covered" is closer phonetically to *ehneth* etc., and would fit with the sense of "old church". If the earlier name ended with *Cill Eidhneach* "ivied church", the later spellings could represent the dative of this, *Cill Eidhnigh*.

However, there is an extra vowel *e/i/y* following *kill* in the early 17th-century spellings, which may have to be read as *Baile Seanchille*, "townland of the the old church", with proper genitive inflection, making the correct form of the adjective *eidhní*. Thinking the vowel might indicate an Irish surname, Mooney considered *Ó hEidhnigh* or *Ó hAdhnaidh*, although the prefixed *h* should be omitted after genitive *Uí*. The Galway family of O'Hanny, anciently chieftains, was scattered by the 16th century and the surname is rare (Woulfe 1923, 547). The surname *Ua hEignigh*, of Fermanagh or *Clann Chearnaigh* in east Co. Armagh (Arthurs 1954(c), 52) developed a form *Ua hÉighnigh*, and sometimes *Ua hÉinigh* (Hegney to Heaney: Woulfe 1923, 565, 567) which would fit reasonably well with the development here. The older pronunciation of Heaney would have been ['henï], as also suggested for **Balleny** in Dromore. Nevertheless it is simpler to accept *Cill Eidhnigh*, bearing in mind that after anglicized *Bally* Irish place-names are not always correctly inflected.

Knockgorm
J 1945

Cnoc Mhig Uidhrín
"McGivern's Hill"

1. Cnocgwrnis	Reg. Cromer ii §54	1546
2. Lo. Knock Gorre	Bartlett Map (Greenwich)	1602
3. Lo & Kno Gorrhe	Bartlett Maps (Esch. Co. Maps) 2	1603
4. Knockgurryn	CPR Jas I 395b	1609
5. Ballylisidimehevaghe	CPR Jas I 395b	1609
6. L. Gorrhe (at head of Bann)	Speed's Ireland	1610
7. L. Knock Iormy	Speed's Ulster	1610
8. Knockgurrin	CPR Jas I 190b	1611
9. Ballylisidunehevagh	CPR Jas I 191a	1611
10. Knockgurrin	CPR Jas I 266a	1614
11. Knockagurrin	CPR Jas I 309a	1616
12. Ballylisdunehevaghie	CPR Jas I 309a	1616
13. Knockaguerin 4tds	Buckworth (EA) 310	1622
14. Knockagnerin 4 towne lands	Buckworth (Atkinson) 127	1622
15. Ballylysdunevaghy (Knockaguerin)	Buckworth (EA) 310	1622
16. Knockryne	Civ. Surv. x §72	1655c
17. Knockgorin	Hib. Reg. Up. Iveagh	1657c
18. Knocknegaren	Census 75	1659c
19. Knockquirin	BSD 116	1661

20. Knocknegorm	Sub. Roll Down 277	1663
21. Knockgorin	Hib. Del. Down	1672c
22. (?)Carny L. (S of Garvaghy ch)	Harris Hist. map	1743
23. Knocknogorm	Deeds & Wills (Mooney) 112 [Will]	1746c
24. Knocknagorm [Will?]	Mooney MS 112	1769
25. Knocknagorm	Ir. Wills Index 70	1798
26. Knocknagorin	Wm. Map (OSNB) NB12	1810
27. Knocknagorm	Tombstone (OSNB) NB12	1828
28. Knockgorm	Bnd. Sur. (OSNB) NB12	1830c
29. Knockgorum	Cess Book (OSNB) NB12	1834c
30. lake of same name (ie Knockgorm)	OSNB NB12	1834c
31. [Knock-'gorm]	OSNB Pron. NB12	1834c
32. Cnoc gorm "Blue hill"	J O'D (OSNB) NB12	1834c
33. Cnoc Mhic Uidhrín "MacGivern's hill"	Mooney 111	1950c
34. lios dún (Uí h)Eachadha, Haffy = Ua hEachach	Mooney 111	1950c
35. nɔk'gɔrm	Local pronunciation	1991
36. nɔk'gɔrəm	Local pronunciation	1991

The present form of Knockgorm might well lead one to assume, with O'Donovan, that it represented *Cnoc Gorm* "blue hill". However 18th-century spellings and even Williamson's map of Co. Down (form 26) have an extra syllable after Knock, and final *-in* appears regularly in the 17th-century forms. The 16th-century form *Cnocgwrnis* (1), which presumably contains an English possessive *-s*, indicates that it is possibly *cnoc* "hill" plus a reduced form of the surname *Mag Uidhrín* "son of the little dun one", now anglicized McGivern. There were many clergymen of the family of *Mag Uidhrín* in the diocese of Dromore in the 15th century (*Swanzy's Dromore, Mooney MS* 110) and Philip *McGwryryn* who died in 1428 was rector of Magherally (*Reg. Swayne* 100). In 1427 Peter *McGyryn* was granted the church lands in another neighbouring parish, Annaclone (*Reg. Swayne* 76), some of which were still held by the family in the early 17th century (*CPR Jas I* 195b, 191a, 395a).

The spellings of the surname in these 17th-century references include *Maguirin* and *McGuiverin*, the antecedent of the modern form McGivern (Woulfe 1923, 427-8). O'Rahilly also gives examples of the change from dental *dh* to labial *bh* (O'Rahilly 1930, 185). There is no evidence for the form with *v* in the place-name, and Mooney's suggestion that McGivern appeared in another townland name *Edengwiran* in Co. Down has been rejected (*PNI* i 139). However the context makes it reasonably likely here, though an alternative would be *Cnoc Goirín* "hill of the lump or pimple". The proprietor in 1663 was an O'Sheil, the same family who were confirmed in the erenagh lands in 1526, and were also church tenants in Annaclone parish, where they gave their name to the townland of **Ballysheil**.

Knockgorm was used as the general name for the Bishop's mensal of four townlands. The four each have their own name, and three can be identified as church townlands round Knockgorm (Killaney, Castlevennon, Balloolymore). Dean Mooney, expecting Garvaghy townland to be church land, suggested that it was included in Knockgorm as *Ballylisidunehevagh* (forms 5,9,12,15). In this name *dún* "hill-fort" seems later to have been explained as *lios* "enclosure/fort" before the unhistorical addition of *baile*. The final element is more complicated. It is unlikely to be the tribal name *Uí Echach* as in (**Knock) Iveagh**, as the anglicized form used as the barony name never includes the final syllable appearing here (*-evaghie*). However, if it is based on the surname *Ó hEochadha* (O'Haughey, O'Haffy) as suggested by Mooney, there is no explanation of the *v*. As to his identification, there is no record of a hill-fort on Garvaghy Hill, which, with its neighbouring townlands, had been church land before 1609 and seems to have been called *Fergone*. It is likely that *Ballylisdunevaghie* is the particular name of Knockgorm townland.

The gentle slope of Knockgorm Hill is the chief feature of the townland, 507 feet high with an extensive view. In 1834 there was "an old fort, partly defaced" on the summit of Knockgorm hill, probably the *Dunevaghie* of the older name, and below it a shallow lake of 11 acres in the centre of the townland, 428 feet up, with a swamp of the same extent at the southern end which had been part of the lake before being drained. The drainage work had left an "island", presumed to be artificial, which was formerly in the middle of the lake, standing 10-12 feet above the south edge of the water (*OSM* xii 79ab, 81a). The site seems to have been important enough to be recorded on the first maps of the area, even though the spelling is corrupt and only Bartlett and Speed's Ulster have the location correct (forms 2,3,6,7). On the modern map (OS 1:10,000 series, sheet 221), Knockgorm Lough, so-named, is shown as rough grassland to the left of the Knockgorm road. Nothing more is known about the fort, or the possible crannog (*ASCD* 184 no. 734).

Shanrod	*Seanród*	
J 2145	"old road"	
1. Ballymonymore als Shan Raddie	CPR Jas I 395b	1609
2. Ballinmunnimore, Pat. O'Kearney of	CPR Jas I 195b	1610
3. Ballymonymore als Shaneradda	CPR Jas I 191a	1611
4. Shaneradda	CPR Jas I 191a	1611
5. Shanrade	Inq. Ult. (Down) xliii	1618
6. Shanrade	CPR Jas I 305a	1623
7. Shanrad	Civ. Surv. x §72	1655c
8. Shamerad	Census 75	1659c
9. Shanread (Bally Elly &)	BSD 116	1661
10. Shanrade	Sub. Roll Down 276	1663
11. Shinrod	Wm. Map (OSNB) NB12	1810
12. Shanrod	Tombstone (OSNB) NB12	1828
13. Shinrod	Bnd. Sur. (OSNB) NB12	1834c
14. [Shan-'rod]	OSNB Pron. NB12	1834c
15. Shenrod... Shenrod Water	OSM xii 84	1837
16. Sean Rod "Old road"	J O'D (OSNB) NB12	1834c
17. Sean-rod "old road"	Joyce iii 553	1913
18. Sean-raid/Seanroide		
"former bogland"	Mooney 115	1950c
19. Baile Móna Móire: old name before		
bog cut out	Mooney 115	1950c
20. 'ʃanrɔd	Local pronunciation	1991
21. ˌʃan'rɔːd	Local pronunciation	1994

The initial element of Shanrod seems to be *sean* "old", but there is doubt about the second element, which varies in pronunciation between short and long *o*. Shanrod could be on an "old road" *Seanród* (form 16, John O'Donovan) perhaps leading to an "old ford" *Seanáthán* (*Mooney MS* 35) across the river Bann in the townland of **Shannaghan**, which belonged to Newry parish (*PNI* i 35–6). Local tradition in the early 19th century claimed that the nearby townland of Tullintanvally in Annaclone parish was on an old road from Armagh to Downpatrick (*Mooney MS* 37). The important modern roads in the area are often on low ground, and are probaby recent, but the minor road from south to north in Shanrod follows a ridge to a crossroads on the summit of the hill in Fedany, after which its direction is less certain.

The alias *Ballymonymore* given in 1609-1611 (forms 1–3) could indicate a "great bog" by then cut out or reclaimed, so that the present name might be *Seanraid* "former bogland" (*Mooney MS* 115), although the spelling -*munni*- in 1609 indicates *muine* "thicket" rather than *móin* "bog" (Toner 1991–3, 55). Even with this interpretation there is still difficulty with the second element, which could represent either *raid* "bog-myrtle" or *roda, roide* "bog-stuff, bog". The final syllable in the earliest forms could be from this word or *Sean-raid(each)* "old boggy place". However, early Irish had a word *raite* (*DIL* sv.) which like *ród* signified "road". Although this meaning does not appear in later dictionaries, *raide*, explained by Ó Dónaill as an alternative form of *roide* "bog mud", may have still kept the meaning "road" when Shanrod was named.

Shanrod Lough is south-east of the crossroads in the townland. A settlement remembered near Shanrod Lough was known as Laketown, a name which does not appear on either the 1:50,000 or 1:10,000 map.

Tullinisky	*Tulaigh Abhann Eascannaí*	
J 2349	"hillock of the Eel Burn"	
1. Ballytullyneskeine	CPR Jas I 395a	1609
2. Ballytullyneskeine	CPR Jas I 190b	1611
3. Ballytollyneskenie	CPR Jas I 191a	1611
4. Ballytullyneskeyne	CPR Jas I 191b	1611
5. Ballitullineskine or		
Ballytollyneskeyneye	CPR Jas I 266a	1614
6. Ballytulleniskie	Inq. Ult. (Down) §13 Car. I	1629
7. Ballintullenuske	Inq. Ult. (Down) §13 Car. I	1629
8. Balletulleneskan	Inq. Ult. (Down) §85 Car. I	1639
9. Tulliskin, Robt Walsh of	Wars Co. Down x 76	1641
10. Tilliniskie	Ir. Wills Index 94	1719
11. Tulliniskie	Ir. Wills Index 94	1719
12. Tulliniskin	Ir. Wills Index 9	1758
13. Tullyniskey	Wm. Map (OSNB) NB12	1810
14. [Tull-in-'is-ky]	OSNB Pron. NB12	1834c
15. Tulaigh an uisce "hill of the water"	J O'D (OSNB) NB12	1834c
16. Tulach nEasconach (neut.) "well-watered hill"	Mooney 119	1950c
17. Tulach Abhann Easconaighe "height of the Eel Burn"	Mooney 119	1950c
18. ˌtọlˈnəski	Local pronunciation	1991
19. ˌtọliˈnəski	Local pronunciation	1994

Tullynisky is one of the Garvaghy group of townlands held by William Worseley from Sir Art Magennis. From the modern form the name could be simply *Tulach an Uisce* "hillock of the water", as suggested by O'Donovan, or possibly *Tulaigh Naoscán* "hillock of the snipe", but the additional final syllable of 17th-century forms such as *Ballytollyneskeyneye* (5) suggests a longer final element originally. It is possible that the name of the **Eel Burn**, which forms the southern boundary of the townland, may have been translated from Irish *Abhainn Eascann* "river of eels" or *Abhainn Eascannach* "eely river" (*Mooney MS* 119). Although internal *n* is all the evidence in the spellings for the element *abhainn*, it is unlikely that the stream was called simply *An Eascannach* as this would give *na hEascannaí* in the genitive.

Tullyorior	*Tulaigh Oirir*	
J 1743	"hillock of the boundary"	

1.	Ballytullagherier	CPR Jas I 395b	1609
2.	Ballytolloghanere, Gilleduffe McBryn of	CPR Jas I 195b	1610
3.	Ballytullyorire	CPR Jas I 191a	1611
4.	Tulliorier	Hib. Reg. Up. Iveagh	1657c
5.	Tulliorior	Inq. Ult. (Down) §1 Interreg.	1658
6.	the said Talliorie	Inq. Ult. (Down) §1 Interreg.	1658
7.	Tolliorie	Census 75	1659c
8.	Tulliorier	BSD 116	1661
9.	Tulliorier	Hib. Del. Down	1672c
10.	Tullyorey	Tombstone (OSNB) NB12	1778
11.	Tullyory	Tombstone (OSNB) NB12	1810
12.	Tullyauriar	Wm. Map (OSNB) NB12	1810
13.	Tullyorier	Tombstone (OSNB) NB12	1815
14.	Tullyorier	Reg. Free. (OSNB) NB12	1829
15.	Tullyoriour	Bnd. Sur. (OSNB) NB12	1830c
16.	[Tul-ly-'o-ry]	OSNB Pron. NB12	1834c
17.	pronounced Tully'ory	OSM xii 81b	1834
18.	Tullyor	OSM xii 82	1837
19.	Tulaigh Oirthear "hill of Oriors" people of Oriel	OSNB Inf. NB12	1834c
20.	"Hill of the Oriors" collis Orientalium	J O'D (OSNB) NB12	1834c
21.	ˌtɔlˈɔrï	Local pronunciation	1991
22.	ˌtïliˈɔrï	Local pronunciation	1995

The current local pronunciation of Tullyorior omits the final syllable of the written form, and this is of long standing. At the time of the first Ordnance Survey the local pronunciation was [Tul-ly-'o-ry] (16), appearing in written form on two local tombstones: *Tullyorey* (1778) in Seapatrick graveyard, and *Tullyory* (1810) in Annaclone graveyard (10, 11). There are two 17th-century examples: *Talliorie* as an alias in 1658, *Tolliorie* in 1659 (forms 6, 7). However most of the early forms, from the first attestation in 1609, contain the final *-r*. The townland then belonged to the bishop of Dromore, and was held by Gilleduffe *MacBrien*. It was Gilleduffe McHugh McPatrick *MacBrien* who had to surrender *Ballytolloghanere*, probably the fullest form (2). The townland was escheated at the time of the interregnum (5, 6), but there are still various families of Byrnes in the area. In this townland there are two house clusters called Byrnestown as well as **Kearneystown**, locally Kearney, and Shawstown, all south of the Bann (OS 1:10,000 sheet 221). The last Shaw of Shawstown died in 1939, but a Byrne of Kearney claims the family have been there for 300 years.

Mount Hill on the southern boundary was possibly the *tulach* of the townland name. O'Donovan's informant for Tullyorior was a man in Downpatrick gaol, who took the second element to refer to the people of Orior barony in Armagh, but this is surely too far away. Four miles to the west along the Bann, outside Banbridge, is Tullyear townland in Seapatrick, part of the Magennis district of Loughbrickland, taken by Dean Mooney to be the "western hillock" in relation to Tullyorior, which he interpreted as *Tulaigh Oirthir* "eastern hillock". However neither hill seems to be notable enough to be contrasted like this.

Tullyorior is in the west of Garvaghy and borders the three parishes of Annaclone, Seapatrick and Magherally. The boundary between Tullyorior and the townlands of Tullintanvally, Cappagh and Tullyconnaught is also the boundary between the Lower Half and Upper Half of Upper Iveagh, and the boundary between Tullyorior and the Corbet is also the boundary between Upper and Lower Iveagh. It must have been in this area that the Bann, which flows through Tullyorior, began to be treated as the barony bound (see introduction to Seapatrick parish). This makes it likely that the second element of the name is *oirear* "border region", hence *Tulaigh Oirir*. The modern pronunciation is thus close to the original, except for loss by haplology of the final *-r*. The spelling *-orior* was influenced by the supposed connection with **Orior** in Co. Armagh (forms 19, 20).

In the south of Tullyorior the Bann is crossed by **Poland's Bridge** into the parish of Annaclone (OS 1:10,000 sheet 221). Further north the same map reveals that a meander in the Bann has left an oxbow lake behind, west of the present channel, near the inn called the Anglers' Rest. This may have been the place called The Loop in 1834 (*OSM* xii 79b).

OTHER NAMES

Chips Corner	An English form	
['t'ʃips 'kɔːrnər]	see parish introduction	
Eel Burn	*An Abhainn Eascannach*	
J 2147	"the eely river"	
1. Abhainn Easconach "Eel Burn"	Mooney 120	1950c
2. An Easconach	Mooney 120	1950c
3. 'il 'bərn	Local pronunciation	1991

From the 1:50,000 map it looks as if one stream, the Eel Burn, divides the hills which form Garvaghy and Fedany townlands, but in fact there is a watershed between two streams flowing north and south, and the Eel Burn is the stream which flows northwards through Tullynisky and under Eel Burn bridge just outside Waringsford. As suggested under **Tullynisky** this may be a translation of an Irish name.

Flow Bog	An English form	
J 1846		
1. the Flow Bog (Killaney)	OSNB NB12	1834c
2. the Flow Bog	OSM xii 80, 81, 113, 114, 115	1834

3. ˌðə ˈflau ˈbɔːg	Local pronunciation	1991
4. ˌðə ˈfləu ˈrod	Local pronunciation	1991

The Flow Bog is not named even on the 1:10,000 map (sheet 221), but lies between the parishes of Magherally and Garvaghy, and is a continuation to the south of the Gall Bog. It was spelled Flow by the Ordnance Survey in the 1830s, when it was used for fuel (*OSM* xii 114a) and by local custom. Flow bog (as in English "flow") is a geographical technical term, signifying its semi-liquid state. However the road sign at the southern end (Corbet) calls the road through the bog the Flough Road, and this spelling appears on the 1:10,000 map sheet 221. Water lies in pools on each side of the road even in summer (June '94), but despite the spelling the pronunciation (4) is against Irish *fliuch* "wet".

Gall Bog   An English form
J 2148

1. Gall Bog (Ednego, Tullyglush)	OSNB E125	1834c
2. Gall Bog (Balloolly)	OSNB NB12	1834c
3. ˌðə ˈgɔːl ˈbɔg	Local pronunciation	1994

The Gall Bog forms a large part of the northern boundary of the parish. The Ordnance Survey Memoir preserved a tradition that the road from Banbridge to Dromara, which runs through it, was "formerly a racecourse" (*OSM* xii 80a). It is "almost dead straight in places" and has been used more recently for testing motorbikes. However along much of its length there are pools on each side of the road, which are locally rumoured to be bottomless. There is no earlier record of the name, which may be English from the colour: "as black as gall" (bile). English field names containing the element *gall* have been derived from Old English *galla* meaning "barren, wet land" (Field 1989, 85).

Kearneystown   An English form

1. ˈkɛrnï	Local pronunciation	1995

Kearney, as it is known locally, is a house cluster in the townland of Tullyorior, where fifty or so people are supposed to have lived at one time. However their surnames were Byrne and O'Hagan, so that the place-name does not seem to have been the standard compound of surname plus -*town*. For other names with the element *kearney* etc, see **Carney Hill**, Moira; **Tullycarn**, Donaghcloney. There is now only one family left in Kearney.

Legnabeepa   *Lag na bPiopa*
J 179435   "the hollow of the pipes"

1. ˌlɛgnəˈbipə	Local pronunciation	1995
2. ˌlognəˈbipə	Local pronunciation	1995

This is a marsh west of the Bann in the townland of Tullyorior, named on OS 1:10,000 sheet 221. In local use Legnabeepa includes the hollow crossed by the northern part of Circular Road, where there is a piped drain which is held to account for the name. There are no earlier forms, but it is also possibly a place where old clay pipes had been found.

Lough Cock *Loch Caoch*
J 203458 "blind lough"

1. Loch Koch (Killaney)	OSNB NB12	1834c
2. marsh called Loch Kock (Shanrod)	OSNB NB12	1834c
3. Lough Kock or Lough Caig	OSM xii 79b	1834
4. Loch Caoch (under Knockgorm)	Mooney 112	1950c

This name has only been recorded since the early 19th century (forms 1–4) and seems now to be forgotten, but the English equivalent Blind Lough is also found as a term for shallow lakes, possibly meaning "overgrown with weeds" as Lough Cock was in 1834 (*OSM* xii 79b). There were **Blind Lough**s in the west of Ballymoney and east of Tullyhinan townlands, parish of Magherally (OS 1:10,000 sheet 202, J 1348, J 1648). Lough Cock is now shown as a marsh with several ponds, between Balloolymore, Knockgorm and Shanrod townlands (1:10,000 sheet 221). The stream between these two marshes is called *The River* locally.

Lough Doo *Loch Dubh*
J 203455 "black lough

1. Loughnotowe	Inq. Ult. (Down) xliii	1618
2. Loghtoe	BSD 116	1661
3. Logh Dugh or the Black Lough (Shanrod)	OSNB NB12	1834c
4. Lough Dugh or Dhu, the black lake	OSM xii 79b	1834
5. Loch Dubh "Black lake"	J O'D (OSNB) NB12	1834c
6. 'lɔx 'du	Local pronunciation	1996

Loughnotowe was mentioned in the bounds of **Ballooly** in 1618, and the name appears as *Loughtoe* in the *Books of Survey and Distribution* in 1661 (forms 1, 2). From the early 19th-century forms *Lough Dugh, Lough Dhu* the Ordnance Survey deduced that it was *Loch Dubh* "the black lake" (forms 3, 4), presumably so understood from the blackness of the water. However the 17th-century forms indicate that the name may have been earlier *Loch (na d)Tua* "lake of (the) axes", perhaps from an archaeological find at the lake. Loughdoo is now a marsh between the townlands of Ballooly, Knockgorm, and Shanrod (OS 1:10,000 sheet 221).

Scion Hill Of uncertain origin
J 2449

1. Sion Hill (in Tullinisky)	OSNB NB12	1834c
2. Sion Hill	OSM xii 80b	1834
3. 'skɑjən 'hïl	Local pronunciation	1994

The house named Scion Hill is on the slope of a hill in Tullynisky townland, with a rath close by. In the early 19th century the name was written as *Sion* Hill, which looks like the fairly common anglicization of *sídheán*, modern Irish *sián*, the diminutive of *sídh* "otherworld dwelling" or "fairy hill" (cf. **Sion Mills**), used of a small isolated hill. There is a Zion Hill in the parish of Moira, on the northern bank of the Lagan where it is crossed by the motorway (OS 1:10,000 sheet 183). However on the modern map the name is now spelt Scion, with the *c* sounded as [k] in local pronunciation (1:10,000 sheet 203). The change is difficult to explain, and in the English word *scion* "offspring" the *c* is silent.

Waringsford   An English form
J 2348

1. Waringsford	Harris Hist. map	1743
2. Waringsford seat of Henry Waring		
Esq.	Harris Hist. 98	1744
3. Waringsford (McMechan)	Ir. Wills Index 99	1771
4. Waringsford	Statist. Sur. Dn 24	1802
5. Waringsford	OSM xii 80b	1834
6. demesne of Waringsford	OSM xii 80b, 81b	1834
7. village of Waringsford = Milltown	OSM xii 80b	1834
8. Waringsford (house in ruins		
Tullynisky)	OSNB NB12	1834c
9. Áth an Bhairínigh	GÉ 8	1989
10. 'warïŋz,ford	Local pronunciation	1991
11. 'wɛrïnz,fo:rd	Local pronunciation	1994

Waringsford, on a tributary of the Lagan joined by the Eel Burn, had been a "gentleman's seat" but was in ruins by 1834, leaving only a plantation of trees in the demesne. By then the village beside it was known both as Waringsford and Mill Town (form 7). However Harris in 1744 recorded the house as "the seat of Henry Waring Esq." (form 2), so that the house and village were clearly named from the proprietor's surname.

The village is well-known locally because of Ervines's mill buildings beside the river. The Ervines are commemorated in Ervines Close in the village, but often the Waringsford mills are known as Tullinisky mills, from the townland in which they are situated.

KILOMETRES 1   0   1   2   3

STATUTE MILES 1   0   1   2

Parish of Magheralin
Barony of Iveagh Lower, Upper Half
Barony of Oneilland East, Co. Armagh★ (3 townlands)

Townlands	Ballymakeonan	Drumo and Drumcro	Lisnashanker
Ballykeel	Ballynadrone	Edenballycoggill	Lisnasure
Ballyleny	Clankilvoragh★	Edenmore	Taughlumny
Ballymacanally	Clogher	Feney	Taughrane
Balymacateer	Derrylisnahavil★	Gartross	Tullyanaghan
Ballymacbredan	Donagreagh★	Gregorlough	Tullynacross
Ballymacbrennan	Drumlin	Kilfullert	
Ballymacmaine	Drumnabreeze	Kircassock	*Town*
Ballymagin	Drumnaferry	Lismaine	Magheralin

THE PARISH OF MAGHERALIN

The parish is on the most western reach of the river Lagan, before it turns east to flow through Lisburn and Belfast. It consists of 33 townlands in Co. Down, and three across the border in Co. Armagh: Clankilvoragh, Derrylisnahavil and Donaghreagh.

In the past much of the parish was church land, and the medieval parish church was in the townland of Ballymakeonan, where the ruins still stand across the road from the 19th-century Church of Ireland church. The present village of Magheralin is in the south part of Ballymagin, and the south-west corner of Ballymakeonan, with the replacement church in the west of Ballynadrone. The parish was once much larger. All the townlands were included in the parish register of 1715, but 20 townlands were divided off in 1725 to form the parish of **Moira**. However, these did not reflect exactly the 17th-century usage of the district name *Moyragh*, which included the townlands of Drumnabreeze, Feney, Gartross and Taughlumny still in the modern civil parish of Magheralin (*CPR Jas I* 395a, 190b). During most of the 18th century the Anglican bishops of Dromore resided in a see house on the site of the modern Roman Catholic church, and the now-ruined parish church was used as "a sort of pro-cathedral for the diocese" (*Atkinson's Dromore* 64), until a new bishop's house was built to replace that destroyed in 1641 in the cathedral town of Dromore.

The church lands of Magheralin included the 10 modern townlands (called "six towne lands" in 1622) of Ballymakeonan, Ballymacateer, Ballymagin, and (earlier half-towns of) Ballymacbredan, Ballymacmaine, Ballynadrone, Drumlin, Edenballycoggill, Lismaine, and Tullynacross. In 1609 this group of townlands was rented by the bishop to William Worseley, and in 1622 to Thomas Coats (*CPR Jas I* 395b, 190b; *Buckworth (Atkinson)* 127), although they had clearly been held earlier by erenagh families. Many of the townland names in Magheralin contain surnames of families important in the area in the past.

In 1609 the McBredan erenagh family still held four church lands, called *Tullyanahie* and *Clondonnelmcbriddon* as well as Donaghcloney and *Ballyemtyshewin* (*CPR Jas I* 395a, 191a). The last is probably the townland of Clogher lying near Donaghcloney and otherwise unaccounted for. These lands were later held from the bishop of Dromore by George Sexton, as recorded in 1632 (*Inq. Ult. (Down)* §30 Car. I). The first two names look like the contiguous townlands of Tullyanaghan and Ballymacbredan further north in Magheralin, but Ballymacbredan was also listed under William Worseley's holding in 1609, while Sir Art Magennis had Tullyanaghan: *Ballytullyannaghy*, with *Ballyclonegillmurry* (Clankilvoragh in Co. Armagh, also contiguous) and *Ballylaghdermott* (*CPR Jas I* 395b; 396a). This last appears to have been modern Tullyloob which became part of Moira parish.

Sir Art Magennis' holdings in the area seem to have been the reason for Clankilvoragh and the other two townlands of Co. Armagh being included in Magheralin parish. Listed also as in Sir Art's possession nearby in 1609 were *Ballyraconnell, Ballytullydagan, Ballydownegreigh, Ballydrumnekerny*, and *Knockineighter*. Tullydegan, Donagreagh, and Drumnykerne are townlands in the modern north-east corner of Co. Armagh, Donagreagh also being included in Magheralin. Unfortunately for Sir Art, as part of the confusion concerning the county boundary in this area, a similar list of townlands was granted in 1610 to John Brownlow in Co. Armagh: *Clan Igollavorist, Dunnagreih*, which are Clankilvoragh and Donagreagh in this parish, *Corakinegeir, Killaghy, Tollidegon, Tollyconally, Dromonikeherny*, which are Cornakinnegar, Killaghy, Tullydagan, Tullyronally, and Drumnykerne in Shankill parish in Armagh (*CPR Jas I* 165a). Derrylisnahavil, the third Armagh townland in this parish, was first mentioned in 1629, as part of Clankilvoragh owned by Brownlow. The other lands held by Sir Art can be shown to be subdivisions of the large modern townland of **Kilmore**, in north-west Co. Down but counted as part of Shankill parish. As well as the north-west there were scattered townlands belonging to Sir Art Magennis in the south of the parish: Ballymacbrennan, Drumo and Drumcro, Edenmore, and Gregorlough.

The parish included the western part of the Magennis district of **Lequirin**: containing Ballykeel, Ballyleny, Ballymacanally, Drumnaferry, Kircassock, Lisnashanker and Lisnasure. Ballykeel is next to Islandderry Lough, which contains the island which was probably the key fortification of Lequirin (**Islandderry**, parish of Dromore). In 1609 Lequirin was divided between three Magennis holders. Art Oge McGlasney Magennis, the son of the holder of **Clanconnell**, had Islandderry in Dromore with Ballymacanally, Drumnaferry, Lisnasure, and eventually Ballykeel, held from the King, James I. Brian McDonell McBrien Magennis had Ballyleny and Donell Oge McEdmond Boy Magennis held Kircassock and Lisnashanker, held from Sir Art.

At first individual townlands of the parish were sublet or transferred to settlers by their Magennis holders. By 1632 George Sexton held Drumnaferry and Ballykeel (*Inq. Ult. (Down)* §30 Car. I). The other portions of Lequirin were listed among the lands of the Magennis chief in 1629 and 1639, but seem to have been divided subsequently. In 1667, after the forfeiture of the Magennis lands, a large part of the parish, with lands in Donaghcloney and Dromore, belonged to John Magill: Drumo and Drumcro, Clogher, Kilfullert, Lisnashanker, also Taughlumny which had belonged to the O'Laverys of Moira. These lands were made into the manor of **Gilford**, named after Magill (*ASE* 112a). Sir George Rawdon also got a large estate further north: Ballymacbrennan, Gortross, Gregorlough, other parts of Drumcro and Taughlumny, also Tullyanaghan (part) and Edenmore in Magheralin, with Magherahinch, Aughadrumman, Derrydrummult, Balloonigan, Ballymagaraghan, Ballyconnell, and Tullyloob in Moira (*ASE* 61b). Subsequent references to the place-names appear in the records of these incoming proprietors.

When John O'Donovan visited Magheralin in 1834 he met a schoolmaster called McVeagh who was a native of the place, and who remembered when Irish had been spoken there although it was not understood any more. McVeagh also showed him the site of a rath levelled before he was born (he could remember 24 being levelled in his lifetime) and took him to a cabin to hear stories about one in the east of Ballymakeonan (*OSL Dn* vii 15). There are now no raths marked in the townland on the 1-inch or the 1:50,000 maps, or on 1:10,000 sheets 182-3. Unfortunately for us O'Donovan did not write these local traditions down. Information on the current local pronunciation of names was received from Messrs Tommy Banks of Magheralin and James Blaney and Kieran Clendinning of Lurgan.

PARISH NAME

Magheralin	*Machaire Lainne*	
J 1359	"plain of the church"	
1. Ronani Find ó Lainn Ruadain (corr.		
to Ronain)	Mart. Tal. May 22 p45	830c
2. Ronán Find Cille Lainde	CSH 48n	1125c
3. Bebil... i lLaind Rónáin Fhind	CSH 318.2	1125c
4. ó Laind Rónáin Fhinn i n-Uibh		
Eachach Uladh	Mart. Gorm. May 22 p102n	1170c
5. Lann Ronain Finn, ardneimadh		
Uladh uile	Miscell. Ann. §7 p66	1178
6. Cell Luinni/Lainni	Buile Suibhne §3	1350c
7. land Ronain Fhind meic Beraig	L.Lec. 88v b15	1397c

8. ó Laind Ronain Fhind in n-Uaib Echach Ulad	Fél. Óeng. May 22 p134n	1453
9. lann Ronain Finn in nUibh Eachach Uladh	Mart. Don. May 22 p137	1630
10. ecc'ia de Lan	Eccles. Tax. 110-1	1306c
11. par. ch., canonry, preb. of St Ronan de Land	Cal. Papal Letters vi 117,123-4	1407
12. Land	Reg. Dowdall §129 275	1422
13. par. ch. of St Ronan de Land	Cal. Papal Letters vii 250	1422
14. perp.vic. par.ch. St Ronan de Land	Cal. Papal Letters vii 264	1422
15. canonry, preb. St Ronan de Land	Cal. Papal Letters viii 123	1429
16. Lawronan (Oranaga)	Reg. Swayne 184	1440
17. prebenda de Lanronan	EA 313	1440
18. Land	Reg. Prene (EA) 111n	1442
19. praebenda de Land	Reg. Prene (EA) 111n	1443
20. Lend, can. preb. de	Annates Ulst. 290	1480
21. canonry, preb. of Land	Cal. Papal Letters xv §863	1492
22. Laune	Reg. Cromer ii §47	1526
23. prebend of Lanne	Reg. Cromer (EA) 111n	1526
24. Layn	Reg. Dowdall §113 80	1546
25. Mahelin	Hondius Map	1591
26. M. Moghlyne	Mercator's Ulst.	1595
27. Moghlyne	Mercator's Ire.	1595
28. Tempell Magharlin	Bartlett Maps (Esch. Co. Maps) 2	1603
29. Lann	Jas I to Dromore Cath. 314	1609
30. Maharla	Speed's Ireland	1610
31. Maharla	Speed's Ulster	1610
32. Magheryawleylan al. Magherilin	CPR Jas I 190b	1611
33. Magherilin 6tds	Buckworth (EA) 310	1622
34. Magherlin parish, Tagharan the Gleabe (sess)	Inq. Down (Reeves1) 85	1657
35. Magharalin	Census 80	1659c
36. Magherelin Parish (twice)	BSD 72 74	1661
37. Magheralin Parish	BSD 73	1661
38. Magherillin Parish	BSD 82	1661
39. (?)Magherau[?]	Trien. Visit. (Margetson) 24	1664
40. (?)Magherel[?]	Trien. Visit. (Margetson) 25	1664
41. Magherlin	Brownlow LB 122	1673
42. Magheralin Rectoria	Trien. Visit. (Boyle) 46	1679
43. Magherelin	Lamb Maps Co. Down	1690c
44. Mahrylen	Ir. Wills Index 62	1700
45. Meigheralin	Reg. Magheralin (OSNB) E8.59	1715
46. Maheralin	Reg. Deeds abstracts i §708	1737
47. Maralin	Harris Hist. map	1743
48. Magherelin now called Maralin	Harris Hist. 102,83	1744
49. Magherelin ie Waterfield... agreeable to nat. situation, from Maghere "a field" lin "a pool of water"	Harris Hist. 102n	1744

50. Magheralin	Map of Down (OSNB) E8.59	1755
51. road from Maharalin	Rocque's Map (Coote)	1760
52. road from Magherlin	Rocque's Map (Coote)	1760
53. Marling (bp's res.)	UJA ser.3 48 (1985) 114	1760
54. Magheralin	Wm. Map (OSNB) E8.59	1810
55. Maralin	Cess Book (OSNB) E8.59	1825
56. Maheralin	Bnd. Sur. (OSNB) E8.59	1830c
57. Maralin village (Ballymakeonan)	OSNB E8.59	1834c
58. Nicholson's Hill Head	OSNB E8.59	1834c
59. Maralin	Post Chaise Comp. (OSNB) E8.59	1834c
60. Magheralin	Post Chaise Comp. (OSNB) E8.59	1834c
61. Maraghlin	Post Chaise Comp. (OSNB) E8.59	1834c
62. [Maralin]	OSNB Pron. E8.59	1834c
63. Magheralin	J O'D (OSNB) E8.59	1834c
64. Machaire Linne "plain of the pool"	J O'D (OSNB) E8.59	1834c
65. Machaire-linne "the plain of the linn or pool"	Joyce iii 496	1913
66. Machaire Lainne / Magheralin	Éire Thuaidh	1988
67. Machaire Lainne	GÉ 132	1989
68. ˌmɑrəˈlən	Local pronunciation	1991
69. ˌmɑxərˈlən	Local pronunciation	1991
70. ˈmɑrəˌlən	Local pronunciation	1991

The sources make clear that the earlier name of Magheralin was *Lann Rónáin Fhinn* "church of (St) Ronan Finn", using the uncommon early Irish term *Lann* "church". In ecclesiastical sources the parish of Magheralin is called both *Lan* (forms 10–15, 18–24, 29: 1306 to 1609 AD) and *LanRonan*, in Irish *Lann Rónáin* "Ronan's church" (forms 16–7, probably the same source). These names probably indicate the same foundation, although Atkinson (*Dromore* 214–5) listed them separately for fear of confusing the evidence. In the Irish forms *Lann Rónáin* is more common (1, 3–5, 7–9), but there are two examples of *Cell Lainne* "the church of *Lann*" (2, 6). "The church of Rónán Fionn (Ronan the fair) in Iveagh of the Ulaid" is mentioned at May 22nd in four Irish martyrologies (1, 4, 8, 9), and the marking out of the church of *Cell Lainne* "the church of *Lann*" in *Dál Araidhe* by St Ronan son of Berach is described in the 12th-century tale *Buile Suibhne* "The Frenzy of Sweeney" (form 6, §§2–3). In the 7th century there were two saints called Ronan who are often confused, and it is more likely that the saint was originally Ronan the Fair son of Sárán, *Rónán Fionn mac Sáráin*, the Ronan the Fair of *Airthir*, i.e. Orior, descent (Ó Riain, P. 1974(b), 178–9; *CSH* 48, 487, 662.87–8, 707.913, but not associated with this church). Also associated with *Lann Rónáin Fhinn* was a saint called *Bebil*, sister of St Telle of Tihelly, Durrow, Co. Offaly (form 3: Ó Riain 1974(b), 181; *CSH* 318.2). St Petrán of *Cell Lainne* may belong here or to another church of the same name (*CSH* 181.11).

It is clear from this history that the derivation of the current name must be *Machaire Lainne* "plain of the church" and that the second element is not *Linne* "of the pool" (49, 64), despite the association with water, also seen in the townland name **Ballynadrone** "the townland between two rivers" by Magheralin village, and the song mentioning the "ducks of Magheralin". Atkinson provides a good summary of why Magheralin cannot be the same place as *Linn Duachaill* "Duachall's pool", actually at Annagassan Co. Louth, despite the earlier guess of Reeves (*Atkinson's Dromore* 212–3; *EA* 111n, 313n). Likewise the river at Annagassan, not the Lagan, was the *Casán Linne* up which the Vikings sailed.

Even though Magheralin means the "plain of the church" the exact site of the early church at Magheralin is unknown. The Book of Lecan located it in *Corco Ruisen* in *Magh Rath*, Moira (form 7), but we do not know how extensive the district of Moira then was. The church was called *ardneimheadh Uladh uile*, "the chief sanctuary of all Ulster" in AD 1178 (*Miscellaneous Irish Annals* 64–7 §7, 1) when it was attacked by John de Courcy and the ere-nagh *Tomás Ó Corcráin* was beheaded. In the same year the Ulaid and allies had attacked De Courcy at Downpatrick and lost many relics of the saints in battle, including *bachall Rónáin Fhinn*, St Ronan Finn's crozier (form 5). By 1422 the parish church was "much collapsed" and penitents were offered special privileges if they visited the church on St Ronan's feast day and gave alms for its repair (form 13). In 1442 John *McGynd*, Canon of Dromore, was allowed the stone tower he had built on to the church of *Land* to store his personal library, free from disturbance by the rector (*Reg. Prene* 69, *EA* 111n). The tower on the ruined early 15th-century church is probably post-medieval, although there is also a wall which could have been part of McGinn's library. There are no remains of any older building, and an "early foundation on this site must remain doubtful" (*ASCD* 307–8, site 951). Mooney recorded St Ronan's Well in a field in the townland of Ballymakeonan (*Mooney MS* 188).

Maps from 1591 give various spellings of the parish name, looking at first as though it were derived from *Magh Lainne* (forms 26–7), but by 1603 (form 28) clearly from *Machaire Lainne*, Magheralin. In church sources the "rectory and vicarage" was referred to by this name in 1611 (form 32), and Magheralin was used subsequently for both the village now containing the church (in Ballymakeonan) and the parish. A common spelling by the early 19th century was *Maralin*, still in use locally and reflected in the local pronunciation, where the stress may shift to the first syllable. The traveller Pococke's form *Marling* in 1760 (53) shows how early the name was shortened in speech. However, the Ordnance Survey restored the fuller form Magheralin used on its maps and in the Topographical Index.

TOWNLAND NAMES

Ballykeel   *Baile Caol*
J 1555   "narrow townland"

1. Ballykeile in the Lequirin	CPR Jas I 394b	1609
2. Ballykeise (in Ballinderrie/Lequirin)	CPR Jas I 193a	1611
3. Ballikeyle	Magennis Paps (O'Sullivan) 68	1632
4. Ballikeole	Hib. Reg. Lr. Iveagh	1657c
5. Ballykeele	Census 80	1659c
6. Ballikeele	BSD 73	1661
7. Ballykeele	ASE 174a 38	1668
8. Ballikeele	Hib. Del. Down	1672c
9. Ballykeel	DS (Mooney) 185	1679c
10. Ballykeel	Wm. Map (OSNB) E8.59	1810
11. Ballykeel	Bnd. Sur. (OSNB) E8.59	1830
12. Baile Caol "narrow town"	J O'D (OSNB) E8.59	1834c
13. ˌbɑliˈkiːl	Local pronunciation	1991

217

Ballykeel is a common townland name, regularly referring to the shape, and this "narrow townland" consists of a strip of land extending along each side of a stream (the Shanker Burn) flowing from Islandderry Lake. The earliest forms for this townland of Ballykeel, as distinct from townlands of the same name in Dromore, Donaghmore, and Seapatrick parishes, can be distinguished by being situated in Lequirin. Ballykeel was held as an outlier, detached from his other lands, by the lord of Clanconnell, Glasney McAugholy Magennis, but was granted in 1611 to Glasney's son Art with the "five towns of *Ballinderrie*" (**Islandderry**, Dromore), held from the King (forms 1, 2). Like Islandderry, it came into the hands of the Waddell family. Springfield House in Ballykeel seems to be in the same place as *Springhall* held by Waddell Esq. in 1777, close to Islandderry (*Taylor & Skinner* maps 5a, 15, 284b). In 1827 Springfield was "not inhabited and apparently falling to decay" (*OSNB* E8.59).

Ballyleny	*Baile Léana*	
J 1455	"townland of the wet meadow"	
1. Ballylinne in Leighquirin	CPR Jas I 395a	1609
2. Ballylyenna in Leighquirrin	CPR Jas I 190b	1611
3. Ballylyenny	Inq. Ult. (Down) §13 Car. I	1629
4. Ballelrany	Inq. Ult. (Down) §85 Car. I	1639
5. Ballineny & Drumtire	Hib. Reg. Lr. Iveagh	1657c
6. Ballineny	Par. Map (Mooney) 185	17thc
7. Ballylynny	Census 81	1659c
8. (?)Ballineny	BSD 74	1661
9. Ballyneny	S & D Ann. (Mooney) 185 (25)	17thc
10. Ballenny D'tire	Hib. Del. Down	1672c
11. Ballyleny	Reg. Magheralin (OSNB) E8.59	1715
12. Ballylany	Map of Down (OSNB) E8.59	1755
13. Ballylaney	Wm. Map (OSNB) E8.59	1810
14. Ballylenny	Reg. Free. (OSNB) E8.59	1834c
15. Ballyleany	Meersman (OSNB) E8.59	1834c
16. Baile Léanaidh "town of the meadow"	J O'D (OSNB) E8.59	1834c
17. Baile Léana, ʔlaighinigh	Mooney 185 (cf. p.95)	1950c
18. 'balï'lenï	Local pronunciation	1991

On the 1:50,000 map this name is spelled Ballyleny, though a different spelling is used for Ballyleaney House in the townland. Ballyleny is on low hills, sloping down from east to west, and is well-watered by streams which form the north and west boundaries. On the 1:10,000 map two raths and Gooleystown are marked in the townland. Ballyleny was in Lequirin, and was held by Brian McDonell McBrien Magennis from Sir Art Magennis (*CPR Jas I* 395a).

Ballymacanally	*Baile Mhic an Fhailigh*	
J 1354	"McNally's townland"	
1. Ballinelurganvickenawly (in Lequirin)	CPR Jas I 394b	1609
2. Ballenlurganvickenawlie (in Lequirin)	CPR Jas I 193a	1611
3. Ballimacknalinge	Par. Map (Mooney) 186	17thc

218

4. Bally McKanollan	Census 81	1659c
5. Ballymc naling	BSD 74	1661
6. Ballimcnaling	Hib. Del. Down	1672c
7. Ballymacanolly [o underlined]	Mooney MS 186	1715
8. Ballymcanally	Reg. Magheralin (OSNB) E8.59	1715
9. Ballymcanally	Vestry Reg. (OSNB) E8.59	1715
10. Linganvicknawhy	Lodge (Mooney) 186	1717
11. Ballymcanalie	Ir. Wills Index 94	1754
12. Ballymacanallen	Wm. Map (OSNB) E8.59	1810
13. Ballymacanally	Reg. Free. (OSNB) E8.59	1829
14. Ballymcnally	Bnd. Sur. (OSNB) E8.59	1830c
15. Baile Mhic an Fhailghe "MacAnally's town"	J O'D (OSNB) E8.59	1834c
16. Baile Mhic an Fhailghigh "MacNally's td"	Mooney 185	1950c
17. 'balï,makə'nalï	Local pronunciation	1991

The name Ballymacanally, in the south of the parish, clearly includes a surname formed with *mac*. The Irish form of the surname McAnally is generally given as *Mac an Fhail(gh)igh* "son of the poor man", "common in parts of Ulster in the 16th century" (Woulfe 1923, 312; Ó Droighneáin 1966, 11), as chosen by O'Donovan and Mooney (15–6). However some similar anglicized spellings have also been used for the East Ulster surnames of *Mac an Fhileadh* "son of the poet" and *Mac Con Uladh* "son of Cú-Uladh", a personal name meaning "hound of Ulster" (Woulfe 1923, 313, 343), and it has been suggested that the names *Mac Con Allaidh* of Tyrone and *Mac Con Uladh* of Clandeboye are the source of McNally in those areas (*GUH* 115n). One possible example of *Mac Con Uladh* is *McAnully*, in south Co. Antrim in 1618 (*CPR Jas I* 373b), and the McNallys were "numerous and important in the barony of Antrim" (*O'Laverty* iii 451n). The early history of the name Ballymacanally adds further complications. If it is the same place as *Ballinelurganvickenawlie* it was part of Lequirin (with Lisnasure to the east of it) and was held by Art Oge McGlasney Magennis of Islandderry from King James (*CPR Jas I* 394b, 193a). This form (1, 2) appears to represent a form like *Baile na Lorgan Mhic an Fhailigh*, "townland of McNally's long ridge", but is ungrammatical in Irish, which could have either *Baile na Lorgan* or *Lorgain Mhic an Fhailigh*, but would omit *na* if the two were combined.

The element *lorgain* "ridge" is replaced by *baile* in the later 17th-century forms, which more certainly refer to this townland, and have a final nasal, spelt *-n* or *-ng*. These forms are difficult to distinguish by spelling from forms of **Ballymacanallen** in Tullylish, held in 1609 by Sir Art Magennis. In 1659 this townland was *Bally McKanollan* and the Tullylish one was called *B: McNally*. The modern ending in *-y* does not appear until 1715 (forms 7, 8, 9), and Williamson's 1810 map of Co. Down still had the spelling *Ballymacanallen* here, and *Ballymacanallon* in Tullylish. The two place-names are still sometimes confused locally. The early spellings of Ballymacanallen in Tullylish are generally consistent, and it appears to contain a rare surname *Mac an Ailín*.

However a final *-n* could be expressed by a suspension stroke, which might be added as a flourish in one document and written out as *-n* in documents copied from it. If *n* had been added by mistake before form 3, forms 7, 8, 9 might represent a return to writing the name as pronounced. Local evidence for the surname in the past includes *McAnnolly*, attested in

Co. Down in 1605 (*CPR Jas I* 86b, 87a, pardoned with others of *Slught McONeile*) and Felomie *McAnnallie* in a pardon for Iveagh Co. Down in 1610 (*CPR Jas I* 175a). *McAnnallie* was the nearest surname geographically, and the closest in form to *Mac an Fhailgigh*, now spelt *Mac an Fhailigh*. However if the evidence of the place-name were not so firmly in favour of an *a* vowel, *Baile Mhic Con Uladh* would be the preferred form, as Mooney seems to have thought in his note to form (7).

Ballymacateer　　　　　　　　*Baile Mhic an tSaoir*
J 1157　　　　　　　　　　　　　"McAteer's townland"

1. bog Moonmoreballymickytire	Inq. Moyry Castle 1	1608
2. BallymcEntire al. Mewvrayne	CPR Jas I 395b	1609
3. Ballemcentire, Brian McP 　McH McEntire of	CPR Jas I 195b	1610
4. BallymcEntire al. Mewvranye	CPR Jas I 190b	1611
5. BallymcEntire al. Newevrany	CPR Jas I 266a	1614
6. Ballymacentire	Inq. Ult. (Down) §4 Jac. I	1616
7. Ballymckentire al. Neworaine	CPR Jas I 309a	1616
8. BallymcEnter	CPR Jas I 373b	1618
9. Ballymcentire (Magherilin 6tds)	Buckworth (EA) 310	1622
10. td of Corcreeny and BallymcIteere	Civ. Surv. x §73	1655c
11. Ballimentire	Hib. Reg. Lr. Iveagh	1657c
12. Ballymackinteare	Census 80	1659c
13. Ballimentyre	BSD 72	1661
14. Mallym'Tntier	Sub. Roll Down 274	1663
15. Ballinmacteere	Brownlow LB 100	1669
16. Ballimenteir	Hib. Del. Down	1672c
17. BallymTeere	Reg. Magheralin (OSNB) E8.59	1715
18. BallymcTeere	Vestry Reg. (OSNB) E8.59	1715
19. Bally McAteer	Map of Down (OSNB) E8.59	1755
20. Ballymacateer	Wm. Map (OSNB) E8.59	1810
21. [Bal-ly-'mac-a-teer]	OSNB Pron. E8.59	1834c
22. Baile Mhic a'tSaoir "MacAntire's 　town"	J O'D (OSNB) E8.59	1834c
23. Baile Mhic an tSaoir "MacAteer's tn"	Mooney 189	1950c
24. ˌbɑliməkə'tiːr	Local pronunciation	1991

The "great bog" of McAteer's townland, *Móin mhór Bhaile Mhic an tSaoir*, was on the border between Cos Down and Armagh (1). The surname *Mac an tSaoir* translates as "son of the craftsman" and like *Mac an Ghabhann* "son of the smith" etc. may have arisen at different times and places (Woulfe 1923, 318). The Scottish family of the name are always anglicized as *McIntyre*, as were an Irish family in Co. Sligo, from whom Carrickmacintyre in Co. Mayo was named. The anglicized spelling *Macateer*, now usually McAteer, is mainly found in the Ulster counties of Armagh, Antrim and Donegal, although there is a place-name Carrickmackateer in Clare (MacLysaght 1982, 25–6). Sixteenth-century records show the name mainly in the Dublin area, but it was found widely in Ulster in the 17th century, especially in Donegal, where it was a "principal Irish name" in the barony of Boylagh and Banagh in 1659 (*Census* 48).

Ballymacateer was a church townland, held in 1609 by William Worseley from the bishop of Dromore (form 2). In the same schedule Brian *McEntire* was recorded as the tenant of the church townland of *Ballycorshillcoghill*, now the townland of **Ballynanny** in Clonduff (*CPR Jas I* 395a; *PNI* iii 81). However, there were people of the name in this townland: Brian McPatrick McHenry *McEntire* of *Ballemcentire*, probably the same Brian as in Clonduff, was required to surrender his lands in 1610 (form 3), and Shane *McEntere* of *BallymcEnter* was pardoned in 1618 (form 8).

There is no record of any earlier ecclesiastical associations for the family in the diocese of Dromore. However the bishop of Clogher in 1268-87 AD was Michael *Mac-an-tSaoir*, and the founding saint of Clonmacnoise (before the age of surnames) was known as Ciarán *mac an tsaoir* "the son of the craftsman" (MacLysaght 1982, 25–6).

The element *Mew* in the alias name (2, 4, 5, 7) is one of the anglicized forms of Irish *magh*, *maigh* "a plain". At the cross-roads in the townland *Sloane's map* of Co. Down (1739) marks Mathers's Fort, still shown as a farm-name Mathersesfort on OS 1:10,000 sheet 182. The surname *Mathers*, still well-known in the area, probably derives from the Scottish place-name Mathers near Montrose (Black 1946, 586–7). It also appears in the minor name Mathers Close in Dromore (J 2155). In the west Sloane's map also marks Hobbs Kesh where the road to Lurgan crosses into Co. Armagh: *kesh* is Irish *ceis* "wattled causeway" but the name is now unknown.

Ballymacbredan	*Baile Mhic Bhrídín*	
J 1158	"McBredan's townland"	
1. (?)Clondonellvickbridden	CPR Jas I 395b	1609
2. Ballymcbriddon al. Knockterson	CPR Jas I 395b	1609
3. Ballemcbridden, Jas McArt Magin of		
	CPR Jas I 195b	1610
4. Ballymcbriddon al. Knockterson	CPR Jas I 190b	1611
5. (?)Clandonellvickbridden x2	CPR Jas I 191a	1611
6. Ballymcbredden al. Knocktersonna	CPR Jas I 266a	1614
7. Ballydiridine al. Knock[illeg.]	Inq. Ult. (Down) §4 Jac. I	1614
8. Ballymcbreedon al. Knocktersona	CPR Jas I 309a	1616
9. Ballymcbreeden half-td (Magherilin 6tds)	Buckworth (EA) 310	1622
10. (?)Clandonnellmacbridden x2	Inq. Ult. (Down) §30 Car. I	1632
11. Ballymackelbredan	OSNB E8.59	1653
12. Ballimackbredew, 3/4 of	BSD 72	1661
13. Ballimcbredew 1/4 of	BSD 73	1661
14. Ballym'Briden	Sub. Roll Down 273	1663
15. Ballymacbridan	Reg. Magheralin (OSNB) E8.59	1715
16. Ballymacbredan	Map Douglas Estate (OSNB) E8.59	1812
17. Bally McBredan	Bnd. Sur. (OSNB) E8.59	1830c
18. Baile Mhic Brighdín "MacBreedan's town" (ref. Bredian)	J O'D (OSNB) E8.59	1834c
19. Baile-Mic-Bhríghdeáin "McBredan's town"	Joyce iii 102	1913
20. Baile Mic (Ghiolla) Bhrighidín "MacBridden's town"	Mooney 189	1950c
21. ˌbɑlïmək'bri:dn̩	Local pronunciation	1991

It is clear that the name Ballymacbredan, another church townland, contains a surname, although a surname McBredan is not listed in Woulfe or MacLysaght. However it was found among the medieval clergy of Dromore: Marcus *MacBridyn* rector of Clonduff, Canon of Dromore, and Prebendary of St Ronan of *Land* in 1428 (*Annates* 290, 295n), Christinus *McBrydyn* or *McBrydy* around 1441 (*Reg. Swayne* 187). In the early 17th century Shane and Jenkin *McBriddie* or *McBriddan* held church lands in Donaghcloney (*CPR Jas I* 395b, 191a, 195b). Thus they seem to have been an ecclesiastical family. The spellings of the surname with and without final -*n* may be significant, also the spelling of the place-name as *Ballymackelbredan* recorded in 1653 (form 11). If the final element in the surname is *Brídín*, a diminutive of *Bríd* (earlier *Brighid*), then McBredan may have been shortened from *Mac Giolla Bhrídín* in the same way that McBride has been shortened from *Mac Giolla Bhríde* "son of the servant of St Brigid" (Woulfe 1923, 368). The element *giolla* has been dropped in the anglicized spelling of many other surnames, such as MacAvoy from *Mac Giolla Bhuí* (also MacIlwee). In 1834 O'Donovan recorded in Drumballyroney that "the MacIlwees as soon as they can scrape a little money together change their name to Macavoy" (*OSNB* E63 sv. Katesbridge).

MacLysaght says that the family called *Mac Giolla Bhríde* first appeared as erenaghs of Raymunterdony in Donegal, the parish which includes Tory Island (MacLysaght 1957, 61). According to the 15th-century *Annates* there were several churchmen of the name in Derry, one being Dean, and MacLysaght mentions several bishops of Raphoe bearing the name. He also says that "A branch of the sept was established in Co. Down" (MacLysaght 1957, 61). A pardon of Magennis followers in 1602 included Owen and Patrick *McGilbridie* (*Fiants Eliz.* §6616) and in 1616 Rory *McGilbridey* (*CPR Jas I* 299a). In 1663 **Ballybrick** in Drumballyroney parish was called *Ballym'ilebrige* and Arte M'ilebrige was in Barnmeen nearby (*Sub. Roll Down* 12). Unfortunately there is not enough information to connect them with the Magheralin McBredans. Possibly the diminutive form of the name was used by the branch of the family which retained its church connections. Likewise the families of *Ó Broin*, *Ó Duinneagáin* seem to have had ecclesiastical branches called *Mac Broin* and *Mac Duinneagáin* in Iveagh, see **Ballintagart** Aghaderg, **Ardbrin** Annaclone; **Ballygunaghan** Donaghcloney, **Balloonigan** Moira. O'Donovan noted that the surname *Bredian*, possibly anglicized from *(Mac) Brídín*, was "common in Kilwarlin" (form 18) but elsewhere included it among the "old families of Ulster... This family is almost extinct" (*OSL Dn* 44). In 1659 McBride formed a "principall Irish name" in Lecale and mid-Antrim (*Census* 72; 7 bis).

The church lands held in the early 17th century by Shane and Jenkin McBriddie or McBriddan were: "four half towns or parcels called *Ballytullyhannahie* and *Clondonellvickbridden*, Donaghcloney and *Ballyemtyshewin*" which may be the old name of Clogher (forms 1, 5; *CPR Jas I* 395b, 191a). The first two names look as if they might refer to Ballymacbredan and Tullyanaghan next to it in this parish. However, in the same source a townland called *Ballymcbriddon alias Knockterson* is listed under William Worseley's holding of church lands (forms 2, 4). It also seems that Sir Art Magennis may have had Tullyanaghan, since *Ballytullyannaghy* was listed among his lands next to *Ballyclonegillmurry*, that is Clankilvoragh townland in Co. Armagh to the west of Tullyanaghan (*CPR Jas I* 396a).

There are two solutions to this problem, which affects the identification of the names. Either the current townlands were divided between the McBredans and others (maybe William Worseley held only a part of Ballymacbredan called *Knockterson*), or by 1609 the McBredans held church lands other than the townland to which their surname had become fixed, like the McAteers and McCormicks (**Ballymacateer, Ballymacormick**). In this case their surname may be part of two place-names, leaving the location of *Clondonellvickbridden*, which seems to derive from *Clann/Cluain Dónaill Mhic Bhrídín* "offspring/meadow of Dónall McBredan" uncertain. There is no published genealogy of the McBredans to assist in identifying or locating this Dónall. The only resident of *Ballemcbridden* named was James McGinn, pardoned in 1611 (form 3).

Ballymacbrennan	*Baile Uí Bhranáin*	
J 1657	"Brennan's townland"	

1. Ballybrynan	CPR Jas I 396a	1609
2. Ballybrinan	CPR Jas I 235a	1612
3. Ballybrenan	Inq. Ult. (Down) §13 Car. I	1629
4. Ballylybrenan	Inq. Ult. (Down) §60 Car. I	1635
5. Ballybrynan	Inq. Ult. (Down) §85 Car. I	1639
6. Ballimc-Brenan	Hib. Reg. Lr. Iveagh	1657c
7. Bally McBrenan	Census 81	1659c
8. Ballimackbrenan	BSD 73	1661
9. Ballymackbrenan or Ballynebrenan	ASE 61b 39	1666
10. B'mcbrenan	Hib. Del. Down	1672c
11. Ballymcbreenan	Vestry Reg. (OSNB) E8.59	1715
12. Ballymacbrenan	Wm. Map (OSNB) E8.59	1810
13. Bally McBrennan	Bnd. Sur. (OSNB) E8.59	1830c
14. Baile Mic Braonáin "Mac Brennan's town"	J O'D (OSNB) E8.59	1834c
15. Baile Mhic Bhranáin/Mac Braonáin	Mooney 191	1950c
16. mac Brianán, dim of Mac Briain	Mooney 191	1950c
17. ˌbalïməkˈbrɛndn̩	Local pronunciation	1991

Although the name Ballymacbrennan looks at present as if it includes a surname, the earliest forms (1–5), all in two sources, do not include the element *mac*, which first appears in the Down Survey in the mid 17th century (form 6). Ballymacbrennan belonged to Sir Art Magennis with a group of townlands which extended north into the modern parish of Moira. The existence of another townland of the same modern name in Drumbeg parish makes it look as if McBrennan had been an old surname once prevalent in north-west Co. Down. However the earliest forms for it also are *Ballybrinan, Ballybrennan*, with *mac* first appearing in 1632 (*CPR Jas I* 73a; *CPR* Chas I ed. Morrin 66; *Inq. Ult. (Down)* §29 Car. I).

There are no references to people called McBrennan in Co. Down, but the surname McBrennan was found in the 16th century in Co. Roscommon (*Fiants Eliz.* §§4240, 4741, 4944). Despite the early anglicized forms all being spelt *Bren-*, Woulfe gives only *Mac Branáin* "son of little raven" as the Irish form of the surname, the name of a family who were also erenaghs of Elphin (Woulfe 1923, 323). The Roscommon family of *Mac Branáin*, who were chiefs of *Corcu Achlann*, were noted regularly in the Annals from the mid-12th to the 15th century, and, according to John O'Donovan, were descended from a druid who had given his land to St Patrick (*AFM* ii 1134, iii 358n, iv 772; 1159, 1256, 1401 AD).

However it appears that the *mac-* element in Ballymacbrennan has been added later, possibly by analogy with Ballymacbredan with which it is still associated locally. MacLysaght also mentions a Fermanagh erenagh family called *Ó Branáin*, anglicized Brannon and Brennan (MacLysaght 1957, 60; 1985, 25). The name was also borne by two 12th-century erenaghs of Derry, where Woulfe thinks the family also used a diminutive form of the surname, *Ó Branagáin* (1923, 440). *Dál mBuinne* (the tribal group from which the local dean-ery of Dalboyn was named) was equated with *Muinntir Bhranáin* "people of Branán" in an annal reference in 1176 AD (*AFM* iii 22), but Séamas Ó Ceallaigh has shown that this is a mistake for the area south of Coleraine, where the surname *Ó Branáin* is still known (now Brennan), and where it appears in the townland name **Moneybrannon** (*GUH* 46–7,17 and genealogy). The family were chieftains of *Cinéal Binnigh* (*Topog. Poems* (*J O'D*) 16, 24n), and were mentioned in *Ceart Uí Néill* "The Right(s) of O'Neill" (*LCABuidhe* 43 §7; Ó Doibhlin 1970, 342–3), and it is likely that any northern instances of the surname Brennan are derived from them. Ballymacbrennan is probably one example.

Ballymacmaine	*Baile Mhic Mhiacháin*	
J 1258	"McMain's/McMechan's townland"	

1. BallymcMeaghan al. Knockneangle	CPR Jas I 395b	1609
2. Ballymcmeaghan al. Knockneangle	CPR Jas I 190b	1611
3. Ballimicmeaghan al. Knockneangle	CPR Jas I 266a	1614
4. Ballymcmeghan al. Knockneangle	CPR Jas I 309a	1616
5. Ballimcmean half-tn (Magherilin 6tds)	Buckworth (EA) 310	1622
6. Ballynagmeane	Census 80	1659c
7. Ballimcnean	Par. Map (Mooney) 189	17thc
8. Ballimacknean	BSD 72	1661
9. Ballym'Mean	Sub. Roll Down 274	1663
10. Ballymackneen	S & D Ann. (Mooney) 189 (22)	1680c
11. BallymcMean	Reg. Magheralin (OSNB) E8.59	1715
12. Ballymcmean	Reg. Deeds abstracts i §324	1722
13. Bally McMene	Map of Down (OSNB) E8.59	1755
14. Ballymacmena	Wm. Map (OSNB) E8.59	1810
15. BallymcMain	Bnd. Sur. (OSNB) E8.59	1830c
16. [Bal-ly-'Mac-Main]	OSNB Pron. E8.59	1834c
17. Baile Mhic Main "McMain's town"	J O'D (OSNB) E8.59	1834c
18. Baile Mac Miadhachain "Mac Mayne's townland"	Mooney 189	1950c
19. ˌbalïməkˈmeṇ	Local pronunciation	1996

Ballymacmaine clearly contains a surname formed with *mac*, and one would expect it to be the name of the church tenants at some period before 1600, since Ballymacmaine was a church townland in 1609 (*CPR Jas I* 395b). According to MacLysaght the name *Mac Miadhacháin* (now spelled *Mac Miacháin*) was "numerous in Cos Antrim and Down under eight different spellings", including *McMeghan, McMeekin, Meegan* and *Meehan* (MacLysaght 1964, 148–9; 1982, 155b; 1985, 212–3). There was a family called McMain in Garvaghy in 1774 (*Ir.Wills Index* 98). Despite a reference to Patrick *McMagin* as a church tenant in Iveagh in 1611 (*CPR Jas I* 191a), there do not seem to be any 17th-century occur-rences of *Mac Miacháin* locally, since his name was given in 1609 as simply *Magyn*, the well-attested local ecclesiastical family (*CPR Jas I* 395b; **Ballymagin**). Some of the forms of Ballymacmaine are very similar to the second element of **Lismaine**, which may possibly be *Lios Miacháin*.

In the four citations of this name in the patent rolls (forms 1–4), *BallymcMeaghan* has an alias *Knockneangle*, not found subsequently. This looks as if it could be *Cnoc na nAingeal* "hill of the angels", like the hill where St Columba was visited by angels on Iona: "*colliculus angelorum Scotice cnoc aingeal*" (*Adomnán (Atkinson)* 117b, 99a). In Scotland there were two further examples of the name in Ross-shire, both at graveyards, and there is a similar name *Ard na nAingeal* "height of the angels" for a burial place in the Irish Finn-cycle (*Acallam (Stokes)* l.7734; Watson 1959, 331 l.6265n). *Cnoc nan Aingeal* at Lochalsh was the burial ground of the MacDonalds of Glengarry, taken over from the Mathesons, where the name had another, less Christian, significance: "hill of the May-day fires" (Watson 1959, 237 l.6265; Rev. Wm Matheson pers. comm.). Scottish Gaelic and Manx preserved an alternative meaning "fire" (as in Scots *ingle*) for the word *aingeal*, although the only Irish reference is that a burnt-out cinder sent as protection with children faring out at night might be called *aingeal* (*Dinneen*).

Ballymagin		*Baile Mhig Fhinn*	
J 1259		"McGinn's townland"	

1.	Ballymagin in Evagh	Inq. Moyry Castle 1	1608
2.	Ballymageyn al. Shanmallaghballymagny		
		CPR Jas I 395b	1609
3.	Ballymagin al. Shanmullagh-Ballymagin		
		CPR Jas I 190b	1611
4.	Ballymagin al. Shanemullagh-Ballymagin		
		CPR Jas I 266a	1614
5.	Ballymcginn al. Shannulla Ballymcginn		
		CPR Jas I 309a	1616
6.	Ballimagin (Magherilin 6tds)	Buckworth (EA) 310	1622
7.	lands of Ballymagin	Civ. Surv. x §73	1655c
8.	Ballimcgin	Hib. Reg. Lr. Iveagh	1657c
9.	Ballymagin	Census 80	1659c
10.	Ballemackgin	BSD 72	1661
11.	B'mcgin	Hib. Del. Down	1672c
12.	Ballymagin	Reg. Magheralin (OSNB) E8.59	1715
13.	Ballymagin	Sur. Brownlow Estate (OSNB) E8.59	1751
14.	Bally McGinn	OSNB E8.59	1834c
15.	[bally-'mag-in]	OSNB Pron. E8.59	1834c
16.	Baile Meg Fhinn "Maginn's town"	J O'D (OSNB) E8.59	1834c
17.	Baile Mic Fhinn "Maginn's town"	Joyce iii 105	1913
18.	Baile Mag Fhinn "homestead of the Maginns"		
		Mooney 191	1950c
19.	ˌbalïmə'gïn	Local pronunciation	1991

Ballymagin was a church townland, and has been said to contain the ruins of the medieval parish church, rebuilt in the 17th century (*Atkinson's Dromore* 211), although OS 1:10,000 and the townland index map (1970) include the site in Ballymakeonan. Members of the McGinn family had had a long association with the diocese of Dromore, where they appeared as churchmen in ecclesiastical records from the early 15th century, connected especially with Magheralin (1407, 1422, 1442, 1477, 1526 AD), Clonduff (1407, 1530 AD) and Dromara (1504, 1530, 1539 AD), as well as the parishes of Donaghcloney, Kilbroney,

Seagoe, Shankill, and Tullylish (*Swanzy's Dromore*). In 1442 one of them was allowed to build a tower on to the parish church of the day to use as a library (*EA* 111n).

The earliest reference to *Ballymagin* alias *Shanmullagh-Ballymagin* appears in the 1609 Schedule of Iveagh, where it was held by William Worseley from the bishop of Dromore (*CPR Jas I* 395b, 191a). *Seanmhullach* "the old summit" only appears as an alias in the patent rolls. However the McGinns were still in the area. In the same schedule James McArt McGilleduff McIdeganagh *Magyn* was the tenant of church land in Dromara (*CPR Jas I* 395a, 191a). Probably the same man James McArt *Magin* was then required to surrender his lands in Dromara and in Ballymacbredan in this parish (*CPR Jas I* 195b). In 1641 the list of those cited as rebels included McGinns of Tullynacross in Magheralin.

Ballymakeonan   *Baile Mhic Eoghanáin*
J 1359   "McKeonan's townland"

1. Ballyvickewnan	CPR Jas I 395b	1609
2. Ballevickonenan, Nicholas McHugh McOwenan of	CPR Jas I 195b	1610
3. Ballyvickeonan	CPR Jas I 190b	1611
4. Ballyvickeonan	CPR Jas I 266a	1614
5. Ballyvickeneuaw	Inq. Ult. (Down) §4 Jac. I	1616
6. Ballyvickenonan	CPR Jas I 309a	1616
7. Ballymcceownan (Magherilin 6tds)	Buckworth (EA) 310	1622
8. Ballym'crouman	Buckworth (Atkinson) 127	1622
9. (?) 3 qrs of Ballecoman	Hib. Reg. Lr. Iveagh	1657c
10. Ballymackeoman 3qrs, Carone McKonigan qr	Par. Map (Mooney) 188	17thc
11. Ballimackcoman al. Carone McKingan	BSD 72	1661
12. (?)Ballicoman, ¾ of	BSD 73	1661
13. Ballicomon	Hib. Del. Down	1672c
14. Ballymackoman al. Carone Mc Kingan	S & D Ann. (Mooney) 188 (22)	1680c
15. Baile McKeonan	Reg. Magheralin (OSNB) E8.59	1715
16. Ballymaconan	Reg. Deeds abstracts i §324	1722
17. Ballymakeownan	Map, Douglas Estate (OSNB) E8.59	1754
18. Ballymackonan	Wm. Map (OSNB) E8.59	1810
19. St Ronan's Well in a field	Mooney 188	1950c
20. The Nuns' Walk	Mooney 188	1950c
21. Baile Mhic Eoghanáin "MacKeonan's town"	J O'D (OSNB) E8.59	1834c
22. Baile Mhic Comhghain "Mackone's or MacCowan's townland"	Mooney 187	1950c
23. ˌbalimə'kjonən	Local pronunciation	1996

The earliest reference to Ballymakeonan appears in 1609, in the schedule of church lands held by William Worseley from the bishop of Dromore (form 1). In the same documents Nicholas *McKewnan* was listed as the church tenant of Ballyaughian in Clonduff (*CPR Jas I* 395b, 191a). However in 1610 *Ballevickonenan* was to be surrendered by Nicholas

226

McHugh *McOwenan* (*CPR Jas I* form 2). In 1620 Owen *McOwnan* of Taughblane townland in Hillsborough was a witness in an investigation of church lands in Blaris and Drumbo (*CPR Jas I* 455b). The surname was unknown to Woulfe and MacLysaght, although, according to Breandán Ó Buachalla, Arthur Brownlow of Shankill in Armagh "was patron of Eoghan *Mac Oghannain*, the main Irish scribe in south-east Ulster in the last quarter of the 17th century" (Ó Buachalla 1982, 25). John O'Donovan listed among the "old families of Ulster" "*Mac Eoghanáin*, now McConan and McKeonan. This family is almost extinct" (*OSL Dn* 44). **Annaghmakeonan** further south in the parish of Donaghcloney, called Keonan Bog on the 1:50,000 map, also preserves the same surname.

According to the 1851 Census, the townland had two parts of 500 acres and 99 acres, described in the Ordnance Survey Name Book as "one in the north end of the parish having the village of Maralin on its south-eastern boundary, the other is situated about one mile west of Maralin" (*OSNB* E8.59). The western part does not appear on the modern map. The river Lagan now forms its boundary on the extreme south-east, and it borders Ballynadrone on the south, south of the village of Magheralin. According to the townland index and the 1:10,000 map, the old churchyard lies within it (Co. Down sheet 1, 1970), although Atkinson located the church in Ballymagin (*Atkinson's Dromore* 211), before the apparent boundary changes to Ballymakeonan.

Ballynadrone	*Baile idir Dhá Abhainn*	
J 1358	"townland between two rivers"	
1. Ballyadderowen	CPR Jas I 395b	1609
2. Ballyadderowen	CPR Jas I 190b	1611
3. Ballyaderdowan half-td (Magherilin		
6tds)	Buckworth (EA) 310	1622
4. Ballederowen	Hib. Reg. Lr. Iveagh	1657c
5. Ballyderowen	BSD 73	1661
6. Ballidro Owen	Hib. Del. Down	1672c
7. Ballyndrone	Reg. Magheralin (OSNB) E8.59	1715
8. Ballynderone	Vestry Reg. (OSNB) E8.59	1715
9. Ballynadrone	Map of Down (OSNB) E8.59	1755
10. Ballyveddrone	Wm. Map (OSNB) E8.59	1810
11. Ballynadrone	Bnd. Sur. (OSNB) E8.59	1830c
12. Ballynadrone	Cess Book (OSNB) E8.59	1834c
13. Ballybogland	Parl. Rept (EA 310n)	1833
14. Kilbogland	Parl. Rept 1868 x 574	1868
15. Baile na dtruaghán "town of the		
meagre people"	J O'D (OSNB) E8.59	1834c
16. "the town between the two rivers"	EA 310n	1847
17. ˌbalˈinaˈdron	Local pronunciation	1995
18. ˌbalənəˈdrɔn	Local pronunciation	1996

Ballynadrone was a church townland, lying just south of the village of Magheralin. It extends west to cross the Donaghcloney road, taking in the modern parish church, while the medieval church site opposite is in Ballymakeonan. In 1847 Reeves said that the name Ballynadrone was "now obsolete", and the area appeared as *Ballybogland* in the

Parliamentary Return of Established Church lands in 1833 (form 13). In the 1868 Report, Coslet Waddell held four acres called *Kilbogland* from the diocese (14). However, the earlier name continued in use by the Ordnance Survey.

John O'Donovan's suggestion was based on 19th-century spellings (15). *Baile idir Dhá Abhainn* "townland between two rivers" fits the early forms, and was originally put forward by Reeves (16) and followed by Mooney. However, the only river shown on the maps is the Lagan, which forms part of the eastern boundary, where it is crossed by Steps Bridge, apparently a replacement for stepping stones. There may have been problems with flooding which caused the name Ballynadrone. The watery reputation of the place is referred to in the song where King William ordered a thousand pairs of clogs for the local ducks, giving rise to the English nick-name Ducks' Town for the village of Magheralin (Parish Magazine for Magheralin/Kilwarlin, 1977 p. 6).

Clankilvoragh Co Armagh *Clann Ghiolla Mhuire*
J 0959 "offspring of Giolla Muire"

1. ClonIgolourrif	Esch. Co. Map 5.29	1609
2. Ballyclonegillmurry	CPR Jas I 396a	1609
3. Clan-Igollavorist 1 bal (Doughcoron)	CPR Jas I 165a	1610
4. Clan-Igollaworist al. Clan-Igollavorisse	Mooney MS 197	1629
5. villages & hamlets of Derrylisnehawly, Clonygillvore: reputed parcels of Cloonygallavoriffe	Mooney MS 197	1629
6. Clangillovoriff	Brownlow LB 152	1635
7. bounded by Outer Drom	Brownlow LB 95	1652
8. td Clankillwory (Shankhill)	Inq. Arm. (Patterson) 235	1657
9. Clongillnorriffe (Magherelin)	BSD 51	1661
10. Clangollevorist 1 b'bo	Inq. Ult. (Armagh) §7 Car. II	1661
11. Clonygillavorist & Tawghrany, reputat' pcell de Clonygillavorist	Inq. Ult. (Armagh) §7 Car. II	1661
12. Outerdrom (inc Piper Hill?)	Brownlow LB 155	1665?
13. Clangillovoriff + Derrilisnehawie	Brownlow LB 53	1667
14. half sess Outer Drom pt of Clangill Voriff	Brownlow LB 87	1667
15. half sess Clangillvory	Brownlow LB 93	1667
16. Outer Druma	Brownlow LB 100	1669
17. part Outerdrom 16a	Brownlow LB 73	1701
18. Clonegillivore	Deeds & Wills (Mooney) 197	1712
19. Clankillvory	Vestry Reg. (OSNB) E8.59	1715
20. Clankilwoory	Deeds & Wills (Mooney) 197	1723
21. Clankillvorragh	Rocque's Map (Coote) 2	1760
22. Clonkillvoragh	Rocque's Map (Coote)	1760
23. Clankilworif	Ir. Wills Index 89	1799
24. Clankilworagh	Ir. Wills Index 85	1803
25. Clanygellavorriffe	Reg. Free. (OSNB) E8.59	1829
26. Clankillvoragh	Bnd. Sur. (OSNB) E8.59	1830c
27. ['voragh]	OSNB Pron. E8.59	1834c

28. Cluain Ghiolla Mhuire "Gilmorie's lawn or meadow"	J O'D (OSNB) E8.59	1834c
29. ˈklaːnkəlˈvɔːra	Local pronunciation	1991

The three north-western townlands of Magheralin, Clankilvoragh, Derrylisnahavil and Donagreagh, are now regarded as part of Co. Armagh. Clankilvoragh was held by Sir Art Magennis in 1609 (form 2), but was mapped as being in Oneilland and granted in 1610 to John Brownlow with other lands in Co. Armagh (1, 3). The final -gh of the modern spelling of the name is not pronounced, and the final -s of some of the historical forms may be taken as an English possessive ending, written -ʃ, misread as -f or -g. The kin-group indicated in the place-name would seem to be the family whose name, meaning "servant of Mary", was anglicized as Gilmore in Co. Down, although there was another family called *Mac Giolla Mhura* "servant of Mura" (of Fahan, Co. Donegal) connected with the church in Armagh. The family of *Mac Giolla Mhuire* was prominent in Co. Down before the Plantation, and by the 16th century held Holywood and the Great Ards, under the O'Neills of Castlereagh (*EA* 339n; *O'Neill Fun. Oration* (1744) 267; *Bagenal's Descr. Ulst.* 1586). I have assumed above that the first element in this place-name is *Clann* "offspring", as in **Clanconnell** and **Clanbrassil** which were districts of Iveagh. This name refers to just one townland and may begin *Cluain* "meadow", but see further below.

The Gilmores were given two alternative pedigrees, one to the royal (Dál Fiatach) line of Lecale, over which they sometimes ruled (*Descendants Ir* xiii 344–5; *AFM* iii 426, iv 722, years 1276, 1391 AD), the other to the tribal group called *Uí Dearca Chéin*, whose link with Dál nAraide has been described by Byrne (1994–5, 54–5; *Descendants Ir* xiv 88f). In 1273 *MaGillamory* was listed as king of *Anderken*, an anglicized form of the name (*Inq. Earl. Ult.* i 40 n2 = *CDI* ii §953). The tribal name was used as a place-name as early as the 7th-century genealogical poem on the descendants of Dubthach Doeltenga, who were said to have been scattered by the inundation of Lough Neagh "towards [Uí] Dearca Chéin" (*dochum Derco chén, Laud Gens.* 308 l.10); and in later sources, where a "raid into *Uí Earca Chéin*" was mentioned in 1199 AD (*crech in Ua nEarca Chéin: AFM* iii 118).

Reeves thought it referred to "a tract in the north of Co. Down, or on the confines of Down and Antrim" (*EA* 339n), although the reference in the *Tripartite Life* of St Patrick lists it after Island Magee, further north and east (*Trip. Life (Stokes)* i 164). Reeves' area would suit the location of Clankilvoragh, and *Clann Ghiolla Mhuire* were still in Iveagh in the 15th century. Members of the family raided alongside the Magennises (*Misc. Irish Annals* 172 §6, 1404 AD), or were even Lords of Iveagh (*A. Conn.* 400, 1407 AD, killed by Magennis), and some were clergymen in Dromore diocese: Magnellus *McGylmor* was vicar of Aghaderg in 1413 (*EA* 113 from *Reg. Flem.* 49; *Reg. Flem.* §210), Mauritius *McGilmore* vicar of Clonduff died in 1416 (*EA* 115 from *Reg. Prene* 345). Éamonn Ó Doibhlin, in his edition of *Ceart Uí Néill*, said that "at a comparatively late date, Holywood (*Ard Mhic Nasca*) was given to this family by the lords of *Clann Aodha Buidhe*", but that little was known about *Mac Giolla Mhuire* or his territory before that (Ó Doibhlin 1970, 334).

The size of the townland may have been reduced since the 17th century. In the 1629 grant from the *Records of the Rolls* discovered by Dean Mooney it contained both Derrylisnahavil and Taughrane, the glebe of Magheralin. Taughrane, to the south and in Co. Down, was still thought to be part of it in 1661 (form 11). In the Brownlow leasebook of 1669 *Clangillvory* was bounded by "*Donnagregh* north, *Tulliana* east, *Taghrane* south and *Derrilisnehawly* west", without mentioning Cornakinnegar to the north, while it is implied that the *half sessiagh of Outer Drom*, up to or including Piperhill in Cornakinnegar, was part of Clankilvoragh (forms 7, 12, 14, 16, 17: *Brownlow LB* 93; 87, 95, 155).

Clogher　　　　　　　　　　　　*Clochar*
J 1454　　　　　　　　　　　　　　"stony place"

1. (?)Ballyemtyshewin	CPR Jas I 395b	1609
2. (?)Ballydentishewnie, half-tn	CPR Jas I 191a	1611
3. (?)Ballyedentishewny, half-vil	Inq. Ult. (Down) §30 Car. I	1632
4. (?)Ballyedentilshewny	Inq. Ult. (Down) §30 Car. I	1632
5. Crogher	Hib. Reg. Lr. Iveagh	1657c
6. Crogher	BSD 73	1661
7. Cregher	S & D Ann. (Mooney) 197 (23)	16??
8. Clogher al. Crogher	DS (Mooney) 197	1666
9. Crogher	Hib. Del. Down	1672c
10. Crogher	ASE 112a 34	1679
11. Clogher	Reg. Magheralin (OSNB) E8.59	1715
12. Clougher	Map of Down (OSNB) E8.59	1755
13. Clochar "stony land"	J O'D (OSNB) E8.59	1834c
14. 'klɔxər	Local pronunciation	1991

The only source to call this townland Clogher before the 18th-century (forms 11, 12) is Mooney's form (8) from 1666, while all the others read *Crogher*. *Crothar* "shaking bog", seems unlikely on account of the terrain. There is a word *cróchar* "bier" (*Ó Dónaill*) or *cnochaire* "heap of footed turf", but it is more likely that a short *l* was misread as *r*. Joyce seems to translate the element *clochar* always as "a stony place" (*Joyce* iii 206–7), like O'Donovan here (form 13). This townland has Clogher Hill in the centre (*OSNB* E8/59), with a road across it, and a height of 297 feet (*Townland index map* 1970, Down sheet 1).

Since there are no references to the name earlier than Petty this townland might have been a new subdivision, or there might be an older name. The suggestion that it could have been the church townland of *Ballyemtyshewin*, held in 1609 by the McBredan family with Donaghcloney, rests on Clogher being the only townland nearby not documented at the period. By 1632 the McBredan church lands had been let by the bishop to George Sexton, and in 1678 both Clogher (69 acres) and Donaghcloney (178 acres) belonged to Captain John Magill (*ASE* 112a). From the few citations of the earlier name it seems it might contain the words *éadan tí* "hillface of the house (of)" as with **Edentiroory** in Dromore. *Shewin* might represent the uncommon personal name *Seaán*.

Derrylisnahavil Co Armagh　　　　*Doire Lios na hAbhla*
J 0959　　　　　　　　　　　　　　"fort/enclosure of the apple-place"

1. the villages & hamlets of.. Derrylisnehawly, reputed parcels of Cloonygallavoriffe	Mooney MS 197	1629
2. half tn Derylysinehavill (Shankhill)	Inq. Arm. (Patterson) 235	1657
3. Derrylishnehaule (Magherelin)	BSD 51	1661
4. hamlet ter' Derrylyshehawly	Inq. Ult. (Armagh) §7 Car. II	1661
5. Derrylisnehanle	Mooney MS 199	1661
6. Derrylishehawle	Mooney MS 199	1661

7. Derylisnehawle	HMR Arm. (PRONI) 35	1664
8. Derrilisnehawie	Brownlow LB 53	1667
9. turf in Derrylisnehawley	Brownlow LB 64,69,72-3	1667
10. Derrilisnehawly	Brownlow LB 93	1669
11. Derrilisnehawley	Brownlow LB 100	1669
12. Derrilisnehawly	Brownlow LB 70	1693
13. Derrylisnahavill	Vestry Reg. (OSNB) E8.59	1715
14. Derrylisna	Rocque's Map (Coote)	1760
15. Derrylisnehavil	Reg. Free. (OSNB) E8.59	1829
16. Derrylisnhavel	Bnd. Sur. (OSNB) E8.59	1830c
17. Derrylisnahavel	Bnd. Sur. (OSNB) E8.59	1830c
18. Doire lios na h-aibhil "oakwood of the fort of the orchard"	J O'D (OSNB) E8.59	1834c
19. Doire lis na h-abhaille	Mooney 200	1950c
20. 'dɛrï,ləsnə'havəl	Local pronunciation	1991

Derrylisnahavil is a townland of Magheralin across the border in Co. Armagh. Apart from the 1629 grant (form 1), the name appears earliest as a half-town of Shankill parish in the 1657 inquisition on Armagh parishes (2). However, in the Armagh *Book of Survey and Distribution* the three Armagh townlands of Magheralin are listed separately after Drumcree and before Shankill parishes, as "part of *Magherelin*" belonging to Sir William Brownlow (3).

In 1669 AD the townland was defined as: "all that parcell of land known by the name of *Derrilisnehawley* bounded by *LorginItarry, Dromnemoe, Ballinmacteere, Outer Druma* and *Taghe Rany*" (11, *Brownlow LB* 100). This name seems to be *Doire* "oakwood" plus uninflected *Lios na hAbhla* "fort/enclosure of the apple-place", with *lisnahavla* later metathesized to *lisnahavil*. Alternatively the final element could be the variant genitive *na hAbhaille* with the final syllable dropped in pronunciation. Another "apple" name locally is **Magherally** *An Mhachaire Abhlaigh*, but earlier *Abhaill*, spelled *Awall* etc. The site of a rath was shown on Armagh 6-inch sheet 6.

Donagreagh Co. Armagh *Dún na Greá*
J 1060 "fort of the stud"

1. Dounagrugh	Esch. Co. Map 5.29	1609
2. Ballydownegreigh	CPR Jas I 396a	1609
3. Dunnagreih 1 bal (Doughcoron)	CPR Jas I 165a	1610
4. Donnaghreigh	Mooney MS 201	1629
5. pt Donagreigha[n] (nr Tullidagon)	Brownlow LB 153	1635
6. pt Donagreigha[n]	Brownlow LB 153	1635
7. Donnagreth	Mooney MS 201	1636
8. Dunegreath	Mooney MS 201	1654
9. td Donagreeagh (Shankhill)	Inq. Arm. (Patterson) 235	1657
10. Donnaghgreagh (Magherelin)	BSD 51	1661
11. vil et ter de Donaghreigh 1 b'bo	Inq. Ult. (Armagh) §7 Car. II	1661
12. Dunnegreagh	HMR Arm. (PRONI) 35	1664

13. Donacreigh..Donagreigh	Brownlow LB 154	1665?
14. qr Donnagregh	Brownlow LB 52-3	1667
15. 3 qrs Donegreigh	Brownlow LB 67	1667
16. Donnagregh	Brownlow LB 93	1669
17. Donaghreigh	Deeds & Wills (Mooney) 201	1712
18. Donagreagh	Vestry Reg. (OSNB) E8.59	1715
19. Donygreagh	Rocque's Map (Coote)	1760
20. Donygragh	Rocque's Map (Coote) 201	1760
21. Donagreigh	Reg. Free. (OSNB) E8.59	1829
22. Donygreagh	Bnd. Sur. (OSNB) E8.59	1830c
23. field Kilmocummog in Gallery's farm	Mooney 201	1950c
24. Dun na gcreach "Fort of the preys"	J O'D (OSNB) E8.59	1834c
25. Domhnach Riach	Mooney 201	1950c
26. ˌdǫnïˈgre:	Local pronunciation	1991
27. ˌdɔnïˈgre:	Local pronunciation	1991

The earliest forms of Donagreagh have either the spelling *u* in the first syllable, or *ow*, as in *dún* "hill-fort" which has become in some cases **Down**. There is no surviving hill-fort and the only suitable site is Carrigans Hill, 50 metres, in the south of the townland. O'Donovan suggested *Dún na gCreach* "fort of the raids", but the current pronunciation does not have the final [x] and is more likely to represent *Dún na Greagha* (an old genitive of *grai*), referring to horse-rearing in the area. Mooney thought the name might indicate an early church site named *Domhnach Riach* "speckled church", since there was a field called Kilmocummog in Gallery's farm with "traces of an ancient graveyard" (*Mooney MS* 201-2). The original name of this site might be *Cill Mo-Chommóg* or *Mo-Cholmóg* "my little Colmán's church", rather like the townland called **Kilminioge** "my little Finn's church" in Moira. The tradition of a burial ground in Donagreagh is still remembered locally. However Donagreagh was not church land, and it seems unlikely that a church site important enough to be called a *domhnach* would have been forgotten (see **Tullindoney**; *Liber Angeli (Bieler)* 188–9). No ancient remains are listed by the Archaeological Survey (in *ASCD* or *NISMR*).

Like Clankilvoragh, Donagreagh was listed in the 1609 schedule of Iveagh lands held by Sir Art Magennis (2), but it also was mapped on the 1609 Escheated County map of Oneilland in Armagh, granted to John Brownlow in 1610 and listed among the lands in that county held at his death (forms 1, 3, 4). The 1657 inquisition of parishes in Armagh placed all three Armagh townlands of Magheralin in the parish of **Shankill**. However subsequently the Armagh Book of Survey and Distribution gave them under *Magherelin* parish (form 10), where they have remained.

Drumlin
J 1255

Droimlín
"drumlin"

1. Ballydromlyn	CPR Jas I 395b	1609
2. Ballydromlin	CPR Jas I 190b	1611
3. Ballidromlin	CPR Jas I 266a	1614

4. Ballydromlyn	Inq. Ult. (Down) §4 Jac. I	1616
5. Ballydromlin	CPR Jas I 309a	1616
6. Ballydrumlin half-td (Magherilin 6tds)		
	Buckworth (EA) 310	1622
7. Drumlin	Hib. Reg. Lr. Iveagh	1657c
8. Drumlin	Census 80	1659c
9. Drumlin	BSD 72	1661
10. Drumlin	Sub. Roll Down 274	1663
11. Drumlin	Hib. Del. Down	1672c
12. Drumlin	Reg. Magheralin (OSNB) E8.59	1715
13. Drumlin	Map of Down (OSNB) E8.59	1755
14. Drumlin	Wm. Map (OSNB) E8.59	1810
15. ['Drum-lin]	OSNB Pron. E8.59	1834c
16. Druim Lín "Ridge of the flag" [sic, = flax?]	J O'D (OSNB) E8.59	1834c
17. Druim Fhlainn	Mooney 203	1950c
18. 'drǫmlən	Local pronunciation	1992

The main geographical feature of the townland of Drumlin is a ridge of higher ground jutting out westwards towards the Lagan.

In 1609 Drumlin was a church townland, which might suggest a church site with the etymology *Droim Lainne* "ridge of the church", including the early term *lann* as in the parish name *Machaire Lainne*, Magheralin. Reeves did not give his reasons why neither this townland nor a hill called Drumlin in Seagoe could be "admissible" as the parish called *Drumlyn* listed next to Dromara in the 1306 papal taxation. *Drumlyn* more likely stood for either **Drumballyroney** or Drumgooland (*EA* 105n).

However a two-word etymology for the townland name is unlikely, since, as early as the 1830s, "the accent is on the first syllable" (*OSNB*). This townland name seems most likely to be an early example of the Irish word giving the Irish-English geographical term *drumlin*, attested in English only since 1833. The history of this word has been studied by E.G. Quin and T.W. Freeman (Quin and Freeman 1947, 86). They found an Irish word *droimlinn* explained by Latin *dorsum* "ridge" in an unpublished 17th-century vocabulary by Richard Plunkett, and Eleanor Knott suggested this might be better written *druimlín*, since it arose as a by-form of *druimnín*, a diminutive of *druimne/droimne* meaning the same as *droim* "ridge". Magheralin parish contains the only townland in Ireland called Drumlin, although there is Drumleene in the parish of Clonleigh, Raphoe Co. Donegal, but there are nine examples of Drumneen in Ireland. Reeves' example of Drumlin Hill does not appear as such in the list of minor place-names from the 6-inch map, but there is a Drumlyn House in the townland of Ballydonaghy in Seagoe, near where the Bann flows from Co. Down to Armagh (Flanagan, L. 1981–2, 79). Mr Copeland of Donaghcloney, the modern informant for this area, thought this townland name must be the word *drumlin*, but pointed out that it does not contain any notable hills of drumlin type.

Drumnabreeze
J 1456

Dromainn Bhris (?)
"ridge of (the) high ground"

1. Dromvrishe sessiagh/ half-tn	CPR Jas I 395a	1609

2. Drumvrishe sessiagh/ half-tn	CPR Jas I 190b	1611
3. Dromanurees sess.	Inq. Ult. (Down) §13 Jac. I	1624
4. Drumvriske	Inq. Ult. (Down) §16 Car. I	1631
5. Drumbrice	Hib. Reg. Lr. Iveagh	1657c
6. Drumbree	Census 81	1659c
7. Drumbrice	BSD 74	1661
8. Drommenevrisse	BSD 82	1661
9. Drumbrice	S & D Ann. (Mooney) 200 (25)	17thc
10. Drommeneurisse	S & D Ann. (Mooney) 200 (26)	17thc
11. Drumnebree	Sub. Roll Down 273	1663
12. Drumneriske al. Drumneris	Lodge (Mooney) 200 (AS iii 72)	1666
13. Drumbric	Hib. Del. Down	1672c
14. Drumnabreeze	Reg. Magheralin (OSNB) E8.59	1715
15. Drumnabreeze	Vestry Reg. (OSNB) E8.59	1715
16. Drumnebreeze	Map of Down (OSNB) E8.59	1755
17. Drumnebreeze (Stothard's map)	Map of Down (OSNB) E8.59	1765
18. Drumnabreese	Wm. Map (OSNB) E8.59	1810
19. Druim na Bri "Ridge of the hillocks/hummocks"	J O'D (OSNB) E8.59	1834c
20. Dromanna Bhrígheacha / Drom Brígheach (+ Eng. pl. s)	Mooney 199	1950c
21. Breese family Dromore dist early 17thc	Mooney 199	1950c
22. Droimne Bríos	GÉ 94	1989
23. ˌdrọmnəˈbriːz	Local pronunciation	1992

Drumnabreeze was part of the O'Lavery district of **Moira** in 1609 (1), and although it was let to Stephen Haven of Dromore by 1631 (4), Laughlin Roe O'Lawry was still resident in 1663 (11). It is on rising ground east of the Lagan valley, with a hill in the centre 297 feet high, from which the view "ranges considerably over the flat ground adjoining the Lagan" (*OSNB*). The first element seems to be one of the words for "ridge", *droim* or its derivatives *dromainn* or *droimne*.

John O'Donovan suggested that the final element was *brí* "upland" (gen. plural *breg* later *brígh*). As noted by the editor, Margaret Dobbs, a name like *Droim na mBrígh* invites comparison with *Druimne Breg* "ridge of the high ground", the location of *Uachtar*, the earliest chief site of Dál Fiatach in east Ulster (*Descendants Ir* xiii 324, 336, 338). However, there is no archaeological evidence for an important historical settlement in this area, and **Dromorebrague** in Aghaderg is a more likely location.

If the element *brí* is accepted, it is possible that the final [z] of the modern pronunciation is due to the addition of English plural -*s*, which is usually pronounced as [z] after a vowel. There are forms without -*s* in the *Census* of 1659 and the Down subsidy roll (forms 6,11). A plural -*s* has been added to this element in English spelling in other place-names, for example *Mac Muiris na mBrígh*, "MacMorris of Brees" Co. Mayo (*Misc. Ir. Annals* 1406). Dean Mooney mentioned Brees Castle from *Caisleán na mBrí*, Brees in Clanmorris, Mayo, referred to as *(is) na Brighibh hi ccloinn Muiris* in 1595 AD (*AFM* vii 1988). Another possibility is that [z] represents the genitive ending [ʃ] of *bríoghas*, an unattested collective form of *brí* (cf. Ó Máille 1989-90). This would be *bríos* in modern spelling.

Final [ʃ] or [z] of whatever origin might have then been associated with the family of *de Bros*, which became Brush or Breese, attested in the parish of Dromore from 1622. In the late 18th century the Brush family were associated with Bishop Percy of Dromore, whose robes were presented to the cathedral by Mr Augustus Brush of Drumnabreeze House (*Atkinson's Dromore* 91). The Brush family came to Drumnabreeze about 1800 and are still in the townland, but they do not believe that there is any connection between their surname and the townland name. There was an obsolete Irish man's name *Bress*, gen. *Breisse*, not used in the historical period (*CGH*), but there is no Irish record of *Brios* (23). The Scottish surname Bryce (Reaney 1958, 110) is derived from the medieval personal name *Bricius* which was also used in Ireland (*EA* 108–10n). The surname is now fairly common in Co. Down, though not listed by Bell, and was borne by "the first Presbyterian minister who settled in Ireland", the Rev. Edward Brice who came to Templecorran near Larne in 1611 (*OSM* x 45b). In Britain the surname Breeze is often derived from Welsh *ap Rhys* "son of Rhys" (Reaney 1958, 45b), although because of the [z] Welsh scholars disagree (Morgan P.& T. 1985, 186). The Norman family of *de Braose* settled in Wales (McKinley 1990, 41). It is unlikely that a Plantation surname would have been incorporated into a townland name beginning with Irish elements.

Some of the earlier forms are similar to forms for **Maddydrumbrist** in Donaghmore, which end *-drombrisk, -dromvrish, -drombrish*, and have been interpreted as *droma bhrisc* "of the easily-broken/ friable ridge" (*PNI* i 104–5). The combination *sk* in handwriting is quite often confused with *sh*. *Droim* is now masculine and thus should not lenite *b* in the nominative, as apparently happens in the earliest forms here. Drumnabreeze therefore might have been *Dromainn Bhriosc*, with the final *-n* of *dromainn* fem. reinterpreted to look like the article. Forms with an internal *-n-* appear in 1624 and 1666 (3, 12). However the weight of the evidence is against *-sk* as the original spelling here.

| **Drumnaferry** | *Dromainn Tí Fhearaigh* | |
| J 1455 | "ridge of Ferry's house" | |

1. Ballendromentiogery in Lequirin	CPR Jas I 394b	1609
2. Ballydromentiogery (in Ballinderrie in Lequirin)	CPR Jas I 193a	1611
3. Dromentioyry in Iveagh	CPR Jas I 194b	1611
4. Ballydromerkiorry al. Ballydromentiogerye	Inq. Ult. (Down) §30 Car. I	1632
5. Dromintiogry	Magennis Paps (O'Sullivan) 68	1632
6. Drumtire	Hib. Reg. Lr. Iveagh	1657c
7. Drumtyre	Par. Map (Mooney) 201	17thc
8. Drummunteferry	Census 81	1659c
9. Drumtire	BSD 74	1661
10. Drumtyre	S & D Ann. (Mooney) 202 (25)	17thc
11. Dromintiogrie al. Dromnaiogrie	Lodge (Mooney) 202 (AS III 74)	1661
12. D:tire	Hib. Del. Down	1672c
13. Dromintrogry al. Dromnatriogrie al. Dromodoffry	Deeds & Wills (Mooney) 201	1714
14. Drominstroigery al. Drominstriogue al. Dromadoffer	Deeds & Wills (Mooney) 201	1714
15. Dromonhory al. Drumnagery al. Dronmacogry	Deeds & Wills (Mooney) 201	1714
16. Drumnafery	Reg. Magheralin (OSNB) E8.59	1715
17. Drumnafery	Vestry Reg. (OSNB) E8.59	1715

18. Dromintiogrie al. Dromonoferry al.		
Dromneferry	Deeds & Wills (Mooney) 201	1717
19. Drumnafeery	Wm. Map (OSNB) E8.59	1810
20. Drumnaferry	Bnd. Sur. (OSNB) E8.59	1834c
21. Druim na fiaire "Ridge of the grassy		
surface"	J O'D (OSNB) E8.59	1834c
22. Droman Thigh Uí Fearadhaigh		
"hill of O'Ferry's house"		
/Mac Fearadaigh/Ó Giorraidh	Mooney 201	1950c
23. ˌdrọmnəˌfɛrï	Local pronunciation	1992

Drumnaferry, in the Magennis district of Lequirin, had passed to George Sexton by 1632 (form 4). It was described as a "small hilly townland" in 1834 (*OSNB*). The name has produced some odd forms, apparently alternating spellings with internal *-f-* and *-g-*. John O'Donovan based his etymology on the later spellings, though it is not clear what word he had in mind, since the relevant ones are all masculine, and would not have *f* following the article *na*: *féar* "grass" gen. *féir*; *féarach* "pasture" gen. *féaraigh*; *fiagar, -air* "grassland" (Ulster, *Dinneen*); *fiaire (fiadhaire)* "rambler". Although the name later seems to begin with *droim* "ridge", the early spellings indicate *dromainn tí* "ridge of the house" which would be most likely to be followed by the owner's name.

Dean Mooney suggested (22) the Ulster family *Mac Fearadhaigh* (becoming *Mac Fearaigh*, McFerry), which has sometimes been corrupted to *Ó Giorraidhe*, via a form *Mag Fhearadhaigh* (Megarry) and the confusion of *mac* and *Ó* in surnames. According to Woulfe it was found "chiefly in East Ulster" (1923, 541). *McGary* was attested in south Co. Antrim in 1606, and there is a settlement called **Megarrystown** in the parish of Moira. The *o* in the spelling *tiogery* (1–2, 4) looks as if it might be intended to indicate a surname, but would require *Ó Giorraidhe* to be the form of the surname current in 1609.

Another possible surname is *Ó Fiodhabhra*, later *Ó Fíobhra* anglicized Furey, borne by a bishop of Armagh in the 13th century (Woulfe 1923, 419, 526). The spelling *Dromentioyry* (3) might represent *Dromainn Tí (Uí) Fhiodhabhra* [ˌdrọmənti:ˈïɣurə], with Irish *dh*, phonetically [ɣ], represented by *g* in other early spellings (1, 2, 4b, 5). However one might expect the Irish *bh* to be included in the anglicized form, and Ferry not Furey appears in later forms of the name. Since "house" in place-names is usually followed by a personal name, the *g* in early spellings could also represent the old form of gen. *tighe* "house", with *gh* preserved before the personal name *Fhearaigh* "of Fearaíoch/Ferry" standing alone. Initial *F* sometimes resists lenition in place-names (**Tirfergus, Kilfullert**) and later forms show it restored here. The Petty spellings (forms 6, 7, 12) must have been abbreviated for simplicity, although they are not followed in the 18th-century deeds.

Drumo and Drumcro	*Droim Eo* "ridge of yews" and
J 1358	*Droim Cró* "ridge of huts"

1. Dromchroe Dromewe	CPR Jas I 395b	1609
2. Dromchrooe half td and		
Drommoe half td	CPR Jas I 235a	1612
3. half vil. Dromchrowe	Inq. Ult. (Down) §13 Car. I	1629
4. sessiagh Drommewe	nq. Ult. (Down) §13 Car. I	1629

5. Dromchro & Dromowe	Inq. Ult. (Down) §85 Car. I	1639
6. Drumcroe Drumoe	Hib. Reg. Lr. Iveagh	1657c
7. Drumore Drumcroe	BSD 73	1661
8. Drumore, Drumcree	S & D Ann. (Mooney) 204 (23)	17thc
9. Drumcroe	Sub. Roll Down 272	1663
10. Drumro	Sub. Roll Down 273	1663
11. Dromcroe	ASE 61b 39	1666
12. Drumoe Drumcroe	ASE 112a 34	1667
13. Drumcroe Drumoe	Hib. Del. Down	1672c
14. Drum & Dromcro	Reg. Magheralin (OSNB) E8.59	1715
15. Dromo and Dromcro	Vestry Reg. (OSNB) E8.59	1715
16. Drom & Dromcro	Ir. Wills Index 1	1739
17. Dromo & Drumcrow	Map of Down (OSNB) E8.59	1755
18. Dromo & Drumcrow	Wm. Map (OSNB) E8.59	1810
19. Drumo Drumcrow	Bnd. Sur. (OSNB) E8.59	1830c
20. Druim Cro "Ridge of the hut"	J O'D (OSNB) E8.59	1834c
21. Druim Eo "Ridge of the yew"	J O'D (OSNB) E8.59	1834c
22. Druim Muadh & Druim Cruadh "soft v. hard ridge"	Mooney 203	1950c
23. dṛọ'mo ən drọm'kro	Local pronunciation	1996

Dromewe and *Dromchroe* belonged to Sir Art Magennis in 1609 (form 1). The citation in 1612 (form 2) made it clear that each was only half a townland, and they are normally quoted together. In the words of the *OSNB* (E8.59), "Dromo and Drumcrow are 2 townlands united and is always used in the parish", and Drumo and Drumcrow was described to me locally as a "split townland". The river Lagan, presumably the boundary between the original two units, runs through the middle of the current townland, spanned by Forge Bridge (*OSM* xii 110a). The present Drumcro House was called New Forge House in 1833 (*ASCD* 361). In 1837 there were four mills run by Coslet Waddle for Lord Clanwilliam (*OSM* xii 110a).

John O'Donovan's suggestion that Drumo meant "ridge of the yew-tree" would require a late form, since the old genitive singular of *eo* was *i*, but it may represent "of yews" from gen. plural *eo*. The word *cró*, less remarkably, is "enclosure, cattle-pen, hut" and also earlier had genitive singular *crai* (*DIL*). Since there are no traditions of local battles it is unlikely to be the homonym meaning "gore". Other possible etymologies are *Droim mBó* "ridge of the cow", preserving nasal mutation after *droim* as in *Droim mBearach* **Dromara**, and *Droim Cnó* "ridge of the nuts", with later change of *n* to *r*. Because of the close association of the two names Dean Mooney assumed there would be a contrast between the two "ridges": he thought the second elements could be the adjectives *cruadh* "hard" (usually *cruaidh* in Ulster), and (a less common word) *muadh* "soft" (22). This is phonetically possible since there are many place-names where *ruadh* "reddish" has been anglicized as *-roe*, but the adjectives are not really opposites. In the dictionary of Early Irish (*DIL*) *muad* is a poetic word of uncertain, although complimentary, meaning, explained as "soft, noble" in *Dinneen*, and now little used (*Ó Dónaill*). O'Donovan's suggestions, but in the plural, seem to be the most likely.

Edenballycoggill
J 1156

Éadan Baile Chogail
"hillface of the townland of corn-cockle"

1. Ballyaden Ballycoggall	CPR Jas I 395b	1609
2. Ballyaden Ballycoggall	CPR Jas I 190b	1611
3. Balliaden Ballicoggall	CPR Jas I 266a	1614
4. Ballyaden Ballyroggall	Inq. Ult. (Down) §4 Jac. I	1614
5. Ballyaden Ballycoggall	CPR Jas I 309a	1616
6. Ballyedentoggall half-td (Magherilin 6tds)	Buckworth (EA) 310	1622
7. Edenballigoll	Hib. Reg. Lr. Iveagh	1657c
8. Edenballigall	BSD 72	1661
9. Edenballigol	Hib. Del. Down	1672c
10. Edenballycogill	Reg. Magheralin (OSNB) E8.59	1715
11. Edenballycogill	Vestry Reg. (OSNB) E8.59	1715
12. Edenballycoggen	Reg. Deeds abstracts i §324	1722
13. Edenballycoghill	Map of Down (OSNB) E8.59	1755
14. Edenballycoghill	Maps (Mooney) 205	1767
15. Edenballycoghill	Wm. Map (OSNB) E8.59	1810
16. Edenballycoghill	Bnd. Sur. (OSNB) E8.59	1830c
17. Edenballycoggill	Cess Book (OSNB) E8.59	1834c
18. Edenballycoggill	J O'D (OSNB) E8.59	1834c
19. Edenballycoggle	Ir. Wills Index 92	1843
20. Éadan Baile Uí Chogail "Brae of Cogglestown"	J O'D (OSNB) E8.59	1834c
21. Éadan Baile Mhic Chomhghaill "McCole"	Mooney 205	1950c
22. ˈidn̩ˌbɑliˈkɑxəl	Local pronunciation	1991
23. ˈidn̩ˌbɑliˈkagəl	Local pronunciation	1992

Edenballycoggill appears to begin with the common term *éadan* "hill-face". However in the early 17th century (forms 1-5) it was clearly in two parts, and when *Ballyaden* and *Ballycoggall* were joined their names were combined to create the modern name, first seen in 1622 (6: *t* is a misreading of *c*). It is not stated where the original division would have been, but Edenballycoggill is bordered on the east by the Lagan, and part of the western boundary is formed by two streams which flow into the ponds at Milltown in the middle of the townland and thence into the river. One of these streams from north and south was probably the boundary between *Baile Éadain* "townland of the hill-face" and the area called *Ballycoggill*. Both parts were church land in 1609, and the schedule refers to another church townland called *Ballycorshillcoghill* (*CPR Jas I* 395a, 191a, 266a), now **Ballynanny** in Clonduff (*PNI* iii 81, no attempt to translate the earlier name). However, here the spelling *coghill* only appears in the 18th century, though local pronunciations support both it and *coggill* with a hard *-g-*. Some of the forms contain *r* and *t*, which are well-known misreadings of *c*.

Both O'Donovan and Mooney thought that *-coggill* might be a surname (20, 21). Dean Mooney suggested McCole, formed from the personal name *Comhghall*, noting the Petty forms which have a second element of one syllable. As evidence, Mooney found a local 17th-century surname spelled *McCowell* (*CPR Jas I* 320a). However, Woulfe says *Mac Comhghaill* is "extremely rare", and McCowell more likely represents *Mac Cathmhaoil*, known in Tyrone and Co. Down (Woulfe 1923, 336, 329). The forms here show hard *g* and also provide no evidence for *mac*. Other possible words are *cogal* masc. "cockle, tares", a word not found in early sources, and *coigeal* fem. "distaff, churn-dash". As regards the second, the spellings provide no evidence for the final syllable of gen. *coigile*, unlike **Ballyvally** in Clonallan (*PNI* i 63), where *coigeal* seems to be the final element in the early forms. The name *Ballycoggall* probably meant "townland of corn-cockle".

Edenmore	*Éadan Mór*	
J 1457	"great hill-face"	

1.	Edenmore	CPR Jas I 396a	1609
2.	Edenmore half td	CPR Jas I 235a	1612
3.	Edinmore	Inq. Ult. (Down) §13 Car. I	1629
4.	Edenmore	Inq. Ult. (Down) §85 Car. I	1639
5.	Edenmore	Hib. Reg. Lr. Iveagh	1657c
6.	Edenmore	BSD 74	1661
7.	Edenmore (56a of)	ASE 61b 39	1666
8.	Edenmore	Hib. Del. Down	1672c
9.	Edenmore	Rent Roll Down 5	1692
10.	Edenmore	Reg. Magheralin (OSNB) E8.59	1715
11.	Edenmore	Deeds & Wills (Mooney) 205	1716
12.	Adenmore	Map of Down (OSNB) E8.59	1755
13.	Edenmore	Wm. Map (OSNB) E8.59	1810
14.	Eadan Mór "great brae or brow of a hill"	J O'D (OSNB) E8.59	1834c
15.	ˌidən'mɔr	Local pronunciation	1991

Edenmore is a long thin townland of 241 acres, with one end running down to the Lagan, overlooking the Lagan valley. It belonged in 1609 to Sir Art Magennis but had passed to Sir George Rawden by 1666 (forms 1,7). Form 11 is from a Rawden deed of 1716. The current pronunciation is like English *Eden*, but a pronunciation more like Irish *éadan* is suggested by the form *Adenmore* on the 1755 map of Down.

Feney	*Fíonaigh*	
J 1458	"(place of) twigs"	

1.	(?)maidm Finnmuighi for Uib Meith... ria nUib Eachach	AU (Mac Airt) 490	1054
2.	(?)maidhm Finnmhaighe... ria nUibh Eathach (translated "Finvoy, Down")	AFM ii 864-5n	1054
3.	Fermoy (in Moyragh)	CPR Jas I 395a	1609
4.	Fenney in Moyragh	CPR Jas I 190b	1611
5.	Fleighny (sessiagh)	Inq. Ult. (Down) §13 Jac. I	1624
6.	Fynny	Inq. Ult. (Down) §65 Car. I	1636
7.	Fennye; Fenye; Fenney (sessiagh)	Inq. Ult. (Down) §93 Car. I	1640
8.	Ffowny, Rory Curragh O'Lawy of	Wars Co. Down x 81	1641
9.	Cartragh & Fenny	Hib. Reg. Lr. Iveagh	1657c
10.	Feany	Census 81	1659c

11. Ffanny (Cortragh &)	BSD 74	1661
12. Cortragh & Fanny	S & D Ann. (Mooney) 208 (25)	17thc
13. Cartra & Fenny	Hib. Del. Down	1672c
14. Feny	Reg. Magheralin (OSNB) E8.59	1715
15. Feny	Map of Down (OSNB) E8.59	1755
16. Feney	Wm. Map (OSNB) E8.59	1810
17. 'Faney' by the common people	OSNB Pron. E8.59	1834c
18. ['Fenny]	OSNB Pron. E8.59	1834c
19. Fiodhnaighe "woody"	J O'D (OSNB) E8.59	1834c
20. Fiadhanach "wild, uncultivated place"	Mooney 207	1950c
21. 'finï	Local pronunciation	1992
22. 'fenï	Local pronunciation	1996
23. ðə 'fenï 'len	Local pronunciation	1996

In 1609 Feney, then a sessiagh, was part of the O'Lavery (*O'Lowry*) holding of **Moira** (form 3). The 1640 inquisition shows it was let to Edward Trevor, although "Rory Curragh *O'Lawy* of *Ffowny*" was implicated in the rebellion in 1641 (forms 7, 8). In the later 17th century another name, *Cartragh*, also appears, clearly not as a mistake for Gartross on the south of Feney, which is also named in the same documents. Feney is now 185 acres.

The Ordnance Survey in the early 19th century recorded two pronunciations, 'Fen-ny, and 'Faney "by the common people" (17, 18). Fennagh in Co. Carlow is traced back to *Fionnmhach* (*AGBP* 30; *GÉ* 221) meaning "white plain", and it might be wondered if this Feney could be the place named *Finnmagh* "white plain" which was the site of an Uí Eachach battle in 1054 (forms 1–2). However the losers were the people of Omeath and *Uachtar Tíre* (**Watertirry**, the Castlewellan area), and the battle was probably fought further south. There is no place called Finvoy in Down (2) but there is a townland now called Finvoy, *Fionnmhaigh*, in Co. Louth (*L. Log. Lú* 15). A word *fidnach* "twigs used for fuel or bedding" is attested in early Irish (*DIL*) and the modern spelling *Fíonach* was suggested as the origin of Feenagh in Co. Cork (*AGBP* 83). The dative or locative form, spelt *Fiodhnaigh > Fíonaigh*, seems more appropriate for Feney.

Gartross *Gort Rosa*
J 1558 "Ross's field/field of the promontory"

1. Gortroise (in Moyragh)	CPR Jas I 395a	1609
2. Gortroisse in Moyragh	CPR Jas I 190b	1611
3. Gortrosse sessiagh	Inq. Ult. (Down) §13 Jac. I	1624
4. Gurtroshe sessiagh	Inq. Ult. (Down) §93 Car. I	1640
5. Gortrosse ½ town land	BSD 74	1661
6. Gortrosse	BSD 75	1661
7. Gortrosse	S & D Ann. (Mooney) 208 (24)	17thc
8. Gartrosse	ASE 61b 39	1666
9. Gorterosse	DS (Mooney) 207	1666
10. (?)Gortglasse, sessiagh of	Rent Roll Down 6	1692
11. Gartross	Reg. Magheralin (OSNB) E8.59	1715
12. Gortross	Deeds & Wills (Mooney) 207	1717
13. Cartrosse	Deeds & Wills (Mooney) 208	1717

14. Gartross	Map of Down (OSNB) E8.59	1755
15. Gartross	Ir. Wills Index 53	1804
16. Gartross	Wm. Map (OSNB) E8.59	1810
17. Gort Rossa "Ross's garden"	J O'D (OSNB) E8.59	1834c
18. Gort Ruis (17thc pers name Dn)	Mooney 207	1950c
19. gɑrt'rɔs	Local pronunciation	1996

In 1609 Gartross was a sessiagh of *Moyragh* (form 1). It was called a half-townland in 1661 (5), and in 1666 it was held as a sessiagh of 118 acres by Sir George Rawden (form 8). The area is now 237 acres. *Gart* is a variant of *gort*, "a field used for crops", which occurs widely in place-names, and there are over 200 examples of townlands in Northern Ireland with it as the first element. The second element is usually descriptive, but can be the owner's name: **Gortdonaghy** in Cleenish, **Gortmaconnell** in Killesher parish, Fermanagh. In this case *Ros* gen. *Rois* could either be a personal name Ross or the word meaning "promontory" or "wood". In *Táin Bó Cuailnge* three Ulster warriors, Rus, Dáire and Imchad, grandsons of King Conchobar mac Nessa, are called "the three great champions of *Cuib* (**Iveagh**)... the three chiefs of *Roth*" (**Moira**) (*TBC Rec. I* 1.3778). Although *-roshe* appears in the 17th century (form 4), the final *-s* in the current anglicized spelling might indicate *Rosa*, the older alternative genitive of the personal name. *Clann Rosa* "offspring of Ross (son of Rudhraighe)" was used in bardic poetry to signify both the Ulster Cycle heroes and their supposed descendants the Magennises (Ó Concheanainn 1974, 246-7).

However, the difference between *-s* and *-sh* (pronounced [ʃ]) is often not made clear in 17th-century documents, and without further evidence it is difficult to be sure if the name Ross is involved. There are no trees to suggest "field of the wood" as the meaning, but Gartross House with a rath marked beside it is on a spur of higher ground (50 metres), a possible promontory, in the south of the townland. There is a townland with the similar name of **Gortrush** in Drumragh, Tyrone.

Gregorlough
J 1656

Grágarlach
"place of tree-stumps"

1. Balligrogallagh	CPR Jas I 396a	1609
2. Balligragolagh	CPR Jas I 235a	1612
3. Ballygragologh	Inq. Ult. (Down) §13 Car. I	1629
4. Graige-irlagh half vil	Inq. Ult. (Down) §85 Car. I	1639
5. Garagulagh, Donald & Ferdoragh Magennis of	Wars Co. Down x 79	1641
6. Gragulaghe, Donell Oge Magennis of	Wars Co. Down x 81	1641
7. Gragerloch	DS (Mooney) 208	1653
8. Gragarlagh	Hib. Reg. Lr. Iveagh	1657c
9. Geagrelagh and Traghlomny	Census 81	1659c
10. Gragarlagh	BSD 73	1661
11. Gragerlagh (part)	ASE 46b 26	1666
12. Gragerlagh	ASE 61b 39	1666
13. Gragarlagh	Hib. Del. Down	1672c
14. Gragertagh	Rent Roll Down 5	1692
15. Gregerlagh	Rent Roll Down 7	1692

16. Gregollogh	Reg. Magheralin (OSNB) E8.59	1715
17. Gregorlough	Vestry Reg. (OSNB) E8.59	1715
18. Gragerlagh	Deeds & Wills (Mooney) 207	1716
19. Cragerlagh	Deeds & Wills (Mooney) 207	1717
20. Gregorlogh	Map of Down (OSNB) E8.59	1755
21. Gregorlogh	Wm. Map (OSNB) E8.59	1810
22. Gregor-lough	Reg. Free. (OSNB) E8.59	1830
23. Gregorlough	Bnd. Sur. (OSNB) E8.59	1830c
24. Loch Griogoir "Gregory's Lough"	J O'D (OSNB) E8.59	1834c
25. Gragallach/Gragarnach "place of fowl-screeching"	Mooney 207	1950c
26. 'grɛgərlɔx	Local pronunciation	1991
27. 'gjihərlɔx	Local pronunciation	1991
28. ˌgrɛgər'lɔx	Local pronunciation	1992

In 1609 Gregorlough was held by Sir Art Magennis (forms 1, 2), but was divided between Sir George Rawden, who acquired many of Sir Art's lands in the area, and John Bennett of Seapatrick by 1666 (forms 11, 12). The north of the townland rises to Sally's Hill (443 feet), while Simpson's Fort is on its western slope, on the boundary with Taughlumny. The southern boundary, with Islandderry, is formed by the Shanker Burn. Although O'Donovan said "there is a small lough" (*OSNB* E8.59), all the townland is on high ground and no lough or marsh is shown on the OS 1:10,000 map (sheet 183). It seems likely that the spelling -*lough* is a suffix -*lach* (as in **Drumlough**, Dromore). The personal name Gregor(y) seems a plausible element from the later spellings, but before the 19th century the vowel in the first syllable is almost always -*a*-, and the second *r* is not in the three earliest forms.

Dean Mooney provided a different etymology, based on such descriptive words as *grágalach* "croaking", *grágarlach* "raucous person" (*Ó Dónaill*). However it is unlikely that such a term would become a place-name on its own, and another possibility would be that *grág* is the word meaning "tree-stump", diminutive *grágán* "bush" (*Ó Dónaill*). *Gráglach* "place of tree-stumps" could be pronounced with an epenthetic vowel between *g* and *l* as ['grɑ:gələx]. In modern Irish the forms *grágánach* and *grágarlach*, with different suffixes, can both be used of a person with bushy hair (*Ó Dónaill*) and, if a short *r*-stroke had been misread as *l* in forms 1-3, this place-name could also be derived from *Grágarlach* with the meaning "bushy place". The whole area was well-wooded before the Plantation. The prefixed *Bally*- in the three earliest forms is probably unhistorical. The stress in the current pronunciation maybe influenced by the modern spelling (form 28). One informant recorded the name as ['gjihərlɔx] (27).

Kilfullert
J 1355

Coill Fulachta
"wood of the cooking place"

1. Ballykillyfollyat	CPR Jas I 395b	1609
2. Ballykillyfollyat	CPR Jas I 235a	1612
3. Ballyfolliat (sessiagh?)	Inq. Ult. (Down) §13 Car. I	1629
4. half vil de Kiltefollagh 60a	Inq. Ult. (Down) §85 Car. I	1639
5. Kilfallotty	Hib. Reg. Lr. Iveagh	1657c
6. Kilfallatty	DS (Mooney) 209	1666

7. Killfalty	S & D Ann. (Mooney) 209 (23)	17thc
8. Kilfalloty	Hib. Del. Down	1672c
9. Killfallaty 85a	ASE 112a 34	1679
10. Kilfallert	Reg. Magheralin (OSNB) E8.59	1715
11. Kilfollart	Map of Down (OSNB) E8.59	1755
12. Kilsollart	Wm. Map (OSNB) E8.59	1810
13. Kilfolard	Ir. Wills Index 101	1826
14. Kilfullart	Reg. Free. (OSNB) E8.59	1830
15. Kilfalert	Meersman (OSNB) E8.59	1834c
16. Coill Folachtaigh "Folaghty's wood"	J O'D (OSNB) E8.59	1834c
17. Coill Folachta "wood of the cooking place"	Mooney 209	1950c
18. Coill Fochlochta "wood of the brooklime"	Mooney 209	1950c
19. Coill Fulachta	GÉ 73	1989
20. ˌkilˈfulərt	Local pronunciation	1991
21. ˌkjəlˈfolərt	Local pronunciation	1992

   Kilfullert belonged to Sir Art Magennis and had no ecclesiastical associations, so that the first element is more likely to be *coill* "wood" than *cill* "church". The second element supports this, since it appears to be *fulacht*, an outdoor cooking-place. Although lenition would normally be expected after *Coill*, *f* appears in all the historical forms and sometimes seems to resist lenition. The *fulacht* appears widely as an archaeological feature, usually as a raised piece of land in wet ground beside a spring or stream, consisting of fragments of burnt stones. Large stones were heated in a fire and then put into water to boil meat placed in it, being discarded when they began to break up. According to J.P. Mallory (1991, 109) they are rare in Ulster, though he describes an excavated example in Co. Down. However, recently many have been found by deliberate searching in Fermanagh. The element shows loss of *-ch-* before *t*, as often happens in east Ulster Irish, for example **Ballybot** in Newry, from *Baile Bocht* (*PNI* i 39–40). In Kilfullert *ch* was replaced by *-r-*, as also happens in **Tartaraghan** parish in Armagh, from *Teach Tíreacháin* "Tíreachán's house" (Arthurs 1956–7, v 41–2), and in some modern Donegal dialects (Ó Dochartaigh 1987, 132f).

Kircassock
J 1456

Cor Cosógaí
"bend of the bulrushy place"

1. (?)Kyllosci	Reg. Swayne 45	1426
2. Ballecartaske in Leighquirrin	CPR Jas I 395a	1609
3. Ballecarcassegie in Leighguyrrin	CPR Jas I 235b	1612
4. Ballycarrcaslegie	Inq. Ult. (Down) §13 Car. I	1629
5. Ballycarcassagy	Inq. Ult. (Down) §85 Car. I	1639
6. Corcasokye	Par. Map (Mooney) 211	1657c
7. Corcassaky	Hib. Reg. Lr. Iveagh	1657c
8. Corcossocke	Census 81	1659c
9. Corkasokie	BSD 74	1661
10. Corkasokie	S & D Ann. (Mooney) 211 (24)	17thc

11. Corkasokey al. Kirkasoke	ASE 46 b 26	1666
12. Corcasokie	DS (Mooney) 211	1666
13. Corkasoky	Hib. Del. Down	1672c
14. Curkanekay als Kirkasoke	Rent Roll Down 7	1692
15. Kirkasoky al. Kirkasoke	Deeds & Wills (Mooney) 212	1709
16. Kircassogue	Reg. Magheralin (OSNB) E8.59	1715
17. Kircassock	Harris Hist. map	1743
18. Kircassog	Map of Down (OSNB) E8.59	1755
19. Kircussock (corr. to Kircassock)	Statist. Sur. Dn 62,124	1802
20. Kirsassog	Wm. Map (OSNB) E8.59	1810
21. Kirkessock	Meersman (OSNB) E8.59	1834c
22. "The Flooded Meadow" in the centre	Mooney 211	1950c
23. Corchachóga "small concaves or morasses"	J O'D (OSNB) E8.59	1834c
24. Corach Coiseogach "rushy or reedy bog or marsh"	Mooney 211	1950c
25. ˌkər'kasək	Local pronunciation	1991
26. 'kɛr'kasək	Local pronunciation	1991

In the *Register of Archbishop Swayne* the editor's equation of form (1) "*Kyllosci*, the lands of O'Donnacon", with Kircassock seems to have been based on the idea that this name had once begun *Kil-* (from *cill* "church") and later became *Kirk-*. But it clearly began as *Cor-* (until 1666), and was not church land, so that *Kyllosci*, church land, meaning possibly "burnt church", can hardly be the same place. Kircassock was part of the secular district of Lequirin, and by 1666 it was held by John Barrett of Lisnafiffy in Seapatrick. Dean Mooney mentioned a place called "the Flooded Meadow" in the centre of this small flat townland (22). Streams form the southern, eastern and northern borders. Both Mooney and O'Donovan suggested forms from *corrach* "marsh", and Mooney suggested an adjective from *coiseog* "reed, bulrush" for the second element. The variant *cosóg* with broad *s* is given by *Dinneen*. The first element may have been *corrach*, shortened in the anglicized form, or, more likely, *cor* "bend (in a stream)".

Lismaine
J 1256

Lios Miacháin
"Meehan's fort"

1. Ballilismean	CPR Jas I 395b	1609
2. Ballylismean	CPR Jas I 190b	1611
3. Ballilismeaghan	CPR Jas I 266a	1614
4. Ballylismehan	Inq. Ult. (Down) §4 Jac. I	1614
5. Ballilisnehan	CPR Jas I 309a	1616
6. Ballilismean half-td (Magherilin 6tds)	Buckworth (EA) 310	1622
7. Lismea	Hib. Reg. Lr. Iveagh	1657c
8. Lismea	BSD 72	1661
9. Lismean	Sub. Roll Down 274	1663
10. Lismea	Hib. Del. Down	1672c
11. Lismean	Reg. Magheralin (OSNB) E8.59	1715

12. Lismean	Vestry Reg. (OSNB) E8.59	1715
13. Lismene	Map of Down (OSNB) E8.59	1755
14. Lismene	Wm. Map (OSNB) E8.59	1810
15. Lismain	Bnd. Sur. (OSNB) E8.59	1830c
16. [-'mane]	OSNB Pron. E8.59	1834c
17. Lios Meadhoin "middle fort"	J O'D (OSNB) E8.59	1834c
18. Lios Miadhacháin "Meehan's fort"	Mooney 213	1950c
19. ləs'me:n	Local pronunciation	1991

In the 1830s there were three forts in Lismaine (*OSNB*), and O'Donovan suggested *Lios Meadhóin* "middle fort" (17), in modern spelling *Lios Meáin*. However, the 17th-century forms with internal -*h*- are probably best explained by *ch* [x] in Irish, and the townland name could be from *Lios Miacháin* "Miachán's fort". *Miachán* is the same personal name as in the surname in nearby **Ballymacmaine**, from which Lismaine is separated only by the townland of Ballymacateer. Lismaine was a church townland in 1609 (form 1), and still belonged to the Church of Ireland in 1868 (*Parl. Rept* x 574). Ballymacmaine was also a church townland. Although there is no evidence for the family as 17th-century erenaghs, the original *Miachán* could have been an offshoot from some other family. The usual local anglicization of *Mac Miacháin* seems to be McMeekin (MacLysaght 1985, 212–3), but according to local tradition c. 1834 "a family of the name Maines had property here" (*OSNB* E8.59).

Lisnashanker   *Lios na Seanchraobh*
J 1756   "fort/enclosure of the old trees"

1. Ballylisncrivie	CPR Jas I 395a	1609
2. Ballelisnecrivie	CPR Jas I 235b	1612
3. Shanker (Bryan M'Ever Magines of)	Ham. Copy Inq. [1623] xxix	1623
4. Lissnecreevy	Inq. Ult. (Down) §13 Car. I	1629
5. Lissnehancree	BSD 73	1661
6. Lisneehancree	DS (Mooney) 213	1666
7. Lisnehanree	ASE 112a 34	1667
8. Lisneshacre	Hib. Del. Down	1672c
9. Lisnashankry	Reg. Magheralin (OSNB) E8.59	1715
10. Lissnashanger	Ir. Wills Index 55	1719
11. Lisnashancre	Map of Down (OSNB) E8.59	1755
12. Lisnashanker	Wm. Map (OSNB) E8.59	1810
13. Lisnashankard	Reg. Free. (OSNB) E8.59	1829
14. Lios na Sean-chroi "Fort of the old hovel"	J O'D (OSNB) E8.59	1834c
15. Lios na sean-chraoibhe	Mooney 213	1950c
16. ˌləsnə'ʃaŋkər	Local pronunciation	1991
17. lə'ʃaŋkər	Local pronunciation	1992
18. 'ʃaŋkər 'bọrn	Local pronunciation	1992

Lisnashanker was in the Magennis district of Lequirin (forms 1, 2), but by 1679 was held with the whole area round about by Captain John Magill and became part of the manor of

Gilford (form 7). The early 17th-century spellings make it clear that the original name included the word *craobh* "tree": *Lios na Seanchraobh* "fort of the old trees". This evidence for the final element was not available to John O'Donovan, but the later 17th-century spellings (forms 5-7,9,11) link the earlier and later forms. Four "forts" were noted in 1834 (*OSNB*). One rath survives, but there were four others marked on the 1835 6-inch Ordnance Survey map in the north of the townland (sheet 20, *ASCD* 166b). Trees were cultivated at or near settlement enclosures in the past: in an early Irish story the Ulster warrior Fergus pulled up as a weapon "the big oak in the centre of the *lios*" (*SMMD I* §18), and the annals describe Cenél nEogain and the Ulaid cutting down the trees at each other's inauguration sites of **Crew Hill** and **Tullahogue** (*AU* AD 1099, 1111). Similarly named townlands are **Lisnacreevy** in Drumballyroney, **Lisnacreeve** Tyrone. **Movilla** (*PNI* ii 233–5) and **Shankill** in Aghaderg are other places in Co. Down named from important trees.

The Shanker Burn (18), which flows through Islandderry Lake and forms the southern boundary of the townland, has been named from the later form of the townland name. However the abbreviation Shanker was in use as early as 1623, when it was given as Brian mac Ever Magennis' "address" (form 3).

Lisnasure *Lios na Saor*
J 1454 "fort/enclosure of the craftsmen"

1. Ballylissneseer (in Lequirin)	CPR Jas I 394b	1609
2. Ballilisseneseere, Arte Oge McG McA Magenis of	CPR Jas I 195b	1610
3. Ballylinesteere (in Lequirin)	CPR Jas I 193a	1611
4. Lisnishur	Hib. Reg. Lr. Iveagh	1657c
5. Lisneshure	Par. Map (Mooney) 214	17thc
6. Lisnegsewer	Census 81	1659c
7. Lisnehure	BSD 74	1661
8. Lisnehure	S & D Ann. (Mooney) 214 (25)	17thc
9. Lisnasure	Reg. Magheralin (OSNB) E8.59	1715
10. Lisnesure	Map of Down (OSNB) E8.59	1755
11. Lisnashure	Atkinson's Donaghcloney 129	1762
12. Lisnasure	Wm. Map (OSNB) E8.59	1810
13. Lisnashure	Ir. Wills Index 76	1815
14. [-'shure]	OSNB Pron. E8.59	1834c
15. Lios na Siur "Fort of the sisters"	J O'D (OSNB) E8.59	1834c
16. Lios na Síobhrogha "of the fairy house"	Mooney 213	1950c
17. Lios na Síor "Fort of the broomrape"	Mooney 213	1950c
18. ˌləsnə'ʃiːr	Local pronunciation	1992
19. ˌləsnə'ʃuːr	Local pronunciation	1992

Lisnasure is the first of "chief-four towns in the Lequirin", held in 1609 by Art Oge mcGlasney McAugholie Magennis, son of the holder of Clanconnell, from King James (form 1). The three early 17th-century forms (1–3) all contain -ee- in the final syllable, while -u- becomes regular from the mid-17th-century on. Lisnasure is not a church townland, so that the name is unlikely to have been *Lios na Siúr* "fort of the (religious) sisters" (15). The other suggestions by Dean Mooney are also based on the later forms. The Irish vowel *ao* is often anglicized *ee*, so that the early forms could represent *Lios na Saor* "fort of the craftsmen", in the same way as the neighbouring townland name of **Ballykeel** is here and elsewhere derived from *Baile Caol*. The spelling *-u-* is either a misreading from *-ee-* written without loops, or represents the "high back unrounded" pronunciation of Irish *ao* (ʌ), as in **Carnew** from Irish *Carn Aodha*, while [s] has become [ʃ] in pronunciation by analogy with *sure* in English. This pronunciation was indicated by the *OSNB* spelling *-shure*, but had developed by 1657, as attested by Petty's maps (forms 4, 5). It is also attested in 1762 (form 11) in the spelling *Lisnashure* from Waringstown graveyard. If the element *saor* had any connection with the family called *Mac an tSaoir* of **Ballymacateer**, it seems it was soon forgotten. Three "forts" were noted in 1834 (*OSNB*). There are now two raths in the townland, one beside Lisnasure school and a smaller one 500 yards south-east (*ASCD* 160, pl. 31; 166).

Taughlumny
J 1456

Teach Lomna
"Lomna's house"

1. Taghlomney (in Moyragh)	CPR Jas I 395a	1609
2. Taghlomney in Moyragh	CPR Jas I 190b	1611
3. Teaghlomny	Inq. Ult. (Down) §13 Jac. I	1624
4. Taghlomny	Inq. Ult. (Down) §96 Car. I	1640
5. Taghlomney, Dermot O'Lawry of	Wars Co. Down x 81	1641
6. Taughlomeny	Hib. Reg. Lr. Iveagh	1657c
7. Tonaghlomeny, al. third Toughlominy		
	Par. Map (Mooney) 219	17thc
8. Traghlomny, Geagrelagh and	Census 81	1659c
9. Taughlomony	BSD 74	1661
10. Taugh[?l]emney	BSD 82	1661
11. Toghlinnyn	Sub. Roll Down 273	1663
12. Taughlumney al. Taughlemony	ASE 61b 39	1666
13. (?)Gough or Gaughlomeny	ASE 112a 34	1667
14. Tullomony	Hib. Del. Down	1672c
15. Farraghlumny	Rent Roll Down 5	1692
16. Toughlemeny	Rent Roll Down 7	1692
17. Taughlomny	Reg. Magheralin (OSNB) E8.59	1715
18. Toughlomny	Map of Down (OSNB) E8.59	1755
19. Taughlumney	Wm. Map (OSNB) E8.59	1810
20. Toughlomney	Reg. Free. (OSNB) E8.59	1830
21. Taughalumny	Ir. Wills Index 70	1855
22. [Tagh-'loam-ney]	Mooney MS 220	1950c
23. Teach Lomna "Lumny's house" a druid's name	J O'D (OSNB) E8.59	1834c
24. Teach Luimnigh "house of the bare spot"	Joyce iii 568, i 50	1913
25. ˌtɔːxˈlọmnï	Local pronunciation	1992

The name Taughlumny appears to begin with *teach* "house", like **Taughblane** Hillsborough, and **Taghnevan** in Shankill Co. Armagh. The second element is more difficult. A suitable word phonetically might be *luman* "cloak, shield", gen. sing. *luimne*, which is used to explain two place-names in the *Dindsenchas* (*Met. Dinds.* iii 272, iv 328). Joyce suggested that the second element was *luimneach* "bare spot", the same word as the name of the city of Limerick (*Joyce* i 50, iii 568). This name, initially applied to the mouth of the Shannon, could be differently translated "cloaked, shielded (place)", using the etymology given in the *Metrical Dindshenchas* (Ó Maolfabhail 1990, 213b). However, one would expect *Teach Luimnigh* "house of the bare spot" to be spelled *-lumny* in the early as well as later forms, rather than *-lomny*.

Apart from a few late examples such as *Teach an Teampaill* "house of the church", *Teach na mBráthar* "house of the brothers", names in *teach* are usually followed by a personal name, most often that of an ecclesiastical founder or revered abbot (Flanagan 1981-2(c), 74). *Lomán* "little bare one" was a well-known saint of Portloman, once *Teach Lomáin*, in Meath (Walsh 1957, 141–3). A derivative form of the name *Teach Lománaigh* might give Taughlomny, with loss of a syllable (cf. 6, 7, 9, 12, 16). A saint called *Lomchú* "bare hound" was commemorated in the martyrologies on Jan. 9th, explained as "from Lomchú's church among the Ulaid", *ó Cill Lomchoin i nUlltoibh* (*Mart. Gorm.* 12; *Mart. Tall.* 6; *Mart. Don.* 11). However, even though the general area is plausible, a name like "Lomchú's house", *Teach Lomchon*, would require metathesis in the final syllable and loss of *ch* [x] to give the form Taughlumny. *Teach* with a saint's name would imply that the place so-named was a church, but no church site is known nor was Taughlumny church land. In 1609 it was part of the holding of Murtagh McTirlogh O'Lowry (form 1), and Terilogh Roe O'Lawry was resident in 1663 (form 11).

There are also places which begin with *teach* followed by the names of pagan supernatural figures, such as *Tech gCuilind* on **Slieve Gullion** Co. Armagh, *Tech Duinn*, the Bull Island off Bantry Bay, Co. Kerry (*Onom. Goed.* 622–627). As suggested by O'Donovan (form 23), there is a character called *Lomna* in early Irish mythology, who is noteworthy for foreknowledge and his severed head. The element *lom* "bare" in his name may well refer to this aspect of the story (*TBDD* §142). Taughlumny could preserve a literary reference as *Teach Lomna*, "Lomna's House", though the stories are not connected with this area.

Taughrane　　　　　　*Tóchar Rathain*
J 1058　　　　　　　　"causeway of bracken"

1. (?)Rónán Tigi Rónáin	CSH 707.916	1125c
2. (?)Skerogath	CPR Jas I 395b	1609
3. (?)Skerogath	CPR Jas I 190a	1611
4. (?)Skerogath	CPR Jas I 266a	1614
5. (?)Skerogath	CPR Jas I 309a	1616
6. (?)Skerogathe	Inq. Ult. (Down) §4 Jac. I	1616
7. Teaghrayne, townland of	Civ. Surv. x §73	1655c
8. Tagharan, the Gleabe being a sessiagh of land called	Inq. Down (Reeves1) 87	1657
9. Taghrane	Hib. Reg. Lr. Iveagh	1657c
10. Tony Eranny	Census 80	1659c
11. Tawghrany p'cell de Clonygillavorist	Inq. Ult. (Armagh) §7 Car. II	1661
12. Taughrane	BSD 72	1661
13. (?)Taughemney	BSD 82	1661
14. Taughrany sessiagh	Inq. Ult. (Down) §5 Car. II	1662

15. Taghran	Sub. Roll Down 273	1663
16. Taghrane	Brownlow LB 93	1669
17. Taghe Rany	Brownlow LB 100	1669
18. Taghran	Hib. Del. Down	1672c
19. Taughran	Reg. Magheralin (OSNB) E8.59	1715
20. Taughran	Vestry Reg. (OSNB) E8.59	1715
21. Taugheran	Sur. Brownlow Estate (OSNB) E8.59	1751?
22. Togheraine	Map Douglas Estate (OSNB) E8.59	1754
23. Taughrain	Map of Down (OSNB) E8.59	1755
24. Taugheraine	Ir. Wills Index 50	1769
25. Toughrain	Wm. Map (OSNB) E8.59	1810
26. Taughran	Bnd. Sur. (OSNB) E8.59	1830c
27. [Taghe'ran, Tagharaan]	OSNB Pron. E8.59	1834c
28. Teach Ráth**á**in "house of the small fort"	J O'D (OSNB) E8.59	1834c
29. ˌtɔxə'rɑːn	Local pronunciation	1991
30. ˌtaxə'rɑːn	Local pronunciation	1991

The forms for the name Taughrane only date back to the mid-17th century, but there was possibly an earlier name for the townland among the church lands held by William Worseley in 1609: *Skerogath* (1–5). By analogy with the spelling of other church lands (see **Drumneath**, Magherally) this might be Gaelicized *Scorógach* and referred to *corróg* "hip, angle" (*Ó Dónaill, Dinneen*; see **Glasker** Aghaderg, **Corrog** *PNI* ii 60).

The current name apparently begins *teach* "house". Taughrane is adjacent to the early 17th-century church lands, though not to the site of the medieval and later parish church. The 1657 inquisition of church lands makes clear that Taughrane was originally the name of the sessiagh which formed the glebe land. It is not clear when it became the glebe, and whether it already bore this name, although early names beginning *teach* "almost invariably" refer not to ordinary dwellings but to religious sites of some kind. A personal name usually forms the second element (Arthurs 1956–7, v 42; **Taughlumny** above). If this were an old name, despite the lack of early references, could it have been *Teach Rónáin* "Ronan (Fionn)'s house/church", with the local saint's name reduced to [rɑːn] by haplology? "Ronan of *Teach Rónáin*" appears in the lists of Irish saints (form 1). However haplology would be likely to preserve the long *o* of the first syllable of *Rónán* rather than the long *a* of the second, to give something like *Taughrone*. Taughrane was held by Brownlow by 1662 and was not listed as church land in the 19th century.

O'Donovan's suggestion makes the second element refer to a (little) fort, *ráthán*, a variant of *Ráithín*, Raheen, common as a townland name in the south of Ireland (*Joyce* i 276). The pronunciations recorded include a middle syllable (27, 29–30), which could represent the article: *Teach an Rátháin*. No monuments have been recorded by the Archaeological Survey (*ASCD, NISMR, PSAMNI*). Alternatively this name could be *Teach Raithin* "house of bracken", with an epenthetic vowel between the two elements. Perhaps a building from an earlier time had been overgrown. Although *raithin* "of bracken" is pronounced [reːn] in two townlands near Banbridge called **Tullyrain**, and in **Coleraine** (*Cúil Raithin, Tírechán (Bieler)* 160 §48), occasionally Coleraine is spelled *Cúil Rathain* (*Fél. Óeng.* 240, Nov. 11n), a form which may account for the difference in pronunciation here. The extra syllable recorded in some of the forms since 1657 (8, 10, 17?, 21–2, 24) as well as in the local pronunciation (27, 29–30) could indicate that the first element was *tóchar* "causeway", which has a variant *táchar* (MacNeill 1962, i 146; *PNI* v 158-9). *Tóchar Rathain* "causeway of bracken" seems equally likely.

Tullyanaghan　　　　　　　　　*Tulaigh Uí Anaithe*
J 1059　　　　　　　　　　　　　　"O'Hanhy's hillock"

1. Ballytullyannaghy (Sir A.)	CPR Jas I 396a	1609
2. Ballytullyhannahie (McBriddon)	CPR Jas I 395b	1609
3. Ballytullyhanahie	CPR Jas I 191a	1611
4. Ballytullyhannaghie (church)	CPR Jas I 191a	1611
5. Ballycullyanaghie (Sir A.)	CPR Jas I 235a	1612
6. vil' de Ballytulleannaghy	Inq. Ult. (Down) §13 Car. I	1629
7. Ballytullyhannaghie, half-vil	Inq. Ult. (Down) §30 Car. I	1632
8. Ballytullyhanaghie x2	Inq. Ult. (Down) §30 Car. I	1632
9. Tullyancher, towneland of	Civ. Surv. x §73	1655c
10. Tulli-ancher	Hib. Reg. Lr. Iveagh	1657c
11. Tollyamcor	Census 80	1659c
12. Tulliagher	ASE 61b 39	1666
13. Tulliaugher	DS (Mooney) 217	1666
14. Tulliana	Brownlow LB 93	1669
15. Tulliancher	Hib. Del. Down	1672c
16. Tullyanaghan	Reg. Magheralin (OSNB) E8.59	1715
17. Tullyanachan	Vestry Reg. (OSNB) E8.59	1715
18. Tullyanaghan par. Magheralyn	Reg. Deeds abstracts i §324	1722
19. Tullyanaghan	Sur. Brownlow Estate (OSNB) E8.59	1751
20. Tullyanaghan	Map Douglas Estate (OSNB) E8.59	1754
21. Tullyenoghan	Map of Down (OSNB) E8.59	1755
22. Tulaigh Eanacháin "Hill of the small marsh"	J O'D (OSNB) E8.59	1834c
23. Tulach Eunacháin "Hill above the mossy place"	Mooney 217	1950c
24. ˌtọliˈanaxən	Local pronunciation	1996

Tullyanaghan seems to be no longer well-known as a townland name and its early history is a problem. In 1609 the McBredan family held four church lands called *Ballytullyhannahie* and *Clondonellvickbriddon* as well as *Ballyemtyshewin* and Donaghcloney. The first two names look as if they might be Tullyanaghan and, from the final element, Ballymacbredan, which is next to it in this parish, but Ballymacbredan was listed under William Worseley's holding of church lands, and Sir Art Magennis had Tullyanaghan, which is also beside Clankilvoragh: *Ballytullyannaghy Ballyclonegillmurry* (*CPR Jas I* 395b, 396a). There are no other obvious lands to which the duplicate names could be applied. It cannot be proved from evidence collected so far, but the most likely interpretation is that Tullyanaghan was divided between Sir Art Magennis and the church. In 1632 (forms 7, 8) the inquisition on George Sexton shows he held the four McBredan townlands from the bishop, and by the 19th century these lands had no connection with the church. However in 1666 Sir George Rawdon held 59 acres of *Tulliagher* along with various other lands in the area which had once belonged to Sir Art (form 12).

The earliest forms, from the 17th-century patent rolls and inquisitions, all end in a vowel (forms 1-8), like *Ballytullyhanahie* in 1611 (form 3). A spelling of this kind recurs in the Brownlow rental (form 14). Late 17th-century forms, beginning with the *Civil Survey* barony bounds (form 9, *Tullyancher* 1655), end in *-r*. The Magheralin register (16) and sources thereafter show the modern form with final *-n*. This renders unlikely O'Donovan's suggestion that *eanachán* "little marsh" was the original final element, although the name may have been re-interpreted later. A possibility based on the early forms is the family name *Ó hAinbhith*, from the Armagh/Down border and Omeath (MacLysaght 1957, 173), in the form *Ó hAnaithe* whence O'Hanhy. In Cos Cork and Kerry there was also a diminutive form *Ó hAinbhtheáin* (Woulfe 1923, 550, 553).

Tullyanaghan contains Grace Hall, the seat in 1834 of the Douglas family who made their estate maps available to the Ordnance Survey (*Statist. Sur. Dn* 52; *OSNB* E8.59; form 20).

Tullynacross
J 1255

Tulaigh na Croise
"hillock of the cross"

1. Ballynacrosse	CPR Jas I 395b	1609
2. Ballynecrosse	CPR Jas I 190b	1611
3. Tullinecrosse half-td (Magherilin 6tds)	Buckworth (EA) 310	1622
4. Tullynecross, Magin of	Wars Co. Down x 81	1641
5. Tollenecros	Hib. Reg. Lr. Iveagh	1657c
6. Tullenggrosse	Census 80	1659c
7. Tollenecross	BSD 72	1661
8. Tullenecros	Hib. Del. Down	1672c
9. Tullynecross	Reg. Magheralin (OSNB) E8.59	1715
10. Tullynacross	Vestry Reg. (OSNB) E8.59	1715
11. Tullynecross	Map of Down (OSNB) E8.59	1755
12. Tullynacross	Wm. Map (OSNB) E8.59	1810
13. Tulaigh na croise "Hill of the cross"	J O'D (OSNB) E8.59	1834c
14. ˌtɒlnəˈkrɔːs	Local pronunciation	1991

Tullynacross probably took its name from the crossroads at **Moorefield**, where the old road between Magheralin village and Donaghcloney, known locally as the **Stonybatter**, crosses that between Lurgan and Dromore. However Tullynacross was a church townland, and there may have been an ecclesiastical termon cross or crosses now lost. One form (6) indicates that the final element may have been plural. Although not named on maps, there was a hill nearby called Moore's Hill. This may have been the *tulach* "hillock" of the first element, although the highest ground in the townland (70 metres) is near the eastern border, by the farm called Watties Hill. The Lagan forms the north-west boundary, over which the road to Lurgan crosses by Geehan's Bridge. The earlier forms have a different first element, *Bally*nacross, but can be distinguished by their church associations from forms of modern Ballynacross, the chief townland of the secular district of Glasquirin in Magherally.

OTHER NAMES

Dollingstown
J 1058

An English form

1. Baile Dhollainn/Dollingstown	Éire Thuaidh	1988

2. ˈdɔlïŋzˌtəun	Local pronunciation	1991
3. ˈdɔlənzˌtəun	Local pronunciation	1991

According to Atkinson, the village of Dollingstown on the road from Magheralin to Lurgan was named from the Reverend Boughey Dolling, "in 1651" rector of Magheralin (*Atkinson's Dromore* 212). In the 1830s the *Ordnance Survey Name-Book* gives forms from "the Rev. Boghey Dolling, rector of the parish" and the Memoir refers to the Glebe house as his residence (*OSNB* E8.59; *OSM* xii 110a), so that either there was a long line of Dollings or Atkinson's date is a misprint. Dollingstown is not shown on 18th-century maps and so probably did not exist at that date (*Sloane map*; *Harris Hist.* map). The road from Lurgan to Dollingstown is known locally as the Cottage Road.

Forge Bridge　　　　　　　　　An English form
J 1258

1. ðə ˈfɔːrdʒ ˈbrïdʒ	Local pronunciation	1991

The Forge Bridge is a road bridge over the Lagan just south of Magheralin village in the townland of Drumo and Drumcro. Presumably there was a forge at the bridge but I have found no specific references. The present Drumcro House was called New Forge House in 1833 (*ASCD* 361), and must be the reason for the road south to Donaghcloney being named New Forge Road on maps, although the older name **The Stonybatter** has survived in local use.

Gamblestown　　　　　　　　　An English form
J 1454

1. ˈgambəlzˌtəun	Local pronunciation	1991

The settlement of Gamblestown in the townland of Clogher preserves a local surname, probably of English origin. There are still Gambles in Steps Road, Magheralin, and Taughlumny Road, a little to the north.

Geehan's Bridge　　　　　　　An English form
J 1256

1. Gihon of Gihonsbridge	Ir. Wills Index 48	1801
2. bridges of... Gihon	Statist. Sur. Dn 24	1802

3. ˈgihənz ˈbrïdʒ	Local pronunciation	1991

Geehan's Bridge is a bridge over the river Lagan which carries the road from Lurgan to Dromore. The surname Geehan is derived by Woulfe from *Ó Gaoithín*, of Leinster and Connaught, although *Mac Gaoithín* was "almost peculiar to the Cos of Down and Donegal" (Woulfe 1923, 539, 365). Geehan is not a common surname in the north-east, from the evidence of the Northern Ireland telephone directory 1994, but was recorded near the bridge in 1801 (form 1).

Milltown　　　　　　　　　　　An English form
J 1255

1. ˈməltəun	Local pronunciation	1991

Milltown, a common and easily interpreted name, grew up from a mill village on the west bank of the Lagan in the townland of Edenballycoggill, near ponds and two streams which enter from the west. A pool in the river was used for baptisms.

Moorefield J 1256	An English form	
1. Moorefield a neat farmhouse	OSNB E8.59	1834c
2. 'muːrz 'fild	Local pronunciation	1992
3. 'muːr'fild	Local pronunciation	1992
4. ˌhɛzəz 'pəip	Local pronunciation	1992

Moorefield is the name given on the current Ordnance Survey maps to the stepped cross-roads where the old road called the Stonybatter over the Forge Bridge from Magheralin intersects with the road from Lurgan to Dromore. This important crossroads seems to be that referred to in the name **Tullynacross**, the local townland. The crossroads was described in 1834, when Moorefield, then "a neat farmhouse", was occupied by Mr Blizard (*OSNB*). The Moore element seems to have been a surname, and as well as Moorefield there was also Moore's Hill, probably the *tulach* of the townland name. However even Moorefield seems to have been overtaken in local usage by Hayes Pipes (3), the name given to Hayes' pipe-making factory beside the crossroads. The Hayes family were mill owners near Banbridge in the 19th century (*OSM* xii 126–7, 134; *Bassett's Down* 240–3).

Orange Lane	An English form	
1. ðï 'ɔrənʒ 'leːn	Local pronunciation	1991

The Orange Lane is a country road in the townland of Drumo and Drumcro connecting with Steps Road to the north east. There is no Orange hall but it is said to have been the route for Orange marchers from their assembly place beside the Lagan to a larger field owned by the Small family. The Orange Lane was also a popular walk for local people.

Redhill J 1556	An English form	
1. ˌrɛd'həl	Local pronunciation	1991

Red Hill is in Lisnashanker, due east of Sally's Hill in Gregorlough which has Simpson's Fort and a trigonometrical point on it. Red Hill or Red Hills seems to be used as the name of a farm, a road, and the summit over which the road passes. No reason is given locally for the name.

Shanker Burn J 1655	A hybrid form See **Lisnashanker** townland	
1. Shankersburn bridge	OSNB E8.59	1834c
2. Shankerburn Bridge (Greenoge)	OSNB E125	1834c
3. 'ʃaŋkər 'bɒrn	Local pronunciation	1992

Steps Bridge　　　　　　　　　　　　An English form
J 1358

1. ðə 'stɛps　　　　　　　　　　　　Local pronunciation　　1996

Steps Bridge is a bridge over the Lagan on the road east from Magheralin towards the Red Hill in Lisnashanker, carrying a road called Steps Road (OS 1:10,000 sheet 183). The bridge is now some distance above the water, with steps down to the river, but there was probably a ford with stepping stones here at one time, like Bateman's Steps further downstream in Feney townland.

The Stonybatter　　　　　　　　　　A hybrid form
J 1256, 1257, 1258

1. ðə ˌstonï'batər　　　　　　　　　Local pronunciation　　1991

The old name of the road from Magheralin to Donaghcloney, the Stonybatter, is not marked on maps but is well known in the locality. It crosses the Lagan by the Forge Bridge, and is marked as New Forge Road on the OS 1:10,000 map, sheets 182 and 183. It must have been an important routeway for a long time, as the crossroads where it meets the road from Lurgan to Dromore seems to have provided the -*cross* in the townland name **Tullynacross**. Irish *bóthar* "road" was borrowed as *batter* etc. in English, here qualified by the English adjective *stony*. "The Irish word *bóthar* was... borrowed into the vocabulary of the early English-speaking settlers, and was at one time in common use". Anglicized examples of *bóthar* can be quoted from the 14th to the 17th centuries (O'Rahilly 1930, 180–1).

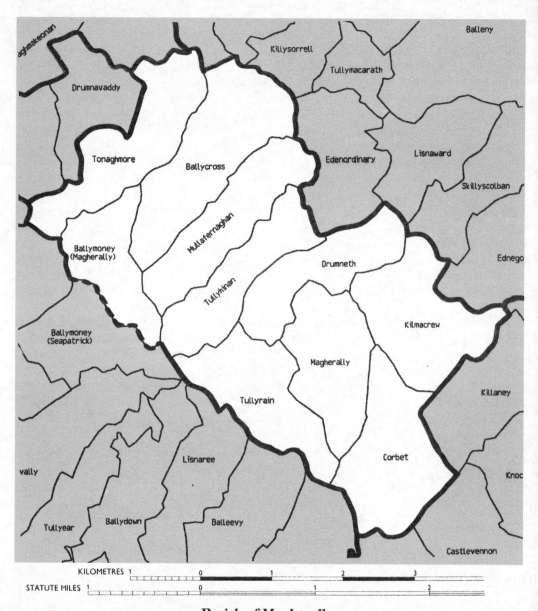

Parish of Magherally

Barony of Iveagh Upper, Lower Half

Townlands
Ballycross
Ballymoney (shared with Seapatrick)
Corbet
Drumneth
Kilmacrew

Magherally
Mullafernaghan
Tonaghmore
Tullyhinan
Tullyrain

THE PARISH OF MAGHERALLY

The parish of Magherally consists of 10 townlands, including part of Ballymoney shared with Seapatrick parish. Ballymoney is in the northern end of the parish, which formed the major part of the Magennis district of **Glasquirin** (Ballycross, Ballymoney, Mullafernaghan and Tonaghmore in Magherally; to the north Ballygunaghan in Donaghcloney and Drumnavaddy in Seapatrick; and detached to the west the Seapatrick townlands of Ballykeel and Drumnagally). The southern part of Magherally was church land (Corbet, Drumneth, Kilmacrew, Magherally townland, Tullyhinan and Tullyrain) adjacent to the church lands of Dromore and Garvaghy parishes.

In 1834 there seemed to be two crannogs in lakes in the north of the parish. Old forts were still numerous, there being 36 in the parish, while the highest point was "a fort in the townland of Kilmacrew, about 480 feet above the sea". The parish church on the summit of Magherally Hill, 450 feet, was "the most conspicuous object in this and the surrounding parishes". The older church site was 30 feet to the south, with no remains visible by 1834 (*OSM* xii 112–3).

On one of Bartlett's maps the parish name was used as an alternative for Iveagh: "*Evaghe Magenis his contrie, the ancyent name thereof Maghra-yllie*" (on cover, *Bartlett (Esch. Co. Maps)* 2). There is no further evidence for this, but a possible explanation lies in the various names in this part of Iveagh which recall the Ulster Cycle tales: Rossconor, Tirfergus, Loughbrickland, Clanconnell, Edentiroory. The ancient Ulster capital of *Eamhain Mhacha*, Navan Fort near Armagh, was given an Otherworld equivalent, *Eamhain Abhlach* "Eamhain of the apple trees", sometimes located on islands like the Isle of Man and Scottish Arran (Ó Cuív 1956–7). Magherally was also associated with apple trees, both by etymology and by continuing tradition (see below). Bartlett may have been told of a poem (which maybe also mentioned the inauguration site near Knock Iveagh included on his map) containing the poetic theory that Magennis' country was another *Eamhain Abhlach*.

Mr William Nat. McFadden, originally of Drumneth, helped with the pronunciation of names from a wide area round about.

PARISH NAME

Magherally	*An Mhachaire Abhlaigh*	
J 1647	"the apple-tree plain"	
1. (?)Colmani episcopi <Ablae>	Mart. Tal. 70 Sept 12	830c
2. Analle, ecc'ia de	Eccles. Tax. 106-7	1306c
3. Anyll	Reg. Dowdall §129 275	1422
4. Anvall	Reg. Swayne 100	1428
5. Awall	Reg. Dowdall §113 81	1546
6. T. Maghrallye	Bartlett Map (BM)	1600
7. Magherawly	EA 309 King's Bks	1601c
8. Evagh... the ancyent name		
Maghra yllie	Bartlett Maps (Esch. Co. Maps) 2	1603
9. Ballynemagheryhawly (from Bp)	CPR Jas I 395b	1609
10. Ballemagheryawlegh,		
Shane & Donell Oge O'Sheale of	CPR Jas I 195b	1610
11. Mt Aghle	Speed's Ireland	1610

12. Mahamly	Speed's Ulster	1610
13. Ballynemagherihauley (from Bp)	CPR Jas I 190b	1611
14. Magheriawley ch, 60a glebe for	CPR Jas I 191a	1611
15. Magherhawle, Manus O'Bryne of	Ulst. Roll Gaol Deliv. 263	1613
16. Ballynemagherie-Auley	CPR Jas I 266a	1614
17. Ballynemaghtrawloy	Inq. Ult. (Down) §4 Jac. I	1616
18. Ballynemagheriawlie	CPR Jas I 309a	1616
19. Magherawly 6 towns viz. Ballyenemaheriawly...	Buckworth (EA) 310	1622
20. Magharawly	Inq. Down (Reeves1) 85	1657
21. Magherally td	Hib. Reg. Lr. Iveagh	1657c
22. Magherallie par	Hib. Reg. Lr. Iveagh	1657c
23. Macherally	Census 78	1659c
24. Magherally	BSD 80	1661
25. Magherawly Parish	BSD 82	1661
26. (?)Rector de Magharowly	Trien. Visit. (Bramhall) 14	1661
27. Vicaria de Magherawly	Trien. Visit. (Bramhall) 17	1661
28. Rector de Magheradrawly	Trien. Visit. (Bramhall) 17	1661
29. Magherawly	Sub. Roll Down 274	1663
30. (?)Magherau[?]	Trien. Visit. (Margetson) 24	1664
31. (?)Magherel[?]	Trien. Visit. (Margetson) 25	1664
32. Magherivalley	Hib. Del. Down	1672c
33. Magherevally	Hib. Del. Ulster	1672c
34. Magherawly Rectoria	Trien. Visit. (Boyle) 46	1679
35. Magherawly vicaria	Trien. Visit. (Boyle) 47	1679
36. Magherawly	Trien. Visit. (Boyle) 48	1679
37. Magherevalli	Lamb Maps Co. Downe	1690c
38. Magheranly	Reg. Deeds abstracts i §387	1727
39. Maharally	Belfast News Letter (OSNB) NB107	1785
40. Maharally	Dubourdieu's Map (OSNB) NB107	1802
41. Church Bog, Green Bog	OSNB NB107	1834
42. [magh-er-'al-ly]	OSNB Pron. NB107	1834c
43. Machaire Abhla, campus pomorum "field of the apple trees/ apple	J O'D (OSNB) NB107	1834c
44. ˌmaxə'ralï	Local pronunciation	1991

The parish of Magherally appears as *Analle* in the papal taxation of 1302–6 (2). 15th- and 16th-century forms of the parish name also show the frequent spelling confusion between *u,w* and *n: Anvall, Awall, Anyll* (3–5). It seems clear that the original church name must have been *Abhaill* "apple-tree", as in the reference to "Colmán bishop of *Abhaill*" in the Martyrology of Tallaght for Sept. 12th (form 1), which does not necessarily refer to this place.

Magherally is now both the name of the parish and of the townland containing the parish church. In 1834 O'Donovan called Magherally townland "the finest townland probably in all the county Down", and reported the tradition that it was "said to have derived its name from... apple trees... in a field adjoining the graveyard" (*OSNB* 107). *Machaire* "plain" appears as part of the name in the 17th century (form 6). At the same period references to the townland begin to include *baile* and the article, as *Ballynemagherihauley* in 1609 (form 9).

This spelling apparently represents *Baile na Machaire Abhlai* "townland of the apple-tree plain", where the older name has been given an adjectival suffix, becoming *Abhlach* "abounding in apple-trees". *Machaire* is usually masculine (cf. **Magherabeg**, Dromore), so one might expect *Baile an Mhachaire Abhlaigh*. However it has been treated as feminine in **Magherabeg** in Drummaul and in **Ballymaghery** in Clonduff (*PNI* iv 53, iii 80). Without *baile* the spellings with final *-y*, *-ie* (6-8,14,19 etc.) indicate either that the name *Machaire Abhlach* (fem.) became fixed in its dative form, or that *Abhlach* was a collective noun, making the name *Machaire Abhlai* "plain of the apple-tree place". As often, it is not clear if *baile*, even followed by the article as here, is a genuine part of the name or an addition in English. If one ignored *Ballyne-* the name could be simply *Machaire Abhla* (43), "plain of the apple-tree", with *machaire* qualified by the original name *Abhaill*.

TOWNLAND NAMES

Ballycross   *Baile na Croise*
J 1449   "townland of the cross"

1. 8 towns in Ballynecrosse...		
Ballyrecrosse	CPR Jas I 395a	1609
2. Ballynacrosse	CPR Jas I 395b	1609
3. 8 towns in... Glassequirrin...		
Ballynecrosse	CPR Jas I 190a	1611
4. Ballynecrosse	CPR Jas I 190b	1611
5. Ballynecrosse	Inq. Ult. (Down) §34 Car. I	1632
6. (?)Ballinegrosse, O Magullaghan of	Wars Co. Down x 77	1641
7. (?)Ballynegross	Wars Co. Down x 78	1641
8. Ballycrosse	Census 78	1659c
9. Ballynecrosse (Tawnaghmore &)	BSD 82	1661
10. Ballycross	Wm. Map (OSNB) NB107	1810
11. Skelton's Cut	OSNB NB107	1834c
12. Baile Crois "town of the cross"	J O'D (OSNB) NB107	1834c
13. ˌbaliˈkrɔːs	Local pronunciation	1991

The elements if not the exact significance of the name Ballycross seem clear: *Baile na Croise* "townland of the cross". The presence of the article is confirmed by the 17th-century forms, but there is a problem as often in interpreting the "cross". The townland is not church land which might have had termon crosses. It is traversed by three minor roads, but there is no particular cross-roads within it, although near the middle road there are two forts overlooking the crannog in Patterson's Lake, and there are two further forts near the road after it crosses the bog into Tonaghmore. In 1611 (form 3) *Ballinecrosse* was one of "eight towns within the precinct of *Glassequirrin*", while in the 1609 schedule the same eight are said to be in *Ballynecrosse*, used as an alternative to the older district name (form 2). Ballycross thus seems to have been the chief townland within **Glasquirin**.

In the same two sources the name Ballycross also appears as a townland belonging to the Bishop of Dromore, but this can be identified as modern Tullynacross in Magheralin parish.

In the account of the 1641 wars (forms 6,7) *Ballinegrosse* is given as the address of several rebel "yeomen"; the following address is Tullyhinan, the next townland to the south of Glasquirin. However this form could refer to **Ballynagross** townland in Annaclone parish further south. The names of several of the Magennises of Clanconnell were cited as rebels (*Wars Co. Down* x 79-81), and their lands in Donaghcloney and Tullylish were surveyed by Petty and confiscated. Ballynagross also appears on Petty's maps (*Hib. Del.* Co. Down). Neither Ballycross nor any of the eight towns of Glasquirin was surveyed on Petty's maps, which indicates that the rebels were probably from Ballynagross in Annaclone.

Ballymoney
J 1348

Baile Muine
"townland of the thicket"

1. Muneleightgarire (in Ballynecrosse)	CPR Jas I 395a	1609
2. Munnielaghtgarvie	CPR Jas I 190a	1611
3. Monylettygarvye	Inq. Ult. (Down) xliv	1618
4. Monylettegarnye	CPR Jas I 305a	1623
5. Ballymony in Lower Iveagh	Civ. Surv. x §72	1655c
6. half td Ballimony [M'ally]	Par. Map (Mooney) 297	1657c
7. Ballymony (Macherally)	Census 78	1659c
8. qr of B:Mony (Sea Patrick)	Census 79	1659c
9. Ballymonylattgarvey (Sepatrick)	BSD 78	1661
10. Ballymonylatgarvy al. Tullyroshane half towne [M'ally]	BSD 82	1661
11. Ballymonylattgarvy [Seapatk]	S & D Ann. (Mooney) 297 (f. 30)	1661
12. Ballymonylatgarvy al. Tullyrashane half town	S & D Ann. (Mooney) 298 (33)	1661
13. Ballymony	Sub. Roll Down 273	1663
14. Ballymoney	Tombstone (OSNB) NB107	1786
15. Ballymoney	Wm. Map (OSNB) NB107, E11, E135	1810
16. the Blue Lough, a small marsh	OSNB NB107 M'ally	1834c
17. [Bally-'mo-ney]	OSNB Pron. E11,E135 Seapatk	1834c
18. Baile Muine "td of the brake"	J O'D (OSNB) NB107 M'ally	1834c
19. Baile Móna "townland of the bog"	J O'D (OSNB) E11,E135 Seapatk	1834c
20. Baile Muine "townland of the brake or shrubbery"	Mooney 297	1950c
21. Muine leaicht Uí Gharbheith "O'Garvie"	Mooney 297	1950c
22. lucht tighe/ leath-taobh Garbhaith	Mooney 297	1950c
23. ˌbalə'mọnï	Local pronunciation	1991

Ballymoney townland is divided between two parishes, the north-eastern part being in Magherally, the south-west in Seapatrick. The townland name is discussed here, with local details only under Seapatrick. In the early 17th century the name was *Munnielaghtgarvie*, and both modern divisions were probably included in Con Boy Magennis' precinct of **Glasquirin** along with seven other townlands of the parishes of Donaghcloney, Magherally and Seapatrick.

O'Donovan was undecided between *muine* "shrubbery" and *móin* "bog" (forms 18,19). The spelling *munnie* shows that the older form of the name consisted of *muine* "shrubbery, thicket" plus further elements, for which Dean Mooney suggested the Irish form *Leacht Uí Gharbheith* "O'Garvey's grave" (*Mooney MS* 297, forms 21, 22). However *Leacht* has genitive *leachta*, and the final element is more likely to be the personal name Gairbhíth, from *garbh-shíth* "rough peace" (Woulfe 1923, 537). *Gairbhíth rí H. nEchdach* "Garvey king of Uí Echach" was killed at the battle of *Craeb Telcha* (Crew Hill on the east side of Lough Neagh) in AD 1004 (*AU*). Although there might be some memorial where he died he would surely have been buried in consecrated ground. Similar names in Iveagh are *Ballylaghtdermod*, now **Tullyloob**; and **Letalian**, *Leacht Aillín*, in Kilcoo (*PNI* iii 111).

It is not clear if this Gairbhíth founded a family. According to Woulfe (1923, 537) there were two families called *Ó Gairbhíth* in the area, one "of the same stock as the Maguinnesses, who were chiefs of Uí Ethach Cobha", the other "anciently chiefs of *Uí Bhreasail*, in... Co. Armagh". They were chiefs of *Uí Bhreasail Macha*, and related to the O'Herons (Arthurs 1954(c), 48–9). MacLysaght treated the Armagh family as the principal sept, the Iveagh family second, adding that "the name is not uncommon today in Co. Down" (MacLysaght 1957, 156). The annals also mention chieftains called Gairbhíth in Co. Louth (*Conaille Muirthemne: AFM, AU* 848,875,908,1027 AD) where the name also gave rise to a surname.

The townland is divided in later 17th-century sources, where the 1659 *Census* has both *Ballymony* in Magherally and *qr B:mony* in Seapatrick, and the Book of Survey and Distribution has *Ballymonylattgarv(e)y* listed in both parishes, with an alias *Tullyrashane* (a half-town) under Magherally (forms 7–12). After 1661 the name is generally Ballymoney.

Corbet	*An Carbad*	
J 1845	"the jaw/boulder"	

1. Corbudd containing 2 tds	CPR Jas I 395b	1609
2. Corbud	CPR Jas I 190b	1611
3. Corbudd containing 2 tds	CPR Jas I 266a	1614
4. Corbudd containing 2 towns	CPR Jas I 309a	1616
5. Corbad 2 tds (M'lly 6 tds)	Buckworth (EA) 310	1622
6. Carbett	Civ. Surv. x §72	1655c
7. the Corbott	Civ. Surv. x §73	1655c
8. Corbet	Hib. Reg. Lr. Iveagh	1657c
9. Corbett	Census 78	1659c
10. Corbett	BSD 80	1661
11. Corbett	Sub. Roll Down 274	1663
12. Corbett	Hib. Del. Down	1672c
13. Corbud	Reg. Deeds abstracts i §387	1727
14. Corbit	Tombstone (OSNB) NB107	1793
15. Corbut	Wm. Map (OSNB) NB107	1810
16. Corbitt	Wm. Little (OSNB) NB107	1834c
17. the Corbet bridge	OSNB NB107	1834c
18. Eliza Hill, the Flow Bog	OSNB NB107	1834c
19. Corbit Milltown (Tullyconnaught)	OSNB E135	1834c
20. Corbit is a family name	OSNB E135	1834c
21. the Corbet Milltown (Tullyconnaught)	OSNB E135	1834c
22. "Cranes' Nest" (<corr)	OSNB NB107	1834
23. ['cor-bet]	OSNB Pron. NB107	1834c
24. Cor beith "round hill of the birch"	J O'D (OSNB) NB107	1834c

25. Corach Baidhte "submerged bog"	Mooney 301	1950c
26. An Carbad = Corbet Milltown	Éire Thuaidh	1988
27. Carbad, An	GÉ 45	1989
28. ðə ˈkɔrbət	Local pronunciation	1991

Corbet was a church townland belonging to the bishop of Dromore, said in some early 17th-century sources (forms 1, 3–5) to contain two towns. The second was probably **Tullyrain**, which is first named c. 1655. *The Corbott* is cited as part of the barony bounds of Lower Iveagh c. 1655, and the next name on the bounds is *Lough Feagh*, presumably Corbet Lough on the border with Garvaghy parish. It seems therefore that in native nomenclature Corbet was a noun with the article and that the lough had its own name. The surname Corbet appears in Co. Derry in the 17th century (*CPR Jas I*) and seems to occur in several place-names in Co. Down: Corbetts Hillhead in the parish of Clonduff and another in Dromara, Corbet Head in Rathmullan parish, and possibly Corbet Milltown beside the Bann in Seapatrick parish. The village of Corbet Milltown is close to the boundary with the townland of Corbet and on a stream running from Corbet lake, so despite the comment in 1834 that "Corbit is a family name" (OSNB E135) it is most likely to take its name from the townland.

The Irish word *carbad*, originally "framework, chariot" or "jaw", also appears in place-names. Hogan has three examples of it as an initial element, including *Carbad na nAbadh* burned in 1020 in the town of Armagh (*Onom. Goed.* 156; *ALC* i 20, where it is translated: "lit. 'the chariot of the abbots'"). Joyce discussed the element under "articles of manufacture", with examples which he interpreted as exercise grounds for the chariot warriors of early Irish literature (*Joyce* ii 175–7), including **Duncarbit** in Co. Antrim *Dún Carbaid* (*SMMD II* 43 §14). In most of these names *carbad* could be translated "chariot", but it seems it might also refer to a topographical feature, a "boulder" (*Ó Dónaill* 191). The pass between Fintown and Glenleheen in Co. Donegal is called *An Carbad* (O'Kane 1970, 83). The examples quoted so far preserve the original *a* vowel in *carbad*, but there is also the parish of Tullycorbet in Co. Monaghan, referred to in the 9th century as *o Thulaig Carpait* (*Mart. Tal.* 12, Jan. 26). Corrabul in Co. Limerick was originally *Baile an Charbaid*, translated "the town of the boulder" (Ó Maolfabhail 1990, 14).

Drumneth *Droim Niadh* (?)
J 1648 "ridge of the warrior"

1. (?)Dromma Faindle, Mael Tolaig ó	Mart. Tal. Sep. 14, 71	830c
2. (?)Druim Niadh i nUltaibh (Maol Tolaig ó)	Mart. Gorm. Sep.13n 176	1170c
3. (?)co beinn Slébhe Niadh	Buile Suibhne 68 §40	1350c
4. (?)Druim Niadh i nUltoibh, Maoltoligh ó	Mart. Don. Sep 13 p248	1630c
5. Ballynedrumeeth	CPR Jas I 395b	1609
6. Ballynedrumneth	CPR Jas I 190b	1611
7. Ballinedromny	CPR Jas I 266a	1614
8. Ballynedroneneth	Inq. Ult. (Down) §4 Jac. I	1616
9. Ballynedromneth	CPR Jas I 309a	1616
10. Ballydroometh (M'lly 6tds)	Buckworth (EA) 310	1622
11. Druminit	Hib. Reg. Lr. Iveagh	1657c

12. Drumoth	Census 78	1659c
13. Drummitt	BSD 80	1661
14. Drumneth	Sub. Roll Down 274	1663
15. Druminie	Hib. Del. Down	1672c
16. Drumneth	Reg. Deeds abstracts i §387	1727
17. Drumnaith	Ir. Wills Index 34	1771
18. Druimneth	Ir. Wills Index 74	1771
19. Drumneth	Wm. Map (OSNB) NB107	1810
20. Drumneath	Tombstone (OSNB) NB107	1826
21. Dronneth	Ir. Wills Index 96	1831
22. Drumneth	Wm. Little (OSNB) NB107	1834c
23. the Blind Lough (Drumneth)	OSNB NB107	1834c
24. [drum-'neth / drum-'neeth]	OSNB Pron. NB107	1834c
25. Druim Neid "Ridge of the nest"	J O'D (OSNB) NB107	1834c
26. Druim nIothach "Corn ridge"	Mooney 301	1950c
27. Droman Iothach "Corn ridge"	Mooney 301	1950c
28. drọm'niθ	Local pronunciation	1991
29. drọm'nɛθ	Local pronunciation	1991

Drumneth was church land, and can be distinguished from *Dromineigh*, also granted in 1611 to William Worseley, by being always held from the bishop. It appears that Sir Art Magennis acquired some lands originally belonging to the church, including **Enagh** earlier *Dromineigh* in Garvaghy parish.

The stress has been on the second syllable since at least the 1830s (form 24), but there are two different local pronunciations of the vowel (28, 29), reflected in the spellings *-neth* (29, used by older people now) and *-neath*. The first element is clearly *droim* "ridge", but the second (stressed) element is more difficult to determine. The current pronunciation with final *th* [θ] must have been restored from the anglicized spelling. *Th* appears at the end of various 17th-century anglicized spellings of church townlands, such as **Drumbroneth** in Dromore, **Fedany** in Garvaghy, and **Tullylish** townland, as an alternative to *gh* [x]. An original Irish *th* would have been reduced to [h] in pronunciation by 1600, while an original *dh*, once pronounced like *th* in English "this" [ð], would have become [ɣ] or been vocalized.

Since Drumneth was a church townland, Hogan suggested it might have been earlier *Druim Niadh i nUlltaib*, which was the provenance of a holy man called Mael Tolaig according to two of the Irish martyrologies (*Onom. Goed.* 367b; forms 2, 4). Another has *Druim Faindle* "ridge of the swallow" (1). *Druim Niadh* would mean the "ridge of the warrior" (*nia*, gen. *niadh*), and *i nUlltaib* "among the Ulaid" probably sets it in the reduced Ulster, east of the Bann. Pádraig Ó Riain, in suggesting that Mael Tolaig may have been the same as Mael Tuile of Bangor who died in AD 820 (*AU*), seems to accept the identification of *Druim Niadh* with Drumneth (Ó Riain 1990, 36). The story *Buile Suibhne*, which is partly set in this area (see the parish name of **Magheralin**), mentions a *Sliabh Niadh* "mountain of the warrior" (3), which could be connected in some way, although it more likely refers to the hill-top cairn in the Fews mountains called *Finncharn na Foraire*, attended by Cormac Conloinges, called *Nia an Chairn* "warrior of the cairn" (Toner 1991, 60n).

It is also possible that Drumneth has a different origin. O'Donovan and Mooney suggested second elements ending in *-d* or *-ch* (forms 25, 26–7). Maynooth and Louth, which now end in *th*, were *Maigh Nuadhad* and *Lughmhadh* in Irish (*Onom. Goed.* 528a, 507b), while the modern Irish forms are *Maigh Nuad, Lú* (*GÉ* 251, 249). Among 17th-century spellings locally, **Fedany** in Garvaghy was spelt *Foydeneth*, where the final syllable apparently represented Irish – *ach* or -*aigh*; and **Drumbroneth** in Dromore seems to derive from *Droim Bróncha*. The anglicized spelling *th* seems to have been used to indicate [h]. The initial *n*- in -*neth* or -*neath* need not have been part of the second Irish word but may have been prefixed by *droim*, an old neuter, since in the parish name of Dromara, *Droim mBearach* "ridge of heifers", *droim* has caused the nasalization of the following word. A name like *Droim/Dromán* followed by the the adjective *iothach* (forms 26, 27), or *Droim nEatha* "ridge of corn" (nom. *ioth*), could also have been anglicized Drumneth.

Kilmacrew	*Coill Mhic Riabhaigh*	
J 1747	"McGreevy's wood"	
1. Ballykillmagrewre	CPR Jas I 395b	1609
2. Ballykilmagrewie	CPR Jas I 190b	1611
3. Ballikilmagrewy	CPR Jas I 266a	1614
4. Ballykillmene[+illeg]	Inq. Ult. (Down) §4 Jac. I	1616
5. Ballykillmagrue	CPR Jas I 309a	1616
6. Ballykilmagrewy (M'lly 6tds)	Buckworth (EA) 310	1622
7. Killmagrye	Civ. Surv. x §72	1655c
8. Killmacreevy	Civ. Surv. x §73	1655c
9. Kilmacreevy	Hib. Reg. Lr. Iveagh	1657c
10. Kilmacrane	Census 78	1659c
11. Killmacreeny	BSD 80	1661
12. Kilmacnew	Sub. Roll Down 274	1663
13. Ballimccrivy	Hib. Del. Down	1672c
14. Killmacrew	Reg. Deeds abstracts i §387	1727
15. Kilmacrue	Belfast News Letter (OSNB) NB107	1785
16. Kilnecrew	Wm. Map (OSNB) NB107	1810
17. "wood or burial ground of red-haired man"	OSNB NB107	1834
18. Coill na craoibhe "Wood of the bush or wide spreading tree"	J O'D (OSNB) NB107	1834c
19. Coill Magh-Chraoibhe "of the famous tree"	Mooney 303	1950c
20. Coill Mhic Craoibhe "MacCreevy's wood"	Mooney 303	1950c
21. Coill Mhic Riabhaigh "Reavy's wood"	Mooney 303	1950c
22. 'kəlmə'kru:	Local pronunciation	1991

Kilmacrew was a church townland, one of the six townlands of Magherally listed by Bishop Buckworth in 1622 (6). The forms show considerable variation in spelling, probably mainly due to misreadings of *n,u,v,w,r*: *Ballykilmagrewie* (1), *Killmacreevy* (8), *Kilmacreeny* (11), *Kilmacnew* (12); and both the *OSNB* (17, 18) and *Mooney* (19–21) made several attempts at interpretation. There is no record of a church site in the townland and although there was an early bishop *Mac Ríme* (*CSH* 704.101) his provenance is unknown. The first element then may as well be *coill* "wood" as *cill* "church", both being equally common with surnames.

If the second part of the name is a surname, the possibilities are *Mac Riabhaigh* (Woulfe 1923, 401) or *Mac Craoibhe,* which is unattested. There are still people bearing the anglicized surname McGreevy in Banbridge nearby in Co Down. There is also a townland of **Tullymacreeve** in Forkill, South Armagh, but all but one of the 17th-century forms have *-mulcreeve* etc., indicating the surname *Ó Maolchraoibhe,* "common throughout east Ulster but generally anglicized as Rice" (Woulfe 1923, 608). *Ó Maolchraoibhe* may also have formed part of the townland name of **Rockmacreeny** in Kilmore, Co. Armagh. In 1744 *Cloinn Í Mhaolchraoibhe* were listed as dependents of the Clandeboye O'Neills, holding the area round Groomsport near Bangor in north Down, although O'Laverty noted that the O'Mulcreevys or Rices "were located along the Co. Down side of the Lagan" (*O'Neill Fun. Oration* iii 268–9). There is however no record of the element *maol* in the earlier spellings of Kilmacrew.

Magherally   *Baile na Machaire Abhlaí*
J 1647   "townland of the apple-tree plain"

See the parish name.

Mullafernaghan   *Mullach Fearnacháin*
J 1549   "hilltop of the little aldery place"

1. Ballyrallyarnoge (in Ballynecrosse)	CPR Jas I 395a	1609
2. Ballyvulliarnoge	CPR Jas I 190a	1611
3. Ballyvulyanoge	Inq. Ult. (Down) §34 Car. I	1632
4. Mullatornegah	Census 78	1659c
5. Mullaghfernegee	BSD 82	1661
6. Malapharnachan	Ir. Wills Index 51	1732
7. Mullaghfernaghan	Wm. Map (OSNB) NB107	1810
8. Mullaghfarnahan	Bnd. Sur. (OSNB) NB107	1830c
9. Mullyfarnan	Wm. Little (OSNB) NB107	1834c
10. Mullafernan	Clergyman (OSNB) NB107	1834c
11. ['Mul-lagh-'far-na-han]	OSNB Pron. NB107	1834c
12. Mullach Fearnachain "summit of the alder wood or grove"	J O'D (OSNB) NB107	1834c
13. Mullach Fearnachain "hilltop of the alder grove'	Mooney 305	1950c
14. Baile Mhullaigh Fhearnogaigh	Mooney 305	1950c
15. Mullach Fearnóige	Mooney 305	1950c
16. ˌmọlə'fərnəhən	Local pronunciation	1991

Mullafernaghan is first referred to as one of the eight towns of **Glasquirin** in 1609 (1). The early 17th-century forms are variants of *Ballyvulliarnoge,* later there is *Mullaghfernegee* (form 5), and ultimately the modern form with final *-n.* It seems that the composition of the name has changed, though not the meaning, based on *fearn* "alder". The earliest form seems to represent *Baile Mhullaigh Fhearnóige* "townland of the hilltop of the (little) alder". Later another possibility for the second element was *Fearnógach* "aldery (place)" (forms 4–5), and *Fearnachán,* another collective or diminutive formation, not attested in dictionaries, seems to be represented in the modern form. In the area the place is now called jokingly Money-fer-nuthin'. Mr Copeland of Donaghcloney had a story about the halt in the townland on the old Dromore - Banbridge railway line, which was near a mill-dam:

The station up here on the railway line was a place called Mullafernaghan and apparently there was a farmer close by it who had a lot of ducks. And they had a duck pond, so they didn't call it Mullaghfernaghan, they called it the Duck Hole. In fact if you had a gone into the Great Northern in Belfast and asked them for a ticket for Mullafernaghan, they would probably have said, "Oh, you're going to the Duck Hole".

Now my late uncle was a soldier in the First World War and he asked a porter in London, "I want to get a connection through to a place called Blackscull". "Right" he says "let me see". He said, "you'll get the boat train from here, from Euston and you'll get the boat to Belfast, across the city to the Great Northern Station, it's in Great Victoria Street. And you'll get a ticket", he says, "you could stop at Dromore, but", he says, "walking from Dromore, it's about four miles to Blackscull. But you could get closer to it", he says, "get within two miles of it. Aye," he says, "get a ticket to the Duck Hole!"

| **Tonaghmore** | *Tamhnach Mór* | |
| J 1350 | "big field" | |

1. Tawnaghmore al. Loughcurran (in Ballynecrosse)	CPR Jas I 395a	1609
2. Tawnaghmore al. Loughcurran	CPR Jas I 190a	1611
3. Tawnaghmore al. Loughkearan al. Loughcarran	Inq. Ult. (Down) §34 Car. I	1632
4. Tawnaghmore & Ballynecrosse	BSD 82	1661
5. Taghnaghmore	Sub. Roll Down 273	1663
6. Tonaghmore	Wm. Map (OSNB) NB107	1810
7. Tanamoa	Ir. Wills Index 73	1816
8. Pattersons Lake, Blind Lough	OSNB NB107	1834
9. Tanaghmore	Wm. Little (OSNB) NB107	1834c
10. [To-'nagh-more]	OSNB Pron. NB107	1834c
11. Tamhnach Mor "Great field"	J O'D (OSNB) NB107	1834c
12. Tamhnach Mór	Mooney 307	1950c
13. Loch Mhig Uidhrinn (Loughcurran)	Mooney 307	1950c
14. ˌtɔnəxˈmoːr	Local pronunciation	1991

The interpretation of the modern townland name is clearly *Tamhnach Mór* "big field". Tonaghmore is a long thin townland with a hill at the southern end. According to the earliest citations, from 1609 to 1632, Tonaghmore while still held by the Magennises was one of the eight towns of **Glasquirin** (forms 1–4). The same sources give *Loughcurran* etc. as an alias name (1–3). In the 1830s Tonaghmore townland contained two loughs called Pattersons Lake and Blind Lough (form 8). Patterson's Lake on the north-eastern boundary, which was then "a mere swamp... with a small pool of water in the centre", had contained an island "built on fir piles" which "consisted almost entirely of masses of bones of horses, sheep etc." destroyed while Lieut. G.A. Bennett watched in 1834 (OSM xii 112b;

ASCD 182–3). *Loughcurran* is presumably Patterson's Lough with the crannog, although it could also be Drumnavaddy Lough on the western bound with Seapatrick or Blind Lough on the extreme south. Drumnavaddy Lake, shown on the 1:50,000, covered 12 acres in 1834 and apparently also had a crannog: "It contains one of those islands which may be seen in nearly every lake or marsh and which is now dry in consequence of the lake having been partially drained" (*OSM* xii 112b Magherally, 124a Seapatrick; *ASCD* 184). A habitation site or crannog would have made both lakes important in the past.

Loughcurran was interpreted by Mooney as *Loch Mhig Uidhrín*, "McGivern's lough" (13), although there is no evidence for the first syllable of the surname. The family of McGivern were church tenants in the nearby parish of Annaclone in the early 17th century, and their name may also appear in the church townland of **Knockgorm** in Garvaghy parish (which see for Dromore clerics of the name). However Loughcurran is more likely to be *Loch Curráin* "lake of the swamp", from a diminutive of *currach* "marsh" (O'Kane 1970, 77, *PNI* v 181). Another possible word would be *Coirrín* "little hollow".

Tullyhinan	*Tulach Uí Aonáin*	
J 1648	"Heenan's hillock"	

1. Ballytollyhenvane	CPR Jas I 395b	1609
2. Ballytollyheuvane	CPR Jas I 190b	1611
3. Ballytollyhewnan	CPR Jas I 266a	1614
4. Ballytullyhewbane	Inq. Ult. (Down) §4 Jac. I	1616
5. Ballytollehewvane	CPR Jas I 309a	1616
6. Ballytullieheenane (M'lly 6tds)	Buckworth (EA) 310	1622
7. Ballytullichnvane	Buckworth (Atkinson) 127	1622
8. Tullyhunion, Jas Welsh of	Wars Co. Down x 76	1641
9. Tullyhinnon, Walsh of	Wars Co. Down x 78	1641
10. Tullyhunan	Civ. Surv. x §72	1655c
11. Tulleheauenan	Hib. Reg. Lr. Iveagh	1657c
12. Tollehennan	Census 78	1659c
13. Tolleheavenan	BSD 80	1661
14. Tullihenan	Sub. Roll Down 274	1663
15. Tolleavenan	Hib. Del. Down	1672c
16. Tullyheinen	Reg. Deeds abstracts i §387	1727
17. Tullyhinean	Wm. Map (OSNB) NB107	1810
18. Tullyhenan	Bnd. Sur. (OSNB) NB107	1830c
19. Tullyhinan	Wm. Little (OSNB) NB107	1834c
20. Tulaigh Sheanain "Sinane's hill"	J O'D (OSNB) NB107	1834c
21. Tulach Uí hEidhneáin "O'Hinane's hill" (Hynan, Heenan)	Mooney 307	1950c
22. ˌtolɪˈhinən	Local pronunciation	1991

Tullyhinan was a church townland in 1609, belonging to the bishop of Dromore. The first element is clearly *tulach* "hillock, mound" but the early spellings of the second element vary widely, *-heuvane, -hewnan, -henvane, -heenane* (forms 1–7, 1609–1622), either due to misreadings of *n* as *u,v,w*, or from uncertainty about the first vowel. The later forms regularly end in *-nan*, with some variation of the vowel. At any rate a surname seems a likely second element, with elision of *Uí*. The *-h-* might result from the final *-ch* of *tulach*, or from a final element beginning with lenited *c*.

MacLysaght (1964, 111) said there are Heenans (from Irish *Ó hAonáin*) in Co Down, while Woulfe (1923, 562,565) gave Heenan from *Ó hÉanáin*, sometimes anglicized as Bird, or *Ó hEidhneáin*, "a scattered surname". It is difficult to say which of these Irish surnames existed in Co. Down. There is a reference in 1605 to Henry *O'Hynane*, yeoman, of *Slught McONeile* in north Co. Down (*CPR Jas I* 86b). However in 1431 Michael *O'Henean* was priest of Dromore diocese, and vicar of Drumgath, and in 1435 Michael *O'Kaunan* (the same man according to Swanzy) was vicar (*Swanzy's Dromore: Reg. Octavian* 92, *Reg. Sweteman* 405). According to Woulfe, O'Keenan (*Ó Cianáin*) was "the name of a literary family in Ulster, who were hereditary historians to the Maguires; still numerous in that province" (1923, 462). This surname is much better attested. Cormac Oge *O'Kenan* was pardoned in 1602 among followers of Sir Art Magennis (*Fiants Eliz.* §6616); and in 1659 *O'Kenane* was a "principall Irish name" in Lecale, three baronies of Armagh, north Fermanagh, and south Co. Derry (*Census* 72; 27, 29, 139; 120; 139). Some of the learned and ecclesiastical family of *Ó Cianáin* may have been settled here on church land. However the spellings in *-heu* and *-hew* could be explained as attempts to spell the initial vowel [ʌ] of *Aonáin,* otherwise often spelled as *ee*.

It is possible that the surname Heenan, whatever its local origin, was at one time also part of the name of the church townland of **Balleny** in Dromore. Dougan Place in Tullyhinan was named after a local councillor in the 1950s.

| **Tullyrain** | *Tulaigh Raithin* | |
| J 1546 | "hillock of bracken" | |

1. Tullyran	Civ. Surv. x §72	1655c
2. Tulliraine	Hib. Reg. Lr. Iveagh	1657c
3. Tulliraine	Census 78	1659c
4. Tulleraine	BSD 80	1661
5. Tollycain	Sub. Roll Down 274	1663
6. Tulleraine	Hib. Del. Down	1672c
7. Tullyreine	Reg. Deeds abstracts i §387	1727
8. Tulaigh Rathain "Ferny hill"	J O'D (OSNB) NB107	1834c
9. Tulach Raithín "Ferny hill-top"	Mooney 307	1950c
10. ˌtolɪˈreːn	Local pronunciation	1991

There is no record of this name before 1655, when *Tullyran* appeared in the Civil Survey barony bounds of Upper Iveagh (1). It was church land in the early 19th century (*OSNB*), and in 1727 *Tullyreine* appeared in the will of Thomas Knox listing the lands he held from the See of Dromore. Apart from this addition these church lands are the same as given by Bishop Buckworth in 1622, where the "six townes" are five names, including "*Corbad* being two townes". Since Tullyrain borders on Corbet on the north-west it is probably the second town. Although none of the early forms preserves the two syllables of *raithen* "bracken", as in *Cúil Raithin*, Coleraine (*Trip. Life (Stokes)* i 166; *GÉ* 85) the etymology "hillock of bracken" seems clear enough. The forms should be compared with those for another town-land of the same name, five miles north-west in Tullylish parish.

OTHER NAMES

Blind Lough
J 1348, J 1648

An English form

1. Blind Lough (Tonaghmore)   OSNB NB107   1834

There are two Blind Loughs in the parish, named only on the OS 1:10,000 map, sheet 202, and apparently no longer so-called. One is in the south of Tonaghmore townland bordering Ballymoney, and the other further east between Tullyhinan and Drumneth. Lough Cock in Garvaghy is the anglicized form of the probable Irish original of the name, *Loch Caoch. Caoch*, "half-blind", seems to have been applied to a lake with rushes growing in it, covering the water. The idea that loughs are "eyes" appears in early Irish and Welsh literature, where two "loughs" seen moving in the distance are interpreted as the eyes of an approaching giant or warrior (*TBDD* §88; Thomson 1961, ll.267, 280).

Corbet Lough
J 1845

Loch Feá
"lough of rushes"

1. Loghfeagh   Civ. Surv. x §73   1655c
2. the Corbet Lough (Castlevennon,
   Tullyorior)   OSNB NB12   1834c
3. the Corbet Lough (Tullyrain)   OSNB NB107   1834c

4. ðə ˈkɔrbət ˌlɔx   Local pronunciation   1991

The Corbet Lough has taken its current name from the townland called the **Corbet** on its western side. *Loghfeagh* in the Civil Survey barony bounds between Upper and Lower Iveagh must be an old name for Corbet Lough, which is close to the Bann on the border with Garvaghy parish. There is another Lough Fea on the border of Cos Derry and Tyrone, which Hogan suggested might be *"Loch Fidaigh* in Ulster" (*Onom. Goed.* 498: Book of Fermoy 67, 49a). However, in both cases the forms which can be allocated without doubt indicate *Loch Feagh* "lough of rushes". *Feagh* (now *feá*) is the Ulster variant of Standard Irish *feag*.

Skelton's Cut
J 1550

An English form

1. Skelton's Cut (Ballycross)   OSNB NB107   1834c

2. ˈskɛltənz ˈkọt   Local pronunciation   1996

In 1834 it was recorded that a drain dug from Big Bog at the north end of Ballycross into Patterson's Lake, organized c. 1825 by Col. Fortescue, was called Skelton's Cut "from a person of that name having been killed by falling into it" (*OSM* xii 113a). At that period Skelton was a "prevalent name" in the parish (*OSM* xii 114a). Skelton's Cut is still marked at the north end of Ballycross, with a road named after it along the east side of Patterson's Lough. Further south in the north of Mullafernaghan there is a crossroads called Skelton's Lane Ends (OS 1:10,000 sheet 202).

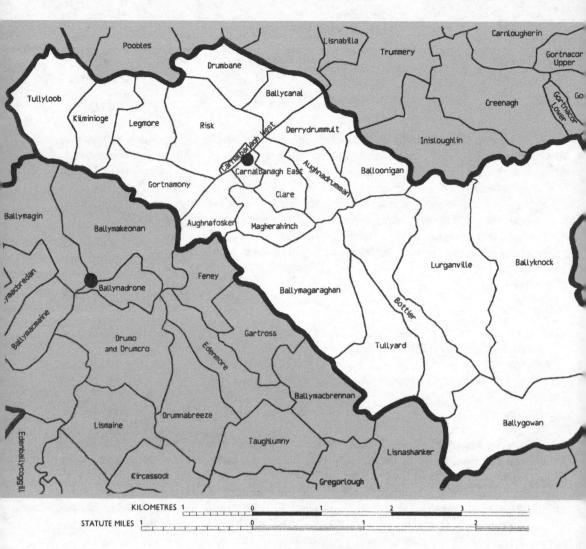

KILOMETRES 1   0   1   2   3

STATUTE MILES 1   0   1   2

Parish of Moira

Barony of Iveagh Lower, Upper Half

Townlands
Aughnadrumman
Aughnafosker
Balloonigan
Ballycanal
Ballygowan
Ballyknock
Ballymagaraghan
Bottier
Carnalbanagh East
Carnalbanagh West
Derrydrummult

Drumbane
Gortnamony
Kilminioge
Legmore
Lurganville
Magherahinch
Risk
Tullyard
Tullyloob

Town
Moira

THE PARISH OF MOIRA

The civil parish of Moira is situated in the north-west corner of Co. Down, although it does not include the large townland of Kilmore, linking Down with Lough Neagh, which belongs to the Armagh parish of Shankill. The 21 townlands lie across the river Lagan, which becomes the boundary between Cos Antrim and Down at the north end of the townland of Lurganville in the north-east of the parish, a mile and a half east of the village of Moira. There is no townland bearing the parish name. Moira village, like Magheralin a mile further south, is not built directly on the river, but on higher ground a mile from its western bank, occupying the small townlands of Carnalbanagh East and West.

Moira was only created a parish in 1725, when it was divided from the parish of Magheralin. Nevertheless the district name was already well known, largely because of the famous battle fought at *Mag Rath* in AD 637. The contestants were Congal *Caech* or *Claen* "one-eyed", the Dál nAraide over-king of east Ulster, with Domnall Brecc, king of Scottish Dál Riata, against the forces of the high-king Domnall son of Aed mac Ainmirech of the Uí Néill (Byrne 1973, 112–4). Congal, who may have hoped to regain the lordship of all Ulster (*CMR II* (FDG) 28, *CMR* II 218f), was defeated and killed. This event is noted in the Irish annals (forms 1–6; *AU* 637, *A. Tigern.* 637, *AFM* 634, *Chron. Scot.* 636 AD) and king-lists (*LL* 11.5796, 5923: forms 16, 17), in an earlier passage, from Cumméne, incorporated into Adomnán's Latin life of St Columba (form 7 *Adomnán* 108a p.47; Byrne 1973, 257), and made much of in early Irish literature: the tales "Feast of the Fort of the Geese", "Battle of *Mag Rath*", and the "Madness of Sweeny" (*Fled Dún na nGéd, Cath Maige Rath, Buile Suibhne*). The first two were edited together (*CMR* II), but there are two versions of *Cath Maige Rath*, one much earlier than the date of the manuscript (*CMR I*).

Some doubt has been expressed whether the place-name is correctly located, mainly because in the later version of the "Battle of *Mag Rath*" a foster-son of the Irish king Domnall is sent to join him in the battle from *Tír Ó mBreasail* in *Oirthear*, Orior, by way of *Iobhar Chinn Trágha*, Newry (*CMR* II 274–7). J.W. Hanna, taking *Tír Ó mBreasail* as "*Clann Breasail* near Lurgan... only a few miles east", thought that the reference to Newry "twenty miles south-south-west" was the clearest indication that *Mag Rath* must be nearer Newry, and suggested the area of the Crown Mound, with its traditions of ancient battles and bones dug up in the fields (Hanna 1856, 57, 59, 61). The editor of the story, John O'Donovan, admitted that various minor names mentioned in the battle tale were no longer known in the area of Moira (*CMR II: Tulchán na dTailgenn* "hillock of the clerics" 118-9n, *Daire an (Fh)latha* "oakwood of the prince" 174n, *Cnocán in Choscair* "hill of the slaughter" 216n, *Áth an Ornaimh* "ford of the *Ornamh*" 226). However, J. Arthurs, while accepting Hanna's main point, thought some of these names "open to the suspicion of being fictions of the story-teller" and thus unlikely to be found in either area (Arthurs 1952-3(a), 9). Dean Mooney finally pointed out that the family of *Uí Breasail* were indeed located in Orior and not in *Clann Breasail* around Lurgan which was a different place (**Clanbrassil**, Mooney 1952-3(b), 12; 1954(a), 6–10). O'Donovan had also noted the 14th-century association of *Magh Rath* with the family of *Uí Labhradha*, the O'Laverys of Moira, in his edition of Seaán Ó Dubhagáin's poem on the rulers of the north of Ireland (*Topog. O'Donovan* 38, notes xxvi, xxviii; *Topog. Poems* ll.421–2, also 376). It thus seems clear that all the events of the battle had long been associated with this parish, which is on the course of the old routeway called *Slige Midluachra* between Newry and the north coast (Hamilton 1913–4; Lawlor 1938, map).

After publishing his edition of the tale, in 1842, John O'Donovan received a letter from a Moira antiquary, John Rogan, giving further local traditions of the battle (*Topog. O'Donovan* xxviii). O'Rogan is described in the Ordnance Survey Letters (*OSL Dn* viii 19–21). Apparently the townland of **Carnalbanagh** "the Scotsmen's cairn" was associated with the burial of Scots killed at the battle (*Dublin University Magazine*, Feb. 1848; quoted Mooney 1952-3(b), 13; Hanna 1856, 58). However, such local knowledge is not apparent in the written versions of the "Battle of Magh Rath". Carnalbanagh is not mentioned, and "red-pooled" *Magh Rath* was equated with "wooded" *Magh Comair* (*CMR* II 110, 226). Although this was taken up by Reeves (*EA* 369; *Adomnán* 201), it is more likely to be a confusion caused by lack of local knowledge, since *Magh Comair* "plain of the confluence" is another well-known plain in Dál nAraide, that is (with change of stress) modern **Muckamore**, some miles north at the north-east corner of Lough Neagh (*EA* 197).

Unlike the "Battle of Magh Rath", the place-names in the "Madness of Sweeney" seem to show considerable local knowledge of the territory of Dál nAraide (in which it locates *Magh Rath*) although the hero is unhistorical. Suibhne, called "king of Dál nAraide", is said to have quarrelled with St Ronan who was marking out a church called *Cell Lainne*, most likely at nearby **Magheralin**. Suibhne then heard a shout summoning him to the battle at Magh Rath, the place where he had already killed the king of Uí Faoláin. St Ronan followed to try and make peace, but cursed the unrepentant Suibhne, who fled in madness back to the area of Rasharkin in Co. Antrim, where his own royal residence was (*Buile Suibhne* §§3, 4, 7, 12, 26).

There is a reference to *Magh Cobha* in one of the poems attributed to Suibhne, but none of the stories associate *Magh Rath* with *Uí Echach Cobha* i.e. Iveagh, although the traditional date for Eochu, the eponymous ancestor of the tribe, is at least a century earlier, and Uí Echach would have become important by the time the tales of the battle were written. References to the clearing of Magh Rath in the "Age of the World" year 3549 (*AFM; LL (L. Gabála)* l.1916) did place it in Iveagh, and it was called "*Rothmag* in the district of *Cuib*" in a poem in the *Book of Invasions* (forms 1,15,28). A medieval tract on Tara (*STTemra* §26) described the good things from the east of Ireland as coming from both plains: *a Cuib... a Maig Roth*. Máire Herbert thinks that the political background for the composition of the story giving the causes of the battle of *Magh Rath* (*CMR II* (FDG), dated from its language to the early 12th century) was the battle at *Magh Cobha* in AD 1103, another link between *Magh Cobha* and *Magh Rath* (Herbert 1989, 75–87).

The church of Rónán Finn, however, was said both to be in the lands of a tribe called *Corco Ruisen* in *Mag Rath* (*Corco Ruisen i Muig Rath, is fuiri ita Land Ronain Find*: MacFirbis' genealogies *L.Lec.* 88v col.b 14), and to be in Iveagh (*i nUib Echach Ulad, Descendants Ir* xiv 111; martyrologies: *Fél. Óeng.* 134n, *Mart. Tal.* 45, *Mart. Gorm.* 102n, *Mart. Donegal* 137; *Onom. Goed.* 295b). This seems to be the church of the parish of **Magheralin**, from which Moira was later divided. **Kilminioge** in Moira, a name which may preserve a pet form of the name of saint Rónán Finn, was no longer church land or contained a church, and the church to serve the new parish of Moira was built in the village in the townland of Clare (*OSM* xii 118a).

As already mentioned, the family of O'Lavery, *Ó Labhradha*, have a long history in the district of Moira. The origins of the family are unknown. In 1039 a son of Flaithbhertach Ó Néill was killed by *Uí Labhradha*, understood by O'Donovan as the family in Iveagh (*AFM* ii 836). Another possible connection is *Etru mac Lobradha*, "chief of the *Monaig*, a pillar of glory of Ulaid", who died in penitence in 1056 AD (*AU (Mac Airt)* 492). The tribal group called *Monaig*, from whom Fermanagh is named, were mostly around Lough Erne, but there were others in east Ulster (Walsh, P. 1960, 2–8). In the Ulster genealogies Labraid son of Amalgaid, whose descendants might be called *Uí Labhradha*, was the latest representative of

Clann Ruairc of the *Monaig* (*Descendants Ir* 74, *L. Lec.* 88v c 12). The Book of Lecan describes *Monaich Ulad* "the Monaig of (east) Ulster" in the text which locates *Corcu Ruisen* in *Magh Rath* (*L. Lec.* 198 = 88v a 50). However a Labraid son of Cairpre son of Ollam Fótla of Dál nAraide was the ancestor of *Cland Labrada* who were called *rígrad Ulad* "the royal house of Ulster" (*Descendants Ir* xiii 320). Since this Labraid is far more remote in the pedigree than Rudraige of the Ulster Cycle connection or Fiacha Araide, the regular eponymous ancestor, this may be a piece of special pleading by *Uí Labrada*.

The O'Laverys remained prominent in the area in the 16th and 17th centuries, when the name was anglicized as both O'Lavery and O'Lawry (pardons in *Fiants Eliz.* §§6616, 6714, 6724). In the 1609 Schedule of Iveagh the western half of the modern parish was held as a freehold by Murtagh McTirlogh O'Lawry *of Moyragh*: "the 14 sessiaghs" of Kilminioge, Legmore, Gortnamony, Aughnafosker, Risk (2 sessiaghs), Drumbane, Ballycanal, Carnalbanagh east and west, Clare, with Feney, Drumnabreeze, Gartross and Taughlumny south of the Lagan in the parish of Magheralin. The chief seat of the O'Laverys was in the townland of Risk, on the north side of the modern village of Moira (*CPR Jas I* 395b, 190b). Members of the family accused of rebellion in 1641 had their addresses in *Moyragh* and the various townlands, and *O Lawry* was still one of the principal names in Lower Iveagh in 1659 (*Census* 81). In the early 19th century Laverys were "very numerous, especially round Magheralin and Moira"; John O'Donovan was also told that Lavery and *O'Lowry* were different names, which is unlikely (*OSL Dn* 43). Lavery was one of three "most numerous names" in the parish of Aghagallon in 1838 (*OSM* xxi 18a). At this period there were different epithets, including *Baun-* ("white") -Lavery, *Roe-* ("red") -Lavery and *Trin-* ("strong") -Lavery, to distinguish the different branches of the name. None of them would recognize any relationship with each other, while Trin-Lavery was often "translated" into Armstrong (*Surnames Matheson* 7–8). Bann-Lavery still survives as a surname. As a place-name, there was a Lavery's Bridge over the Lagan Canal (*OSM* xii 119a), which is now replaced by Nut Hill Bridge over the motorway, though the road leading to it is still called Lavery's Bridge Road (OS 1:10,000 sheet 183).

The eastern part of Moira, also stretching across the river, was held by Sir Art Magennis of Rathfriland: Tullyard, Bottier, Ballymagaraghan, Magherahinch, Derrydrummult, Aughnadrumman, Balloonigan, with Ballymacbrennan, Gregorlough and Edenmore in Magheralin (*CPR Jas I* 396a). These 10 names are called half-townlands in his grant (*CPR Jas I* 235a), so that it appears that all the land denominations in this north-west corner of Co. Down were less than the usual size. Of the townlands already listed in Moira, 13 are still 202 acres or smaller. All the Magennis townlands and three of the O'Lavery townlands were acquired by Sir George Rawdon (*ASE* 61b §39, 1666 AD).

The three furthest east townlands, Ballygowan, Ballyknock and Lurganville, were part of the MacRory Magennis territory of **Kilwarlin**. They passed in 1611 to Moses Hill (*Inq. Ult. (Down)* §25 Car. I), and are all 500 acres or more. According to O'Laverty, before 1725 they had been part of the parish of Cromlin (Hillsborough) in the diocese of Down, rather than of Dromore (*O'Laverty* ii App.lx). In 1834 they were held by the Marquis of Downshire, and all the other townlands of the parish by Sir R. Bateson (*OSM* xii 120–1). After 1840 the eastern end of Moira parish was incorporated into the new Church of Ireland parish of **Kilwarlin**. The first Ordnance Survey made use of a survey of Bateson's estate done in 1810 (*OSNB*).

The *towne of Moyrath* was first mentioned in 1692 (*Rent Roll Dn*), but may be intended by the 1659 *Census* (form 54), which included *Moyrough*, with 36 prosperous inhabitants, among the townlands of Magheralin. A planter house was built here in 1651 (*ASCD* 417 site 416; *CSP Ire.* 1647–60, 385).

PARISH NAME

Moira   *Maigh Rath*
J 1560   "plain of streams/wheels" (?)

1. Magh Roth la hUibh Eachdach	AFM i 38 (prehistoric)	3549
2. cath Maighe Rath	AFM i 252	634
3. cath Maighe Rath	Chron. Scot. 84	636
4. Bellum Roth	AU (Mac Airt) 118	637
5. cath Muighe Rath	A. Tigern. 183	637
6. Cath Roth	AI 90	639
7. in bello Roth	Adomnán 108a	700c
8. da cath i Maig Roth	B. in Scáil xx 226 §32	900c
9. Sluag fri rōi Roth	B. in Scáil xii 238 §64	900c
10. Adhaigh dhuin im Muigh Rath redh	Circ. of Ireland 30 l.33	942
11. (?)do laech Muman a Muig Ráth	Lebor na Cert 131	1050c
12. co hIeth co Roth	TBC (Rec. I) l.3455	1100c
13. Trí meic Fiachna, Trí ruirig Roth	TBC (Rec. I) l.3778	1100c
14. Eocho mac Dáre din Róth (:lóc)	LL 21b/i l.2650 LG (verse)	1160c
15. Mag Roth la hU Echach Coba	LL 16a/i l.1916 LG	1160c
16. Congal Caech... i Cath Roth	LL 41c/i l.5796	1160c
17. (?)i Cath Roth	LL 42a/i l.5923	1160c
18. comaidm catha Raith/Roith roruaid	Trip. Life (Stokes) ii 538 §39	1160c
19. Cath Maige Roth	Trip. Life (Stokes) ii 516 l.29	1160c
20. cath ar Muig Roth (:moch)	Clann Ollaman 64 §20	1165c
21. Tulach na nArm re nabar Magh Rath		
	Acallam (Stokes) l.2939	12thc
22. a Muig Rath (Dal nAraide)	Descendants Ir xiv 111	1200c
23. Mhuigh Rath, o	Topog. Poems l. 421	1350c
24. Magh Rath	Buile Suibhne §§4,7,8,20,22,27ff	1350c
25. Magh Rath (:cath, :dath)	Buile Suibhne §§6,16,75 (verse)	1350c
26. a cath Roth (:moch)	Buile Suibhne §75 (verse)	1350c
27. a Maig Roth	ST Temra §26	1392c
28. Rothmag a crích Coba cian	L. Gabála v 430, poem xci	1397c
29. co Dun Roith co Leidhe	Cath Aen. Macha §5	14thc
30. Cath Muigi Rath andso	CMR I 232	1392c
31. Macan docing sligi rath/ imma tuarad lechta roth	CMR I 240 ll.139-40 (verse)	1392c
32. Macan docing sligi roth	CMR I 240 l.144 (verse)	1392c
33. (?)cath roth	CMR I 242	1392c
34. tucait Catha Muige Rath	CMR II 86 (FDG)	1392c
35. Cath Muighe Rath	CMR II 90	1392c
36. Cath Mhuigi ruadh-linntige Rath	CMR II 110,168	1392c
37. Magh Comair risi raiter Magh ruaid-lintech Rath	CMR II 226	1392c
38. Mag cuanach Muigi Ratha (:latha)	CMR II 174 (verse)	1392c
39. Bid Mag Rath o'n roth-mal sa	CMR II 174 (verse)	1392c
40. for Muig Rath	CMR II 210,312	1392c
41. ar Cath Muige Rath	CMR II 260, 270	1392c

42. Magh Rath x3	CMR II 276	1392c
43. Ar Muig Rath na ríghraidhe	CMR II 304 (verse)	1392c
44. Corco Ruisen i Muig Rath,		
is fuiri ita Land Ronain Find	L.Lec. 88v b14	1397
45. cath Muige Rath x2	Trip. Life (Stokes) ii 552 l.30	1400c
46. Dúin Róith 7 Tulach na nArm	Cogadh F. C. 408 §3	1715
47. do sgélaibh Catha Muighi Rath	CMR II 321	1720c
48. Myra	Fiants Eliz. §4218	1583
49. Moyragh	CPR Jas I 395a	1609
50. Moyragh, Mortagh McTirlagh		
O'Lawrie of	CPR Jas I 195b	1610
51. Moyragh	CPR Jas I 190b	1611
52. Moyragh	CPR Jas I 373b	1618
53. Moyragh	CPR Jas I 576b	1624
54. Moyrough	Census 81	1659c
55. Moyrath, Towne of	Rent Roll Down 6	1692
56. Moyra	Maps Down (Mac Aodha) 68	1712
57. Moyragh	Deeds & Wills (Mooney) 215	1717
58. Moirah [inscrip.]	OSM xxi 30b	1719
59. Moyrah	Harris Hist. map	1743
60. Moyra, Moyrah	Harris Hist. 83, 103	1744
61. Moyra	Map of Down (OSNB) E4	1755
62. Moira	Maps Down (Mac Aodha) 68	1776
63. Moira	Wm. Map (OSNB) E4	1810
64. Moira	J O'D (OSNB) E4	1834c
65. Magh Ráth "plain of the fort"	OSNB Inf. E2	1834c
66. Magh rath "plain of prosperity"	J O'D (OSNB) E4	1834c
67. Magh Ráth	Post-Sheanchas 97	1905
68. Maigh Rath	AGBP 118	1969
69. Maigh Rath/Moira	Éire Thuaidh	1988
70. Maigh Rath	GÉ 134	1989
71. 'marə	Local pronunciation	1991
72. 'maïrə	Local pronunciation	1991
73. 'mɛːrə	Local pronunciation	1991
74. 'mo̤irə	Local pronunciation	1992

As mentioned above, Moira was originally a district name, not corresponding exactly to the parish. The name was well-known in Irish (forms 1–47), and probably more could be added. The first element is *magh* (*má*) "a plain", probably anglicized from the dative or locative form *maigh*, which has more recently been used as the nominative. The traditional interpretation of the rest of the name has been either *Magh Ráth* "plain of forts" or *Magh Rath* "plain of prosperity" (John O'Donovan: *Circuit of Ireland* 31; cf. forms 65–6). Several forts such as Rough Fort, Pretty Mary's Fort, survive near the village of Moira. Atkinson assumed the name meant "plain of the fort" (*Atkinson's Dromore* 216), but this would require the second element to be spelled *rátha*, and there is little evidence in the Irish sources for a final vowel, the only example being *mag cuanach Muigi Ratha* "the beautiful plain of Magh Rath", to rhyme with the artificial place-name *Daire in [Fh]Latha* "oakwood of the prince" (form 38: *CMR II* 174n–5). Likewise the internal vowel of *Rath* is rarely marked long, and a short vowel is confirmed in verse, where the name is frequently, and predictably, made to rhyme with *cath* "battle" (*Buile Suibhne* §6 v4, §16 vv1, 13; *CMR II* 210, 312). Form 14 has been identified with *Magh Roth* (i.e. Moira) by Macalister (*L. Gabála* v 463 l.3560), and other copies of the poem do not mark the vowel as long: the patronymic *mac Loc* among the early kings of Emain may have been confused with the name *Lóch* (*CGH* 157.3) and the accent added to both rhyming words. *Ráth* "fort" is thus excluded. If the second element were *rath* "prosperity", the form would have to be genitive plural, an unusual formation unless *rath* could be understood in a more concrete sense, e.g. "of bounties".

Many of the early forms, up to the 14th century (1, 4, 6–9, 12–17, 19, 20, 26–9, 33), give the vowel in the second element as *o* not *a*, in some cases confirmed by the rhyme-scheme used in verse (20, 26), so that *ar Muig Roth* "at Moira", and *a cath Roth* "from the battle of Moira", rhyme with *moch* "early" (*Clann Ollaman* 64 §20; *Buile Suibhne*: §75 v9 p140 top). The ordinary meaning of *roth* is "wheel". The earlier version of the "Battle of Magh Rath" includes the phrase *cath roth* in a verse predicting that the battle will be a story in the future (form 33). *Cath roth* is translated by the editor, Marstrander, as "*renowned* battle" (*CMR I* 242; *DIL*), but it seems to me that it is the title of the story "Battle of Magh Rath". Some of the earliest sources use *Roth* without *magh* as the place-name (4, 6, 7, 9, 12, 13; cf. *Magh Cobha*, earlier *Cuib*, **Iveagh**). Almost all these examples are in the genitive, which makes it likely that the element is genitive plural (Appendix A §16), although it appears to be used as accusative singular in form (12).

A poem in the later version of "The Battle of Magh Rath" (form 39) gives a derivation of the name, translated by O'Donovan, "It shall be called *Magh Rath* from this prosperous battle, the plain over the brink of the ford" (*CMR II* 174). However the word *rothmal*, translated "prosperous battle", has since been interpreted as a compound of *roth* "wheel" and *mol* "shaft", describing the revolving machinery of an early watermill, and thus developing the meaning "whirling movement", which was also attributed in early Irish literature to warriors in the frenzy of battle (*DIL*). The association with *rothmal* supports the idea that the name was originally *Mag Roth*.

The earlier version of the story contains a prophetic verse dialogue between king Congal and his fool which appears to play on the two spellings *roth* and *rath*, or *Roth* and *Rath* (*CMR I* 240 l.139: forms 31–2). It begins *Macan docing sligi rath*. The first couplet is translated by the editor Marstrander as "A boy walks the road of raths/ around which were dug the graves of *roth*" (*CMR I* 241). Marstrander did not translate *roth*, but the phrase *lechta roth* is reworded as *lechta loech* "graves of heroes" in the second couplet (l.145) and there is some evidence, despite the reinterpretation of *rothmal* above, for *roth* as an honorific term (*DIL*). However *rath* in the first line is corrected by the king to *roth*, this time translated "A boy walks the road of wheels".

The place-name element *roth* has been discussed by J.B. Arthurs (1952–3(a), 10–11). The meaning "wheel" had been suggested in names like *Rouen* in France, which seems to be a parallel formation to *Mag Roth*, as *Rotumagos* "wheel plain". Arthurs thought this unlikely, and quoted Welsh and Gaulish names which suggest that *roth* could be connected either with the Irish verb *rethid* "runs", or with Welsh *rhyd* "ford" and Latin *portus* "harbour". If *Mag Roth* once meant "plain of rivers" or "fords" this might provide one explanation why it was given *Magh Comair*, "plain of the confluence" as an alias name (37; Arthurs 1952–3(a), 10; *CMR II* 110, 226; noted *EA* 369; though I doubt if the name was still "understood"). Apart from the river Lagan, there is a stream in Tullyard, ponds in Risk and in Legmore, and probably a stream preceding the Lagan canal ("the going of the water called the ford of *Hakar*" between Aghalee and Blaris, *Fiants Eliz.* §4327). A "small stream" formed the chief part of the boundary between Aghagallon and Moira parishes (*OSM* xxi 26b), and several streams join the Lagan near the old ford at **Spencer's Bridge**. On the other hand this area was at the meeting of routeways north and south, and east and west, and thus could be called "the plain of wheels".

Giolla Caemáin's poem on the history of Ireland gave the second element genitive singular inflection: *Cath Raith/Roith*, translated as "the full-red rout of the battle of *Rath*" (form 18). In two late Ulster Cycle tales (*Cath Aen. Macha* §5, *Cogadh FC* §3: forms 29, 46) lists of place-names include a *Dún Roith* "hill-fort of *Roth*", associated in (46) with *Tulach na nArm* "hillock of the armies", which is given in *Acallam na Senórach* (form 21) as an alias for Moira. A personal name *Roth* appears in a list of warriors in the *Táin* (*TBC Rec. I* 1.1558). Whoever invented the name *Dún Roith* "Roth's fort" seems to have been reinterpreting the second element in *Magh Roth*, which it seems was no longer understood. In more recent times *Magh/Maigh Rath* became the standard spelling in Irish, and would have been pronounced eventually [maï'ra], with the stress on the second element. This form, but with initial stress, is the most common local pronunciation (72), though outsiders usually say ['mɔïrə].

After the 1583 form (48) the later anglicized spellings have a final *-gh*, but I doubt if this was intended to show that the name ended with [x] in pronunciation. Although it is not clear when the current stress on the first syllable **Moi**ra developed, I suspect it had not changed in the 17th century and that the *-gh* was added to the second syllable to indicate that it bore the stress in pronunciation. One could contrast the name, stressed on the first syllable, of the Moyry Pass on the old route from Dundalk to Newry (Lawlor 1938(a), 3,map), which was anglicized from *Bealach an Mhaighre* (*AFM* vi 2222n, 2256n: AD 1600–1).

TOWNLANDS

Aughnadrumman	*Achadh na Dromann*	
J 1660	"field of the ridge"	
1. Aghenedromayne	CPR Jas I 396a	1609
2. Aghenedrouran	CPR Jas I 235a	1612
3. Aghnedromon	Inq. Ult. (Down) §13 Car. I	1629
4. Aghenedroman	Inq. Ult. (Down) §85 Car. I	1639
5. Aghedroma	Hib. Reg. Lr. Iveagh	1657c
6. Aghedroma	BSD 74	1661
7. Aghadroman	ASE 61b 39	1666
8. Sessiagh of Aghadroma	Rent Roll Down 5	1692
9. Aughnadrumond	Reg. Magheralin (OSNB) E4	1715
10. Aghandrumman	Deeds & Wills (Mooney) 183	1716
11. Aghnadromon	Wm. Map (OSNB) E4	1810
12. Aghnadromon	Sur. Bateson Estate (OSNB) E4	1810
13. Agnadrummen	Bnd. Sur. (OSNB) E4	1830c
14. Aughnadrumman	J O'D (OSNB) E4	1834c
15. Achadh dromainn "Field of the ridge"		
	J O'D (OSNB) E4	1834c

16. Athan a'dromáin "Ford of the ridge"   Mooney 183   1950c

17. ˌaxnəˈdrọmən   Local pronunciation   1996

Aughnadrumman was originally held by Sir Art Magennis. The forms suggest *Achadh na Dromann* "field of the ridge", although in two mid-17th-century forms (5, 6) the second element has been shortened, possibly via a mis-read abbreviation, so that it looks more like *droim*, the basic word for "ridge" from which *dromainn* derives. There is no final vowel in the anglicized forms to suggest the more usual genitive *dromainne*. *Aghene*- (forms 1, 2, 4) looks like *Achadh* plus article, but it could represent *Áthán* "(small) ford" plus article, (as suggested by Dean Mooney, form 16), since the Lagan forms the southern border of the townland, now crossed by Newmill Bridge. There is no visible ridge, only the rising ground as one leaves the river, and an alternative Irish form might be *Achadh na dTromán* "field of the dwarf elders".

Aughnafosker   *Achadh Ghiolla Choscair*
J 1459   "Gilkosker's field"

 1. Aghakillfosker   CPR Jas I 395a   1609
 2. Aghakillifoster   CPR Jas I 190b   1611
 3. Aghgallifosker   CPR Jas I 373b   1618
 4. Aghigillfausker   Hib. Reg. Lr. Iveagh   1657c
 5. Aghigill ffausker   BSD 74   1661
 6. Ahigilfancer   Hib. Del. Down   1672c
 7. Aughnafosker   Reg. Magheralin (OSNB) E4   1715
 8. Aghillfosket   Deeds & Wills (Mooney) 183   1716
 9. Aghillfoskett   Deeds & Wills (Mooney) 183   1717
10. Aughlafosker   Wm. Map (OSNB) E4   1810
11. Aughlafosker   Sur. Bateson Estate (OSNB) E4   1810
12. Aghlafosker   Bnd. Sur. (OSNB) E4   1830c
13. Aughnafosker   J O'D (OSNB) E4   1834c

14. Achadh na foscair "Field of the shelter"
                                J O'D (OSNB) E4   1834c
15. Ath giolla fuascraigh/fuascair
    "ford of the panic-stricken fellow"   Mooney 183   1950c

16. ˌanəˈfɔskər   Local pronunciation   1996

Aughnafosker lies immediately south of **Carnalbanagh** and the village of Moira. Dean Mooney recorded a local theory "not traditional but now popular" that Aughnafosker is *Achadh an Choscair* "field of the slaughter", in his view a "learned but misguided attempt" to link the name with the place-name *Cnocán an Choscair* "little hill of the slaughter" in the story of the battle of *Magh Rath* (*CMR II* 216; Mooney 1952–3(b), 13). This etymology would require the fairly common change of an internal [x] to [f] in the anglicized form, as in Murphy from *Ó Murchú*. However, the early spellings also show a middle element containing *l* which survived till the 19th century. In 1834 it was noted, "It is generally pronounced Augh*l*afosker", but the early forms disprove the conclusion there that "the registry of 1715 is good authority for Aughna" (*OSNB*). Mooney thought the name "certainly contained the word *giolla* "servant" (1952–3(b), 13), and linked the suggestion in his manuscript (form 15) with "some incident in the Battle of Moyrath, perhaps the 'flying Scotchman' with the dead man strapped to his foot" (cf. *CMR II* (FDG) 84–7,282n). Since the Lagan forms the southern boundary of the townland, Mooney assumed the first element was *Áth* "ford", then followed by the article and *giolla* plus an adjective.

However there was also a personal name *Giolla Coscair.* Woulfe gave the surname *Mac Giolla Choscair*, without any provenance, translating it "son of Lad of Victory" (Woulfe 1923, 71). McGilcosker appeared occasionally at the Plantation period in Meath and Fermanagh (*Fiants Eliz.* §6389; *CPR Jas I* 276b) and, spelt *McGilosker*, was a "principall Irish name" in three north Fermanagh parishes in 1659 (*Census* 120). However there is no evidence for the *mac* element here, and the development seems to have been from *Achadh Ghiolla Choscair*, anglicized as six syllables *Aghakillifoster* in 1611 (form 2), reduced to four syllables in the 18th century, as in *Aghillfosket* (form 8), metathesized to *Aughlafosker*, as in form (10), giving Aughnafosker by interchange of *l* and *n*.

Aughnafosker belonged to the O'Lavery holding. It includes two-ringed Pretty Mary's Fort, though the Mary who was the origin of the name is now unknown (*ASCD* 151 site 451).

Balloonigan   *Baile Uí Dhuinneagáin*

J 1760   "O'Donegan's townland"

1. Belaballidonoghan, the ford in a bog called (Bnds CAB)	CPR Jas I 74a	1605
2. Balledonegan	CPR Jas I 396a	1609
3. Belaballidonegan, a ford in a bog called (Bnds CAB)	CPR Jas I 146b	1609
4. Balledownegan	CPR Jas I 235a	1612
5. Ballydonegan	Inq. Ult. (Down) §13 Car. I	1629
6. Ballynedonegan	Inq. Ult. (Down) §85 Car. I	1639
7. Ballydonnegan, half towneland of	Civ. Surv. x §73	1655c
8. Balliuonagan	Hib. Reg. Lr. Iveagh	1657c
9. Balumigan	Census 81	1659c
10. Ballivonegan al. Ballyvonygan	Par. Map (Mooney) 193	1660c
11. Ballyvonygan	BSD 74	1661
12. Ballyvingane	ASE 61b 39	1666
13. Ballirongan	Hib. Del. Down	1672c
14. (?)Ballyvingham	Rent Roll Down 5	1692
15. (?)Ballyvorgan	Rent Roll Down 6	1692
16. Ballunagan	Reg. Magheralin (OSNB) E4	1715
17. Ballunagan	Vestry Reg. (OSNB) E8.59	1715
18. Ballionegan	Deeds & Wills (Mooney) 193	1716
19. Ballyunegan	Deeds & Wills (Mooney) 193	1717
20. Balloonigan	Wm. Map (OSNB) E4	1810
21. Balloonigan	Sur. Bateson Estate (OSNB) E4	1810
22. Balloonigin	Bnd. Sur. (OSNB) E4	1830c
23. [Ball'unagan]	OSNB Pron. E4	1834c
24. Balloonigan	J O'D (OSNB) E4	1834c
25. Baile Lughnagain "Lunagan's town"	J O'D (OSNB) E4	1834c

26. Baile Uí Dhonnagáin "O'Donnegan's
    townland'   Mooney 193   1950c

27. ˌbəˈlunəgən   Local pronunciation   1996

Balloonigan, bordered on the south by the Lagan, belonged to Sir Art Magennis, although immediately east of it were the lands of *Clann Aodha Buí*, Clandeboye in Co. Antrim (forms 1,3; *PNI* ii 169–171). Despite the abbreviation of the modern place-name form, on which O'Donovan based his guesses, the spellings from the first half of the 17th century (1–7) clearly show the surname *Ó Donnagáin*, derived from the personal name meaning "little brown one", apparently in the variant *Ó Duinneagáin* (Woulfe 1923, 518). The later spellings show that the initial *D* of this name must have been lenited to [ɣ] and subsequently lost, probably in the genitive case of the surname, *Uí Dhuinneagáin*. Woulfe (1923, 502) stated that "there were in early times three distinct families of the name *Ó Donnagáin* in Ulster", and MacLysaght (1964(a), 67) located one of these in Co. Monaghan. In the early 17th-century there were O'Donegans in Antrim and Tyrone (*CPR Jas I* 110b, 373b Ant., 136a Tyr.).

The surname O'Donegan is attested in the 15th century in the diocese of Dromore, when *McKynnyryn* (McGivern?) was erenagh in "part of the lands of *Odonnacon* and *Kyllosci*" in 1426 (*Reg. Swayne* 45, 97). These must be church lands, and in the early 14th century Florence McDonnegan (*Mac Donnagáin*) had been bishop of Dromore. During the 15th century members of the family were clergymen in the parishes of Clonallan, Clonduff and Kilbroney (*Swanzy's Dromore*). In the 17th century the surname McDonegan was promi-nent among tenants of church land in Co. Down in the area around Banbridge and of other unidentified lands (*CPR Jas. I*: 191a, 395b; 195b), and was borne by the erenagh of Galloon Co. Fermanagh (*CPR Jas I* 384a). It may be that the ecclesiastical branch of the family decided to standardize their surname as *Mac*Donegan. Both forms of the surname have now become Donegan.

Ballygunaghan in Donaghcloney, like Balloonigan not a church townland but part of Magennis territory, seems also to have been named from *Ó Duinneagáin*. The daughter of George Sexton, who acquired lands in Aghaderg and Seapatrick, was married to Mic[hael] *Doinegan*, apparently of that area (*Inq. Ult. (Down)* §30 Car. I, 1632).

Ballycanal   *Baile Uí Chon Allta* (?)
J 1561   "Conalty's townland"

1. Ballyconnalt	CPR Jas I 395a	1609
2. Balleconnalt	CPR Jas I 190b	1611
3. Balliconallity	Inq. Ult. (Down) §13 Jac. I	1624
4. Ballyconall	Inq. Ult. (Down) §93 Car. I	1640
5. Ballackanall	Census 81	1659c
6. Ballyconnell ½ towne	BSD 74	1661
7. Ballicanelle	BSD 75	1661
8. Ballyconnell	ASE 61b 39	1666
9. Ballyconnell, sessiagh of	Rent Roll Down 6	1692
10. Ballykanall	Reg. Magheralin (OSNB) E4	1715
11. Ballyconnell	Deeds & Wills (Mooney) 185	1716
12. Ballycanal	Wm. Map (OSNB) E4	1810
13. Ballycanal	Sur. Bateson Estate (OSNB) E4	1810

14. Ballycanal	Bnd. Sur. (OSNB) E4	1830c
15. [Ballaghanaul] by the old people	OSNB Pron. E4	1834c
16. Bealach an fhail "Road of the hedge"	J O'D (OSNB) E4	1834c
17. Bealach an aille "Rock road"	J O'D (OSNB) E4	1834c
18. Baile/Bealach Congbháile/Coinnealta "The townland or road of the habitation or guest-house"	Mooney 185	1950c
19. Baile Ui Chon-allaidh or Ui C[h]on-allta	Mooney 185	1950c
20. ˌbalïkə'naːl	Local pronunciation	1991
21. ˌbalïkə'nɔːl	Local pronunciation	1996

Ballycanal once belonged to O'Lavery. The spellings suggest *Baile* plus a second element beginning with a hard *c*, the sound [k]. However, in the early 19th century the name was pronounced [Ballaghanaul] by the old inhabitants (form 15 *OSNB*), and the stress is on the final syllable now (20, 21). In Irish this would suggest that the final syllable was a separate word. O'Donovan's and the other Name-Book suggestion, *Bealach an Fháil* or *an Aille* "routeway of the hedge", or "rock" (16, 17), seem to be based on the 1834 pronunciation, but although they reproduce the stress they are unlikely unless the final fricative of *bealach* was regularly represented by *c*. The three earliest 17th-century forms have a *-t-* towards the end of the second element. *Baile Coingilte*, "townland of shared grazing", like Mooney's *Baile Congbháile* "townland of maintenance", or "of an establishment" (18), does not have the correct stress. Another suggestion of Mooney's (19, also with [x] not [k]) is *Baile Uí Chon-allaidh* or *Uí Chon-allta*, anglicized Conalty, a rare Ulster surname (Woulfe 1923, 475). Although only the 1624 form (3) has the final vowel, the stress would have been right, although the anglicized form is now pronounced 'Conalty. Presumably *-lt* was later misread as *-ll*, as has happened in reverse in **Clonmakate** in Co. Armagh, in 1609 *Clonvckolla*.

If *lt* were considered as a mistake for *ll*, Ballycanal could have been earlier simply *Baile Conaill* "Conall's town" (see **Clanconnell** for background to the name Conall in Iveagh). The Lagan canal which connected Belfast with Lough Neagh forms the northern border of Ballycanal, and could have influenced both spelling and pronunciation in recent times.

Ballygowan   *Baile an Ghabhann*
J 1857   "townland of the smith"

1. Balliengowen (Kilwarlin)	Fiants Eliz. §4650	1585
2. (?)Ballyvickegowan, containing 2 towns		
	CPR Jas I 395b	1609
3. Ballengowen (Kilwarlin)	CPR Jas I 396a	1609
4. Ballingowen (Kilwarlin)	CPR Jas I 181b	1610
5. (?)Ballyvickegowan	CPR Jas I 190b	1611
6. (?)Ballyvickegowne othw. Ballyreagh or Ballynemagheriebegg	CPR Jas I 266a	1614
7. (?)Ballyvickgowan, containing 2 towns		
	CPR Jas I 309a	1616
8. Ballynegowen al. Smithestowne	Inq. Ult. (Down) §25 Car. I	1631
9. Ballingawen	Inq. Ult. (Down) §60 Car. I	1635

10. Ballygowone	Census 81	1659c
11. Ballygowen	BSD 82	1661
12. Ballygown al. Smithstown	CSP Ire. 1660-2 p459	1661
13. Ballygorran	Hib. Del. Down	1672c
14. Ballygown	Wm. Map (OSNB) E4	1810
15. Ballygowne al. Ballymagowne al. al. Ballygowan al. Smiths town	Marriage Downshire (OSNB) E4	1811
16. Ballygowan	Reg. Magheralin (OSNB) E4	1715
17. Ballygowan	Bnd. Sur. (OSNB) E4	1830c
18. Baile Ui Ghabhain	OSNB Inf. E4	1834c
19. Baile Ui Gabhann "O'Gowan's town"	J O'D (OSNB) E4	1834c
20. (?)Baile Mhic Ghabhann "Mac Gowan's townland'	Mooney 187	1950c
21. ˌbaliˈgəuən	Local pronunciation	1991

Ballygowan in the north-east of the parish was part of the MacRory Magennis territory of Kilwarlin, and the definite early 17th-century forms are those listed next to Lurganville in Kilwarlin. After *Baile* the second element could be the surname *Ó Gabhann* (see **Ballygowan** in Kilkeel, *PNI* iii 23). However the earliest forms show clear evidence of the article and Ballygowan probably includes the common noun *gabha* gen. *gabhann* "smith", as in **Ballygowan**, parish of Aghaderg.

The queried examples (2, 5, 6, 7) from the patent rolls of King James I refer to church land held initially by William Worseley from the bishop of Dromore, which contained "two towns": *Ballyreogh alias Ballymagerybegg, Ballymackormocke* (*CPR Jas I* 395b) *Ballireagh otherwise Ballimagheribeg and Ballinaries* (*CPR Jas I* 309a). **Magherabeg**, in the parish of Dromore, is once said to be an alias of *Ballyvickegowne* (form 6). These examples make it clear that the second part of the name of the church unit was the surname *Mac an Ghabhann* "son of the smith", and a similar spelling is found in form 15. However, the townland of Greenoge lies between modern Ballygowan and Magherabeg, and since Greenoge is not named as one of the denominations making up Ballygowan it seems most likely that *Ballyvickegowne* is an obsolete alias name for a nearby part of Dromore parish.

Ballyknock
J 1959

Baile an Chnoic
"townland of the hill"

1. Ballienknoick (Kilwarlin)	Fiants Eliz. §4650	1585
2. Ballyknocke (Kilwarlin)	CPR Jas I 396a	1609
3. Ballyenknoicke (Kilwarlin)	CPR Jas I 181b	1610
4. Ballinknock al. Hilltowne	Inq. Ult. (Down) §25 Car. I	1631
5. Ballycnocke	Inq. Ult. (Down) §60 Car. I	1635
6. Baliknoske	Census 81	1659c
7. Balliknocke	BSD 82	1661
8. Ballyknocke al. Hillstoun (manor of Hillsborough)	CSP Ire. 1660-2 p459	1661
9. (?)Ballyknok, Hugh Cleries of	Sub. Roll Down 275	1663
10. B:Knoche	Hib. Del. Down	1672c

11. sessiagh of Halfe Towne of Ballymacknocan	Rent Roll Down 5	1692
12. Ballyknock	Reg. Magheralin (OSNB) E4	1715
13. Ballynock	Wm. Map (OSNB) E4	1810
14. Ballyknock al. Ballynock al. Hilltown	Marriage Downshire (OSNB) E4	1811
15. Ballyknock	Bnd. Sur. (OSNB) E4	1830c
16. Baile an chnuic "hill-town"	J O'D (OSNB) E4	1834c
17. ˌbalïˈnɔk	Local pronunciation	1996

Ballyknock formed part of the McRory Magennis holding of Kilwárlin, and was translated as *Hilltown* as early as 1631 (form 4). However it does not have the same origin as **Hillsborough** (8) and **Hilltown**, which are named after the Hill family (*PNI* iii 96). There is a fine view of the Lagan valley from the high ground in Ballyknock and a foothill called the Nut Hill in the townland.

Ballymagaraghan
J 1558

Baile Mhig Aracháin
"McGaraghan's townland"

1. Ballymcgarraghan	CPR Jas I 396a	1609
2. Ballymacgarraghan	CPR Jas I 235a	1612
3. Ballymac-Garraghan	Inq. Ult. (Down) §13 Car. I	1629
4. Ballymagarchan	Inq. Ult. (Down) §85 Car. I	1639
5. Ballimagracha	Hib. Reg. Lr. Iveagh	1657c
6. Bally McGarchan	Census 81	1659c
7. Ballimagarcha	BSD 74	1661
8. Ballymackgarchans or Ballynagarrahans	ASE 61b 39	1666
9. Ballimagarcha	Hib. Del. Down	1672c
10. 2 Sessiaghs of Ballinmackoraham	Rent Roll Down 5	1692
11. Ballymc garahan, Upper & Lower	Reg. Magheralin (OSNB) E4	1715
12. Ballymcgarthary	Deeds & Wills (Mooney) 191	1717
13. Ballymagarahan	Wm. Map (OSNB) E4	1810
14. Ballymagarrahan	Sur. Bateson Estate (OSNB) E4	1810
15. Ballymagaraghan	Bnd. Sur. (OSNB) E4	1830c
16. Baile Mic Garacháin "Magarahan's town"	J O'D (OSNB) E4	1834c
17. Baile Mag Aracháin/Mag Garacháin "MacGarraghan's town"	Mooney 191	1950c
18. ˌbalïməˈgranaɣən	Local pronunciation	1996

Ballymagaraghan belonged to Sir Art Magennis. The name seems to be based on a surname formed with *mac* "son (of)", which often becomes *Mag* when the second element of the surname begins with a vowel. The name *Mag (Mac) Arachán* occurs in the annals in the 15th century, associated with Lisgool abbey, Co. Fermanagh (*AU* 1431, 1456 AD; *AFM* iv 882: a canon). Woulfe called them "an ecclesiastical family at Lisgoole" (1923, 421). In the 17th century the name Magaraghan was found at Termonmagrath and Boho; and

Clanmcgarraghan "the family of Magaraghan", as "another sept in the nature of an here-nagh" were under the erenaghs O'Fellan at Boho (*CPR Jas I* 144a, 384a). The surname in the townland name may have arisen independently, or come from a branch of the same family, but no longer exists in the area.

Bottier   *Bochtír*
J 1659   "poor land"

1. Ballybotyre	CPR Jas I 396a	1609
2. Ballybotyre	CPR Jas I 235a	1612
3. Ballybotier	Inq. Ult. (Down) §13 Car. I	1629
4. Ballybotrie half vil.	Inq. Ult. (Down) §85 Car. I	1639
5. Bolere	Civ. Surv. x §73	1655c
6. Botlyre, woody bog of	Hib. Reg. Lr. Iveagh	1657c
7. Botlyre al. Cregeenigh	Hib. Reg. Lr. Iveagh	1657c
8. Bottyre	Census 81	1659c
9. Bottyre al. Creggenagh	BSD 73	1661
10. Botteir	Sub. Roll Down 273	1663
11. Bottire or Crigineagh al. Creganeagh	ASE 61b 39	1666
12. Boltier	Hib. Del. Down	1672c
13. halfe Towne of Crigeneagh als Battyre	Rent Roll Down 5	1692
14. Booteere, Upper & Lower	Reg. Magheralin (OSNB) E4	1715
15. Botier al. Rotier al. Creganeagh	Deeds & Wills (Mooney) 195	1716
16. Creageagh al. Rotier	Deeds & Wills (Mooney) 196	1717
17. Boteer	Reg. Deeds abstracts i §708	1737
18. Bottear	Wm. Map (OSNB) E4	1810
19. Bottear	Sur. Bateson Estate (OSNB) E4	1810
20. Bowteer	Ir. Wills Index 77	1811
21. Buttear	Ir. Wills Index 75	1828
22. Battear	Bnd. Sur. (OSNB) E4	1830c
23. Battier or Boultier	Clergyman (OSNB) E4	1834c
24. Bottier	J O'D (OSNB) E4	1834c
25. Both tiar "western tent or hut"	J O'D (OSNB) E4	1834c
26. Bocht thír "Poor land'	Mooney 195	1950c
27. bo'tir	Local pronunciation	1996

Bottier belonged to Sir Art Magennis. It is a long, almost hour-glass shaped, townland, stretching roughly north to south. In the later 17th-century sources the lost name *Cregenagh* occurs in connection with Bottier, and, Mooney thought, provided a clue to its meaning: *Creagánach*, a "place of little rocks", which would indicate poor soil. Bottier might then be a compound meaning "poor land", *Bocht-tír* (26) although this would have been stressed on the first syllable. *Ch* [x] is regularly lost before *t* in east Ulster, as in **Ballybot** in Newry, from *Baile Bocht* (*PNI* i 39); **Ott** mountain in the Mournes (*PNI* iii 146). Bottier was a "woody bog" in 1657 (6), and although called a "half townland" of 60 acres in 1639 (form 4) contains 489 acres today.

Carnalbanagh East and West   *Carn Albanach*
J 1560, J 1460   "cairn of (the) Scotsmen"

1. Cornalbanagh	CPR Jas I 395a	1609

2. Carnalbonagh	CPR Jas I 190b	1611
3. Carrnenasbanagh	Inq. Ult. (Down) §13 Jac. I	1624
4. Carnalbanagh	Inq. Ult. (Down) §47 Car. I	1634
5. Carnealbeanagh	Inq. Ult. (Down) §96 Car. I	1640
6. Carnealbannagh	BSD 82	1661
7. Carnalbanagh	Reg. Magheralin (OSNB) E4	1715
8. Carnalbanagh	Deeds & Wills (Mooney) 195	1716
9. Carnalbana	Sur. Bateson Estate (OSNB) E4	1810
10. Canalbana	Bnd. Sur. (OSNB) E4	1830c
11. Carnalbanagh	J O'D (OSNB) E4	1834c
12. Carn Albanach "Scotch carn"	J O'D (OSNB) E4	1834c
13. ˌkarnəlˈban	Local pronunciation	1996

Carnalbanagh was part of the lands of the O'Lavery family, and the village of Moira is built on these two very small townlands, now 11 and 22 acres. The name is no longer in general use. The mound in Carnalbanagh East may be what was known in the mid-19th-century as the Rath of Moira (OS 1:10,000 sh. 183). In the 19th century, according to local popular tradition apparently collected by Samuel Ferguson, *Carn Albanach* "cairn of the Scotsmen" was the burial place of the Scottish princes who fell in the battle of *Magh Rath*, and a pillar stone engraved with a cross formerly marked the site, a partly-artificial eminence levelled in improving the farm (O'Laverty 1905, 119; Mooney 1952–3(b), 13; Hanna 1856, 58; *UJA* 1855, 292–4, which illustrated the stone). Of course, the Scotsmen commemorated by the name may have arrived at a much later date, whether as Scottish mercenaries (gallowglasses) or planters. However the sources show the name existed in 1609, so gallowglasses are more probable.

The townland appears as one unit (a *sessiagh*) in the sources, but the two parts are now divided by the main road from Lurgan to Lisburn, as are Gortnamony and Aughnafosker to the south; Risk and Clare, Ballycanal and Derrydrummult to the north. It is unusual to find a man-made feature such as a road used as a townland boundary, which either illustrates the historical significance of the route or suggests that local townland boundaries have been redrawn.

Clare
J 1660

Cláraigh
"level land"

1. Clarey	CPR Jas I 395a	1609
2. Clarey	CPR Jas I 190b	1611
3. Crary	Inq. Ult. (Down) §13 Jac. I	1624
4. Clary	Inq. Ult. (Down) §65 Car. I	1636
5. Clary(e)	Inq. Ult. (Down) §93 Car. I	1640
6. Clare	Census 81	1659c
7. Clare	Sub. Roll Down 273	1663
8. Clare	Reg. Magheralin (OSNB) E4	1715
9. Clare	Wm. Map (OSNB) E4	1810
10. Clare	Sur. Bateson Estate (OSNB) E4	1810
11. Clare	Bnd. Sur. (OSNB) E4	1830c

12. Clár "a board; a level plain"	J O'D (OSNB) E4	1834c
13. Clarach	Mooney 197	1950c
14. 'klɛr	Local pronunciation	1996

Clare belonged to the O'Lavery holding. The final syllable -y in the early 17th-century forms (1–5) shows that the name was originally *Clárach* "flat land", a derivative from *clár* "a board, a plain", here in the dative form *Cláraigh*. Clarehill in the townland represents the rise of the ground as one approaches from the river Lagan.

Derrydrummult   *Doire Droma Molt*
J 1661   "oakwood of the ridge of the wethers"

1. Dromulte	CPR Jas I 396a	1609
2. Dromulte	CPR Jas I 235a	1612
3. Drommulte	Inq. Ult. (Down) §13 Car. I	1629
4. Derrydromoylt	Inq. Ult. (Down) §85 Car. I	1639
5. Derydrumult	Hib. Reg. Lr. Iveagh	1657c
6. Derry Drummust	Census 81	1659c
7. Deridrumult	BSD 74	1661
8. Derrydrumulte	ASE 61b 39	1666
9. Deridrumut	Hib. Del. Down	1672c
10. Sessiagh of Dordrumull	Rent Roll Down 5	1692
11. Derrydromald part	Rent Roll Down 6	1692
12. Derrydrumult	Reg. Magheralin (OSNB) E4	1715
13. (?)Derrydrummuske	Deeds & Wills (Mooney) 199	1716
14. Derrydrummult	Wm. Map (OSNB) E4	1810
15. Derrydrummult	Sur. Bateson Estate (OSNB) E4	1810
16. Derrydrumult	Bnd. Sur. (OSNB) E4	1830c
17. Derrydrummult	J O'D (OSNB) E4	1834c
18. Doire droma molt "Oak-wood of the ridge of the wethers" Roboretum dorsi vervecum	J O'D (OSNB) E4	1834c
19. Doire-droma-molt "derry of the hill-ridge of wethers"	Joyce iii 295	1913
20. Doire droma molt	Mooney 199	1950c
21. ˌdɛrïdrọ'mọlt	Local pronunciation	1996
22. ˌdɛrï'drọmlət	Local pronunciation	1996

Derrydrummult belonged to Sir Art Magennis, and was referred to in the earliest forms (1–3) as *Dromulte*. From 1629 on, *Derry* was prefixed to the name. The extent is given as 60 acres in 1639 (4) and in 1666 (8) it was called a sessiagh. The two forms (10, 11) from the Down Rental of 1692 are intriguing in that one, *Derrydromald*, is much more accurately preserved than the other, which has been reduced to *Dordrumull*. *Molt* "wether" appears in other place-names such as **Drummilt**, a townland of Loughgilly parish Co. Armagh, Benwilt *Beann Mhoilt* "wether's peak", a notable hill in Co. Cavan (*Onom. Goed*. 110b). In

Derrydrummult the spelling -*mult* indicates the genitive plural rather than the singular. For a similar formation, see **Derrydrummuck** in Aghaderg.

Drumbane *Droim Bán*
J 1461 "white ridge"

1. Drombane	CPR Jas I 395a	1609
2. Drombar	CPR Jas I 190b	1611
3. Drombane	Inq. Ult. (Down) §13 Jac. I	1624
4. Drombane	Inq. Ult. (Down) §96 Car. I	1640
5. Drumbane	Census 81	1659c
6. Drombane	BSD 82	1661
7. Drumbane	Reg. Magheralin (OSNB) E4	1715
8. Drumbane al. Drumbar	Deeds & Wills (Mooney) 203	1716
9. Drumbane, Stothard of	Harris Hist. 104	1744
10. Drumbane	Sur. Bateson Estate (OSNB) E4	1810
11. Drumbane	Wm. Map (OSNB) E4	1810
12. Drumbane	Bnd. Sur. (OSNB) E4	1830c
13. Druim bán "white ridge" dorsum album	J O'D (OSNB) E4	1834c
14. ˌdrəmˈbɑːn	Local pronunciation	1992

Drumbane was in the O'Lavery district of Moira, and is now largely to the north of the M1 motorway and bordered on the north by Co. Antrim. The minor road that crosses the motorway by Drumbane Bridge then runs along a small ridge, probably the original *droim bán*, and on to what were once Sir Art Magennis' townlands in Aghalee. Local pronunciation has maintained the original sound of *bán* "white", as in **Kinbane** in north Antrim, [kïnˈbɑːn], rather than turn it into English *bane*, pronounced [beːn].

Gortnamony *Gort na Mónadh*
J 1360 "enclosed field of the bog"

1. Gortnemoney	CPR Jas I 395a	1609
2. Gortnemoney	CPR Jas I 190b	1611
3. Gortnamony	Inq. Ult. (Down) §13 Jac. I	1624
4. Gortemony	Inq. Ult. (Down) §96 Car. I	1640
5. Gurtingmony	Census 81	1659c
6. Gortmcmony	Par. Map (Mooney) 209	1660c
7. Gortmony	BSD 82	1661
8. Gortmonybeg	Sub. Roll Down 273	1663
9. Gartnamony	Reg. Magheralin (OSNB) E4	1715
10. Gortnemoney	Deeds & Wills (Mooney) 209	1716
11. Gortnamoney	Wm. Map (OSNB) E4	1810
12. Gartnamoney	Sur. Bateson Estate (OSNB) E4	1810
13. Gortnamony	Bnd. Sur. (OSNB) E4	1830c
14. Gort na móna "field of the bog"	J O'D (OSNB) E4	1834c

15. Gort na muine/móna "the field
    of the brake or shrubbery"   Mooney 209   1950c

16. ˌgɔrtnəˈmonï   Local pronunciation   1991

Gortnamony belonged to O'Lavery, and is bounded on the south by the former church lands of Magheralin. There is nothing remarkable in the forms. The element *gort* usually refers to an enclosed field used for cultivation. The form of the second element may be either *na Móine* or *na Mónadh*, since the spelling *y* which usually represents [ə] also represents Irish [u] in names like **Finaghy** and **Garvaghy**. The townland is now 205 acres.

Kilminioge   *Cill M'Fhionnóg*
J 1361   "My little Finn's church"

1. Killinmeog   CPR Jas I 395a   1609
2. Killinmeoge   CPR Jas I 190b   1611
3. Killmoinoge   Inq. Ult. (Down) §13 Jac. I   1624
4. Kilmonyoge   Inq. Ult. (Down) §96 Car. I   1640
5. Kilmonyoge, sessiagh of   Census 81   1659c
6. Killmonioge   BSD 82   1661
7. Hazelhill   Ir. Wills Index 61   1701
8. Kilmineoge   Deeds & Wills (Mooney) 211   1711
9. Killmonioagg   Ir. Wills Index 31   1712
10. Killmonyoge   Reg. Magheralin (OSNB) E4   1715
11. Killmineoge al. Killmineogh   Deeds & Wills (Mooney) 211   1716
12. Kilminiog   Wm. Map (OSNB) E4   1810
13. Kilminioge   Sur. Bateson Estate (OSNB) E4   1810
14. Kilminioge   Bnd. Sur. (OSNB) E4   1830c

15. Cill Fionóg "St. Winog's church"   J O'D (OSNB) E4   1834c
16. Cill Wionóg   J O'D (OSNB) E4   1834c
17. Cill Mo Fhíonóg   J O'D (OSNB) E4   1834c
18. Cill Mo Finneóg "St (Ronan?)
    Finn's church or church of St Finnóg" Mooney 211   1950c

19. ˌkïlməˈnog   Local pronunciation   1996

Kilminioge belonged to the O'Laverys. It was not church land, but the name appears to represent *Cill* "church" followed by a personal name ending in the diminutive suffix *-óg*. The initial *M* could be the prefix *Mo* "my" sometimes prefixed to saints names in Early Irish. Although the earlier forms (1–2) suggest *Maedhóg* "my little Aedh", it would seem that Mooney (form 18; 1952–3(b), 12–3) is generally correct in deriving Kilminioge from Irish *Cill M'Fhinneóg*, "My little Finn's church", and equating the founder with the saint called *Rónán Fionn* "Ronan the Fair-haired", who is commemorated at Magheralin, the neighbouring parish which once included Moira. The only difficulty is that the expected Irish form is *Cill Mo Fhionnóg* abbreviated *Mionnóg*, as in the lost early place-name *Ráth Moinnóc* (*CSH* 707.415), while the anglicized forms from 1624 (form 3ff) have *i* or *y* following *n*, indicating a palatalized *n* as in Mooney's spelling. The Archaeological Survey recorded a graveyard and well "not precisely located" (*NISMR* Down, sheet 13 no.36). O'Laverty described it as a church site, "on a little eminence in a field belonging to Charles Byrne", where human bones had been found near "an ancient well called Tubber" (O'Laverty 1905, 119). Tubber must be Irish *tobar*, which means "well". Although townlands containing church sites usually continued to be held by the Church, there were old graveyards in **Donagreagh** in Magheralin and **Magherana** in Donaghcloney which were also secular lands.

The site of Ronan Finn's original church in the area has not been ascertained. The 14th-century Book of Lecan says it was in *Magh Rath*, in the lands of a tribe called Corco Ruisean: *Corco Ruisean i Muigh Rath, is fuiri itá Lann Rónáin Finn*, "Corco Ruisean in Magh Rath, on which is Ronan Finn's church" (*L.Lec.* fol.88v b14; *EA* 378). In *Buile Suibhne*, one of the stories relating to the battle of *Magh Rath*, St Ronan Finn marked out the site of a church called *Cell Lainne* "the church of *Lann*" (*Buile Suibhne* §3). These references can be linked with the early church of the parish of **Magheralin**, which included Moira till 1725. In the story Suibhne king of Dál nAraide tried to prevent St Ronan from marking out the church in his territory by throwing the saint's psalter into a lake nearby, from which an otter retrieved it. If the story is topographically accurate, and Kilminioge had been the earlier church site, this would have to be the lake in the neighbouring townland of Legmore (*Buile Suibhne* 4 §4).

Reeves stated that the Church of Ireland parish church built for Moira was known as St. Inn's, but did not cite any source (*EA* 378). Mooney in checking this found a reference to St. Inn's in the "Parliamentary Gazetteer" of 1835, but discovered that it was consecrated St. John's according to the "Dromore Register", 2 May 1732. He believed, therefore, that St. Inn's might have begun as a copyist's error for St. John's (Mooney 1952-3(b), 12–3). According to a 1725 indenture from the vestry book the rector and churchwardens of the "parish of Saint John *Moyrah*" were given an acre of the townland of Clare on which to build the church (*OSM* xii 117). The house called Hazel Hill (7) has disappeared.

Legmore	*Lag Mór*	
J 1361	"big hollow"	

1. Legvallevicaske	CPR Jas I 395a	1609
2. Leighvallyvicaske	CPR Jas I 190b	1611
3. Legballye Mc Cahie	Inq. Ult. (Down) §13 Jac. I	1624
4. Leyge	Inq. Ult. (Down) §47 Car. I	1634
5. Leage	Inq. Ult. (Down) §96 Car. I	1640
6. Leballimakaske	BSD 82	1661
7. (?)Lothualunaske al. Leigh	Lodge (Mooney) 212	1681
8. Legmore	Reg. Magheralin (OSNB) E4	1715
9. (?)Lothnalmuke al. Lothualmuske al.		
Leigh	Deeds & Wills (Mooney) 211	1716
10. Legmore	Wm. Map (OSNB) E4	1810
11. Legmore	Sur. Bateson Estate (OSNB) E4	1810
12. Legmore	Bnd. Sur. (OSNB) E4	1830c
13. Lag mór "great hollow"	J O'D (OSNB) E4	1834c
14. Leith(bhaile) Mhic Eochadha		
"MacKeogh's or MacCahy's half town"	Mooney 211	1950c
15. ˌlɛgˈmoːr	Local pronunciation	1991

The townland of Legmore belonged to O'Lavery. O'Donovan's suggestion *Log* or *Lag Mór* (13) "big place or hollow", reflects the modern form. However Legmore is considerably shorter than the form used till 1661 (6, with corrupt forms as late as 1716, form 9) which seems to contain *leathbhaile* "half-town" plus a surname formed with *mac*. Alternatively the first element may have been *Léig* "stone" (dative), once followed by *baile*. The element *mór* "great" does not appear until the 18th century. The 1:50,000 map shows a small lake in the townland, marked as a "pond" (but with no name) on OS 1:10,000 sheet 163.

Several of the earlier forms clearly contain a surname (1–3, 6, 7, 9). *Mac Ascaidh* is a "rare North of Ireland surname, probably of Norse origin" (Woulfe 1923, 321), or, if *h* has been misread as *k*, the name may contain a surname apparently *Mac Cais* which appears in several names between the Lagan and the Bann: **Derrymacash** (parish of Montiaghs, Co. Armagh), **Ballymacoss** (parish Derryaghy, Co. Antrim). This could be connected with the Airgialla grouping called *Uí Mac* (earlier *Moccu*) *Uais* (descendants of *Colla Uais*) which existed in *Brega* in Meath and in Co. Derry (*GUH* 18, 23). However there seems little connection with this area. Woulfe gives without provenance *Mac Coise*, as in the surname of the 10th-century Irish poet *Irard mac Coise*, anglicized MacCush or Legge. He says the name also existed in Scotland (1923, 334–5). *McCassye* was a "principall Irish name" in Monaghan in 1659 (*Census* 160). One could also suggest *g* has been misread as *ʃ*, as in reverse in one of the forms of **Coolsallagh**, parish of Dromore. In this case McCahie would be *Mac Eochadha*, but the bulk of the evidence is against it.

Lurganville
J 1859

Lorgain an Mhíl
"ridge of the hare"

1. Ballilorgan Evile (Kilwarlin)	Fiants Eliz. §4650	1585
2. Ballylurgan, Evile (Kilwarlin)	CPR Jas I 396a	1609
3. Ballilorganevile (Kilwarlin)	CPR Jas I 181b	1610
4. Ballelurganveile	Inq. Ult. (Down) §25 Car. I	1631
5. Ballilorgen Eville	Inq. Ult. (Down) §60 Car. I	1635
6. Lurgan Veele	Census 81	1659c
7. Lurgonvile	BSD 82	1661
8. Ballylurganveil (manor of Hillsborough)	CSP Ire. 1660–2 p459	1661
9. Lurganveile	Hib. Del. Down	1672c
10. Lurganavilla	Deeds & Wills (Mooney) 214	1696
11. Ballylurgan Veile	Deeds & Wills (Mooney) 214	1711
12. Lurganaveel	Reg. Magheralin (OSNB) E4	1715
13. Lurganofeel	Ir. Wills Index 59	1799
14. Lurganavill	Wm. Map (OSNB) E4	1810
15. Ballylurganveale al. Ballylurganveele al. Lurganville	Marriage Downshire (OSNB) E4	1811
16. Lurganaville	Bnd. Sur. (OSNB) E4	1830c
17. Lurganville	J O'D (OSNB) E4	1834c
18. Lurgainn a bhile "long hill of the old tree"	J O'D (OSNB) E4	1834c
19. (?)Lurgan a' Bhile	Mooney 213	1950c
20. L. mhaol	Mooney 213	1950c
21. ˌləːrgənˈvil	Local pronunciation	1996
22. ˈləːrgənˌvil	Local pronunciation	1996

Lurganville, one of the three most easterly townlands of Moira, was part of the MacRory Magennis district of Kilwarlin. However no attempt was made to translate this name in the Inquisition (*Inq. Ult. (Down)* §25 Car I) which gave English translations of the names of the other two townlands, Ballygowan and Ballyknock. The first element is clearly *lorgain* "shin" often used of a long ridge, apparently followed by the article in the three earliest and several later spellings (1–3, 5, 10, 12–14, 16). The townland stretches from the Lagan on the north boundary, gently rising towards Ballygowan on the hills to the south. The ridge is probably that from Fort William (south) to Cherry Valley (north), to the east of which a stream forms the townland boundary, running down from Maryvale. The final element, following the article, is likely to have begun with palatalized *b* or *m*, which would lenite to [v] as in the anglicized spellings. *Lorgain an Mhíl*, from *míol (má)* "hare" (*Ó Dónaill*), does not have the final vowel shown in some forms, but which may simply indicate a preceding long vowel. John O'Donovan's suggestion *Lorgain an Bhile* "ridge of the notable tree" seems unlikely in view of the many early spellings (*ee, ei*) indicating a long vowel in the final syllable (4, 6, 8, 9, 11–13). However there is no evidence for a long vowel in the current pronunciation.

| **Magherahinch** | *Machaire na hInse* | |
| J 1559 | "plain of the watermeadow" | |

1.	Magheryne-Inchye	CPR Jas I 396a	1609
2.	Magherinehinchy	CPR Jas I 235a	1612
3.	Maghere-Inchye	Inq. Ult. (Down) §13 Car. I	1629
4.	Magharnahensie	Inq. Ult. (Down) §85 Car. I	1639
5.	Magherenihinch	Hib. Reg. Lr. Iveagh	1657c
6.	Magharalinch	Census 81	1659c
7.	Magherenehinch	BSD 74	1661
8.	Maghernehinch	ASE 61b 39	1666
9.	Mahernihinch	Hib. Del. Down	1672c
10.	Mahernefinch	Rent Roll Down 5	1692
11.	Magherahinch	Reg. Magheralin (OSNB) E4	1715
12.	Mar.Inch	Harris Hist. map	1743
13.	Maghereinch	Harris Hist. 104	1744
14.	Marahinch	Wm. Map (OSNB) E4	1810
15.	Magherahinch	Sur. Bateson Estate (OSNB) E4	1810
16.	Magherahinch	Bnd. Sur. (OSNB) E4	1830c
17.	Machaire na hinse "plain of the holm or strath"	J O'D (OSNB) E4	1834c
18.	Machaire na h-inse "plain of the island i.e. holm"	Mooney 215	1950c
19.	ˌmahərəˈhïntʃ	Local pronunciation	1996

Magherahinch belonged in 1609 to Sir Art Magennis. The name is apparently missing from the list in the 1639 Inquisition on the lands of the Magennis chief (*Inq. Ult. (Down)* §85 Car. I), but it is probably one of the illegible names there, as it is mentioned with Edenmore further on in the same document. By 1659 it belonged to Symond Bateman (form 6). The river Lagan forms the southern border of Magherahinch. O'Donovan stated that "there is a holm from which *inis*". *Inis* means both "island" and land liable to flood. Most of the town-land consists of low-lying flat land beside the river. A bell called the *Clog Ruadh* "red bell" was held by a family of O'Lavery in Magherahinch, but then passed to the Earl of Moira. The O'Laverys asked for it back when the new Roman Catholic chapel was dedicated in 1815, but according to local tradition it was never returned (O'Laverty 1905, 121–2).

Risk	*Riasc*	
J 1461	"marsh"	
1. Reske	CPR Jas I 395a	1609
2. Reske, containing 2 sessioghs	CPR Jas I 190b	1611
3. Roske	CPR Jas I 190b	1611
4. Re(a)ske	Inq. Ult. (Down) §13 Jac. I	1624
5. Riske	Inq. Ult. (Down) §16 Car. I	1631
6. Riske	Ex. Inq. (Dn) 8 Car. I (DF)	1633
7. Reaske	Inq. Ult. (Down) §47 Car. I	1634
8. Reske	Inq. Ult. (Down) §96 Car. I	1640
9. Reaske	Census 81	1659c
10. Reiske al. Lisscorrane	BSD 82	1661
11. Resk	Reg. Magheralin (OSNB) E4	1715
12. Reske	Deeds & Wills (Mooney) 217	1716
13. Risk	Wm. Map (OSNB) E4	1810
14. Resk	Sur. Bateson Estate (OSNB) E4	1810
15. Risk	Bnd. Sur. (OSNB) E4	1830c
16. Riasg "a morass"	J O'D (OSNB) E4	1834c
17. Riasg "a morass or marsh"	Mooney 217	1950c
18. 'rəsk	Local pronunciation	1991

Risk was the main land unit (two sessiaghs) belonging to the O'Laverys, who were described either as being *of Moyragh* or *of Reske*, which was "held free" from King James (*CPR Jas I* 190b). Risk stretches north from the Lurgan–Lisburn road to the Co. Antrim border, around the small townland of Carnalbanagh West which is covered by the village of Moira. There are ponds shown in the townland on OS 1:10,000 sheet 164. Risk "was anciently boggy" according to O'Donovan, and thus apparently chosen as a fastness. It contains Rough Fort (on 1:50,000 sheet 20) and a possible crannog site (*ASCD* 185, site 742).

Tullyard	*Tulaigh Ard*	
J 1758	"high hillock"	
1. Ballytullyard	CPR Jas I 396a	1609
2. Ballytullyard	CPR Jas I 235a	1612
3. Ballytullearde	Inq. Ult. (Down) §13 Car. I	1629
4. Balletulleard	Inq. Ult. (Down) §85 Car. I	1639
5. Tulliard, woody bog of	Hib. Reg. Lr. Iveagh	1657c
6. Tollyard	Census 81	1659c
7. Tulliard	BSD 73	1661
8. Tullyard	ASE 223a 2	1669

9. Tulliard	Hib. Del. Down	1672c
10. Tullyyard	Rent Roll Down 5	1692
11. (?)Tullogher	Rent Roll Down 5	1692
12. Tullyard	Rent Roll Down 10	1692
13. Tullyard	Reg. Magheralin (OSNB) E4	1715
14. Tullyard	Reg. Deeds abstracts i §708	1737
15. Tullyard	Wm. Map (OSNB) E4	1810
16. Tullyard	Bnd. Sur. (OSNB) E4	1830c
17. Tulaigh Árd "high hill"	J O'D (OSNB) E4	1834c
18. Tulach ard "high hill"	Mooney 217	1950c
19. ˌtolïˈɑrd	Local pronunciation	1996

Tullyard townland is on rising ground south of the Lagan, including Tullyard House beside a rath on a spur, and the summit of **Carney Hill** (397 feet) at the southern end. This was probably the *tulach* of the name. Tullyard was part of the holding of Sir Art Magennis (forms 1–4).

Tullyloob　　　　　　　　　　　*Tulaigh Lúb*
J 1161　　　　　　　　　　　　　　"hillock of the bends"

1. (?)Ballylaghdermott	CPR Jas I 396a	1609
2. (?)Ballylaghdermott	CPR Jas I 235a	1612
3. (?)Ballylaghdermod	Inq. Ult. (Down) §13 Car. I	1629
4. (?)Tullylogh	Inq. Ult. (Down) §85 Car. I	1639
5. Tullelubb	BSD 75	1661
6. the p'cell of Tullylub or Tullybabe	ASE 61b 39	1666
7. (?)Tullagheke	Rent Roll Down 6	1692
8. Tullyloobe	Reg. Magheralin (OSNB) E4	1715
9. Tullylobe	Deeds & Wills (Mooney) 219	1716
10. Tullyloob	Wm. Map (OSNB) E4	1810
11. Tullyloob	Sur. Bateson Estate (OSNB) E4	1810
12. Tullyloob	Bnd. Sur. (OSNB) E4	1830c
13. Tulaigh na lúb "hill of the loops or windings"	J O'D (OSNB) E4	1834c
14. Tulaigh-lúb "of the windings"	Joyce iii 591	1913
15. ˌtolïˈlub	Local pronunciation	1996

Tullyloob is the furthest west townland of the parish, on the far side (west) of the O'Lavery holding, and next to the townland of Kilmore which connects Co. Down with Lough Neagh. The name does not appear until 1661 (listed next to Ballycanal), and again among Sir George Rawdon's possessions in 1666 (forms 5, 6). Sir George acquired many of Sir Art Magennis' lands. The highest ground, 70 metres, is in the north-east of the townland, by Moira Station. There are no particular streams and it is difficult to see to what feature *lúb* "bend" refers, possibly winding paths.

Tullyloob seems to be a late name for the townland. A form *Tullylogh* appears once in 1639 among the lands of Sir Art's son Sir Hugh Magennis, between Edenmore and

Ballymagaraghan (form 4). It is not a mistake for Tullyard, or for Gregorlough in Magheralin, which also appear in the list. It could be an intermediate form from the name *Ballylaghdermott* found in earlier lists of the lands of the Magennis chief. When the early 17th-century landholding in the area is plotted on to the townland index map, it appears likely that either Derrylisnahavil in Magheralin or Tullyloob in Moira was held by Sir Art Magennis under this older name. However *Ballylaghdermott* still belonged to Sir Art in 1629, the date *Derrylisnehawly* is first mentioned as belonging to Brownlow, so that it is more likely to have been Tullyloob. The Irish form of *Laghdermott* would be *Leacht Diarmada* "Diarmaid's grave" (*Joyce* i 66, sv. *slaght*).

The name Diarmaid does not occur in Magennis pedigrees (*TCD Gens*; *Céitinn, AFM* index). It was used by 17th-century O'Laverys, of Gartross and Taughlumny (*Wars Co. Down* x 81b). Clandermot, which became a district name in south Antrim, was *Clann Diarmada* "descendants of Diarmaid" (Morton 1956–7, v 6), a branch of Dál Fiatach, of the same vintage as Clann Gormley of **Glengormley**. Both names were derived in the 9th century from grandsons of the king of east Ulster, Eochaid son of Fiachna son of Aed Róin, who died in 810 AD (*EA* 180, 360; *Descendants Ir* xiv 82; Byrne 1973, 285). **Clankilvoragh** nearby in Magheralin seems to preserve the name of the Gilmore or *Mac Giolla Mhuire* family. In 1276 Irish annals recorded the death of *Diarmaitt Mag Giolla Muire*, lord of Lecale (*AFM* iii 426), who might have been important enough to get a monument. There is no record of where he died, but it could have been in this area.

OTHER NAMES

| **Carney Hill** | Of uncertain origin |
| J 1657 | |

| 1. 'karnï 'hïl | Local pronunciation | 1996 |

Carney Hill, 397 feet high, is in the townland of Tullyard. The name may preserve a local surname, as often with minor names.

The surname Carney or Kearney in Ireland can be the anglicized form of *Ó Catharnaigh*, a Meath family, *Ó Cearnaigh* or, as is often the case in Ulster, *Mac Cearnaigh* (*lez McKearnyes, Inq. Ult. (Down)* §2 Jac. I), and *Ó* or *Mac Ceithearnaigh* (Woulfe 1923, 63,99). The names *Ó Cearnaigh*, erenaghs of Derry, and *Mac Cearnaigh*, from Meath, were derived from *cearnach* "victorious" (Woulfe 1923, 330, 460). Bell has a rather inaccurate note on the Ulster surname McKearney: "The latter were a branch of the Cenél Eoghain [sic] and took their name from Cearnach, one of the O'Hanlons of Armagh". Bell refers to the village of Kearney in the Ards but does not postulate the original form of the name (Bell 1988, 108–9).

The northern family of *Ó* or *Mac Ceithearnaigh*, derived from *ceithearnach* "a foot-soldier", was from Roscommon, but there were probably others, as "the name (with Ó) in the 16th century was rather widespread" (Woulfe 1923, 331, 461). Both O'Kearney and MacKearney were known in Iveagh (*CPR Jas I* 197a; 395b, 195b). The surname *Ó Ceithearnaigh* or *Ó Cearnaigh* may form part of the townland name **Tullycarn** in Donaghcloney, where no cairn is visible.

The element Carney variously spelt is common in the North, in names of both townlands and minor features. **Kearneystown** in Garvaghy is locally called Kearney and does not appear to contain a surname. There is another **Carney Hill** in Drumgooland, a **Kearney's Hill** in Bangor, a townland called **Carneyhill** in Donaghadee, and one in Ballytrustan called **Kearney** (*PNI* ii 174, 188–9, 61–2). For this last O'Donovan suggested *Carnach* "full of cairns" and the editor decided on *Cearnach* "area of the angular rocks".

Flatfield	An English form	
J 1859		

1. Flat-field	Downshire Direct. 322	1823
2. An Gort Réidh/Flatfield	Éire Thuaidh	1988
3. 'flat'fild	Local pronunciation	1996

In the *Downshire Directory* Flatfield is said to be in the postal district of Hillsborough, but as this is the neighbouring parish, and as "Flat-field" is also said to be owned by a James Megarry (see **Megarrystown** below), it is clear that the Moira place-name is intended. Flatfield is in the north of the townland of Ballyknock, where the ground levels out towards the Lagan. An Irish translation was given on the bilingual map *Éire Thuaidh* (2).

Irwinstown	An English form	
J 1360		

1. əːrnzʹtəun	Local pronunciation	1996

Irwinstown is in the east of the townland of Ballymakeonan (OS 1:10,000 sheet 183), and there was a farmer of the same surname in the next townland Gortnamony in 1886 (*Bassett's Down* 277). The current Northern Ireland telephone directory contains many Irwins in Moira, Dollingstown and Magheralin.

Lagan, River	*Abhainn an Lagáin*	
	"river of the low-lying district"	

1. Logia "female calf"	Ptolemy 3	150c
2. super fluvium vocabulo Locha	VSSH (Heist) 358 §6	14thc
3. fluminis cui nomen Locha	VSSH (Heist) 357 §1	14thc
4. a river called Venelaggan	Cal. Carew MSS 1515-74 §207 25	1556
5. Ryver Leggane	S-E Ulster Map	1580c
6. fl. Laghan	Hondius Map	1591
7. Lagand flu	Mercator's Ulst.	1595
8. (?)Malagand	Mercator's Ulst.	1595
9. (?)Malaganda	Mercator's Ire.	1595
10. Legan flu	Goghe's Map	1601
11. Knock Benelegen [?]	Bartlett Map (Greenwich)	1602
12. Logan flu	Bartlett Maps (Esch. Co. Maps) 2	1603
13. (?)Knocke Bonalegan	Bartlett Maps (Esch. Co. Maps) 1	1603
14. (?)Fort Enish Alaghon taken from Bryan McArte	Bartlett Maps (Esch. Co. Maps) 2	1603
15. Forte Enislaghon	Bartlett Maps (Esch. Co. Maps) 1	1603
16. The river Lagan	CPR Jas I 73a	1605
17. the Lagan x3	CPR Jas I 74a	1605
18. ford Bealanilaghan near an old fort	CPR Jas I 74a	1605
19. the midst of the Lagan called Owenmore	CPR Jas I 74a	1605

20. flumen de Lagan	Inq. Ult. (Down) §2 Jac. I	1605
21. the whole river Lagan	CPR Jas I 89a	1606
22. the river Lagan	CPR Jas I 121b	1608
23. the Lagan water	CPR Jas I 146b	1609
24. the banks of the Lagan	CPR Jas I 146b	1609
25. Legan Water	Speed's Antrim & Down	1610
26. Logan flu	Speed's Ulster	1610
27. Logan flu	Speed's Antrim & Down	1610
28. the river Lagan	CPR Jas I 216b	1611
29. fishing and weirs of the river Lagan	CPR Jas I 236a	1612
30. the river... Lagan	CPR Jas I 271a	1614
31. the river Lagan	CPR Jas I 523b	1621
32. all fishing in... the Lagan	CPR Jas I 523b	1621
33. a ferry on the Lagan	CPR Jas I 524b	1621
34. the Laggan Water x2 (barony bound Lr Iveagh/Co. Antrim)	Civ. Surv. x §73	1655c
35. Luggan River	Inq. Down (Reeves1) 117	1657
36. Legan Water	Hib. Del. Down	1672c
37. Legan Water	Hib. Del.	1672c
38. Lagan Water	Lamb Maps	1690
39. River Laggan	UJA 3 48 (1985) 114	1760
40. Lagan R.	Taylor & Skinner 5	1777
41. Abhainn an Lagáin	Éire Thuaidh	1988
42. Abhainn an Lagáin	GÉ 1	1989
43. ðə 'lagən	Local pronunciation	1992

The original name of the river Lagan was *Laogh* (modern *Lao*) "calf", as can be seen from the former name of Belfast Lough where the Lagan enters the sea, anciently *Loch Laoigh* (*Onom. Goed.*). The Greek geographer Ptolemy compiled his Cosmography c. 150 AD, although the manuscripts are all later than 1200. Nevertheless many of his Irish place-names can be identified. If Ptolemy's river *Logia* is included, the original name was feminine, "female calf", or "heifer" (form 1; O'Rahilly 1946, 3). Alan Mac an Bhaird, however, thinks Ptolemy's original represented the masculine genitive singular, as in *Loch Laoigh* (1991–3, 12, 18).

The present name of the Lagan is derived from the low-lying district, *lagán*, through which the river flows from Moira to its mouth at Belfast, the part of its course which forms the boundary between Cos Antrim and Down, and the stretch of the river most often mentioned in the sources. In 1835 the Lagan regularly flooded the lands on each side for half a mile in autumn in the parish of Blaris (Lisburn) (*OSM* viii 19a). In 1605 the river in this area was also called *Owenmore*, in Irish *Abhainn Mhór* "big river" (form 19). Form 4 in 1556 makes the development plain: the river was then called *Venelaggan* or *Abhainn an Lagáin*, "river of the lowlying district". The process may have been made easier by the rough similarity in sound of *laogh* and the first syllable of *lagán* (initial *l*, syllable closed by *g* or [ɣ]).

I have found no other source for the place-name (forms 8,9) given by the continental map-publisher Mercator on the north bank of the Lagan south of Belfast, between the river and the hills. *Malagand* could represent *Magh an Lagáin* "plain of the Lagan". The name of a Lagan ford (form 18), probably that later crossed by **Spencer's Bridge**, is similar to Bartlett's map spellings (14, 15) of **Inisloughlin**, site of a fortification surrounded by bog on the north bank of the river, and a townland name in the parish of Magheramesk. Apparently the name was understood as *Inis an Lagáin* "island of the Lagan". The name Bartlett calls a hill near Belfast (forms 11, 13) looks like *Cnoc Buna an Lagáin* "hill at the foot of the Lagan". The name *Bun an Lagáin* for the river mouth is parallelled by **Bunamargy** and the recent Irish forms of **Cushendun** and **Cushendall** in Co. Antrim (*Joyce* i 528; *GÉ* 212).

Lany	*Léana*	
J 1960	"water-meadow"	
1. 'lanï	Local pronunciation	1995
2. 'lenï	Local pronunciation	1996

The name Lany or Laney (Laney House) is apparently Irish, possibly from *Léana* masc. "water-meadow", since it is on low ground near the Lagan in the north of Ballyknock. Lany seems to be a building on 1:10,000 sheet 183, with Laney House near it. There was an enclosure called Lany Fort in the townland of Ballyknock (*NISMR* Dn, 6-inch sheet 14). Lany Road crosses the Lagan at Spencer's Bridge.

Megarrystown	An English form	
J 1958		
1. ˌmi'garïztəun	Local pronunciation	1995

Megarrystown is in the west of the townland of Ballyknock, and many Magarrys or Megarrys were in the Ballyknock area between the years 1773 and 1855 (*Ir. Wills Index* iv, 103, 111). Megarry is a form of Gaelic *Mag Fhearadhaigh*, later *Mag Fhearaigh*, a "not uncommon" surname found in east Connaught, Tyrone and Antrim (Woulfe 1923, 420–1). Gilglasse *McGary*, husbandman, was noted in Co. Antrim in 1606 (*CPR Jas I* 92b). The Gaelic surname has been suggested as a possible component in the townland name **Drumnaferry** four miles south-west in the parish of Magheralin.

There was a tradition of a lost village called McGarry's-town in the parish of Ballymartin, Co. Antrim. According to the story in the Ordnance Survey Memoirs the McGarrys were a "powerful sept" and "unrelenting enemies of the early invaders", whose town was destroyed in the reign of Elizabeth as punishment for having attacked a detachment of her artillery (*OSM* ii 12b, map 14).

Spencers Bridge	An English form	
J 1860		
1. ford of Bealanilaghan nr an old fort	CPR Jas I 74a	1605
2. Spencer's Br.	Harris Hist. map	1743
3. Spence's Bridge	Harris Hist. 145	1744
4. Spencer's-bridge	Statist. Sur. Dn 24	1802
5. Spencer's Bridge	Downshire Direct. 329	1823
6. Spence's Bridge	OSM xxi 115b	1835
7. Spincer's Bridge x2	OSM xxi 118b	1835
8. 'spensəz 'brïdʒ	Local pronunciation	1996

Spencers Bridge is a bridge over the Lagan, carrying Lany Road from the townland of Ballyknock to Inisloughlin in the Antrim parish of Magheramesk, on the old route between Moira and Hillsborough. The bridge with its additional arches to cope with floods in the Lagan was described in 1837 (*OSM* xxi 118b). It must have been there since the 18th century, since Harris mentioned it, called *Spence's Bridge* in the text, but *Spencer's* on his map (forms 2–3). Its site seems to be the ford by an old fort recorded in the bounds of the district of Killultagh in 1605, the fort being that of Inisloughlin (form 1).

In the late 19th century G.& M. Spence were lime-burners at Moira, and there were farmers of the name in the Magheralin townlands of Ballymagin, Edenmore, Drumo and Drumcro (*Bassett's Down* 276). Local forms of both surnames, Spence and Spencer, were well-known in Magheramesk across the Lagan. In 1837 John Spence or Spince of Maghaberry was a local informant for the Ordnance Survey Memoir, and in 1832 there was a Spence's Fort in that townland (*OSM* xxi 113, 118b, 120b). However, the family of *Spincer* were said to have been granted the townland of Inisloughlin for ever in return for the service of Major Spincer to Cromwell in 1641. In the 18th century they swapped Inisloughlin for a lease of Trummery townland which had expired by 1837 (*OSM* xxi 117, 120, 125–6). Petty's map of Co. Down supports this account, since he gave *Castl. Spencers* as the name of Inisloughlin fort (*Hib. Del.*, c. 1672 AD).

Stannus Grove An English form
J 1957

1. 'stanəs,grov Local pronunciation 1996

The farm of Stannus Grove in the townland of Ballyknock is believed to have been named after a sailor, and the surname is no longer known locally. A James Stannus of Ballyknock occurs in the *Irish Wills Index* (iv 142) for the year 1835. At the same period Dean Stannus was rector of Blaris (Lisburn), and on the committee of the Lisburn Free School (*OSM* viii 11a, 32a, 33b). The surname occurs in the Carlingford area at the beginning of the 18th century (*Prerog. Wills* 437). In 1617 a Will. *Stanehouse* of Carbolzie, from Co. Down (a Scot) was granted the rights and privileges of an English subject (*CPR Jas I* 326a). He may have been the ancestor of the 19th-century Stannus family.

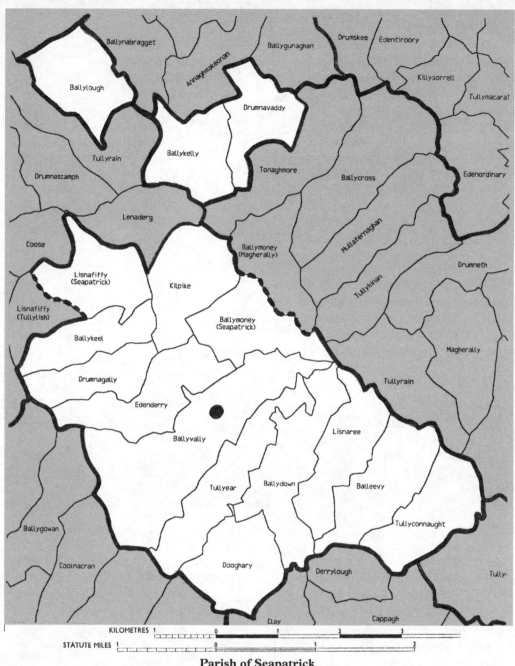

KILOMETRES 1 0 1 2 3

STATUTE MILES 1 0 1 2

Parish of Seapatrick

Barony of Iveagh Lower*, Lower Half (8 townlands)
Barony of Iveagh Lower*, Upper Half (1 townland)
Barony of Iveagh Upper†, Upper Half (7 townlands)

Townlands
Balleevy†
Ballydown†
Ballykeel*
Ballykelly* (detached)
Ballylough* (Upper half, detached)

Ballymoney* (shared with Magherally)
Ballyvally†
Dooghary†
Drumnagally*
Drumnavaddy* (detached)
Edenderry†

Kilpike*
Lisnafiffy* (shared with Tullylish)
Lisnaree†
Tullyconnaught†
Tullyear†

Town
Banbridge

The civil parish of Seapatrick, centred on the town of Banbridge, contains 16 townlands, none of which bears the parish name. The old site of the parish church is in the townland of Kilpike, on the east bank of the Bann, but the church itself was described as "old walls and out of repaire" in 1657 when the parish was reckoned at "13 townes and a half" (*Inq. Down (Atkinson)* 135). The river Bann runs through the parish, as did the barony bound between Iveagh Upper, Upper Half (Balleevy, Ballydown, Ballyvally, Dooghary, Edenderry, Lisnaree, Tullyconnaught, Tullyear) and Iveagh Lower, Lower Half (Ballykeel, Ballykelly, Ballymoney, Drumnagally, Drumnavaddy, Kilpike, Lisnafiffy). From the barony bounds of Lower Iveagh given in the *Civil Survey* of 1654-6 it seems that in this parish the Bann formed the original boundary between Upper and Lower Iveagh. 17th-century confusion about the river's function as a boundary was continued by Petty, who made it the boundary between Cos Down and Armagh (*Civ. Surv.* x §73). The Bann would not have formed a major barrier in this area, except in winter weather. The Ordnance Survey description said in 1834:

> The average breadth is about 60 or 70 feet... it is in summer nearly dry... After heavy rains in the mountains it overflows its banks, rising in a few hours to 8 or 9 feet (*OSM* xii 124b).

The Bann flows through the middle of the modern townlands of Tullyconnaught, Balleevy, Lisnaree, Ballydown, Tullyear, Ballyvally and Drumnagally, but in the Civil Survey their northern extremities were given as the boundary between Lower and Upper Iveagh (*Civ. Surv.* x §72). The townland boundaries must have changed somewhat, as Ballydown and Tullyear were said to meet Tullyhinan, but the eastern extremities of Ballyvally and Ballymoney now come between.

Subsequently Upper and Lower Iveagh were each also divided in two. Most of the northern townlands of this parish were in Iveagh Lower, Lower Half. The detached townland of Ballylough to the north is in Iveagh Lower, Upper Half, so that the parish was in three baronies before Ballylough was transferred to Tullylish. Ballykelly and Drumnavaddy are also detached, but in Iveagh Lower, Lower Half (see the parish map). Two townlands are divided between this and other parishes: Ballymoney with Magherally on the east, Lisnafiffy with Tullylish on the north-west.

Seapatrick formed part of four native districts: **Clanconnell**, in which Ballykelly was one of 14 townlands, mostly in the parishes of Tullylish (north) and Donaghcloney (*CPR Jas I* 394b, 193a), **Glasquirin** or Ballycross, in which there were 8 townlands: Ballykeel, Ballymoney, Drumnagally, Drumnavaddy in this parish, Ballygunaghan in Donaghcloney, Ballycross, Mullaghfernaghan, Tonaghmore in Magherally; **Loughbrickland** containing 10 townlands: Balleevy, Ballydown, Ballyvally, Dooghary, Lisnaree, Tullyear in this parish, Brickland, Caskum, Coolnacran and Drumnahare in Aghaderg; **Shankill** containing 12 townlands: Tullyconnaught in Seapatrick, the rest in the parishes of Aghaderg and Annaclone to the south (*CPR Jas I* 394b–395a, 190a). At the beginning of the 17th century all these were freeholds held from the King by subgroups of the Magennises (see the introduction to **Iveagh**). Some individual townlands were also part of the lands held by Sir Art Magennis of Rathfriland: Ballylough, Edenderry, and Lisnafiffy.

Many of the townlands in Seapatrick were acquired c. 1618 by Marmaduke Whitchurch: Ballyvally, Tullyear, Dooghary, Ballydown (Loughbrickland), Ballykeel and Drumnagally (the western detached part of Glasquirin), Ballylough from Sir Art Magennis, and Ballykelly in the south of Clanconnell.

Apart from Balleevy and Lisnaree, Whitchurch gained all the old district of

Loughbrickland, which controlled the route north via Newry to the crossing of the Bann at **Ballyvally** *Baile an Bhealaigh* "townland of the way", the site of the town of **Banbridge**. Other townlands were acquired by Sir Edward Trevor (Balleevy, Ballymoney) and Sir George Sexton (Lisnaree). When the land came into other hands the boundaries of several townlands were set down in detail for the new owners: the boundary of Balleevy with Lisnaree, Ballydown with Lisnaree, Ballykeel with Lisnafiffy, and Ballymoney with Edenderry (recorded in 1618/1623). Each bound was demonstrated by local experts, "according as yt had, by consent of both parties, beene formerly meered, trodden and sett forth by very auntient men" (*Inq. Ult.* xlii). Unfortunately the landmarks they mention, namely fords, bogs, streams, hills, groves, and *lysse* monuments, many with individual names, are difficult to identify today.

By 1834 N. C. Whyte of Loughbrickland House (Coolnacran townland) in Aghaderg held seven townlands in the parish: four from Loughbrickland district: Balleevy, Ballydown, Dooghary, Tullyear; plus Ballykeel and Drumnagally, from Glasquirin, and Tullyconnaught, from Shankill. Most had belonged to Whitchurch. From 18th-century estate maps quoted it seems that the family had also held Ballyvally and Lisnafiffy (*OSM* xii 123–4, 126a). Dean Mooney in his research made extensive use of the Whyte family's unpublished papers in the Public Record Office for Northern Ireland.

The only church land in Seapatrick was the townland of Kilpike in which the old parish church was situated, next to Lenaderg, one of the two church townlands of Tullylish. Church land in the area called the "manor of *Desertmoy*" was held in the early 15th century by the *McKewyn* family (*Reg. Swayne, EA* 106n). In the 17th century Bishop Buckworth said the church lands were relet to the ancient tenants, paying a chief rent to the bishop of Dromore (*EA* 311). Owen McDonegan held *Sipatrick* alias the sessiagh of *Killpatrick* as part of the "manor of Dromore" in the early 17th century, when Cormac O'Sheale also had land there (*CPR Jas I* 395b, 191a, 195b). Sir Art Magennis and his son Sir Hugh held the advowson of the parish (*Inq. Ult. (Down)* §§13,85 Car. I). However by 1834 Kilpike was secular land, part of the estate of Lord Dungannon, having been let to the James family about 1693 (*OSM* xii 126a).

PARISH NAME

Seapatrick   *Suí Phádraig*
J 1247   "St Patrick's seat"

1.	(?)i nOenuch Descirt Maige	CGH 409 330c53	1125c
2.	(?)a nDescert Maigi	Descendants Ir xiii 340	1200c
3.	(?)Disertunde	Eccles. Tax. (CDI) 211	1306c
4.	(?)Desertmoygh, eccl.de, pert. ad mensam Episcopi	Reg. Dowdall §129 275	1422
5.	(?)Dysertmoygh	Reg. Dowdall (EA) 106n	1422
6.	(?)Disertmoy	Reg. Swayne 85	1428
7.	(?)Dysertmoy Manor	Reg. Swayne 101	1428
8.	(?)church of Dysertmogy	Reg. Prene (EA) 106n	1433
9.	(?)rectory of Dissertdubunnugi	Reg. Prene (EA) 106n	1442
10.	Samgpadrig	Annates Ulst. 292	1505
11.	Soyge-Patrick	Reg. Dowdall §113 80	1546
12.	Sea St Patrick	Bartlett Maps (Esch. Co. Maps) 2	1603

13. Sipatrick al. Sessiagh Killpatrick	CPR Jas I 395b	1609
14. Carrowentample, to parson of Sipatricke	CPR Jas I 396a	1609
15. Sipatrick, Cormock McManus O'Sheale of	CPR Jas I 195b	1610
16. Patrick	Speed's Ulster	1610
17. Sipatrick al. Sessioghkilphekin	CPR Jas I 191a	1611
18. Sipatrick al. Sessioghkilpeacke	CPR Jas I 191a	1611
19. qr or parcel called Carrow-tample to rector of Sipatricke	CPR Jas I 191b	1611
20. Sye Patrick	Inq. Ult. (Down) §13 Car. I	1629
21. Seapatrick vic. et capell.	Inq. Ult. (Down) §85 Car. I	1639
22. Seapatrick	Civ. Surv. x §73	1655c
23. Seapatrick	Inq. Down (Reeves1) 79	1657
24. Seapatrick	Hib. Reg. Up. Iveagh	1657c
25. Sepatrick Parish	BSD 78	1661
26. Rector de Seapatrick	Trien. Visit. (Bramhall) 17	1661
27. Seapatrick	Trien. Visit. (Margetson) 26	1664
28. Seapatrick Rectoria	Trien. Visit. (Boyle) 46	1679
29. Seapatrick vicaria	Trien. Visit. (Boyle) 47	1679
30. Seapatrick	Lamb Maps Co. Downe	1690c
31. Sea-Patrick	Harris Hist. map	1743
32. Seapatrick	Dubourdieu's Map (OSNB) E11	1802
33. Seapatrick	Wm. Map (OSNB) E11, E135	1810
34. Suidhe Phádraig "Patrick's seat or sitting place"	OSNB E11, E135	1834c
35. Suidhe Phatraic, Sedes Patricii	J O'D (OSNB) E135	1834c
36. Suí Pádraig/Seapatrick	Éire Thuaidh	1988
37 ˌsiˈpatrïk	Local pronunciation	1991

Reeves suggested that *Dysertmoygh* (form 5), a name which occurs in early ecclesiastical documents, referred to this parish (*EA* 106, 309). The name *Desertmoy* was used from 1306 to 1433 (forms 4–8; the earliest, *Disertunde* form 3, is presumably a corruption). The spellings indicate that this represents *Díseart Maighe* (now *Maí*) "hermitage of the plain", and *díseart*, which was derived from Latin *desertum* "lonely, deserted place", seems to have been a formative element in ecclesiastical place-names by the 8th century (Flanagan 1981–2 (c) 72). The queried Irish forms (1, 2), the place of a murder among the Dál Fiatach royal line in the early 7th century, are given from the Ulster genealogies at Margaret Dobbs' suggestion (M. Dobbs ed. *Descendants Ir* xiii 340 n4), but have a different first element *deisceart* "south". The corresponding form *tuaisceart* "north" was anglicized as the Anglo-Norman district of *Twescard* in Co. Antrim, which makes it unlikely that *deisceart* would be anglicized as *desert* here. Another scholar linked *Descert Maige* instead to *Descert Maige ind Óendruind*, mentioned in a place-name poem on the view from *Sliab Fuait* (the hills of south Armagh) and this is more plausible (E. Gwynn, *Met. Dinds* iv 162, 420n; *Onom. Goed.* Hogan 289a).

Forms of the name Seapatrick appear from 1505 to the present. The 1505 form (10) may have misread *Saug-* as *Samg-*, but form 11 (1546) makes it plain that the name was derived from *Suidhe Pádraig*, in modern Irish *Suí P(h)ádraig*, "Patrick's seat", which was latinized as

Sessio Patricii by Colgan (*EA* 106n). The element *suí* is quite common in the name of various hills throughout Ireland called Seefin: *Suí Finn* "seat of Fionn (mac Cumhaill)" (for example, **Seafin** in Drumballyroney). The patron of the church thus appears to have been St Patrick, a shrine to whom was mentioned in the neighbouring parish of Tullylish in AD 809 (*AU*).

At present Seapatrick is also the name of the village around the site of the original church of the parish. In the past Seapatrick was sometimes used as the name of a land unit (forms 13, 15, 17, 18) equivalent to *sessiagh Kilpatrick*, which is probably the modern townland of **Kilpike** in which the church is situated. *Carrowentample*, which must be in Irish *Ceathrú an Teampaill* "church quarter", occurs (14, 19) as the name for the glebe land of the parish, which was 60 acres in 1657, and *Glebe House* was shown in 1777 on Taylor and Skinner's map 15 on the opposite side of the road a little south of Seapatrick church.

TOWNLAND NAMES

Balleevy   *Béal Átha Aobhdha*
J 1544   "approach to a pleasant ford"

1.	Ballyivee (10 towns of Loughbrickland)	CPR Jas I 394b	1609
2.	Bally-Ivee (10 towns of Loughbrickland)	CPR Jas I 190a	1611
3.	Beleeve, Aughdavanny parcell of	Inq. Ult. (Down) xlii	1618
4.	Beleeve inc Aughnadavanny	Inq. Ult. (Down) xlii	1618
5.	Beleeve towne, Bande, Lisnelanno	Inq. Ult. (Down) xlii	1618
6.	Bally-Ivy (in Loughbrickland)	CPR Jas I 373b	1618
7.	Beleeve, Aughdavany parcel of	CPR Jas I 304b	1623
8.	Beleeve inc Aghnadavanny	CPR Jas I 304b	1623
9.	Beleeve, Bande, Lisnelanno	CPR Jas I 304b	1623
10.	Ballyvie	Civ. Surv. x §72	1655c
11.	Ballyivy	Census 73	1659c
12.	Ballivey	Map of Down (OSNB) E11, E135	1755
13.	Ballevey	Sur. Whyte Estate (OSNB) E11,E135	1762
14.	Bellievy	Ir. Wills Index 99	1783
15.	Bally-vey	Wm. Map (OSNB) E11, E135	1810
16.	Balleivy	Wm. Little (OSNB) E11, E135	1834c
17.	[bal-'lee-vy]	OSNB Pron. E11, E135	1834c
18.	Baile aoibhe "pleasant town"	J O'D (OSNB) E135	1834c
19.	Baile aoibhe "pleasant, a lovely townland"	Mooney 295	1950c
20.	ˌbəˈliːvï	Local pronunciation	1991

John O'Donovan suggested that Balleevy was simply *Baile Aoibhe* "pleasant townland" (18). Since *aoibhe* means literally "of pleasantness" one could replace *aoibhe* with the adjective *aobhdha* of the same meaning. However, the townland once formed part of Loughbrickland precinct, which controlled the route north from Newry across the Bann

(1, 2). In 1618 a "parcel of land called" *Aughdavanny* beside the (west bank of) the Bann was allocated to Balleevy in a border dispute between Edward Trevor, who had acquired Balleevy, and George Sexton, who had acquired Lisnaree. The name *Augh(na)davanny* (3, 4, 7, 8) may begin with the element *áth* "ford", possibly the ford that has been replaced by the current bridge over the Bann just inside Lisnaree (Lisnaree Road). The boundary south-west of the Bann then included *Lisnelanno* as another minor name, though there is now no fort (Irish *lios*) on the boundary between Lisnaree and Balleevy. Finally both townlands met, then as now, the boundary of Ballydown.

There is a modern crossing of the Bann in the east of Balleevy (below Balleevy House), and the approach road from the south passes a large rath on the left-hand side, which may indicate an old route. The boundary description in 1618 (forms 3–5, 7–9) consistently called the townland *Beleeve*, although all the other sources call it *Bally-*. The modern spelling can be traced from *Ballyvie* c. 1655 (another boundary description) to the local pronunciation in 1834, though there is an alternative spelling *Ballievey* as used for Ballievy Road in the townland (Crowe 1969, 108, 119–123; OS 1:10,000 sheet 221). Boundary descriptions sometimes seem to employ more local forms of names than those fixed in grants etc. which were copied from other documents. Could it be *Béal Átha Aobhdha* "pleasant approach (to a ford)" or "approach to a pleasant ford", as *Baile Aobhdha* "pleasant townland" seems unlikely in its vagueness. Before the days of bridges it would be important for travellers to know if a ford became dangerous or impassable in bad weather. Joyce commented that *béal* "approach" was so common in the phrase *béal átha* "approach to a ford" that it could also bear that meaning when standing alone (*Joyce* i 357).

Ballydown	*Baile an Dúin*
J 1444	"townland of the hill-fort"

1. Ballyndowne (10 towns of Loughbrickland)	CPR Jas I 394b	1609
2. Ballyndowne (10 towns of Loughbrickland)	CPR Jas I 190a	1611
3. Ballendowne	CPR Jas I 409b	1618
4. Ballendowne	Inq. Ult. (Down) xlii	1618
5. Ballindowne	Inq. Ult. (Down) xliv	1623
6. bogge Fowleinany, hill Nyany	Inq. Ult. (Down) xliv	1623
7. hill Knocknecree, Lisnesillagh	Inq. Ult. (Down) xliv	1623
8. hill Knocknecarr	Inq. Ult. (Down) xliv	1623
9. Lisvane & hill Dronaghy	Inq. Ult. (Down) xliv	1623
10. foarde Abyogg, ryver Bonde	Inq. Ult. (Down) xliv	1623
11. thro' Tullynegarlisse to Munarley	Inq. Ult. (Down) xliv	1623
12. Ballidowne	CPR Jas I 304b	1623
13. Ballydowne	CPR Jas I 305b	1623
14. Fowlemany bog, hill Nyany	CPR Jas I 305b	1623
15. Knocknecree hill, Lisnesillagh,	CPR Jas I 305b	1623
16. Knocknecarr hill	CPR Jas I 305b	1623
17. Lissvane hill, Dronaghy hill	CPR Jas I 305b	1623
18. ford Abyogge, river Bande	CPR Jas I 305b	1623
19. thro' Tullynegarlisse to Munarley	CPR Jas I 305b	1623
20. Ballindowne	Inq. Ult. (Down) §39 Car. I	1633
21. Ballindowne	Inq. Ult. (Down) §62 Car. I	1635

22. Ballydoon	Civ. Surv. x §72	1655c
23. Ballydowne	Census 74	1659c
24. Belidonn	Ir. Wills Index 1	1712
25. Balleendown al. Ballindown	Deeds & Wills (Mooney) 295	1719
26. Ballydowne	Sur. Whyte Estate (OSNB) E11, E135	1727
27. Ballydown	Reg. Deeds abstracts ii §243	1758
28. Ballydown	Wm. Map (OSNB) E11, E135	1810
29. [bal-ly-'down]	OSNB Pron. E11, E135	1834c
30. Baile an dúin "Town of the dun or fort"	J O'D (OSNB) E135	1834c
31. Baile an dóin "townland of the fort"	Mooney 295	1950c
32. ˌbɑlïˈdəïn	Local pronunciation	1991

Ballydown in Upper Iveagh, stretching across the Bann on the west side of Lisnaree, also formed part of Loughbrickland precinct. In 1618 the boundaries of Balleevy and Lisnaree met Ballydown at the same point, presumably the same point at which the three townlands now meet south-west of the Bann. The boundary between Ballydown, held by Marmaduke Whitchurch, and Lisnaree, held by George Sexton, was given at the end of the same document, trodden by Tyrlogh McConwell and Ferdorogh McArt Oge Magenise (*Inq. Ult.* xlii, xliv). The series of named boundary markers (forms 6-11,14-19) seems to begin in the north, where the townlands now meet, along with Ballyvally, Ballymoney and Tullyrain, at a hill of 346 feet, possibly the "little hill called *Nyany*". Or, since Ballydown, Lisnaree and Ballyvally are in Upper Iveagh and Ballymoney and Tullyrain are in the barony of Lower Iveagh, maybe this hill was that called *Knocknechree* next in the list. This name could be anglicized from *Cnoc na Críche*, or, with a variant modern genitive, *Cnoc na Crí*, "hill of the boundary". **Lisnacree** in Kilkeel, *Lios na Crí* "fort of the boundary", contains a fort near the boundary of the half-barony of Mourne (*PNI* iii 46-7), and in Co. Donegal a stream called *Sruhannacree*, *Sruthán na Crí* "stream of the boundary" marks the limit of the parish of Templecrone (Mac Aodha, B. 1989-90, 177). The *foarde of Abyogg*, which was possibly *Áth Beag* "little ford", across the Bann was perhaps the place where the railway embankment crosses, and the junction with Balleevy, where the boundary ends in the south, must have been *Munarly* (*Inq. Ult.* xliv).

The name Ballydown clearly contains the element *dún* "hill-fort", which, although most often anglicized *dun*, can also be anglicized *down*, as in the county name of **Down**. There are two forts remaining on the borders of the townland (not mentioned in *ASCD*). The one south of the Bann is on a hill of 110 metres, actually just inside the boundary with Lisnaree, due south of a farm called The Hill. The minor names listed in 1623 on the border with Lisnaree include two (7,9,15,17) with the element *lios* "fort/enclosure", but these also cannot be identified.

Ballykeel
J 1047

Baile Caol
"narrow townland"

1. Ballykeele (in Ballynecrosse)	CPR Jas I 395a	1609
2. (?)Ballikeile (Bp, Laughlin O'Fegan)	CPR Jas I 395b	1609
3. (?)Ballekehill, Laughlin O'Fegan of	CPR Jas I 195b	1610

4. Ballykeill (8 towns of Glassequirrin)	CPR Jas I 190b	1611
5. Ballikeile:	Inq. Ult. (Down) xliv	1618
6. Lisnegeragh, streame Edenoconchy	Inq. Ult. (Down) xliv	1618
7. bogge betw Carricullyn & B'keile	Inq. Ult. (Down) xliv	1618
8. moore of Derryinsillee	Inq. Ult. (Down) xliv	1618
9. Ballikeole	CPR Jas I 409b	1618
10. Ballykeile:	CPR Jas I 305b	1623
11. Lisnegeragh, stream Edenoconchy	CPR Jas I 305b	1623
12. Ballykeile & Carrickcully bog	CPR Jas I 305b	1623
13. mearing/moor of Derrynysillee	CPR Jas I 305b	1623
14. Ballykeele 60a (Whitchurch)	Inq. Ult. (Down) §39 Car. I	1633
15. Ballekeele 60a (Whitchurch)	Inq. Ult. (Down) §62 Car. I	1635
16. half vil. de Ballykeele x2 (Wh.)	Inq. Ult. (Down) §91 Car. I	1640
17. half towne of Ballykeil (Seaptk)	Census 79	1659c
18. Balliceile	Par. Map (Mooney) 297	1660c
19. Ballykeele (Drumnegally &)	BSD 78	1661
20. Ballykeele; Chynawly, posson of	Rent Roll Down 11	1692
21. Ballykeele	Sur. Whyte Estate (OSNB) E11,E135	1727
22. Ballykeel	Wm. Map (OSNB) E11, E135	1810
23. [bal-ly-'keel]	OSNB Pron. E11, E135	1834c
24. Baile Caol "narrow town"	J O'D (OSNB) E135	1834c
25. Baile Caol "slender town"	Mooney 297	1950c
26. ˌbalï'kil	Local pronunciation	1991

Ballykeel, with Drumnagally in the north-west of the parish, formed a detached part of **Glasquirin** precinct (or *Ballynecrosse*), and was held in 1609 by Con Boy Mc Phellym McHugh Magennis (forms 1, 4). It can thus be distinguished from a church townland of Ballykeel held by Laughlin Oge O'Fegan (forms 2, 3) which was probably part of Ballykeel in Clanawly, parish of Drumgath (*PNI* i 118–9, forms 4–6). Ballykeel in Seapatrick is a long narrow townland, stretching west from the Bann and including the highest hill in the parish (519 feet) at its western end, surmounted by the fort of **Listullyard**.

Ballykeel came into the hands of Marmaduke Whitchurch and the bounds between it and Lisnafiffy, held by Sir Art Magennis, were "trodden and sett forth by Cormucke oge O'Sheale, clarke, and Concher Boy McConwah" in 1618 (*Inq. Ult.* xliv; *CPR Jas I* 305b). The places named (forms 6–8,11–13) go from east to west. *Lisnageragh*, probably *Lios na gCaorach* "fort of the sheep", must have been on the west side of the Bann opposite Seapatrick church, near Hill House; and a stream which forms part of the townland boundary near Ballykeel House, after the golf course, must be that named *Edenoconchy*, which possibly represents *Éadan Mhic Dhonnchaidh* "McConaghy's hill-face". The name would have transferred from a hill to the stream. The OS 1:10,000 map (sheet 220) shows a long narrow bog stretching north and south at the west end of Ballykeel, which could be the *moore of Derryinsillee*, the last name in the bounds. This may be *Doire na Sailí* "(oak)wood of the willow".

Ballykeel is not said to be a half-townland until 1633 (forms 14–17). Since it now measures 318 acres these references may only be to half of it. **Chinauley** (20) is in the northern part of Balleevy close to the Bann.

Ballykelly   *Baile Mhic Ceallaigh*
J 1249   "McKelly's townland"

1. Ballyvickeally in Clanconnell	CPR Jas I 193a	1611
2. Ballinekelly + Ballicollran	CPR Jas I 409b	1618
3. Ballevickealy	Inq. Ult. (Down) §9 Car. I	1627
4. Ballymackeale al. Ballyvickeale	Inq. Ult. (Down) §35 Car. I	1632
5. Ballmackelly	Inq. Ult. (Down) §39 Car. I	1633
6. BallyKelly	Census 79	1659c
7. Ballymycelley	Par. Map (Mooney) 297	1660c
8. Ballymc cally (Dromnevoddy &)	BSD 78	1661
9. Ballynekelly al. BallymacKelly	Deeds & Wills (Mooney) 297	1719
10. Ballykelly	Wm. Map (OSNB) E11, E135	1810
11. Baile Uí Cheallaigh "O'Kelly's town"	J O'D (OSNB) E135	1834c
12. Baile Mhic Cheallaigh "(Mac)Kelly's townland"	Mooney 297	1950c
13. ˌbaliˈkjalï	Local pronunciation	1994

Ballykelly was in Lower Iveagh and formed part of Clanconnell. The forms for the name make it quite clear that the surname *Mac Ceallaigh* (McKelly, later Kelly) is involved, as in the townland of **Carnacally** in Newry (*PNI* i 11), and possibly **Ballyvicknacally** beside Dromore, and **Drumnagally** in this parish. Woulfe gives *Mac Ceallaigh* in Cos Galway and Leitrim, and also in the Isle of Man (Woulfe 1923, 330), sometimes confused with *Ó Ceallaigh*, from Roscommon, Meath, Loughinsholin Co. Derry, etc. (Woulfe 1923, 330, 457–8). There were several O'Kellies in **Ballyvicknacally** in 1641 and eight households of the name in Lower Iveagh in 1659 (*Census* 81). If they were the people located at Drumbo as *Clann Cheallaigh* by the Ulster genealogies, derived from an 8th-century *Ceallach* son of Bécc Bairche of Dál Fiatach (*Descendants Ir* xiv 80), and who appeared on 16th- and 17th-century maps as the district of **(Slut) Kellies** (see **Clanbrassil McGoolechan**), the family seem to have had a long history in north Co. Down.

Ballylough   *Baile an Locha*
J 1051   "townland of the lake"

1. Ballelaghe	Fiants Eliz. §4218	1583
2. Ballelagh	Fiants Eliz. §4327	1583c
3. Balleenlagh	CPR Jas I 395b	1609
4. Balleenlagh, Brian Oge & Brian Carragh Magenis of	CPR Jas I 195b	1610
5. Ballinlagh	CPR Jas I 235b	1612
6. Ballenlagh	Inq. Ult. (Down) §85 Car. I	1639
7. Ballilogh	Hib. Reg. Lr. Iveagh	1657c
8. halfe towne of Ballyloch	Census 79	1659c
9. Ballylough	BSD 78	1661
10. Ballylogh	Sub. Roll Down 273	1663
11. Ballenlogh	ASE 61b 35	1666
12. Ballenlough	Lodge (Mooney) 331	1666

13. Ballilogh	Hib. Del. Down	1672c
14. Ballylough	Wm. Map (OSNB) E11	1810
15. Ballylough	County Warrant (OSNB) E61	1826
16. Baile an Locha "town of the lough or lake"	J O'D (OSNB) E135	1834c
17. ˌbali'lɔːx	Local pronunciation	1991

Ballylough formed a detached townland to the north of the main part of Seapatrick, in the barony of Lower Iveagh, Upper Half. It belonged to the patrimony of the chief Magennis in Rathfriland, and in 1609 was held from him, with Ballynabragget and Moygannon, adjoining townlands north-east of it in Donaghcloney, by Brian Carragh McBrien Roe Magennis (forms 3, 4, 5). It is sometimes difficult to separate the references from those to the townland of **Loughans** (Tullylish) on the Armagh border, but both were mentioned (as districts) in 1583 (form 1): *Loghan, Clare, Ballelaghe*, where **Clare** is the chief townland of Clanconnell, contiguous with Ballylough (*Fiants Eliz.* §4218). The townland of Ballylough, held by Daniel Monroe in 1659, was grouped with the other two townlands until 1666, which differentiates it from another **Ballylough** in Iveagh which was part of the district of **Clanagan**, parish of Donaghmore (*PNI* i 93). It is unclear why this Ballylough, without its two associated townlands, was attached to the parish of Seapatrick.

There is no lough on the 1:50,000 map, but on the OS 1:10,000 series, sheet 201, rough grassland is shown south-west of Boggle Hill, with high ground on three sides. This elevated site must be that described in 1834: "the swamp on Ballylough Hill, formerly a lake (from whence the name of the townland Ballylough), was partly drained in 1756 and has left an island now dry". The island had been raised on fir piles, and a dugout canoe of oak was found there in 1826 (*OSM* xii 124b). There is no further archaeological information on the site, another possible crannog (*ASCD* 183).

Ballymoney	*Baile Muine*
J 1348	"townland of the thicket"

1. Monylettygarvye:	Inq. Ult. (Down) xliv	1618
2. Lisboyoge Lyssynurgher Lysnetretemeall	Inq. Ult. (Down) xliv	1618
3. Awltnekirke, Tollyne Cerlessyn	Inq. Ult. (Down) xliv	1618
4. Aughe Coolefowle, Lissnetresheragh	Inq. Ult. (Down) xliv	1618
5. ˌbalə'mǫnï	Local pronunciation	1991

Ballymoney, in Lower Iveagh and part of Glasquirin, was divided between Seapatrick and Magherally parishes. The name has been discussed under Magherally, which see. The older form of the name seems to have been in Irish *Muine Leachta Ghairbhith* "shrubbery of Garvey's grave" (form 1). By 1618 this (whole?) townland belonged to Sir Edward Trevor, and the boundary between his land and Sir Art Magennis' townland of Edenderry, in Upper Iveagh, gave a series of minor names along the south-western boundary of Ballymoney within Seapatrick, probably now occupied by the town of Banbridge (2–4, repeated *CPR Jas I* 305a, 1623). Although four names include the element *lios* "fort", no forts survive on the modern map, and although fords are mentioned in the bounds the river which they cross is never named. The modern townland boundary skirts the north east of Banbridge, partly along Big Kiln Loaning in the area of Brick Row north of Banbridge Academy. There are no obvious streams and the whole description may refer to the time when the river Bann functioned as townland, and barony, bound in the parish (see introduction). *Cormucke* (Cormac) *O'Sheale*, the expert who "trod and set forth" this boundary in 1618, was a member of the O'Sheil family, well-known ecclesiastical tenants in Iveagh, who gave their name to **Ballysheil**, parish of Annaclone.

Ballyvally	*Baile an Bhealaigh*	
J 1245	"townland of the routeway"	

1. Ballyvalee al. Ballaghanharree (Loughbrickland)	CPR Jas I 394b	1609
2. Ballynvally al. Ballaghnaharde (Loughbrickland)	CPR Jas I 190a	1611
3. Ballibally al Ballaghnaharee	CPR Jas I 409b	1618
4. Ballyvally al. Ballaghnehary al. Tullyvolke al. Dromenergill	Inq. Ult. (Down) §39 Car. I	1633
5. Ballyvally al. Ballaghnahare al. Tulli- al. Drom-	Inq. Ult. (Down) §62 Car. I	1635
6. Ballyvally	Civ. Surv. x §72	1655c
7. Ballyvally	Census 74	1659c
8. Ballyvally	Sub. Roll Down 276	1663
9. Ballyvally al. Ballaghnaharee al. Tullyalke al. T'ake al. Drumenergill	Deeds & Wills (Mooney) 300	1719
10. Ballyvally al. Ballaghnaharee al. Tullyake al. Dromenergill	Deeds & Wills (Mooney) 300	1720
11. Ballyvaly	Sur. Whyte Estate (OSNB) E11	1762
12. Ballyvally	Wm. Map (OSNB) E11	1810
13. Ballyvalley	County Warrant (OSNB) E11	1827
14. The Rough Fort	Bassett's Down 256	1886
15. Baile an bhealaigh "town of the road or pass"	J O'D (OSNB) E135	1834c
16. Bealach na h-aithrighe "penance"	Mooney 299	1950c
17. ˌbalə'valï	Local pronunciation	1991

Ballyvally in Upper Iveagh formed part of Loughbrickland precinct (1, 2), but had come into the hands of Marmaduke Whitchurch before 1633 (4). It is a long townland, stretching for over two miles along what was, before the bypass, the main road from Newry to Dromore. The name seems to refer to the road, crossing over the Bann at Banbridge: *Baile an Bhealaigh* (15) "townland of the routeway". However, according to Lewis in 1837, the present road through the town and the bridge built in 1712 did not use the old ford, which was by **Huntly** a little to the north-west, and was the route used in 1690 by William III on his march to the Boyne (*Lewis' Top. Dict.* i 177a).

The alternative names survived to the 18th century, in deeds noted by Dean Mooney. *Ballaghnehary* clearly includes the element *bealach* "pass" and Mooney suggested *na haithrighe* (modern *na haithrí*) "of penance" for *nehary*, thinking of a pilgrim route (form

16). The third name begins *Tulach* "hillock". *Drumenergill* may be *Droim an Eargail* "ridge of the oratory".

The fort called the Rough Fort (form 14) is still well known, on the Yellow Hill to the east of the Old Newry Road leading south out of Banbridge (OS 1:10,000 sheet 220).

Dooghary   *Dúchoire*
J 1343   "black hollow"

1.	(?)Drominbekawly	CPR Jas I 394b	1609
2.	(?)Dromynleckawlie	CPR Jas I 190a	1611
3.	(?)Dromnecawly	CPR Jas I 409b	1618
4.	(?)Dromneleckawly	Inq. Ult. (Down) §39 Car. I	1633
5.	(?)Dromenelekeawly	Inq. Ult. (Down) §62 Car. I	1635
6.	Duchory	Census 74	1659c
7.	(?)Ballyjuige	Sub. Roll Down 276	1663
8.	Ditchry al. Dughory al. Diuhry	Deeds & Wills (Mooney) 299	1719
9.	Diughry al. Dughory	Deeds & Wills (Mooney) 299	1726
10.	Duchery	Sur. Whyte Estate (OSNB) E11,E135	1727
11.	Dughgary	Map of Down (OSNB) E11	1755
12.	Dughary	Deeds & Wills (Mooney) 300	1759
13.	Dughgarry	Maps (Mooney) 299	1767
14.	Duchery	Ir. Wills Index 55	1800c
15.	Doochrey	Ir. Wills Index 55	1800c
16.	Doochry	Ir. Wills Index 15	1808
17.	Duchry	Reg. Free. (OSNB) E11,E135	1810
18.	Doughry	Wm. Map (OSNB) E11,E135	1810
19.	Duchery	Ir. Wills Index 64	1825
20.	Duckery	Reg. Free. (OSNB) E11,E135	1829
21.	Duchery, Dughery	Reg. Free. (OSNB) E11,E135	1830c
22.	Dughery	Bnd. Sur. (OSNB) E11	1830c
23.	Duchry	Wm. Little (OSNB) E11,E135	1834c
24.	['Dugh-er-y]	OSNB Pron. E11,E135	1834c
25.	Duckerry	Ir. Wills Index 18	1843
26.	[Deoghary] + d slender	Mooney 299	1950c
27.	Dubh-chaire/Dubhgharraidh "black weir"	J O'D (OSNB) E11,E135	1834c
28.	Dubh-charaidh "black weir"	Joyce iii 307 (Don.& Dn)	1913
29.	Dromann leac Amhalgaidh	Mooney 299	1950c
30.	Dubhdhoire & Doire-loch "black"	Mooney 299	1950c
31.	Dubh-choirthe "grave-stone"	Mooney 299	1950c
32.	Diugha-/diogha-rach "the "worst" land in the district"	Mooney 299	1950c
33.	Dubh-cháthraigh "black, broken, mossy ground"	Mooney 299	1950c
34.	'djǫxrï	Local pronunciation	1991
35.	'djɔxrï	Local pronunciation	1992
36.	'djǫxərï	Local pronunciation	1994

There are no forms of Dooghary earlier than 1659, but it is likely that the townland is referred to earlier as *Dromonleckawly* in Loughbrickland precinct, listed regularly between Tullyear and Ballydown, the townlands which border Dooghary on the north-west and north-east (forms 1–5). Dean Mooney suggested (form 29) this name was *Dromainn Leac Amhalghaidh* "ridge of Aulay's flagstone", but if so the site of such a monument is unknown. The townland rises to 419 feet, the second highest hill in the parish (*OSM* xii 124a). It is bordered on the east by a stream flowing towards the Bann.

Dooghary is still pronounced, as Dean Mooney noted earlier this century, with a palatal-ized *d* approaching an English *j* (cf. the English word *dew*), which explains the unusual spellings in the Subsidy Roll (form 7, listed next to Tullyear), and the deeds which Mooney collected (8, 9). The palatal *d* is not remarked on in the *OSNB*, which suggested a compound with *dubh* "black": and the meaning "black weir". This last was also put forward by Joyce (form 28), on the analogy of other Irish places called Dooghary etc., for instance Doochary in Donegal. However there is no suitable site for a weir. Mooney suggested further com-pounds of *dubh* (31, 30) *Dúchoirthe*, *Dúdhoire* "black pillarstone, black oakwood", the latter to fit his theory that this townland was once united with Derrylough "black oakwood" using the obsolete *loch* "black" (*DIL*). Another possibility would be *dúchoire* "black hollow", from *coire* "cauldron" (*Joyce* ii 431). These still seem unlikely, given the *dj*. Mooney's alternative suggestion was *Diogharach* "the worst land in the district", derived from Irish *díogha* "the worst" (*Ó Dónaill, Dinneen*), although this form is not attested elsewhere (32). Mooney also referred to a compound of *dubh* with *càtharach*, a Scottish Gaelic term for boggy ground (33; *Dwelly*), although the equivalent *cáthar* is not known in Ireland. O'Rahilly considered that *càthar* was borrowed from English (1932, 185), presumably from *carr* "woody fen".

There is nothing in Irish compounds with *dubh* to cause the change from initial *d* to palatal [dj]. The very occasional variation between palatal and non-palatal consonants in Irish words seems most often to involve a consonant cluster: e.g. *drúcht/driúcht* "dew", though it also occurs with single consonants, as in *tuig/tig* "understand".

However Scottish placenames such as Deuchar, Deuchrie, pronounced with palatal *d'*, have been derived by Watson from *dubh-chàthar* or *dubh-chàthraigh* "black, broken, mossy ground" (Watson 1926, 138, 141). There are several Scottish names, some of which seem to alternate between palatalized and non-palatalized forms (collected by Simon Taylor) includ-ing Deuchar in Yarrow parish, Selkirk, *Dewchir* in 1520 AD; Deuchary Hill, Dunkeld parish Perthshire, *the Dwchyre* 1584; Duchra, Inch parish, Wigtownshire, *Dewchra* 1545. In Aberdeenshire "the dialect pronunciation is [Dyochry] (with open *o*, the first syllable like Gaelic *deoch* "drink"); but the sounds [Dyoochry] and [Doochry] are frequent" (Alexander 1952, 265–6). This sounds very similar to Dooghary in Seapatrick.

There is no problem with this derivation in Scotland, or with the palatalization of *d* in a Scots context (Simon Taylor, pers. comm.), but the linguistic situation in Ireland was not the same. Mooney may be right in involving the Gaelic element *díogha* to explain palatal *d*, but without the borrowed *càthar* the most likely second element is *coire*. Irish Gaelic names beginning with a consonant followed by *u*, such as Tuam Co. Galway, have often had the ini-tial consonant palatalized by English-speakers in Ireland. This may have happened with the anglicized form of Dooghary while it was spelled *Du-*, the usual form before the 20th cen-tury (6,10-14,19-25), unconnected with the development of the similar Scottish Gaelic names. It is also possible that Scottish settlers in north-west Co. Down used the same pro-nunciation for Dooghary as for names like Deuchrie in Scotland.

Drumnagally   *Dromainn Ó gCeallaigh*
J 1046   "O'Kellys' ridge"

1. Ballydromengally (in Ballynecrosse)	CPR Jas I 395a	1609
2. Ballydromengally (8 towns of Glassequirrin)	CPR Jas I 190ab	1611
3. (?)Dromneskawlagh in Clanconnell half town	CPR Jas I 193a	1611
4. (?)Dromnecawly	CPR Jas I 409b	1618
5. Dromynigally	CPR Jas I 409b	1618
6. Dromynegally	Inq. Ult. (Down) §39 Car. I	1633
7. Dromenegally	Inq. Ult. (Down) §62 Car. I	1635
8. Dromongally	Civ. Surv. x §72	1655c
9. Drominigally	Civ. Surv. x §73	1655c
10. half towne of Drummunagally	Census 79	1659c
11. Drumnegally & Ballykeele	BSD 78	1661
12. Drumnegally	Sub. Roll Down 273	1663
13. Drumnagally	Sur. Whyte Estate (OSNB) E11, E135	1705
14. Dromynigally al Dromnegally	Deeds & Wills (Mooney) 301	1719
15. (?)Dromneawly al. Dromnecawly al. Dromeneakeawly	Deeds & Wills (Mooney) 301	1719
16. Dromymgally al. Drumingally	Deeds & Wills (Mooney) 302	1720
17. Drumnagalley	Sur. Whyte Estate (OSNB) E11	1727
18. Drumnagally	Sur. Whyte Estate (OSNB) E11	1775
19. Drumnagelly	Wm. Map (OSNB) E11, E135	1810
20. Drumnagally	Bnd. Sur. (OSNB) E11, E135	1830c
21. [Drum-na-'gal-ly]	OSNB Pron. E11, E135	1834c
22. Mr Dunbar's... thread manufactory (Drumnagally)	OSNB E11	1834c
23. Druim na gCailleach "ridge of the nuns or hags"	J O'D (OSNB) E135	1834c
24. Dromann Mhig Amhalghaidh "Mac Cauley's Hill"	Mooney 301	1950c
25. Dromann Mhig Eachmhilidh	Mooney 301	1950c
26. ˌdrʊmnəˈgjalï	Local pronunciation	1991

Drumnagally (although west of the Bann) was in Glasquirin, which provides a useful means of distinguishing the early 17th-century forms from the similarly named lost land unit of *Drumnecawly*, which was in Clanconnell (near Ballykelly and marked with (?) above, forms 3, 4), and from *Dromonleckawly* (later **Dooghary**) in Loughbrickland precinct. Separate identity though not ownership continues in later sources: apparently both Drumnagally and *Drumnecawly* passed to Whitchurch and then to Whyte (forms 4/5, 14/15).

The earlier forms of Drumnagally indicate that the first element was *dromainn*, often with a following vowel that might indicate a surname. Surnames in Irish townland names are usually in the genitive singular, but this seems to be in the plural, like Derrygonnelly *Doire Ó gConaíle* Co. Fer. (App. A §21; *GÉ* 89): and was probably *Dromainn Ó gCeallaigh* "ridge of O'Kellys". **(Slut) Kellies** (*Sliocht Ceallaigh* "offspring of Ceallach") was a district in north

Co. Down according to 16th-century sources (see **Clanbrassil McGoolechan**). There is no evidence for *mac*, and *Ó Ceallaigh* could be a different surname from *Mac Ceallaigh* as found in **Ballykelly** two miles away; on the other hand variation between *Ó* and *Mac* seems to have occurred in other surnames in Co. Down (Ó Casaide S. 1930, 5), as in the names *Ó Broin, Mac Broin; Ó Duinneagáin, Mac Duinneagáin*.

Ballyvicknacally in Dromore may also contain the surname *Mac Ceallaigh*, confused with the word *cailleach* "old woman". The spellings of Drumnagally after 1660 AD indicate the name had become *droim na* "ridge of the". O'Donovan suggested the word *cailleach* "old woman" here (form 23), but although the plural *Droim na gCailleach* would give internal *g*, none of the spellings indicate the final consonant [x].

Drumnavaddy	*Dromainn an Mhadaidh*	
J 1350	"ridge of the dog"	

1. Dromenevoddie al. Doromenlissnegogie (in Ballynecrosse)	CPR Jas I 395a	1609
2. Dromenevoddy, Con Boy McP McHugh Magenis of	CPR Jas I 195b	1610
3. Dromenevaddie al. Drummenlisnigoggie (8 towns of Glassequirrin)	CPR Jas I 190a	1611
4. Dromenevoddy (Glassequirrin)	CPR Jas I 190b	1611
5. Dromravaddy, Con Modder Magenise of	CPR Jas I 373b	1618
6. Dromnevoddy al. Dromballissegoggye	Inq. Ult. (Down) §34 Car. I	1632
7. Drumnovoddry	Census 79	1659c
8. Dromnevoddy & Ballymc cally	BSD 78	1661
9. Drumnamadie	Sub. Roll Down 273	1663
10. Drumnavady	Harris Hist. map	1743
11. Drumnavaddy	Map of Down (OSNB) E11, E135	1755
12. Druminavady	Ir. Wills Index 54	1781
13. Drumnevaddy	Wm. Map (OSNB) E11, E135	1810
14. old fort called Diamond Camp	OSNB E135	1834c
15. [Drum-na-'vad-dy]	OSNB Pron. E11, E135	1834c
16. Dromainn a'mhadaidh "the dog's ridge"	J O'D (OSNB) E135	1834c
17. ˌdrọmnə'vadï	Local pronunciation	1991

Drumnavaddy, a detached townland in the north of the parish (Iveagh Lower) formed part of Glasquirin precinct, Ballykelly beside it being in Clanconnell. The early 17th-century forms make it clear that the first element was *dromainn*, probably followed, as O'Donovan suggested (form 16), by *an mhadaidh* "of the dog". The alias name given till 1632 includes *dromainn*, *lios* "fort/enclosure" and a further element, possibly *na (n)gogaí(the)* "of the eggies", which may have been a local nickname for an ancient monument (1, 3, 6). Another possible interpretation of this element would be *na gcogaí* "of the battles". There is a farm called Diamond's Fort on a hill in the north of the townland, probably the site of the "old fort called Diamond Camp 389 feet above the sea" in 1834 (form 14), but no remains are marked (OS 1:10,000 sheet 202). In 1834 there was also an island "built probably on piles" in Drumnavaddy Lake, left dry by recent drainage (*OSM* xii 124a). This lake may have been that earlier called *Lough Curran*: see **Tonaghmore** in Magherally parish.

Edenderry		*Éadan Doire*	
J 1046		"hill-face of the oakwood"	
1.	Ballyedenderny	CPR Jas I 396a	1609
2.	Ballyedenderrie	CPR Jas I 235a	1612
3.	Edenderry	Inq. Ult. (Down) xliv	1618
4.	Lisboyoge Lissynurgher		
	Lysnetretemeall	Inq. Ult. (Down) xliv	1618
5.	Awltenekirke Tollyne-Cerlessyn	Inq. Ult. (Down) xliv	1618
6.	Aughe-Coolefowle Lisnetressheragh	Inq. Ult. (Down) xliv	1618
7.	Edenderie	CPR Jas I 305a	1623
8.	Bally-Edenderry	Inq. Ult. (Down) §13 Car. I	1629
9.	Ballyedenderry	Inq. Ult. (Down) §85 Car. I	1639
10.	Edenderry	Civ. Surv. x §72	1655c
11.	Edenderry	Civ. Surv. x §73	1655c
12.	Edenderry	Hib. Reg. Up. Iveagh	1657c
13.	Edenderie	Census 74	1659c
14.	Edenderry	BSD 115	1661
15.	Edendery	Hib. Del. Down	1672c
16.	Edenderry	ASE 274a 29	1681
17.	Eddenderry	Rent Roll Down 11	1692
18.	Edenderry	Wm. Map (OSNB) E11, E135	1810
19.	Edenderry	County Warrant (OSNB) E11	1827
20.	[eden-'der-ey]	OSNB Pron. E11	1834c
21.	Eadan a'doire "Brae or hill-brow of the oakwood"	J O'D (OSNB) E135	1834c
22.	Éadan Doire "hill-brow of the oakwood"	Mooney 303	1950c
23.	ˌidən'dɛrï	Local pronunciation	1991

Edenderry is a common name-formation: borne, for example, by seven townlands in Northern Ireland, in Armagh, Down and Tyrone. This one is the most northerly of the townlands in this parish which extend across the Bann, and the bridge from Huntly is on its northern boundary. Edenderry was held by Sir Art Magennis, and is frequently listed next to townlands of his in Aghaderg, but must not be taken as the modern townland of **Edenderry** in that parish, which then bore a different name.

This is the only reference to woodland in the names of the parish. In the early 19th century it was reported that there were "no natural woods or remains", while "there is much young planting, principally fir on the steep banks of the Bann river, but the parish can scarcely boast of a single full-grown forest tree" (*OSM* xii 127b, 126a). However, Petty's maps of the area show a large number of trees beside the Bann in the late 17th century. The minor names in forms 4–6 (repeated *CPR Jas I* 305a) were on the border with **Ballymoney** in this parish, but can no longer be identified.

Kilpike
J 1248

Cill Phádraig
"St Patrick's church"

1. Sipatrick al. Sessiagh Killpatrick	CPR Jas I 395b	1609
2. Sipatrick al. Sessioghkilphekin	CPR Jas I 191a	1611
3. Sipatrick al. Sessioghkilpeacke	CPR Jas I 191a	1611
4. (?)Kilphekan al. Kilpheighan (to J.Keyres)	CPR Jas I 191a	1611
5. Killspeake half town	Par. Map (Mooney) 303	1657c
6. half towne of Kilpick	Census 79	1659c
7. Killpeake	BSD 78	1661
8. Kilpike	Tombstone (OSNB) E11	1793
9. Kilpike	Wm. Map (OSNB) E11, E135	1810
10. [kil-'pike]	OSNB Pron. E11, E135	1834c
11. The Glebe	OSNB E11	1834c
12. Coill a'Phíce "wood of the pike"	J O'D (OSNB) E135	1834c
13. Cill Phéice "Peake's (ie Fiacha's?) church"	Mooney 303	1950c
14. ˌkəl'pəik	Local pronunciation	1994

The reference to St Patrick in the name of Seapatrick parish is not clear in the surviving forms of Kilpike, which is the townland that contains the site of the early parish church, and a later church built close by. The first element is probably *cill* "church". At first glance the form Kilpike implies dedication to a saint of a different name, possibly *Fíacc*. There was a saint Fíacc, but connected with Leinster (*CSH* 286, 662.169). The parish of Kilpipe in Co. Wicklow, *Cellpichi* in 1179, has been connected with the personal name *Pich* or *Píc* (Price 1946, 76–7). There is no evidence here for the syllable *mac* of the surname McPeake, in Irish "*Mac Péice*... 'son of Péic' (a variant of the Anglo-saxon Pic); a rare West Ulster surname" (Woulfe 1923, 399).

However, if one examines the versions of the name Kilpike given as an alias for **Seapatrick** (forms 1–3), where Seapatrick is clearly being used to refer to church land being held from the Bishop of Dromore, rather than to Seapatrick parish, *Sessiagh Kilpeake* is identified with *Sessiagh Killpatrick*. *Cill Phádraig* "St Patrick's church" must have been the original name, with a shortened form of Patrick replacing the full name of the saint at some stage in written documents. *Sessiagh* also explains the reference to Kilpike as a half-town. Presumably the rector's glebe called *Carrowentample*, *Ceathrú an Teampaill*, "the church's quarter", was also near the church. In 1834 the glebe was "included in the townland of Kilpike... bounded on the west by the river Bann. Its northern extremity terminates in a point" (*OSNB* E135).

The queried form, although similar and listed with other church lands nearby in north-west Co. Down, can be shown to refer to the church townland of **Kilfeaghan** much further south in the parish of Kilbroney (*PNI* i 144–6).

Lisnafiffy
J 1047

Lios na Faiche
"fort/enclosure of the green"

1. Lisnefie half td in Kallydromad	CPR Jas I 396a	1609
2. Lesmefefie (Ballydromad; 4 half tds:)	CPR Jas I 235a	1612

3. Lisnepheagh	Inq. Ult. (Down) xliv	1618
4. Lisnegeragh, stream Edenoconchy	Inq. Ult. (Down) xliv	1618
5. Carricullyn, moore Derryinsillee	Inq. Ult. (Down) xliv	1618
6. Lisnepheagh	CPR Jas I 305b	1623
7. Lisnegeragh, Edenoconchy, Carrickcully, Derrynysillee	CPR Jas I 305b	1623
8. Balledromadd al. Lissnefefye	Inq. Ult. (Down) §13 Car. I	1629
9. Silvefefy, Ballehedromad	Magennis Paps (O'Sullivan) 63 §93	1632
10. Ballelisneffeffy	Inq. Ult. (Down) §85 Car. I	1639
11. Lisneery 6 tds	DS (Mooney) 305	1657c
12. Lisnaferry 2 sess	Hib. Reg. Lr. Iveagh	1657c
13. Lisnaferry 1 sess.	Hib. Reg. Lr. Iveagh	1657c
14. half Lisnefuthy	Census 79	1659c
15. Lisneferry 2 sessiaghs	BSD 78	1661
16. Lisneferry 1 Sessiagh (T'lish)	BSD 79	1661
17. Lissneffeeffee al. Lissneferry	ASE 49b 19	1666
18. Lisnafery	Hib. Del. Down	1672c
19. Lisnafectowne als Lissneferry	Rent Roll Down 6	1692
20. Lisnafifey	Map of Down (OSNB) E11, E135	1755
21. Lisnafiffey	Wm. Map (OSNB) E11, E135	1810
22. Lisnafiffy	Reg. Free. (OSNB) E11, E135	1829
23. (in English) Fivey's Fort	OSNB E11, E135	1834c
24. [lis-na-'fif-fy]	OSNB Pron. E11, E135	1834c
25. Lios na faithche "Fort of the green or lawn"	J O'D (OSNB) E135	1834c
26. Liosán Uí Fiacha "O'Fyffes'/Fivey's Fort"	Mooney 303	1950c
27. faithche/féarmhaighe "of the grassy plain"	Mooney 303	1950c
28. fiodhbhach/fiodhradh "wooded district"	Mooney 303	1950c
29. ˌləsnə'fəfi	Local pronunciation	1991

Lisnafiffy is partly in the parish of Seapatrick (431 acres), partly in Tullylish (209 acres). The division was first noted on Petty's barony map (12, 13), explained in 1661 as two sessiaghs in Seapatrick, one in Tullylish. In 1609 Lisnafiffy was owned by Sir Art Magennis. In the lists of his property the name is often associated with that of *Ballydromad* (1, 2, 8, 9). However the order is very confused, and what seems at first to be a district name: "*Kallydromad* containing four half townlands viz. *Lisnefie, Ballyannaghanckeonan* and *Ballykowsie*" (form 1), separates later into three half townlands with *Balledromadd al' Lissnefefye* further on in the list (*Inq. Ult. (Down)* §13 Car. I, form 8). Ballydromad, *Baile Droma Fhada* "townland of the long ridge", seems to be a lost alias name for one part of the townland. For the places on the boundary between Lisnafiffy and Ballykeel to the south in 1618 (forms 4–5, 7) see **Ballykeel**.

The historical spellings vary between Lisnafiffy and *Lisnaferry* (11–13, 15, 16, 18, 19), leading Mooney to suggest words with variants including *r* (27, 28), but *-ferry* is more likely a mistake repeated in related documents (Petty's maps, *BSD*). The name Lisnafiffy seems likely to represent *Lios na Faiche* "fort/enclosure of the green", with interchange of *ch* [x] and *f*, as in the names Murphy from *Ó Murchadha*; *Beannyborfy* from *Beanna Boirche*, **Mourne Mountains**; **Fofanny** related to *feochadán* "thistle" (*PNI* iii 110, 119–25). The interchange would have to have taken place while the syllable following [x] was still strongly pronounced, as *-faiche* has usually resulted in *-feigh, -fey,-foy* in anglicized forms (as in forms 1, 3, 6 here; **Ballynafoy**, parish of Annaclone). Dean Mooney and the *Ordnance Survey Name-Book* noted the name of Fivey's Fort in Lisnafiffy. This fort, not mentioned in *ASCD*, may well be the *lios* from which the townland was named, but the English version of its name is possibly a later interpretation. The surname Fivey was known locally, as landlords in the parish of Aghaderg, where the family lived at Union Lodge. One of them was responsible for the draining of Loughadian (*OSM* xii 6a, 3b). However the name Fivey in Co. Down was often an anglicized form of *Ó Cuaig*, a Co. Derry family, by confusion with Irish *cúig* "five" (MacLysaght 1985, 250; Bell 1988, 215).

Lisnaree
J 1545

Lios na Rí
"fort/enclosure of the kings"

1. (?)Carra Lissen Ree	Cal. Carew MSS 1515-75, 259	1556
2. (?)Lisenrie	Cal. Carew MSS 1515-75, 259	1556
3. (?)Lise-ne-ree	Bartlett Maps (Esch. Co. Maps) 2	1603
4. Ballylissnery (10 towns of Loughbrickland)	CPR Jas I 394b	1609
5. Lisnahirie	CPR Jas I 194b	1611
6. Ballynlisnery (10 towns of Loughbrickland)	CPR Jas I 190a	1611
7. Lisnerewe (bnds Balleevy)	Inq. Ult. (Down) xlii	1618
8. Ballylisnerigh (bnds B'down)	Inq. Ult. (Down) xliv	1618
9. Lisnerew (bnds Balleevy)	CPR Jas I 304b	1623
10. Ballylisnerigh (bnds B'down)	CPR Jas I 305b	1623
11. Ballylissnerikie (G. Sexton)	Inq. Ult. (Down) §30 Car. I	1632
12. Ballylissnerehye	Inq. Ult. (Down) §30 Car. I	1632
13. town of Lisnarihi	Magennis Paps (O'Sullivan) 68	1632
14. Lissnerye	Civ. Surv. x §72	1655c
15. Lisnaree	Census 73	1659c
16. Lisnery, six towne lands +	BSD 115	1661
17. Liseneare	Sub. Roll Down 276	1663
18. Lisneree	Map of Down (OSNB) E11	1755
19. Lisnaree	Wm. Map (OSNB) E11, E135	1810
20. [Lis-na-'ree]	OSNB Pron. E11, E135	1834c
21. lios na ríogh "fort of the kings"	J O'D (OSNB) E135	1834c
22. Lios na ri, in English Kingsfort	J O'D (OSNB) E135	1834c
23. leasanna a'ríogh "the forts of the king"	Mooney 305	1950c
24. ˌləsnə'ri:	Local pronunciation	1994

Lisnaree, again on both sides of the Bann, formed part of Loughbrickland precinct. The boundary commission on Iveagh (forms 7–8, 9–10) gives minor names on the border between Lisnaree and Balleevy and Ballydown east and west of it, discussed under those townland names. From forms (11, 12, 13) it appears that the name was modernized at one time from earlier *Lios na Ríogh* (now *Rí*) to *Lios na Ríthe*, both meaning "fort/enclosure of the kings". There are forts, one cut into by the road beside Ballydown primary school in this townland, but the site intended in the name cannot be determined.

The significance of the name is problematical. Like **Lisnatierny** "fort of the lords" in Aghaderg it may just be a popular supposition about the occupants of an abandoned site. However Bartlett's map of south-east Ulster added beside **Knock Iveagh** (Drumballyroney parish) the note "*Lise-ne Ree* where the McGenis is made". This may refer to the Newry townland of **Lisnaree** south of Knock Iveagh (*PNI* i 31), or it could be the lost name of a fort nearer to the hill. There is nothing further to support the identification of this townland with Bartlett's site, and it may refer to a mound now in **Lisnacroppan**.

An earlier source gives the Earl of Sussex's itinerary from Newry to Belfast in 1556, which passed through *Carra Lissen Ree* and *Lisenrie* (forms 1, 2, quoted *O'Laverty* ii 251). The itinerary is confused, apparently giving the beginning and end of each day's march, then listing the places between, though many of the spaces for place-names were left blank. However both Sunday's and Monday's travels start at *Bellahe Clare* (**Jonesborough**), followed on Monday by *Morres Va-* and *Carra Lissen Ree*, though that day's real starting point must be *Mahere Carran* or *Molloughe Cloughlan Carran beyond the Nurie* (probably **Carnbane** or *Moycarn, PNI* i 12; Mooney 1956(b), 206–7), which was reached on Sunday. *Lisenrie* then began Tuesday's journey, which went through the "great pass called *Kelleultahe*" (**Killultagh**) and ended at *Blarras* (**Lisburn**). The main road north from Newry, as shown by Harris' map and by Taylor and Skinner, passed, as it still does, about four miles west of the Newry Lisnaree, but the Seapatrick Lisnaree would provide a crossing of the Bann and be nearer to Killultagh, which was a district along the Lagan between Cos Antrim and Down (introduction xx). The return journey appears to go by a different route from Hillsborough (*Cromlin*) over a hill called *Banne Rory* to arrive at *Mahere Carran* again.

Tullyconnaught	*Tulaigh Chú Chonnacht*	
J 1644	"Cú Chonnacht's hillock"	
1. Ballytullyconnogh (in Shanchall)	CPR Jas I 394b	1609
2. Ballitullyconnagh (12 towns, precinct		
of Shanchall)	CPR Jas I 190a	1611
3. Tullycoonagh	Civ. Surv. x §72	1655c
4. Tullycomagh	Civ. Surv. x §73	1655c
5. Tollyconagh	Census 73	1659c
6. Tillyconough	Ir. Wills Index 99	1714
7. Tulliconnough	Ir. Wills Index 84	1745
8. Tullyconagh	Map of Down (OSNB) E11, E135	1755
9. Tullyconaght	Wm. Map (OSNB) E11, E135	1810
10. Tullyconaght	Tombstone (OSNB) E11, E135	1819
11. Tullyconnet	County Warrant (OSNB) E11, E135	1827
12. Tullyconnaught	Reg. Free. (OSNB) E11	1830
13. Corbit Milltown (a family name)	OSNB E135	1834c
14. [tully-'con-out]	OSNB Pron. E11, E135	1834c
15. Tulaigh Conchonnacht		
"Constantine's hill"	J O'D (OSNB) E135	1834c

16. Tulach Cuchonnacht "Constantine's hilltop'	Mooney 307	1950c
17. ˌtol̪iˈkɔnət	Local pronunciation	1994

Tullyconnaught in the south-east corner of Seapatrick was part of **Shankill** precinct, the only such townland in the parish. Until the 19th century the forms did not have a final -*t*. However the present form looks likely to contain the personal name *Cú Chonnacht* "hound of Connaught", which is attested in Co. Down among the O'Roneys in the 17th century (*CPR Jas I* 195b) and in the parish of Drumgath (**Lurgancahone**, *PNI* i 124). Maybe the place-name was written down before Ulster Irish dropped *ch* before *t*, and -*t* was only restored to the spelling when *ch* had gone. One would also expect some evidence for the first syllable of the personal name, whether *cú* undeclined, as in later usage in such names, or its genitive form *con*. In the earliest spelling of Lurgancahone, *Lurganconnaght* (1609), the element as shown in *Lurgancoconaght* in 1611 had dropped out by haplology. However subsequently Lurgancahone had a very different development, as shown by the current form.

The schoolhouse of Tullyconnaught, called Mulligan's in 1836, was founded by a Miss Mulligan in 1824 (*Lewis' Top. Dict.* ii 549a), probably the same family who had mills on the Bann, and are also commemorated by the bridge built in 1826 over the river at Corbet Milltown, called Mulligan's or The Corbet Bridge, near **Corbet** in Garvaghy (*OSM* xii 125b, 126a, 132a, 134, 135).

Tullyear
J 1245

Tulaigh Eirre
"hillock of the boundary"

1. Tullyerch (10 towns of Loughbrickland)	CPR Jas I 394b	1609
2. (?)Balletolloghonere, Gilleduffe McBryn of	CPR Jas I 195b	1610
3. Tullyerie (10 towns of Loughbrickland)	CPR Jas I 190a	1611
4. Tullyery	CPR Jas I 409b	1618
5. Tullyery	Inq. Ult. (Down) §39 Car. I	1632
6. Tullery	Inq. Ult. (Down) §62 Car. I	1635
7. Tullyerr	Civ. Surv. x §72	1655c
8. Tollyear	Census 74	1659c
9. Tullyeare	Sub. Roll Down 276	1663
10. Tullery al. Tullyeare	Deeds & Wills (Mooney) 307	1719
11. Tullery al. Tullyar [Exch. Bill]	Mooney MS 308	1724
12. Tullyear	Sur. Whyte Estate (OSNB) E11	1727
13. Tullyere/Tullyears/Tullyeire	Mooney MS 308	1755
14. Tullyeary	Wm. Map (OSNB) E11	1810
15. Tullyear/Tullyere	Reg. Free. (OSNB) E11	1830
16. [Tully-'ear]	OSNB Pron. E11, E135	1834c
17. Tulaigh fhéir "Grassy Hill"	J O'D (OSNB) E135	1834c
18. Tulach Iar(ach) "Western hill"	Mooney 307	1950c
19. ˌtol̪iˈir	Local pronunciation	1995

Tullyear is a long thin townland, lying east of the Banbridge bypass on both sides of the Bann. In the 17th century it formed part of Loughbrickland precinct. There seem to have been alterations to the boundary at the northern end, as the 1655 barony bounds say it met the south end of Tullyhinan in Magherally, whereas the eastern ends of Ballymoney and Ballyvally in this parish now come between (*Civ. Surv.* x §72). The first element is clearly *tulach* or *tulaigh* "knoll, hillock". The most likely hill is that surmounted by a rath in the north-east of the townland, where the townland boundary follows the ramparts of the rath for most of its circumference (J 1346, height 100 metres), although further south "a slight bluff of the high ground overlooking the valley of the river Bann to the north" also bore a rath (*ASCD* 167).

The later forms without a final vowel in the second element would support O'Donovan's suggestion "grassy hill". (The queried form, 2, can be shown by its proprietor to refer to **Tullyorior** in Garvaghy). However, a final vowel is represented in several early spellings, and the two versions are given as alternatives in the 18th century. Because of this Dean Mooney suggested the name was *Tulaigh Iar(ach)* "western hill", compared to **Tullyorior** which he thought was *Tulaigh Oirthir* "eastern hillock". However the relationship between the two is more accurately north-west and south-east of each other, and Tullyorior is clearly *Tulaigh Oirir* "hillock of the boundary", since it lies between Garvaghy and three other parishes, and between Upper and Lower Iveagh. Tullyear could be *Tulaigh Eirre*, also "hillock of the boundary", using the word *earr* fem. "end" (*Ó Dónaill*), since its northern extremity once lay on the barony bound between Upper and Lower Iveagh.

OTHER NAMES

Banbridge
J 1345

Droichead na Banna
"bridge of the Bann"

1. ciúin-Mheall na Banna	SCtSiadhail 73 §xxiv, 98n	1854c
2. Droichead na Banna	Omeath Infs (GJ) 157	1901
3. Droichead na Banna	SCtSiadhail 98n	1904
4. Bann Br.	Harris Hist. map	1743
5. Bann-Bridge	Harris Hist. 145	1744
6. Bannon Bridge, a very small town	UJA 3 48 (1985) 114	1760
7. Banbridge	Statist. Sur. Dn 223,233	1802
8. Banbridge	Wm. Map (OSNB) E11, E135	1810
9. Droichead na Banna, Pons Bannae	J O'D (OSNB) E135	1834c
10. Droichead na Banna/Banbridge	Éire Thuaidh	1988
11. Droichead na Banna	GÉ 91	1989
12. ˌbaːnˈbrədʒ	Local pronunciation	1991

The first bridge in Banbridge was built in 1712, the town laid out after 1767, and a new bridge built in 1832 (*ASCD* 393 §403). By 1834 the town had "entirely superseded Loughbrickland, the old port [*leg.* post] town two miles distant" *OSM* xii 124b). The Irish form of the name above is attested as that used by Irish speakers in Omeath and Monaghan at the beginning of this century (forms 2,3), and has the same meaning as the English name. However one of Laoide's reciters of the Irish traditional song *Seachrán Cairn tSiadhail*

321

explained *Meall na Banna* (form 1), "lump/mound by the Bann", as Banbridge. The local name Millmount may preserve something of this name but it is unlikely, as *mill* is appropriate in its English meaning. Since the town grew up in Ballyvally, the "townland of the routeway" (like **Ballynavally** near Shaws Bridge over the Lagan), one might assume that the bridge which gave the town its name was built near the old crossing point or ford. However this is said to have been at **Huntly** to the north of the town, although the records suggest that several fords were in use in the parish, as represented by the modern bridges.

Bann, River	*An Bhanna*	
J 2333	"the goddess"	

1.	Búas, Bóann, Banna	Cath MT §79	O.Ir.
2.	Búas, Boand, Bandai	TBDD §154	O.Ir.
3.	soir co Banna	AFM ii 604	919
4.	sair co Bandai	AU i 372	921
5.	ar bru Banna i nUib Echach	CSH §707.282	1125c
6.	for Banna, iar nUactur, for Glend Ríge	Imm. Dá T §5 =LL l.24224	1160c
7.	ota Bernus Tire hAeda co Banna	Geneal. Tracts Ba §14, A §112	MidIr
8.	Banna	Buile Suibhne 32	1350c
9.	Banna	LCABuidhe 51	1680c
10.	lands between.. Strangforde and the Banne	Fiants Eliz. §1530	1570
11.	ryver of the Bande	Inq. Ult. (Down) xlii	1618
12.	foarde Abyogg, ryver Bonde	Inq. Ult. (Down) xliv	1623
13.	river of the Bande	CPR Jas I 304b	1623
14.	river Bann ... northward ... to Seapatrick	Civ. Surv. x §73	1655c
15.	an Bhanna	J O'D (OSNB) E11, E135	1834c
16.	ðə 'ba:n	Local pronunciation	1991

Early references to the river name *Banna* "goddess" have been collected and discussed already in this series (*PNI* iii 175, 136), since the Bann rises in Deers' Meadow in the parish of Clonduff. It was treated as a major river, and was included with the Bush and the Boyne in an Old Irish list of the 12 chief rivers of Ireland (forms 1, 2), and the versified place-name legend or *dindsenchas* of Tara (*Met. Dinds* i 42). In the Irish *Triads* (4 §40), the Shannon, Boyne and Bann are the "three rivers of Ireland".

The citations above refer particularly to the Bann in this area. Form 5 (see **Drumhorc** in Tullylish) refers to a lost church called *Cluain Torc* beside the river in Iveagh. Form 6 is on an itinerary between south Co. Antrim and the city of Armagh (*Imm. Dá T.*). The Irish Annals refer most often to the Lower Bann, but forms 3–4 have a reference to an attack on Armagh in 919/921 AD where the plundering spread "eastwards to the Bann", which must mean the upper Bann. The Upper Bann was also used as a boundary marker, for example in the genealogical tracts on the *Aithechthuatha*, "vassal tribes", where *Tuath Chruithnech in tuaiscirt*, the Cruthin of the north, are said to stretch from Barnismore in the south of Donegal to the Bann (7), or in the Book of Clandeboy (form 9) where the "four noblest rivers in Ulster" marked out the land of the Collas (or *Airgialla*): *.i. Bóinn, Banna, an Éirne, an Fhionn* "that is, Boyne, Bann, the Erne, the Finn". Sir William Petty was misled in thinking that the river, once the western limit of Iveagh, still formed the boundary between Cos Down and Armagh, with the result that his maps show the river entering Lough Neagh at the present county boundary in the south-east, rather than farther west (*Hib. Del.* Ireland, Down, Armagh).

Boggle Hill   An English form
J 1051

1.	Buggle Hill	Sloane map	1739
2.	'bɒgəl 'hïl	Local pronunciation	1992

Boggle Hill is the highest point in Ballylough, a detached townland in the north of the parish. The modern pronunciation reflects the spelling of 1739 (1) rather than the present. Mr Copeland of Donaghcloney linked the name with the family name *Bodle*, attested in the area since the 18th century (1760 in Ballycross, *Ir. Wills Index* iv 13). However it is not clear that Boggle Hill took its name from them, especially as the pronunciation ['bodəl] is rather different. It is unlikely to be from Irish *buachaill* "lad" which is usually anglicized in place-names as *boghil* or *bohil* but might have become *bogle*. Alternatively *bogle* is a northern English dialect term for a supernatural creature similar to the Irish *púca* "hobgoblin", which appears in place-names in the south of Ireland (Ó Cearbhaill 1987, 96–113), as well as **Pollaphouca** in the Mournes (*PNI* iii 148).

Chinauley   An English form (?)
J 1545

1.	posson of Chynawly	Rent Roll Down 11	1692
2.	ʃən'ɔːlï	Local pronunciation	1991

Chinauley, a house and estate near the Bann in Balleevy townland (OS 1:10,000 sheet 221) was shown on the 1-inch map, although it is not on the 1:50,000 map. The name is well known in the area, and has also been given to a housing development in the east of Banbridge. If it began as the house name, the pronunciation of *Ch* as *sh* [ʃ] could indicate French origin, but no such place-name is known in France. There is one 17th-century form, listed next to Ballykeel (form 1). If it were an old name for the district one could suggest an Irish form *Sídh nAmhalaidh* "Aulay's otherworld hill", but there are no other historical references.

Huntly   Of Scottish origin
J 1146

1.	Huntley Glen	Lewis' Top. Dict. i 177a	1837
2.	Huntley Glen	Bassett's Down 219	1886
3.	'hɒntlï	Local pronunciation	1995

Early and later 19th-century sources name *Huntley Glen* as the place where King William

III forded the Bann on his march to the Boyne in 1690 (forms 1,2), described as "Huntly ford near Huntly House" (Haughton Crowe 1969, 15). This ford, near the old parish church, was on the main road from Newry to Belfast before the bridge was built in Banbridge. Huntly is marked on OS 1:10,000 sheet 220 (Co. Down townland index map sheet 2; *LGD* sheet 9) across the river from Millmount, on the west bank of the Bann in the townland of Drumnagally. The name is apparently from Scottish Huntly, from the title of the powerful Gordon family, which had been transferred to Aberdeenshire from the extinct hamlet of Huntlie in Berwickshire (Black 1946, 371a). Huntly is not recorded as a surname in Ireland (MacLysaght 1985, Bell 1988), but Gordon, in Ireland since the 14th century (Woulfe 1923, 259), has become "a Scottish surname very numerous... in Ulster" (MacLysaght 1985, 132) although it does not appear in Ulster plantation sources (*Fiants Eliz.* or *CPR Jas I*).

Listullyard Fort	*Lios Tulai Airde*		
J 1046	"fort of the high knoll"		

1. (?)Lissetolloh Arde	Cal. Carew MSS 1515-75, 259	1556
2. Listillyard	Sur. Whyte Estate (OSNB) E11,E135	1755
3. Lesleyard Fort	Bnd. Sur. (OSNB) E11	1830c
4. Listullyard Fort	OSM 124b, 125b	1834
5. Lesleyard Fort / Lios-li-aird	Wm. Little (OSNB) E11,E135	1834c
6. Listullyard	OSNB E11, E135	1834c
7. Lesleyard Hill & Fort (Ballykeel)	OSNB E11	1834c
8. Listullyard	J O'D (OSNB) E11	1834c
9. Lios liath ard "high grey fort"	OSNB Inf. E11, E135	1834c
10. Lios Tulaigh Aird "fort of the high hill"	J O'D (OSNB) E135	1834c
11. ˌləsli'aːrd	Local pronunciation	1991
12. ˌləsto̥li'aːrd	Local pronunciation	1991

The fort called Listullyard is on a hill beside the road in the west end of Ballykeel. This is the highest hill in the parish (519 feet), and is marked with a triangulation station although not named on the 1:50,000 map. Although there are no definite early forms, the name seems to be *Lios Tulai Airde* "fort of the high hillock (or knoll)", sometimes pronounced Lesleyard (forms 3, 5, 7, 11) by omitting the syllable -*tu*. Listullyard is well known as a local landmark. In 1834 the fort was "the largest and most perfect in the parish" with an extensive view of "the distant mountains of Louth, Armagh, Tyrone, Derry and Antrim", as well as "the mountains of Mourne and Iveagh and the range above Newry" (*OSM* xii 124a, 125b). The fort was levelled about 1850 to a platform some 5 feet above the surrounding ground, but remained "visible from forts for many miles around" (*PSAMNI* 103). It is not mentioned in *ASCD*. Haughton Crowe in his book "The Ring of Mourne" called the fort *Lisnaward*, and said it was visible from Balleevy (1969, 26, 123). In 1993 I was given the name Lisnaward for a wooded mound visible in the direction of Banbridge from the top of Knock Iveagh.

Despite the prominence of this fort near Banbridge, the place *Lissetolloh Arde* passed the day after *Lisenrie* by the English Lord Deputy on his route north in 1556 (form 1) is to be identified with the townland of **Low Wood** beside Skegoneil, Belfast (Morton 1957(b), 50; *Census* 8; *PSAMNI* 39). However the etymology of the two names appears to be the same.

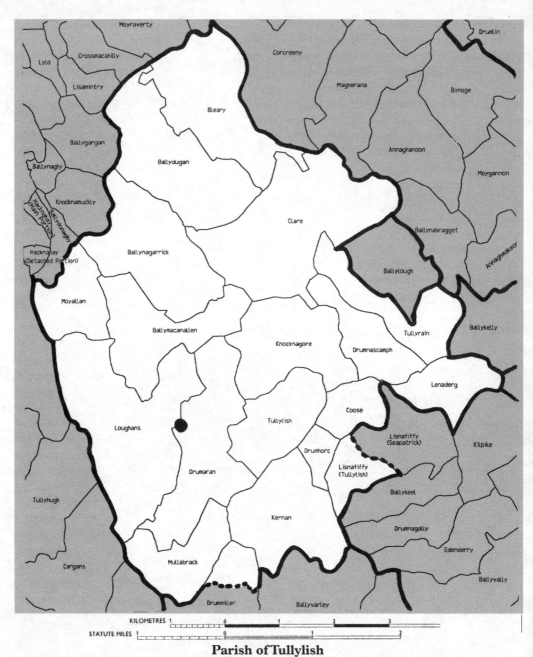

Parish of Tullylish
Barony of Iveagh Lower, Upper Half

Townlands
Ballydugan
Ballylough
Ballymacanallen
Ballynagarrick
Bleary
Clare
Coose
Drumaran
Drumhorc

Drummiller (shared with
  Aghaderg)
Drumnascamph
Gilford
Kernan
Knocknagore
Lenaderg
Lisnafiffy (shared with
  Seapatrick)
Loughans

Moyallan
Mullabrack
Tullylish
Tullyrain

Towns
Gilford

THE PARISH OF TULLYLISH

The parish of Tullylish now contains 19 townlands, reckoned as 14 in 1657 (*Inq. Down (Atkinson)* 134). The church site which gave the parish its name was first mentioned in the Irish annals in 809 AD, when its superior Dunchú, *princeps Telcha Leiss*, was killed "beside the shrine of Patrick in the house of the abbot of Tullylish" (*i tigh abad Telcha Liss, AU*: form 1 below). A reference to an another holy man, Erc Nasca, appears in the martyrologies for May 12th, where the entry is translated "Erc of the fetter, i.e. in *Telach Léis*" (*Mart. Tal.* 42); "hallowed Erc Nascai", glossed "from Tullylish in Ulster Iveagh" (*Fél. Óeng.* 124, 130n; *Atkinson's Dromore* 100). The medieval notes to the Calendar of Oengus explain the epithet by saying that St Erc wore a fetter in the river, when he was praying (an early Irish penitential practice) or washing (*Féil. Óeng.* 130–1). The river must have been the Bann, which flows close to the parish church.

The parish name later appears in the registers of the Archbishops of Armagh: *Tullaghlyss* in 1422, *Tolachlys* in 1526, and in the foundation charter for the diocese (1609) as *Tullaghlisse* (forms 8,9,11 below). Tullylish townland and Lenaderg, listed in 1427 as if it were a parish name (*Reg. Swayne*), were church lands. The earliest ruins of the old church in Tullylish are late 17th-century, but it is on the earlier site, placed "eccentrically within an oval earthwork about 150 ft by 130 ft across, the enclosing ditch and outer bank of which can be traced" (*ASCD* 336). It is beside the river Bann, close to the bridge at **Banford**. This was the largest fort in the parish (*Lewis' Top. Dict.* ii 659b), out of nine forts left in 1834 (*OSM* xii 142a). The graveyard is mentioned along with that of Hillsborough (*Croimghlinn uachtrach*) by the 18th-century Co. Armagh poet Art Mac Cumhaigh as being a burial place of the Magennises (*Marbhna Airt Óig Uí Néill* §32, form 7 below).

In the north the parish contained part of the large Magennis freehold of **Clanconnell** (Bleary, Ballydugan, Ballynagarrick, Moyallan, Clare, Drumnascamph, Tullyrain: see introduction to **Donaghcloney**) based on the townland of Clare and held in 1609 by Glasney McAugholy Magennis (*CPR Jas I* 394b, 193a). Landholding in Clanconnell was distinguished by giving the names of two "hamlets", apparently sessiagh subdivisions, along with each of the land units. Sometimes the modern townland has derived not from the major unit but from one of the sessiagh names, as with **Ballydugan** and **Bleary**.

Further south some sessiagh divisions listed in the 17th century have now become townlands, as with **Drumhorc**, or been lost, as with *Downemoyle*, only mentioned early in the century (*CPR Jas I* 396a, 235a), and *Creevy* and *Aghnekenny*, which although in Lower Iveagh were counted as being in the neighbouring parish of **Aghaderg** in 1666 (*BSD Dn* 78; *Hib. Del.* Down). Petty's atlas showed the last two to the east of Drummiller and north of Ballyvarley townland (*Hib. Del.* Down, c. 1672). All these lands had belonged to Sir Art Magennis, who owned the southern part of the parish including the smaller Magennis district of Loughans, held from Sir Art by Edmund Roe Magennis (*Inq. Ult. (Down)* §87 Car. I).

By 1618 Marmaduke Whitchurch had acquired the south of Clanconnell: Ballykelly (in Seapatrick), and two contiguous townlands in Tullylish, Drumnascamph (20 acres, another sessiagh) and Tullyrain (*CPR Jas I* 409b, 1618; *Inq. Ult. (Down)* §§39, 62 Car. I). Whitchurch died in 1633.

In the aftermath of 1641 many other lands changed hands. In Clanconnell George Rawdon acquired part of Magherana (Donaghcloney) and several lands in Tullylish: Bleary, Shanes Hill, Ballydugan, Clare, part of Ballynagarrick etc. (*ASE* 61b, 1666). Captain John Magill got Ballymacanallen, Drumaran, Drummiller, Kernan (60 acres), Loughans and Mullaghbrack in the south of Tullylish (*ASE* 112a). Most of these had been Sir Art's lands, and are followed in the list by the Dromore townlands of Killysorrell, not mentioned before, and Lisnaward, which had also belonged to the Magennis chief. In 1678 Magill's grandson, also called John Magill, had his lands created into the manor of Gilford, for which Gilford became the fair and market town (*ASE* 112a 1667). John Barrett also got lands in Tullylish: Knocknagore, Coose, *Crever* and *Aghenekenny*, and Kernan, all possibly from Sir Art Magennis, plus lands once his in Magheralin, Dromore, and Aghaderg (*ASE* 46b 26). Magill acquired *Crevy* by 1681 (*ASE* 274a). Knocknagore (now 712 acres) and Mullaghbrack (436 acres) have no forms before the mid 17th century (survey of Sir William Petty), but seem likely to have earlier been Sir Art's townlands. They cannot be *Creevy* or *Aghnekenny*, which changed hands under these names, but could be later names for lands listed as his and otherwise unknown. Between the names Drumaran and Ballymacanallen was *Ballytullylevin*, followed by *Downemoyle*, *Ballydownedrenny* and then Gargarry and Drumlee in Drumgooland (*CPR Jas I* 396a, 235a). Mullaghbrack was listed between Drumaran and Ballymacanallen in Barrett's lands in 1667 and seems likely to be a later name for *Ballytullylevin*, although its small size then (146 acres) may indicate it was the name of a sessiagh (*ASE* 112a). Knocknagore, which lies to the east of Ballymacanallen, was 340 acres when acquired by Barrett, along with *Crever* 60 acres and *Aghenekenny* 105 acres (*ASE* 46b). Since *Downemoyle* was only a sessiagh, Knocknagore may have been *Ballydownedrenny*.

The two most northerly townlands of Aghaderg were included in Lower Iveagh, one of them, Drummiller, being now part in Aghaderg, part in Tullylish. The reasons for the barony bound following this course are obscure, but the disappearance of several land units in the area may well be connected. It is likely that one of *Creevy*, *Aghnekenny* and possibly *Downemoyle* became the part of **Drummiller** which for some reason was included in Tullylish (cf. Myles 1936, 5, 16).

By 1834 the Johnston family had large holdings in the south of the parish: Drumaran, including the village of Gilford; Loughans, Moyallen, Mullabrack, with a clergyman of the same surname holding Drummiller (*OSM* xii 143). Sir William Johnston Bart. lived at Gilford Castle (*Bassett's Down* 259-60), and the ruins of Tallyho House, another former dwelling of the family, were in Mullabrack (*OSM* xii 142a). *Tullyhoa* was rumoured to have once been an abbey (*Lewis' Top. Dict.* ii 659b). In 1834 Alexander Stewart "of Ards House, Co. Donegal" owned the townlands of Ballynagarrick (part), Bleary, Clare, Coose, Drumnascamph, Kernan (part), and Lenaderg. Thomas Waring owned Drumhorc and Lisnafiffey (*OSM* xii 143).

A history of the parish was compiled by the Rev. E.A. Myles, Church of Ireland rector of Tullylish for 60 years from 1896, and published in 1936 as an anonymous pamphlet titled *Historical notes on the parish of Tullylish* (Myles 1936).

PARISH NAME

Tullylish	*Tulaigh Lis*	
J 0848	"knoll of the fort/enclosure"	
1. Occisio Dunchon principis Telcha Leiss, i tigh abad Telcha Liss, i fail scríne Patraicc	AU (Mac Airt) 264	809
2. Herc Nasci .i. i Tilaig Léis	Mart. Tal. 42n May 12	830c
3. ó Thilaig Lis ind Huaib Echach Uladh	Fél. Óeng. 130n May 12	1453
4. i Telaig Lis.. i n-Uaib Ethach Ulad	Fél. Óeng. 130n May 12	1453
5. ó Thelaigh Lis i n-Úaib Eachdach Uladh	Mart. Gorm. 94n May 12	1630c

6. ó Tulaig Lis i nUaibh Eachach Uladh		
	Mart. Don. 125 May 12	1630c
7. Dá scaoileadh Tulach Lis cumhra a léagaibh	Mac Cumhaigh (b) 21 l.187	1769
8. Tullaghlyss	Reg. Dowdall §129 275	1422
9. Tolachlys	Reg. Cromer ii §47	1526
10. Tulaglys	Reg. Dowdall §113 80	1546
11. Tullaghlisse	Jas I to Dromore Cath. 314	1609
12. T. Tullash	Speed's Ireland	1610
13. Tullash	Speed's Ulster	1610
14. Tollilish	Inq. Down (Reeves1) 79	1657
15. Tullelish	Hib. Reg. Lr. Iveagh	1657c
16. Tollelistes	Census 79	1659c
17. Tullelish par.(twice)	BSD 79/80	1661
18. Rector de Tullalish	Trien. Visit. (Bramhall) 14	1661
19. Tullylish	Sub. Roll Down 273	1663
20. Tullalish	Sub. Roll Down 273	1663
21. Tullalish	Trien. Visit. (Margetson) 24	1664
22. Tullylish al. Tullyneslatt	ASE 112a 38	1667
23. Tullelish	Hib. Del. Down	1672c
24. Tullalish Rectoria	Trien. Visit. (Boyle) 46	1679
25. Tullalish vicaria	Trien. Visit. (Boyle) 47	1679
26. Tullelist	Lamb Maps Co. Downe	1690c
27. Tullaleish als Tullanesla	Rent Roll Down 9	1692
28. Tullalish	Ir. Wills Index 75	1704
29. Tullelish	Harris Hist. map	1743
30. Tullelish	Harris Hist. 9,105,106,145	1744
31. Tullyleish Ch. (beside bridge)	Taylor & Skinner 15	1777
32. Tullylish	Wm. Map (OSNB) E61	1810
33. [Tul-ly-lish]	OSNB Pron. E61	1834c
34. Tulaigh Lis "fort hill/ hill of the fort"	J O'D (OSNB) E61	1834c
35. Tulaigh-lis "hill of the lis or fort"	Joyce iii 591	1913
36. Tulach Léis	AU (Mac Airt) 265 (AD 809 trans.)	1983
37. ˌtol̬iˈliʃ	Local pronunciation	1991
38. ˌtol̬əˈliʃ	Local pronunciation	1995

The later Irish references to the early church are clear evidence for the etymology suggested for the parish name, earlier *Tulach Lis*, and later the dative form *Tulaigh Lis* (2–6). The early forms use *telach*, an old by-form of *tulach* "hillock" (1–5). The occasional spellings with *-leiss, -léis* (forms 1, 2) suggest an alternative second element *lías*, gen. *léis* "fold, pen" (36), presumably referring to the same earthwork. The alternative may have continued in use, as suggested by occasional spellings and one local pronunciation of the name (forms 27, 31, 38). If the knoll is the one on which the church ruins stand, it is surrounded by a large ancient enclosure or *lios*, which apparently also guarded the ford nearby (**Banford**).

The place-name now also belongs to the townland in which the old church was situated. However it appears the townland of Tullylish originally had another name, discussed below.

TOWNLAND NAMES

Ballydugan　　　　　　　　　　*Baile Uí Dhuagáin*
J 0652　　　　　　　　　　　　　"O'Dugan's townland"

1. Ballydromneskie & hamlet Shian & hamlet of Dowgane in Clanconnell	CPR Jas I 193a	1611
2. Balledromnesky Shyane Dowgan	Inq. Ult. (Down) §9 Car. I	1627
3. (?)Ballidogan, Harrison & Crooke of	Wars Co. Down x 81	1641
4. td of Ballydoogan	Civ. Surv. x §73	1655c
5. Druneskie al. Ballido-gan, Shiane	Hib. Reg. Lr. Iveagh	1657c
6. B:Dugan (Tollelistes parish)	Census 79	1659c
7. Dromiskey al. Ballydoogan (Tullelish)	BSD 79	1661
8. Drumisky al. Ballydowigan, Drumiske sess, Shyane or Skeane sess	ASE 61b §39	1666
9. Shian Ballidogan Drumhesky	Hib. Del. Down	1672c
10. Ballydougan sessiah (Rawdon)	Atkinson's Donaghcloney 132	1691
11. td Ballydogan al. Dromniskee = 3 sess Ballydogan Dromniskee Sheean	Atkinson's Donaghcloney 132	1691
12. Drumisky als Ballydowryan: Drumusky sessiagh, Skyan sessiagh	Rent Roll Down 6	1692
13. Ballydugan	Atkinson's Donaghcloney 46	1703
14. Ballydowigan al. Ballydonagan	Deeds & Wills (Mooney) 329	1716
15. B.Dugan	Map of Down (OSNB) E61	1755
16. Ballyduggan	Bnd. Sur. (OSNB) E61	1830c
17. [Bal-ly-'du-gan]	OSNB Pron. E61	1834c
18. Ballydugan pronounced Bally'doogan	OSM xii 143a	1834
19. Baile Uí Dubhagain "O'Dugan's town"	J O'D (OSNB) E61	1834c
20. Baile Uí Dhubhagáin "(O')Dougan's td"	Mooney 329	1950c
21. ˌbali'dugən	Local pronunciation	1991
22. ˌbali'dɒgən	Local pronunciation	1992

Modern Ballydugan lies on the boundary between Cos Down and Armagh. The forms illustrate how this name, at first a subdivision of a townland, ended up replacing the original townland name. The *hamlet of Dowgane* first appears in 1611 as part of an area in Clanconnell called *Ballydromneskie* (form 1). By the middle of the century (form 4) the "townland of Ballydoogan" is cited on the boundary of Lower Iveagh, while it is given as an alias for the older name in the sources following Petty's barony map (5, 7, 8, also 11, 12). The division called *Shian* is preserved in the name of **Shanes Hill** in the townland.

The spelling *Ballydowigan* (forms 8, 14) indicates a further syllable in the second element. Despite the early occurrences without *Baile-* (forms 1, 2) it seems likely, as O'Donovan and Mooney have taken it, that *Dugan* represents a family name, anglicized from *Ó Du(bh)agáin*. Woulfe (1923, 509) gives five distinct families. In Ulster the name is most likely an offshoot

330

of the family who were hereditary historians (*De Script. Hib.* 91) to the O'Kellys, compilers of the Book of Uí Mháine, from Ballydugan near Loughrea. **Ballydugan** is also the name of a townland near Downpatrick, as possibly in form 3. There is no 17th-century record of the surname in Down, but "some of the sept of Duganes" were established tenants of some archbishop lands near Armagh city in 1609 (*CPR Jas I* 374a).

The surname is now Dougan and Duggan, pronounced with [u/ǫ] respectively. Although Ballydugan is generally pronounced Dougan in the area, the immediate local inhabitants may say Duggan (22).

Ballymacanallen	*Baile Mhic an Ailín*	
J 0650	"McEnallen's townland"	

1.	Ballyvickinallin	CPR Jas I 396a	1609
2.	Ballyvickinallin	CPR Jas I 235a	1612
3.	Ballevickenallin	Inq. Ult. (Down) §13 Car. I	1629
4.	Ballyvicknallyn	Inq. Ult. (Down) §85 Car. I	1639
5.	Ballimackenallin	Hib. Reg. Lr. Iveagh	1657c
6.	B:McNally	Census 79	1659c
7.	Ballimackenallen	BSD 79	1661
8.	Ballym'Mullan	Sub. Roll Down 273	1663
9.	Ballymackkenallan or konallan	ASE 112a 34	1667
10.	Ballimcanallen	Hib. Del. Down	1672c
11.	Ballymackenellan	Rent Roll Down 8	1692
12.	BallymcAnallen	Map of Down (OSNB) E61	1755
13.	Ballymacanallan	Ir. Wills Index 94	1776
14.	Ballymacknallan	Ir. Wills Indcx 94	1778
15.	BallymcAnallan	Ir. Wills Index 94	1800
16.	Ballymackanallin	Ir. Wills Index 90	1808
17.	Ballymeanelan	Ir. Wills Index 94	1808
18.	Ballymacanallon	Wm. Map (OSNB) E61	1810
19.	[Bal-ly-'mac-a-nal-lin]	OSNB Pron. E61	1834c
20.	Baile Mhic Conalláin "Macconnallan's town"	J O'D (OSNB) E61	1834c
21.	Baile Mhic an Ailín	Mooney 329	950c
23.	ˌbalïmakəˈnalən	Local pronunciation	1991

Ballymacanallen was part of the lands of the Magennis chief. The earliest forms, from the 1609 Schedule of Iveagh to the 1639 inquisition (1–4), show what is clearly a surname formed with *mac-* "son", lenited in the genitive singular according to the rules for proper names: *Ballevickenallin*. In later examples, such as the Petty maps, the surname is no longer lenited, and *-mac-* appears in the place-name: *Ballimackenallin* (5); this may be a gen. plural form but is more likely an anglicization of the familiar form of the surname. Despite two forms which appear to show a different surname, *B:McNally* 1659 (6), *Ballym'Mullan* 1663 (8), and the lack of historical references in the area, it seems we must have here an example of what Woulfe called "a rare surname in Ulster and Connaught, the origin of which I cannot trace. *Mac an Ailín* represents the pronunciation as I heard it" (Woulfe 1923, 308). The forms of this townland name can normally be distinguished by the final *-n* from those of

Ballymacanally townland in the nearby parish of Magheralin, but confusion is possible even today.

The Glass Moss, so called since 1797 (Myles 1936, 39), is presumably named from Irish *glas* "green" plus English *moss*, used to mean "turf-bog" in northern dialects.

| **Ballynagarrick** | *Baile na gCarraig* | |
| J 0551 | "townland of the rocks" | |

1. Ballynegaricke in Clanconnell & hamlets Browkishe Clonly	CPR Jas I 193a	1611
2. Ballinegarrick Browkish Cowley	Inq. Ult. (Down) §9 Car. I	1627
3. Ballinegarrick, Arthur Oge McGlasney Magennis of	Wars Co. Down x 81	1641
4. Ballynegarrick, Hugh Magennis of	Wars Co. Down x 81	1641
5. Ballynegarrick, McArt Oge Magennis of	Wars Co. Down x 81	1641
6. towne td of Ballynagarick	Civ. Surv. x §73	1655c
7. Clonclee Bruher Ballinegarig	Hib. Reg. Lr. Iveagh	1657c
8. Ballygarricke	Census 79	1659c
9. Ballinegaricke	BSD 79	1661
10. Brugher Ballynegarick	S & D Ann. (Mooney) 332 (31)	17thc
11. Ballynegarick	Sub. Roll Down 273	1663
12. Ballynegarricke	ASE 61b 35	1666
13. BallymcGarrick	ASE 61b 39	1666
14. Ballynegarricke	ASE 112a 34	1667
15. Clonclee Brugher Ballinegarig	Hib. Del. Down	1672c
16. tn Ballynegaricke = 3 sess: Brohish Clonlee Ballynegaricke	Atkinson's Donaghcloney 132	1691
17. Ballymackgarrick, sess Chomlee	Rent Roll Down 6	1692
18. Ballynegaricke, half towne land of	Rent Roll Down 8	1692
19. Ballygarrick	Deeds & Wills (Mooney) 331	1716
20. Ballynegarrick	Map of Down (OSNB) E61	1755
21. Ballynagarrick	Wm. Map (OSNB) E61	1810
22. Ballymagabrick	Bnd. Sur. (OSNB) E61	1830c
23. [Bal-ly-na-'gar-rick]	OSNB Pron. E61	1834c
24. Baile na gCarrag "town of the rocks"	J O'D (OSNB) E61	1834c
25. 'bɑlnə'garïk	Local pronunciation	1991
26. 'bɑlənə'gɑrək	Local pronunciation	1991

Ballynagarrick on the border with Co. Armagh was part of the Magennis holding of Clanconnell, and the earliest reference gives it two "hamlets" called *Browkishe* and *Clonly* (1). The forms of the townland name clearly indicate "townland of the rocks" but I am not sure where the rocks are. The 1:10,000 map sheet 201 shows a house called Craigmore (in Irish *Creag Mhór* "big rock") and quarries in the south of the townland. The hamlets are referred to throughout the 17th century and appear on the Petty maps (forms 7, 15).

In 1641 several members of the Magennis family named as rebels were said to come from *Ballinegarrick* (3,4,5). Arthur Oge McGlasney Magennis, with his two sons Phelim McArt Oge Magennis and Brian Crossagh McArt Oge Magennis, seems to have been the Art Oge son of Glasney Magennis of Clanconnell who held **Islandderry** in **Lequirin** in 1609. A letter survives from 1691 from Daniel Magennis, conveying the family interest in *Brughis*, which must have been one of the divisions of this townland (*Atkinson's Donaghcloney* 44). Most of the forms of this name suggest a final *-s* and there is a townland of Brughas in the parish of Tartaraghan in Co. Armagh (and another nearby in the 17th century). The name appears to derive from *briugas* meaning "hospitality, abundance", used as the name of an imaginary fort (*dún*) in the 12th century (*DIL* sv., *LL* i l.3914) in its later form *brughachas* (Dinneen) which might now be spelt *brúchas*. Alternatively the *-k-* spellings may indicate *brocais* "(badger) den". The latest form of *Clonelee* is in the *Rent Roll* of 1691. It appears to be *Cluain Liath* "grey meadow". Another *Clonlee* was a hamlet of Tullyrain.

Bleary	*Bladhraigh*	
J 0754	"portion"(?)	

1. (?)Carracc Blaraighe	AFM i 26-8 (prehist.)	3501
2. (?)Bladraidi la Dal Riada	Geneal. Tracts 158, C §99 (Lec.)	1397c
3. (?)Bladraige (Aithechthuatha)	Geneal. Tracts 107, Ba §1 (BB)	14thc
4. Ballytullyconely & hamlet Longert & hamlet of Blyery in Clanconnell	CPR Jas I 193a	1611
5. Balletallewnnelly Lougert Bleire	Inq. Ult. (Down) §9 Car. I	1627
6. td of Bleery	Civ. Surv. x §73	1655c
7. half tn of Bleary	Hib. Reg. Lr. Iveagh	1657c
8. Blearby, Bleary	Par. Map (Mooney) 333	17thc
9. B:Lerry	Census 79	1659c
10. Bleary ½ Towne of	BSD 79	1661
11. ½ Bleary	BSD 80	1661
12. Bleary (half & qr)	ASE 61b 39	1666
13. Bleary	Hib. Del. Down	1672c
14. half ye tn Bleary	Atkinson's Donaghcloney 132	1691
15. td Blearey al. Bally Tully Conell 3 sess: Blearey al. Taliconely & Gortgeney & Corhillis al. Longford	Atkinson's Donaghcloney 132	1691
16. Qr Towne Bleary, Bleary, half Bleary	Rent Roll Down 5	1692
17. Bleerey	Ir. Wills Index 78	1711
18. Bleary	Deeds & Wills (Mooney) 333	1716
19. Bleery	Map of Down (OSNB) E61	1755
20. Dean's Turn (road) at Bleary Cross	Atkinson's Donaghcloney 63	1800c
21. Bleary	Wm. Map (OSNB) E61	1810
22. ['Blea-ry / Blary / Blayry]	OSNB Pron. E61	1834c
23. pron. by old people Blairey	Mooney 334 (ex Myles p.2)	1936
24. Bla Righ "field of the king"	J O'D (OSNB) E61	1834c
25. Bleodhrach "clamorous, noisy place"	Mooney 333	1950c
26. Bléithrach "corn-land"	Mooney 333	1950c

27. 'blɛːrï   Local pronunciation   1991
28. 'blïrï   Local pronunciation   1991
29. 'bliːrï   Local pronunciation   1994

Bleary like Ballydugan appears in 1611 as the name of a subdivision (hamlet) of a town-land in Clanconnell (4), and later takes over from the original townland name. However here the transfer seems to have happened earlier and the subdivisions were not mapped by Petty. The earliest spelling (anglicized) which clearly refers to this location is *Blyery* (form 4), but from the late 17th century the spelling *Bleery* or *Bleary* becomes standard. Pronunciations collected in the 19th century, *Blary*, in the 1930s "from the old people" *Blairey* (22, 23), and occasionally at the present (27) indicate [ɛː] not [iː] as the earlier vowel sound of the first syllable here. Dean Mooney suggested a connection with *bleithech* "corn for grinding" (i.e. "place of corn-grinding"), or with a word with the forms *bladhrach/ blaidhreach/ blaodhrach* "shouting" (*Dinneen*). However these seem unlikely to stand alone as a place-name, and *-ry* in anglicized names like Kerry, **Cary** represents early Irish *-raige*, a suffix indicating a tribal name.

Myles' anonymous pamphlet on the history of Tullylish first suggested the population name *Bladraige*, one of the scattered *aithechthuatha* or "subject tribes" (forms 2, 3). References to the tribe put them on the north-east coast of Co. Antrim: "*Bladraige* in the ter-ritory of Dál Riada descend from Bladchú of the Britons of Man" (form 3). However the name may also be connected with the character called *Blai Briugad* "Blai the hospitaller" in the Ulster Cycle tales. He kept a *bruiden* or house of hospitality somewhere in Ulster (*SMMD I* §1n, *CMR II* 52), but the only time his dwelling is located it is at **Tara** at the tip of the Ards peninsula (*Mesca Ulad* 1.714; *PNI* ii 131–2). Séamas Ó Ceallaigh noted that there was a tribe in Co. Derry called *Tuath Rois Blai* and a mountain *Blaishliabh*, possibly connected with *Bladraige* or Blai Briugad, and that Dál Riada may have once extended further to the west over the Bann (*GUH* 42n). A fort called *Carraig Bladraide* appears in three lists of the build-ings erected in Ireland in the time of the legendary invader Éremón, said to be "in the north-east of Ireland" or at *Murbolg* on the north coast (*L. Gabála* v 166 §483, 170 §487). These references are admittedly rather far away from the area in question here.

O'Donovan in discussing the fort (form 1) said the only similar modern place-name was Blyry in Westmeath (*AFM* i 28 n.t), and Hogan accepted Blyry as its location (s.v. *Blarach*). In the Field Namebook, however, Blyry was given the Gaelic form *Bladhraidh* and translated as "flowery land" (Walsh 1957, 112). Such a Gaelic form would be derived from *bláth* "flower" with suffix *-rach* (*Joyce* ii 7–8), in the dative *bláthraigh*. The only historical form calls Blyry "half a cartron called *the Bloyery*" and Bleary in Tullylish is occasionally called The Bleary. Since Bleary too was originally a subdivision name, the Irish form could be from *blogh* fem. variant *bladh* "portion" (*DIL, Dinneen*) with suffix *-raigh*, i.e. "portion place."

Bleary replaced the townland name *Ballytullyconally*, apparently either *Baile Tulaí Conaille* "townland of the hillock of the *Conaille*" or *Baile Tulaí Uí Chonghaile* "townland of the hillock of O'Connelly" (4, 5, 15). The tribal name *Conaille* might be associated with the district name **Clanconnell**, also indicating the descendants of an ancestor called Conall. Two sur-names Ó *Conghaile*, an ecclesiastical family in Fermanagh, and Ó *Conghalaigh*, a branch of the southern Uí Néill in Monaghan, have been confused in both English and Irish (Woulfe 1923, 478). As for the "hillock", the highest ground in Bleary lies east of Wells Cross on the road from Gilford to Lurgan, and consists of several hillocks of 80 metres, one of which is beside Summerhill (OS 1;10,000 sheet 201).

The other hamlet or subdivision *Longert* may be in Irish *An Longfort*, earlier *An Longphort*, "the camp, stronghold", often anglicized Longford, as recorded here in 1691.

Clare   *An Clár*
J 0852   "the level plain"

1. Clare	Fiants Eliz. §4218	1583
2. Clare	Fiants Eliz. §4327	1584
3. Ballenclare in Clanconnell, hamlet Dromenkenan	CPR Jas I 193a	1611
4. Ballyenclare (twice)	CPR Jas I 193a	1611
5. Ballenclare Dromenkenan	Inq. Ult. (Down) §9 Car. I	1627
6. Clare, Edm Boy McGlasney Magennis of	Wars Co. Down x 81	1641
7. Clare, Brian McEdmund Boy Magennis of	Wars Co. Down x 81	1641
8. Clare	Hib. Reg. Lr. Iveagh	1657c
9. Clare	Par. Map (Mooney) 333	17thc
10. Clare	Census 79	1659c
11. Clare	BSD 79	1661
12. Clare	ASE 61b 35	1666
13. Claire al. Claris	ASE 61b 39	1666
14. Clare	Hib. Del. Down	1672c
15. townland Clare	Atkinson's Donaghcloney 132	1691
16. townland Clare = 3 sess: Dromenkenan Derinaran Edenard	Atkinson's Donaghcloney 132	1691
17. Clare als Clareipp [for -ss?]	Rent Roll Down 6	1692
18. Clare	Deeds & Wills (Mooney) 333	1716
19. Clare	Map of Down (OSNB) E61	1755
20. Clare	Civ. & Ecc. Top. (OSNB) E61	1806
21. Clare	Wm. Map (OSNB) E61	1810
22. Clare of Clenconnell	Ir. Wills Index 41	1814
23. The Clare Street (Clare)	OSNB E61	1834c
24. Clare Street a... small village	OSM xii 141a	1834
25. the Clare bog	OSM xii 140b, 142a	1834
26. Clár "a board or plain" campus	J O'D (OSNB) E61	1834c
27. Baile an cláir "a plain'	Mooney 333	1950c
28. Clár, An	GÉ 63	1989
29. ðəˈklɛːr	Local pronunciation	1991

Clare first appears in 1583 as part of the lands held by Hugh Magennis of Iveagh, where the name probably represents the whole district of **Clanconnell**. Three succeeding references, in 1611 and 1627 (3–5), give the name as *Ballenclare*, held by Glasney McAgholy Magennis whose address was "of *Clare*", after which the name is regularly Clare once again. In 1641 Glasney's son and grandson "of Clare" were named as rebels (forms 6, 7). All the modern informants testified that local people preserve a reflex of the Irish article, seen in the middle of the anglicized form *Ballenclare* "townland of the plain", by using the form *The Clare* (29). Clare is a large townland of 1335 acres, containing Clare Bog in the north east. Mooney described the area as "large and very flat" (27). On Sir William Petty's barony map of Lower Iveagh, Clare is shown as surrounded on three sides by bog, between two strips of bog which joined at Clare Bog: one to the east, which seems to link Clare Bog, via a stream on the modern map, with the bog now called the Glass Moss in the townland of Knocknagore, one to the west along the stream which rises near Crowhill, on the modern map, and still forms the boundary between Clare and Ballydugan. The centre of Clanconnell must have been well-protected from outside attack.

The village in the townland was known as Clare Street in 1834 (*OSM* xii 141a). A hamlet was mentioned in 1611 (form 3, 5), and three sessiaghs were named in 1691 (16): *Dromenkenan, Derinaran, Edenard,* but these names are long obsolete.

Coose　　　　　　　　　　　*An Cuas*
J 0948　　　　　　　　　　　　 "the cave"

1. Ballykowsie in Kallydromad	CPR Jas I 396a	1609
2. Ballycowse (half td)	CPR Jas I 235a	1612
3. Ballycouse	Inq. Ult. (Down) §13 Car. I	1629
4. Cowes al. Ballycowes half vil.	Inq. Ult. (Down) §85 Car. I	1639
5. 2 vil de Cowes	Inq. Ult. (Down) §85 Car. I	1639
6. Cows, Agholy O'Musty of	Wars Co. Down x 81	1641
7. Coose	Hib. Reg. Lr. Iveagh	1657c
8. Cooselaraderke	Census 79	1659c
9. Coose	BSD 79	1661
10. Coose al. Couse	ASE 46b 26	1666
11. Coose	Hib. Del. Down	1672c
12. Coose als Couse	Rent Roll Down 7	1692
13. Cowes [?Cowas]	Map of Down (OSNB) E61	1755
14. Coozes	Wm. Map (OSNB) E61	1810
15. Coose	Bnd. Sur. (OSNB) E61	1830c
16. ['Coose]	OSNB Pron. E61	1834c
17. Coose pronounced Koose	OSM xii 143b	1834
18. Cuas "a cave"	J O'D (OSNB) E61	1834c
19. Cuas "hollow, cave"	Mooney 333	1950c
20. 'kus	Local pronunciation	1994

In the early part of the 17th century Coose was part of the holding of the Magennis chief. Early forms of the name have *Bally-* prefixed (1–4). Some lists of the Magennis lands call it a half-town (2, 4), but the 1639 inquisition also says that Sir Hugh Magennis (*Hugo Iveagh*) granted two townlands of *Cowes* to Agholy O'*Mustey* "chirugeon" (form 5). The learned family of Ó *Maoilsté*, McStay, were also well-known as churchmen in Iveagh, and gave their name to **Carrickmacstay** in Clonallan (*PNI* i 69–70). This medical doctor is named again as a rebel from *Cows* in 1641 (form 6).

Coose is now a small townland of 232 acres. The identity of the second townland in 1639 (form 5) is a problem, complicated by the reference to *Kallydromad* in form 1. In the 1609 Schedule of Iveagh as calendered *Kallydromad* looked like the name of a district, but in the 1612 list of Magennis lands (2) the name *Ballydromad* simply preceded others called "four half towns". The 1659 *Census* (8) ran the name together with the nearby townland of Lenaderg, although the boundaries now meet at one point only. The adjacent small townland of Drumhorc (now 117 acres) to the south of Coose, also held by Magennis, is not a possibility, as it was mentioned independently in 1639.

An apparently plural anglicized form appears on the Williamson map, *Coozes*. However the basic form appears to be singular, *Cowes* becoming Coose, probably from *cuas* "a cave". *Cuas* has genitive *cuais*, but there is an alternative *cuasa* to explain the final syllable of *-cowsie* (form 1). *Cabhas* "stepping-stones" cf. *cabhsa* "path" (*Dinneen*), which might be appropriate beside the Bann, is not attested in early Irish (*DIL*).

Drumaran *Droim Árann*
J 0747 "kidney ridge"

1. Ballydromarran	CPR Jas I 396a	1609
2. Ballydromaran	CPR Jas I 235a	1612
3. Ballydromdram	Inq. Ult. (Down) §13 Car. I	1629
4. Ballydrinnarran	Inq. Ult. (Down) §85 Car. I	1639
5. Drummarren	Hib. Reg. Lr. Iveagh	1657c
6. Drumaran	Census 79	1659c
7. Drummarran	BSD 79	1661
8. Drummarran	ASE 112a 34	1667
9. Drummarran	Hib. Del. Down	1672c
10. Drummearren	Rent Roll Down 8	1692
11. Drumaran	Map of Down (OSNB) E61	1755
12. Drumaran	Wm. Map (OSNB) E61	1810
13. Dromarin	Reg. Free. (OSNB) E61	1830
14. Drumarron	Bnd. Sur. (OSNB) E61	1830c
15. Drummarron Lake	OSM xii 140a	1834
16. [Drum-'ma-ron]	OSNB Pron. E61	1834c
17. Druim Aráin "Ridge of the bread"	OSNB Inf. E61	1834c
18. Druim Arain "Aran's Ridge"	J O'D (OSNB) E61	1834c
19. ˌdrəmˈarən	Local pronunciation	1994

Drumaran clearly begins with *droim* "ridge", with *baile* prefixed in the early 17th-century forms (1–4). After 1650 (form 5) the vowel in the first syllable is regularly spelt *-u-* and there is negligible variation from the modern spelling. There are low hills in Drumaran both south and north of the Bann, but the highest is in the north where a hill rises to 70m near the **Scrog**. Hogan lists *ára* gen. *árann* "kidney" as a second element, whatever its meaning, qualifying *dún* "hill-fort", *mag* "plain" and *tipra* "well", as in the name of the county town of Tipperary *Tiobraid Árann* (*Onom. Goed.* 377a, 513a, 634a; *GÉ* 277). *Ára* is more likely as a topographic element than *arán* "bread" (17), and there is no direct evidence for a longer element like *achrann* "tangled growth" or for a surname.

One possible surname might be *Ó Fearáin*, "a branch of the Cinel Eoghain in Ulster" (Woulfe 1923, 523). A man surnamed *O'Farrane* was pardoned in 1608 in Co. Antrim (*CPR Jas I* 110b), and MacLysaght mentions *O'Fearon* as an Oriel sept (1982, 95b; 1985, 105). In 1663 a man called Shane *O'Ffarran* was taxed in Knocknagore in this parish (*Sub. Roll Down* 273). The *f* would not be pronounced in the lenited form *Droim Uí Fhearáin*. Mooney suggested the Donegal surname *Ó (F)aracháin* which may also be anglicized as Farren (*Mooney MS* 337; Woulfe 1923, 522), but the *ch* would be unlikely to disappear in 17th-century spellings. Another possibility is the family of *Ua hEaradháin*, later *Ó hEaráin*, anglicized O'Heron or Haran, who were chieftains of *Uí Bhreasail Macha* in Co. Armagh (Woulfe 1923, 562; *AFM* ii 792–3 1017 AD), and were closely related to *Ó Gairbhíth* (Arthurs 1954(c),

48–9; **Ballymoney** in Magherally). **Tullyherron** in Donaghcloney may be *Tulach Uí Earáin* but the forms there all have *e* not *a*. A Hugh *O'Hawran* appears associated with Sir Art Magennis in the 17th century (*CPR Jas I* 299a, 1616), although Woulfe gives *Ó hAmhráin* (usually anglicized with a *-v-* e.g. Havern) as a family "anciently chiefs of Dál Fiatach; still extant in East Ulster" (Woulfe 1923, 553). Drumaran belonged to the Magennis chief, transferred by 1666 to John Magill.

| **Drumhorc** | *Droim Thorc* | |
| J 0947 | "ridge of (the) boars" | |

1. (?)Cluain torc ar bru Banna		
i nUib Echach	CSH 707.282	1125c
2. (?)Cluain Torc	Descendants Ir xiv 95,n	1200c
3. Dromhorke (Tyrfarish)	CPR Jas I 395b/396a	1609
4. Dromhorke (and Terfarishe) 2 qrs	CPR Jas I 235a	1612
5. qr de Dromhorke	Inq. Ult. (Down) §13 Car. I	1629
6. qr de Dromhorke	Inq. Ult. (Down) §85 Car. I	1639
7. half sess de Dromorck	Inq. Ult. (Down) §85 Car. I	1639
8. Dromhursk	BSD 79	1661
9. Dromhurske	S & D Ann. (Mooney) 338 (30)	17thc
10. Dromhurcke (part)	ASE 49b 19	1666
11. Dromhurcke	Lodge (Mooney) 337	1666
12. Drumharke	Rent Roll Down 6	1692
13. Drumhirk	Map of Down (OSNB) E61	1755
14. Drumturk	Wm. Map (OSNB) E61	1810
15. Drumhork	Wm. Little (OSNB) E61	1834c
16. [Drum-horc (-hurk)]	OSNB Pron. E61	1834c
17. Drumhork pronounced Drum'hurk	OSM xii 143b	1834
18. Druim Thuirc "Ridge of the hog"	J O'D (OSNB) E61	1834c
19. ˌdrəm'hoərk	Local pronunciation	1995

Drumhorc was part of Sir Art Magennis' lands, called a quarter in 1612 (along with Tirfergus in Drumballyroney), and further subdivided in 1639 (forms 4–7). It is the "smallest townland in the parish", being 114 acres (*OSM* xii 143b). The first element is clearly *droim* "ridge", and the second is most likely *torc* "boar", probably genitive plural and lenited after the dative case of *droim*.

The Ulster genealogies refer to a family called *Clann Laitir* of Dál nAraide, descended from Angus son of Crund Ba Druí, from *Cluain Torc* "meadow of boars" (form 2). The tract on saints of the same name lists Colmán son of Derggan at a church called *Cluain Torc* beside the Bann in Iveagh (form 1). These references are probably to the same place, established before Uí Echach rather than Dál nAraide achieved dominance in north-west Down. There may also be a connection with the second element of Drumhorc. Drumhorc is not now church land or next to the Bann, but, given its size, it could have once been part of the adjacent townland of Tullylish, which contains the parish church beside the river. There is only one Drumhorc but 11 townlands called **Drumhirk** *Droim Thoirc* "ridge of the boar", singular, in Northern Ireland (e.g. *PNI* ii 229).

Drummiller (part)   *Droim Iolair*
J 2352   "eagle's ridge"

1. (?)i Craibig	Descendants Ir xiv 115	1200c
2. (?)Downemoyle	CPR Jas I 396a	1609
3. (?)Ballynecrivie	CPR Jas I 396a	1609
4. (?)Downemoyle half-town or sessiagh	CPR Jas I 235a	1612
5. (?)Ballynecrivie	CPR Jas I 235a	1612
6. (?)le sessiagh, vil et ter' de Creevy 40a	Inq. Ult. (Down) §85 Car I	1639
7. (?)le sessiagh de Aghnekeny, Ptk Deery	Inq. Ult. (Down) §85 Car I	1639
8. (?)Creeve, Agnekem	Hib. Reg. Lr Iveagh	1657c
9. (?)Creeue, Aghenekenny, Aghaderigg par. & Lr Iveagh	BSD 78	1661
10. (?)Crever 60a, Aghenekenny 105a	ASE 46b	1666
11. (?)Kenney, Hugh Roe Magenis of	ASE 61b 35	1666
12. (?)Creeve, Aghnekeene (Aghaderrig)	Hib. Del. Down	1672c
13. (?)Crever, Aghenkenny	Rent Roll Down 7	1692
14. drə'mələr	Local pronunciation	1991

The townland of Drummiller, a further portion of Sir Art Magennis' lands, was shared with the parish of Aghaderg to the south. Two sessiaghs of Drummiller were referred to as being in the parish of Aghaderg in 1661 (*BSD* 78), and the name Drummiller appears on each side of the parish boundary on Petty's atlas (*Hib. Del.* Down). The connection with Tullylish is not made explicit before 1834, and the townland name has been discussed under **Drummiller** in Aghaderg.

The Tullylish part of Drummiller is the north-eastern corner beside Drummiller Lough and away from Co. Armagh. It contains one hill of 100 metres, while the Aghaderg part, which is larger, rises twice to this height. Drummiller Lough and the stream which flows west from it form the boundary between Drummiller and Mullabrack.

Although *Downemoyle* has been linked with **The Scrog** north of the Bann in Drumaran (Myles 1936, 5), it is possible that parts of Drummiller may have borne the name of any of the lost units of *Downemoyle*, *Creevy*, or *Aghnekenny*, all of which belonged to the Magennis chief (forms 2–7). *Creevy* may be the place of a Dál nAraide sept mentioned in the Ulster genealogies (form 1). *Creevy* and *Aghnekenny* were shown in the right area, south of the Bann, by Petty (forms 8, 12), while the name *Aghnekenny* (7–13) may have replaced *Downemoyle* (2, 4). *Creevy* must be in Irish *Craobhaigh* "place of trees", *Aghnekenny* may be *Achadh an Cheana* "field of the portion", and *Dún Maol* is probably "incomplete, dilapidated fort". Possibly one of the monuments referred to in earlier sources but now completely destroyed (**Drummiller**) might have been called *Dún Maol*, but the exact sites are unknown.

Drumnascamph   *Dromainn na Scamhthai*
J 1049   "ridge of the bare patch of rocks"

1. half-td Dromneskawlagh (Clanconnell)	CPR Jas I 193a	1611
2. Drominskanighin, sessiogh	CPR Jas I 409b	1618

3. Dromeskewagh	Inq. Ult. (Down) §9 Car. I	1627
4. Dromyneskaughin 20a	Inq. Ult. (Down) §39 Car. I	1632
5. Drumneskaugh	Hib. Reg. Lr. Iveagh	1657c
6. Drummeskaugh	BSD 79	1661
7. Drummeskaugh	S & D Ann. (Mooney) 337 (31)	17thc
8. Drumneskagh	Sub. Roll Down 273	1663
9. Drumnaskaghnagh	DS (Mooney) 337	1666
10. (?)half-td Drommcskeagh	ASE 92a 26	1667
11. Drumneskagh	Hib. Del. Down	1672c
12. Drumnaskaughin	Deeds & Wills (Mooney) 337	1719
13. Drourmuskoughin al. Dranneskaughin	Deeds & Wills (Mooney) 337	1719
14. Drimnascamph	Ir. Wills Index 72	1754
15. Drumneskaff	Map of Down (OSNB) E61	1755
16. Drumnaschamp	Wm. Map (OSNB) E61	1810
17. Druminascamph	Ir. Wills Index 94	1816
18. Drumnascamph	County Warrant (OSNB) E61	1827
19. Drumnascamp	Bnd. Sur. (OSNB) E61	1830c
20. Drumnascamp	Wm. Little (OSNB) E61	1834c
21. [Drum-na-'scamp]	OSNB Pron. E61	1834c
22. Drumnascamp pronounced Drumna'scamp	OSM xii 143b	1834
23. Druim na sgeamh "ridge of the polypody or wall fern"	J O'D (OSNB) E61	1834c
24. ˌdrọmnəˈskamf	Local pronunciation	1991

Drumnascamph, misspelt as "the half-townland of *Dromneskawlagh*", was part of Clanconnell in the early 17th century (1), but the "sessiogh commonly called *Drominskanighin*" was passed by Glasney Magennis to Marmaduke Whitchurch in 1618 (form 2). The first element seems to vary between *droim* and *dromainn*, both meaning "ridge", while the various spellings with final *n* suggest a nasal as well as a fricative in the second element. O'Donovan's suggestion was *Druim na sgeamh* "ridge of the wall ferns" from *sceamh* fem., gen. sing. *sceimhe* "wall-fern, polypody" (*Dinneen*). Another possibility might be *scamh* masc. "lungs", but this would not explain the forms where this element had two syllables (forms 1–4, 9, 12, 13).

The various spellings suggest the same etymology as the identically named townland of **Drumnascamph** in Clonduff: *Dromainn na Scamhthaí* "ridge of the bare patch of rocks" (*PNI* iii 86–7). There are similar minor names in the townland of Brockagh near Doochary, Co. Donegal: *Cnoc na Scamhthaí, Loch na Scamhthaí* "hill, lough of the bare patch of rocks" (Mac Aodha 1989–90, 175). The element has been anglicized as Scaufey, but is now locally pronounced ['skawi]. *An Scamhthach* was given as a part of the townland "where the rocks on the hillside have been stripped by the westerly wind so that it can be noticed from miles away" (Ó Dónaill 1952, 182).

Kernan
J 0746

Caorthannán
"rowans"

Kernan Lake
J 0746

Loch Chaorthannáin
"the lake of Caorthannán"

1. Ballykirman	CPR Jas I 396a	1609
2. Ballykirinan	CPR Jas I 235a	1612
3. Ballykerenan	Inq. Ult. (Down) §13 Car. I	1629
4. Ballekerynan	Inq. Ult. (Down) §85 Car. I	1639
5. Lough Kearnan	Wars Co. Down x 85	1641
6. Lough Kearne	Wars Co. Down x 85	1641
7. Kesenan	Hib. Reg. Lr. Iveagh	1657c
8. Keerinan	Census 79	1659c
9. Kesenan	BSD 79	1661
10. Kesenan	S & D Ann. (Mooney) 340 (30)	17thc
11. Kerenan al. Kesenan	ASE 46b 26	1666
12. Keerenan	ASE 82b 40	1666
13. Kessenan al. Kerdnan	ASE 112a 34	1667
14. Kesenen	Hib. Del. Down	1672c
15. Keereenan	Rent Roll Down 4	1692
16. Kerrenen als Kesenan	Rent Roll Down 7	1692
17. Kessenan als Kerdian	Rent Roll Down 7	1692
18. L.Kernan	Harris Hist. map	1743
19. Lough-Kearnan Lough-Kernan	Harris Hist. 106-7	1744
20. Kerdnan	Map of Down (OSNB) E61	1755
21. Kornan	Ir. Wills Index 76	1783
22. Kernon	Tombstone (OSNB) E61	1803
23. Kernan	Wm. Map (OSNB) E61	1810
24. Kearnan	County Warrant (OSNB) E61	1827
25. Kernan Lake	OSM xii 140a	1834
26. ['Ker-non]	OSNB Pron. E61	1834c
27. Kernan properly Carnan	J O'D (OSNB) E61	1834c
28. Kirdnon	Ir. Wills Index 86	1855
29. Carnán "heap of stones"	J O'D (OSNB) E61	1834c
30. Caorthannáin "place of rowans"	Mooney 339	1950c
31. 'kɛrnən	Local pronunciation	1991
32. 'karnən	Local pronunciation	1991

The townland of Kernan is perhaps best known for the lake of the same name within it, but the two names will be dealt with together here. Early 17th-century spellings prefix *baile*- to the name (1-4), and clearly show an extra syllable in Kernan which continued throughout the century (2-3, 7-17), although after Petty's barony map (7) many of them show the common written confusion of *s* for *r*. The extra syllable makes *carnán* "heap of stones" (29, 27) unlikely. Hogan lists a *Caislén Caerthennáin* in Mayo, where the second element is a derivative of *caorthann* "rowan tree", and this word would fit the evidence here (*Onom. Goed.* 145b).

Kernan townland contains the highest ground in the parish, rising at the southern end to 423 feet (*OSM* xii 140a). The lake in the middle of the townland, Lough Kernan, which is 266 feet high, became notorious in 1641 as the site of a massacre of Protestant settlers, though the exact circumstances are unknown. Phelim McBrinn was alleged to have driven families on to thin ice on the lake, where they all, or all but two, drowned (*Wars Co. Down* x 85–6, 74). There is also Drumaran Lake in the north of the townland, on the border with the townland of Drumaran. The stream flowing from Kernan Lough down to Drumaran Lake (not shown on the 1:50,000) supported mills in 1834 (*OSM* xii 140b, 146a).

Knocknagore *Cnoc na nGabhar*
J 0849 "hill of the goats"

1.	(?)Balledownedrenny	CPR Jas I 396a	1609
2.	(?)Ballydowney-Dremyne or Ballydownedremny	CPR Jas I 235a	1612
3.	Knocknegare	Hib. Reg. Lr. Iveagh	1657c
4.	Knocknajor	Census 79	1659c
5.	Knocknegare	BSD 79	1661
6.	Knocknegann, Shane O'Ffarran of	Sub. Roll Down 273	1663
7.	Knocknagor	ASE 46 b 26	1666
8.	Knocknagow	Rent Roll Down 7	1692
9.	Knocknagor	Wm. Map (OSNB) E61	1810
10.	Knocknagor	County Warrant (OSNB) E61	1827
11.	Knockagore	Wm. Little (OSNB) E61	1834c
12.	['Knock-na-gor]	OSNB Pron. E61	1834c
13.	in English "Goats Hill"	OSNB Inf. E61	1834c
14.	Cnoc na gcorr "Hill of the cranes"	J O'D (OSNB) E61	1834c
15.	Cnoc na ngabhar "hill of the goats"	Mooney 339	1950c
16.	ˌnɔknəˈgoər	Local pronunciation	1991
17.	ˌnəknəˈgɔːr	Local pronunciation	1991

The name Knocknagore first appears, on Petty's barony map, as *Knocknegare* (3). There is a 1663 citation (6) as *Knocknegann*, after which *-gore* became standard as the final syllable. Since other anglicized names such as Donegal, *Dún na nGall*, do not spell the nasalization of *g*, it seems best to accept the suggestion of an informant to the Ordnance Survey (13) that this was "in English Goats Hill" (Irish *Cnoc na nGabhar*). Possibly the earlier name was *Ballydownedrenny* held by Sir Art Magennis in 1609 (1–2), although if this is to be identified with *Drumendowne* near Glenloughan in Aghaderg (*Inq. Ult. (Down)* xliv; *CPR Jas I* 305a) it would more likely be a name for part of Drummiller. In that case another possible early name among Sir Art's lands would be *Downemoyle* (see **Drummiller**).

Lenaderg *Láithreach Dearg*
J 1149 "red site"

1.	Laireachtdyke	Reg. Swayne 73	1427
2.	Laireacht, Dyrke (dioc Dromore)	Mooney MS 341 (Reg. Swayne)	1427
3.	Ballinlaraderricke	CPR Jas I 395b	1609
4.	Ballyelaraderricke	CPR Jas I 191a	1611
5.	Ballylaraderricke	CPR Jas I 191a	1611
6.	Laradericke	Hib. Reg. Lr. Iveagh	1657c
7.	Laragh-Deirke halftown	Inq. Ult. (Down) §1 Interreg.	1658
8.	Cooselaraderke	Census 79	1659c
9.	Laderick	BSD 79	1661

10. Larahderisk al. Ladarick	ASE 92a 26	1667
11. Larahderisk al. Laderick	Lodge (Mooney) 342	1667
12. Laraderick	Hib. Del. Down	1672c
13. Laradery[?]	Deeds & Wills (Mooney) 342	1714
14. Laraderg al. Lenidarge al. Lanederg	Deeds & Wills (Mooney) 342	1717
15. Milltowne al. Laraderry	Deeds & Wills (Mooney) 342	1732
16. Lenaderrig	Map of Down (OSNB) E61	1755
17. Lenaderg	Map of Down (OSNB) E61	1755
18. Lenederg	Tombstone (OSNB) E61	1796
19. Leniderrig	Wm. Map (OSNB) E61	1810
20. Lenniderg	Ir. Wills Index 57	1814
21. Linnadirg	Bnd. Sur. (OSNB) E61	1830c
22. Linnadirg	Clergyman (OSNB) E61	1834c
23. Lenaderg	Wm. Little (OSNB) E61	1834c
24. [Len-na-'der-rig/Lin-na-'der-rig]	OSNB Pron. E61	1834c
25. pronounced Lin- by inhabitants	Mooney 342	1950c
26. Léana Dearg "red meadow/ swamp/pool"	J O'D (OSNB) E61	1834c
27. Leana-dearg "red wet meadow"	Joyce iii 468	1913
28. Láithreach Dair-thighe "ruins of the oratory"	Mooney 341	1950c
29. Láithreach Dearg "red meeting-place"	Mooney 341	1950c
30. ˌlɛnəˈdɛːrg	Local pronunciation	1991
31. ˌlanəˈdɛrəg	Local pronunciation	1994

Lenaderg was one of two church townlands in the parish, the other being Tullylish. The modern form looks as if the etymology would be from *Léana Dearg* "red water-meadow", and this may have been a recent alternative Irish name for the place (26, 27). However the place was first referred to as the "lands of *Laireachtdy[r]ke*" in Swayne's Register in 1427, granted by the Archbishop of Armagh to the erenagh McCryn or *McBryn* (forms 1, 2). Although the McBrins were the erenagh family in **Ballintaggart** in Aghaderg parish in 1609, Reeves was wrong to take what he read as *Lachreachtdyrke* as a misspelling of Aghaderg (EA 114n, 309). In 1611 Ballylaraderricke was held by Patrick McDonegan of the same (4–5) and in 1658 another McDonegan held Laragh-Deirke halftown from the Bishop of Dromore (7). Dean Mooney found a 1717 source as the earliest evidence for the replacement of the first *-r-* by the modern *-n-* in alias forms (14). He would have liked the church connection to be apparent in the etymology as "site of the oratory" (28) but, while *láithreach* seems likely, the evidence favours the adjective *dearg* 'red' (29). Lenaderg contains **Milltown** (15), **Broken Bridge** and **Five Lights Hill**.

Lisnafiffy
J 1047

Lios na Faiche
"fort/enclosure of the green"

1. Lios na faithche "Fort of the green (plateau)"	J O'D (OSNB) E61	1834c
2. ˌləsnəˈfəfi	Local pronunciation	1991

343

The historical forms of the name **Lisnafiffy** are given and have been discussed in the parish of Seapatrick. Lisnafiffy is divided between the parishes of Tullylish (209 acres) and Seapatrick (431 acres), a division first recorded in 1657 and 1661, when Seapatrick had two sessiaghs and Tullylish one (*Hib. Reg., BSD*, forms 12–13, 15–16). In 1834 the area of the Tullylish portion was given as 213 acres (*OSM* xii 143b).

Loughans	*Na Locháin*	
J 0548	"the little lakes /pools"	

1.	(?)Art an Locháin... Muinntir an Locháin	TCD Gens 144a §261c	1666c
2.	Loghan	Fiants Eliz. §4218	1583
3.	(?)Deyrloghan	Fiants Eliz. §4327	1584
4.	Ballynloghan	CPR Jas I 396a	1609
5.	Ballynloghan	CPR Jas I 235a	1612
6.	Loughan	CPR Jas I 373b	1618
7.	Ballinloghan	Inq. Ult. (Down) §13 Car. I	1629
8.	Loghan	Inq. Ult. (Down) §87 Car. I	1640
9.	Loghan, Rory Magennis of	Wars Co. Down x 77	1641
10.	Loghin	Hib. Reg. Lr. Iveagh	1657c
11.	Laughan	Census 79	1659c
12.	Loggans	Sub. Roll Down 273	1663
13.	Loughin	ASE 112 a 34	1667
14.	Loghin	Hib. Del. Down	1672c
15.	Loghin	Rent Roll Down 8	1692
16.	Loughends	Ir. Wills Index 1	1747
17.	Birch, the Grove, Loughans	Ir. Wills Index 9	1773
18.	Loughans	County Warrant (OSNB) E61	1827
19.	['Logh-ans]	OSNB Pron. E61	1834c
20.	The swamps of Loughans	Mooney 342 < Myles 1936, 15	1950c
21.	Locháin "little loughs"	J O'D (OSNB) E61	1934c
22.	'lɔxənz	Local pronunciation	1994

Loughans is situated on the western boundary of Co. Down, between the rivers Bann and Cusher, plus the Newry canal, which flow together at its northern end. The anglicized name *Loghan* first appears in 1583, between *Deyne* (Loughadian, in Aghaderg) and Clare, chief townland of Clanconnell, in a list of lands surrendered by Hugh Magennis (form 2). The two names Loughans and **Loughadian** are misread as one in form (3). The name of a Magennis holding in form (1), to be translated "Art of the little lough, people of the little lough" may not be the same place, although it is implied that *Lochán* was a district name.

Loughans is a very large townland, being 1,338 acres (*OSM* xii 143b). In the list in 1583 most of the names refer to districts, not individual townlands, and it is evident that the southern half of the parish of Tullylish all belonged to the Magennis chief in the early 17th century, apart from Knocknagore and Mullabrack for which there are no references before Petty. These are again large areas (714 acres, 435 acres, *OSM* xii 143b) so are unlikely to be later subdivisions. An old name *Aughnakeeran* has been linked with the Whinney Hill southwest of Gilford (Myles 1936, 16).

The early form *Ballynloghan* (forms 4, 5, 7) is listed next to *Ballydromaran*, Drumaran townland contiguous in this parish, and thus is clearly not **Ballylough** in Donaghmore (PNI i 93) or Seapatrick parishes. The final element seems to be singular, *Baile an Locháin* "townland of the little lough" but probably represents *Baile na Lochán* "townland of the lakelets". The English -*s* plural marker first appears in the 1663 *Subsidy Roll* form (12): *Loggans.* Before the land was drained "Redmond O'Hanlon's horse could find its way in the darkest nights through the swamps of Loughans" (20). On the 1:10,000 map ponds are shown in the townland in the Park Bog, which in 1837 was normally "covered with water" in the winter season (*OSM* xii 144b). Given the boggy nature of part of the townland to this day, "pools" seems an appropriate meaning, though there is also one small lake on the 1:50,000 map to the south of Stramore House.

| **Moyallan** | *Maigh Alúine* | |
| J 0550 | "plain of alum" | |

1. river of town of Menalone	Fiants Eliz. §4327	1583c
2. Menalone	Fiants Eliz. §4327	1583c
3. half td of Moynalbin al. Moynallon in Clanconnell	CPR Jas I 193a	1611
4. Moynalvin al. Moynallon	Inq. Ult. (Down) §9 Car. I	1627
5. Monyallen	Par. Map (Mooney) 343	1657c
6. The towne of Drumnost & Ancly & Menalon	Census 79	1659c
7. Moneallen	BSD 80	1661
8. Munalune	ASE 61b 35	1666
9. Monalune	Lodge (Mooney) 343	1666
10. Moneallen	Hib. Del. Down	1672c
11. Moneallen [Comm. Grace]	Mooney MS 343	1686
12. Monallan	Harris Hist. map	1743
13. Monallen	Harris Hist. 113,115-6	1744
14. Moyallon	Map of Down (OSNB) E61	1755
15. Moyallan	Statist. Sur. Dn 145,241	1802
16. Moyallen	Wm. Map (OSNB) E61	1810
17. Magh Alainn "beautiful plain"	J O'D (OSNB) E61	1834c
18. Magh (n)Álainn "lovely plain'	Mooney 343	1950c
19. Maigh Alúine	GÉ 132	1989
20. ˌmɔiˈaln̩	Local pronunciation	1994

The earliest form of Moyallen, *Menalone*, appears in a 1583 fiant listing the bounds of Iveagh (forms 1–2), and in 1611 the *half-townland of Moynalbin alias Moynallon in Clanconnell* was held by Glasney Magennis of Clare (form 3). The internal -*n*- persists until the mid-18th-century (forms 12–13), and shows that this is an example of fossilized nasalization after the nominative of *magh* "a plain", which was neuter in Old Irish. The form in a 1627 inquisition, *Moynalvin* (4), provides the best clue to the second element. Latin *alumen* "alum" was borrowed into early Irish as a feminine *n*-stem, *alamha* gen. *alamhan*, and this genitive would fit the spellings here, with *mh* of *Magh nAlamhan* anglicized as *v* and *b* (4, 3). However, in the *Irish Grammatical Tracts* a new nominative *alamhuin* appeared, described as "faulty", but developing into the modern *alúin* gen. *alúine* "clay" (*DIL: IGT* ex. 318). The name of the Hill of Allen in Leinster, *Almhu* gen. *Almhaine*, does not occur in the north (*Onom. Goed.* 29b). *Munalune* was held by Fardarragh Magennis in 1628 (8).

"The clean and well-wooded townland of Moyallen (which is inhabited entirely by Quakers) would perhaps be reckoned beautiful in any country". The wooden bridge over the Bann mentioned in 1834 in Moyallan seems to be that now called the White Bridge (*OSM* xii 142, 1834).

Mullabrack	*Mullach Breac*	
J 0646	"speckled summit"	
1. (?)Ballytullylevin	CPR Jas I 396a	1609
2. (?)Ballytullylevin	CPR Jas I 235a	1612
3. (?)Balletullelevin	Inq. Ult. (Down) §13 Car. I	1629
4. Mulloghbrack	Hib. Reg. Lr. Iveagh	1657c
5. Mullebracke	Census 79	1659c
6. Mulloughbrack	BSD 80	1661
7. Mullaghbracke 146a	ASE 112a 34	1667
8. Mullabrack	Hib. Del. Down	1672c
9. Mullaghbrake	Rent Roll Down 8	1692
10. Mullaghbrack	Map of Down (OSNB) E61	1755
11. (?)Moybrick	Tombstone (OSNB) E61	1803
12. Mullabrack	Wm. Map (OSNB) E61	1810
13. Tallyho House (Mullaghbrack)	OSNB E61	1834c
14. [Mul-la-'brack]	OSNB Pron. E61	1834c
15. Mulla'brack so pronounced	OSM xii 143b	1834
16. Mullach Breac "speckled summit"	J O'D (OSNB) E61	1834c
17. Tulach Leibhinn "hill of the bank"	Mooney 347	1950c
18. ˌmɔlə'brak	Local pronunciation	1994

There seems to be no record of the name Mullabrack earlier than the Petty maps, *Mulloghbrack* (form 4). Many of the lands created into the manor of Gilford by Sir John Magill had earlier belonged to Sir Art Magennis, and it is noteworthy that *Mullaghbracke* appeared in the list of Magill's lands in 1667 between the names of Drumaran and Ballymacanallen, the same position occupied by the name *Ballytullylevin* in the lists of Sir Art's lands earlier (forms 7; 1–2). *Ballytullylevin* cannot be the same place as Tullyrain as suggested by Dean Mooney (17), as Tullyrain was in Clanconnell. *Ballytullylevin* would be *Baile Tulaí Léibhinn* "townland of the knoll of the bank". The knoll or hillock may be the same height described in the name *Mullach Breac*, the "speckled summit", apparently the ridge that rises to 80 metres east of Drummiller Lough. Many of the earlier spellings preserve the *gh* which represented the [x] of *mullach*, but there are also *Mullebracke* (form 5), *Mullabrack* (8, 12), which indicate the loss of the fricative as in the present pronunciation and spelling.

Tullylish	*Tulaigh Lis*	
J 0848	see the parish name	
1. Balletotleneslott al. Ballieno	CPR Jas I 395b	1609
2. Ballytollyneslott al. Ballyen	CPR Jas I 191a	1611

3. Ballintolleneslott al. Ballinken al. Balliens	CPR Jas I 191a	1611
4. Tullineslat al. Tullieyne	Hib. Reg. Lr. Iveagh	1657c
5. Tolleneslatt al. Tollein	Inq. Ult. (Down) §1 Interreg.	1658
6. Tullenslatt	BSD 80	1661
7. Tullylish al. Tullyneslatt	ASE 112a 38	1667
8. Tullieyne	Hib. Del. Down	1672c

The townland of Tullylish which contains the parish church now bears the same name as the parish. However in the past it had its own name, or names. In 1611 Patrick McDonegan held the church townland of *Ballintolleneslott alias Ballinken alias Balliens* (form 3). Three names appear on Petty's barony maps, presumably as townland (*Tullineslat al. Tullieyne*, form 4) and parish (*Tullelish*, the surviving name). In 1667 William Lesley owned *Tullylish alias Tullyneslatt* (form 7). *Tullyneslatt* seems to have been from *Tulaigh na Slat* "hillock of the rods". *Tullieyne* may have been *Tulaigh Eidhinn* "hillock of ivy".

Tullyrain　　　　　　　　　　　*Tulaigh Raithin*
J 1049　　　　　　　　　　　　　　 "hillock of bracken"

1. Ballytullyrane in Clanconnell	CPR Jas I 193a	1611
2. Ballytullyrahine in Clanconnell	CPR Jas I 193a	1611
3. Ballentullerane	Inq. Ult. (Down) §9 Car. I	1627
4. Tullyerane	Inq. Ult. (Down) §39 Car. I	1633
5. Tulleraine	Par. Map (Mooney) 347	17thc
6. Tollerine	BSD 80	1661
7. Tuliran 3 sess: Clonley Tulirane Killiusles	Atkinson's Donaghcloney 133	1691
8. Tullyrine al. Tullarene	Lodge (Mooney) 347 [Bk IV]	1719
9. Tullyrain	Map of Down (OSNB) E61	1755
10. Tullyrean	Tombstone (OSNB) E61	1791
11. Tullyrain	Wm. Map (OSNB) E61	1810
12. [Tul-ly-'rain]	OSNB Pron. E61	1834c
13. Tulaigh Rathain "Ferny hill"	J O'D (OSNB) E61	1834c
14. Tulach Raithin "Ferny hill"	Mooney 348	1950c
15. ˌtɒliˈreːn	Local pronunciation	1994

As with other townlands in Clanconnell, Tullyrain was divided into three sessiaghs, now long obsolete (form 7). The name *Clonley* also appears as a sessiagh of Ballydugan in the west of the parish. Up to 1627 the prefix *Bally-* was added to the townland name (forms 1–3). From the single occurrence of *-rahine* (form 2) the etymology of the townland name is fairly clear, although the Irish dictionaries contain only *raith* "bracken" and *raithneach*, the modern form, not *raithean*. Nevertheless this is the form in *Cúil Raithin*, modern Coleraine (*GÉ* 206), and in the compound *raitheanmhagh* (Dinneen) "bracken plain". Tullyrain had passed to Marmaduke Whitchurch by 1633 (form 4). There is another townland called **Tullyrain**, church land not named before 1655, in Magherally parish five miles south-east.

OTHER NAMES

Banford	An English form	
J 0748	"ford over the Bann"	
1. Banford (Knocknagore)	OSNB E61	1834c
2. Banford	Lewis' Top. Dict. ii 658-9	1837
3. Banford... the river pass, now		
spanned by a stone bridge	Bassett's Down 260	1886
4. Banford Bleach Works	Bassett's Down 261	1886
5. Mount Pleasant adjoining Banford	Bassett's Down 261	1886
6. Banford House	Bassett's Down 266	1886
7. "Black Castle" lodge to		
Banford House	Bassett's Down 260	1886
8. 'ban 'fɔrd	Local pronunciation	1995

Banford Green on the 1:50,000 map is the modern place-name beside an old ford on the Bann close to the old church site of Tullylish. At this point the bed of the river consists of sheets of rock, but the river is now spanned by Tullylish Bridge carrying a minor road south past the church towards Loughbrickland. In the late 19th century this was the site of Banford Bleach Works, in existence since 1795, "beautifully situated near the historical river pass from which the name is derived", and of Banford House. There were also flour mills at Mount Pleasant adjoining Banford (*Bassett's Down* 260, 261, 266). A small square older building in view of the ford, called the "Black Castle", was then used as the lodge to Banford House. The importance of the crossing was evident to Bassett, who also described the large earthen fort at Banford "upon the site of the old parish church... used to guard the river pass" (*Bassett's Down* 260). The bridge was built in 1698 "on one of the outer defences of an ancient fort or field-work, raised to defend the pass of the river" (*Lewis' Top. Dict.* ii 659a), and rebuilt in 1818 (*OSM* xii 142a).

Broken Bridge	An English form	
J 1149		
1. 'brokən 'brədʒ	Local pronunciation	1992

Broken Bridge in the south-west corner of Tullyrain is on a stream flowing down into the Bann, formed from the confluence of a stream which forms the border between Tullyrain and Ballykelly, and another which forms the border between Ballykelly and Lenaderg. It carries the road from Milltown which joins the main road from Lawrencetown to Lurgan. The bridge was not mentioned in 1834 (*OSM* xii 142a) and the background to the name is unknown.

Civiltown	An English form	
J 1049		
1. Civiltown, division of Laurencetown	Bassett's Down 260	1886

Although Civiltown appears on the modern map the name is no longer used locally: "I never heard tell of Civiltown". It was one of the three divisions of **Laurencetown**, and contained the Presbyterian church, noted as the burial place of the Rev. Samuel Morell, a Presbyterian minister who died in 1772 defending Gilford Castle and its owner Sir Richard Johnston from an attack by the land campaigners "Hearts of Steel" (*Bassett's Down* 260, 267). A contemporary poem blames Morell's death on his cutting of a fairy thorn (Myles 1936, 32).

Cranny	*Crannaigh*	
J 0553	"place of trees"	
1. 'kranï 'len	Local pronunciation	1996
2. ðə 'kranï 'len	Local pronunciation	1996

Cranny, including Cranny Road and Cranny Lane, is in the west of Ballydugan townland near the boundary with Co. Armagh. Although there are no earlier forms it appears to be an Irish name, the dative/locative of *crannach* "place of trees".

Dunbarton	An English form	
J 0649	"Dunbar's town"	
1. Dunbarton Ho., Hugh Dunbar		
McMaster JP	Bassett's Down 260,266	1886
2. Dún Breatan/Dunbarton	Éire Thuaidh	1988
3. ˌdǫn'bartən	Local pronunciation	1995

Dunbarton is not a borrowing of the name Dumbarton beside the Clyde in Scotland, which is from Gaelic *Dún Breatan* "fort of the Britons" (form 2; Watson 1926, 15), but a 19th-century example of an invented place-name consisting of the surname Dunbar with the suffix *-town*. In 1834 a Mr Dunbar had a thread mill in Drumnagally in Seapatrick parish (*OSNB* E11), and Messrs Dunbar and Co. had been tenants of two mills in Loughans (*OSM* xii 147a). The "immense thread mills" of Messrs Dunbar McMaster and Co. Ltd at Gilford were founded about 1838 by Hugh Dunbar of **Huntly**, Banbridge, who soon after formed a partnership with John McMaster of Armagh (*Bassett's Down* 262–3). Before his death in 1847 Hugh Dunbar had given the land for the Roman Catholic church, and John McMaster contributed to the cost of the local Church of Ireland. The firm also set up schools and reading rooms. In 1886 Hugh Dunbar McMaster JP, son of John McMaster, was head of the firm, and lived in Dunbarton House in the town. A branch of the firm was set up in New York in 1880, also called Dunbarton Mills (*Bassett's Down* 263, 260).

Five Lights Hill	An English form	
1. ðə 'fɑiv 'ləits ˌhïl	Local pronunciation	1992

The Five Lights Hill is near Lenaderg, three miles from Banbridge, going out towards Lurgan on a link road. It got the name from a row of houses on the very summit which you could see from a distance.

Gilford	An English form
J 0748	"Magill's ford"

1. a Monday market at Gilford	ASE 112a	1678
2. ye manor of Gilford	ASE 112a	1678
3. Guilford, Towne of	Rent Roll Down 9	1692
4. Gillford	Ir. Wills Index 95	1734
5. Gillford	Harris Hist. map	1743
6. Gilford on r.Bann	Harris Hist. 105	1744
7. Gillford	Taylor & Skinner 15	1777
8. Gilford	Dubourdieu's Map (OSNB) E61	1802
9. Gilford	Wm. Map (OSNB) E61	1810
10. ['Gil-ford]	OSNB Pron. E61	1834c
11. "Gill's Ford" from McGill of Gill Hall	J O'D (OSNB) E61	1834c
12. Áth Mhic Giolla	GÉ 9	1989
13. 'gəlfərd	Local pronunciation	1995

Gilford on the river Bann is at the junction of roads leading to Banbridge, Tanderagee, Portadown and Lurgan. The town was founded and given its name by Captain, later Sir, John Magill, who acquired parts of Donaghcloney, Tullylish and Dromore parishes in the 17th century, and who lived at **Gill Hall** in Dromore (*Atkinson's Donaghcloney* 24). In 1678 his grandson had the lands created into the manor of Gilford, with provision to hold courts, fairs and markets (forms 1,2). Form (12) is a translation of the name. In 1743 Harris' map does not show clearly if a bridge had been built at the ford, but there appears to have been one by 1777 (*Taylor and Skinner* map 15). In 1834 the bridge was described as having 22 small arches (*OSM* xii 142a). Gilford was a busy mill village in the late 19th century, but had given up its entitlement to hold fairs and markets, as being too near Portadown on one side and Banbridge on the other (*Bassett's Down* 259). Gilford Castle, in ruins by 1886, stood near the river bank on the road to Banbridge, but had been replaced by another building in the same grounds (*Bassett's Down* 260). Lewis mentioned a chalybeate spring in the town (*Lewis' Top. Dict.* i 653a). The 1886 directory stated, "Mr Benjamin Dickson J.P. and Messrs Dunbar McMaster and Co., Limited, own the town" (*Bassett's Down* 259). The Dunbar family left their name in **Dunbarton**.

Lawrencetown
J 0949

An English form

1. Halls Mill	Sloane map	1739
2. Hall's Mill	Harris Hist. map	1743
3. Halls-mill	Harris Hist. 105	1744
4. Halls-Mill, Halsmill	Taylor & Skinner 15	1777
5. Hall's-mill	Statist. Sur. Dn 24	1802
6. Laurencetown formerly Hall's Mill (Knocknagore)	OSNB E61	1834c
7. Laurence Town formerly... Hall'smill	OSM xii 141a	1834
8. Hall's Mill	J O'D (OSNB) E61	1834c
9. Lorton's Town is now the name	OSNB E61	1834c
10. to be altered to Laurencetown	J O'D (OSNB) E61	1834c

11. Hall's Mill	Lewis' Top. Dict. ii 659a	1837
12. Springvale Bleach Works, Lawrencetown	Bassett's Down 269	1886
13. Baile Labhráis	GÉ 20	1989
14. 'lɑrəns,təun	Local pronunciation	1991
15. 'lɔrəns,təun	Local pronunciation	1991

Lawrencetown was called Hall's Mill in the 18th century, and Harris (forms 2, 3) showed a bleach-yard run by Mr John Nicholson where "a village is beginning to make its appearance already". Lewis referred to the village as *Hall's Mill* in 1837 (form 11), although the Ordnance Survey said "Lorton's Town is now the name", and O'Donovan improved the spelling to Laurencetown (forms 9,10). Atkinson (*Donaghcloney* 25, *Dromore* 244) explained this name as referring ultimately to Colonel Lawrence, who married the widow of Captain Barrett, the original Cromwellian settler who died without children. In 1674 the Lawrences let the property for 99 years to Francis Hall, whence the name *Hall's Mill*, but in the late 18th century a descendant returned to live in Lawrencetown House (Myles 1936, 10,22). In 1886 Bassett said of the village of Lawrencetown:

> It consists of three divisions. The first is Civiltown, in which is Tullylish Prebyterian church... The second village division, The Point, contains the Roman Catholic church and schools. The third division, Hall's Mill, contains the Post Office and a number of workmen's cottages. (*Bassett's Down*, 267).

On the 1:10,000 map, sheet 201, Civiltown is shown at the east end of Lawrencetown and The Point in the middle, opposite Lawrencetown Bridge, but there is no sign of Hall's Mill.

Madden
J 0547

Maide na hEascainne
"footstick of the eel"

1. Maddenascone Passe	Map Newry Canal	1690c
2. Madenhony Br.	Harris Hist. map	1743
3. Madenehony Bridge (on canal)	Harris Hist. 117	1744
4. Maden Brige	Rocque's Map (Coote)	1760
5. the Madden Bridge (Gilford)	OSNB E61	1834c
6. Madden Bridge	OSM i 10b (18b)	1835
7. The Madden (railway station)	Bassett's Down 259	1886
8. ˌðə 'madən	Local pronunciation	1995

Madden Bridge crosses the canal in the townland of Loughans and is not named on the map, although Madden Hill is shown to the north-east of it on OS 1:10,000 sheet 220 and the road west into Tanderagee is called Madden Road. The local railway station was also called The Madden (form 7). The crossing over bog and later the bridge over the canal was the primary place-name, shown in form 1 (the map-survey for the canal) to contain the word *eascann* "eel". Joyce says "sometimes *maide* means a strong stick placed across a little stream, by which you might cross", with reference to Maddyboy in Limerick, **Maddydoo, Muddyderg** in Co. Antrim (*Joyce* iii 494–5, *PNI* iv 73). There is no reference to *madadh* "dog" in this name (*pace* Myles 1936, 15).

Milltown J 1148	An English form	
1. Milltowne al. Laraderry	Deeds & Wills (Mooney) 342	1732
2. Milltown bleach green & mills (Lenaderg)	OSNB E61	1834c
3. Milltown Bleach Works, Lenaderg	Bassett's Down 255	1886
4. 'məltəun	Local pronunciation	1992

Mooney found a 1732 deed giving *Milltowne* as an alias of the townland name *Lenaderg* (form 1). This is the Milltown of the modern map (2), and seven mills beside the Bann in the townland were described in 1837 (*OSM* xii 146). Bassett also described Milltown in 1886, including Bannville beetling mills (*Bassett's Down* 255).

Newmills J 0651	An English form	
1. Newmill	Sloane map	1739
2. 'nju'mĭlz	Local pronunciation	1996

Newmills was noteworthy enough in 1739 to appear on Sloane's map of Co. Down (1), and a meeting house at *New-Mills* was burned in 1797, in a period of bitter civil disturbance (Myles 1936, 42). By 1834 the place was described without a name: "On a small stream from the Clare bog is a corn mill situated in the townland of Ballynagarrick" (*OSM* xii 142a). Another mill shown by Sloane was *One-mile Mill*, apparently Millfield in **Lisnaward** townland south of Dromore.

The Park Bog J 0547	An English form

Park Bog is in the southern end of Loughans townland. In the early 19th century it was known for containing timber: "It is said by the inhabitants of the neighbourhood that the greater part of the timber used in the building of their houses was raised out of this bog... mostly oak and what is usually called tree sally by the natives". In February 1837 the memoir-writer J.R. Ward found the bog covered with water, but saw a block of oak at the south-western edge "seven and a half feet in diameter... part of a large tree recently raised" (*OSM* xii 144–5).

Rose Hall J 1049	An English form	
1. Rose Hall al. Drumski[?]	Deeds & Wills (Mooney) 342	1732
2. Rose Hall	Sloane map	1739
3. (?)Monroe's Grove	Harris Hist. 106	1744
4. Rosehall, Daniel Monroe Esq.	Taylor & Skinner 15	1777
5. Rose Hall (Drumnascamph)	OSNB E61	1834c
6. Rose Hall	Bassett's Down 269	1886
7. 'roz ˌhɔl	Local pronunciation	1995

Rose Hall is in Drumnascamph townland just north of Lawrencetown. Rose Hall may have been earlier called *Monroe's Grove* (form 3, *Harris Hist.*), since it continued to belong to the family of Monroe (4). In the pamphlet on Tullylish the name is given as Roe's Hall (Myles 1936, 25), and the present spelling of the name may have been intended as a floral pun on this form, which uses only the second syllable of the surname. Black quotes the traditional Scottish Gaelic explanation of the surname Monroe/Munroe as a family who came from the river Roe in Co. Derry in Ireland: in two words *Bun Rotha* "foot of the Roe" (Black 1946, 619b). However it is unlikely that this derivation was known to the Tullylish Monroes, who were Cromwellian settlers from Scotland (Paterson 1938, 196n).

In 1659 the first Daniel Monroe held the townland of Ballylough which borders Drumnascamph to the north (*Census* 79), and in 1667 the half-townland of *Drommcskeagh* (*ASE* 92a 26). According to one of Dean Mooney's sources Rose Hall was used as an alias for a place called *Drumski* in 1732. Petty's county map shows the name *Drumhesky* next to Ballydugan three miles to the north-west (*Hib. Del.* c. 1672). *Ballydromneskie* was originally the townland name, later replaced by the name of the sessiagh **Ballydugan**. Because of the Monroes, there seems to have been confusion between *Drumski*, meaning the townland of Ballydugan, and the townland name Drumnascamph.

The Scrog   An English form (?)
J 0749

1. ðə ˈskrɔː	Local pronunciation	1991
2. ðə ˈskrɔg	Local pronunciation	1996

The Scrog is in the northern part of Drumaran, north of the Bann, where a hill rises to 70 metres (OS 1:10,000 map sheet 201). There was a football team called The Scraw Gelties (1). The English (dialect) term *scrog* means a stunted bush (2). On the other hand, the Irish term *scraith*, anglicized *scraw*, refers to a grassy layer on top of bog. Maybe this name represents *scrathóg*, a diminutive of *scraith*.

Shanes Hill   *An Sián*
J 0653   "the small fairy dwelling"

1. Hamlet Shian (Ballydromneskie)	CPR Jas I 193a	1611
2. Shyane	Inq. Ult. (Down) §9 Car. I	1627
3. Shiane	Hib. Reg. Lr. Iveagh	1657c
4. Shyane or Skeane sess.	ASE 61b §39	1666
5. Shian	Hib. Del. Down	1672c
6. Sheean, sess. of Ballydogan	Atkinson's Donaghcloney 132	1691
7. sessiagh of Skyan	Rent Roll Down 6	1692
8. Shane's hill Ballydugan, 336'	OSM xii 140a	1834
9. the Shanes Hill, highest point Ballydugan	OSNB E61	1834c
10. the Shane Hill, on rd Gilford to Lurgan	Mooney 330	1950c
11. Siodhán	Mooney 329	1950c
12. ˈʃenz ˈhïl	Local pronunciation	1996

353

Shanes Hill is shown on the 1:50,000 map as the name of a hill, the second highest in this low-lying parish: "Shane's Hill in the townland of Ballydugan, 336 feet above the sea. From this point there is an extensive view" (*OSM* xii 140a). At present Shane is regarded as a personal name, representing Shane O'Neill. In the 17th century similar forms (1–7) were used as the name of one of three land divisions within the townland of **Ballydugan**: the hamlet of *Shian* in the grant of Clanconnell (form 1), the sessiagh of *Sheean* in a will (form 6). Forms with *sk* must be a misreading of *sh* (4, 7), and the name is clearly from *sián* "small otherworld dwelling". It was recorded by Dean Mooney pre-1950 as *the Shane Hill* (form 10), without the current final (possessive?) -*s*. Hills called in Irish *sí, sián* (earlier *síodh, síodhán*) are generally isolated and with a good view, like this.

Stramore *Srath Mór*
J 0548 "big valley-bottom"

1. Stran-more	Harris Hist. map	1743
2. Stranmore	Harris Hist. 113	1744
3. Stramore marshes (Loughans)	OSNB E61	1834c
4. Stramore marshes	Mooney 342	1950c
5. Srath Mór	Mooney 341	1950c
6. ˌstrəˈmɔr	Local pronunciation	1995

Harris provides the earliest reference to Stramore, in the west of Loughans townland near the canal, which he spells with an internal -*n*-, *Stran-more* (forms 1, 2). *Stran-* would suggest *sruthán* "stream(let)", as in Stranmillis, Belfast (Uí Fhlannagáin 1982, 59), whereas *Stra-* would suggest *srath* "valley-bottom" as in **Strabane** in Tyrone (*GÉ* 273) and various Scottish place-names, such as Strathearn, Strathfillan and Strathpeffer (Watson 1926, 113, 284, 452). In 1834 the area was described: "Stramore marshes... apparently reclaimed bog... where numerous cattle are grazed in the summer" (*OSNB* E61). Stramore House is situated on a low rise between the rivers Bann and Cusher.

APPENDIX A

ASPECTS OF IRISH GRAMMAR RELEVANT TO PLACE-NAMES

The following types of place-names can be identified:

1. Those which consist of a noun only:

> Sabhall "a barn" (Saul, Dn)
> Tuaim "a tumulus" (Toome, Ant.)

There is no indefinite article in Irish, that is, there is no word for *a*, e.g. *Sabhall* means "barn" or "a barn".

English nouns generally have only two forms, singular and plural, and the plural is normally formed by adding s, e.g. *wall, walls; road, roads*. Occasionally a different ending is added – *ox, oxen* – and occasionally the word is changed internally – *man, men;* sometimes there is both addition and internal change – *brother, brethren*. Irish nouns have not only distinctive forms for the plural but also for the genitive singular and sometimes for the dative and vocative as well. These distinctive forms are made by addition, by internal change and sometimes by both. Five principal types of noun change are identified in Irish and nouns are therefore divided into five major groups known as *declensions*. Examples of change will be seen later.

2. Singular article + masculine noun:

> An Clár "the plain" (Clare, Arm.)
> An Gleann "the valley" (Glen, Der.)

The only article in Irish is the definite article, that is, the word corresponding to *the* in English.

The singular article *an* "the" prefixes *t* to masculine nouns beginning with a vowel in certain cases. The nouns *éadan* "front, forehead" and *iúr* "yew tree", for example, appear in the place-names:

> An tÉadan "the face (of a hill)" (Eden, Ant.)
> An tIúr "the yew tree" (Newry, Dn)

3. Singular article + feminine noun:

> An Chloch "the stone" (Clough, Dn)
> An Bhreacach "the speckled place" (Brockagh, Der.)

The article *an* aspirates the first consonant of a following feminine noun.

Aspiration is indicated by putting *h* after the consonant *(cloch* "a stone"; *an chloch* "the stone")* and the sound of that consonant is modified, just as in English the sound of *p*, as in the word *praise*, is changed when *h* is added, as in the word *phrase*. Only *b, c, d, f, g, m, p, s,* and *t* are aspirated. The other consonants, and vowels, are not aspirated.

The singular article *an* does not affect feminine nouns beginning with a vowel, e.g.

> An Eaglais "the church" (Eglish, Tyr.)

4. Masculine noun + adjective:

> Domhnach Mór "great church" (Donaghmore, Tyr.)
> Lios Liath "grey ring fort" (Lislea, Arm.)

In Irish the adjective normally follows the noun (but see §8).

5. Feminine noun + adjective:

> Bearn Mhín "smooth gap" (Barnmeen, Dn)
> Doire Fhada "long oak-wood" (Derryadd, Arm.)

The first consonant of the adjective is aspirated after a feminine noun.

6. Singular article + masculine noun + adjective:

> An Caisleán Riabhach "the brindled castle" (Castlereagh, Dn)
> An Baile Meánach "the middle town" (Ballymena, Ant.)

7. Singular article + feminine noun + adjective:

> An Charraig Mhór "the large rock" (Carrickmore, Tyr.)
> An Chloch Fhionn "the white stone" (Cloghfin, Tyr.)

Note that the first consonant of the feminine noun is aspirated after the definite article as in §3 above and that the adjective is aspirated after the feminine noun as in §5 above.

8. Adjective + noun:

> Fionnshliabh "white mountain" (Finlieve, Dn)
> Seanchill "old church" (Shankill, Ant.)

Sometimes an adjective precedes a noun. In such cases the two words are generally written as one and the second noun is usually aspirated. In compounds aspiration sometimes does not occur when d, t or s is preceded by d, n, t, l or s.

9. Article + adjective + noun:

> An Seanmhullach "the old summit" (Castledawson, Der.)
> An Ghlasdromainn "the green ridge" (Glasdrumman, Dn)

Dromainn is a feminine noun and the initial consonant of the compound is aspirated in accordance with §3 above.

10. Masculine noun + genitive singular of noun:

> Srath Gabhláin "(the) river valley of (the) fork" (Stragolan, Fer.)
> Port Rois "(the) harbour of (the) headland" (Portrush, Ant.)

These two examples contain the genitive singular forms of the nouns *gabhlán* and *ros*. Many nouns form the genitive singular by inserting *i* before the final consonant.

11. Feminine noun + genitive singular of noun:

> Maigh Bhile "(the) plain of (the) sacred tree" (Movilla, Dn)
> Cill Shléibhe "(the) church of (the) mountain" (Killevy, Arm.)

Note that in these examples the qualifying genitive is aspirated after the feminine noun. However the forms *maigh* and *cill* are also both old datives, and in the older language aspiration followed any dative singular noun.

Two other types of genitive are illustrated here: many nouns which end in a vowel, like *bile*, do not change at all, whereas others, like *sliabh*, form their genitive by adding *e* (and sometimes an internal change is necessary).

12. Noun + *an* + genitive singular:

> Léim an Mhadaidh "(the) leap of the dog" (Limavady, Der.)
> Baile an tSéipéil "(the) town of the chapel" (Chapeltown, Dn)

The noun *an madadh* "the dog" has a genitive *an mhadaidh* "of the dog". Note that, as well as the end of the noun changing as in §10 above, the genitive is aspirated after *an*.

   Instead of aspirating *s* the article *an* prefixes *t* to it: *an sac* "the sack", *an tsaic* "of the sack"; *an séipéal* "the chapel", *an tséipéil* "of the chapel".

13. Noun + *na* + genitive singular:

> Muileann na Cloiche "(the) mill of the stone/the stone mill" (Clogh Mills, Ant.)
> Cúil na Baice "(the) corner/angle of the river bend" (Cullybackey, Ant.)

The genitive singular feminine article is *na*. It does not aspirate the following noun: *an chloch* "the stone", *na cloiche* "of the stone".
   It prefixes *h*, however, to words beginning with a vowel e.g.

> Baile na hInse "(the) town of the water-meadow" (Ballynahinch, Dn)

The genitive in all these examples is formed by adding *e* to the nominative singular and making a slight internal adjustment.

14. Plural noun:

> Botha "huts" (Boho, Fer.)

The plural form of a substantial group of nouns in Irish is formed by adding -a. In the examples in §15 below an internal adjustment has also to be made.

15. *Na* + plural noun:

> Na Creaga "the rocks" (Craigs, Ant.)
> Na Cealla "the churches" (Kells, Ant.)

Na is also the plural article. *Creaga* and *cealla* are the plural forms of the nouns *creig* "rock" and *cill* "church".

16. Noun + genitive plural:

> Droim Bearach "(the) ridge of (the) heifers" (Dromara, Dn)
> Port Muc "(the) harbour of (the) pigs" (Portmuck, Ant.)

As in the case of *bearach* "a heifer" and *muc* "a pig" the genitive plural form is the same as the nominative singular.

17. Noun + *na* + genitive plural:

> Lios na gCearrbhach "(the) fort/enclosure of the gamblers" (Lisburn, Dn)
> Lios na nDaróg "(the) fort/enclosure of the little oaks" (Lisnarick, Fer.)

After *na* the first letter of the following genitive plural is eclipsed. Eclipsis involves adding to the beginning of a word a consonant which obliterates the sound of the original consonant, e.g.

bó "a cow", pronounced like English "bow" (and arrow)

(na) mbó "(of the) cows", pronounced like "mow"

The following are the changes which take place:

Written letter	Is eclipsed by
b	m
c	g
d	n
f	bh
g	ng
p	b
t	d
vowel	n

The other consonants are not eclipsed, e.g.

Áth na Long "(the) ford of the ships" (Annalong, Dn)

18. Noun + genitive of personal name:

Dún Muirígh *"Muiríoch's* fort" (Dunmurry, Ant.)
Boith Mhéabha "Maeve's hut" (Bovevagh, Der.)

In the older language the genitive of a personal name was not aspirated after a masculine noun but it was after a feminine noun. In the above examples *dún* is masculine and *boith* is feminine. In current Irish aspiration of the personal name is also usual after a masculine noun and this is reflected in many place-names in areas where Irish survived until quite recently, e.g.

Ard Mhacha, interpreted as "the height of *Macha*" (Armagh, Arm.)

19. Noun + genitive singular of *Ó* surname:

Baile Uí Dhonnaíle "Donnelly's townland" (Castlecaulfield, Tyr.)
Coill Uí Chiaragáin "Kerrigan's wood" (Killykergan, Der.)

Surnames in *Ó*, e.g. Ó Dochartaigh "(O') Doherty", Ó Flannagáin "Flanagan", etc. form their genitive by changing *Ó* to *Uí* and aspirating the second element – Uí Dhochartaigh, Uí Fhlannagáin .

20. Noun + genitive singular of *Mac* surname:

Lios Mhic Dhuibhleacháin *"Mac Duibhleacháin's* fort/enclosure" (Lisnagelvin, Der.)
Baile Mhic Gabhann *"Mac Gabhann's* town (angl. McGowan, Smith, etc.) (Ballygowan, Dn)

Surnames in *Mac*, e.g. Mac Dónaill "McDonnell", Mac Muiris "Morrison, Fitzmaurice", etc. form their genitive by changing *Mac* to *Mhic* and aspirating the second element (except those beginning with *C* or *G*).

21. Noun + genitive plural of *Ó* surname:

Doire Ó gConaíle "the oak-wood of the *Ó Conaíle* family (angl. Connelly)" (Derrygonnelly, Fer.)

In the genitive plural of *Ó* surnames the second element is eclipsed.

22. Neuter noun + genitive or adjective:

Sliabh gCuillinn "mountain of (the) steep slope" (Slieve Gullion, Arm.)
Loch gCaol "(the) narrow lake" (Loughguile, Ant.)

The neuter gender no longer exists in Irish but traces of it are found in place-names. The initials of nouns and adjectives were eclipsed after neuter nouns.

APPENDIX B

LAND UNITS

TERRITORIAL DIVISIONS IN IRELAND

The old administrative system, used in the arrangement of these books, consisted of land units in descending order of size: province, county, barony, parish and townland. Theoretically at least the units fit inside each other, townlands into parishes, parishes into baronies, baronies into counties. This system began piecemeal, with the names of the provinces dating back to prehistoric times, while the institution of counties and baronies dates from the 13th to the 17th century, though the names used are often the names of earlier tribal groups or settlements. Parishes originate not as a secular land-unit, but as part of the territorial organization of the Christian Church. There they form the smallest unit in the system which, in descending order of size, goes from provinces to dioceses to deaneries to parishes. Some Irish parishes derive from churches founded by St Patrick and early saints, and appear as parish units in Anglo-Norman church records: parish units are thus older than counties and baronies. Townlands make their first appearance as small land units listed in Anglo-Norman records. However the evidence suggests that land units of this type (which had various local names) are of pre-Norman native origin.

The 17th-century historian Geoffrey Keating outlined a native land-holding system based on the *tríocha céad* or "thirty hundreds", each divided in Ulster into about 28 *baile biadhtaigh* "lands of a food-provider" or "ballybetaghs", and about 463 *seisrigh* "six-horse plough-teams" or "seisreachs" *(Céitinn* iv 112f.). The term *tríocha céad,* which seems to relate to the size of the army an area could muster, is not prominent in English accounts, though there is a barony called Trough *(Tríocha)* in Co. Monaghan. The ballybetagh (land of a farmer legally obliged to feed his lord and retinue while travelling through the area) is mentioned in Plantation documents for west Ulster, and there is some evidence, from townlands grouped in multiples of three and four, that it existed in Armagh, Antrim and Down (McErlean 1983, 318).

Boundaries of large areas, such as provinces and dioceses, are often denoted in early Irish sources by means of two or four extreme points (Hogan 1910, 279–280; *Céitinn* iii 302). There was also a detailed native tradition of boundary description, listing landmarks such as streams, hills, trees and bogs. This can be demonstrated as early as the 8th century in Tírechán's record of a land grant to St Patrick *(Trip. Life (Stokes)* ii 338–9),[1] and as late as the 17th century, when native experts guided those surveying and mapping Ireland for the English administration. The boundary marks on the ground were carefully maintained, as illustrated in the *Perambulation of Iveagh* in 1618 *(Inq. Ult.* xliii), according to which the guide broke the plough of a man found ploughing up a boundary. However very often Irish texts, for example the "Book of Rights" *(Lebor na Cert),* the "topographical" poems by Seaán Mór Ó Dubhagáin and Giolla-na-naomh Ó hUidhrín *(Topog. Poems),* and "The rights of O'Neill" *(Ceart Uí Néill),* refer to territories by the names of the peoples inhabiting them. This custom has been preserved to the present in some place-names, particularly those of provinces and baronies.

SECULAR ADMINISTRATIVE DIVISIONS

Townlands

Twelfth-century charters provide the earliest documentary evidence for the existence in Ireland of small land units, although we do not know what these units were called. Keating's smallest unit, the *seisreach,* a division of the ballybetagh, is given as 120 acres (the word *acra* is apparently borrowed from English). The size of the *seisreach* seems to have been approximately that of a modern townland, but the word does not occur much outside Keating's *schema.* Many other terms appear in the sources: *ceathrú* "quarter" (often a quarter of a ballybetagh), *baile bó* "land providing one cow as rent" (usually a twelfth of a ballybetagh), *seiseach* "sixth" and *trian* "third" (apparently divisions of a ballyboe). In most of Ulster the ballyboe and its subdivisions are the precursors of the modern townlands, and were referred to in Latin sources as *villa* or *carucata,* and in English as "town" or "ploughland" (the term used for similar units in 11th-century England in the Domesday Book). The Irish term *baile* (see below) seems to have been treated as equivalent to English "town", which had originally meant "settlement (and lands appertaining)"; and the compound term "townland" seems to have been adopted to make the intended meaning clear. It was used in 19th-century Ireland as a blanket term for various local words. In the area of Fermanagh and Monaghan the term for the local unit was "tate". In an English document of 1591 it is stated that the tate was 60 acres in size and that there were sixteen tates in the ballybetagh *(Fiants Eliz.* §5674). Tate appears in place-names in composition with Gaelic elements, but was regarded by Reeves (1861, 484) as a pre-1600 English borrowing into Irish.

There is no evidence for the use of the word *baile* in the formation of place-names before the middle of the 12th century. The earliest examples are found in a charter dating to c. 1150 in the Book of Kells which relates to lands belonging to the monastery of Kells. At this period *baile* seems to mean "a piece of land" and is not restricted to its present-day meaning "hamlet, group of houses", much less "town, village". After the coming of the Normans, *baile* appears more frequently in place-names, until it finally becomes the most prevalent type of townland name. By the 14th century, *baile* had acquired its present-day meaning of "town", probably in reference to small medieval towns, or settlements that had arisen in the vicinity of castles. Price suggests that the proliferation of the use of the word in place-names was a result of the arrival of settlers and their use of the word "town" *(tūn)* in giving names to their lands (Price 1963, 124). When the Irish revival took place in the 14th century many English-language names were translated into Irish and "town" was generally replaced by *baile.* The proportion of *baile* names is greatest in those parts of Ireland which had been overrun by the Anglo-Normans but subsequently gaelicized, and is lowest in the counties of mid-Ulster in which there was little or no English settlement *(ibid.* 125).

Despite attempts at schematization none of the units which predated the modern townlands was of uniform size, and it is clear from the native sources that evaluation was based on an area of good land together with a variable amount of uncultivated land. Thus townlands on bad land are usually larger than those on good land. The average size of a townland in Ireland as a whole is 325 acres, and 357 acres in the six counties of Northern Ireland, though these averages include huge townlands like Slievedoo (4551 acres, Co. Tyrone) and tiny townlands like Acre McCricket (4 acres, Co. Down). There is also considerable local variation: townlands in Co. Down average 457 acres (based on the ballyboe), compared to 184 acres (based on the tate) in Fermanagh (Reeves 1861, 490).

Parishes

Early accounts of the lives of saints such as Patrick and Columcille refer to many church foundations. It seems that land was often given for early churches beside routeways, or on the boundaries of tribal territories. Some of the same church names appear as the names of medieval parishes in the papal taxation of 1302–06 *(Eccles. Tax.).* Some parish names include ecclesiastical elements such as *ceall, domhnach, lann,* all meaning "church", *diseart* "hermitage" and *tearmann* "sanctuary", but others are secular in origin. Parish bounds are not given in the papal taxation, but parishes vary considerably in size, probably depending on the wealth or influence of the local church. The medieval ecclesiastical parishes seem to have come into existence after the reform of the native Irish church in the course of the 12th century; in Anglo-Norman areas such as Skreen in Co. Meath the parochial system had already been adopted by the early 13th century (Otway-Ruthven 1964, 111–22). After the Reformation the medieval parish boundaries were continued by the established Church of Ireland, and used by the government as the bounds of civil parishes, a secular land unit forming the major division of a barony. (The boundaries of modern Roman Catholic parishes have often been drawn afresh, to suit the population of worshippers).

As well as the area inhabited by local worshippers, lands belonging to a medieval church often became part of its parish. These were usually close by, but it is quite common, even in the early 19th century when some rationalization had occurred, for parishes to include detached lands at some distance from the main body (Power 1947, 222–3). Kilclief in the barony of Lecale, Co. Down, for example, has five separate detached townlands, while Ballytrustan in the Upper Ards and Trory in Co. Fermanagh are divided into several parts. While an average parish might contain 30 townlands, parishes vary in the number of townlands they contained; for example, Ballykinler in Co. Down contained only 3 townlands, while Aghalurcher contained 237 townlands (including several islands) in Co. Fermanagh plus 17 townlands in Co. Tyrone. Although most of its townlands are fairly small, Aghalurcher is still much larger than Ballykinler. There were usually several parishes within a barony (on average 5 or 6, but, for example, only 2 in the barony of Dufferin, Co. Down, and 18 in the barony of Loughinsholin, Co. Derry). Occasional parishes constituted an entire barony, as did Kilkeel, for example, which is coterminous with the barony of Mourne. However parish units also frequently extended across rivers, which were often used as obvious natural boundaries for counties and baronies: Newry across the Newry River, Clonfeacle over the Blackwater, Artrea over the Ballinderry River, Blaris over the Lagan. This means that civil parishes may be in more than one barony, and sometimes in more than one county.

Baronies

The process of bringing Irish tribal kingdoms into the feudal system as "baronies" under chieftains owing allegiance to the English crown began during the medieval period, although the system was not extended throughout Ulster until the early 17th century. Many of the baronies established in the later administrative system have population names: Oneilland, Irish *Uí Nialláin* "descendants of Niallán" (Arm.); Keenaght, Irish *Cianachta* "descendants of Cian" (Der.); Clankelly, Irish *Clann Cheallaigh* "Ceallach's children" (Fer.). Others have the names of historically important castles or towns: Dungannon (O'Neills, Tyr.), Dunluce (MacDonnells, Antr.), Castlereagh (Clandeboy O'Neills, Down). The barony of Loughinsholin (Der.) is named after an island fortification or crannog, *Loch Inse Uí Fhloinn* "the lake of O'Flynn's island", although by the 17th century the island was inhabited by the O'Hagans, and the O'Flynn area of influence had moved east of the Bann.

The barony system was revised and co-ordinated at the same time as the counties, so that later baronies always fit inside the county bounds. Both counties and baronies appear on maps from 1590 on. These later baronies may contain more than one older district, and other district or population names used in the 16th and 17th centuries, such as *Clancan* and *Clanbrassil* in Armagh, *Slutkellies* in Down, and *Munterbirn* and *Munterevlin* in Tyrone, gradually fell out of use. Baronies were not of uniform size, though in many cases large baronies have been subdivided to make the size more regular. The barony of Dungannon in Co. Tyrone has three sections (Lower, Middle and Upper) while Iveagh in Co. Down has been divided into four (Lower, Lower Half; Lower, Upper Half; Upper, Lower Half; Upper,

Upper Half). The number of baronies in a county in Ulster varies between five in Co. Monaghan and fifteen in Co. Antrim. Armagh, Fermanagh and Tyrone have eight.

Counties

Over the centuries following the Anglo-Norman invasion the English government created a new administrative system in Ireland, adapting the native divisions of provinces, tribal districts (as baronies), parishes and townlands, and dividing each province of Ireland into counties. The counties were equivalent to the shire in England, where a sheriff exercized jurisdiction on behalf of the King. To begin with the county system applied to only those areas where English rule was strong, but was eventually extended, through the reigns of Elizabeth and James I, to cover the whole of the country. Although a commission to shire Ulster was set up in 1585 *(Fiants Eliz. §4763)*, the situation in 1604 was expressed, rather hopefully, in a document in the state papers:

> "each province, except Ulster and other uncivil parts of the realm, is subdued into counties, and each county into baronies and hundreds, and every barony into parishes, consisting of manors, towns and villages after the manner of England."
> *(CSP Ire.* 1603–6, 231).

Most of the counties created in the north were given the names of important towns: Antrim, Armagh, Coleraine (later Londonderry), Down, Donegal, Monaghan and Cavan. Fermanagh and Tyrone, however, have population names. *Fir Manach* "the men of the *Manaig*" (probably the *Menapii* of Ptolemy's *Geography)* had been important in the area before the Maguires. *Tír Eoghain* "Eoghan's land" derives its name from the *Cenél nEógain* branch of the *Uí Néill*, who had expanded southwards from *Inis Eógain* (Inishowen) during the centuries and whose dominant position continued right up until the Plantation. Counties were generally formed out of an amalgam of smaller territorial units, some of which were preserved as baronies within each county.[2] The bounds of these older units were often of long standing, and usually followed obvious physical features, like the lower Bann, the Blackwater, and the Newry River.

Down and Antrim, as part of the feudal Earldom of Ulster (see below) had been treated as counties since the 13th or 14th century (Falkiner 1903, 189; *Inq. Earldom Ulster* ii 141, iii 60). However other districts within the earldom could also be called counties, and up to the mid-16th-century the whole area was sometimes called the "county of Ulster" *(Cal. Carew MSS* 1515–74, 223–4). The settling of Down and Antrim with their modern bounds began in 1570–1 *(Fiants Eliz. §1530, §1736)*. Coleraine had also been the centre of an Anglo-Norman county *(Inq. Earldom Ulster* iv 127). Jobson's map of 1590 shows *Antrym, Armagh, Colrane, Downe, Manahan, Farmanaugh, Terconnel,* and *Upper and Nether Terone* as the names of counties. However, Ulster west of the Bann was still referred to as "four seigniories" (Armagh? plus *Terreconnell, Tyren, Formannoche)* in 1603 *(Cal. Carew MSS* 1601–3, 446–454), although Tyrone had been divided into baronies from 1591 *(Colton Vis.* 125–130). Armagh was settled into baronies in 1605 *(CSP Ire.* 1603–6, 318). The "nine counties of Ulster" were first listed in 1608: *Dunegal or Tirconnel, Tirone, Colraine, Antrim, Downe, Ardmagh, Cavan, Monoghan,* and *Fermanagh (CSP Ire.* 1606–8, 401), and these counties are shown on Hole's adaptation of Mercator's map of Ireland for Camden's atlas *Britannia* (1610). The county of Coleraine was renamed as a result of the plantation grant to the London companies. Under the terms of the formal grant of the area in 1613, the barony of Loughinsholin, which had hitherto been part of Tyrone, was amalgamated with the old county of Coleraine, and Londonderry was made the new county name (Moody 1939, 122–3).

Provinces

Gaelic Ireland, in prehistory and in early historic times, was made up of many small native kingdoms (called *tuatha*), but a sense of the underlying unity of the island is evident from the name of the earliest division in Ireland, that represented by the four modern provinces of Connaught, Leinster, Munster and Ulster. In Irish each is called *cúige* (older *cóiced*) "a fifth", followed by a district or population name. *Cúige Chonnacht* means "the fifth of the Connaughtmen" *Cúige Laighean* "the fifth of the Leinstermen", *Cúige Mumhan* "the fifth of Munster", *Cúige Uladh* "the fifth of the Ulstermen". The connection between population and place-names is evident at this very early stage. The ancient fifth "fifth" making up the whole was that of Meath, in Irish *Midhe* "middle". The division into these five provinces was taken over when Henry II of England invaded Ireland: Leinster, (North and South) Munster, Connaught, Ulster and Meath *quasi in medio regni positum* (as if placed in the middle of the kingdom), but the number was reduced by the 17th century to the modern four *(CSP Ire.* 1603–6 §402, 231), by incorporating Meath in Leinster.

The Province of Ulster

As mentioned above, the province of Ulster took its name from the tribal name *Ulaid* "Ulstermen" (Flanagan 1978(d)). The earliest record of the tribal name is the form quoted by the 2nd-century Greek geographer Ptolemy, as *Uoluntii* (O'Rahilly 1946, 7). The precise origin of the English form of the name is obscure, though it has been suggested that it derives from something like *Ulaðstir,* an unusual combination of the original Irish name plus the Norse possessive suffix -*s* and the Irish word *tír* "land" (Sommerfelt 1958, 223–227). Ptolemy mentions various other tribes in the north of Ireland, but it appears that the *Ulaid* were the dominant group.

The ancient province of the Ulstermen, according to the native boundary description, stretched south to a line running between the courses of the rivers *Drobaís* (Drowse, on the border between Donegal and Leitrim) and *Bóann* (Boyne, Co. Meath). The "fifth" of the legendary king of the Ulaid, Conchobar, *(Cóiced Conchobair)* thus included modern Co. Louth (Hogan 1910, 279b). It became contracted in historical times, as a result of the expansion of the *Uí Néill* "descendants of Niall", who drove the rulers of the Ulaid from the provincial capital at *Emain Macha* (Navan fort near Armagh) across the Bann into modern Antrim and Down.[3] From the 5th century the area stretching south from Derry and Tyrone to Monaghan and most of Louth belonged to a confederation of tribes called the *Airgialla,* who have been described "as a satellite state of the Uí Néill" (Byrne 1973, 73). Three groups of Uí Néill established themselves in the west, *Cenél Conaill* "Conall's kin" in south Donegal, *Cenél nÉndae* in the area around Raphoe, and *Cenél nEógain* in Inishowen *(Inis Eógain* "Eógan's island"). On the north coast, east of the river Foyle, the *Cianachta* maintained a separate identity, despite continuing pressure from *Cenél nEógain.*

East of the Bann the *Dál Fiatach* (the historic Ulaid) shared the kingship of the reduced Ulster with *Dál nAraide* and *Uí Echach Coba,* both originally *Cruthin* tribes.[4] In the 12th century the Anglo-Norman conquest of Antrim and Down resulted in the creation of a feudal lordship of the area under the English crown called the Earldom of Ulster. During the same period the kings of Cenél nEógain had extended their influence eastward, and after the extinction of the Dál Fiatach kingship in the 13th century they assumed the title of *rí Ulad* "king of the Ulaid" to forward their claim to be kings of the whole of the North. It is this greater Ulster which was the basis for the modern province, although there was some doubt at the beginning of the 17th century as to whether or not this included Co. Louth. By the time of the Plantation in 1609 Ulster had been stabilized as nine counties and Louth had been incorporated into the neighbouring province of Leinster.

ECCLESIASTICAL ADMINISTRATIVE DIVISIONS

Dioceses

Under the Roman Empire Christianity developed an administrative structure of dioceses led by bishops based in the local towns. In early Christian Ireland a bishop was provided for each *tuath*, but since the main centres of population were the monasteries established by the church, the bishop often became part of the monastic community, with less power than the abbot. The invasion of the Anglo-Normans in the 12th century encouraged the re-organization and reform of the native church along continental lines, and by the beginning of the 14th century the territories and boundaries for Irish bishops and dioceses had been settled. Most dioceses are named after important church or monastic foundations: Armagh, Clogher, Connor, Derry, Down, Dromore, Kilmore and Raphoe in the North. The ancient secular province of Ulster was included in the ecclesiastical province of Armagh, which became the chief church in Ireland. The bounds of individual dioceses within the province reflect older tribal areas, for example Derry reflects the development of *Cenél nEógain*, Dromore *Uí Echach Coba*. In the 8th century *Dál Fiatach*, who had settled in east Down, pushed northward into the land of *Dál nAraide*, and the bounds of the diocese of Down reflect their expansion as far north as the river *Ollarba* (the Larne Water). The diocesan bounds differ from those of similarly-named later counties because by the time the county boundaries were settled in the 17th century the leaders of many of the larger native territories had been overthrown. County boundaries were generally not based on large native kingdoms but were put together from an amalgam of smaller districts.

Deaneries

The medieval church divided dioceses into rural deaneries, the names of which often derive from old population names. *Blaethwyc* (modern Newtownards) in the diocese of Down, for example, derives from *Uí Blathmaic* "the descendants of Blathmac", whereas *Turtrye*, in the diocese of Connor, derives from *Uí Thuirtre* "the descendants of (Fiachra) Tort". The deaneries of Tullyhogue (Irish *Tulach Óc*) in the diocese of Armagh and *Maulyne* (Irish *Mag Line*) in Connor are named after royal sites. *Mag Line* was the seat of the *Dal nAraide* and *Tulach Óc* was probably the original seat of the Uí Thuirtre, whose area of influence had by this time moved east across the Bann, as the deanery name reveals. The deanery of Inishowen reflects the earlier homeland of the Cenél nEógain. Deanery names are often a useful source of information on important tribal groups of medieval times. Some of these same population names were used later as the names of baronies, while in other cases the earlier population group had lost its influence and the area had become known by another name.

TRIBAL AND FAMILY NAMES

Many personal or population names of various forms have been used as place-names or parts of place-names in Ireland, from provinces, counties, deaneries and baronies to townlands. As with different types of land divisions, different types of family names have come into being at various times.

The names of early Irish tribal groupings were sometimes simple plurals, for example *Ulaid, Cruthin,* and sometimes the personal name of an ancestor or some other element in composition with various suffixes: *Connachta, Dartraige, Latharna.* Other types prefixed *ui* "grandsons", *cenél* "kin", *clann* "children", *dál* "share of", *moccu* "descendants", *síol* "seed", *sliocht* "line" to the name of the ancestor, for example *Dál nAraide* "share of (Fiacha)

Araide", and *Uí Néill* "grandsons of Niall", who are supposedly descended from the 5th-century *Niall Noígiallach* "Niall of the Nine Hostages".

In early Ireland individuals were often identified by patronymics formed by using *mac* "son of" or *ó* (earlier *ua*) "grandson" plus the name of the father or grandfather, rather than by giving the name of the larger group to which the individual belonged. Thus the most straightforward interpretation of *Eoghan mac Néill* is "Eoghan son of Niall", *Eoghan ó Néill* "Eoghan grandson of Niall". Sometimes the same formation can occur with female names. However, in the course of the 10th and 11th centuries patronymics began to be used as surnames. In Modern Irish orthography surnames are distinguished from simple patronymics by using capital *M* or *Ó*: *Eoghan Ó Néill* "Eoghan O'Neill", *Eoghan Mac Néill* "Eoghan MacNeill". However, in early documents, in either Irish or English, it is often difficult to distinguish between surnames and patronymics. This is particularly true of sources such as the *Fiants* where a name such as Donagh M'Donagh may represent the patronymic Donagh, son of Donagh, or the surname Donagh MacDonagh.

As families expanded it was common for different branches to develop their own particular surnames. Some of these have survived to the present, while others, which may have been important enough in their time to be incorporated in place-names, have either died out or been assimilated by similar, more vigorous surnames. In cases such as this the place-name itself may be the only evidence for the former existence of a particular surname in the locality.

Kay Muhr

(1) See also *Geinealach Chorca Laidhe* (O'Donovan 1849, 48–56); *Críchad an Caoilli* (Power 1932, 43–47).

(2) See *Fiants Eliz.* §1736 (1570) for Co. Down; *Colton Vis.* 125–30 (1591) for Cos Derry and Tyrone.

(3) North-east Derry and Louth were also held by the Ulaid, but their influence had been reduced to Down, Antrim and north Louth by the 7th century (Flanagan 1978(d), 41).

(4) The *Cruthin* were a population group widespread in the north of Ireland. The name is of the same origin as "Briton".

ABBREVIATIONS

acc.	Accusative	**Mod. Eng.**	Modern English
adj.	Adjective	**Mod. Ir.**	Modern Irish
al.	Alias	**MS(S)**	Manuscript(s)
angl.	Anglicized	**n.**	(Foot)note
Ant.	Co. Antrim	**neut.**	Neuter
Arm.	Co. Armagh	**NLI**	National Library of
art. cit.	In the article cited		Ireland, Dublin
BM	British Museum	**no(s).**	Number(s)
c.	About	**nom.**	Nominative
cf.	Compare	**O. Eng.**	Old English
Co(s).	County (-ies)	**O. Ir.**	Old Irish
col.	Column	**op. cit.**	In the work cited
coll.	Collective	**OSI**	Ordnance Survey, Dublin
d.	Died	**OSNI**	Ordnance Survey, Belfast
dat.	Dative	**p(p).**	Page(s)
Der.	Co. Derry	**par.**	Parish
Dn	Co. Down	**pass.**	Here and there
eag.	Eagarthóir/Curtha in	**pers. comm.**	personal comment
	eagar ag	**pl.**	Plural
ed.	Edited by	**PRO**	Public Record Office,
edn	Edition		London
Eng.	English	**PROI**	Public Record Office, Dublin
et pass.	And elsewhere	**PRONI**	Public Record Office,
et var.	And variations (thereon)		Belfast
f.	Following page	**pt**	Part
fem.	Feminine	**r.**	Correctly
Fer.	Co. Fermanagh	**RIA**	Royal Irish Academy,
ff.	Folios/Following pages		Dublin
fol.	Folio	**s.**	Shilling
gen.	Genitive	**sa.**	Under the year
HMSO	Her Majesty's Stationery	**sect.**	Section
	Office	**ser.**	Series
ibid.	In the same place	**sic**	As in source
IE	Indo-European	**sing.**	Singular
iml.	Imleabhar	**SS**	Saints
IPA	International Phonetic	**St**	Saint
	Alphabet	**sv(v).**	Under the word(s)
l(l).	Line(s)	**TCD**	Trinity College, Dublin
lit.	Literally	**trans.**	Translated by
loc.	Locative	**Tyr.**	Co. Tyrone
loc. cit.	In the place cited	**uimh.**	Uimhir
Lr.	Lower	**Up.**	Upper
masc.	Masculine	**viz.**	Namely
Mid. Eng.	Middle English	**voc.**	Vocative
Mid. Ir.	Middle Irish	**vol(s).**	Volume(s)

PRIMARY BIBLIOGRAPHY

Acallam (Ní Shéaghdha) *Agallamh na seanórach*, later version, ed. Nessa Ní Shéaghdha, 3 vols (Baile Átha Cliath, Oifig an tSoláthair, 1942–5).

Acallam (O'Grady) *Acallamh na senórach*, ed. S.H. O'Grady from the Book of Lismore, *SG* vol.i 94-233 (text), ii 101-265, 557-65 (translation and notes).

Acallam (Stokes) *Acallamh na senórach*, ed. Whitley Stokes from the Book of Lismore and Laud 610 (*IT* 4 pt 1, Leipzig 1900), completing the text ed. by O'Grady.

A. Conn. *Annála Connacht: the annals of Connacht (AD1224–1544)*, ed. A. Martin Freeman (Dublin 1944).

Acta SS (Bolland) EA The Bollandist series named *Acta sanctorum*, begun by J. Bollandus (Paris 1643), quoted in *EA*.

Adomnán *Adomnan's life of Columba*, ed. A.O. Anderson and M.O. Anderson (Edinburgh 1961).

Aeidhe ma chroidhe "[*Aeidhe ma chroidhe, ceann Bhriain*:] Poem on the Battle of Dun by Gilla-Brighde Mac Conmhidhe", ed. John O'Donovan, *Miscellany of the Celtic Society* (Dublin 1849) 146–83.

AFM *Annála Ríoghachta Éireann: annals of the kingdom of Ireland by the Four Masters from the earliest period to the year 1616*, ed. John O'Donovan, 7 vols (Dublin 1848–51; reprint 1990).

AGBP *Ainmneacha Gaeilge na mbailte poist*, Oifig an tSoláthair (Baile Átha Cliath 1969).

AIF *The Annals of Innisfallen*, ed. Seán Mac Airt (Dublin 1951).

Ainm *Ainm: bulletin of the Ulster Place-name Society* (Belfast 1986–).

Airne Fíngein *Airne Fíngein*, ed. Joseph Vendryes (*MMIS* vol. xv, Dublin 1953).

ALC *The annals of Loch Cé: a chronicle of Irish affairs from AD 1014 to AD 1590*, ed. William Hennessy, 2 vols (London 1871; reprint Dublin 1939).

Anal. Hib. *Analecta Hibernica* (Dublin 1930–69; Shannon1970–).

Ancient Patent (OSNB)   Ancient patent cited in *OSNB* passim.

Annates Ulst.   *De annatis Hiberniae: a calendar of the first-fruits' fees levied on papal appointments to benefices in Ireland, AD 1400–1535*, vol. i (Ulster), ed. Michael A. Costello and Ambrose Coleman (Dundalk 1909; reprint Maynooth 1912).

Armagh Misc.   *Armagh Miscellanea*, papers of T.G.F. Paterson bound in 25 vols by Armagh County Museum.

ASCD   *An archaeological survey of County Down*, Archaeological Survey of Northern Ireland (Belfast 1966).

ASE   "Abstracts of grants of lands and other hereditaments under the acts of settlement and explanation, AD 1666–84", compiled by John Lodge and published in the appendix to the *15th Annual report from the commissioners... respecting the Public Records of Ireland* (1825) 45–340.

A. Tigern.   "The annals of Tigernach", ed. Whitley Stokes, *Rev. Celt.* xvi (1895) 374–419; xvii (1896) 6–33, 116–263, 337–420; xviii (1897) 9–59, 150–303, 374–91.

Atkinson's Donaghcloney   *Donaghcloney, an Ulster parish*, Edward Dupré Atkinson (Dublin 1898).

Atkinson's Dromore   *Dromore: an Ulster diocese*, Edward Dupré Atkinson (Dundalk 1925).

Atkinson's Tour (OSNB)   Atkinson's Tour, cited in *OSNB passim.*

AU   *Annála Uladh: annals of Ulster; otherwise Annála Senait, annals of Senait: a chronicle of Irish affairs, 431-1131, 1155-1541*, ed. William Hennessy and Bartholomew MacCarthy, 4 vols (Dublin 1887–1901).

AU (Mac Airt)   *The annals of Ulster* (vol. i to 1131 AD), ed. Seán Mac Airt and Gearóid Mac Niocaill (Dublin 1983).

Auraicept na nÉces   *Auraicept na nÉces: the scholar's primer*, ed. G. Calder (Edinburgh 1917).

Bagenal's Descr. Ulst.   "Marshal Bagenal's description of Ulster, anno 1586", ed. Herbert F. Hore, *UJA* ser. 1, vol. ii (1854) 137–60.

Barbour's Bruce   *The Bruce by John Barbour*, ed. M. McDiarmid and J. Stevenson, Scottish Texts Society 4th series, 3 vols: 12,13,15 (Edinburgh 1980–5).

Bartlett Map (BM)

A map of south-east Ulster, AD 1600, by Richard Bartlett, British Museum, Cotton MS, Augustus i, vol. ii, no. 37.

Bartlett Map (Greenwich)

A map of east Ulster c. 1602 derived from Richard Bartlett, containing a drawing of the O'Neill inauguration ceremony at Tullaghoge, reproduced in *UJA* ser.3 vol. 33 (1970). National Maritime Museum, Greenwich, Dartmouth MS 25.

Bartlett Map (TCD)

The descriptione of a parte of Ulster containing the p[ar]ticuler places of the Righte Ho. the Lo. Montjoie now Lo. Deputie of Irelande his jorneies & services in the North part of that kingdome, from his entrie therinto until this present August 1601, by Richard Barthelett (Bartlett), TCD MS 2379 (formerly 21 U 19). Reproduced in reduced form as frontispiece in *Dúiche Néill* vol. 1, no. 2 (1987).

Bartlett Maps (Esch. Co. Maps)

Three maps by Richard Bartlett published together with the *Esch. Co. Maps*: (i) *A Generalle Description of Ulster*; (ii) South-east Ulster; (iii) North-west Ulster, (PRO MPF 35–37; copies in PRONI T1652/1–3). These maps have been dated to 1603 by G.A. Hayes-McCoy, *Ulster and Other Irish Maps, c. 1600*, p. 2, n. 13 (Dublin 1964).

Bassett's Down

County Down 100 years ago: a guide and directory 1886, George Henry Bassett (Dublin 1886, repr. Belfast 1988).

Battle of Airtech

"The battle of Airtech" ed. R.I. Best, *Ériu* viii pt.2 (1916) 170–190.

Belfast News Letter (OSNB)

Belfast News Letter cited by *OSNB* passim.

B. in Scáil

"*Baile in Scáil*", ed. Kuno Meyer, *ZCP* iii (1901) 457–66, 1st pt from MS Harleian 5280; *ZCP* xii (1918) 232–8, 2nd pt from Rawlinson B 512.

BM Cat.

Catalogue of Irish manuscripts in the British Museum, 3 vols., vol.i ed. Standish Hayes O'Grady, vol.ii Robin Flower, vol.iii The British Museum (London 1926–52).

Bnd. Sur. (OSNB)

Boundary Survey sketch maps c. 1830, cited in *OSNB* passim.

Boazio's Map (BM)

Gennerall discription or Chart of Irelande, AD 1599, by Baptista Boazio. Three impressions are known, one in the British Museum, one in TCD, and a third in private hands.

Bodley's Lecale

"Bodley's visit to Lecale, County of Down, AD 1602–3", *UJA* ser. 1, vol. 2 (1854) 73–99.

Brownlow LB

Settlement and survival on an Ulster estate: the Brownlow leasebook 1667–1711, ed. R.G. Gillespie (Belfast 1988).

BSD

Book of survey & distribution, AD 1661: Armagh, Down & Antrim (Quit Rent Office copy), PRONI T370/A.

BSD (Annes.)

The Annesley copy (AD 1680) of the *Book of Survey and distribution, PRONI mic. 532 reel 11*.

Buckworth (Atkinson)

"Bishop Buckworth's report of the diocese [of Dromore], AD 1622", *Atkinson's Dromore* 127–32.

Buckworth (EA)

"Bishop Buckworth's return", AD 1622, *EA* 310–11.

Buile Suibhne

Buile Suibhne (the frenzy of Suibhne): being the adventures of Suibhne Geilt... ed. J.G. O'Keeffe, *ITS* xii (London 1913, reprint 1984).

BUPNS

Bulletin of the Ulster Place-name Society, ser. 1, vols i–v (Belfast 1952–7); ser. 2, vols 1–4 (1978–82).

Cal. Carew MSS

Calendar of the Carew manuscripts preserved in the Archiepiscopal Library at Lambeth, ed. J.S. Brewer and W. Bullen, 6 vols (London 1867–73).

Cal. Papal Letters

Calendar of entries in the papal registers relating to Great Britain and Ireland: papal letters AD 1198-1498, ed. W.H. Bliss, C. Johnson, J.A. Twelmow, Michael J. Haren, Anne P. Fuller, 16 vols (London 1893-1960, Dublin 1978, 1986). In progress.

Cambr. MCS

Cambridge Medieval Celtic Studies (Cambridge 1981–93); *Cambrian Medieval Celtic Studies* (Aberystwyth, 1993–)

Cartae Dun.

"Cartae Dunenses XII-XIII céad", eag. Gearóid Mac Niocaill, *S. Ard Mh.* vol. 5, no. 2 (1970), 418–28.

Cath Aen. Macha

"[Cath Aenaigh Macha:] Battle of the assembly of Macha", ed. Margaret Dobbs, *ZCP* xvi (1926) 145–61.

Cath Leit. Ruibhe

"Cath Leitreach Ruibhe", ed. Margaret Dobbs, *Rev. Celt.* xxxix (1922) 1–32.

Cath MT

Cath Maige Tuired: the second battle of Mag Tuired, ed. E.A. Gray, *ITS* lii (London 1983).

C. Conghail Cláir.   *Caithréim Conghail Cláiringhnigh: Martial career of Conghal Cláiringhneach*, ed. Patrick M. MacSweeney, *ITS* v (London 1904).

CDI   *Calendar of documents relating to Ireland, 1171–1307*, ed. H.S. Sweetman and G.F. Handcock, 5 vols (London 1875–86).

Ceart Uí Néill   "*Ceart Uí Néill*", ed. Myles Dillon, *Stud. Celt.* 1 (1966) 1–18. Trans. Éamonn Ó Doibhlin, "*Ceart Uí Néill*, a discussion and translation of the document", *S. Ard Mh.* vol. 5, no. 2 (1970) 324–58. Text printed in *LCABuidhe* 41–7.

Céitinn   *Foras Feasa ar Éirinn: the history of Ireland by Seathrún Céitinn (Geoffrey Keating)*, ed. Rev. Patrick S. Dinneen, 4 vols, *ITS* iv, viii, ix, xiv (London 1902–14).

Celtica   *Celtica*, Dublin Institute for Advanced Studies (Dublin 1946–).

Census   *A census of Ireland, circa 1659, with supplementary material from the poll money ordinances (1660–1)*, ed. Séamus Pender (Dublin 1939).

Census 1851   *Census of Ireland, 1851. General alphabetical index to the townlands and towns, parishes and baronies of Ireland...* (Dublin 1861, reprint Baltimore 1984–95).

Cess Book (OSNB)   Cess Book cited in *OSNB* passim.

CGH   *Corpus genealogiarum Hiberniae*, vol. 1, Irish genealogies ed. M.A. O'Brien (Dublin 1962).

Chron. Scot.   *Chronicon Scotorum: a chronicle of Irish affairs from the earliest times to AD 1135; with a supplement containing the events from 1141 to 1150* ed. William Hennessy (London 1886).

Church Lands Arm.   "The church lands of (Co.) Armagh" by Michael Glancy, *S. Ard. Mh.* vol.1 (1954) 67–100; vol.2 no.2 (1957) 327–55; vol.3 no.2 (1959) 352–68; "The primates and the church lands of Armagh" vol.5 no.2 (1970) 370–96.

Cín Lae Ó M.   *Cín lae Ó Mealláin*, ed. Tadhg Ó Donnchadha (alias Torna), *Anal. Hib.* iii (1931) 1-61.

Circ. of Ireland   *The Circuit of Ireland by Muircheartach mac Néill, prince of Aileach, composed by Cormacan Eigeas.* Ed. with translation and notes by John O'Donovan in *Tracts relating to Ireland* printed for the Irish Archaeological Society (Dublin 1841).

Civ. & Ecc. Top. (OSNB)   *Topographia Hibernica,* William Wenman Seward (Dublin 1795). Cited in *OSNB passim.*

Civ. Surv.   *The civil survey, AD 1654–6,* ed. Robert C. Simington, 10 vols, Irish Manuscripts Commission (Dublin 1931–61).

Clann Ollaman   "*Clann Ollaman uaisle Emna*", ed. F.J. Byrne, *Stud. Hib.* iv (1964) 54–94.

Clergyman (OSNB)   Local clergyman, cited in *OSNB passim.*

CMR I   "A new version of the Battle of Magh Rath", ed. Carl Marstrander, *Ériu* v (1911) 226–47.

CMR II   *The Banquet of Dun na nGedh and the Battle of Magh Rath, an ancient historical tale...,* ed. John O'Donovan, Irish Archaeological Society (Dublin 1842).

Cogadh FC   "La guerre entre Fergus et Conchobar: *Cogadh Fergusa agus Chonchubhair sonn*", ed. M. Dobbs, *Revue Celtique* xl (1923) 403–23.

Cóir Anmann   "*Cóir Anmann* 'Fitness of names'", ed. Whitley Stokes, IT 3 pt 2, 285–444 (1897).

Colton Vis.   *Acts of Archbishop Colton in his metropolitical visitation of the diocese of Derry, AD 1397,* ed. William Reeves (Dublin 1850).

Comp. CC   *Compert Con Culainn and other stories,* ed. A.G. Van Hamel, *MMIS* iii (Dublin 1933).

County Warrant (OSNB)   *County warrant,* cited in *OSNB, passim.*

CPR Chas. I   *Calendar of patent and close rolls of chancery in Ireland, Charles I, years 1–8,* ed. James Morrin (Dublin 1864).

CPR Jas. I   *Irish patent rolls of James I: facsimile of the Irish record commissioners' calendar prepared prior to 1830,* with a foreword by M.C. Griffith (Dublin 1966).

CPR (Tresham)   *Rotulorum patentium et clausorum cancellariae Hiberniae calendarium,* 2 vols (vol. 2 has no title), ed. Edward Tresham (Dublin 1828–[1830]).

CSH   *Corpus genealogiarum sanctorum Hiberniae,* ed. Pádraig Ó Riain (Dublin 1985).

CSP Ire.   *Calendar of the state papers relating to Ireland, 1509–1670,* ed. H.C. Hamilton, E.G. Atkinson, R.P. Mahaffy, C.P. Russell and J.P. Prendergast, 24 vols (London 1860–1912).

Custom of County	Spelling or pronunciation current in the count[r]y c. 1834, cited in *OSNB, passim*.
Dartmouth Map 5	A map of the north of Ireland dating to 1590 from the National Maritime Museum, Greenwich; Dartmouth Collection no. 5.
Dartmouth Map 6	A maritime chart/map of Ireland dating to 1590 preserved in the National Maritime Museum, Greenwich, Dartmouth Collection no. 6.
Deeds & Wills (Mooney)	A variety of unspecified deeds and wills, largely 18th century, cited in *Mooney, passim*.
Descendants Ir	"The history of the descendants of Ir", Ulster genealogies ed. Margaret Dobbs, *ZCP* xiii (1921) 308–59; xiv (1923) 44–144.
De Script. Hib.	*De Scriptoribus Hibernicis* by An Dubhaltach Mac Firbhisigh, 1657 AD, ed. J. Carney, *Celtica* i pt 1 (1946) 86–110.
Descr. Ire.	*The description of Ireland and the state thereof as it is at this present, in anno 1598...*, ed. Edmund Hogan (Dublin 1878).
DIL	*Dictionary of the Irish language: compact edition* (Dublin 1983).
Dinneen	*Foclóir Gaedhilge agus Béarla: an Irish-English dictionary*, Rev. Patrick S. Dinneen (Dublin 1904; reprint with additions 1927 and 1934).
Downshire Direct.	"Directory to the seats of Downshire, with their respective post towns alphabetically arranged", A. Atkinson, *Ireland exhibited to England, in a political and moral survey of her population*, vol. i, 315–30 (London 1823).
DS (Mooney)	Petty's Down Survey, cited in *Mooney (MS) passim*.
Duan. Finn	*Duanaire Finn: the book of the lays of Finn*, ed. Eoin MacNeill and Gerard Murphy, 3 vols. *ITS* (London 1908–41, vol. iii repr. Dublin 1953).
Dubourdieu's Map (OSNB)	*Dubourdieu's map*, cited in *OSNB, passim*. See *Statist. Sur. Dn.*
Dúiche Néill	*Dúiche Néill: journal of the O'Neill Country Historical Society* (Benburb 1986–).

Dwelly

The illustrated Gaelic-English dictionary, Edward Dwelly (Glasgow 1901–11; reprint 1920 etc.).

EA

Ecclesiastical antiquities of Down, Connor and Dromore, consisting of a taxation of those dioceses compiled in the year 1306, ed. William Reeves (Dublin 1847).

Eachtra CG

"Eine Brüsseler handschrift der *Eachtra Conaill Gulban*", ed. Gustav Lehmacher, *ZCP* xiv (1923) 212–69.

Eccles. Tax.

"Ecclesiastical taxation of the dioceses of Down, Connor, and Dromore", ed. William Reeves, *EA* 2–119.

Eccles. Tax. (CDI)

"Ecclesiastical taxation of Ireland", ed. H.S. Sweetman & G.F. Handcock, *Calendar of documents relating to Ireland...*, *1302–07* (London 1886), 202–323.

Éigse

Éigse: a journal of Irish studies (Dublin 1939–).

Éire Thuaidh

Éire Thuaidh/Ireland North: a cultural map and gazetteer of Irish place-names, Ordnance Survey of Northern Ireland (Belfast 1988).

Ériu

Ériu: the journal of the School of Irish Learning (Dublin 1904–).

Esch. Co. Map

Barony maps of the escheated counties in Ireland, AD 1609, 28 maps, PRO London. Published as *The Irish Historical Atlas*, Sir Henry James, Ordnance Survey (Southampton 1861).

Exch. Accounts Ulst.

"Ancient exchequer accounts of Ulster", *UJA* ser. 1, vol. iii (1855), 155–62.

Ex. Inq. (Dn)

Inquisition of the court of exchequer in Ireland taken at Downpatrick, March 25, 8th year of the reign of Charles I, AD 1633, transcribed by Deirdre Flanagan from PROI.

FB

Fled Bricrenn, ed. George Henderson, *ITS* ii (London 1899).

Féil. Torna

Féilscríbhinn Torna .i. tráchtaisí léanta in onóir don Ollamh Tadhg Ua Donnchadha..., eag. Séamus Pender (Corcaigh 1947).

Fél. Óeng.

Félire Óengusso Céli Dé: the martyrology of Oengus the culdee, ed. Whitley Stokes (London 1905; reprint 1984).

Fiants Eliz.

"Calendar and index to the fiants of the reign of Elizabeth I", appendix to the 11–13th, 15–18th and 21–22nd *Reports of the Deputy Keeper of public records in Ireland* (Dublin 1879–81, 1883–86, 1889–90).

Fragment. Ann.	*Fragmentary annals of Ireland*, ed. Joan. N. Radner (Dublin 1978).
Fragment. Ann. (JOD)	*Annals of Ireland: three fragments*, ed. John O'Donovan (The Irish Archaeological and Celtic Society, Dublin, 1860).
Geneal. Tracts	*Genealogical tracts*, ed. T. Ó Raithbheartaigh (Dublin 1932).
GÉ	*Gasaitéar na hÉireann/Gazetteer of Ireland: ainmneacha ionad daonra agus gnéithe aiceanta*, Brainse Logainmneacha na Suirbhéireachta Ordanáis (Baile Átha Cliath 1989).
GJ	*Gaelic Journal: Irisleabhar na Gaedhilge*, 19 vols (Dublin 1882–1909).
Goghe's Map	*Hibernia: Insula non procul ab Anglia vulgare Hirlandia vocata, AD 1567*, by John Goghe, PRO London MPF 68. Reproduced in *SP Hen. VIII* vol. ii, pt 3.
GOI	*A grammar of Old Irish*, Rudolf Thurneysen, trans. D.A. Binchy and Osborn Bergin (Dublin 1946).
GUH	*Gleanings from Ulster history*, by Séamas Ó Ceallaigh (Cork 1951), enlarged and reprinted by Ballinascreen Historical Society (1994).
Ham. Copy Inq.	"Copy inquisition, dated 13th October, 1623", ed. T.K. Lowry, *Hamilton MSS*, appendix iv, xxix-lvi.
Hamilton MSS	*The Hamilton manuscripts: containing some account of the settlement of the territories of the Upper Clandeboye, Great Ardes and Dufferin, in the County of Down*, by Sir James Hamilton, Knight, ed. T.K. Lowry (Belfast 1867).
Ham. Rent-roll	"Rent-roll of the Jointure Lands of Ann, late Countess of Clanbrassill", ed. T.K. Lowry, *Hamilton MSS* 125–32.
Harris Hist.	*The antient and present state of the county of Down*, Walter Harris (Dublin 1744).
Harris Hist. map	*A new and correct map of ye county of Down partly by an actual survey and partly by observation, 1743*. Reproduced in *Harris Hist.*
Hermathena	*Hermathena: a Dublin University review* (Dublin 1873–).

Hib. Del.

Hiberniae Delineatio: an atlas of Ireland by Sir William Petty comprised of one map of Ireland, 4 maps of provinces and 32 county maps. It was engraved c. 1671–72 and first published in London c. 1685 (Goblet 1932, viii). A facsimile reprint was published in Newcastle-Upon-Tyne in 1968 and a further reprint, with critical introduction by J.H. Andrews, in Shannon, 1970.

Hib. Reg.

Hibernia Regnum: a set of 214 barony maps of Ireland dating to the period AD 1655–59. These maps were drawn at the same time as the official parish maps which illustrated the Down Survey of Sir William Petty. The original parish maps have been lost but the *Hibernia Regnum* maps are preserved in the Bibliothèque Nationale, Paris (Goblet 1932, v-x). Photographic facsimiles of these maps were published by the Ordnance Survey, Southampton in 1908.

Hondius Map

Hyberniae Novissima Descriptio, AD 1591, drawn by Jodocus Hondius and engraved by Pieter van den Keere, reprinted Linen Hall Library, Belfast (1983).

Imm. Dá T.

"*Immaccallam in dá Thuarad*: the colloquy of the two sages", ed. Whitley Stokes, *Revue Celtique* xxvi (1905) 4–64.

Inq. Arm. (Paterson)

"Cromwellian inquisition as to parishes in County Armagh in 1657", ed. T.G.F. Paterson, *UJA* ser. 3, vol. ii (1939) 212–49.

Inq. Down (Atkinson)

An inquisition of Down, AD 1657, ed. E.D. Atkinson, *Atkinson's Dromore*, 133-46.

Inq. Down (Reeves1)

An inquisition of Down, AD 1657, transcribed by William Reeves, PRONI DIO/1/24/8/2.

Inq. Earldom Ulster

"The earldom of Ulster", Goddard H. Orpen, *JRSAI* xliii (1913) 30–46, 133–43; xliv (1914) 51–66; xlv (1915) 123–42.

Inq. Moyry Castle

Inquisition at Moyry castle, August 1608, TCD MS 582 fols 83–92; transcribed by T.G.F. Paterson *Armagh Misc.* xxi 215–39.

Inq. Ult.

Inquisitionum in officio rotulorum cancellariae Hiberniae asservatarum repertorium, vol. ii (Ulster), ed. James Hardiman (Dublin 1829). It contains separate sections for each county.

Irish Geography	*Irish Geography: bulletin of the Geographical Society of Ireland* (Dublin 1944–).
Irish Litanies	*Irish litanies*, ed. Charles Plummer, Henry Bradshaw Society lxii (London 1925).
Ir. Wills Index	*Indexes to Irish wills*, ed. W.P. Phillimore and Gertrude Thrift, 5 vols (London 1909–20; reprint Baltimore, 1970).
IT	*Irische Texte*, Leipzig (1880–1909).
ITS	*Irish Texts Society*, London (1899-).
Jas I to Dromore Cath.	Grant of James I to the cathedral of Dromore, AD 1609, ed. William Reeves, *EA* 313-4.
JDCHS	*Journal of the Down and Connor Historical Society*, 10 vols (Belfast 1928–39).
J Louth AS	*Journal of the County Louth Archaeological Society* (Dundalk 1904–).
Jobson's Ulster (BM)	A map of Ulster by Francis Jobson c. 1590, British Museum, Cotton MS. Augustus i vol.ii no.19.
Jobson's Ulster (TCD)	A set of three maps of Ulster by Francis Jobson, the first of which dates to AD 1590, TCD MS 1209, nos 15–17.
J O'D (OSNB)	Irish and anglicized forms of names attributed to John O'Donovan in the *OSNB*.
Joyce	*The origin and history of Irish names of places*, P.W. Joyce, 3 vols (Dublin 1869–1913).
JRSAI	*Journal of the Royal Society of Antiquaries of Ireland* (Dublin 1849–). 6th ser., vols i-xx [consecutive ser. vols xli-lx] (1911—30); 7th ser., vols i-xiv [consecutive ser. vols lxi-lxxiv] (1931–44); thereafter numbered only as consecutive series vol. lxxv- (1945–).
Kennedy Map (OSNB)	*A map of the county of Downe, with a chart of the sea coast done from actual surveys and accurate observations*, by Dr Kennedy, AD 1755, cited in *OSNB, passim*.
Knox Hist.	*A history of the county of Down from the most remote period to the present day*, Alexander Knox (Dublin 1875; reprint Ballynahinch 1982).

Lamb Maps | *A Geographical Description of ye Kingdom of Ireland Collected from ye actual Survey made by Sir William Petty...Containing one General Mapp of ye whole Kingdom, with four Provincial Mapps, & 32 County Mapps...Engraven & Published for ye benefit of ye Publique* by Francis Lamb (London [c. 1690]).

LASID | *Linguistic atlas and survey of Irish dialects*, Heinrich Wagner and Colm Ó Baoill, 4 vols (Dublin 1958–69).

Laud Gens | "The Laud genealogies and tribal histories", ed. Kuno Meyer, *ZCP* viii (1912) 291–338.

LCABuidhe | *Leabhar Cloinne Aodha Buidhe*, ed. Tadhg Ó Donnchadha alias Torna (Dublin 1931). Contents: *Leabhar Eoghanach* 1–40, *Ceart Uí Néill* 41–7, *Duanaire* 59–290.

Leabharlann | *An Leabharlann*: journal of *Cumann na Leabharlann* (later, the Library Association of Ireland), vols 1–29 (Dublin 1906–71); new ser., vols 1–11 (1972–82); 2nd new ser., vol. 1– (1984–).

Leabhar na gCeart (JOD) | *Leabhar na g-Ceart or the Book of Rights*, ed. John O'Donovan (The Celtic Society, Dublin, 1847).

Lebor na Cert | *Lebor na Cert: the book of rights*, ed. Myles Dillon, *ITS* 46 (Dublin 1962).

Lewis' Top. Dict. | *A topographical dictionary of Ireland, comprising the several counties, cities, boroughs, corporate, market and post towns, parishes and villages with statistical descriptions*, ed. Samuel Lewis, 2 vols and atlas (London 1837; 2nd edn 1842).

L. Gabála | *Lebor Gabála Érenn: the book of the taking of Ireland*, ed. R.A.S. MacAlister, 5 vols. *ITS* 34,35,39,41,44 (Dublin 1938-56). The earliest manuscript is *LL*, i 1-56/99.

LGD Map | *Local government district series showing townlands and wards within the various districts and showing the layout of the OS 1:10,000 sheets*, Ordnance Survey of Northern Ireland (Belfast 1974).

Liber Angeli (Bieler) | *Liber Angeli* ("Book of the angel"), ed. Ludwig Bieler *The Patrician texts in the Book of Armagh, Scriptores Latini Hiberniae* x (1979), 184–91.

Liosta Log. Lú | *Liostaí logainmneacha: Contae Lú/County Louth*, arna ullmhú ag Brainse Logainmneacha na Suirbhéireachta Ordanáis (Baile Átha Cliath 1991).

LL
The Book of Leinster, formerly Lebar na Núachongbála, diplomatic edn R.I. Rest, O. Bergin, M.A. O'Brien and A. O'Sullivan, 6 vols (Dublin 1954–83).

L.Lec.
The Book of Lecan: Leabhar Mór Mhic Fhir Bhisigh Lecáin, facsimile edn K. Mulchrone (Dublin 1937).

Local pronunciation
Local pronunciation recorded by the editors.

Lochlann
Lochlann: a review of Celtic studies (Oslo 1958–).

Lodge (Mooney)
Lodge RR cited by *Mooney, passim.*

Lodge RR
John Lodge's *Record of the Rolls*: being an "exact list of the patent rolls remaining of record in the office of the rolls of His Majesty's high court of chancery in Ireland", transcribed in 1755. Vols ii-x (Jas I–George II) PROI 1a.53.51–1a.53.59 (Dublin).

Longman Dict.
Longman Dictionary of the English language (Harlow 1984, 2nd edn 1991).

Mac Cumhaigh (b)
Art Mac Cumhaigh: Dánta, eag. Tomás Ó Fiaich (Baile Átha Cliath 1973).

MacDonnells Antrim
An historical account of the MacDonnells of Antrim, Rev. George Hill (Belfast 1873, repr. 1978).

Magennis Paps (O'Sullivan)
Documents quoted in a manuscript history of the Magennises of Co. Down by Harold O'Sullivan.

Map Douglas Estate (OSNB)
Map of the Douglas estate based on Grace Hall, Moira, cited in *OSNB.*

Map Kilwarlin
Map of Kilwarlin estate, a true copy of 1640 survey made by G. White for Arthur Hill Esq. 1667. Published *UJA* ser. 3 vol. xii (1949) plate iv; a later copy (1823) in PRONI D671/m8/1.

Map Newry Canal
Late 17th-century map of the route for the Newry canal, PRONI D1248/m/11.

Map of Down (OSNB)
Unspecified map(s) of Co. Down, cited in *OSNB, passim.* Probably from 1739 *Sloane,* 1755 *Kennedy* maps.

Maps Down (Mac Aodha)
"Fianaise chartagrafach i dtaobh ainmneacha bhailte an Dúin, 1573–1864", Breandán S. Mac Aodha, *Ainm* ii (1987), 55–75.

Maps (Mooney)
Unidentified maps, cited in *Mooney, passim.*

Marriage (Downshire)   *Marriage settlement of the Marquis of Downshire, AD 1811*, cited in *OSNB, passim*.

Mart. Don.   *The martyrology of Donegal: a calendar of the saints of Ireland*, trans. John O'Donovan, ed. James H. Todd and William Reeves (Dublin 1864).

Mart. Gorm.   *Félire Húi Gormáin: the martyrology of Gorman*, ed. Whitley Stokes (London 1895).

Mart. Tal.   *The martyrology of Tallaght*, ed. R.I. Best and H.J. Lawlor (London 1931).

Meath (McDonnell)   A Meath phrase-list in Hugh McDonnell's handwriting in Belfast Public Library (MS xviii), ed. É. Ó Tuathail, *Éigse* v (1945-7) 36-44.

Meersman (OSNB)   Documents associated with the boundary survey, cited in *OSNB, passim*.

Mercator's Ire. (1564)   A map of Ireland by Gerard Mercator, first published in his atlas entitled *Angliae, Scotiae et Hiberniae nova descriptio* (Duisburg 1564).

Mercator's Ire. (1595)   *Irlandiae Regnum*, by Gerard Mercator, first published in his atlas entitled *Atlas sive Cosmographicae Meditationes de Fabrica Mundi et Fabricati Figura*, AD 1595.

Mercator's Ulst.   *Ultoniae Orientalis Pars* by Gerard Mercator, first published in his *Atlas sive Cosmographicae Meditationes de Fabrica Mundi et Fabricati Figura*, AD 1595.

Mesca Ulad   *Mesca Ulad*, ed. J. Carmichael Watson, *MMIS* xiii (Dublin 1961).

Met. Dinds.   *The metrical Dindshenchas*, ed. Edward J. Gwynn, 5 vols (RIA Dublin 1903–35).

Miscell. Ann.   *Miscellaneous Irish annals (AD 1114-1437)*, ed. Séamus Ó hInnse (Dublin 1947).

MMIS   *Mediaeval and Modern Irish series*, Dublin Institute for Advanced studies, Dublin.

Mon. Ang.   *Monasticon Anglicanum: a history of the abbies and other monasteries, hospitals and frieries...in England and Wales*, William Dugdale (London 1661). New edn John Caley, Sir Henry Ellis and Bulkeley Bandinel, 6 vols (London 1846).

Montgomery MSS

The Montgomery manuscripts (1603–1706) compiled from family papers by William Montgomery..., ed. Rev. George Hill (Belfast 1869).

Mooney (MS)

An unpublished study of the townlands of the diocese of Dromore and the barony of Iveagh by Bernard J. Mooney (Ballynahinch Library, Co. Down).

Mrs Con Magennis (OSNB)

Informant for Annaclone and Drumballyroney parishes in OSNB.

Muirchú (Bieler)

The Life of St Patrick by Muirchú maccu Machtheni, ed. Ludwig Bieler *The Patrician texts in the Book of Armagh, Scriptores Latini Hiberniae x* (1979), 61-123.

Newry Char. (Flanagan)

"Confirmation charter and grant of protection of Muirchertach Mac Lochlainn, king of Cenél nEógain and high-king of Ireland, to the Cistercian abbey of Newry, Co. Down", ed. M.T. Flanagan, *Monastic charters from Irish kings of the 12th and 13th centuries*, M.A. thesis vol. ii 245-6 (University College Dublin 1973).

Newry Char. (Mon. Ang.)

"Charter of Newry", ed. W. Dugdale, *Mon. Ang.* vi, 1133–4.

Newry Tel. (OSNB)

Newry Telegraph, cited in *OSNB, passim*.

NISMR

Northern Ireland sites and monuments record: stage 1 (1979), published privately by the Department of the Environment (NI) and the Archaeological Survey (Belfast 1979).

Norden's Map

"The plott of Irelande with the confines", formerly included in *A discription of Ireland*, c. 1610, by John Norden. This map had been preserved in the State Paper Office but is now in PRO MPF 67. It is reproduced in *SP Hen. VIII* vol. ii, pt. 3.

Nowel's Ire. (1)

A map of Ireland, c. 1570, attributed to Laurence Nowel, dean of Lichfield (d. 1576). British Museum Cotton MS, Domitian A18, ff. 101–103. Reproduced by the Ordnance Survey, Southampton.

Ó Dónaill

Foclóir Gaeilge-Béarla, eag. Niall Ó Dónaill (Baile Átha Cliath 1977).

OED

Oxford English Dictionary ed. J.A. Simpson, E.S.C. Weiner (2nd edn 1989).

O'Laverty

An historical account of the diocese of Down and Connor ancient and modern, Rev. James O'Laverty, 5 vols. (Dublin 1878–95).

Old Hennan and others (OSNB)   Informants for parishes of Annaclone and Drumballyroney in *OSNB*.

Omeath Infs. (GJ)   "Dinnseanchas: [Irish forms of place-names supplied by two natives of Omeath]", *GJ* xi (1901) 156–7.

O'Neill Fun. Oration   "An Irish funeral oration over Owen O'Neill, of the House of Clanaboy", ed. Douglas Hyde, *UJA* ser. 2 vol. iii (1897), 258–71; vol. iv (1898), 50–5.

Onoma   *Onoma: bibliographical and information bulletin*, International Centre of Onomastics (Louvain 1950–).

Onom. Goed.   *Onomasticon Goedelicum locorum et tribuum Hiberniae et Scotiae*, Edmund Hogan (Dublin 1910).

O'Reilly   *An Irish-English dictionary*, Edward O'Reilly. Revised and corrected, with a supplement by John O'Donovan (Dublin 1864).

Ortelius Map   *Eryn. Hiberniae, Britannicae Insulae, Nova Descriptio. Irlandt* by Abraham Ortelius. Published in the second edition of his *Theatrum Orbis Terrarum* (Antwerp 1573).

OS 1:10,000   *The Ordnance Survey 1:10,000 series maps*, Ordnance Survey of Northern Ireland (Belfast 1968–).

OS 1:50,000   *The Ordnance Survey 1:50,000 series maps*, also known as *The Discoverer Series*, Ordnance Survey of Northern Ireland (Belfast 1978–88).

OS 6-inch   *The Ordnance Survey six-inch series maps*, first published in the 1830s and 1840s with numerous subsequent editions. It has now been superseded by the OS 1:10,000.

OSL Dn   "Letters [written by John O'Donovan] containing information relative to the [history and] antiquities of the County of Down collected during the progress of the Ordnance Survey in 1834", published as a supplement to *Leabharlann* iii (Dublin 1909).

OSM   *Ordnance Survey memoirs of Ireland*, ed. Angélique Day and Patrick McWilliams (Belfast 1990–).

OSNB   Name-books compiled during the progress of the Ordnance Survey in 1834–5 and preserved in the Ordnance Survey, Phoenix Park, Dublin.

OSNB Inf.   Informants for the Irish forms of place-names in the *OSNB*.

OSNB Pron.	Local pronunciation recorded in *OSNB, passim*.
Par. Map (Mooney)	Parish maps of the Down Survey c. 1657 AD, quoted by *Mooney*.
Par. Reg. (OSNB)	Parish register quoted in *OSNB, passim*.
Parl. Rep. 1833	*First report of his Majesty's commissioners on ecclesiastical revenue and patronage, Ireland* (House of Commons, 1833).
Parl. Rep. 1868	*Report of Her Majesty's commissioners on the revenues and conditions of the established church (Ireland)*, with temporalities appendix. Presented to both Houses of Parliament (Dublin 1868).
Pipe Roll John	"The Irish pipe roll of 14 John, 1211–2", ed. Oliver Davies and David B. Quinn, supplement to *UJA* ser. 3, vol. iv (1941) 76pp.
PNI	*Place-names of Northern Ireland* series, (Belfast 1992–)
Pontif. Hib.	*Pontificia Hibernica: medieval papal chancery documents concerning Ireland, 640–1261*, ed. Maurice P. Sheehy, 2 vols (Dublin 1962–5).
Post Chaise Comp. (OSNB)	*Post Chaise Companion*, cited in *OSNB, passim*.
Post-Sheanchas	*Post-Sheanchas i n-a bhfuil cúigí, dúithchí, conntaethe, & bailte puist na hÉireann*, Seosamh Laoide (Baile Átha Cliath 1905).
PRIA	*Proceedings of the Royal Irish Academy* (Dublin 1836–). Published in three sections since 1902 (section C: archaeology, linguistics and literature).
Prerog. Wills Index	*Index to the prerogative wills of Ireland, 1536–1810*, ed. Arthur E. Vicars (Dublin 1897).
PSAMNI	*Preliminary survey of the ancient monuments of Northern Ireland*, ed. D.A. Chart (Belfast 1940).
Ptolemy	Ptolemy's *Geography of Ireland* (4th-century BC–2nd-century AD): names discussed T.F. O'Rahilly 1946, 1-42.
Reg. Cromer	"Archbishop Cromer's register", ed. L.P. Murray, *J Louth AS* vii (1929–32) 516–24; viii (1933–6) 38–49, 169–88, 257–74, 322–51; ix (1937–40) 36–41, 124–30; x (1941–44) 116–27; completed by Aubrey Gwynn, 165–79.

Reg. Cromer (EA)   *Register of Archbishop Cromer* cited in *EA, passim.*

Reg. Deeds abstracts   *Registry of Deeds, Dublin. Abstracts of wills, 1708-1832*, ed. P. Beryl Eustace and Eilish Ellis, 3 vols (Dublin 1954–84).

Reg. Dowdall   "A calendar of the register of Primate George Dowdall, commonly called the *Liber Niger* or 'Black Book'", ed. L.P. Murray, *J Louth AS* vi (1925–8) 90–101, 147–58, 211–28; vii (1929–32) 78-95, 258–75.

Reg. Dowdall (EA)   *Register of Primate George Dowdall*, cited in *EA, passim.*

Reg. Fleming   "A calendar of the register of Archbishop Fleming", ed. Rev. H.J. Lawlor, *PRIA* vol. xxx, sect. C (1912) 94–190.

Reg. Free. (OSNB)   *Register of Freeholders*, cited in *OSNB passim.*

Reg. Magheralin (OSNB)   Parish register of Magheralin, AD 1715, quoted in *OSNB.*

Reg. Mey   *Registrum Johannis Mey: the register of John Mey, Archbishop of Armagh 1443–56*, ed. W.G.H. Quigley and E.F.D. Roberts (Belfast 1972).

Reg. Octavian (EA)   *Register of Octavian de Palatio*, Primate 1478–1513, cited in *EA passim.*

Reg. Prene (EA)   *Register of John Prene*, Primate 1439–43, cited in *EA passim.*

Reg. Swayne   *The register of John Swayne, Archbishop of Armagh and Primate of Ireland 1418–39*, ed. D.A. Chart (Belfast 1935).

Reg. Swayne (EA)   *Register of Archbishop Swayne* cited in *EA, passim.*

Reg. Sweteman   "A calendar of the Register of Archbishop Sweetman", ed. Rev. H.J. Lawlor, *PRIA* vol. xxix, sect. C (1911) 213–310.

Regal Visit. (Reeves)   *Regal visitation of Down, Connor & Dromore, AD 1633–34*, transcribed by William Reeves, and collated and corrected from originals in the Prerogative Office [now the Record Office] Dublin, PRONI DIO/1/24/2/4.

Rennes Dinds.   "The prose tales in the Rennes Dindsenchas", ed. Whitley Stokes, *Rev. Celt.* xv (1894) 272–336, 418–84; xvi (1895) 31–83, 135–67, 269–312.

Rent Roll Down   *Strangford and Lisburn rent roll no. 21, AD 1692*, PRONI T372/E.

Rev. Celt.	*Révue Celtique*, 51 vols (Paris 1870–1934).
RIA Cat.	Catalogue of Irish manuscripts in the Royal Irish Academy, vols i- (Dublin 1926–).
Rocque's Map (Coote)	*John Rocque's map of Co. Armagh*, AD 1760, PRONI D602. Reproduced in part in Charles Coote's *Statistical survey of the county of Armagh* (Dublin 1804).
S & D Ann. (Mooney)	*BSD Annes.* cited by *Mooney, passim*.
S. Ard Mh.	*Seanchas Ard Mhacha: journal of the Armagh Diocesan Historical Society* (Armagh 1954–).
Scéla Cano	*Scéla Cano meic Gartnáin*, ed. D.A. Binchy, *MMIS* xviii (Dublin 1963).
SCtSiadhail	*Seachrán Chairn tSiadhail: amhrán ilcheardhaidheachta agus seanchas síor-chuardhaidheachta...*, eag. Seosamh Laoide (Baile Átha Cliath 1904).
S-E Ulster Map	A map of south-east Ulster (from Olderfleet in the north to Dundrum in the south), c. 1580, PRO MPF 87.
SG	*Silva Gadelica, a collection of tales in Irish,* ed. S.H. O'Grady, 2 vols., vol.i texts, vol.ii translations, London 1892.
Sgéalta Mh. L.	*Sgéalta Mhuintir Luinigh, Munterloney folk-tales*, ed. Éamonn Ó Tuathail (Dublin 1933). [Collection of folktales in Irish from Tyrone with phonological description of dialect].
Shorter OED	*The shorter Oxford English dictionary on historical principles*, prepared by W. Little, H.W. Fowler & J. Coulson; revised and ed. C.T. Onions. 3rd edn revised with addenda (Oxford 1944; reprint 1969 etc.).
Sloane Map	*A map of the County of Down containing an actual survey of all the principal roads and their distances; with the baronys, churches, seats etc. on or near the roads. Survey'd & drawn by Oliver Sloane, anno 1739* (repr. 1992, Linenhall Library, Belfast).
SMMD I	*Scéla Mucce Meic Dathó*, ed. Rudolph Thurneysen, *MMIS* iv (Dublin 1935).
SMMD II	"The early modern version of *Scéla Mucce Meic DaThó - Tempus, Locus, persona et causa scribendi*", C. Breatnach, *Ériu* xli (1990) 37–60.

Speed's Antrim & Down	A map entitled *Antrym and Downe*, AD 1610, by John Speed. Reproduced in *UJA* ser. 1, vol. i (1853) between pp. 123 and 124.
Speed's Ireland	*The Kingdome of Irland devided into severall Provinces and then againe devided into Counties. Newly described*, AD 1610, by John Speed. Also published in his atlas *The Theatre of the Empire of Great Britain* (Sudbury & Humble 1612).
Speed's Ulster	*The Province Ulster described*, AD 1610, by John Speed. Also published in his atlas *The Theatre of the Empire of Great Britain* (Sudbury & Humble 1612).
SP Hen. VIII	*State papers published under the authority of His Majesty's Commission: King Henry VIII*, 11 vols (London 1830–52).
Statist. Sur. Dn.	*Statistical survey of the county of Down, with observations on the means of improvement...*, John Dubourdieu (Dublin 1802).
Stuart's Armagh	*Historical memoirs of the city of Armagh*, James Stuart (Newry 1819).
ST Temra	"[*Suidiugad Tellaig Temra*]: the settling of the manor of Tara", ed. R.I. Best, *Ériu* iv pt 2 (1910), 121–72.
Stud. Hib.	*Studia Hibernica*, journal of Coláiste Phádraig, Drumcondra (Baile Átha Cliath 1961–).
Sub. Roll Down	*Subsidy roll for the county of Down, AD 1663*, PRONI T/307.
Sur. Bateson Estate (OSNB)	Survey of the Bateson estate (Magheralin/Moira) cited in *OSNB*.
Sur. Brownlow Estate (OSNB)	Survey of the Brownlow estate (Magheralin/Shankill) cited in *OSNB*.
Sur. Whyte Estate (OSNB)	Survey of the Whyte estate (Aghaderg) cited in *OSNB*.
Surnames Dn	"Surnames in the County of Down", A. Hume, *UJA* ser. 1 vol. 6 (1858), 77–90.
Surnames Matheson	*Varieties and synonymes of surnames and Christian names in Ireland, for the guidance of registration officers and the public in searching the indexes of births, deaths and marriages,* by R.E. Matheson (Dublin 1890). Part repr. in *Irish Genealogy, a record finder*, ed. D. Begley (Dublin 1987) 195–232.

Swanzy's Dromore

Succession lists of the diocese of Dromore, Henry B. Swanzy, ed. J.B. Leslie (Belfast 1933).

Taylor & Skinner

Maps of the roads of Ireland, surveyed 1777, by George Taylor and Andrew Skinner (Dublin 1778).

TBC (LL)

Táin Bó Cúalnge from the Book of Leinster, ed. Cecile O'Rahilly (Dublin 1967).

TBC (Rec. I)

Táin Bó Cúailnge Recension I, ed. Cecile O'Rahilly (Dublin 1976).

TBDD

Togail Bruidne Da Derga, ed. Eleanor Knott, *MMIS* viii (Dublin 1936).

TCD Gens

Na ginealaigh as LS TCD 1366 (H.4.25), dáta c. 1666, eag. Nollaig Ó Muraíle (neamhfhoilsithe).

Teall. Uí Echach

"Teallach féile Uí Echach", ed. K. Meyer 1919, *Miscellanea Hibernica, Kgl. Preufs. Akad. der Wissensch.* 89–100.

Tombstone (OSNB)

Tombstone inscription cited in *OSNB, passim.*

Top. Index 1961

Census of population 1961: topographical index, Government of Northern Ireland, General Register Office (Belfast 1962).

Topog. Poems

Topographical poems: by Seaán Mór Ó Dubhagáin and Giolla-na-Naomh Ó hUidhrín, ed. James Carney (Dublin 1943).

Topog. Poems (JOD)

The topographical poems of John O'Dubhagain and Giolla na Naomh O'Huidhrin, ed. John O'Donovan for the Irish Archaeological and Celtic Society (Dublin 1862).

Townland Index Map

County index maps showing townlands and other administrative units and the disposition of six-inch sheets and 1:2,500 plans, Ordnance Survey of Northern Ireland (2 series, Belfast c. 1938, c. 1970).

Triads of Ireland

The triads of Ireland, ed. Kuno Meyer, RIA Todd Lecture Series xiii (Dublin 1906).

Trien. Visit. (Boyle)

Boyle's *Triennial visitation of Down, Connor and Dromore, AD 1679*, transcribed by William Reeves, PRONI DIO/1/24/16/1, pp. 34–49.

Trien. Visit. (Bramhall)

Bramhall's *Triennial visitation of Down, Connor and Dromore, AD 1661*, transcribed by William Reeves, PRONI DIO/1/24/16/1, pp. 1–16.

Trien. Visit. (Margetson)	Margetson's *Triennial visitation of Down, Connor and Dromore, AD 1664*, transcribed by William Reeves, PRONI DIO/1/24/16/1, pp. 19–33.
Trip. Life (Stokes)	*The tripartite life of Saint Patrick, with other documents relating to that Saint*, ed. Whitley Stokes, 2 vols (London 1887).
UJA	*Ulster Journal of Archaeology*, 1st ser., 9 vols (Belfast 1853–62); 2nd ser., 17 vols (1894–1911); 3rd ser. (1938–).
ULS	*Ulster Local Studies*: journal of the Federation for Ulster Local Studies (Derry 1975–).
Ulster Map [1570c]	*A plat of Ulster*, c. 1570, annotated by Lord Burghley, AD 1590, PRO London MPF 90. There is a copy in PRONI T1493/6.
Ulst. Roll Gaol Deliv.	"Ulster roll of gaol delivery, 1613–18", ed. James F. Ferguson, *UJA* ser. 1 vol. 1 (1853), 260–70; vol. 2 (1854), 25–8.
Ultach	*An tUltach: iris oifigiúil Chomhaltas Uladh* (1923–).
Vestry Bk D'cloney	Vestry book of the parish of Donaghcloney, *Atkinson's Donaghcloney* pp. 114–9.
Vestry Reg. (OSNB)	Vestry register of the parish cited in *OSNB, passim*.
VSSH (Heist)	*Vitae sanctorum Hiberniae ex codice olim Salamanticensi nunc Bruxellensi*, ed. William W. Heist (Bruxelles 1965).
Wars Co. Down	"The wars of 1641 in County Down: the deposition of High Sheriff Peter Hill (1645)", transcribed and annotated by Thomas Fitzpatrick with additional notes by Rev. Monsignor O'Laverty and Edward Parkinson, *UJA* ser. 2, vol. x (1904) 73–90; "The deposition of Captain Henry Smith of Loghedeyne in the County Down" vol. xi (1905) 58–64; "The fall of Down, 1642" vol. xii (1906) 1–10, 62–77.
Wm. Little (OSNB)	William Little, informant cited in *OSNB passim*.
Wm. Map (OSNB)	James Williamson's map of Co. Down, AD 1810, cited in *OSNB, passim*.
ZCP	*Zeitschrift für Celtische Philologie* (Halle 1897–).

SECONDARY BIBLIOGRAPHY

Alexander, W.   1952   *Place-Names of Aberdeenshire* (Spalding Club, Aberdeen).

Andrews, J.H.   1974   "The maps of the escheated counties of Ulster, 1609–10", *PRIA* vol. lxxiv, sect. C, 133–70.
                       1975   *A paper landscape; the Ordnance Survey in nineteenth-century Ireland* (Oxford).
                       1978   *Irish maps*: the Irish heritage series, no.18 (Dublin).

Arthurs, J.B.   1952-3(a)   "Magh Rath", *BUPNS* ser. 1 vol. i, 7–11.
                       1952-3(c)   "Macha and Armagh" *BUPNS* ser. 1 vol. i, 25–29.
                       1954(b)   "Sliabh Fuaid", *BUPNS* ser. 1 vol. i pt 2, 33–8; pt 3, 67.
                       1954(c)   "Early septs and territories of Co. Armagh", *BUPNS* ser. 1 vol. ii pt 3, 45–55.
                       1955-6   "The Ulster Place-name Society", *Onoma* vi 80–2.
                       1956(a)   "A manuscript note [the Mac Con Coilleadh or Woods family]", *BUPNS* ser. 1 vol. iv pt 2, 24.
                       1956-7   "The place-names of Co. Armagh", *BUPNS* ser.1 vol.iv (1956) 32-7, vol.v (1957) 13–33,40–5.

Bell, Robert   1988   *The book of Ulster surnames* (Belfast)

Black, George F.   1946   *The surnames of Scotland: their origin, meaning and history* (New York).

Brady, J.   1947   "The Irish medical family of O'Sheil", *Irish Book Lover* xxx no. 2, 50–1.

Byrne, F.J.   1973   *Irish kings and high-kings* (London).
                       1994–5   "*Dercu*: the feminine of *Mocu*", *Éigse* xxviii 42-70.

Cahill, M.   1985   "Correspondence relating to the discovery of a later Bronze Age gold torc at Drumsallagh, Co. Down", *UJA* ser. 3 vol. 48, 116–21.

Canavan, Tony   1991   ed. *Every Stoney Acre has a Name: a celebration of the townland in Ulster*, Belfast.

Crowe, W.H.   1969   *The Ring of Mourne* (Dundalk).

Dobbs, Margaret   1912   "The Black Pig's Dyke and the campaign of the Táin Bó Cuailgne", *ZCP* viii 338–46.

Falkiner, C.L.   1903   "The counties of Ireland: an historical sketch of their origin, constitution, and gradual delimitation", *PRIA* vol. xxiv, sect. C, 169–94.

Field, John   1989   *English field names: a dictionary* (Gloucester).

Flanagan, Deirdre   1978(d)   "Transferred population or sept-names: *Ulaidh* (a quo Ulster)", *BUPNS* ser. 2, vol. i, 40–3.

	1979(f)	"Review of *The meaning of Irish place names* by James O'Connell (Belfast 1978)", *BUPNS* ser. 2 vol. iv, 58–60.
	1981-2(b)	"Some guidelines to the use of Joyce's *Irish names of places*, vol. i", *BUPNS* ser. 2, vol. iv, 61–9.
	1981-2(c)	"A summary guide to the more commonly attested ecclesiastical elements in place-names", *BUPNS* ser. 2, vol. iv, 69–75.
Flanagan, L.	1981–2	"An index to minor place-names from the 6" ordnance survey: County Armagh", *BUPNS* ser. 2 vol. iv appendix.
Gamble, Roy	1991	"Farewell to the Knowe", in Canavan 1991, 35–7.
Glancy, M.	1956	"Notes and queries: Armagh – a surmise", *Seanchas Ard Mhacha* vol. 2 no.1, 78.
Goblet, Y.M.	1932	*A topographical index of the parishes and townlands of Ireland in Sir William Petty's Mss barony maps (c. 1655–9) and Hiberniae Delineatio* (c. 1672) (Dublin).
Haley, G.C.	1970	*The topography of the Táin Bó Cúailnge*, unpublished Ph.D. thesis, Harvard.
Hanna, J.W.	1856	"The battle of Magh Rath: its true site determined", *UJA* ser. 1 vol. iv, 53–61.
Hayes McCoy, G.A.	1970	"The making of an O'Neill", *UJA* ser.3 vol.xxxiii, 89–94. Plate viii Dartmouth map 25, c. 1602. (= *Bartlett Map (Greenwich)*).
Herbert, M.	1989	"*Fled Dúin na nGéd*: a reappraisal" *Cambr. MCS* xviii 75–87.
Hogan, Edmund	1910	*Onom. Goed.*.
Hore, H.	1857	"The inauguration of Irish chiefs", *UJA* ser. 1 vol. v 216–42.
Kenney, J.F.	1929	*The sources for the early history of Ireland: an introduction and guide*, (New York; 2nd edn Shannon 1966).
Lawlor, H.C.	1938(a)	"An ancient route: the *Slighe Miodhluachra* in Ulaidh", *UJA* ser. 3 vol. i pt 1, 3–6, map.
	1938(b)	"The identification of the castle of Magh Cobha", *UJA* ser. 3 vol. i, 84–9.
Lett, H.W.	1895	"Ancient canoe found near Loughbrickland, Co. Down" *UJA* ser. 2 vol. i, 153–4.
	1897	"The Great Wall of Ulidia, commonly known as *The Dane's Cast* or *Gleann na Muice Duibhe*", *UJA* ser. 2 vol. iii, 23–9, 65–82, map.

| | 1898 | "Sepulchral cairn on Knock Iveagh", *UJA* ser. 2 vol. iv, 67. |

Lewis, H. and
Pedersen, H.   1937   *A concise comparative Celtic grammar* (Gottingen).

M'Aleer, P.   1936   *Townland names of County Tyrone* (reprint Portadown & Draperstown 1988).

Mac an Bhaird, Alan   1995   "Ptolemy revisited", *Ainm* v 1–20.

Mac Aodha, B.   1989–90   "Some aspects of the topography of the Commeen district, Gweebarra, Co. Donegal", *Ainm* iv 165–79.

McCann, F.   1952-3   "Caille Conaill", *BUPNS* ser. 1 vol. i, 31–2.

McErlean, Thomas   1983   "The Irish townland system of landscape organisation", *Landscape archaeology in Ireland,* ed. Terence Reeves-Smyth and Fred Hamond, 315–39 (Oxford).

McKinley, R.   1990   *A history of British surnames* (Longman).

MacLysaght, Edward   1957   *Irish families, their names, arms and origins* (Dublin, 1st edn Oct. 1957, reprinted with corrections Dec. 1957).
   1964(a)   *A guide to Irish surnames* (Dublin).
   1982   *More Irish families: a new and revised and enlarged edition of More Irish families incorporating Supplement to Irish families, with an essay on Irish chieftainries* (Dublin).
   1985   *The surnames of Ireland* (Dublin, 4th edn revised and enlarged; 1st edn 1957).

MacNeill, Máire   1962   *The Festival of Lughnasa* 2 vols (OUP, reprint Dublin 1982).

Mac Niocaill, G.   1959   *Na manaigh liatha in Éirinn, 1142 – c. 1600* (Baile Átha Cliath).

Mallory, J. and
McNeill, T.   1991   *The Archaeology of Ulster* (Belfast).

Mason, William Shaw   1814–9   *A statistical account or parochial survey of Ireland... in 3 vols* (Dublin, Edinburgh).

Moody, T.W.   1939   *The Londonderry plantation, 1609–41: the city of London and the plantation in Ulster* (Belfast).

Mooney, Bernard J.   1952–3(b)   "Hanna on *Magh Rath*", *BUPNS* ser. 1 vol. i 11–4.
   1952–3(d)   "Sound-change and the shaping of place-names", *BUPNS* ser. 1 vol. i 54–7.
   1954(a)   *The parish of Seagoe - its place-names and history: part 1, the place-names explained* (Newry).

	1955(a)	"The element *derg* in certain place-names", *BUPNS* ser.1 vol. iii pt 1, 1–4.
	1956(a)	"The element *brague* in certain place-names", *BUPNS* ser. 1 vol. iv pt 2, 25–7.
	1956(b)	"Moycarn", *S. Ard Mh.* ii pt 2, 206–7.

Morgan, P.& T. 1985 *Welsh Surnames*, Cardiff.

Morton, Deirdre 1956–7 "Tuath-divisions in the baronies of Belfast and Masserene", *BUPNS* ser. 1 vol. iv pt 2, 38–44; vol. v pt 1, 6–12.

1957(b) "Former townland names in Tuath Cinament", *BUPNS* ser. 1 vol. v pt 2, 46–53.

Munn, A.M. 1925 *Notes on the place names of the parishes and townlands of the County of Londonderry* (reprint Ballinascreen 1985).

Myles, E. A. 1936 *Historical notes on the parish of Tullylish* (Anonymous pamphlet, Belfast; no date, but after *Reg. Swayne* (1935) p2; reviewed *Belfast Newsletter*, Dec. 24 1936).

Ó Buachalla, B. 1979 "Art Mac Bionaid Scríobhaí" *S.Ard. Mh.* ix pt 2, 338–49.

1982 "Arthur Brownlow: a gentleman more curious than ordinary", *Ulster Local Studies* vii pt 2, 24–8.

Ó Casaide, S. 1929 "The Irish language in Belfast and Co Down, 1601–1850", *JDCHS* ii 4–63.

Ó Ceallaigh, S. 1952–3(b) "Queries and suggestions: 1. Ard Macha Bréige", *BUPNS* ser. 1 vol. i, 36–7.

Ó Cearbhaill, P. 1987 "An púca i logainmneacha", *Ainm* ii 96–113.

Ó Concheanainn, T. 1974 "A feature of the poetry of Fearghal Óg Mac an Bhaird", *Éigse* xv pt 3, 235–251.

Ó Corráin, D. and Maguire, F. 1981 *Gaelic personal names* (Dublin).

Ó Cuív, B. 1956–7 "*Baile suthach síth Emhna*: a poem in praise of Raghnall, king of Man", *Éigse* viii 283–301.

Ó Dochartaigh, C. 1987 *Dialects of Ulster Irish* (Belfast).

Ó Doibhlin, É. 1970 "Ceart Uí Néill" translated in *S. Ard Mh.* vol. 5 no. 2, 324–58.

1971(a) "O'Neill's 'Own Country' and its families", *S. Ard Mh.* vol. 6 no. 1, 3–23.

Ó Domhnaill, Niall 1952 *Na Glúnta Rosannacha* (Baile Átha Cliath, repr.1974).

Ó Droighneáin, Muiris 1966   *An sloinnteoir Gaeilge agus an t-ainmneoir* (Dublin 3rd edn 1982).

Ó Foghludha, Risteard 1935   *Log-ainmneacha .i. dictionary of Irish place-names...* (Dublin).

O'Kane, James   1970   "Placenames of Inniskeel and Kilteevoge", *ZCP* xxxi 59–145.

O'Laverty, James   1905   "Antiquarian jottings: Church of St Ronan Finn and the 'Battle of Magh Rath'", *UJA* ser. 2 vol. xi, 118–122.

Ó Máille, T.S.   1989–90   "Irish place-names in *-as, -es, -is, -os, -us*", *Ainm* iv 125–43.

Ó Mainnín, M.B.   1989–90   "The element island in Ulster place-names", *Ainm* iv 200–10.

Ó Maolfabhail, Art   1974   "*Grianán* i logainmneacha", *Dinnsean.* iml. vi uimh. 2, 60–75.

    1990   *Logainmneacha na hÉireann, iml. I: Contae Luimnigh* (Baile Átha Cliath).

O'Rahilly, T.F.   1922   "Irish poets, historians and judges in English documents, 1538–1615", *PRIA* xxxvi sect. C, 86–120.

    1930   "Notes on Middle-Irish pronunciation", *Hermathena* xx 152–95.

    1932   *Irish dialects past and present* (Dublin, reprint 1976).

    1946   *Early Irish history and mythology* (Dublin; reprint 1976).

Ó Riain, Pádraig   1974(a)   "Battle-site and territorial extent in early Ireland", *ZCP* xxxiii 67-80.

    1974(b)   "The materials and provenance of *Buile Shuibhne*", *Éigse* xv pt 3, 173–88.

    1989   "Sanctity and politics in Connacht c.1100: the case of St Fursa", *Cambr. MCS* xvii 1–14.

    1990   "The Tallaght Martyrologies, redated", *Cambr. MCS* xx 20–38.

Otway-Ruthven, A.J. 1964   "Parochial development in the rural deanery of Skreen", *JRSAI* xciv 111–22.

Paterson, T.G.F.   1938   "Lisburn and neighbourhood in 1798", *UJA* ser. 3 vol. i pt 2, 193–8.

    1976   *Harvest Home; the last sheaf:* a selection from the writings of T.G.F. Paterson relating to Co. Armagh, edited with an introduction by E. Estyn Evans (Armagh).

Petty, William   1672   *The political anatomy of Ireland* (1672), reprinted in *Tracts and treatises illustrative of Ireland* ii 72-3 (Dublin 1860–1).

Power, Patrick	1932	*Críchad an chaoilli: being the topography of ancient Fermoy* (Cork).
	1947	"The bounds and extent of Irish parishes", *Féil. Torna* 218–23.
Price, Liam	1946	*The place-names of Co. Wicklow ii: the barony of Ballinacor South* (Dublin).
	1963	"A note on the use of the word *baile* in place-names", *Celtica* vi 119-26.
Quiggin, E.C.	1906	*A dialect of Donegal, being the speech of Meenawannia in the parish of Glenties* (Cambridge).
Quin, E.G. and Freeman, T.W.	1947	"Some Irish topographical terms", *Irish Geography* i pt 4, 85–9.
Reaney, P.H.	1958	*A dictionary of British surnames* (London).
Reeves, William	1861	"On the townland distribution of Ireland", *PRIA* vii 473–90.
Reid, Professor	1957	"A note on *cinament*", *BUPNS* ser. 1 vol. v, 12.
Robinson, T.	1990	*Connemara* Part 1: Introduction and Gazetteer, Part 2: Map (Roundstone, Galway).
Simms, K.	1978	"The O'Hanlons, the O'Neills and the Anglo-Normans in 13th-century Armagh", *S. Ard Mh.* vol. 9 no. 1, 70–94.
Sommerfelt, Alf	1958	"The English forms of the names of the main provinces of Ireland", *Lochlann* i 223–7.
Stockman, G. and Wagner, H.	1965	"Contributions to a study of Tyrone Irish", *Lochlann* iii 43–235.
Stockman, G.	1986	"Giorrú gutaí fada aiceannta i nGaeilge Chúige Uladh", *Féilscríbhinn Thomáis de Bhaldraithe*, ed. Seosamh Watson, 11–7.
	1991	"Focail: athrú béime", *Ultach* 68.11, 19.
Taylor, Isaac	1896	*Names and their histories* (1896), reprinted in the Everyman edition of his *Words and places* (1911).
Thomson, D.	1961	*Branwen uerch Lyr* ed., Mediaeval and Modern Welsh series vol. 2 (Dublin).
Toner, G.	1991	"Cormac Conloinges - the hero of the mound", *Emania* viii 60–2.
	1991–3	"Money in the place names of east Ulster", *Ainm* v 52–8.
Uí Fhlannagáin, D.	1970(k)	"Bóthar na bhFál, Maigh Lón, an tSeanchill, agus Baile na mBráthar", *Ultach*, 47.12, 22.

| | 1982 | "Béal Feirste agus áiteainmneacha laistigh", *Topothesia*, ed. B. Mac Aodha, 45–64 (Gaillimh 1982). |

UJA (Anon.) 1855 "Notices of the round towers of Ulster: Trummery", *UJA* ser. 1 vol. iii 292–300.

Vaughan, T.D. 1960 "Dromore, an urban study in Co. Down", *Irish Geography* iv pt 2, 131–7.

Walsh, Paul 1957 *The place-names of Westmeath* (Dublin; first published in two parts 1915–38).

1960 *Irish chiefs and leaders*, ed. Colm Ó Lochlainn (Dublin).

Waterman, D. 1955 "Excavations at Seafin castle and Dromore motte and bailey", *UJA* ser. 3 xviii, 83–104.

Watson, W.J. 1926 *The history of the Celtic place-names of Scotland* (London and Edinburgh, reprint Shannon 1973).

1959 *Bàrdachd Ghàidhlig: specimens of Gaelic poetry 1550–1900*, 3rd edn (*An Comunn Gaidhealach*, Stirling. 1st edn Inverness, 1918).

Woods, C.J. 1985 "Documents and sources: Pocock's journey through County Down in 1760" *UJA* ser.3 vol.48, 113–5.

Woulfe, Patrick 1923 *Sloinnte Gaedheal is Gall: Irish names and surnames; collected and edited with explanatory and historical notes* (Dublin).

GLOSSARY OF TECHNICAL TERMS

advowson The right of presenting a clergyman to a vacant benefice.

affricate A plosive pronounced in conjunction with a fricative; e.g. the sounds spelt with *(t)ch* or *-dge* in English.

alveolar Pronounced with the tip of the tongue touching the ridge of hard flesh behind the upper teeth; e.g. *t* in the English word *tea*.

analogy The replacement of a form by another in imitation of words of a similar class; e.g. in imitation of *bake – baked, fake – faked, rake – raked* a child or foreigner might create a form *shaked*.

anglicize Make English in form; e.g. in place-names the Irish word *baile* "homestead, townland" is anglicized *bally*.

annal A record of events in chronological order, according to the date of the year.

annates Later known as First Fruits; a tax paid, initially to the Pope, by a clergyman on appointment to a benefice.

apocope The loss of the end of a word.

aspiration (i) The forcing of air through a narrow passage thereby creating a frictional sound; e.g. *gh* in the word *lough* as pronounced in Ireland and Scotland is an aspirated consonant, (ii) the modification of a consonant sound in this way, indicated in Irish writing by putting *h* after the consonant; e.g. *p* aspirated resembles the *ph* sound at the beginning of *phantom;* also called **lenition.**

assimilation The replacing of a sound in one syllable by another to make it similar to a sound in another syllable; e.g. in some dialects of Irish the *r* in the first syllable of the Latin *sermon-* was changed to *n* in imitation of the *n* in the second syllable, giving a form *seanmóin*.

ballybetagh Irish *baile biataigh* "land of a food-provider", native land unit, the holder of which had a duty to maintain his lord and retinue when travelling in the area (*Colton Vis.* 130).

ballyboe Irish *baile bó* "land of a cow", a land unit equivalent to a modern townland, possibly so-named as supplying the yearly rent of one cow (*Colton Vis.* 130).

barony In Ireland an administrative unit midway in size between a county and a civil parish, originally the landholding of a feudal baron (*EA* 62).

benefice An ecclesiastical office to which income is attached.

bilabial Articulated by bringing the two lips together; e.g. the *p* in the English word *pea*.

Brittonic Relating to the branch of Celtic languages which includes Welsh, Cornish and Breton.

calendar A précis of an historical document or documents with its contents arranged according to date.

carrow Irish *ceathru* "a quarter". See **quarter.**

cartography The science of map-making.

cartouche An ornamental frame round the title etc. of a map.

carucate Latin *carucata* "ploughland", a territorial unit, the equivalent of a townland.

Celtic Relating to the (language of the) Irish, Scots, Manx, Welsh, Cornish, Bretons, and Gauls.

centralized Pronounced with the centre of the tongue raised; e.g. the vowel sound at the beginning of *again* or at the end of *the.*

cess Tax.

cinament A territorial unit of lesser size than a **tuogh** (which see). Three derivations have been suggested: (i) from Irish *cine* "a family", (*cineamhain?*) (*EA* 388); (ii) from French *scindement* "cutting up, division" (Morton 1956–7, 39); (iii) from French *(a)ceignement* "enclosure(?)" (Reid 1957, 12).

civil parish An administrative unit based on the medieval parish.

cluster See **consonant cluster.**

coarb Irish *comharba*, originally the heir of an ecclesiastical office, later a high-ranking hereditary tenant of church land under the bishop. The coarb may be in charge of other ecclesiastical tenants called **erenaghs,** which see.

compound A word consisting of two or more verbal elements; e.g. *aircraft, housework.*

consonant (i) An element of the alphabet which is not a vowel, e.g. *c, j, x,* etc., (ii) a speech sound in which the passage of air through the mouth or nose is impeded, e.g. at the lips (*b, p, or m*), at the teeth (*s, z*), etc.

consonant cluster A group of two or more consonants; e.g. *bl* in *blood, ndl* in *handle, lfths* in *twelfths.*

contraction (i) The shortening of a word or words normally by the omission of one or more sounds, (ii) a contracted word; e.g. *good-bye is* a contraction of *God be with you; can not* is contracted to *can't.*

county Feudal land division, equivalent to an English shire, created by the English administration in Ireland as the major subdivision of an Irish province.

deanery Properly called a rural deanery, an ecclesiastical division of people or land administered by a rural dean.

declension A group of nouns whose case-endings vary according to a fixed pattern. (There are five declensions in modern Irish).

delenition Sounding or writing a consonant as if it were not aspirated; see **aspiration.**

dental A sound pronounced with the tip of the tongue touching the upper teeth; e.g. *th* in the English *thumb.*

devoicing Removing the sound caused by the resonance of vocal cords; see **voiced.**

dialect A variety of a language in a given area with distinctive vocabulary, pronunciation or grammatical forms.

digraph A group of two letters expressing a single sound; e.g. *ea* in English *team* or *ph* in English *photograph.*

diocese The area or population over which a bishop has ecclesiastical authority.

diphthong A union of two vowel sounds pronounced in one syllable; e.g. *oi* in English *boil.* (Note that a diphthong cannot be sung on a single sustained note without changing the position of the mouth).

dissimilation The replacing of a sound in one syllable by another to make it different from a sound in another syllable e.g. Loughbrickland comes from an original Irish form, *Loch Bricrenn.*

eclipsis The replacement in Irish of one sound by another in initial position as the result of the influence of the previous word; e.g. the *c* of Irish *cór* "choir" (pronounced like English *core*) is eclipsed by *g* in the phrase *i gcór* "in a choir" due to the influence of the preposition *i,* and *gcór* is pronounced like English *gore*; also called **nasalization.**

elision The omission of a sound in pronunciation; e.g. the *d* is elided in the word *handkerchief.*

emphasis See **stress.**

epenthetic vowel A vowel sound inserted within a word; e.g. in Ireland an extra vowel is generally inserted between the *l* and *m* of the word *film.*

eponymous adjective referring to the real or legendary person from whom a tribe or family etc. has derived its name, for example Niall *Noígiallach,* "of the nine hostages", is the eponymous ancestor of the tribal name *Uí Néill.*

erenagh Irish *airchinnech* "steward", hereditary officer in charge of church lands, later a tenant to the bishop *(ColtonVis.* 4–5).

escheat Revert to the feudal overlord, in Ireland usually forfeit to the English crown.

etymology The facts relating to the formation and meaning of a word.

fiant A warrant for the making out of a grant under the royal seal, or (letters) patent.

fricative   A speech sound formed by narrowing the passage of air from the mouth so that audible friction is produced; e.g. *gh* in Irish and Scottish *lough*.

Gaelic   Relating to the branch of Celtic languages which includes Irish, Scottish Gaelic and Manx.

glebe   The house and land (and its revenue) provided for the clergyman of a parish.

glide   A sound produced when the organs of speech are moving from the position for one speech sound to the position for another; e.g. in pronouncing the word *deluge* there is a *y*-like glide between the *l* and the *u*.

gloss   A word or phrase inserted in a manuscript to explain a part of the text.

Goedelic = Gaelic   which see.

grange   Anglo-Norman term for farm land providing food or revenue for a feudal lord, frequently a monastery.

haplology   The omission of a syllable beside another with a similar sound; e.g. *lib(ra)ry*, *deteri(or)ated*.

hearth money   A tax on the number of hearths used by a household.

impropriator   The person to whom rectorial tithes of a monastery etc. were granted after the Dissolution.

inflect   To vary the form of a word to indicate a different grammatical relationship; e.g. *man* singular, *men* plural.

inquisition   A judicial inquiry, here usually into the possessions of an individual at death.

International Phonetic Alphabet   The system of phonetic transcription advocated by the International Phonetic Association.

labial = bilabial   which see.

lenition   See **aspiration.**

lexicon   The complete word content of a language.

lowering   Changing a vowel sound by dropping the tongue slightly in the mouth; e.g. pronouncing *doctor* as *dactor*.

manor   Feudal estate (Anglo–Norman and Plantation), smaller than a barony, entitling the landowner to jurisdiction over his tenants at a manor court.

martyrology   Irish *féilire*, also translated "calendar", a list of names of saints giving the days on which their feasts are to be celebrated.

mearing   A boundary.

metathesis   The transposition of sounds in a word; e.g. saying *elascit* instead of *elastic*.

moiety   French *moitié*, "the half of", also a part or portion of any size.

morphology   The study of the grammatical structure of words.

nasalization   See **eclipsis.**

oblique   Having a grammatical form other than nominative singular.

onomasticon   A list of proper names, usually places.

orthography   Normal spelling.

palatal   A sound produced with the tongue raised towards the hard palate.

parish   A subdivision of a diocese served by a single main church or clergyman.

patent   (or letters patent), an official document conferring a right or privilege, frequently here a grant of land.

patronymic   A name derived from that of the father.

phonemic   Relating to the system of phonetic oppositions in the speech sounds of a language, which make, in English for example, *soap* a different word from *soup*, and *pin* a different word from *bin*.

phonetic   Relating to vocal sound.

phonology   The study of the sound features of a language.

plosive   A sound formed by closing the air passage and then releasing the air flow suddenly, causing an explosive sound; e.g. *p* in English *pipe*.

ploughland   Medieval English land unit of about 120 acres, equivalent to a townland.

prebend   An endowment, often in land, for the maintenance of a canon or prebendary, a senior churchman who assisted the bishop or had duties in the cathedral.

precinct   *Ad hoc* land division (usually a number of townlands) used in Plantation grants.

prefix   A verbal element placed at the beginning of a word which modifies the meaning of the word; e.g. *un-* in *unlikely*.

proportion   *Ad hoc* land division (usually a number of townlands) used in Plantation grants.

province   Irish *cúige* "a fifth": the largest administrative division in Ireland, of which there are now four (Ulster, Leinster, Connaught, Munster) but were once five.

quarter   Land unit often a quarter of the ballybetagh, and thus containing three or four townlands, but sometimes referring to a subdivision of a townland. See also **carrow.**

raising   Changing a vowel sound by lifting the tongue higher in the mouth; e.g. pronouncing *bag* as *beg.*

realize   Pronounce; e.g. *-adh* at the end of verbal nouns in Ulster Irish is realized as English *-oo.*

rectory   A parish under the care of a rector supported by its tithes; if the rector cannot reside in the parish he appoints and supports a resident vicar.

reduction   (i) Shortening of a vowel sound; e.g. the vowel sound in *board* is reduced in the word *cupboard*, (ii) = **contraction** which see.

register   A document providing a chronological record of the transactions of an individual or organization.

rounded   Pronounced with pouting lips; e.g. the vowel sounds in *oar* and *ooze.*

Scots   A dialect of Anglo-Saxon which developed independently in lowland Scotland from the 11th to the 16th centuries. By the time of the Union of Crowns in 1603 it was markedly different from southern English.

seize   To put in legal possession of property, especially land.

semantic   Relating to the meaning of words.

semivowel   A sound such as *y* or *w* at the beginning of words like *yet, wet,* etc.

sept   Subgroup of people, for instance of a tribe or ruling family.

sessiagh   Irish *seiseach* "a sixth", usually referring to a subdivision of a townland or similar unit. Apparently three sessiaghs were equivalent to a ballyboe (*Colton Vis.* 130).

shift of stress   The transfer of emphasis from one syllable to another; e.g. *Belfast* was originally stressed on the second syllable *fast* but because of shift of stress many people now pronounce it **Bel**fast. See **stress.**

stem   (dental, o-, etc.) Classification of nouns based on the form of their endings before the Old Irish period.

stress   The degree of force with which a syllable is pronounced. For example, the name Antrim is stressed on the first syllable while Tyrone is stressed on the second.

subdenomination   A smaller land division, usually a division of a townland.

substantive   A noun.

suffix   A verbal element placed at the end of a word which modifies the meaning of the word; e.g. *-less* in *senseless.*

syllable   A unit of pronunciation containing one vowel sound which may be preceded or followed by a consonant or consonants; e.g. *I*, *my*, *hill*, have one syllable; *outside*, *table*, *ceiling* have two; *sympathy*, *understand*, *telephone* have three, etc.

syncopation   The omission of a short unstressed vowel or digraph when a syllable beginning with a vowel is added; e.g. *tiger+ess* becomes *tigress*.

tate   A small land unit once used in parts of Ulster, treated as equivalent to a townland, although only half the size.

termon   Irish *tearmann*, land belonging to the Church, with privilege of sanctuary (providing safety from arrest for repentant criminals), usually held for the bishop by a coarb as hereditary tenant.

terrier   A list of the names of lands held by the Church or other body.

tithes   Taxes paid to the Church. Under the native system they were shared between parish clergy and erenagh (as the tenant of the bishop), under the English administration they were payable to the local clergyman of the Established Church.

topography   The configuration of a land surface, including its relief and the position of its features.

toponymy   Place-names as a subject for study.

townland   The common term or English translation for a variety of small local land units; the smallest unit in the 19th-century Irish administrative system.

transcription   An indication by written symbols of the precise sound of an utterance.

tuogh   Irish *tuath* "tribe, tribal kingdom", a population or territorial unit.

unrounded   Articulated with the lips spread or in neutral position; see **rounded**.

velar   Articulated with the back of the tongue touching the soft palate; e.g. *c* in *cool*.

vicarage   A parish in the charge of a vicar, the deputy either for a rector who received some of the revenue but resided elsewhere, or for a monastery or cathedral or lay impropriator.

visitation   An inspection of (church) lands, usually carried out for a bishop (ecclesiastical or episcopal visitation) or for the Crown (regal visitation).

vocalization   The changing of a consonant sound into a vowel sound by widening the air passage; akin to the disappearance of *r* in Southern English pronunciation of words like *bird*, *worm*, *car*.

voiced   Sounded with resonance of the vocal cords. (A test for voicing can be made by closing the ears with the fingers and uttering a consonant sound. e.g. *ssss*, *zzzz*, *ffff*, *vvvv*. If a buzzing or humming sound is heard the consonant is voiced; if not it is voiceless).

voiceless   See **voiced**.

INDEX TO IRISH PLACE-NAMES
(with pronunciation guide)

The following guide to the pronunciation of Irish forms suggested in this book is only approximate. Words are to be sounded as though written in English. The following symbols have the values shown:

ă	as in *above, coma*
ā	as in *father, draught*
ċ	as in *lough, Bach*
ch	as in *chip, church*
ġ	does not occur in English. To approximate this sound try gargling without water, or consider the following: *lock* is to *lough* as *log* is to *loġ*. If you cannot manage this sound just pronounce it like *g* in *go*.
gh	as in *lough, Bach*; not as in *foghorn*
ī	as in *five, line*
ky	as in *cure, McKeown*
ly	at beginning of words as in *brilliant, million*
ō	as in *boar, sore*
ow	as in *now, plough*

Stress is indicated by writing the vowel in the stressed syllable in bold, e.g., Arm**a**gh, Ballym**e**na, L**u**rgan. The few Old Irish names discussed are listed under their Old and Modern Irish spellings.

Place-Name	Rough Guide	Page
Abhainn an Lagáin	ōne ă l**a**ggine	295
Abhainn Eascannach, An	ă nōne **a**skanagh	207
Achadh Dearg	aghoo j**a**răg	21
Achadh Ghiolla Choscair	aghoo yillă ċ**o**skir	278
Achadh na Dromann	aghoo nă dr**u**mmăn	277
Achadh na bhFáinleóg	aghoo nă wīnlog	154
Aonach	**ee**nagh	197
Ard Brain	ard br**i**n	63
Áth an Bhairínigh	ā ăn w**a**reeny	210
Áth Mhic Giolla	ā vick g**i**llă	349
Áth na Cloiche	ā nă cl**i**hă	64
Bac & Mullach	bak, m**u**llagh	108
Baile Ailigh	ballă **a**lly	191
Baile Ailigh Mór	ballă ally m**o**re	193
Baile an Árais	ballăn **ā**rish	114
Baile an Bhealaigh	ballăn v**a**lly	310
Baile an Chnoic	ballăn ċr**i**ck	282
Baile an Dúin	ballăn d**oo**n	305
Baile an Ghabhann	ballăn ġ**ō**ne	281
Baile an Locha	ballăn l**ou**ghă	308
Baile an tSagairt	ballăn t**a**ggirch	23

Place-Name	Rough Guide	Page
Both Bheinéid	bwy vennedge	27
Brega (Breá)	brey	34
Cabhán, An	ă kawan	160
Caiseal Uí Bheannacháin	cashel ee vannaghine	195
Caorthannán	keerhanine	340
Carbad, An	ă karăbăd	261
Carn Albanach	carn alăbănagh	284
Carn Aodha	carn oo	194
Carraig Dhromainne	carrick ġrumminyă	29
Cheapaigh, An	ă ċyappy	69
Chléith, An	ă ċlay	70
Choillidh, An	ă ċălyee	139
Choiscéim, An	ă ċoshcame	29
Chraobhaigh, An	ă ċreewy	31
Cill Eidhnigh	kill aynee	200
Cill Eoghain	kill ōne	12
Cill M'Fhionnóg	kill minnog	288
Cill Mo-Cholmóg	kill măċolămog	232
Cill Phádraig	kill fădrick	316
Cineál nAmhalaidh	kinyal nowly	9
Cionn Álainn, An	ă kin ālin	133
Clann Aogáin	clan oogine	9
Clann Bhreasail	clan vrassil	9
Clann Bhreasail Mhic Dhúileacháin	clan vrassil vick ġoolaghine	10
Clann Chonaill	clan ċonnill	11
Clann Ghiolla Mhuire	clan yillă wirră	228
Clochar	clogher	230
Cluain Chnámharlaigh	clooin ċrowărly	52
Cluain Chrannacháin	clooin ċrannaghine	30
Cluain Locháin	clooin loughine	41
Clár, An	ă klār	335
Cláraigh	klārry	285
Cnoc Mhig Uidhrín	crock vă girreen	202
Cnoc na nGabhar	crock nang ōre	342
Cnoc Uíbh Eachach	crock eev aghagh	183
Coill Bhairrline	kăl wārlinyă	12
Coill Chon Murchaidh	kăl ċon murraghy	199
Coill Fulachta	kăl fullaghtă	242
Coill Mhic Riabhaigh	kăl vick reeăwy	264
Coill Mhór	kăl wōre	12
Coill Során	kăl sorran	132
Coillidh Scolbán	kălyee skullaban	141
Coirneál Mhé	cornyal vay	185
Conaille	connilyă	11
Cor Cosógaí	cor cossogee	243
Corr Chríonaigh	cor ċreeny	89

PLACE-NAME INDEX

Sheet numbers are given below for the OS 1:50,000 map only when the name occurs on that map. Not all the townlands discussed in this volume appear on the published 1:50,000 map and no sheet number appears for those names. The sheet numbers for the 1:10,000 series and the earlier 6-inch series, which is still important for historical research, are supplied for townlands, although not for other names. For these, follow the townland in which they occur.

Place-Name	1:50,000	1:10,000	6 inch	Page
Aghaderg parish			33	21
Altafort	20			145
Annaclone	20			62
Annaghanarva	29			74
Annaghanoon	20	201	20	83
Annaghmakeonan		201	20, 27	85
Annahunshigo		239	42	153
Ardbrin	20	221, 238	34, 35	63
Aughnacloy	20	221	34	64
Aughnadrumman		183	13	277
Aughnafosker		183	13	278
Aughnavallog	29	238, 253	41, 42	154
Backnamullagh	20	183, 184, 203	21	108
Balleevy	20	221	27, 34	304
Balleny	20	202	20, 21, 27, 28	110
Ballintaggart	29	237	33, 34	23
Ballooly	20	202, 221	27, 28	191
Balloolymore	20	221	34, 35	193
Balloonigan	20	164, 183	13	279
Ballybrick	29	238	34, 35, 41, 42	156
Ballycanal	20	164	13	280
Ballycross	20	202	27	259
Ballydown	20	221	27, 34	305
Ballydugan	20	201	19	330
Ballygowan (Aghaderg)	20	220	26, 27, 33, 34	24
Ballygowan (Moira)	20	183	20, 21	281
Ballygunaghan		202	20, 27	86
Ballykeel (Dromore)	20	203	21, 22	111
Ballykeel (Magheralin)		183	20	217
Ballykeel (Seapatrick)	20	220	26, 27	306
Ballykelly	20	201, 202	27	308
Ballyknock	20	164, 183	13, 14, 20, 21	282
Ballyleny	20	183	20	218
Ballylough		201	19, 20, 26, 27	308
Ballyloughlin		240, 255	43	8
Ballymacanallen	20	201	26	331
Ballymacanally	20	183, 202	20	218
Ballymacateer	20	182, 183	13, 19, 20	220

Place-Name	1:50,000	1:10,000	6 inch	Page
Killaney	20	221	27, 28	200
Killowen	29	277	54, 55	12
Killysorrell		202	20, 27	132
Kilmacrew	20	202, 221	27	264
Kilminioge	20	163, 164, 182, 183	13, 13a	288
Kilmocummog				232
Kilmore	20	163	13	12
Kilpike	20	201, 202, 220, 221	27	316
Kilwarlin				12
Kinallen	20	203	28	133
Kircassock	20	183	20	243
Knockgorm	20	221	27, 28, 34, 35	202
Knockiveagh	29			183
Knocknagore	20	201	26	342
Lackan		238, 239	42	167
Lagan Green	20			149
Lagan, River	20			295
Lambs Island	20			100
Lany	20			297
Lappoges	20	203	21, 28	133
Lawrencetown	20			350
Legan, The				12
Legananny	20	220, 237	33	43
Legmore	20	164, 183	13	289
Legnabeepa				208
Lenaderg	20	201	27	342
Lequirin				13
Liscrum				156
Lismaine	20	183	20	244
Lisnabrague	20	220, 237	33	43
Lisnacreevy	29	238	34, 41	168
Lisnacroppan	29	238	41, 42	169
Lisnafiffy (Seapatrick/Tullylish)	20	201, 220	26, 27	316, 343
Lisnagade	20	220	33	44
Lisnagonnell	29	237	33, 34, 41	45
Lisnaree	20	221	27, 34	318
Lisnashanker	20	183	20	245
Lisnasliggan	20	221, 238	34	71
Lisnasure	20	183	20	246
Lisnatierny	29	237	40, 41	47
Lisnavaghrog	29	238	35, 41, 42	170
Lisnaward		202	27	134
Lisnisk		239, 254	42	172
Lissize	29	253	41	172
Listullyard Fort				324
Listullycurran	20	183	20, 21	136

SURNAME INDEX

This index includes surnames involved in place-names and some others mentioned in the book. Apart from obsolete names, the surnames are given in the most familiar anglicized spelling, following the Northern Ireland telephone directory. Since some surnames of Gaelic origin appear to alternate between the prefixes *Ó/O'* and *Mac*/Mc, and since some anglicized spellings use neither, the prefix is ignored in the alphabetical order. Initial *Mag* is treated as *Mc + G.*